PHILIP'S

STRE[obscured by sticker]S
East Yo[obscured by sticker]e
Northern Lincolnshire

www.philips-maps.co.uk
First published in 2002 by
Philip's, a division of
Octopus Publishing Group Ltd
www.octopusbooks.co.uk
2-4 Heron Quays, London E14 4JP
An Hachette UK Company
www.hachettelivre.co.uk

Third edition 2009
First impression 2009
EYLCA

978-0-540-09493-6 (pocket)

Speed camera data provided by
PocketGPSWorld.com Ltd

Printed by Toppan, China

Contents

II Mobile safety cameras
III **Key to map symbols**
IV **Key to map pages**
VI **Route planning**
X **Administrative and Postcode boundaries**

1 **Street maps** at 1⅓ inches to 1 mile
122 **Street maps** at 2⅔ inches to 1 mile
154 **Street maps** at 5⅓ inches to 1 mile

157 **Index** of towns, villages, streets, hospitals, industrial estates, railway stations, schools, shopping centres, universities and places of interest

Digital Data

The exceptionally high-quality mapping found in this atlas is available as digital data in TIFF format, which is easily convertible to other bitmapped (raster) image formats.

The index is also available in digital form as a standard database table. It contains all the details found in the printed index together with the National Grid reference for the map square in which each entry is named.

For further information and to discuss your requirements, please contact
victoria.dawbarn@philips-maps.co.uk

Mobile safety cameras

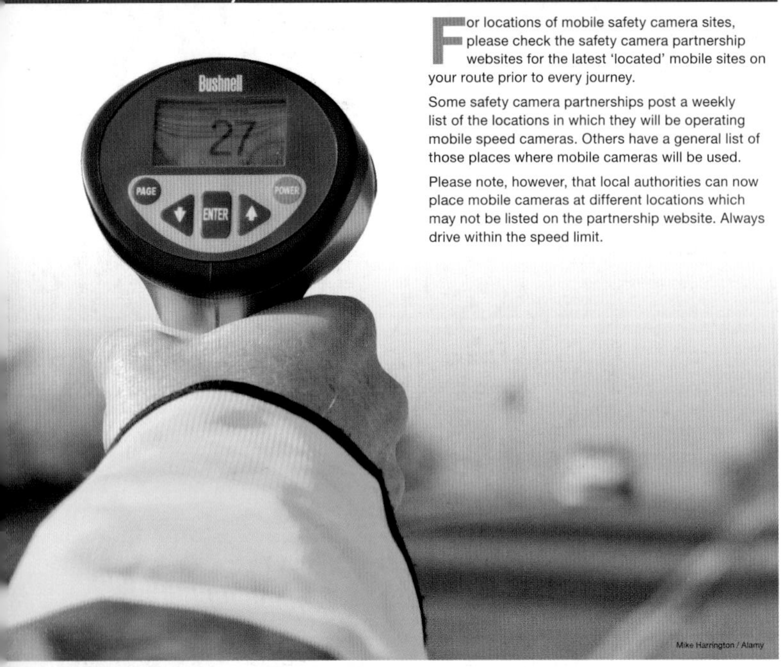

Mike Harrington / Alamy

For locations of mobile safety camera sites, please check the safety camera partnership websites for the latest 'located' mobile sites on your route prior to every journey.

Some safety camera partnerships post a weekly list of the locations in which they will be operating mobile speed cameras. Others have a general list of those places where mobile cameras will be used.

Please note, however, that local authorities can now place mobile cameras at different locations which may not be listed on the partnership website. Always drive within the speed limit.

Useful websites

East Riding safety camera partnership
www.eastriding.gov.uk/safetycamerapartnership

Lincolnshire safety camera partnership
www.lincssafetycamera.com

Nottinghamshire safety camera partnership
http://www.nottspeed.com

South Yorkshire safety camera partnership
www.safetycamera.org/home

West Yorkshire safety camera partnership
www.safetycameraswestyorkshire.co.uk

Further information
www.dvla.gov.uk
www.thinkroadsafety.gov.uk
www.dft.gov.uk
www.road-safe.org

Key to map symbols

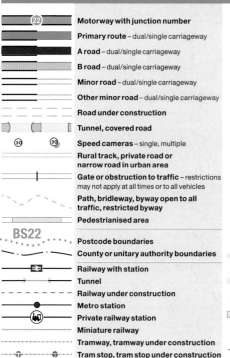

- 22 **Motorway with junction number**
- **Primary route** – dual/single carriageway
- **A road** – dual/single carriageway
- **B road** – dual/single carriageway
- **Minor road** – dual/single carriageway
- **Other minor road** – dual/single carriageway
- **Road under construction**
- **Tunnel, covered road**
- 30 30 **Speed cameras** – single, multiple
- **Rural track, private road or narrow road in urban area**
- **Gate or obstruction to traffic** – restrictions may not apply at all times or to all vehicles
- **Path, bridleway, byway open to all traffic, restricted byway**
- **Pedestrianised area**
- BS22 **Postcode boundaries**
- **County or unitary authority boundaries**
- **Railway with station**
- **Tunnel**
- **Railway under construction**
- **Metro station**
- **Private railway station**
- **Miniature railway**
- **Tramway, tramway under construction**
- **Tram stop, tram stop under construction**
- **Bus, coach station**

- **Ambulance station**
- **Coastguard station**
- **Fire station**
- **Police station**
- **Accident and Emergency entrance to hospital**
- H **Hospital**
- **Place of worship**
- i **Information centre** – open all year
- P **Shopping centre, parking**
- P&R PO **Park and Ride, Post Office**
- **Camping site, caravan site**
- **Golf course, picnic site**
- Church ROMAN FORT **Non-Roman antiquity, Roman antiquity**
- Univ **Important buildings, schools, colleges, universities and hospitals**
- **Woods, built-up area**
- River Medway **Water name**
- **River, weir**
- **Stream**
- **Canal, lock, tunnel**
- **Water**
- **Tidal water**
- 58 87 246 **Adjoining page indicators and overlap bands** – the colour of the arrow and band indicates the scale of the adjoining or overlapping page (see scales below)

The dark grey border on the inside edge of some pages indicates that the mapping does not continue onto the adjacent page

The small numbers around the edges of the maps identify the 1-kilometre National Grid lines

Enlarged maps only

- **Railway or bus station building**
- **Place of interest**
- **Parkland**

Abbreviations

Acad	**Academy**	Meml	**Memorial**
Allot Gdns	**Allotments**	Mon	**Monument**
Cemy	**Cemetery**	Mus	**Museum**
C Ctr	**Civic centre**	Obsy	**Observatory**
CH	**Club house**	Pal	**Royal palace**
Coll	**College**	PH	**Public house**
Crem	**Crematorium**	Recn Gd	**Recreation ground**
Ent	**Enterprise**	Resr	**Reservoir**
Ex H	**Exhibition hall**	Ret Pk	**Retail park**
Ind Est	**Industrial Estate**	Sch	**School**
IRB Sta	**Inshore rescue boat station**	Sh Ctr	**Shopping centre**
Inst	**Institute**	TH	**Town hall / house**
Ct	**Law court**	Trad Est	**Trading estate**
L Ctr	**Leisure centre**	Univ	**University**
LC	**Level crossing**	W Twr	**Water tower**
Liby	**Library**	Wks	**Works**
Mkt	**Market**	YH	**Youth hostel**

The map scale on the pages numbered in green is 1⅓ inches to 1 mile
2.1 cm to 1 km • 1:47 620

0 ½ mile 1 mile 1½ miles **2 miles**
0 500m 1 km 1½ km **2km**

The map scale on the pages numbered in blue is 2⅔ inches to 1 mile
4.2 cm to 1 km • 1:23 810

0 ¼ mile ½ mile ¾ mile **1 mile**
0 250m 500m 750m **1km**

The map scale on the pages numbered in red is 5⅓ inches to 1 mile
8.4 cm to 1 km • 1:11 900

0 220yds 440yds 660yds **½ mile**
0 125m 250m 375m **500m**

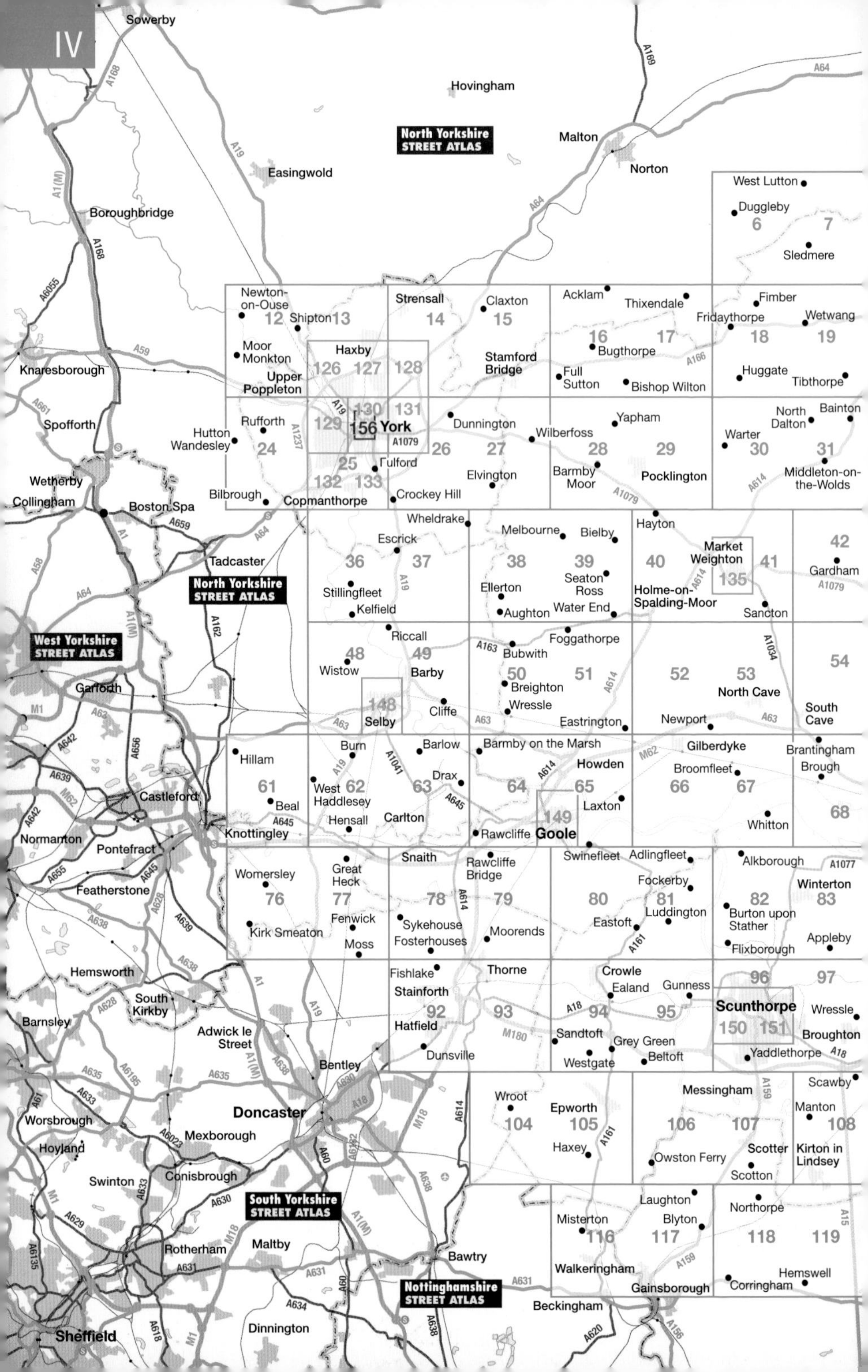
Sowerby
Hovingham
A169
A64
A168
North Yorkshire STREET ATLAS
Malton
Norton
A19
Easingwold
A1(M)
A64
Boroughbridge
West Lutton
Duggleby
6
7
Sledmere
A168
A6055
Newton-on-Ouse
12
Shipton
13
Strensall
14
Claxton
15
Acklam
Thixendale
16
17
Bugthorpe
Fimber
Fridaythorpe
Wetwang
18
19
A59
Moor Monkton
Haxby
126
127
128
Stamford Bridge
Full Sutton
Bishop Wilton
A166
Huggate
Tibthorpe
Knaresborough
Upper Poppleton
A661
Spofforth
Rufforth
A19
129
130
131
156
York
Dunnington
Wilberfoss
Yapham
North Dalton
Bainton
Hutton Wandesley
24
A1237
A1079
26
27
28
29
Warter
30
31
25
Fulford
Elvington
Barmby Moor
Pocklington
Middleton-on-the-Wolds
Wetherby
132
133
A614
Collingham
Boston Spa
Bilbrough
Copmanthorpe
Crockey Hill
A1079
Wheldrake
Hayton
A659
Escrick
Melbourne
Bielby
Market Weighton
42
A1
A64
Tadcaster
36
37
38
39
40
41
A58
North Yorkshire STREET ATLAS
A19
Seaton Ross
135
Gardham
A1079
Stillingfleet
Ellerton
Holme-on-Spalding-Moor
A614
A64
Kelfield
Aughton
Water End
Sancton
A1(M)
A162
Riccall
Foggathorpe
A1034
West Yorkshire STREET ATLAS
48
49
A163
Bubwith
54
Wistow
Barby
50
51
52
53
Garforth
Breighton
A614
North Cave
M1
A63
148
Cliffe
Wressle
South Cave
A642
A656
A63
Selby
A63
Eastrington
Newport
A63
Burn
Barlow
Barmby on the Marsh
Gilberdyke
Brantingham
Hillam
A1041
M62
Brough
A19
Drax
A614
Howden
Broomfleet
A639
Castleford
West Haddlesey
61
62
63
64
65
66
67
M62
Beal
A645
Laxton
68
A642
A645
149
Hensall
Carlton
Whitton
Normanton
Knottingley
Rawcliffe
Goole
Pontefract
Snaith
Rawcliffe Bridge
Swinefleet
Adlingfleet
Alkborough
A1077
A655
A645
Womersley
Great Heck
Fockerby
Winterton
Featherstone
76
77
78
79
80
81
82
83
A614
A628
A639
A638
Fenwick
Sykehouse
Eastoft
Luddington
Burton upon Stather
Kirk Smeaton
Moss
Fosterhouses
Moorends
A161
Appleby
A638
Flixborough
Hemsworth
Fishlake
Thorne
Crowle
96
97
A1
Stainforth
Ealand
Gunness
South Kirkby
A628
A19
92
93
A18
94
95
Scunthorpe
Wressle
Barnsley
Adwick le Street
Hatfield
M180
Sandtoft
150
151
Broughton
Grey Green
Dunsville
Westgate
Beltoft
Yaddlethorpe
A18
A1(M)
A638
Bentley
A635
A6195
A635
A630
A1159
Scawby
Wroot
Messingham
A61
A633
Doncaster
A18
M18
A614
Epworth
Manton
Worsbrough
104
105
106
107
108
Mexborough
A6023
A60
A6182
A161
Hoyland
Haxey
Scotter
Kirton in Lindsey
Owston Ferry
Swinton
A633
Conisbrough
Scotton
M1
A630
A638
Laughton
South Yorkshire STREET ATLAS
Northorpe
A629
Misterton
Blyton
A15
M18
116
117
118
119
A6135
Rotherham
Maltby
A1(M)
Bawtry
A631
A631
Walkeringham
A159
A60
Hemswell
A631
Gainsborough
Corringham
A634
Nottinghamshire STREET ATLAS
Beckingham
A618
M1
A638
A620
A156
Sheffield
Dinnington

Key to map pages

113	Map pages at 1⅓ inches to 1 mile
141	Map pages at 2⅔ inches to 1 mile
156	Map pages at 5⅓ inches to 1 mile

Scale

0 5 10 15 20 km

0 5 10 miles

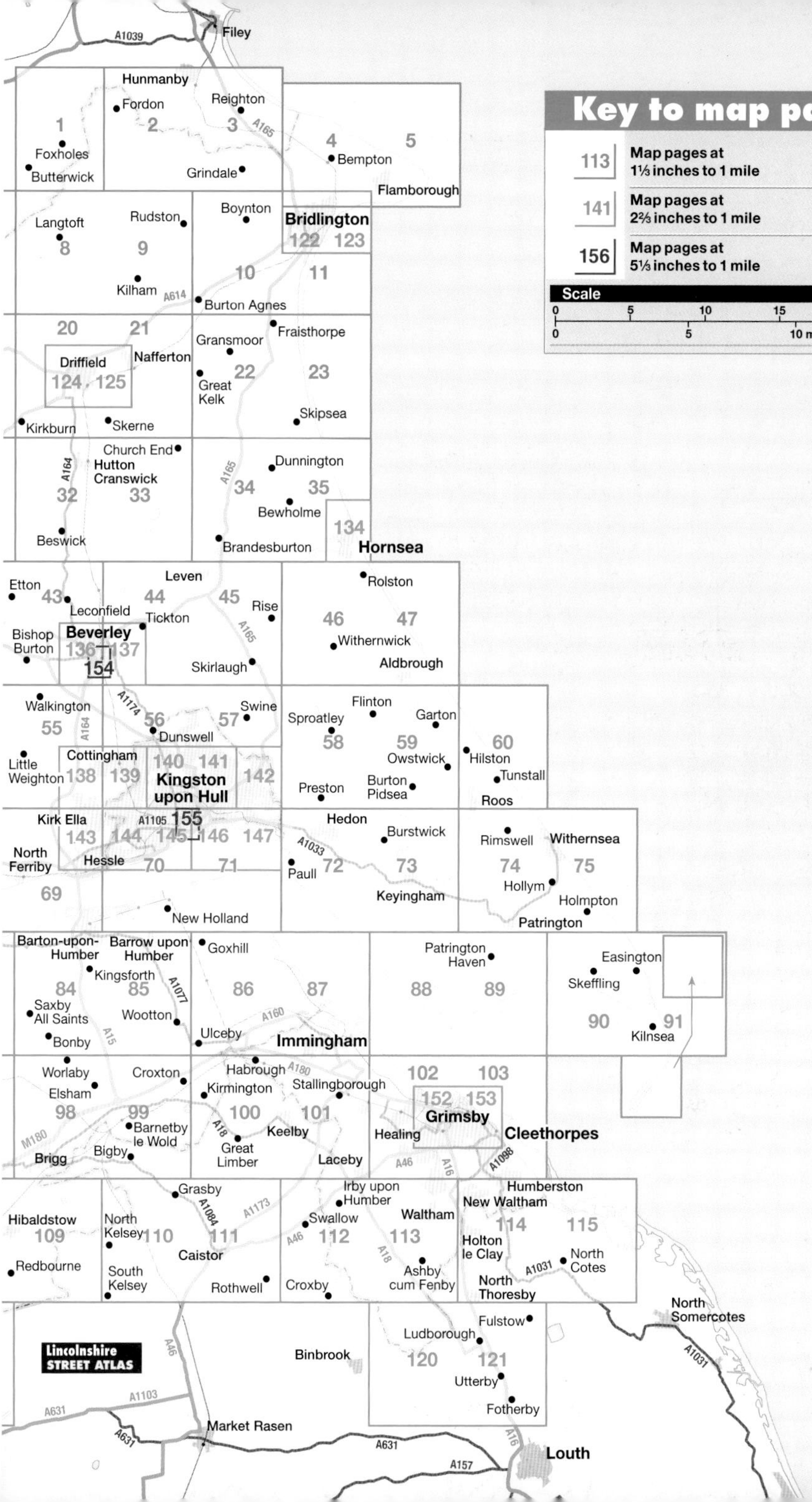
Filey
A1039
Hunmanby
Fordon
Reighton
A165
1
2
3
4
5
Foxholes
Butterwick
Grindale
Bempton
Flamborough
Langtoft
Rudston
Boynton
Bridlington
122
123
8
9
10
11
Kilham
A614
Burton Agnes
20
21
Fraisthorpe
Gransmoor
Driffield
Nafferton
124
125
22
23
Great Kelk
Skipsea
Kirkburn
Skerne
Church End
Hutton Cranswick
A164
32
33
A165
Dunnington
34
35
Bewholme
134
Hornsea
Beswick
Brandesburton
Etton
Leven
Rolston
43
44
45
Leconfield
Rise
46
47
Tickton
Bishop Burton
Beverley
136
137
154
A165
Withernwick
Aldbrough
Skirlaugh
Walkington
A1174
Flinton
Swine
Sproatley
Garton
55
A164
56
57
58
59
60
Dunswell
Owstwick
Hilston
Cottingham
140
141
Little Weighton
138
139
Kingston upon Hull
142
Burton Pidsea
Tunstall
Preston
Roos
Kirk Ella
A1105
155
Hedon
143
144
145
146
147
Burstwick
Rimswell
Withernsea
North Ferriby
Hessle
70
71
A1033
Paull
72
73
74
75
Hollym
69
Keyingham
Holmpton
New Holland
Patrington
Barton-upon-Humber
Barrow upon Humber
Goxhill
Patrington Haven
Easington
Kingsforth
84
85
A1077
86
87
88
89
Skeffling
Saxby All Saints
Wootton
A160
90
91
A15
Kilnsea
Bonby
Ulceby
Immingham
Worlaby
Croxton
Habrough
A180
102
103
Elsham
Kirmington
Stallingborough
98
99
100
101
152
153
M180
Barnetby le Wold
A18
Keelby
Grimsby
Healing
Cleethorpes
Brigg
Bigby
Great Limber
Laceby
A46
A16
A1098
Grasby
Irby upon Humber
Humberston
New Waltham
Hibaldstow
North Kelsey
A1084
A1173
Swallow
Waltham
109
110
111
112
113
114
115
A46
Caistor
Holton le Clay
Redbourne
A18
A1031
North Cotes
South Kelsey
Rothwell
Croxby
Ashby cum Fenby
North Thoresby
North Somercotes
Fulstow
Lincolnshire STREET ATLAS
A46
Ludborough
Binbrook
120
121
A1031
A1103
Utterby
A631
Fotherby
Market Rasen
A631
A631
A16
A157
Louth

VI
Route planning
Scale
0 5 10 15 km
0 5 10 miles
Sproxton
Harome
Normanby
le-Dale
Allerston
Oldstead
Kilburn
High Kilburn
Wass
Muscoates
Little Barugh
Nunnington
West Ness
East Ness
Salton
Great Barugh
Kirby Misperton
Stonegrave
South Holme
Butterwick
Brawby
High Marishes
Low Marishes
Cawton
Little Habton
Great Habton
Ryton
Scampston
West Knapton
Hovingham
Wath
Fryton
Slingsby
Barton-le-Street
Wykeham
Rillington
Coulton
Amotherby
Appleton-le-Street
Swinton
Broughton
Old Malton
Thorpe Bassett
Brandsby
Scackleton
Malton
Norton-on-Derwent
Scagglethorpe
Stearsby
Dalby
Raskel
Skewsby
Terrington
Ganthorpe
Coneysthorpe
Settrington
Crayke
Easingwold
Whenby
Whitewall Corner
Stillington
Farlington
Welburn
High Hutton
North Grimston
Tholthorpe
Bulmer
Low Hutton
Langton
Sheriff Hutton
Whitwell-on-the-Hill
Firby
Flawith
Alne
Huby
Sutton-on-the-Forest
Thornton-le-Clay
Kirkham
Kennythorpe
Birdsall
Wharram le Street
Dunsforth
Cross Lanes
West Lilling
Foston
Crambe
Westow
Burythorpe
Aldwark
Tollerton
Youlton
Leavening
Barton-le-Willows
Howsham
Linton-on-Ouse
Flaxton
Harton
Acklam
Great Ouseburn
Strensall
Bossall
Leppington
Thixendale
Claxton
Scrayingham
Thorpe Underwood
Newton on Ouse
Towthorpe
Sand Hutton
Kirby Underdale
Nun Monkton
Shipton
Wigginton
Buttercrambe
Painsthorpe
Green Hammerton
Beningbrough
Haxby
Earswick
City
Moor End
Upper Helmsley
Bugthorpe
Skirpenbeck
Moor Monkton
Skelton
Stockton on the Forest
Stamford Bridge
Youlthorpe
Overton
Huntington
Gate Helmsley
Kirk Hammerton
Nether Poppleton
West Huntington
New Earswick
Warthill
Full Sutton
Bishop Wilton
Upper Poppleton
Rawcliffe
Holtby
Low Catton
Gowthorpe
Great Givendale
Fangfoss
Hessay
Clifton
of
Murton
High Catton
Tockwith
Knapton
York
Heworth
Osbaldwick
Dunnington
Bolton
Meltonby
Long Marston
Rufforth
Holgate
Grimston
Yapham
Millington
Acomb
Wilberfoss
Hutton Wandesley
Nunthorpe
Heslington
Kexby
Kilnwick Percy
Warter
Bilton in Ainsty
Woodthorpe
Barmby Moor
Askham Bryan
Fulford
Newton upon Derwent
Pocklington
Angram
York
Askham Richard
Bishopthorpe
Elvington
Nunburnholme
Wighill
Healaugh
Crockey Hill
Allerthorpe
Bilbrough
Copmanthorpe
Sutton upon Derwent
Burnby
Catterton
Acaster Malbis
Naburn
Thornton
Hayton
Londesborough
Newton Kyme
Wheldrake
Colton
Deighton
Storwood
Melbourne
Thorpe le Street
Tadcaster
Bielby
Shiptonthorpe
Market Weighton
Appleton Roebuck
Escrick
Everingham
Acaster Selby
Seaton Ross
Bolton Percy
East Cottingwith
Thorganby
Stutton
Kirkby Wharfe
Holme Green
Harswell
Ulleskelf
Stillingfleet
Ryther
Ellerton
Laytham
Towton
Water End
Holme-on-Spalding-Moor
Kelfield
Church Fenton
Aughton
Skipwith
North Duffield
Harlthorpe
Moor End
Cawood
Foggathorpe
Sand Hole
Saxton
Riccall
Bubwith
Highfield
Rascal Moor
Barkston
Wistow
Gunby
Gribthorpe
South Cliffe
Biggin
Willitoft
Sherburn in Elmet
Little Fenton
Barlby
Menthorpe
Breighton
Spaldington
Osgodby
Bursea
Newthorpe
Lund
South Duffield
North Cave
Selby
Cliffe
Thorpe Willoughby
Wressle
North Howden
Portington
Hive
South Milford
Hambleton
East Common
Brind
Lumby
Monk Fryston
Brayton
Hemingbrough
Cavil
Sandholme
Newport
Newsholme
Eastrington
Scalby
Gilberdyke
Hillam
Barlow
Barmby on the Marsh
Howden
Staddlethorpe
Fairburn
Gateforth
Burn
Long Drax
Asselby
Knedlington
Kilpin Pike
Balkholme
Burton Salmon
West Haddlesey
Birkin
Chapel Haddlesey
Kilpin
New Fryston
Brotherton
Drax
Boothferry
Laxton
Beal
Temple Hirst
Camblesforth
Newland
Skelton
Hook
Ferrybridge
Sutton
Kellington
Hirst Courtney
Airmyn
Saltmarshe
Blacktoft
Faxfleet
Kellingley
Eggborough
Yokefleet
Knottingley
Hensall
Carlton
Goole
Ousefleet
Gowdall
Snaith
East Cowick
Rawcliffe
Reedness
Whitgift
Rawcliffe Bridge
Swinefleet
Little Reedness
High Eggborough
Chequerfield
Cridling Stubbs
Whitley
Great Heck
West Cowick
Old Goole
Adlingfleet
Dutch River
Southfield Reservoir
Pollington
Darrington
Womersley
East Hardwick
Balne
Aire and Calder Navigation
Fockerby
Garthorpe
Burton Stather
Wentbridge
Little Smeaton
Walden Stubbs
Burton upon Stather
Luddington
Low Ackworth
Sykehouse
Pincheon Green
Normanby
Kirk Smeaton
Fenwick
Eastoft
Thorpe Audlin
Moorends
Flixborough
Badsworth
Norton
Campsall
Fosterhouses
Amcotts
Upton
Wrangbrook
Moss
Fishlake
Flixborough Stather
Ouse
Derwent
Wharfe
Aire
Went
Don
Trent
Foulness
Rye
Riccal
Selby Canal
Pocklington Canal
Market Weighton Canal
A19
A64
A59
A1237
A1036
A166
A1079
A163
A614
A63
A645
A1041
A1238
A162
A659
A628
A639
A161
A169
A638
A6474
M62
M18
B1257
B1258
B1248
B1363
B1224
B1228
B1222
B1223
B1217
B1230
B1241
B1392
B1430
TOLL
YORK WEST SERVICES
FERRYBRIDGE SERVICES
BARNSDALE BAR SERVICES

Brompton
Lebberston
Gristhorpe
A1039
Filey
Filey Bay
Yedingham
Flixton
Folkton
Willerby
Staxton
Muston
Primrose Valley
East Heslerton
Sherburn
Ganton
Hunmanby
Hunmanby Moor
A64
West Heslerton
Potter Brompton
Reighton Gap
B1249
Fordon
Reighton
Speeton
Wold Newton
Foxholes
Burton Fleming
B1229
Buckton
Bempton
Butterwick
Grindale
A165
B1255
Flamborough
B1259
Helperthorpe
Weaverthorpe
Octon
Thwing
East Lutton
West Lutton
Octon Cross Roads
Boynton
Sewerby
Rudston
B1253
Kirby Grindalythe
Bridlington
Langtoft
Bessingby
Carnaby
West Hill
Hilderthorpe
Sledmere
Haisthorpe
A614
Cottam
Thornholme
Kilham
BRIDLINGTON BAY
B1251
B1252
Burton Agnes
Ruston Parva
Harpham
Fraisthorpe
Fimber
Garton-on-the-Wolds
Lowthorpe
Nafferton
Gransmoor
A166
Wetwang
Barmston
Elmswell
Little Driffield
Driffield
Great Kelk
Lissett
Gembling
Driffield Canal
Ulrome
B1248
Kelleythorpe
Foston on the Wolds
Tibthorpe
Wansford
B1249
Kirkburn
Southburn
Skerne
Skipsea
East Riding of Yorkshire
Church End
Beeford
Skipsea Brough
Brigham
Hutton
North Frodingham
B1242
North Dalton
Bainton
Hutton Cranswick
Rotsea
Dunnington
Hempholme
Middleton-on-the-Wolds
Watton
Bewholme
Atwick
Kilnwick
North Cliff
A164
Watton Beck
Burshill
Hornsea
Lund
Beswick
Holme on the Wolds
Lockington
Baswick Steer
Brandesburton
Hornsea Mere
Seaton
Thorpe
South Dalton
Scorborough
Aike
Leven
B1244
Hornsea Bridge
Rolston
Leven Canal
Catwick
Sigglesthorne
Goxhill
Arram
Etton
Mappleton
Goodmanham
Leconfield
Eske
Little Hatfield
Cherry Burton
Gardham
Routh
A165
B1243
Rise
Great Hatfield
Great Cowden
A1035
Long Riston
Tickton
Arnold
Molescroft
Withernwick
A1079
Beverley
New Ellerby
Meaux
Skirlaugh
Bishop Burton
A1035
Weel
Marton
West Newton
Aldbrough
East Newton
North Newbald
Woodmansey
Walkington
Wawne
Old Ellerby
South Newbald
Thearne
Flinton
A1174
Bentley
Garton
B1230
Swine
Coniston
A1034
Dunswell
Grimston
High Hunsley
A164
Skidby
Thirtleby
Sproatley
Humbleton
Fitling
A1033
Bransholme
Hilston
Kingston-upon-Hull
Sutton on Hull
Ganstead
Little Weighton
Inglemire
B1238
Lelley
Rowley
Owstwick
Cottingham
B1237
Bilton
B1240
Tunstall
Everthorpe
Epplewoth
Sutton Ings
Elstronwick
164
B1233
A1165
B1239
Riplingham
Newland
Stoneferry
Preston
Burton Pidsea
North End
West End
South Cave
A63
Roos
Willerby
Sculcoates
A165
Summergangs
B1242
Kirk Ella
West End
Waxholme
Brantingham
East Ella
A1105
Salt End
Ellerker
West Ella
Marfleet
A1033
Hedon
Anlaby
Rimswell
Swanland
Elloughton
B1231
Haven Side
Welton
B1362
Burstwick
Halsham
A1033
Northfield
Brough
East End
Paull
Hessle
Camerton
North Ferriby
A63
KINGSTON UPON HULL
Thorngumbald
Keyingham
Ryehill
HUMBER
Humber Bridge
Whitton
Goxhill Haven
Ottringham
Redcliff Channel
New Holland
Barton Waterside
Winestead
Read's Island
Little Humber
Winteringham
Barton-upon-Humber
Thorney Crofts
Barrow Haven
Patrington
A1077
West Halton
Goxhill
South Ferriby
Barrow upon Humber
A1077
B1218
South End
Winterton
East Halton
Kingsforth
Sunk Island
B1206
A1077
Horkstow
New River Ancholme
Thealby
Saxby All Saints
B1204
A15
Thornton Curtis
North Killingholme
Burnham
Roxby
Wootton
A160
North
Ulceby Skitter
South Killingholme
Immingham
ROTTERDAM ZEEBRUGGE
Bonby
Ulceby
B1206
Appleby
B1211
Habrough
Dragonby
Worlaby

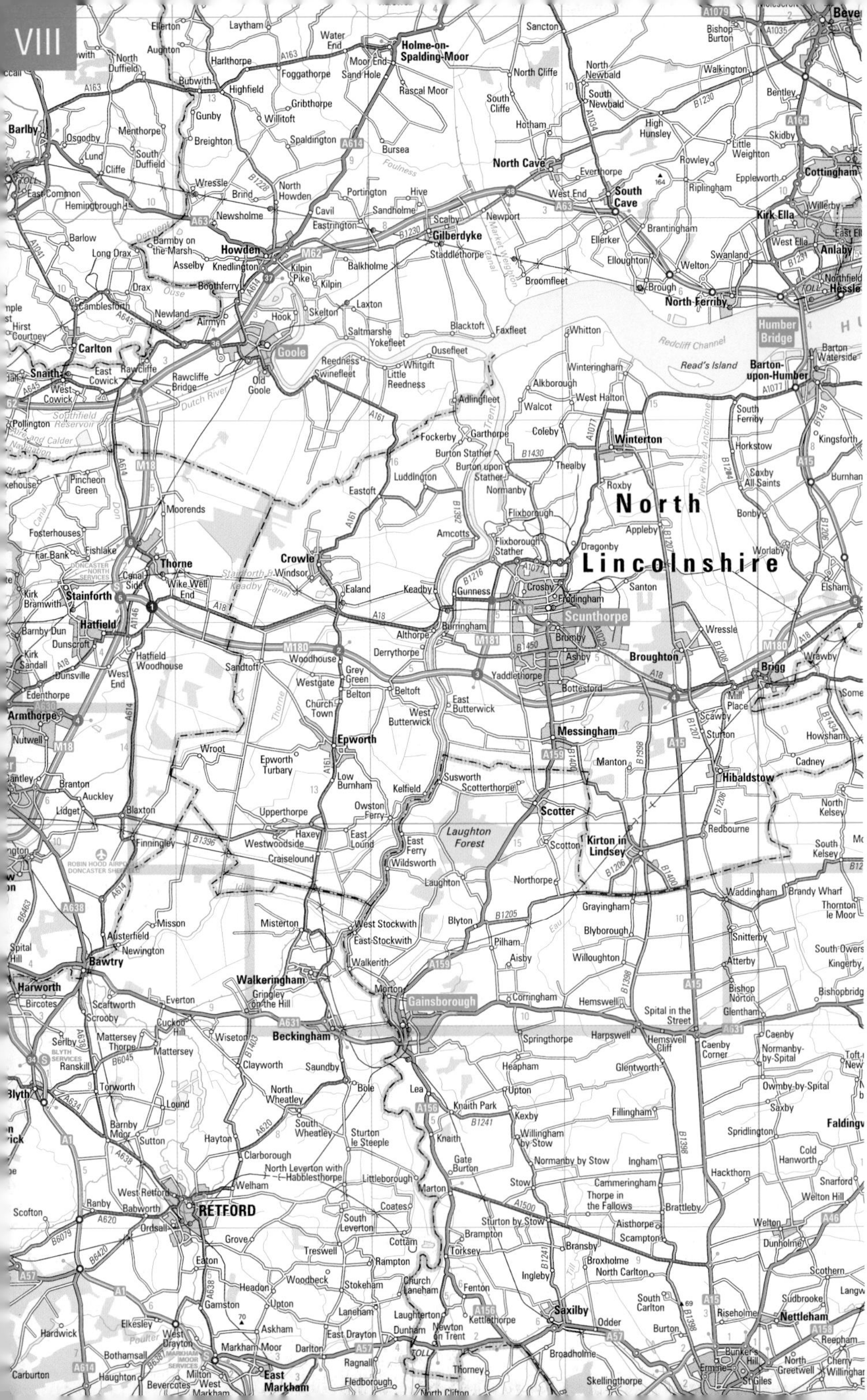
North Lincolnshire
Holme-on-Spalding-Moor
Sancton
Bishop Burton
Beverley
Ellerton
Laytham
Water End
Aughton
North Duffield
Harlthorpe
Foggathorpe
Moor End
Sand Hole
North Cliffe
North Newbald
South Newbald
Walkington
Bubwith
Highfield
Rascal Moor
South Cliffe
Bentley
Gunby
Gribthorpe
Willitoft
Hotham
High Hunsley
Skidby
Barlby
Osgodby
Menthorpe
Breighton
Spaldington
Bursea
Little Weighton
Lund
South Duffield
Cliffe
Foulness
North Cave
Rowley
Everthorpe
Cottingham
Eppleworth
Riplingham
Wressle
Brind
North Howden
Portington
Hive
West End
South Cave
East Common
Hemingbrough
Cavil
Sandholme
Newport
Willerby
Kirk Ella
Newsholme
Eastrington
Scalby
Gilberdyke
Brantingham
West Ella
East Ella
Anlaby
Barlow
Barmby on the Marsh
Howden
Staddlethorpe
Ellerker
Long Drax
Asselby
Knedlington
Kilpin Pike
Balkholme
Market Weighton Canal
Elloughton
Swanland
Welton
Northfield
Hessle
Drax
Boothferry
Kilpin
Broomfleet
Brough
North Ferriby
Camblesforth
Newland
Airmyn
Hook
Skelton
Laxton
Hirst Courtney
Carlton
Saltmarshe
Yokefleet
Blacktoft
Faxfleet
Whitton
Humber Bridge
Goole
Redcliff Channel
Barton Waterside
Snaith
East Cowick
Rawcliffe
Reedness
Swinefleet
Ousefleet
Whitgift
Little Reedness
Winteringham
Read's Island
Barton-upon-Humber
West Cowick
Rawcliffe Bridge
Old Goole
Dutch River
Alkborough
West Halton
Adlingfleet
Walcot
South Ferriby
Pollington
Southfield Reservoir
Aire and Calder Navigation
Fockerby
Garthorpe
Coleby
Winterton
Kingsforth
Burton Stather
Thealby
Horkstow
Luddington
Burton upon Stather
Normanby
Roxby
Saxby All Saints
Burnham
Pincheon Green
Eastoft
North
Moorends
Flixborough
Bonby
Fosterhouses
Amcotts
Appleby
Flixborough Stather
Dragonby
Worlaby
Fishlake
Far Bank
Thorne
Crowle
Lincolnshire
Canal Side
Wike Well End
Windsor
Stainforth & Keadby Canal
Santon
Elsham
Kirk Bramwith
Stainforth
Ealand
Keadby
Gunness
Crosby
Frodingham
Hatfield
Scunthorpe
Barnby Dun
Burringham
Althorpe
Wressle
Dunscroft
Derrythorpe
Brumby
Kirk Sandall
Hatfield Woodhouse
Sandtoft
Woodhouse
Ashby
Broughton
Brigg
Wrawby
Dunsville
West End
Grey Green
Yaddlethorpe
Edenthorpe
Westgate
Belton
Beltoft
Bottesford
Mill Place
Armthorpe
Church Town
East Butterwick
West Butterwick
Scawby
Epworth
Messingham
Sturton
Nutwell
Howsham
Wroot
Epworth Turbary
Manton
Cadney
Cantley
Low Burnham
Susworth
Scotterthorpe
Hibaldstow
Branton
Auckley
Kelfield
Scotter
North Kelsey
Lidget
Blaxton
Upperthorpe
Owston Ferry
Laughton Forest
Redbourne
Finningley
Westwoodside
Haxey
East Lound
East Ferry
Scotton
Kirton in Lindsey
South Kelsey
Craiselound
Wildsworth
Robin Hood Airport Doncaster Sheffield
Laughton
Northorpe
Waddingham
Brandy Wharf
Grayingham
Thornton le Moor
Misson
Misterton
West Stockwith
Blyton
Austerfield
East Stockwith
Pilham
Blyborough
Snitterby
Spital Hill
Newington
Aisby
Willoughton
South Owersby
Bawtry
Walkerith
Atterby
Kingerby
Walkeringham
Harworth
Gringley on the Hill
Morton
Gainsborough
Corringham
Hemswell
Bishop Norton
Bishopbridge
Bircotes
Scaftworth
Everton
Spital in the Street
Glentham
Scrooby
Cuckoo Hill
Wiseton
Beckingham
Springthorpe
Harpswell
Hemswell Cliff
Caenby Corner
Caenby
Serlby
Mattersey Thorpe
Mattersey
Normanby-by-Spital
Blyth Services
Ranskill
Clayworth
Saundby
Heapham
Glentworth
Torworth
Bole
Upton
Owmby-by-Spital
Blyth
Lound
North Wheatley
Lea
Knaith Park
Saxby
Fillingham
Barnby Moor
South Wheatley
Sturton le Steeple
Kexby
Willingham by Stow
Spridlington
Faldingworth
Sutton
Hayton
Knaith
Cold Hanworth
Clarborough
Gate Burton
Normanby by Stow
Ingham
Hackthorn
North Leverton with Habblesthorpe
Littleborough
Stow
Cammeringham
Snarford
West Retford
Welham
Thorpe in the Fallows
Welton Hill
Ranby
Babworth
Retford
Marton
Brattleby
Scofton
Coates
Sturton by Stow
Aisthorpe
Welton
Ordsall
South Leverton
Brampton
Scampton
Dunholme
Grove
Cottam
Torksey
Treswell
Bransby
Eaton
Rampton
Broxholme
Scothern
North Carlton
Woodbeck
Ingleby
Headon
Stokeham
Church Laneham
Fenton
Langworth
Gamston
Upton
South Carlton
Sudbrooke
Laneham
Saxilby
Riseholme
Nettleham
Elkesley
Askham
Laughterton
Kettlethorpe
Odder
Burton
Hardwick
West Drayton
East Drayton
Dunham
Newton on Trent
Reepham
Markham Moor
Darlton
Broadholme
Bunker's Hill
Bothamsall
Markham Moor Services
Ragnall
Thorney
North Greetwell
Cherry Willingham
Carburton
Haughton
Milton
West Markham
East Markham
Fledborough
North Clifton
Skellingthorpe
Ermine
St Giles
Bevercotes

Kingston-upon-Hull
KINGSTON UPON HULL
Bransholme
Sutton on Hull
Sutton-Ings
Stoneferry
Summergangs
Newland
Sculcoates
Marfleet
Dunswell
Thearne
Wawne
Woodmansey
Weel
Meaux
Skirlaugh
New Ellerby
Marton
West Newton
Old Ellerby
Swine
Coniston
Thirtleby
Ganstead
Bilton
Preston
West End
Salt End
Hedon
Haven Side
Paull
Thorngumbald
Camerton
Ryehill
Burstwick
Halsham
Keyingham
Ottringham
Winestead
Patrington
Little Humber
Thorney Crofts
Sunk Island
Aldbrough
East Newton
Garton
Grimston
Hilston
Flinton
Sproatley
Humbleton
Fitling
Lelley
Elstronwick
Burton Pidsea
Owstwick
Tunstall
Roos
North End
Waxholme
Rimswell
East End
Owthorne
Withernsea
Hollym
Holmpton
Out Newton
Welwick
Weeton
Skeffling
Easington
Kilnsea
HUMBER
Goxhill Haven
New Holland
Barrow Haven
Goxhill
Barrow upon Humber
South End
East Halton
Thornton Curtis
North Killingholme
Wootton
Ulceby
Ulceby Skitter
South Killingholme
Immingham
ROTTERDAM ZEEBRUGGE
Habrough
Croxton
Kirmington
Melton Ross
New Barnetby
Barnetby le Wold
HUMBERSIDE (HULL)
Brocklesby
Stallingborough
Keelby
Great Limber
Riby Cross Roads
Riby
Healing
Pyewipe
West Marsh
Grimsby
CLEETHORPES
Old Clee
MOUTH OF THE HUMBER
Great Coates
Aylesby
Laceby
Nunsthorpe
Bradley
Scartho
Humberston
North East Lincolnshire
Irby upon Humber
Barnoldby le Beck
Waltham
New Waltham
Holton le Clay
Tetney Lock
Tetney
North Cotes
Bigby
Searby
Owmby
Grasby
Clixby
North Kelsey Moor
Caistor
Cabourne
Swallow
Beelsby
Brigsley
Ashby cum Fenby
Hatcliffe
Cuxwold
Nettleton
East Ravendale
Waithe
Grainsby
Rothwell
Croxby
Marshchapel
Eskham
Wragholme
Grainthorpe
North Thoresby
Holton le Moor
Thorganby
Thoresway
Swinhope
Wold Newton
Brookenby
Ludborough
Fulstow
Covenham St Bartholomew
Covenham St Mary
Conisholme
North Somercotes
Skidbrooke North End
South Somercotes
Saltfleet
North Owersby
Claxby
Normanby le Wold
Usselby
Osgodby
Kirkby
Stainton le Vale
Binbrook
Utterby
North Ormsby
Yarburgh
Skidbrooke
Kirmond le Mire
Walesby
Fotherby
Little Grimsby
Alvingham
North Cockerington
Saltfleetby St Clements
Tealby
Great Tows
Kelstern
North Elkington
Saltfleetby All Saints
Theddlethorpe St Helen
West Rasen
Middle Rasen
Market Rasen
North Willingham
Ludford
South Elkington
Louth
South Cockerington
Keddington
Grimoldby
Saltfleetby St Peter
Theddlethorpe All Saints
Welton le Wold
Burgh on Bain
Stewton
Manby
Sixhills
Linwood
Grimblethorpe
Gayton le Wold
Little Carlton
Great Carlton
Meers Bridge
Buslingthorpe
Legsby
Hainton
Hallington
Legbourne
Bleasby
South Willingham
Biscathorpe
Raithby
Friesthorpe
East Torrington
Donington on Bain
Withcall
Little Cawthorpe
South Reston
North Reston
Gayton le Marsh
Lissington
West Torrington
Tathwell
Wickenby
Holton cum Beckering
Benniworth
Haugham
Muckton
Tothill
Withern
Strubby
Thorpe
Maltby le Marsh
Beesby
East Barkwith
West Barkwith
Snelland
Fulnetby
Rand
Market Stainton
Stenigot
Cawkwell
Maidenwell
Burwell
Authorpe
Woodthorpe
Stainton by Langworth
Wragby
Bullington
Belleau
White Pit
Swaby
Aby
Saleby
Langton by Wragby
Great Sturton
Ketsby
South Thoresby
Bilsby
Apley
Kingthorpe
Belchford
South Ormsby
Calceby
Haugh
Rigsby
Alford
Farlesthorpe
Tetford
Low Barlings
Baumber
Minting
Hemingby
Fulletby
Salmonby
Brinkhill
Driby
Somersby
Well
Cumberworth
Stainfield
Gautby
Wispington
West Ashby
Bag Enderby
Sutterby
Ulceby
Claxby
Bonthorpe
Scale
0
5
10
15 km
0
5
10 miles

Administrative and Postcode boundaries

County and unitary authority boundaries

Postcode boundaries

Area covered by this atlas

Scale

0 5 10 15 20 25 30 35 40 km

0 5 10 15 20 25 miles

NZ
SE TA
SE
SK
SK TF
North Yorkshire
City of York
East Riding of Yorkshire
Kingston-upon-Hull
North Lincolnshire
North East Lincolnshire
Doncaster
Rotherham
Nottinghamshire
Lincolnshire
YO11 Hunmanby
YO12
YO14
YO15
YO16
YO17
YO25
YO30
YO31
YO32
YO41
YO42
YO43
YO60
YO61
YO1
YO8
YO10
YO19
YO23
YO24
YO26
LS24
LS25
WF8
WF11
DN3
DN6
DN7
DN8
DN9
DN10
DN14
DN15
DN16
DN17
DN18
DN19
DN20
DN21
DN31
DN32
DN33
DN34
DN35
DN36
DN37
DN38
DN39
DN40
DN41
HU1
HU2
HU3
HU4
HU5
HU6
HU7
HU8
HU9
HU10
HU11
HU12
HU13
HU14
HU15
HU16
HU17
HU18
HU19
HU20
LN7
LN8
LN11
Reighton
Fordon
Bempton
Butterwick
Foxholes
Grindale
Flamborough
West Lutton
Rudston
Boynton
Bridlington
Duggleby
Langtoft
Sledmere
Burton Agnes
Kilham
Fraisthorpe
Strensall
Claxton
Acklam
Thixendale
Fimber
Nafferton
Gransmoor
Shipton
Haxby
Stamford Bridge
Bugthorpe
Wetwang
Driffield
Great Kelk
Moor Monkton
Bishop Wilton
Huggate
Kirkburn
Skerne
Skipsea
Dunnington
Full Sutton
Church End
Dunnington
York
Yapham
Warter
Hutton Cranswick
Bewholme
Hutton Wandesley
Elvington
Pocklington
Barmby Moor
Hornsea
Fulford
Bishopthorpe
Beswick
Brandesburton
Bilbrough
Hayton
Leven
Rolston
Wheldrake
Melbourne
Market Weighton
Etton
Leconfield
Bielby
Rise
Escrick
Seaton Ross
Tickton
Withernwick
Ellerton
Gardham
Sancton
Skirlaugh
Kelfield
Beverley
Aldbrough
Riccall
Holme-on-Spalding-Moor
Walkington
Swine
Wistow
Foggathorpe
Humbleton
Breighton
South Cave
Little Weighton
Selby
Cliffe
North Cave
Owstwick
Eastrington
Kingston-upon-Hull
Hillam
Burn
Barlow
Gilberdyke
Kirk Ella
Withernsea
Drax
Barmby on the Marsh
Howden
Hessle
Brough
Keyingham
Beal
Laxton
North Ferriby
Hollym
Hensall
Whitton
Barrow upon Humber
Holmpton
Knottingley
Snaith
Goole
Adlingfleet
Alkborough
Barton-upon-Humber
Patrington
Great Heck
Rawcliffe Bridge
Fockerby
Winterton
Patrington Haven
Easington
Womersley
Sykehouse
Luddington
Wootton
Skeffling
Kirk Smeaton
Fenwick
Moorends
Flixborough
Bonby
Ulceby
Immingham
Kilnsea
Moss
Eastoft
Crowle
Croxton
Thorne
Gunness
Keelby
Healing
Grimsby
Stainforth
Ealand
Scunthorpe
Broughton
Cleethorpes
Hatfield
Dunsville
Brigg
Bigby
Great Limber
Grasby
Laceby
Westgate
Messingham
Humberston
Wroot
Hibaldstow
New Waltham
Epworth
Manton
Swallow
Waltham
Holton le Clay
Scotter
North Kelsey
Caistor
Haxey
Owston Ferry
Kirton in Lindsey
Rothwell
Croxby
North Cotes
Laughton
South Kelsey
North Thoresby
Misterton
Northorpe
Walkeringham
Blyton
Utterby
Hemswell
Fotherby
Gainsborough

Scale: 1⅓ inches to 1 mile
0 ¼ ½ mile
0 250m 500m 750m 1 km

2

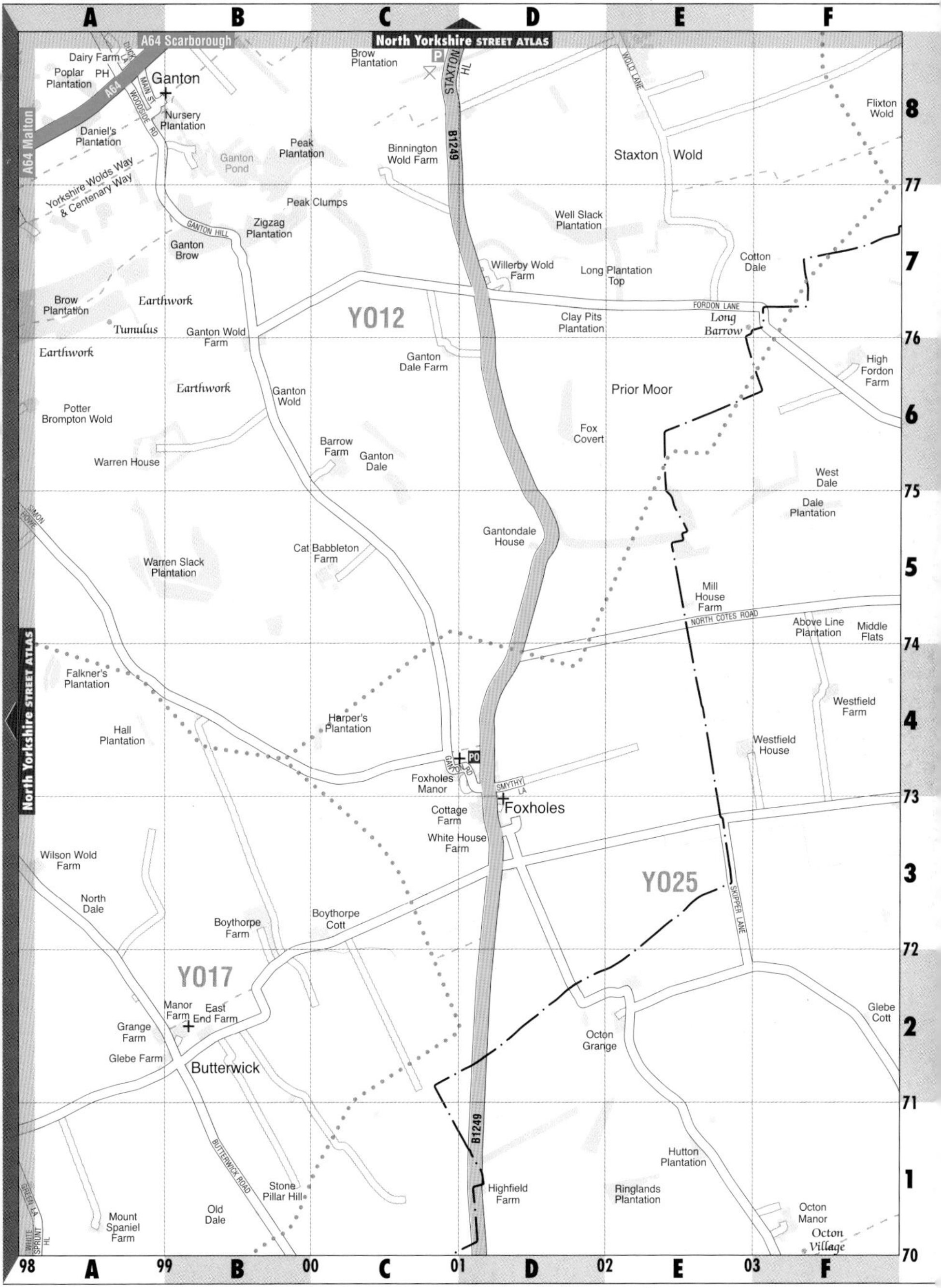
A B C D E F
A64 Scarborough
North Yorkshire STREET ATLAS
A64 Malton
Dairy Farm
Poplar Plantation
PH
Ganton
Nursery Plantation
Daniel's Plantation
Ganton Pond
Peak Plantation
Brow Plantation
Binnington Wold Farm
STAXTON HL
B1249
Staxton Wold
WOLD LANE
Flixton Wold
Yorkshire Wolds Way & Centenary Way
Peak Clumps
Zigzag Plantation
GANTON HILL
Ganton Brow
Well Slack Plantation
Willerby Wold Farm
Long Plantation Top
Cotton Dale
Earthwork
Tumulus
Ganton Wold Farm
YO12
FORDON LANE
Long Barrow
Clay Pits Plantation
Ganton Dale Farm
Ganton Wold
Prior Moor
High Fordon Farm
Potter Brompton Wold
Barrow Farm
Ganton Dale
Fox Covert
Warren House
West Dale
Dale Plantation
SIMON HOWE
Gantondale House
Cat Babbleton Farm
Warren Slack Plantation
Mill House Farm
NORTH COTES ROAD
Above Line Plantation
Middle Flats
Falkner's Plantation
Harper's Plantation
Westfield Farm
Hall Plantation
Westfield House
PO
Foxholes Manor
SMYTHY LA
Foxholes
Cottage Farm
White House Farm
Wilson Wold Farm
YO25
North Dale
Boythorpe Farm
Boythorpe Cott
SKIPPER LANE
YO17
Manor Farm
East End Farm
Grange Farm
Glebe Farm
Butterwick
Octon Grange
Glebe Cott
BUTTERWICK ROAD
Hutton Plantation
Stone Pillar Hill
Highfield Farm
Ringlands Plantation
GREEN LA
WHITE SPRUNT HL
Mount Spaniel Farm
Old Dale
Octon Manor
Octon Village
8 77 7 76 6 75 5 74 4 73 3 72 2 71 1 70
98 99 00 01 02 03

8
2

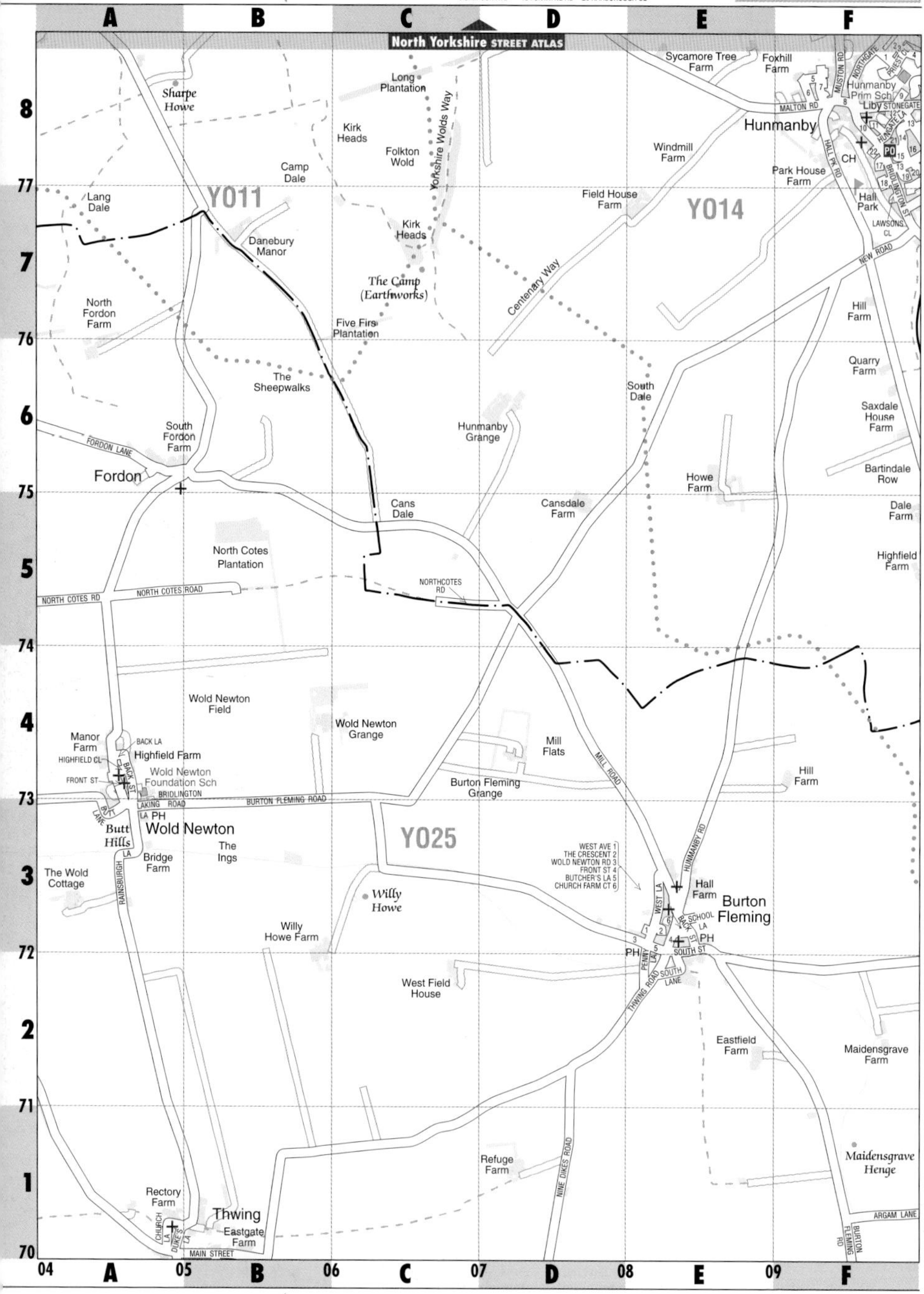
A B C D E F
North Yorkshire STREET ATLAS
8
77
7
76
6
75
5
74
4
73
3
72
2
71
1
70
04 05 06 07 08 09
Sharpe Howe
Long Plantation
Kirk Heads
Folkton Wold
Yorkshire Wolds Way
Camp Dale
Lang Dale
YO11
Danebury Manor
Kirk Heads
The Camp (Earthworks)
North Fordon Farm
Five Firs Plantation
The Sheepwalks
Centenary Way
South Fordon Farm
FORDON LANE
Fordon
Cans Dale
North Cotes Plantation
NORTH COTES RD
NORTH COTES ROAD
NORTHCOTES RD
Sycamore Tree Farm
Foxhill Farm
MALTON RD
MUSTON RD
NORTHGATE
Hunmanby Prim Sch
Liby
STONEGATE
Hunmanby
HALL PK RD
Windmill Farm
Park House Farm
CH
PO
HUNGATE LA
BRIDLINGTON ST
Field House Farm
YO14
Hall Park
LAWSONS CL
NEW ROAD
Hill Farm
Quarry Farm
South Dale
Saxdale House Farm
Hunmanby Grange
Bartindale Row
Howe Farm
Cansdale Farm
Dale Farm
Highfield Farm
Wold Newton Field
Wold Newton Grange
Mill Flats
MILL ROAD
Manor Farm
BACK LA
Highfield Farm
HIGHFIELD CL
FRONT ST
BACK ST
Wold Newton Foundation Sch
BRIDLINGTON
LAKING ROAD
BURTON FLEMING ROAD
Burton Fleming Grange
Hill Farm
BUTT LANE
PH
Wold Newton
Butt Hills
The Ings
YO25
HUNMANBY RD
WEST AVE 1
THE CRESCENT 2
WOLD NEWTON RD 3
FRONT ST 4
BUTCHER'S LA 5
CHURCH FARM CT 6
The Wold Cottage
Bridge Farm
RAINSBURGH LA
Willy Howe
Willy Howe Farm
Hall Farm
WEST LA
SCHOOL LA
BACK ST
Burton Fleming
PH
SOUTH ST
PENNY LA
SOUTH LANE
THWING ROAD
West Field House
Eastfield Farm
Maidensgrave Farm
NINE DIKES ROAD
Refuge Farm
Maidensgrave Henge
Rectory Farm
Thwing
CHURCH LA
DUKE'S LA
Eastgate Farm
MAIN STREET
ARGAM LANE
BURTON FLEMING RD

Scale: 1⅓ inches to 1 mile

0 ¼ ½ mile

0 250m 500m 750m 1 km

A8
1 WRANGHAM DR
2 LENNOX CL
3 BURLYN RD
4 CHERRY RD
5 HAWKE GARTH
6 MANOR GDNS
7 CECIL RD
8 HOWES RD
9 WATSON CL
10 HAMERTON RD
11 HAMERTON CL
12 GRIMSTON RD
13 STRICKLAND RD
14 PERCY RD
15 HAVERCROFT RD
16 COWLINGS CL

4

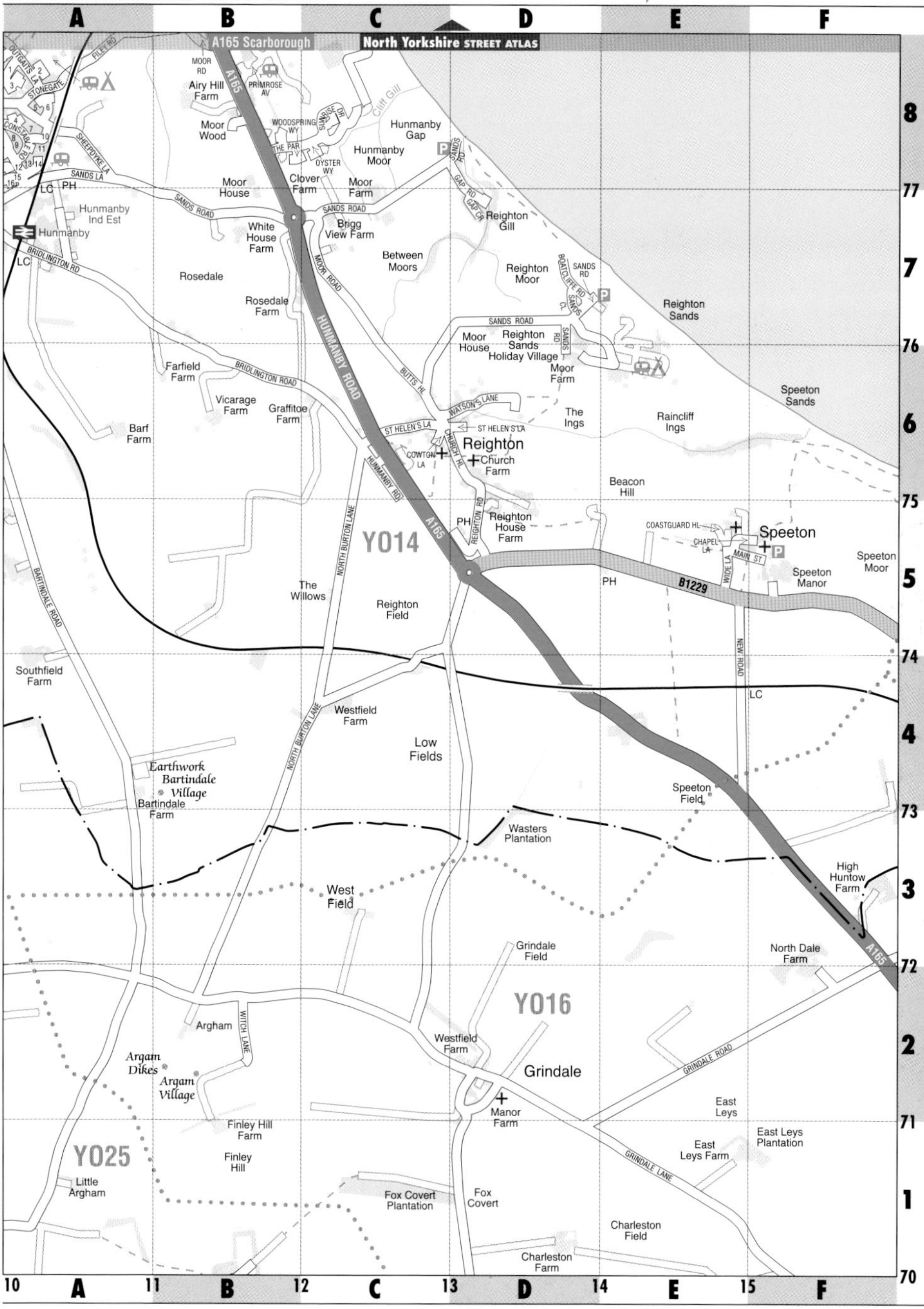

10

4

Scale: 1⅓ inches to 1 mile
0 ¼ ½ mile
0 250m 500m 750m 1 km

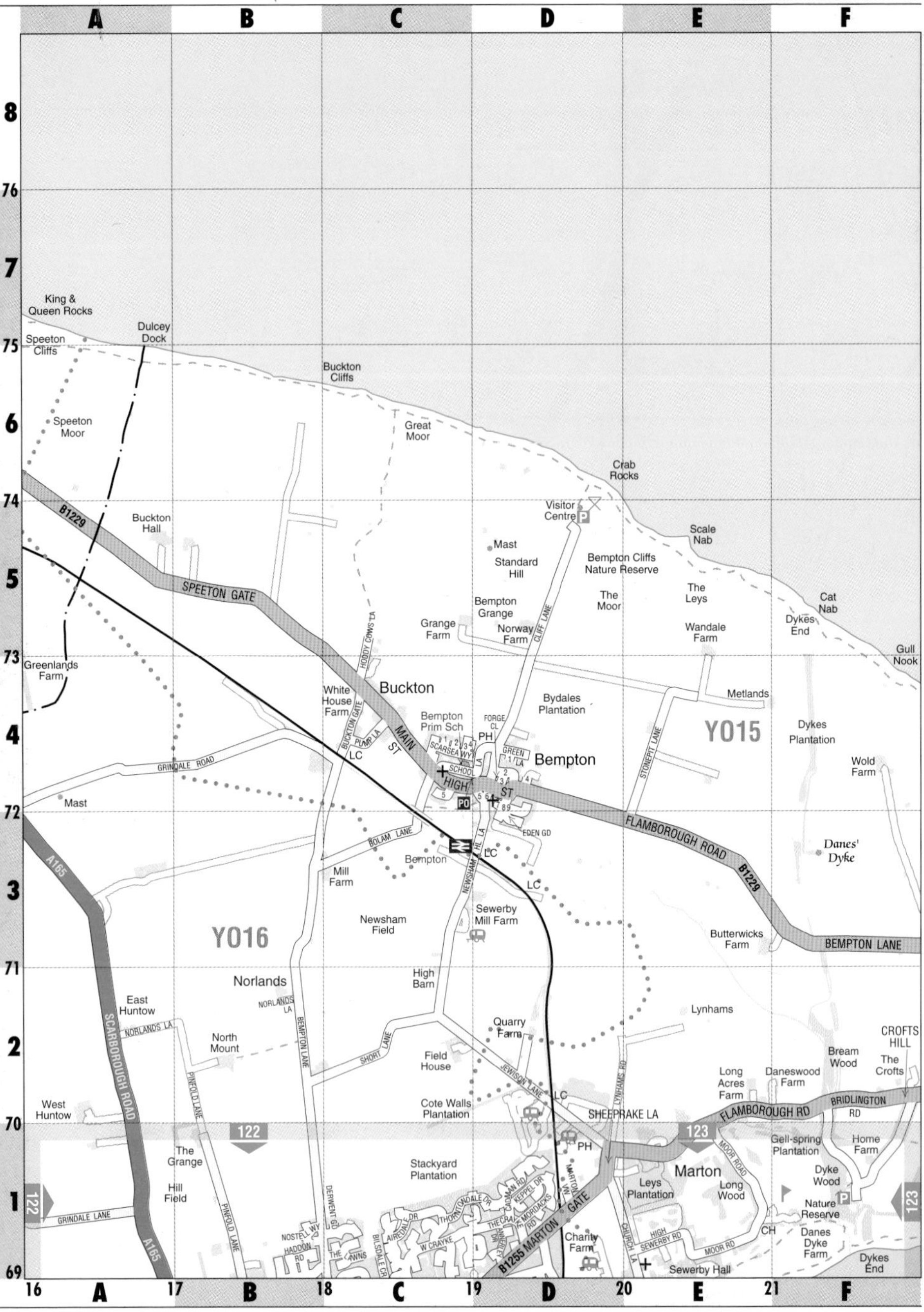
A
B
C
D
E
F
8
76
7
75
6
74
5
73
4
72
3
71
2
70
1
69
16
17
18
19
20
21
King & Queen Rocks
Speeton Cliffs
Dulcey Dock
Buckton Cliffs
Speeton Moor
Great Moor
Crab Rocks
Visitor Centre
Scale Nab
Buckton Hall
Mast
Standard Hill
Bempton Cliffs Nature Reserve
B1229
SPEETON GATE
The Leys
Cat Nab
The Moor
Bempton Grange
Grange Farm
Norway Farm
CLIFF LANE
Wandale Farm
Dykes End
Gull Nook
HODDY COWS LA
Greenlands Farm
Buckton
White House Farm
Bydales Plantation
Metlands
BUCKTON GATE
Bempton Prim Sch
FORGE CL
PH
MAIN ST
PUMP LA
SCARSEA WY
SCHOOL LA
GREEN LA
Bempton
YO15
STONEPIT LANE
Dykes Plantation
Wold Farm
LC
GRINDALE ROAD
HIGH ST
Mast
PO
EDEN GD
FLAMBOROUGH ROAD
BOLAM LANE
NEWSHAM HL LA
Bempton
LC
Danes' Dyke
A165
Mill Farm
LC
Newsham Field
Sewerby Mill Farm
YO16
Butterwicks Farm
BEMPTON LANE
Norlands
High Barn
NORLANDS LA
East Huntow
Lynhams
BEMPTON LANE
NORLANDS LA
Quarry Farm
CROFTS HILL
North Mount
SHORT LANE
Field House
Bream Wood
SCARBOROUGH ROAD
PINFOLD LANE
JEWISON LANE
Long Acres Farm
Daneswood Farm
The Crofts
LYNHAMS RD
West Huntow
Cote Walls Plantation
LC
SHEEPRAKE LA
FLAMBOROUGH RD
BRIDLINGTON RD
122
123
The Grange
Stackyard Plantation
PH
Gell-spring Plantation
Home Farm
Marton
MOOR ROAD
Hill Field
Leys Plantation
Long Wood
Dyke Wood
122
GRINDALE LANE
PINFOLD LANE
DERWENT GD
THORNTONDALE DR
CAYMAN RD
KEPPEL DR
MARTON WY
Nature Reserve
123
NOSTELL WY
HADDON RD
AIREDALE DR
THE CRAYKE
MORDACKS RD
B1255 MARTON GATE
Charity Farm
CHURCH LA
CH
HIGH SEWERBY RD
MOOR RD
Danes Dyke Farm
Dykes End
BILSDALE GR
THE LAWNS
W CRAYKE
Sewerby Hall

C4
1 WALMSLEY CL
2 GRANGE CL
3 COLLINGWOOD RD
4 THE MEADOWS
5 RINGLEY MDWS

D4
1 THE PADDOCK
2 SPRING LA
3 ST MICHAEL'S WK
4 BYEDALES
5 GILLUS LA
6 CHURCH LA
7 ACREDYKES
8 VICARAGE LA
9 CLARK CR

For full street detail of the highlighted area see pages 122 and 123.

Scale: 1⅓ inches to 1 mile
0 ¼ ½ mile
0 250m 500m 750m 1 km
A B C D E F
8 7 6 5 4 3 2 1
76 75 74 73 72 71 70 69
22 23 24 25 26 27
Flamborough Outer Headland Nature Reserve
Scab Scar
Thornwick Bay
Holmes Scar
North Cliff
West Scar
Sixpenny Hill Plantation
Holiday Centre
Thornwick Farm
THORNWICK RD
PH
NORTH MARINE ROAD
ST DAVID LANE
1 NORTH MARINE RD
2 MARINE VALLEY
3 NORTH MOOR RD
Breil Nook
Breil Head
Cradle Head
North Moor
Northcliff Farm
Stottle Bank Nook
The Grange
Hotel
B1255
YO15
Flamborough Head Golf Club
Selwicks Bay
Kindle Scar
CRAIKEWELLS
BEMPTON LA
B1229
EAST SCAR
GULL NOOK
MERESIDE VW
Flatmere Plantation
CH
Tower
Flamborough Outer Headland Nature Reserve
Flamborough Head
Flamborough CE VC Prim Sch
Castle
CARTER LA
PO
TOWER ST
SEA ROAD
CONSTABLE ROAD
Seaways Farm
B1259
SELWICK DR
Lighthouse
LIGHTHOUSE ROAD
Head Farm
Beacon
FLAEN CL
Liby
Ocean View Farm
High Stacks
B1255
DUNNSCROFT
SOUTH SEA MS
SOUTH SEA ROAD
Flamborough
Cattlemere Scar
Old Fall Plantation
Beacon Farm
South Landing Nature Reserve
The Timoneer
Beacon Hill
Visitor Centre
SOUTH SEA RD
South Landing
South Cliff
IRB Sta
Great Scars

A2
1 WOODCOCK RD
2 BEECH GR
3 BEECH AVE
4 GARENDS RD
5 NORTH END
6 CHAPEL ST
7 HIGH ST
8 GREENSIDE
9 MERESIDE
10 SCHOOL LA
11 OGLE RD
12 POST OFFICE ST
13 DOG AND DUCK SQ
14 ALLISON LA
15 STYLEFIELD RD
16 CASTLE CR
17 STOTTLEBINK
18 CONSTABLE CL
19 CHURCH ST
20 WATER LA
21 WEST ST
22 HARTENDALE CL
23 BUTLERS LA
24 CHURCH LA
25 CHURCH CL
26 SOUTH SEA AVE
27 CHAPEL CL

Scale: 1⅓ inches to 1 mile
0 ¼ ½ mile
0 250m 500m 750m 1 km

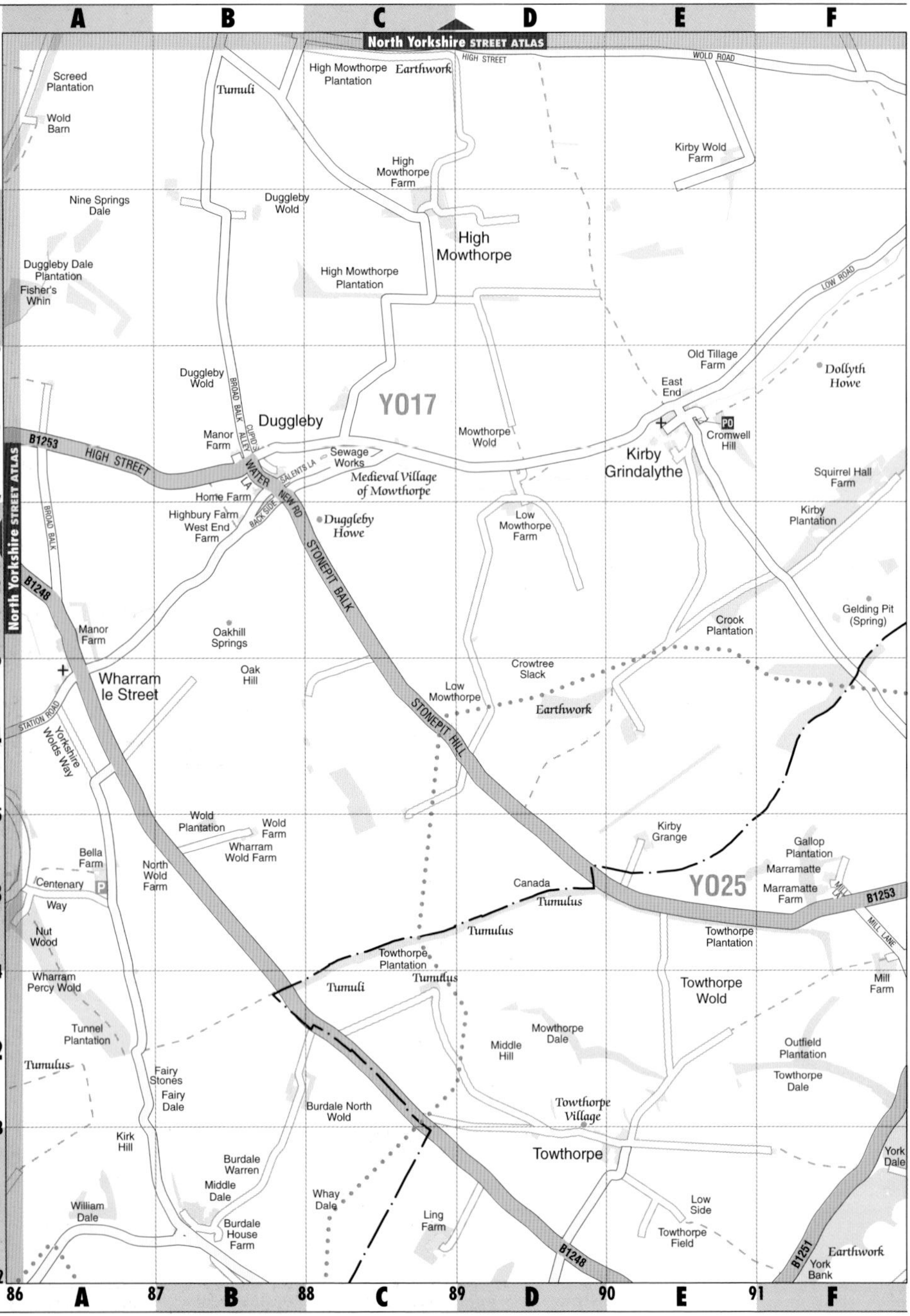
A
B
C
D
E
F
North Yorkshire STREET ATLAS
HIGH STREET
WOLD ROAD
Screed Plantation
Wold Barn
Tumuli
High Mowthorpe Plantation
Earthwork
High Mowthorpe Farm
Kirby Wold Farm
Nine Springs Dale
Duggleby Wold
High Mowthorpe
Duggleby Dale Plantation
Fisher's Whin
High Mowthorpe Plantation
LOW ROAD
Old Tillage Farm
Dollyth Howe
Duggleby Wold
BROAD BALK
CUPIDS ALLEY
Duggleby
YO17
East End
PO
Cromwell Hill
Mowthorpe Wold
Manor Farm
B1253
HIGH STREET
Sewage Works
WATER LA
SALENTS LA
Kirby Grindalythe
Medieval Village of Mowthorpe
Squirrel Hall Farm
Home Farm
NEW RD
BACK SIDE
Highbury Farm West End Farm
Duggleby Howe
Low Mowthorpe Farm
Kirby Plantation
BROAD BALK
STONEPIT BALK
B1248
Gelding Pit (Spring)
Crook Plantation
Manor Farm
Oakhill Springs
Oak Hill
Crowtree Slack
Wharram le Street
Low Mowthorpe
STONEPIT HILL
Earthwork
STATION ROAD
Yorkshire Wolds Way
Wold Plantation
Wold Farm
Kirby Grange
Gallop Plantation
Bella Farm
Wharram Wold Farm
Marramatte
North Wold Farm
Canada
YO25
Marramatte Farm
Centenary Way
P
Tumulus
MILL LA
B1253
Nut Wood
Tumulus
Towthorpe Plantation
MILL LANE
Towthorpe Plantation
Wharram Percy Wold
Tumuli
Tumulus
Towthorpe Wold
Mill Farm
Tunnel Plantation
Mowthorpe Dale
Middle Hill
Outfield Plantation
Tumulus
Fairy Stones
Towthorpe Dale
Fairy Dale
Burdale North Wold
Towthorpe Village
Kirk Hill
Towthorpe
York Dale
Burdale Warren
Middle Dale
Whay Dale
Low Side
William Dale
Burdale House Farm
Ling Farm
Towthorpe Field
B1251
Earthwork
B1248
York Bank
8
69
7
68
6
67
5
66
4
65
3
64
2
63
1
62
86
87
88
89
90
91

Scale: 1⅓ inches to 1 mile
0 ¼ ½ mile
0 250m 500m 750m 1 km

8

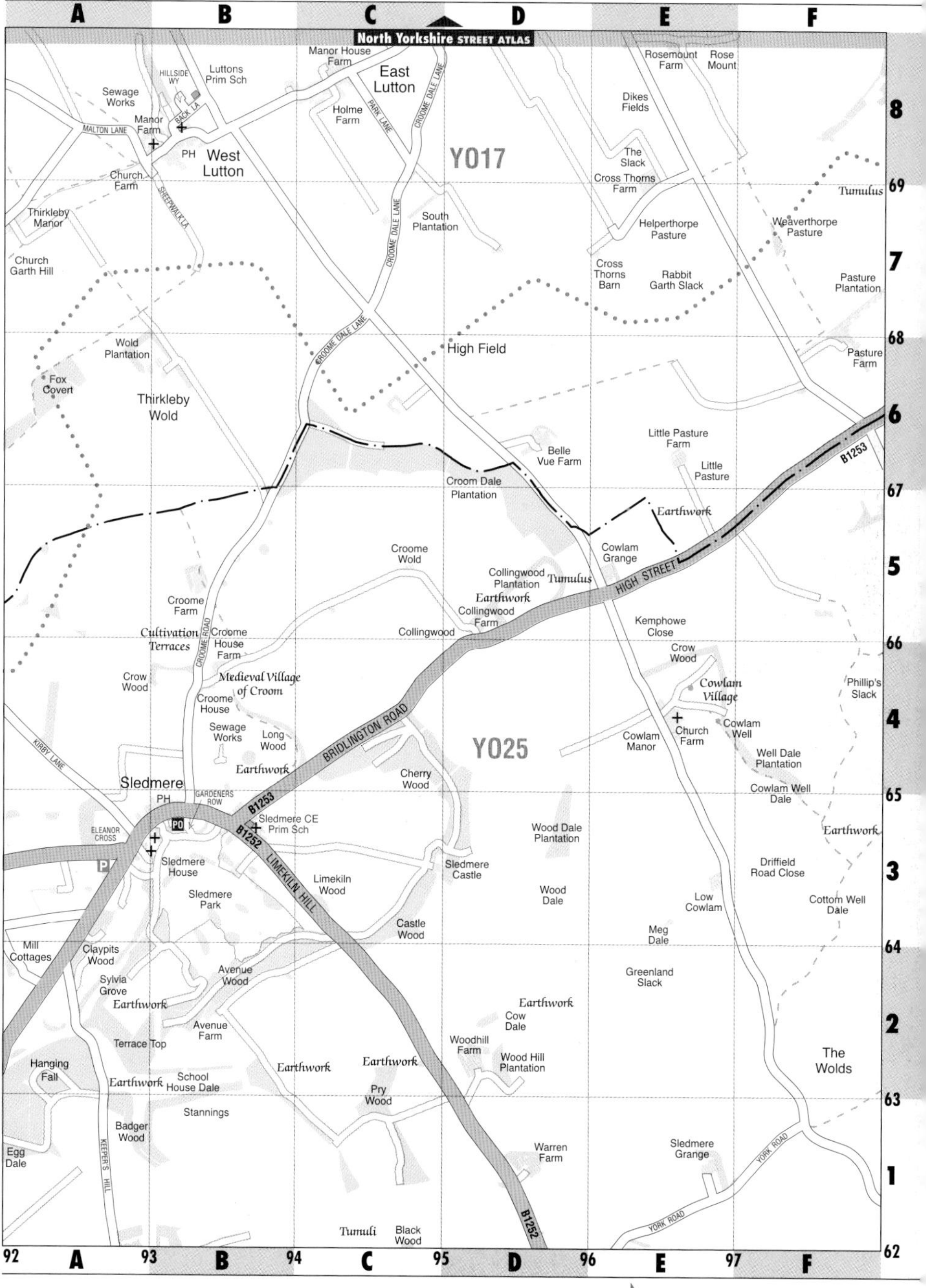

A B C D E F
North Yorkshire STREET ATLAS
Manor House Farm
East Lutton
Luttons Prim Sch
HILLSIDE WY
BACK LA
Sewage Works
Manor Farm
MALTON LANE
PH
West Lutton
Holme Farm
PARK LANE
CROOME DALE LANE
YO17
Rosemount Farm
Rose Mount
Dikes Fields
The Slack
Cross Thorns Farm
Church Farm
SHEEPWALK LA
Thirkleby Manor
Church Garth Hill
South Plantation
Helperthorpe Pasture
Weaverthorpe Pasture
Tumulus
Cross Thorns Barn
Rabbit Garth Slack
Pasture Plantation
Wold Plantation
High Field
Pasture Farm
Fox Covert
Thirkleby Wold
Little Pasture Farm
Belle Vue Farm
Little Pasture
B1253
Croom Dale Plantation
Earthwork
Croome Wold
Cowlam Grange
Collingwood Plantation
Tumulus
HIGH STREET
Croome Farm
Earthwork
Collingwood Farm
Kemphowe Close
Cultivation Terraces
Croome House Farm
CROOME ROAD
Collingwood
Crow Wood
Crow Wood
Medieval Village of Croom
Cowlam Village
Phillip's Slack
Croome House
Cowlam Well
Church Farm
Cowlam Manor
Sewage Works
Long Wood
KIRBY LANE
BRIDLINGTON ROAD
YO25
Well Dale Plantation
Earthwork
Cherry Wood
Sledmere
GARDENERS ROW
Cowlam Well Dale
PH
B1253
PO
Sledmere CE Prim Sch
ELEANOR CROSS
Wood Dale Plantation
Earthwork
B1252
P
Sledmere House
LIMEKILN HILL
Driffield Road Close
Limekiln Wood
Sledmere Castle
Sledmere Park
Wood Dale
Low Cowlam
Cottom Well Dale
Castle Wood
Meg Dale
Mill Cottages
Claypits Wood
Avenue Wood
Greenland Slack
Sylvia Grove
Earthwork
Earthwork
Cow Dale
Avenue Farm
Terrace Top
Woodhill Farm
Wood Hill Plantation
The Wolds
Hanging Fall
Earthwork
Earthwork
Earthwork
School House Dale
Pry Wood
Stannings
Badger Wood
Warren Farm
Sledmere Grange
YORK ROAD
Egg Dale
KEEPER'S HILL
Tumuli
Black Wood
B1252
YORK ROAD
8 69 7 68 6 67 5 66 4 65 3 64 2 63 1 62
92 93 94 95 96 97

19
8

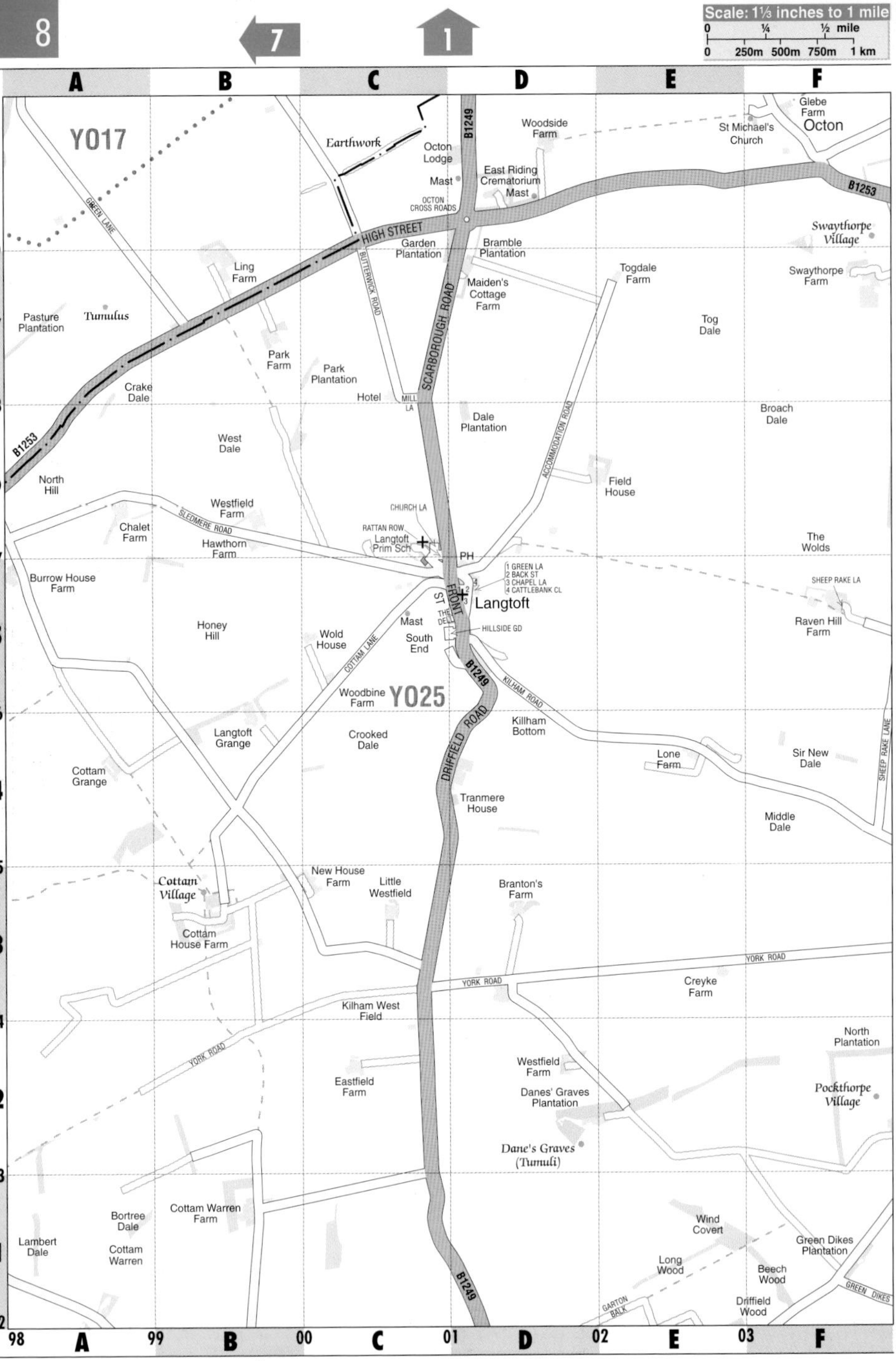
7
1
Scale: 1⅓ inches to 1 mile
0 ¼ ½ mile
0 250m 500m 750m 1 km
A B C D E F
YO17
Earthwork
Octon Lodge
B1249
Woodside Farm
Glebe Farm
Octon
St Michael's Church
East Riding Crematorium
Mast
Mast
OCTON CROSS ROADS
B1253
GREEN LANE
HIGH STREET
Garden Plantation
Bramble Plantation
Swaythorpe Village
Swaythorpe Farm
Ling Farm
BUTTERWICK ROAD
Maiden's Cottage Farm
Togdale Farm
Pasture Plantation
Tumulus
SCARBOROUGH ROAD
Tog Dale
Park Farm
Park Plantation
Crake Dale
Hotel
MILL LA
Dale Plantation
ACCOMMODATION ROAD
Broach Dale
West Dale
North Hill
Field House
Westfield Farm
CHURCH LA
SLEDMERE ROAD
Chalet Farm
RATTAN ROW
Langtoft Prim Sch
PH
The Wolds
Hawthorn Farm
1 GREEN LA
2 BACK ST
3 CHAPEL LA
4 CATTLEBANK CL
Burrow House Farm
SHEEP RAKE LA
FRONT ST
Langtoft
THE DELL
HILLSIDE GD
Honey Hill
Wold House
Mast
South End
Raven Hill Farm
COTTAM LANE
KILHAM ROAD
Woodbine Farm
YO25
Crooked Dale
DRIFFIELD ROAD
Killham Bottom
Langtoft Grange
Lone Farm
Sir New Dale
SHEEP RAKE LANE
Cottam Grange
Tranmere House
Middle Dale
New House Farm
Little Westfield
Branton's Farm
Cottam Village
Cottam House Farm
YORK ROAD
YORK ROAD
Creyke Farm
Kilham West Field
North Plantation
YORK ROAD
Westfield Farm
Eastfield Farm
Danes' Graves Plantation
Pockthorpe Village
Dane's Graves (Tumuli)
Cottam Warren Farm
Bortree Dale
Wind Covert
Green Dikes Plantation
Lambert Dale
Cottam Warren
Long Wood
Beech Wood
GREEN DIKES
GARTON BALK
Driffield Wood
8
69
7
68
6
67
5
66
4
65
3
64
2
63
1
62
98 A 99 B 00 C 01 D 02 E 03 F

Scale: 1⅓ inches to 1 mile
0 ¼ ½ mile
0 250m 500m 750m 1 km

2
10

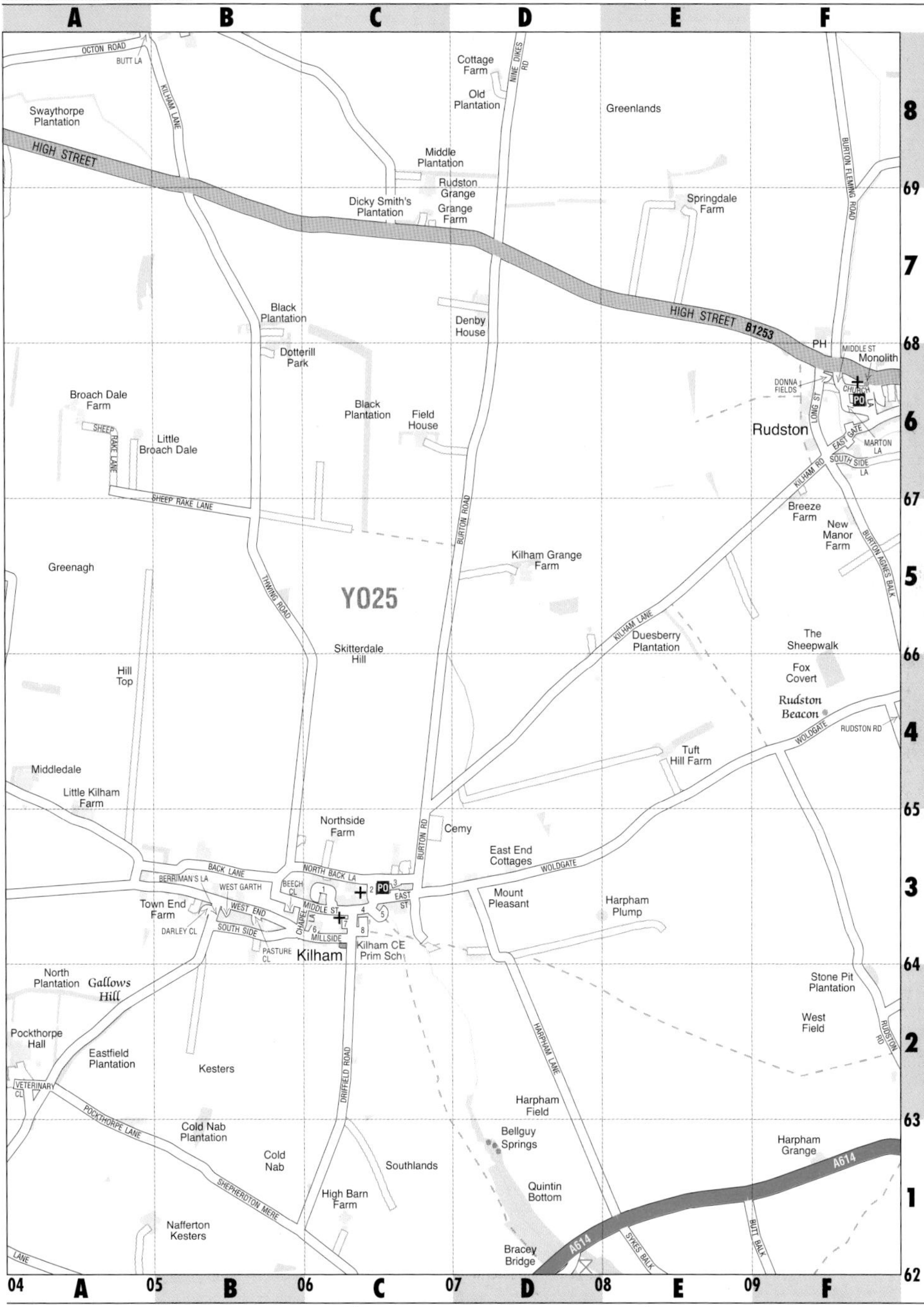

C3
1 CHANTRY MDWS
2 CHURCH LA
3 ROPERY CL
4 CHURCH ST
5 BAKEHOUSE LA
6 MILL SIDE CL
7 SOUTH CL
8 SOUTH GR

21
10

9
3

Scale: 1⅓ inches to 1 mile
0 ¼ ½ mile
0 250m 500m 750m 1 km

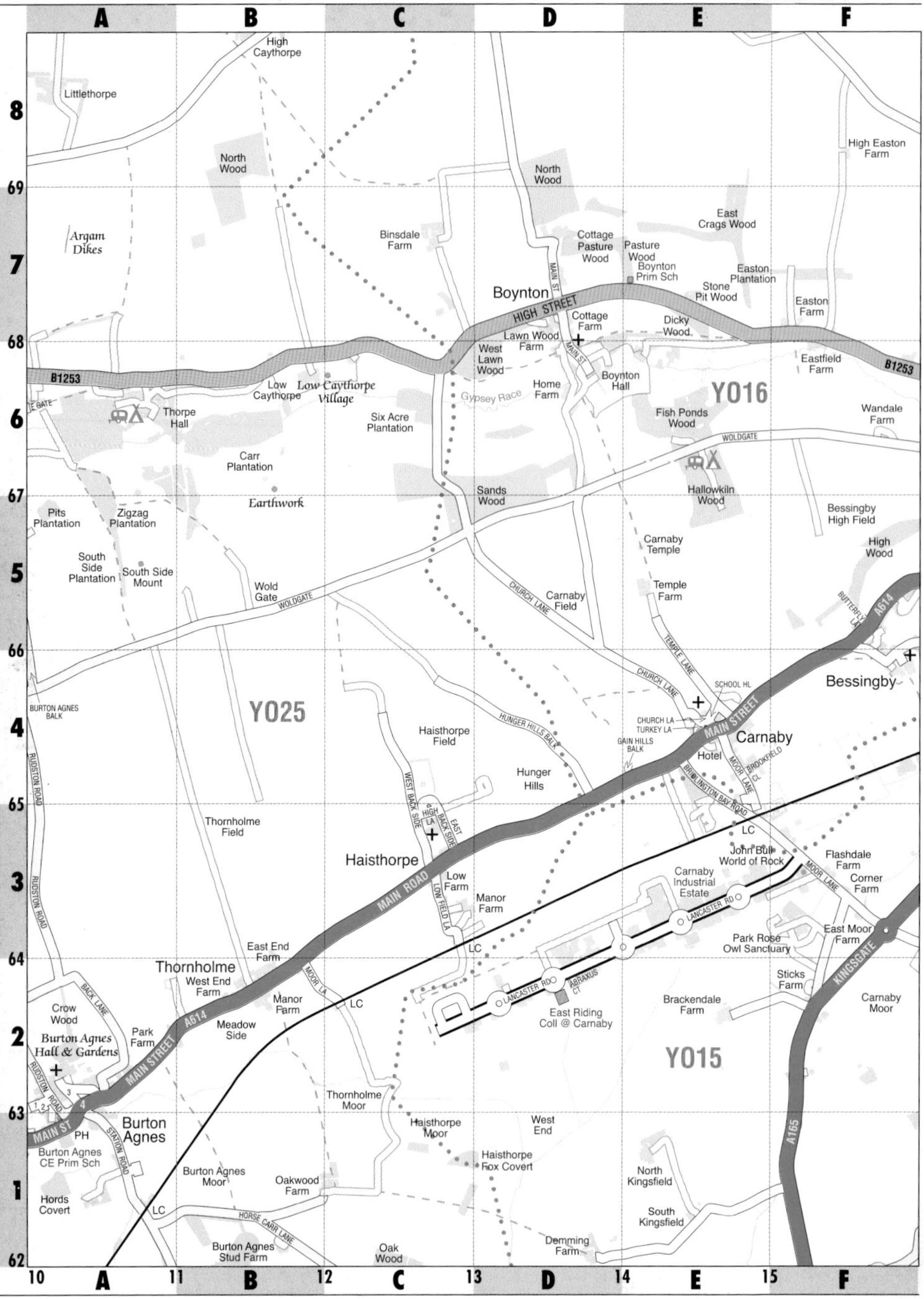
A B C D E F
8
69
7
68
6
67
5
66
4
65
3
64
2
63
1
62
10 A 11 B 12 C 13 D 14 E 15 F
High Caythorpe
Littlethorpe
North Wood
North Wood
High Easton Farm
Argam Dikes
Binsdale Farm
Cottage Pasture Wood
Pasture Wood
East Crags Wood
Boynton Prim Sch
Easton Plantation
Stone Pit Wood
Easton Farm
Boynton
HIGH STREET
MAIN ST
Cottage Farm
Lawn Wood Farm
Dicky Wood
West Lawn Wood
B1253
Low Caythorpe
Low Caythorpe Village
Gypsey Race
Home Farm
Boynton Hall
Eastfield Farm
YO16
Thorpe Hall
Six Acre Plantation
Fish Ponds Wood
Wandale Farm
WOLDGATE
Carr Plantation
Hallowkiln Wood
Sands Wood
Earthwork
Pits Plantation
Zigzag Plantation
Bessingby High Field
Carnaby Temple
High Wood
South Side Plantation
South Side Mount
Wold Gate
Temple Farm
CHURCH LANE
Carnaby Field
BUTTERFLY LA
A614
TEMPLE LANE
Bessingby
BURTON AGNES BALK
YO25
SCHOOL HL
CHURCH LA
TURKEY LA
GAIN HILLS BALK
MAIN STREET
Carnaby
Haisthorpe Field
HUNGER HILLS BALK
Hunger Hills
Hotel
MOOR LANE
BROOKFIELD CL
BRIDLINGTON BAY ROAD
RUDSTON ROAD
WEST BACK SIDE
HIGH LA
EAST BACK SIDE
Thornholme Field
LC
John Bull World of Rock
Flashdale Farm
Haisthorpe
MAIN ROAD
Low Farm
LOW FIELD LA
Carnaby Industrial Estate
Corner Farm
Manor Farm
LANCASTER RD
East Moor Farm
Park Rose Owl Sanctuary
East End Farm
Thornholme
KINGSGATE
Sticks Farm
West End Farm
Manor Farm
MOOR LA
ABRAXUS CT
Brackendale Farm
Carnaby Moor
Crow Wood
BACK LANE
Meadow Side
East Riding Coll @ Carnaby
Park Farm
Burton Agnes Hall & Gardens
YO15
Thornholme Moor
Haisthorpe Moor
West End
MAIN ST
PH
Burton Agnes
STATION ROAD
Burton Agnes CE Prim Sch
Haisthorpe Fox Covert
A165
Burton Agnes Moor
Oakwood Farm
North Kingsfield
Hords Covert
HORSE CARR LANE
South Kingsfield
Burton Agnes Stud Farm
Oak Wood
Demming Farm

A2
1 ST MARTIN'S DR
2 ST MARTIN'S CL
3 SHADY LA
4 HOSPITAL HL

9
22

Scale: 1⅓ inches to 1 mile
0 ¼ ½ mile
0 250m 500m 750m 1 km

4

A
B
C
D
E
F
122
123
The Grange
Hill Field
Grindale Lane
Scarborough Road
A165
Pinfold Lane
Bempton Lane
Stackyard Plantation
Jewison La
Flamborough Rd
Marton
Gell-spring Plantation
Home Farm
Leys Plantation
Long Wood
Moor Road
Dyke Wood
Nature Reserve
Needles Plantation
YO15
Dane Dykes Farm
Dykes End
Marton Gate
B1255
Charity Farm
Church La
Sewerby Hall
Moor Rd
CH
Pinfold La Ind Est
County Farm
YO16
Thoresby Rd
Darwin Rd
Bempton Ovl
Liby
Sandsacre Ave
Beech Dr
Viking Road
Main St
PH
Sewerby Village
Sewerby Rocks
PO
Sch
Mill Lane
B1255 Marton Road
Sewerby Fields
Rock Ends
Sewerby
Prim Sch
Burstall Hl
New Pasture Lane
Sewerby Rd
Old Town
Fortyfoot
Lambert Rd
Queensgate
Harland Rd
Omega Rd
Limekiln Lane
Eighth Ave
Second Av
First Av
North Marine Drive
Easton Rd
Westgate
High St
South Back La
St John's St
Cemy
Coll
St Alban Rd
Brookland Rd
Milner Rd
Bridlington Town FC
Bridlington RUFC
B1254
Promenade
BRIDLINGTON
Bessingby Hl
Bridlington & District
H
LC
Trinity Rd
Tennyson Ave
A1038
Quay Rd
Bessingby Rd
Midway Av
Bridlington
Hilderthorpe Rd
A614
Wright Cr
Windsor Cr
Mus
West Hill
Ind Est
Bessingby Wy
Georgian Wy
St James Rd
East Rd
Richmond St
Horsforth Av
Cardigan Rd
Marine Dr
The Spa
Brick Kiln Balk
Main St
Middle Wood
Kingsgate
Kingston Rd
Hilderthorpe
Church Plantation
Hilderthorpe Village
Belvedere Rd
Belvedere Parade
1 KINGSTON CR
2 TRAFALGAR CRES
3 AVOCET WAY
4 TEAL GARTH
5 HERON MEWS
6 CURLEW GREEN
7 KINGFISHER DR
8 PARTRIDGE CL
9 KINGSTON CL
10 BELVEDERE CL
Bridlington Bay
Southcliff Caravan Park
Wilsthorpe Covert
Bridge Farm
Cliff Farm
Wilsthorpe Village
Wilsthorpe
Sewage
YO15
Auburn Farm
Auburn Village
P
8
69
7
68
6
67
5
66
4
65
3
64
2
63
1
62
16
17
18
19
20
21

23

For full street detail of the highlighted area see pages 122 and 123.

Scale: 1⅓ inches to 1 mile
0 ¼ ½ mile
0 250m 500m 750m 1 km

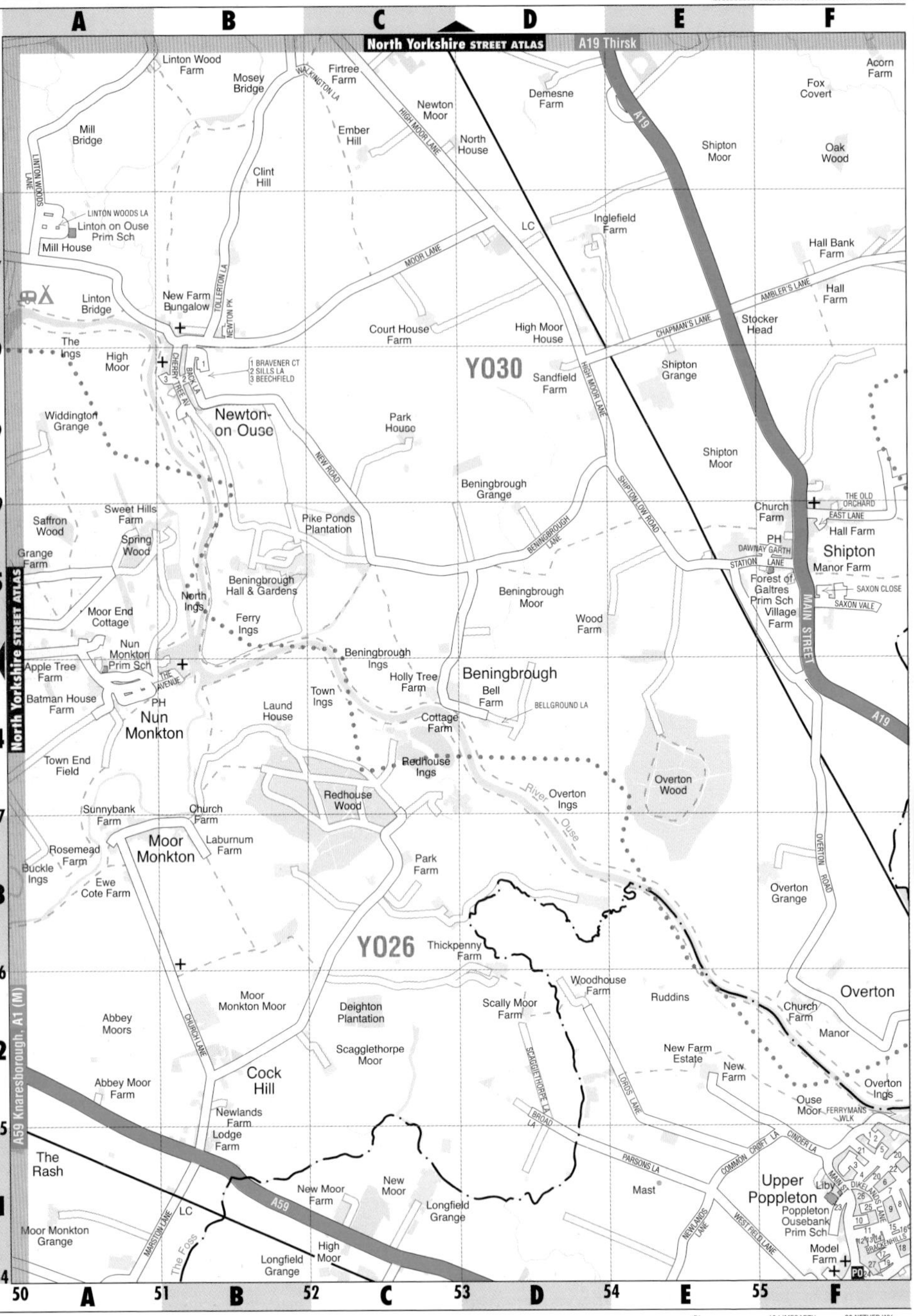
A B C D E F
North Yorkshire STREET ATLAS
A19 Thirsk
8
61
7
60
6
59
5
4
57
3
56
2
55
1
54
50 51 52 53 54 55
Linton Wood Farm
Mosey Bridge
Firtree Farm
WALKINGTON LA
Newton Moor
HIGH MOOR LANE
North House
Ember Hill
Demesne Farm
Fox Covert
Acorn Farm
Mill Bridge
LINTON WOODS LANE
Clint Hill
Shipton Moor
Oak Wood
A19
LINTON WOODS LA
Linton on Ouse Prim Sch
Mill House
LC
Inglefield Farm
Hall Bank Farm
MOOR LANE
TOLLERTON LA
Linton Bridge
New Farm Bungalow
NEWTON PK
Court House Farm
High Moor House
AMBLER'S LANE
CHAPMAN'S LANE
Hall Farm
Stocker Head
The Ings
High Moor
1 BRAVENER CT
2 SILLS LA
3 BEECHFIELD
CHERRY TREE AV
BACK LA
YO30
Sandfield Farm
Shipton Grange
Widdington Grange
Newton-on-Ouse
Park House
NEW ROAD
Shipton Moor
Beningbrough Grange
SHIPTON LOW ROAD
Saffron Wood
Sweet Hills Farm
Pike Ponds Plantation
BENINGBROUGH LANE
Church Farm
THE OLD ORCHARD
EAST LANE
Hall Farm
Spring Wood
PH
DAWNAY GARTH
STATION LANE
Shipton
Manor Farm
Grange Farm
Beningbrough Hall & Gardens
Forest of Galtres Prim Sch
SAXON CLOSE
SAXON VALE
North Ings
Ferry Ings
Beningbrough Moor
Wood Farm
Village Farm
MAIN STREET
Moor End Cottage
Nun Monkton Prim Sch
Apple Tree Farm
THE AVENUE
Beningbrough Ings
Holly Tree Farm
Beningbrough
Town Ings
Bell Farm
BELLGROUND LA
Batman House Farm
PH
Laund House
Cottage Farm
Nun Monkton
A19
Town End Field
Redhouse Ings
River Ouse
Overton Ings
Overton Wood
Redhouse Wood
Sunnybank Farm
Church Farm
Moor Monkton
Laburnum Farm
OVERTON ROAD
Rosemead Farm
Park Farm
Buckle Ings
Ewe Cote Farm
Overton Grange
YO26
Thickpenny Farm
Woodhouse Farm
Moor Monkton Moor
Deighton Plantation
Scally Moor Farm
Ruddins
Overton
Abbey Moors
CHURCH LANE
Church Farm
Manor
Scagglethorpe Moor
SCAGGLETHORPE LA
New Farm Estate
A59 Knaresborough, A1 (M)
Abbey Moor Farm
Cock Hill
LORDS LANE
New Farm
Overton Ings
Newlands Farm
Ouse Moor
FERRYMANS WLK
Lodge Farm
BROAD LA
The Rash
CINDER LA
PARSONS LA
COMMON CROFT LA
New Moor Farm
New Moor
Mast
Upper Poppleton
Liby
MAIN ST
DIKELANDS LANE
A59
Longfield Grange
Poppleton Ousebank Prim Sch
LC
NEWLANDS LANE
WEST FIELD LANE
Moor Monkton Grange
MARSTON LANE
The Foss
High Moor
Model Farm
BRACKENHILLS
Longfield Grange
PO
North Yorkshire STREET ATLAS

24

F1
1 RIVERSIDE WALK
2 RIVERSIDE GDNS
3 BANKSIDE CL
4 SPRINGFIELD RD
5 LITTLEFIELD CL
6 MONTAGUE WALK
7 EBOR WAY
8 PEAR TREE AVE
9 ELM TREE AVE
10 LIMEGARTH
11 CHANTRY GAP
12 GROVE GDNS
13 CHANTRY GR
14 CHANTRY AVE
15 APPLE GARTH
16 CHERRY GROVE
17 SYCAMORE VIEW
18 FAIRWAY DR
19 DIKELANDS CL
20 NETHER WY
21 RIVERSVALE DR
22 ALLERTON DR
23 SCHOOL LA
24 STATION RD
25 BEECH WY
26 THE BEECHES
27 LONGRIDGE GDNS

E5
1 VILLAGE GARTH
2 LONGCROFT
3 RIPLEY GR
4 SOUTHLANDS
5 THE AVENUE
6 REDWOOD DR
7 MULBERRY DR
8 ASH LA
9 ELM END
10 COPPICE CL
11 LITTLE LA
12 HAWTHORN AVE
13 BIRCH LA
14 FLETCHER CT
15 ST MARY'S CL
16 SANDY LA
17 CHURCH LA
18 BROAD OAK LA
19 WESTFIELD PL
20 WESTFIELD RD
21 WESTFIELD CL
22 ST NICHOLAS WY
23 PLANTATION WY
24 MIDDLE BANKS
25 HORNSEY GARTH
26 GLEBE WY
27 FOREST CL
28 CHURCHFIELD DR
29 SANDYLAND
30 HEADLAND CL
31 WANDHILL
32 KENNEDY DR
33 ABELTON GR
34 ORCHARD PADDOCK
35 LARCH WY
36 ACACIA GR
37 CYPRUS GR
38 ELDER GR
39 WALNUT CL
40 MINSTER CL

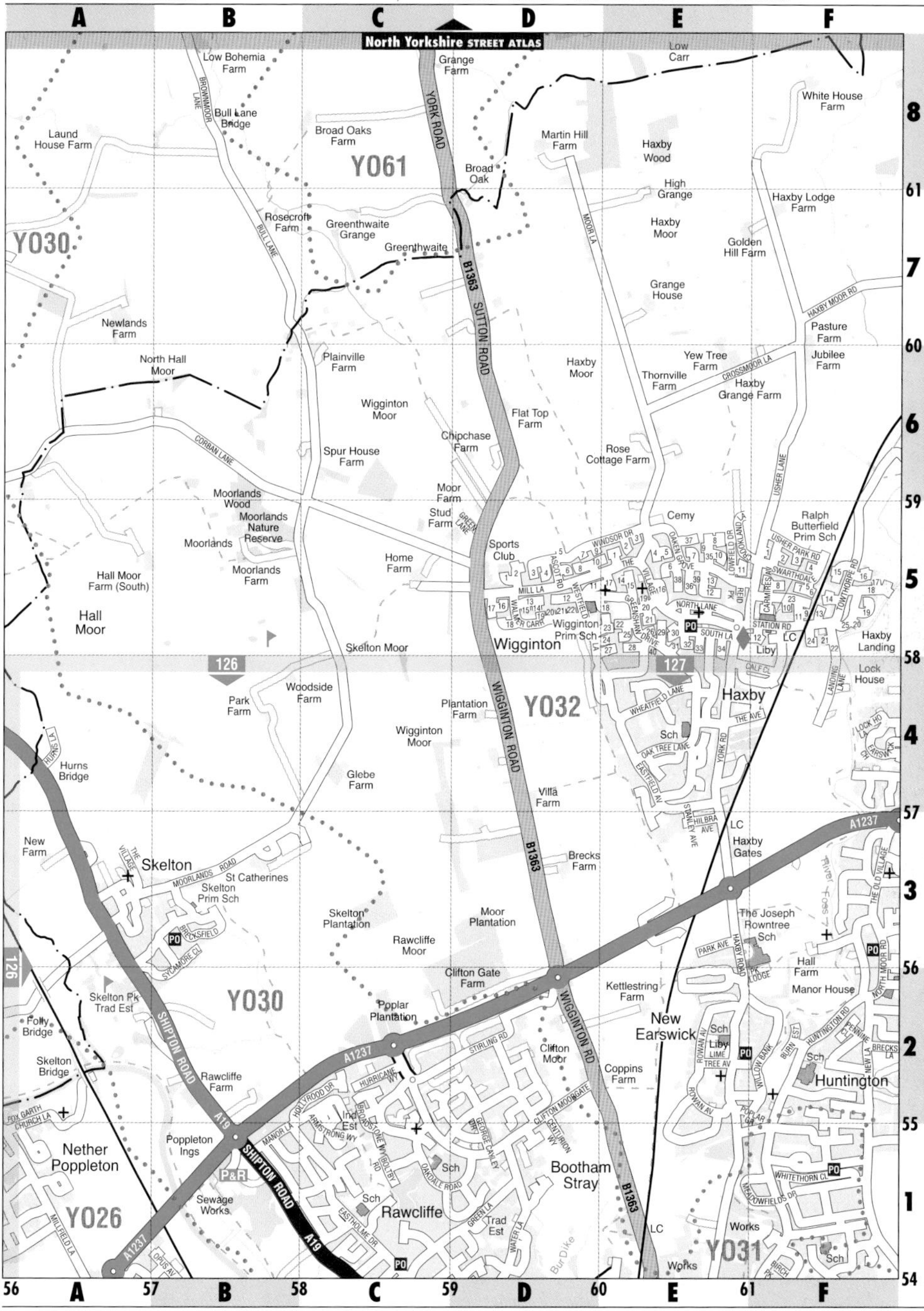
A B C D E F
North Yorkshire STREET ATLAS
Low Bohemia Farm
Grange Farm
Low Carr
White House Farm
BROWNMOOR LANE
Bull Lane Bridge
Laund House Farm
Broad Oaks Farm
YORK ROAD
YO61
Martin Hill Farm
Haxby Wood
Broad Oak
High Grange
Haxby Lodge Farm
YO30
Rosecroft Farm
Greenthwaite Grange
Greenthwaite
BULL LANE
MOOR LA
Haxby Moor
Golden Hill Farm
B1363 SUTTON ROAD
Grange House
HAXBY MOOR RD
Newlands Farm
Pasture Farm
North Hall Moor
Plainville Farm
Haxby Moor
Yew Tree Farm
Jubilee Farm
Thornville Farm
CROSSMOOR LA
Haxby Grange Farm
Wigginton Moor
Flat Top Farm
CORBAN LANE
Chipchase Farm
Spur House Farm
Rose Cottage Farm
USHER LANE
Moorlands Wood
Moor Farm
Moorlands Nature Reserve
Stud Farm
GREEN LANE
Cemy
Ralph Butterfield Prim Sch
Moorlands
Sports Club
WINDSOR DR
USHER PARK RD
Home Farm
Moorlands Farm
Hall Moor Farm (South)
MILL LA
WALMER CARR
NORTH LANE
SOUTH LA
STATION RD
Hall Moor
Wigginton Prim Sch
Wigginton
Haxby Landing
Lock House
Skelton Moor
126
127
CALF CL
Park Farm
Woodside Farm
Plantation Farm
YO32
WHEATFIELD LANE
Haxby
THE AVE
Wigginton Moor
Sch
OAK TREE LANE
YORK RD
HURNS LA
Hurns Bridge
Glebe Farm
WIGGINTON ROAD
Villa Farm
EASTFIELD AV
HILBRA AVE
STANLEY AVE
LC
Haxby Gates
New Farm
A1237
Skelton
MOORLANDS ROAD
St Catherines
Skelton Prim Sch
B1363
Brecks Farm
River Foss
THE OLD VILLAGE
The Joseph Rowntree Sch
Skelton Plantation
Moor Plantation
Rawcliffe Moor
PARK AVE
HAXBY ROAD
Hall Farm
Manor House
Clifton Gate Farm
Kettlestring Farm
NORTH MOOR RD
Skelton Pk Trad Est
YO30
Poplar Plantation
New Earswick
ROWAN AV
LIME TREE AV
WILLOW BANK
HUNTINGTON RD
Folly Bridge
SHIPTON ROAD
A1237
STIRLING RD
Clifton Moor
Coppins Farm
Huntington
Skelton Bridge
Rawcliffe Farm
HURRICANE WY
Ind Est
CLIFTON MOORGATE
CENTURION WY
FOX GARTH
CHURCH LA
Nether Poppleton
Poppleton Ings
HOLLYROOD DR
ARMSTRONG WY
GEORGE CAYLEY DR
Bootham Stray
WHITETHORN CL
MANOR LA
A19
SHIPTON ROAD
P&R
OAKDALE ROAD
B1363
MEADOWFIELDS DR
Sewage Works
Sch
Rawcliffe
GREEN LA
Trad Est
Works
YO26
MILLFIELD LA
EASTHOLME DR
WATER LA
Bur Dike
LC
YO31
Works
A1237
Sch
8 61 7 60 6 59 5 58 4 57 3 56 2 55 1 54
56 A 57 B 58 C 59 D 60 E 61 F

For full street detail of the highlighted area see pages 126 and 127.

129

128

D5
1 CASTLE CL
2 WINDSOR DR
3 TOWN END GDNS
4 STEEPLE CL
5 HAREWOOD CL
6 DELAMERE CL
7 ETON DR
8 SAXFORD WAY
9 CANTERBURY CL
10 HAMBLETON VIEW
11 BACK LA
12 WESTFIELD GR
13 BURRILL DR
14 TWIN PIKE WY
15 STABLER CL
16 HELMSLEY GR
17 CORNER CL
18 LANCAR CL
19 WATERINGS
20 BUTTERS CL
21 CORBAN WY
22 BUTT HILL

F5
1 FARNDALE CL
2 SANDHOLME
3 NEWDALE
4 KELDALE
5 NORTHCROFT
6 RUSHWOOD CL
7 LANSDOWN WY
8 SCRIVEN GR
9 WOODCOCK CL
10 FALCON CL
11 MALLARD WY
12 HALL RISE
13 FOLKS CL
14 OLD COPPICE
15 NEW FORGE CT
16 CHATSWORTH DR
17 RIVERSDALE
18 NETHERWINDINGS
19 THORNHILLS
20 GARTHS END
21 THE LANDINGS
22 LANDING LA
23 WINDMILL WY
24 LINLEY AVE
25 WEST NOOKS

130

A7
1 LEYFIELD CL
2 MOORLAND GARTH
3 WILKINSON WY
4 FOSSLAND VW
5 RIVERSIDE WK
6 LOW CFT
7 WOOD CL
8 ADLINGTON CL
9 FIRBANK CL
10 OSMINGTON GDNS
11 MELCOMBE AVE
12 PORTISHAM PL
13 LADYSMITH MS
14 SUSSEX WY
15 PELHAM PL

B7
1 ORCHARD WY
2 MIDDLECROFT GR
3 GLEBE CL
4 STATION SQ
5 HIGHLANDS AVE
6 OAKLANDS
7 HALLARD WY
8 THE WILLOWS
9 WEST END CL
10 OAK TREE WY
11 HARVEST CL

13

B8
1 LAKESIDE GR
2 THOMPSON DR
3 BLACKLEE CL
4 NORTHFIELDS
5 NETHERWOODS
6 LITTLETHORPE CL

C8
1 CHAPMAN CL
2 BRUNSWICK CL
3 PULLEYN CL
4 STUART CL
5 COULSON CL
6 CUNDALL CL

Scale: 1⅓ inches to 1 mile
0 ¼ ½ mile
0 250m 500m 750m 1 km

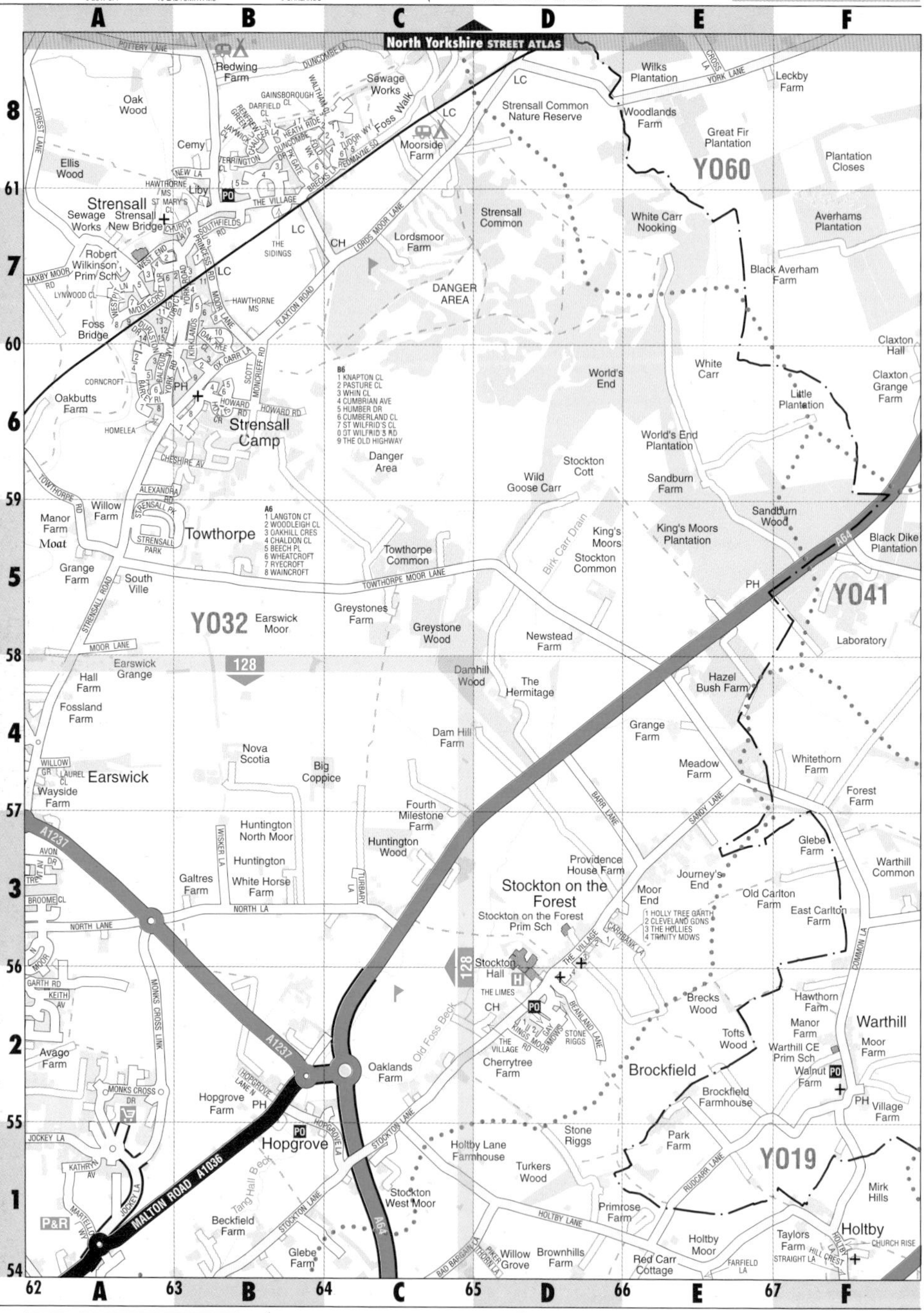

For full street detail of the highlighted area see page 128.
13
131
26

D2
1 CHAUMONT WY
2 MARMIAM DR

Scale: 1⅓ inches to 1 mile
0 ¼ ½ mile
0 250m 500m 750m 1 km

16

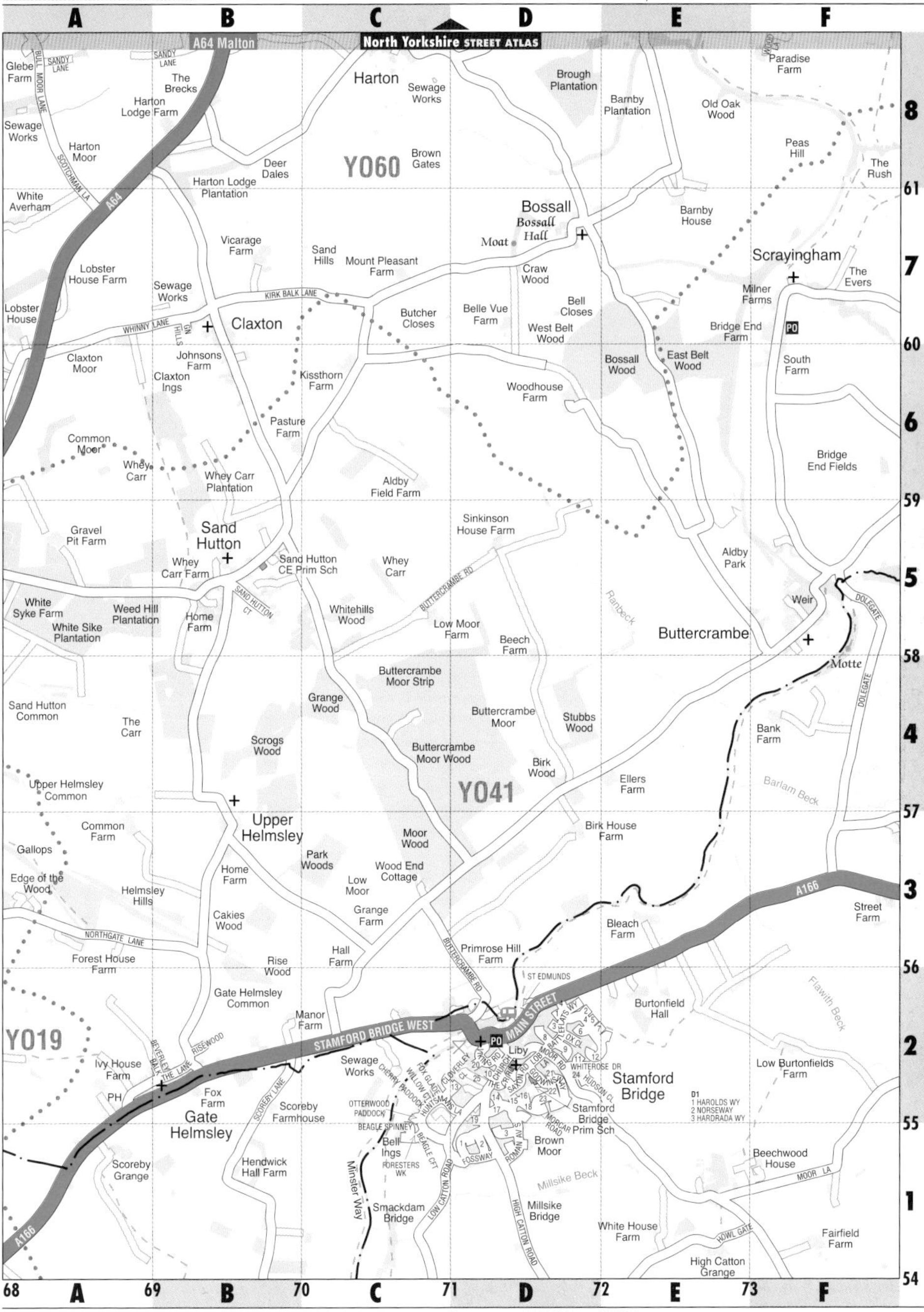

27

D2
1 BRIDLINGTON RD
2 DERWENT CL
3 DANESWELL CL
4 BURTON FIELDS RD
5 GARROWBY VW
6 KINGSWAY
7 DARLEY CL
8 WHARTON RD
9 ST JOHN'S RD
10 CHURCH LA
11 EGREMONT CL
12 BURTON FIELDS CL
13 HEATHER BANK
14 TOSTIG CL
15 FAIRFAX
16 SCHOOL CL
17 ROMAN AVE N
18 GODWINSWAY
19 BUTTS CL
20 VIKING CL
21 MIDGLEY CL
22 BROWN MOOR
23 FURLONG RD
24 ETTY CL
25 STONE WALL COTTAGE LA

16

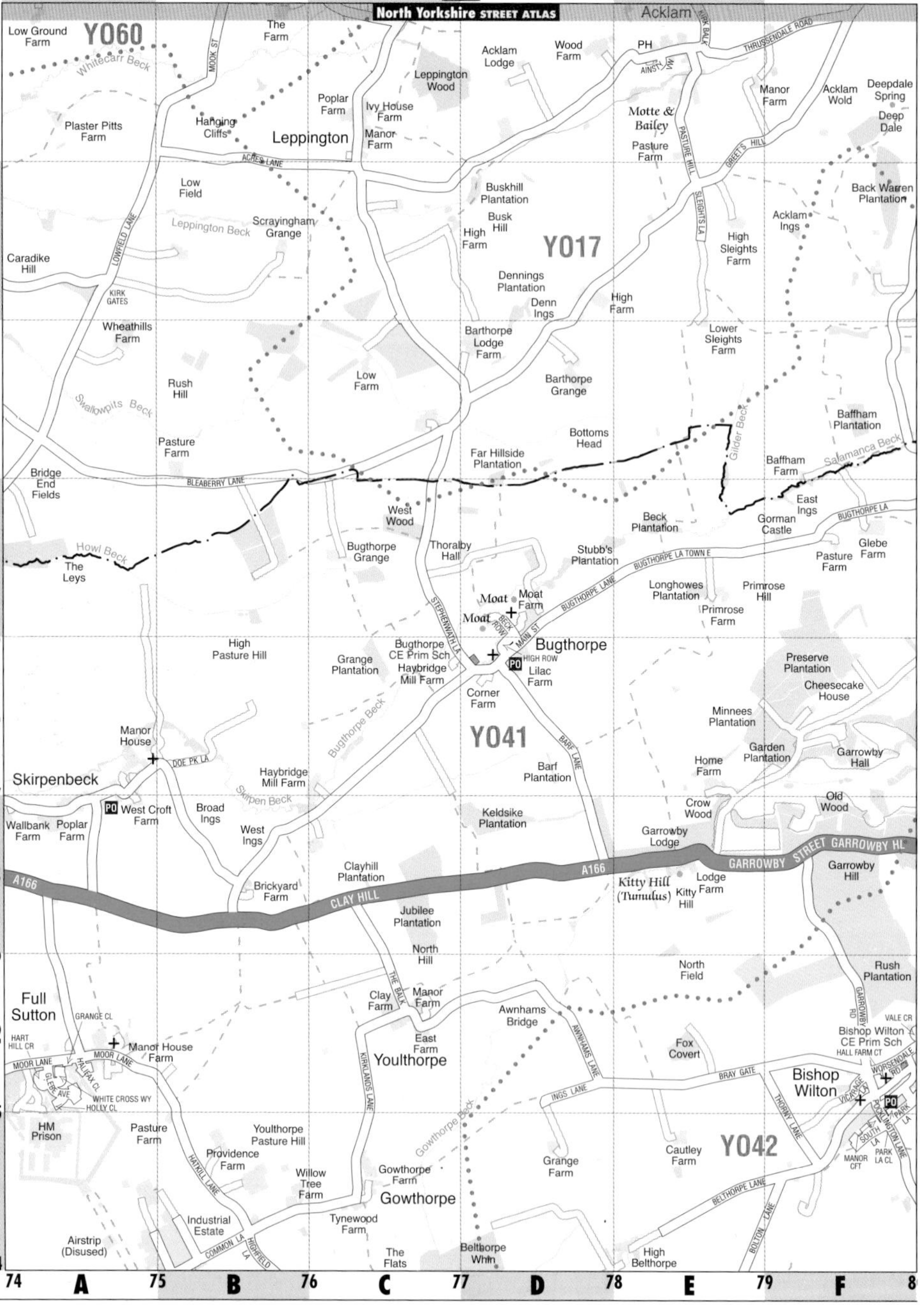
YO60
YO17
YO41
YO42
Low Ground Farm
Whitecarr Beck
The Farm
Acklam
Acklam Lodge
Wood Farm
PH
Leppington Wood
Poplar Farm
Ivy House Farm
Manor Farm
Plaster Pitts Farm
Hanging Cliffs
Leppington
Motte & Bailey
Pasture Farm
Acklam Wold
Deepdale Spring
Deep Dale
Low Field
Leppington Beck
Scrayingham Grange
Buskhill Plantation
Busk Hill
High Farm
Back Warren Plantation
Acklam Ings
High Sleights Farm
Caradike Hill
Dennings Plantation
Denn Ings
Wheathills Farm
Barthorpe Lodge Farm
Lower Sleights Farm
Low Farm
Rush Hill
Swallowpits Beck
Barthorpe Grange
Bottoms Head
Baffham Plantation
Pasture Farm
Far Hillside Plantation
Gilder Beck
Salamanca Beck
Bridge End Fields
Baffham Farm
West Wood
Beck Plantation
East Ings
Gorman Castle
Howl Beck
The Leys
Bugthorpe Grange
Thoralby Hall
Stubb's Plantation
Glebe Farm
Pasture Farm
Longhowes Plantation
Primrose Hill
Moat
Moat Farm
Primrose Farm
High Pasture Hill
Grange Plantation
Bugthorpe CE Prim Sch
Haybridge Mill Farm
Bugthorpe
Lilac Farm
Preserve Plantation
Cheesecake House
Corner Farm
Minnees Plantation
Manor House
Bugthorpe Beck
Home Farm
Garden Plantation
Garrowby Hall
Skirpenbeck
Haybridge Mill Farm
Barf Plantation
Skirpen Beck
West Croft Farm
Broad Ings
Keldsike Plantation
Crow Wood
Old Wood
Wallbank Farm
Poplar Farm
West Ings
Garrowby Lodge
Clayhill Plantation
A166
CLAY HILL
GARROWBY STREET GARROWBY HL
Garrowby Hill
Brickyard Farm
Kitty Hill (Tumulus)
Kitty Hill
Lodge Farm
Jubilee Plantation
North Hill
North Field
Rush Plantation
Full Sutton
Clay Farm
Manor Farm
Awnhams Bridge
Manor House Farm
East Farm
Youlthorpe
Fox Covert
Bishop Wilton CE Prim Sch
Bishop Wilton
HM Prison
Pasture Farm
Youlthorpe Pasture Hill
Providence Farm
Willow Tree Farm
Gowthorpe Farm
Gowthorpe Beck
Gowthorpe
Grange Farm
Cautley Farm
Industrial Estate
Tynewood Farm
Airstrip (Disused)
The Flats
Belthorpe Whin
High Belthorpe
MOOK ST
ACRES LANE
LOWFIELD LANE
KIRK GATES
BLEABERRY LANE
STEPHENWATH LA
BECK ROW
MAIN ST
HIGH ROW
DOE PK LA
BUGTHORPE LANE
BUGTHORPE LA TOWN E
BUGTHORPE LA
BARF LANE
THE BALK
KIRKLANDS LANE
AWNHAMS LANE
INGS LANE
BRAY GATE
THORNY LANE
BELTHORPE LANE
BOLTON LANE
HATKILL LANE
COMMON LA
HIGHFIELD LA
KIRK BALK
THRUSSENDALE ROAD
AINSTY
PASTURE HILL
SLEIGHTS LA
GREET'S HILL
GARROWBY RD
VALE CR
HALL FARM CT
WORSENDALE RD
VICARAGE LA
POCKLINGTON LANE
SOUTH LA
PARK LA
PARK LA CL
MANOR CFT
HART HILL CR
GRANGE CL
MOOR LANE
HALIFAX CL
GLEBE AVE
WHITE CROSS WY
HOLLY CL
PO

Scale: 1⅓ inches to 1 mile
0 ¼ ½ mile
0 250m 500m 750m 1 km

18

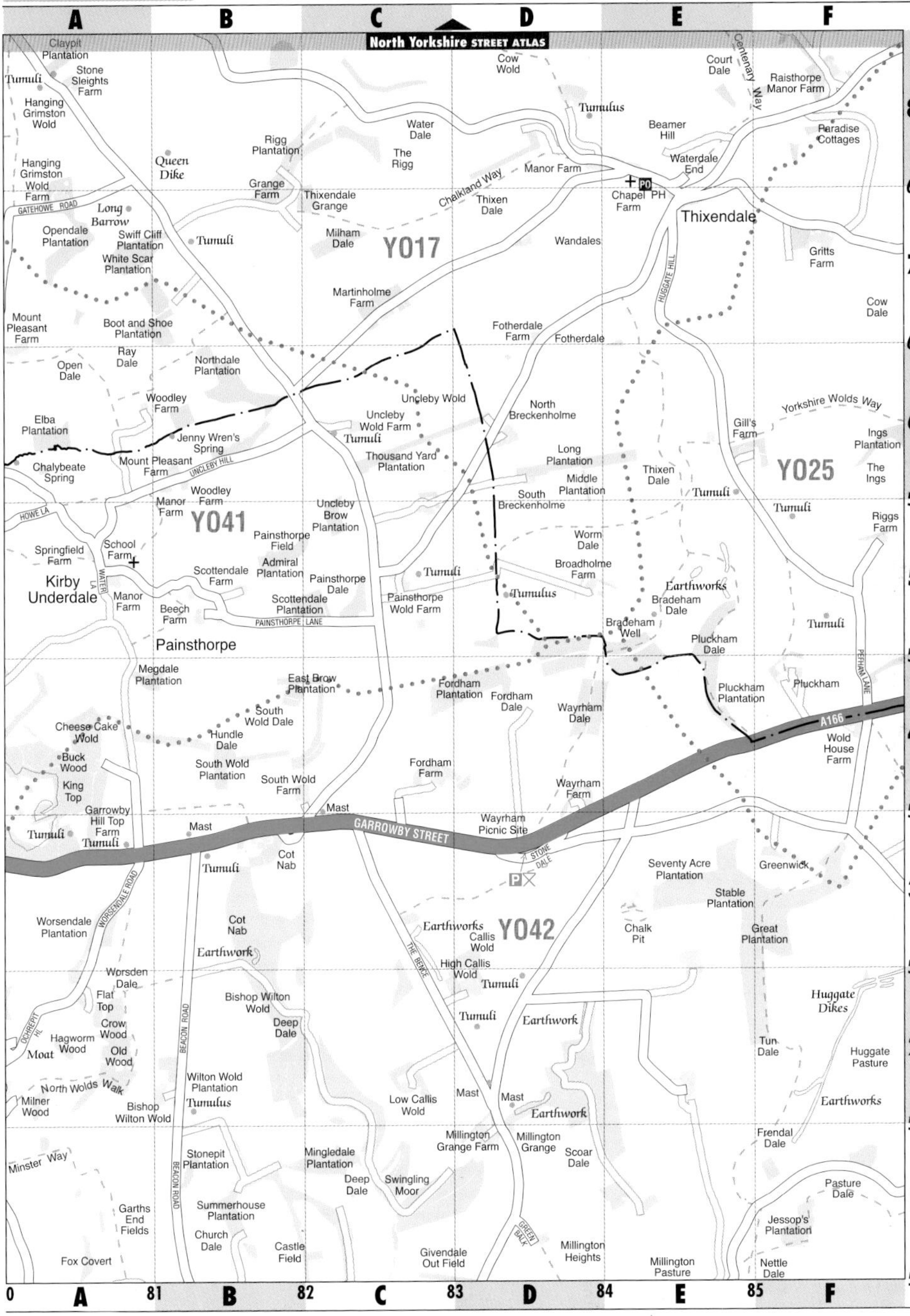

A B C D E F
North Yorkshire STREET ATLAS
Claypit Plantation
Tumuli
Stone Sleights Farm
Hanging Grimston Wold
Hanging Grimston Wold Farm
Queen Dike
GATEHOWE ROAD
Long Barrow
Opendale Plantation
Swift Cliff Plantation
White Scar Plantation
Mount Pleasant Farm
Boot and Shoe Plantation
Ray Dale
Open Dale
Northdale Plantation
Woodley Farm
Elba Plantation
Jenny Wren's Spring
Chalybeate Spring
Mount Pleasant Farm
UNCLEBY HILL
Woodley Farm
Manor Farm
HOWE LA
YO41
Springfield Farm
School Farm
Kirby Underdale
WATER LA
Manor Farm
Beech Farm
Scottendale Farm
Painsthorpe Field
Admiral Plantation
Painsthorpe
PAINSTHORPE LANE
Megdale Plantation
Cheese Cake Wold
Buck Wood
King Top
Garrowby Hill Top Farm
Mast
Rigg Plantation
Grange Farm
Thixendale Grange
Milham Dale
Water Dale
The Rigg
Chalkland Way
YO17
Martinholme Farm
Uncleby Wold
Uncleby Wold Farm
Thousand Yard Plantation
Uncleby Brow Plantation
Painsthorpe Dale
Scottendale Plantation
Painsthorpe Wold Farm
East Brow Plantation
South Wold Dale
Hundle Dale
South Wold Plantation
South Wold Farm
Cot Nab
GARROWBY STREET
Cow Wold
Tumulus
Manor Farm
Thixen Dale
Wandales
Fotherdale Farm
Fotherdale
North Breckenholme
Long Plantation
Middle Plantation
South Breckenholme
Worm Dale
Broadholme Farm
Fordham Plantation
Fordham Dale
Fordham Farm
Wayrham Dale
Wayrham Farm
Wayrham Picnic Site
STONE DALE
Court Dale
Centenary Way
Raisthorpe Manor Farm
Beamer Hill
Waterdale End
Paradise Cottages
Chapel Farm
PH
PO
Thixendale
HUGGATE HILL
Gritts Farm
Cow Dale
Yorkshire Wolds Way
Gill's Farm
Ings Plantation
The Ings
YO25
Thixen Dale
Riggs Farm
Earthworks
Bradeham Dale
Bradeham Well
Pluckham Dale
Pluckham Plantation
Pluckham
PEFHAM LANE
A166
Wold House Farm
Seventy Acre Plantation
Greenwick
Stable Plantation
Great Plantation
Chalk Pit
Worsendale Plantation
WORSENDALE ROAD
Earthwork
Worsden Dale
Flat Top
Crow Wood
Old Wood
Hagworm Wood
Moat
OCHREPIT HL
North Wolds Walk
Milner Wood
Bishop Wilton Wold
BEACON ROAD
Bishop Wilton Wold
Deep Dale
Wilton Wold Plantation
Tumulus
Minster Way
Stonepit Plantation
Garths End Fields
Summerhouse Plantation
Church Dale
Fox Covert
Castle Field
Earthworks
Callis Wold
YO42
THE BENCE
High Callis Wold
Low Callis Wold
Mast
Millington Grange Farm
Millington Grange
Scoar Dale
Mingledale Plantation
Deep Dale
Swingling Moor
Givendale Out Field
GREEN BALK
Millington Heights
Millington Pasture
Huggate Dikes
Tun Dale
Huggate Pasture
Frendal Dale
Pasture Dale
Jessop's Plantation
Nettle Dale
8 61 7 60 6 59 5 58 4 57 3 56 2 55 1 54
0 81 82 83 84 85

29
18

17
6

Scale: 1⅓ inches to 1 mile
0 ¼ ½ mile
0 250m 500m 750m 1 km

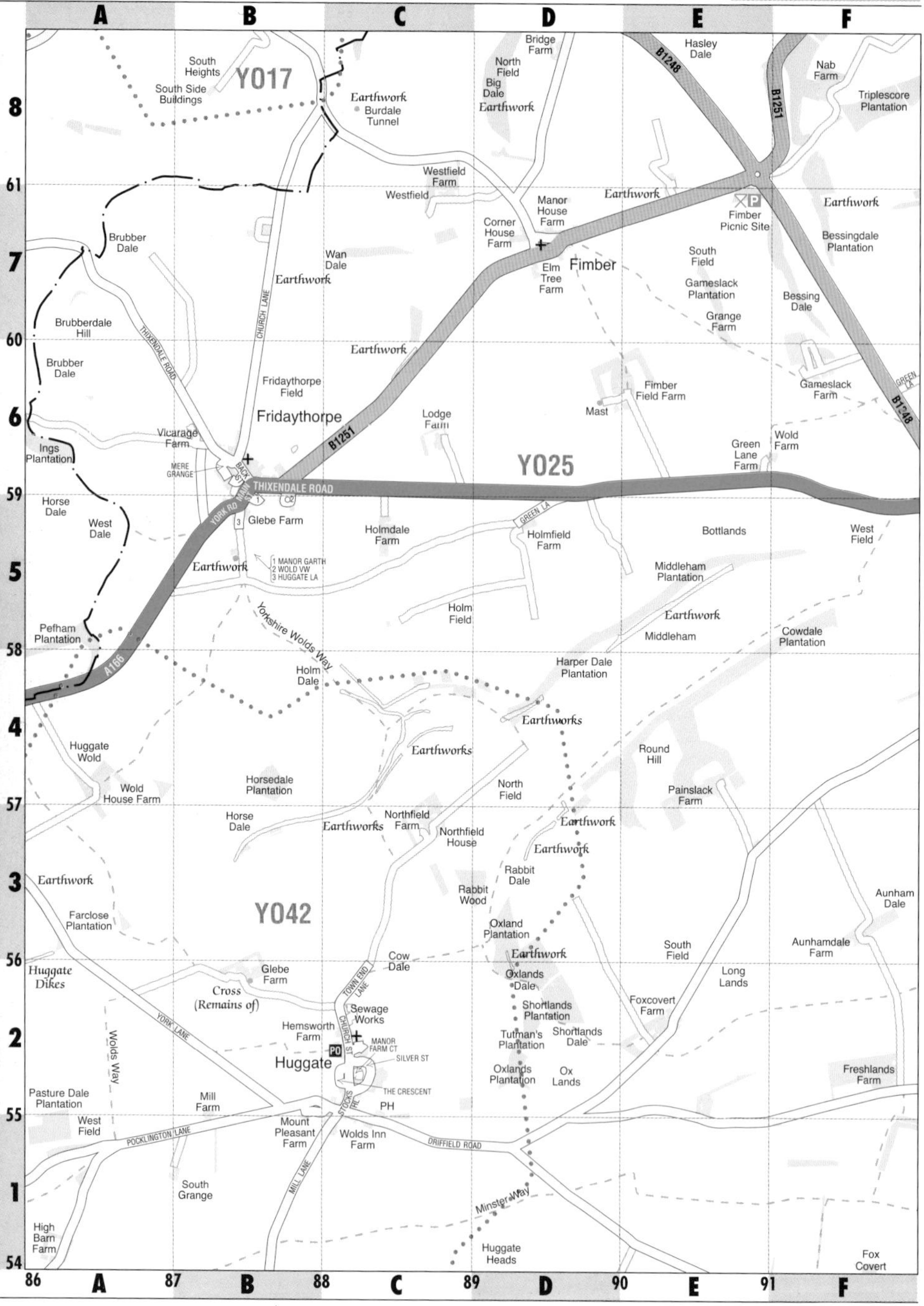
A
B
C
D
E
F
South Heights
South Side Buildings
YO17
Earthwork
Burdale Tunnel
Bridge Farm
North Field
Big Dale
Earthwork
Hasley Dale
B1248
Nab Farm
B1251
Triplescore Plantation
Westfield Farm
Westfield
Manor House Farm
Earthwork
Fimber Picnic Site
Earthwork
Brubber Dale
Wan Dale
Corner House Farm
Elm Tree Farm
Fimber
South Field
Bessingdale Plantation
Earthwork
Gameslack Plantation
Bessing Dale
Grange Farm
Brubberdale Hill
THIXENDALE ROAD
CHURCH LANE
Earthwork
Brubber Dale
Fridaythorpe Field
Fimber Field Farm
Gameslack Farm
GREEN LA
Mast
Lodge Farm
Fridaythorpe
B1251
Vicarage Farm
Ings Plantation
MERE GRANGE
BACK ST
YO25
Wold Farm
Green Lane Farm
THIXENDALE ROAD
YORK RD
MAIN ST
Horse Dale
West Dale
Glebe Farm
Holmdale Farm
GREEN LA
Holmfield Farm
Bottlands
West Field
Earthwork
1 MANOR GARTH
2 WOLD VW
3 HUGGATE LA
Middleham Plantation
Holm Field
Earthwork
Middleham
Pefham Plantation
Yorkshire Wolds Way
Cowdale Plantation
A166
Holm Dale
Harper Dale Plantation
Earthworks
Huggate Wold
Earthworks
Round Hill
Horsedale Plantation
North Field
Painslack Farm
Wold House Farm
Horse Dale
Earthworks
Northfield Farm
Northfield House
Earthwork
Earthwork
Earthwork
Rabbit Dale
Rabbit Wood
Aunham Dale
Farclose Plantation
YO42
Oxland Plantation
South Field
Aunhamdale Farm
Earthwork
Cow Dale
Huggate Dikes
Glebe Farm
Oxlands Dale
Long Lands
Cross (Remains of)
TOWN END LANE
Sewage Works
Shortlands Plantation
Foxcovert Farm
YORK LANE
Wolds Way
Hemsworth Farm
CHURCH ST
MANOR FARM CT
Tutman's Plantation
Shortlands Dale
SILVER ST
PO
Huggate
Oxlands Plantation
Ox Lands
Freshlands Farm
Pasture Dale Plantation
THE CRESCENT
Mill Farm
STOCKS HL
PH
West Field
POCKLINGTON LANE
Mount Pleasant Farm
Wolds Inn Farm
DRIFFIELD ROAD
MILL LANE
South Grange
Minster Way
High Barn Farm
Huggate Heads
Fox Covert
8
61
7
60
6
59
5
58
4
57
3
56
2
55
1
54
86
87
88
89
90
91

17
30

Scale: 1⅓ inches to 1 mile
0 ¼ ½ mile
0 250m 500m 750m 1 km

7
20

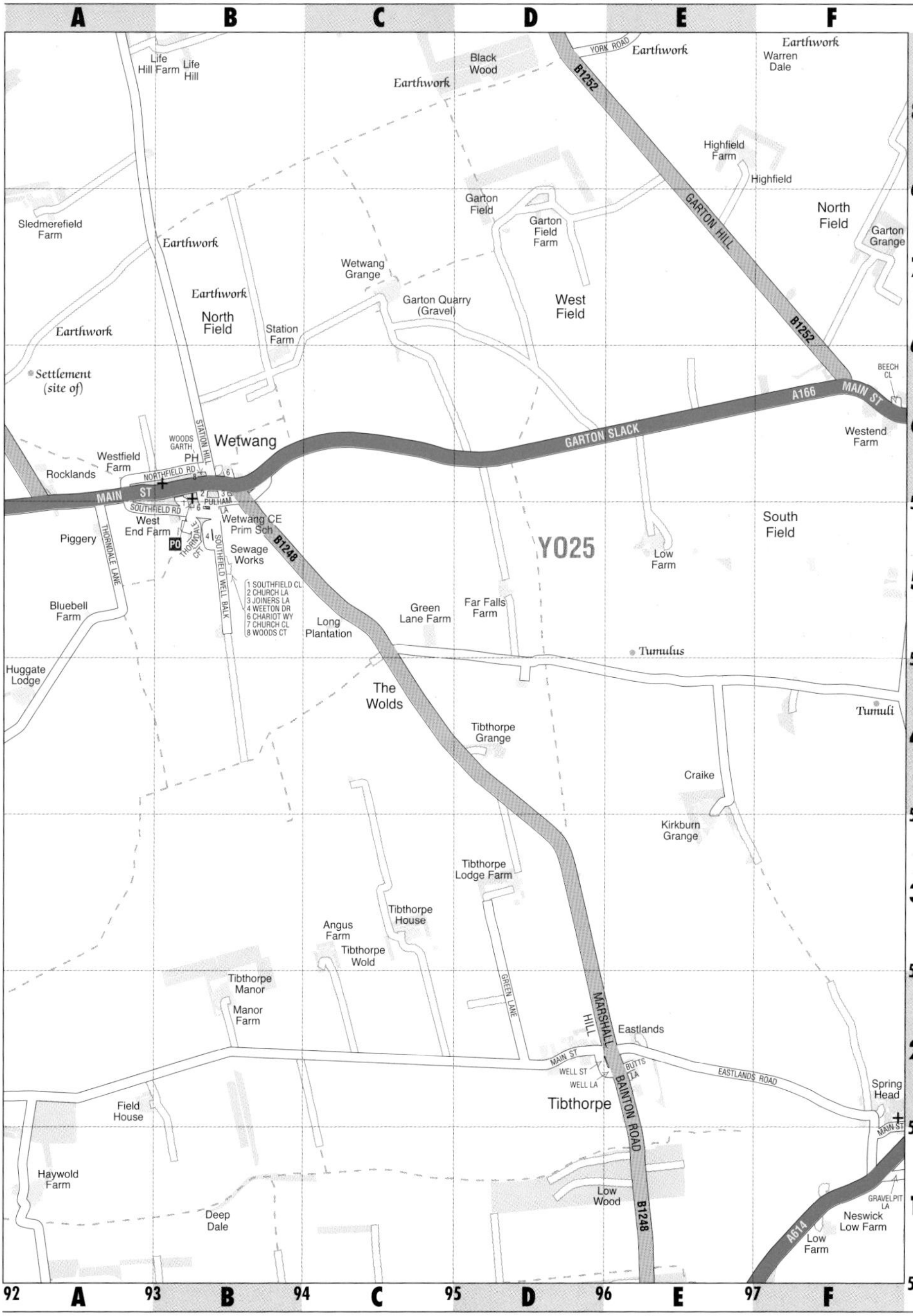

31
20

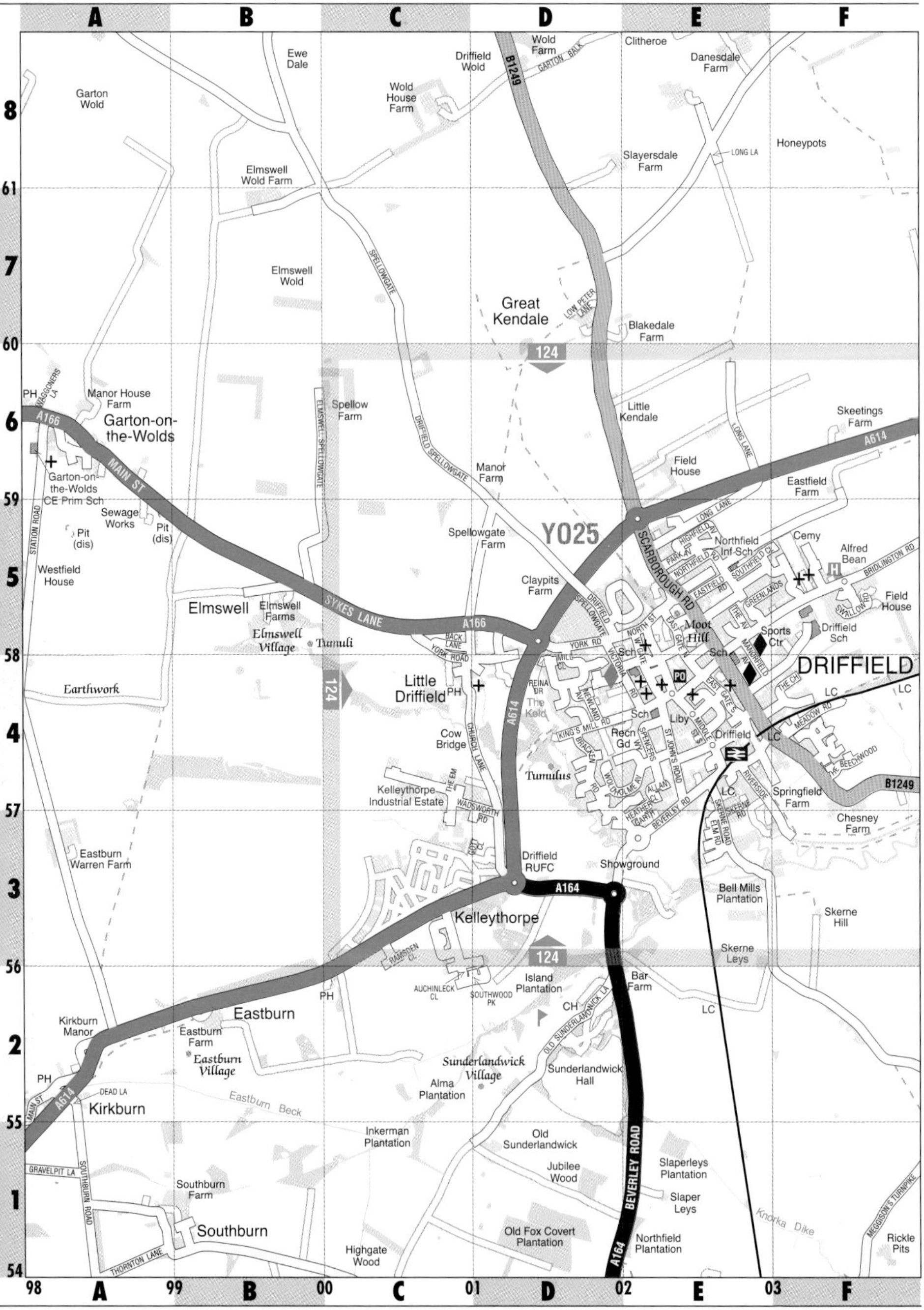

For full street detail of the highlighted area see pages 124 and 125.

Scale: 1⅓ inches to 1 mile
0 ¼ ½ mile
0 250m 500m 750m 1 km

9
22

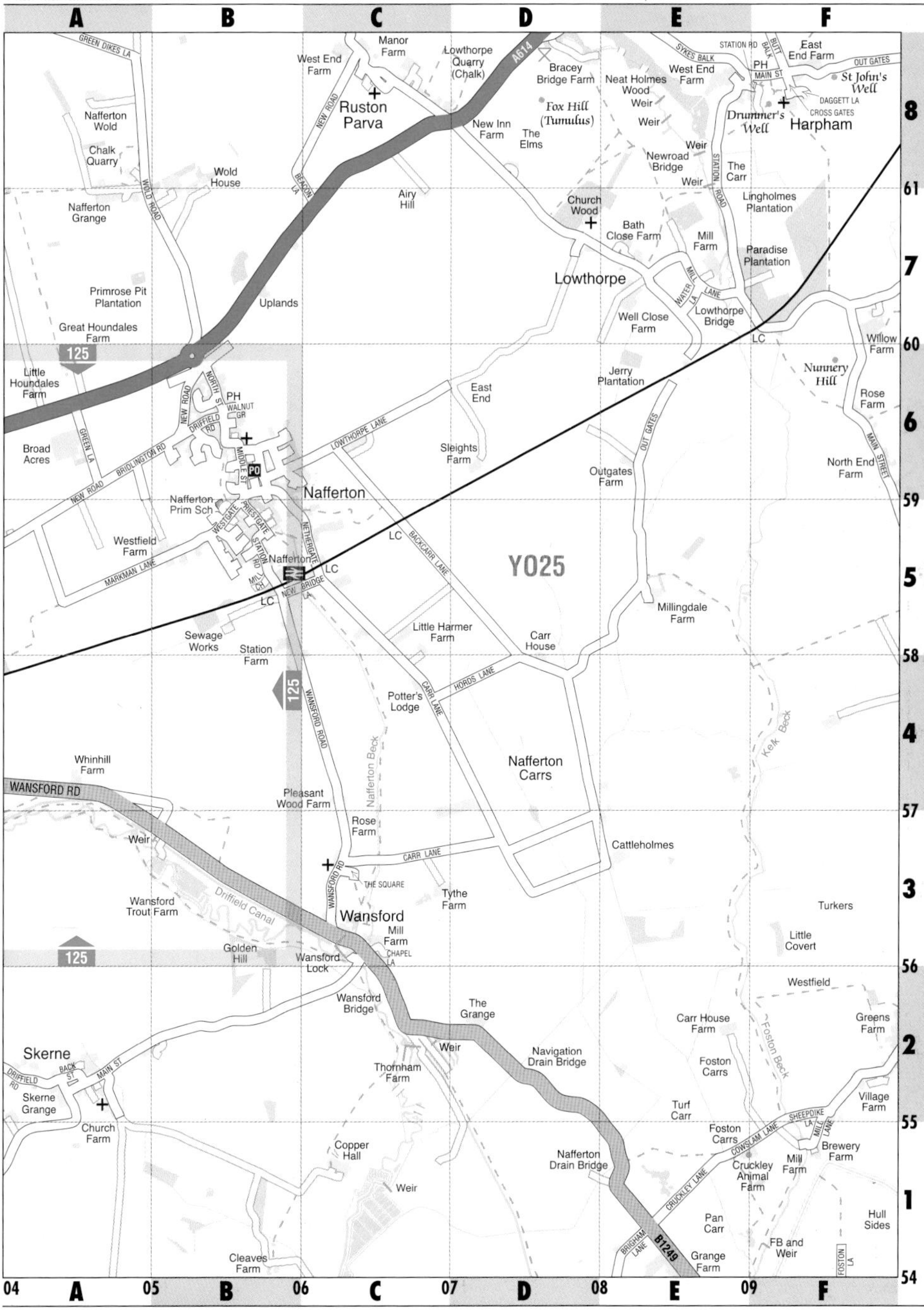
A
B
C
D
E
F
8
61
7
60
6
59
5
58
4
57
3
56
2
55
1
54
04
05
06
07
08
09
GREEN DIKES LA
West End
Farm
Manor
Farm
Lowthorpe
Quarry
(Chalk)
A614
Bracey
Bridge Farm
Neat Holmes
Wood
West End
Farm
STATION RD
BUTT BALK
East
End Farm
SYKES BALK
PH
MAIN ST
OUT GATES
St John's
Well
DAGGETT LA
CROSS GATES
Nafferton
Wold
Chalk
Quarry
NEW ROAD
Ruston
Parva
New Inn
Farm
Fox Hill
(Tumulus)
The
Elms
Weir
Weir
Drummer's
Well
Harpham
Wold
House
Newroad
Bridge
Weir
Weir
STATION ROAD
The
Carr
BEACON LA
Airy
Hill
Nafferton
Grange
WOLD ROAD
Church
Wood
Bath
Close Farm
Mill
Farm
Lingholmes
Plantation
Paradise
Plantation
Primrose Pit
Plantation
Uplands
Lowthorpe
MILL LA
WATER LA
LANE
Lowthorpe
Bridge
Great Houndales
Farm
Well Close
Farm
LC
Willow
Farm
125
Little
Houndales
Farm
NORTH ST
NEW ROAD
PH
WALNUT GR
DRIFFIELD RD
East
End
Jerry
Plantation
Nunnery
Hill
Rose
Farm
GREEN LA
Broad
Acres
BRIDLINGTON RD
LOWTHORPE LANE
MIDDLE ST
PO
Sleights
Farm
OUT GATES
Outgates
Farm
North End
Farm
MAIN STREET
NEW ROAD
Nafferton
Nafferton
Prim Sch
WESTGATE
PRIESTGATE
NETHERGATE
LC
BACKCARR LANE
Westfield
Farm
STATION RD
Nafferton
YO25
MARKMAN LANE
MILL CH
LC
NEW BRIDGE
LA
LC
Millingdale
Farm
Little Harmer
Farm
Sewage
Works
Station
Farm
Carr
House
125
HORDS LANE
CARR LANE
Potter's
Lodge
WANSFORD ROAD
Kelk Beck
Nafferton
Carrs
Whinhill
Farm
WANSFORD RD
Pleasant
Wood Farm
Nafferton Beck
Weir
Rose
Farm
Cattleholmes
CARR LANE
THE SQUARE
WANSFORD RD
Wansford
Trout Farm
Driffield Canal
Tythe
Farm
Turkers
Wansford
Mill
Farm
CHAPEL LA
Little
Covert
125
Golden
Hill
Wansford
Lock
Westfield
Wansford
Bridge
The
Grange
Carr House
Farm
Greens
Farm
Foston Beck
Skerne
BACK ST
MAIN ST
DRIFFIELD RD
Weir
Navigation
Drain Bridge
Thornham
Farm
Foston
Carrs
Skerne
Grange
Church
Farm
Turf
Carr
Village
Farm
SHEEPDIKE LA
MILL LANE
Foston
Carrs
COWSLAM LANE
Brewery
Farm
Copper
Hall
Nafferton
Drain Bridge
Cruckley
Animal
Farm
Mill
Farm
CRUCKLEY LANE
Weir
Hull
Sides
Pan
Carr
BRIGHAM LANE
B1249
FB and
Weir
Cleaves
Farm
Grange
Farm
FOSTON LA

For full street detail of the highlighted area see page 125.

33
22

21
10

Scale: 1⅓ inches to 1 mile
0 ¼ ½ mile
0 250m 500m 750m 1 km

A B C D E F

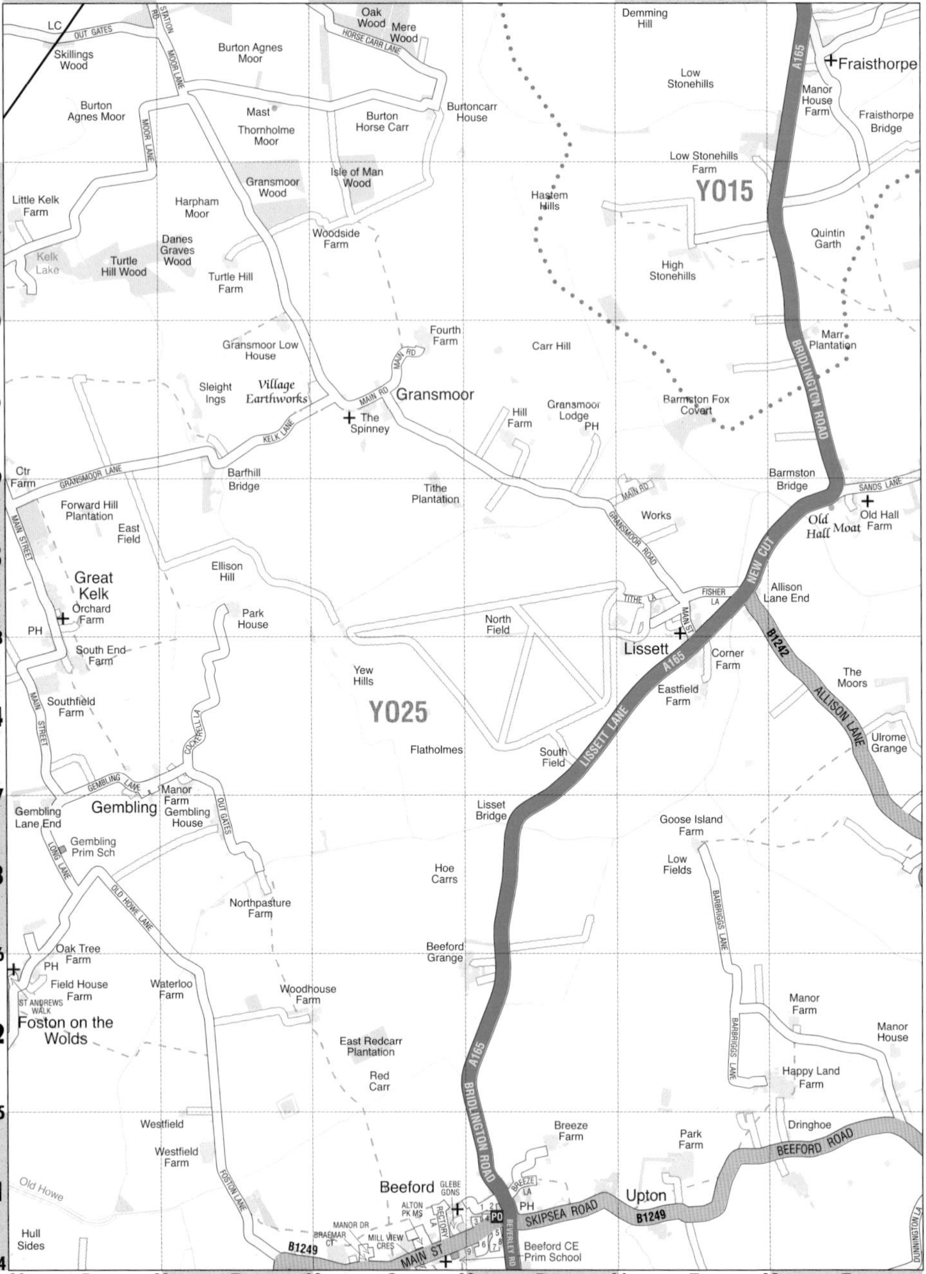

A B C D E F

21
34

D1
1 CHURCH LA
2 ST LEONARD'S CL
3 WHARRAM FIELD
4 NEWSAM CL
5 MEADOW CL
6 ASHLEIGH DR
7 BARONWOOD CR
8 WELBURN CT
9 RECTORY VW

Scale: 1⅓ inches to 1 mile

11

YO15
Sheep Walks
Hamiltonhill Farm
HAMILTON HILL ROAD
BROOMFIELD WY
HOLLYCROFT
SANDS LANE
PO
P
Barmston
CHAPEL LA
PH
SOUTHFIELD LANE
SOUTHFIELD LANE
Trusey Hill
Barmston Main Drain
YO25
North Field
NORTH TURNPIKE
NORTH ROAD
East End
MALLARD CL
MAIN ST
SANDS LA
SOUTHFIELD LA
Ulrome
THIRD AVE 1
FIFTH AVE 2
SIXTH AVE 3
SEVENTH AVE 4
Cliff Farm
West End
Cliff Farm Caravan Site
FOURTH AV
SECOND AV
Cliff House
SOUTHFIELD LANE
SKIPSEA LANE
MILL LANE
Corner Farm
B1242
BRIDLINGTON RD
Sewage Works
Smiddys Farm
Motte and Bailey
CLEETON LA
ROSEDALE
PH
Skipsea
HORNSEA ROAD
PO
MAIN ST
Skipsea Castle
Skipsea Prim Sch
B1249
Great Carr
B1242
HORNSEA ROAD
1 MANOR CL
2 BACK ST
3 CROSS ST
4 TOWN FARM CL
5 LEYS LA
6 CASTLE VW
7 CHAPEL GARTH
Southfield Farm
Brough Carr
BEWHOLME LANE
Stream Dyke
A B C D E F
8 61 7 60 6 59 5 58 4 57 3 56 2 55 1 54
16 17 18 19 20 21

35

12

Scale: 1⅓ inches to 1 mile
0 ¼ ½ mile
0 250m 500m 750m 1 km

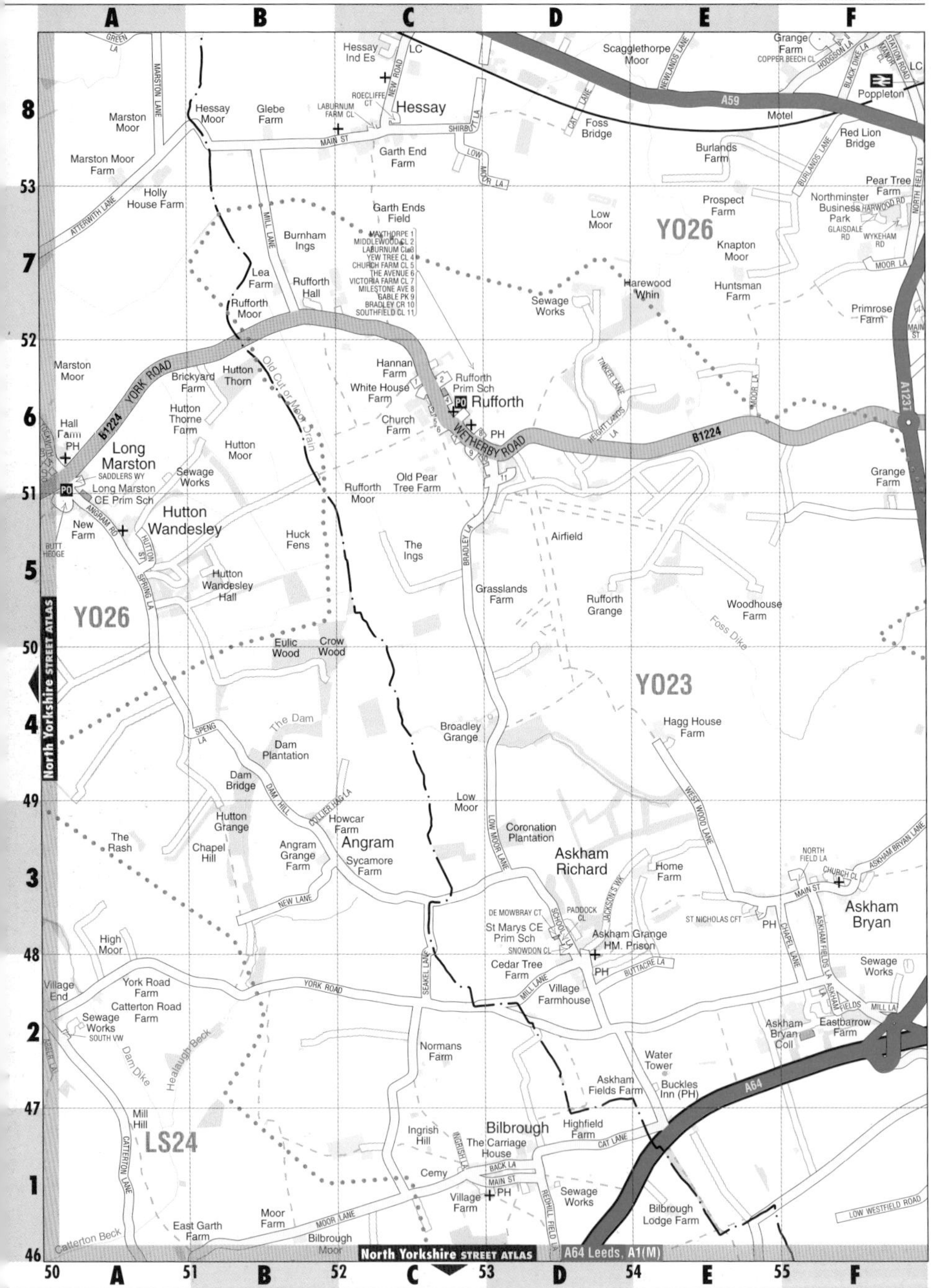

Scale: 1⅓ inches to 1 mile

0 ¼ ½ mile

0 250m 500m 750m 1 km

126 127 131

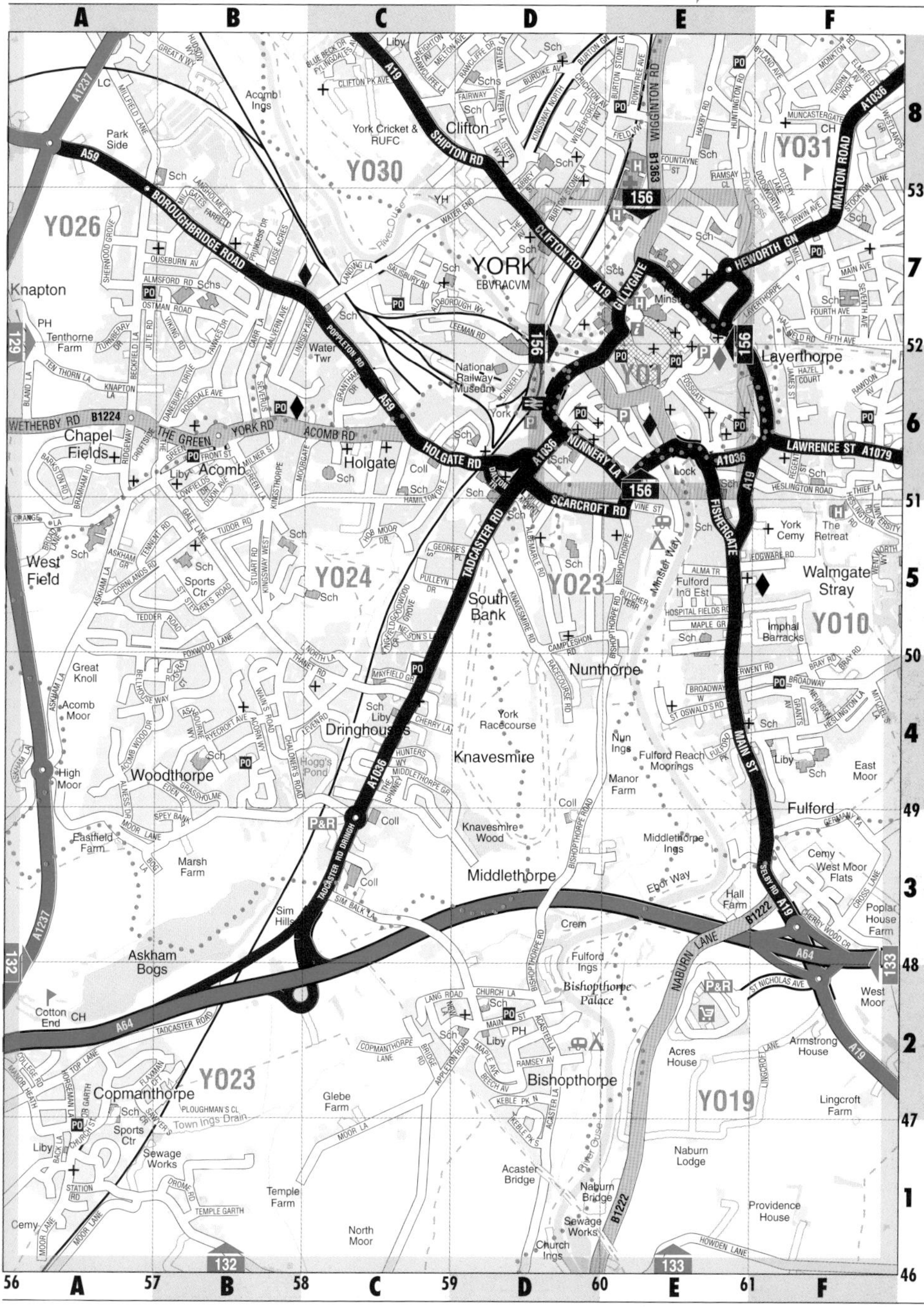
A B C D E F
8
53
7
52
6
51
5
50
4
49
3
48
2
47
1
46
56 57 58 59 60 61
Acomb Ings
Park Side
York Cricket & RUFC
Clifton
YO30
YO26
YO31
YORK
EBVRACVM
Knapton
Tenthorne Farm
Chapel Fields
Acomb
Holgate
National Railway Museum
YO1
Layerthorpe
West Field
YO24
South Bank
YO23
Walmgate Stray
YO10
Fulford Ind Est
Imphal Barracks
Great Knoll
Acomb Moor
Nunthorpe
Dringhouses
York Racecourse
Knavesmire
Woodthorpe
High Moor
Hogg's Pond
Nun Ings
Fulford Reach Moorings
Manor Farm
Fulford
East Moor
Eastfield Farm
Marsh Farm
Knavesmire Wood
Middlethorpe Ings
Middlethorpe
Hall Farm
Sim Hills
Askham Bogs
Crem
Fulford Ings
Bishopthorpe Palace
Poplar House Farm
West Moor
Cotton End
Copmanthorpe
YO23
Glebe Farm
Bishopthorpe
Acres House
Armstrong House
YO19
Lingcroft Farm
Sports Ctr
Sewage Works
Temple Farm
Acaster Bridge
Naburn Bridge
Naburn Lodge
Providence House
North Moor
Church Ings
Cemy
West Moor Flats
York Cemy
The Retreat
A59
A19
A1036
A1079
A64
A1237
B1224
B1222
B1363
156
129
132
133

36 26

For full street detail of the highlighted area see pages 129, 130, 132 and 133.

For full street detail of the highlighted area see page 156.

130
128
14

F7
1 GORSE HL
2 HOLLY TREE CFT
3 ASPEN CL
4 ORCHARD CTS
5 PETERCROFT CL
6 KENDAL CL
7 UNDERCROFT
8 THORNCROFT
9 SAWYERS WK
10 CONEYCROFT
11 KEEPERS WY
12 WESTWOOD MEWS
13 SCAUDERCROFT
14 GREENCROFT CT
15 LIME TREE MEWS
16 OX CALDER CL
17 GREENCROFT LA
18 GREENSIDE
19 ASHDALE RD
20 THE GREEN
21 HUNTERS WOOD WY
22 DEERSTONE WY
23 GREENSIDE WLK
24 GREENSIDE CL

Scale: 1⅓ inches to 1 mile
0 ¼ ½ mile
0 250m 500m 750m 1 km

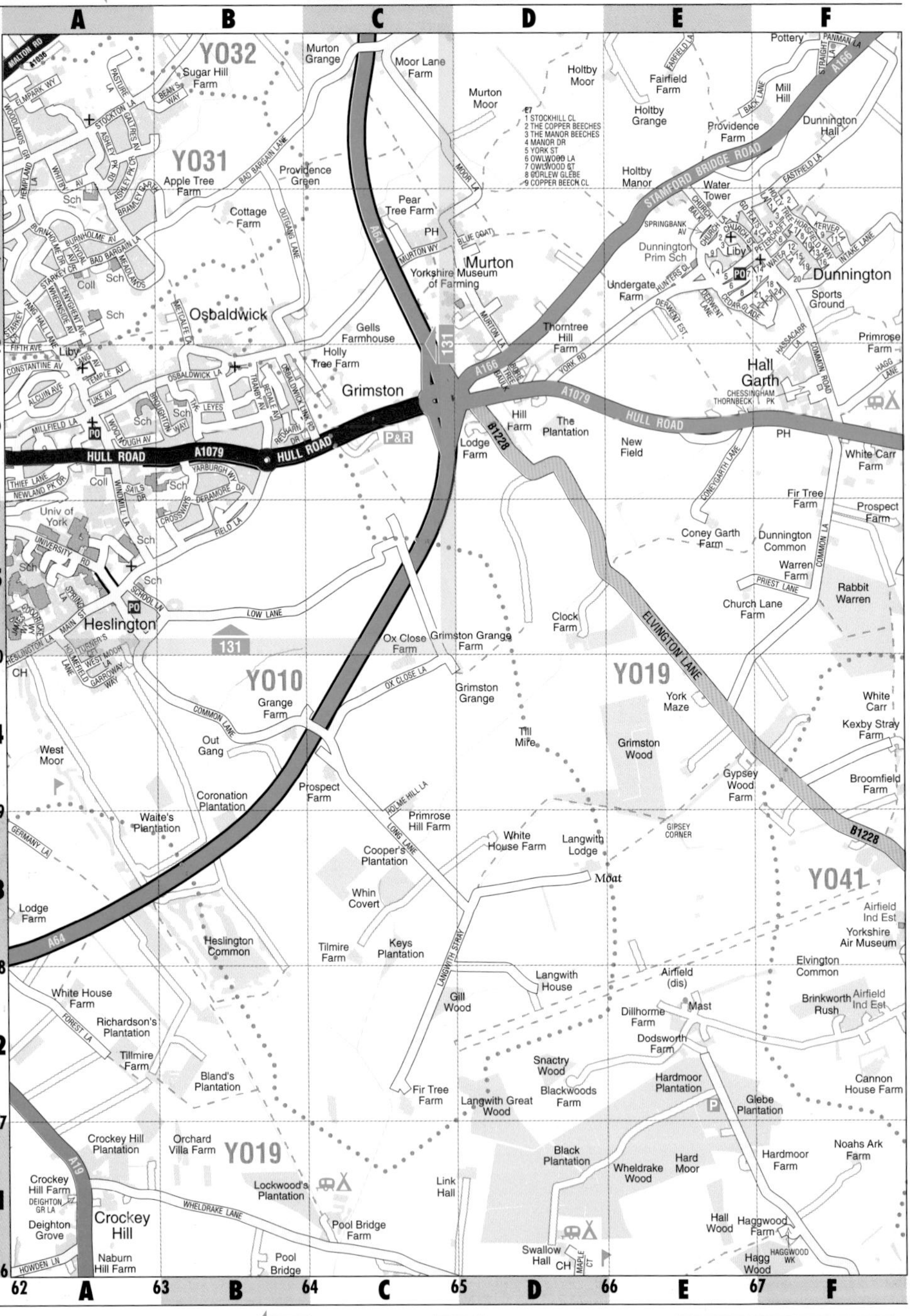

For full street detail of the highlighted area see page 131.

Scale: 1⅓ inches to 1 mile
0 ¼ ½ mile
0 250m 500m 750m 1 km

15 28

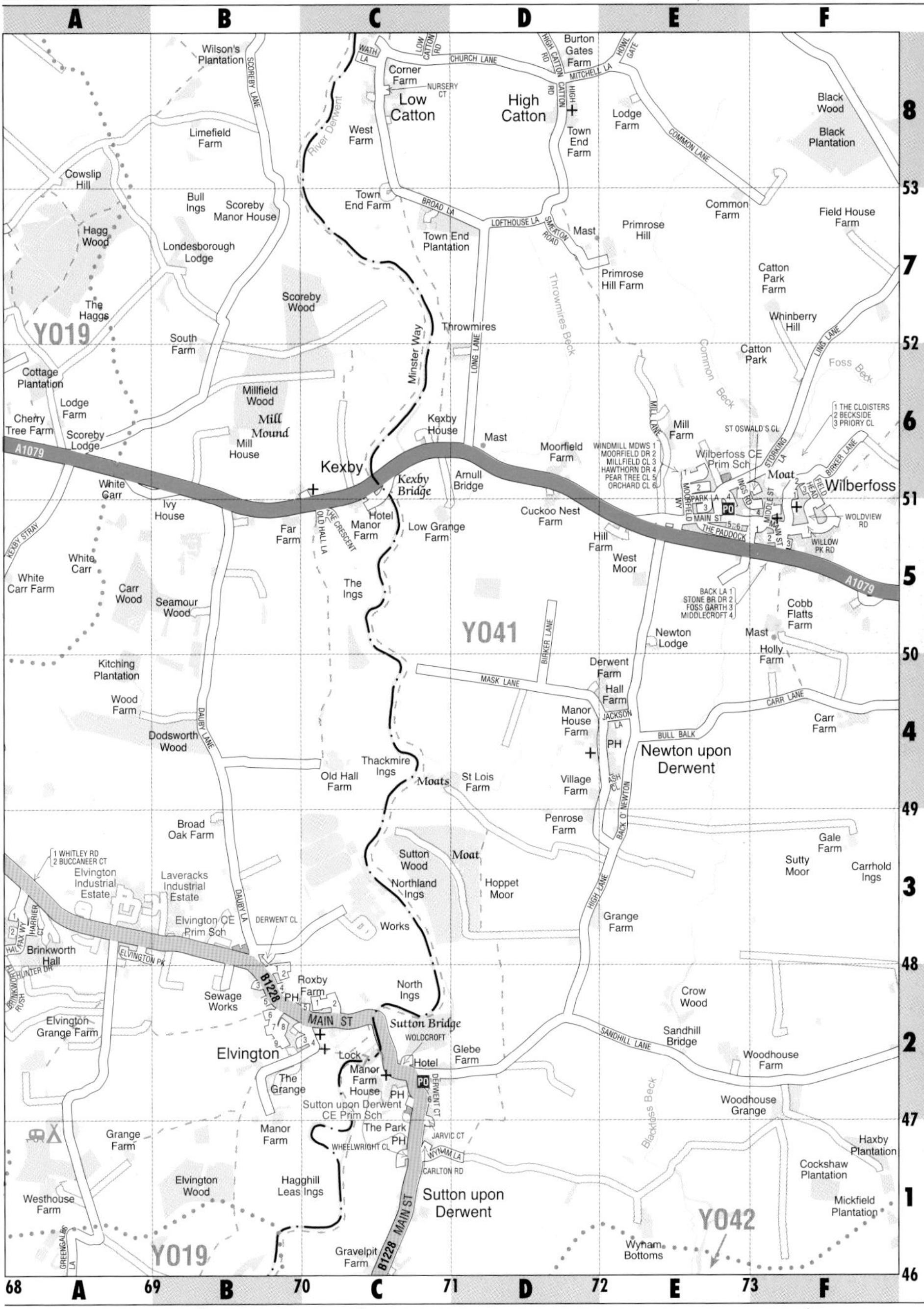

B2
1 WHITE HOUSE GR
2 BEECH CL
3 LORRAINE AVE
4 HILLGARTH CT
5 DOVECOTE GARTH
6 BECK CL
7 BECKSIDE
8 BELVOIR AVE
9 ALVIN WK

C2
1 RIVERSIDE CL
2 RIVERSIDE GDNS
3 CHURCH GN
4 CHURCH LA
5 BLACKSMITHS CL
6 JASMINE GARTH

38 28

27
16

Scale: 1⅓ inches to 1 mile
0 ¼ ½ mile
0 250m 500m 750m 1 km

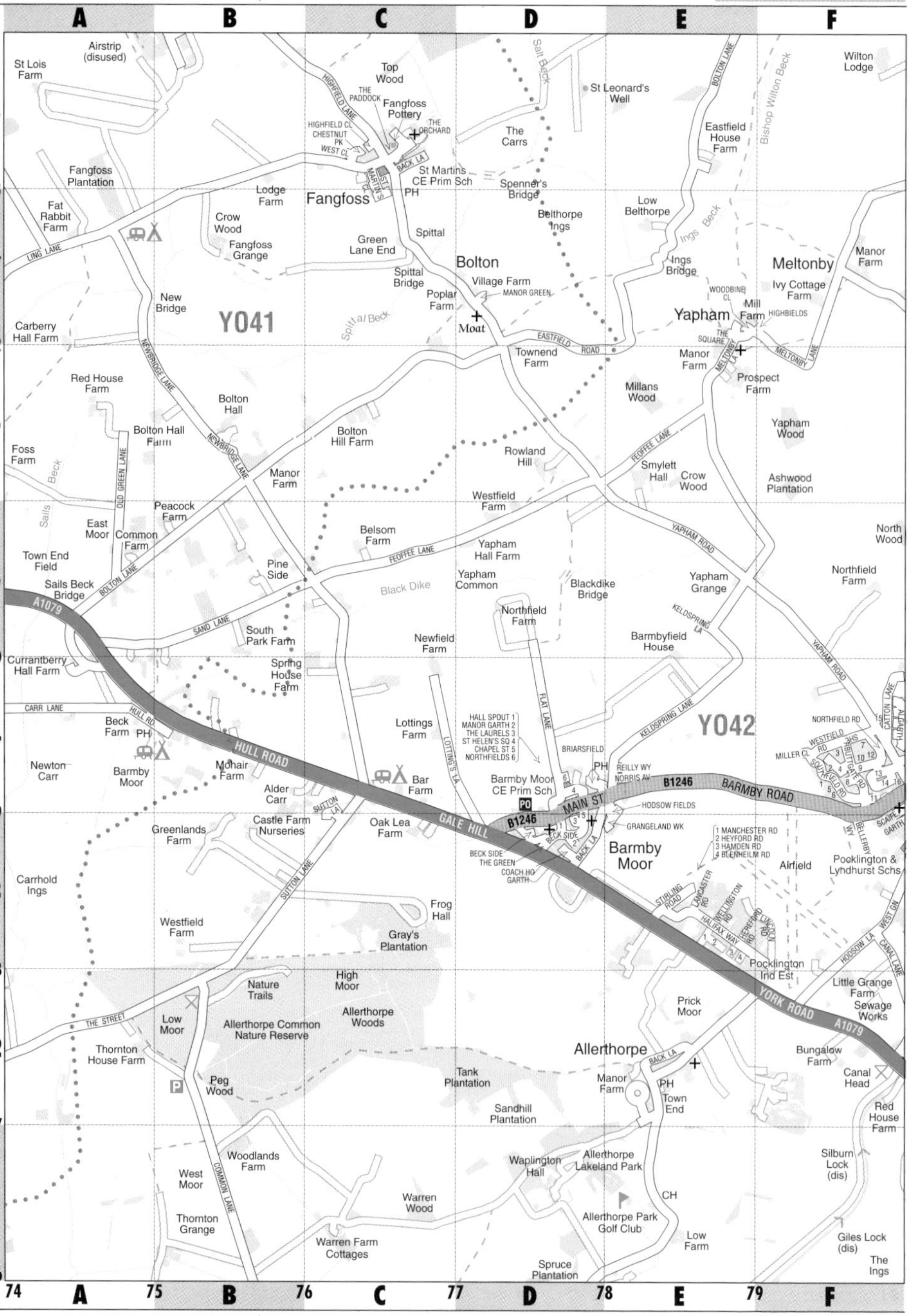

27
39

F4
1 DALMAIS CL
2 BURNS CL
3 WESTFIELD CL
4 ORCHARD GDNS
5 WELLINGTON CL
6 MEADOWFIELD CL
7 NORTHFIELD RISE
8 HALIFAX CL
9 ORCHARD WY
10 ORCHARD CL
11 ST JOHN'S CL
12 NORTHFIELD CL
13 SHERBUTTGATE DR
14 SHERBUTTGATE RD
15 ANDREW'S CT
16 ARCHIBALD CL

Scale: 1⅓ inches to 1 mile
0 ¼ ½ mile
0 250m 500m 750m 1 km

17
30

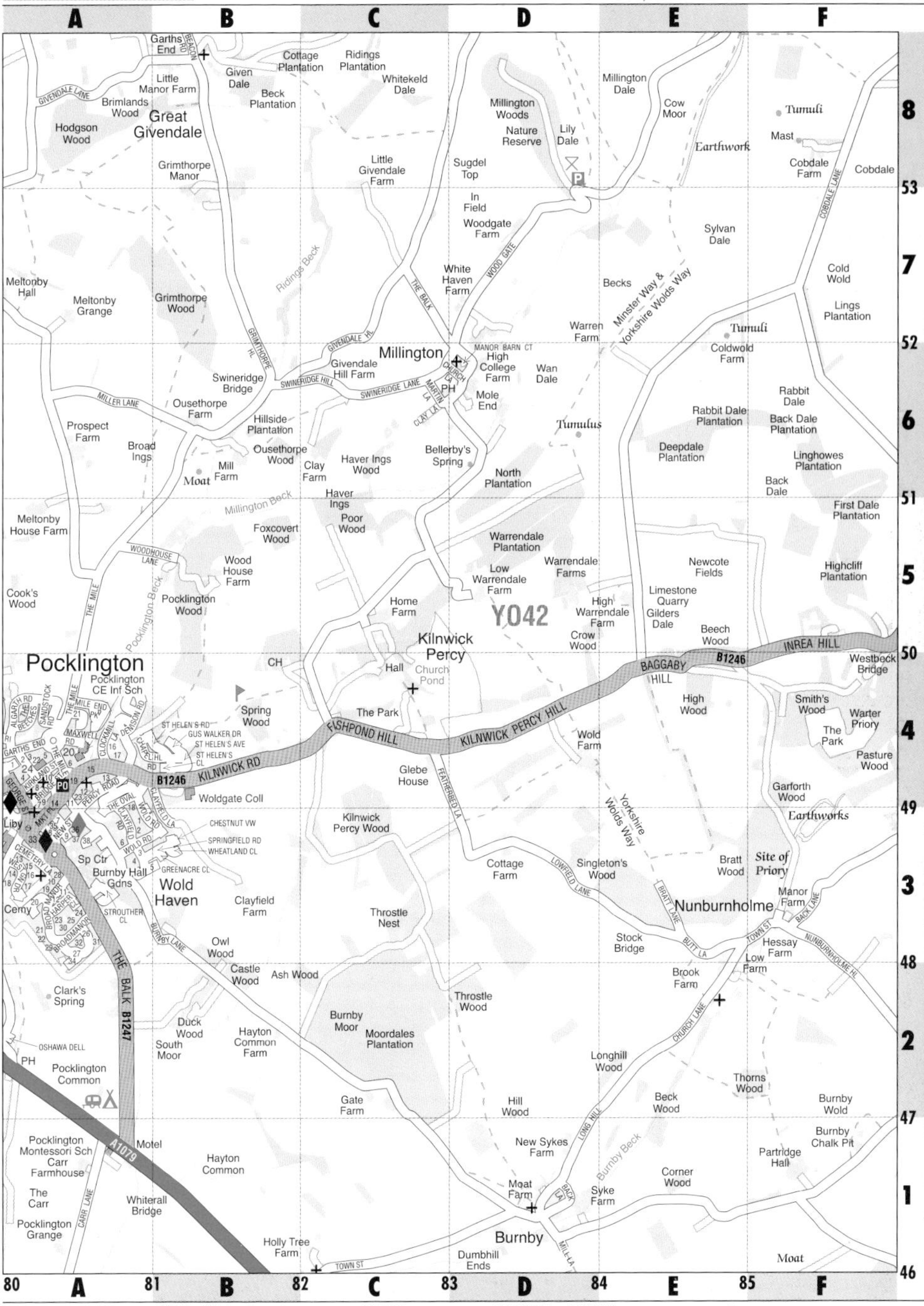

A4
1 EDWARD ST
2 VICTORIA RD
3 MURRAY CL
4 BRINDLEGATE
5 SCHOOL LA
6 BEECH CT
7 PEM LANE
8 KIRKGATE
9 MARKET ST
10 HALLGATE
11 THE AVENUE
12 CHERRY ORCH MEWS
13 VOLAGE CT
14 ST PETER'S SQ
15 LONDON ST
16 TARGET LA
17 PAYTON CL
18 CLAYFIELD CL
19 UNION ST
20 St Mary & St Josephs RC Prim Sch
21 APPERSTON CT
22 PROSPECT RD
23 ST MARY'S CT
24 Pocklington Com Jun Sch

A3
1 WOLDGATE VW
2 KILNWICK GARTH
3 PINEWOOD RD
4 PINEWOOD CT
5 PINEWOOD CL
6 VALENTINE CL
7 DEAN'S LA
8 REGENT ST PAVEMENT
9 WILLOW CT
10 THE LILACS
11 MCSHANE CT
12 MACDONALD CT
13 SYMONS WY
14 BECK VW
15 GARRICK CL
16 COMRIE DR
17 WAITE CL
18 TURNBULL DR
19 FETHERSTON CL
20 BROWNING RD
21 SAUNDERS CRES
22 THURLOW AVE
23 DORRINGTON CL
24 KINGS CL
25 MCGRATH CL
26 HART DR
27 LORD DR
28 MAY CT
29 RUNDLE CT
30 JENKINGS CL
31 ALBRIGHT CL
32 MORGAN CL
33 STA RD
34 NICHOLSON CT
35 BUCK INN YARD
36 ROPERY WLK
37 ROWLEY MEWS
38 WOLD GARTH

40
30

29
18

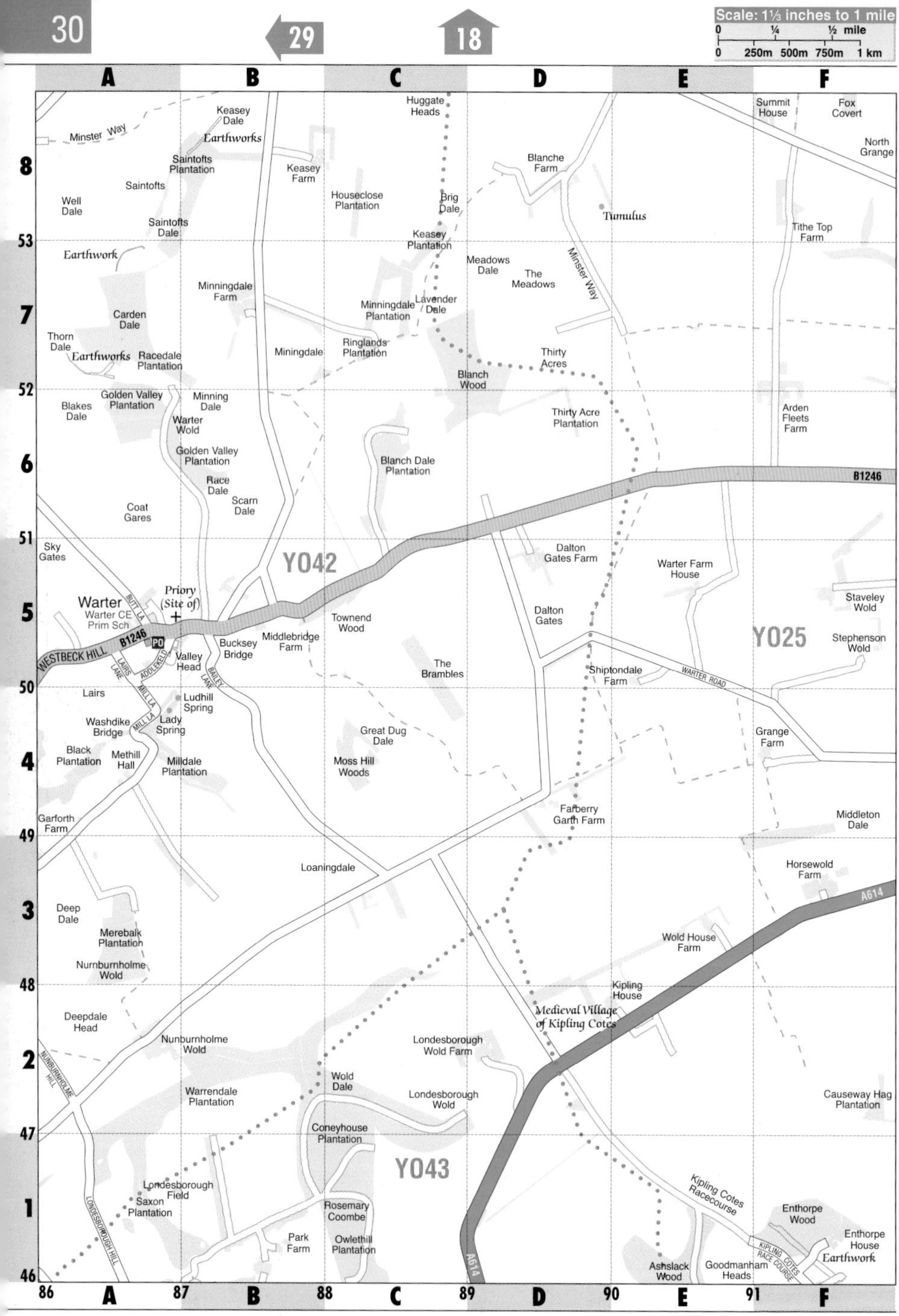
Scale: 1½ inches to 1 mile
0 ¼ ½ mile
0 250m 500m 750m 1 km
A B C D E F
8
53
7
52
6
51
5
50
4
49
3
48
2
47
1
46
86 87 88 89 90 91
Huggate Heads
Keasey Dale
Minster Way
Earthworks
Saintofts Plantation
Saintofts
Well Dale
Saintofts Dale
Earthwork
Keasey Farm
Houseclose Plantation
Brig Dale
Keasey Plantation
Summit House
Fox Covert
North Grange
Blanche Farm
Tumulus
Tithe Top Farm
Meadows Dale
The Meadows
Minster Way
Minningdale Farm
Carden Dale
Minningdale Plantation
Lavender Dale
Thorn Dale
Earthworks
Racedale Plantation
Miningdale
Ringlands Plantation
Thirty Acres
Blanch Wood
Blakes Dale
Golden Valley Plantation
Minning Dale
Warter Wold
Golden Valley Plantation
Race Dale
Scarn Dale
Coat Gares
Thirty Acre Plantation
Arden Fleets Farm
Blanch Dale Plantation
B1246
Sky Gates
YO42
Dalton Gates Farm
Warter Farm House
Warter
Warter CE Prim Sch
Priory (Site of)
BUTT LA
B1246
PO
WESTBECK HILL
Townend Wood
Dalton Gates
Staveley Wold
YO25
Stephenson Wold
Bucksey Bridge
Middlebridge Farm
Valley Head
ADDLEKELD
LAIRS LANE
BAILEY LANE
The Brambles
Shiptondale Farm
WARTER ROAD
Lairs
MILL LA
Ludhill Spring
Washdike Bridge
Lady Spring
Great Dug Dale
Grange Farm
Black Plantation
Methill Hall
Milldale Plantation
Moss Hill Woods
Farberry Garth Farm
Middleton Dale
Garforth Farm
Loaningdale
Horsewold Farm
Deep Dale
A614
Merebalk Plantation
Wold House Farm
Nurnburnholme Wold
Kipling House
Deepdale Head
Medieval Village of Kipling Cotes
Nunburnholme Wold
Londesborough Wold Farm
NUNBURNHOLME HILL
Wold Dale
Warrendale Plantation
Londesborough Wold
Causeway Hag Plantation
Coneyhouse Plantation
YO43
Londesborough Field
Kipling Cotes Racecourse
Saxon Plantation
Rosemary Coombe
Enthorpe Wood
LONDESBOROUGH HILL
Park Farm
Owlethill Plantation
Enthorpe House
Earthwork
KIPLING COTES RACE COURSE
A614
Ashslack Wood
Goodmanham Heads

29
41

Scale: 1⅓ inches to 1 mile
0 ¼ ½ mile
0 250m 500m 750m 1 km

19
32

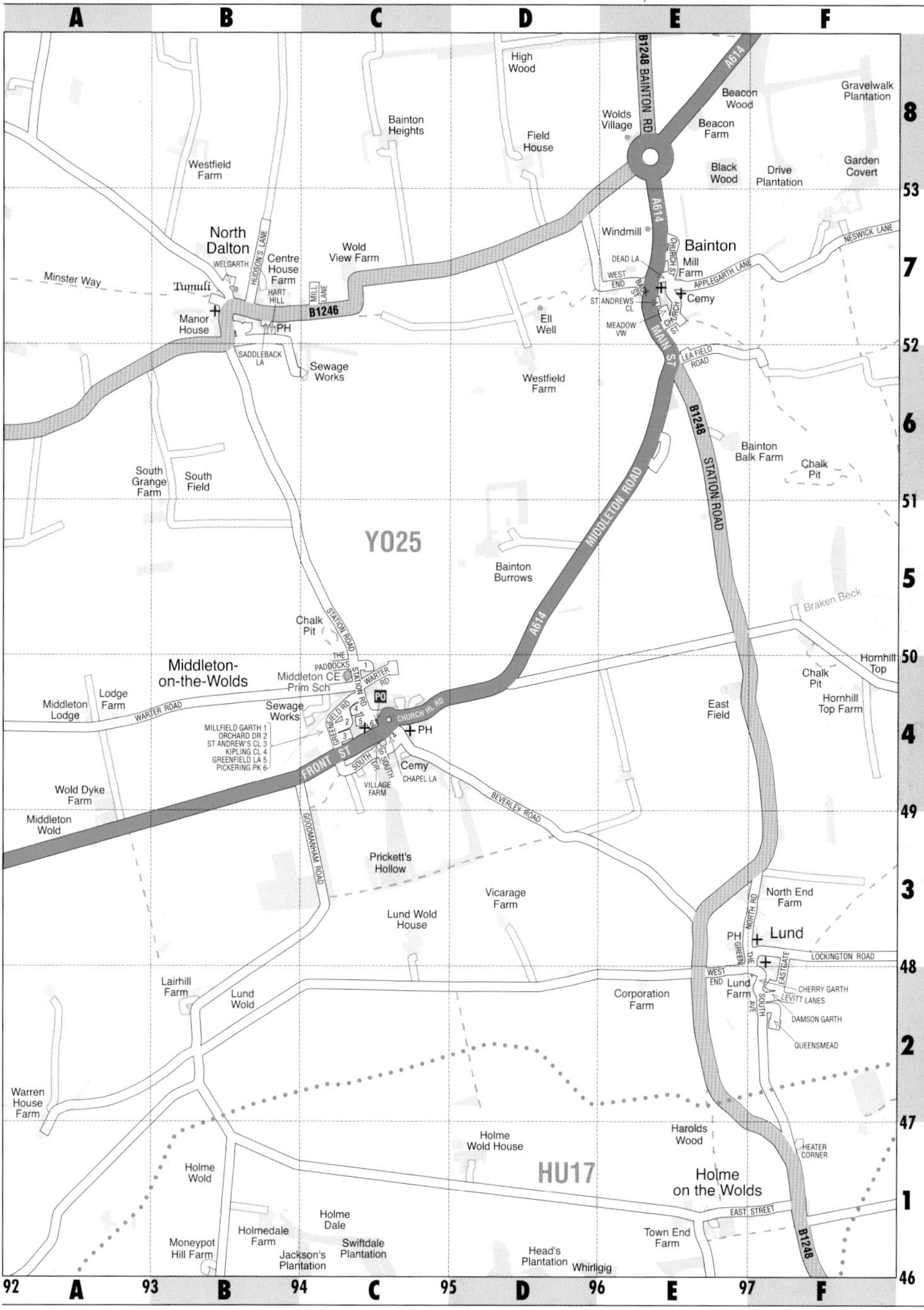

42
32

31
20

Scale: 1⅓ inches to 1 mile
0 ¼ ½ mile
0 250m 500m 750m 1 km

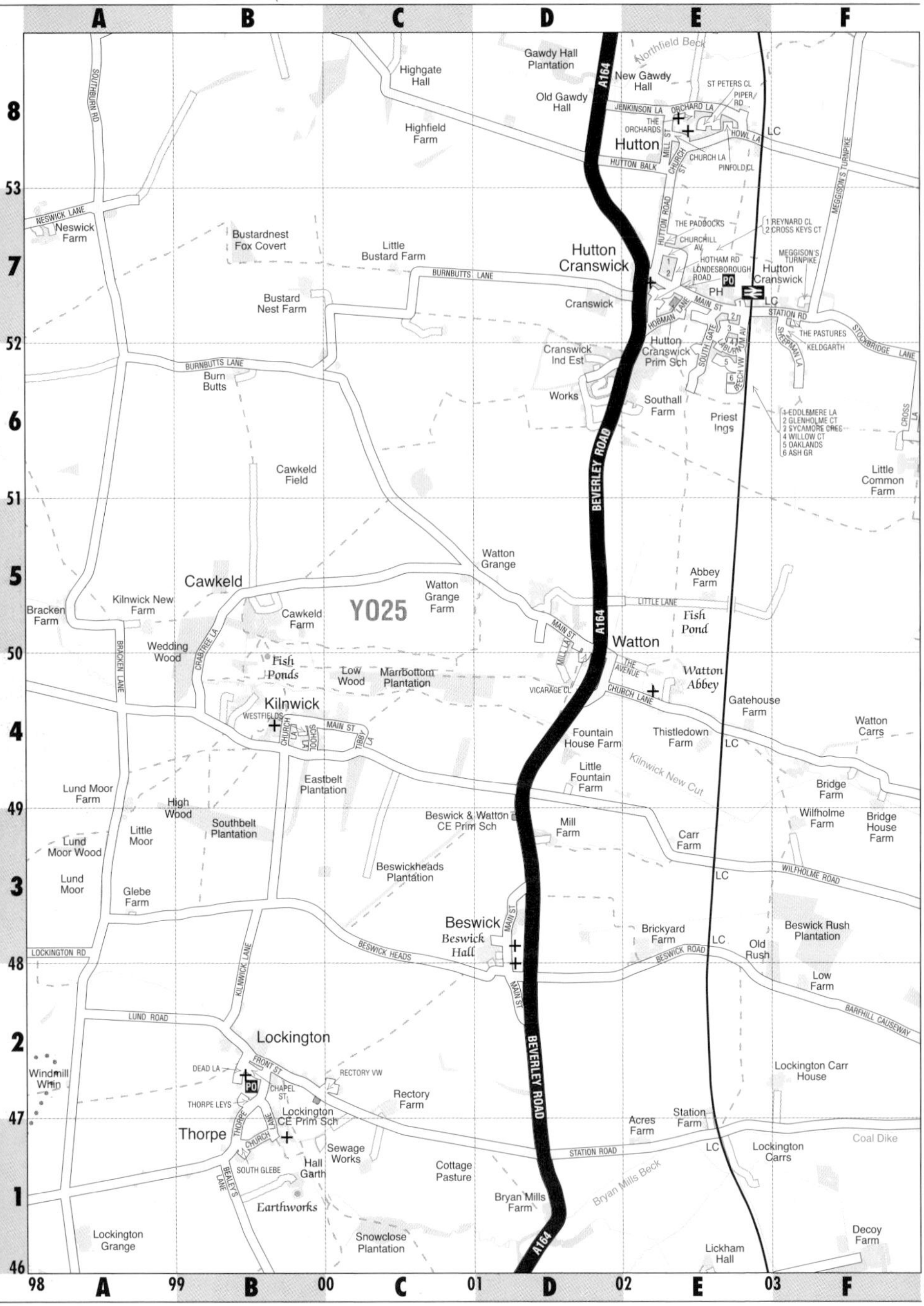

31
43

21
34

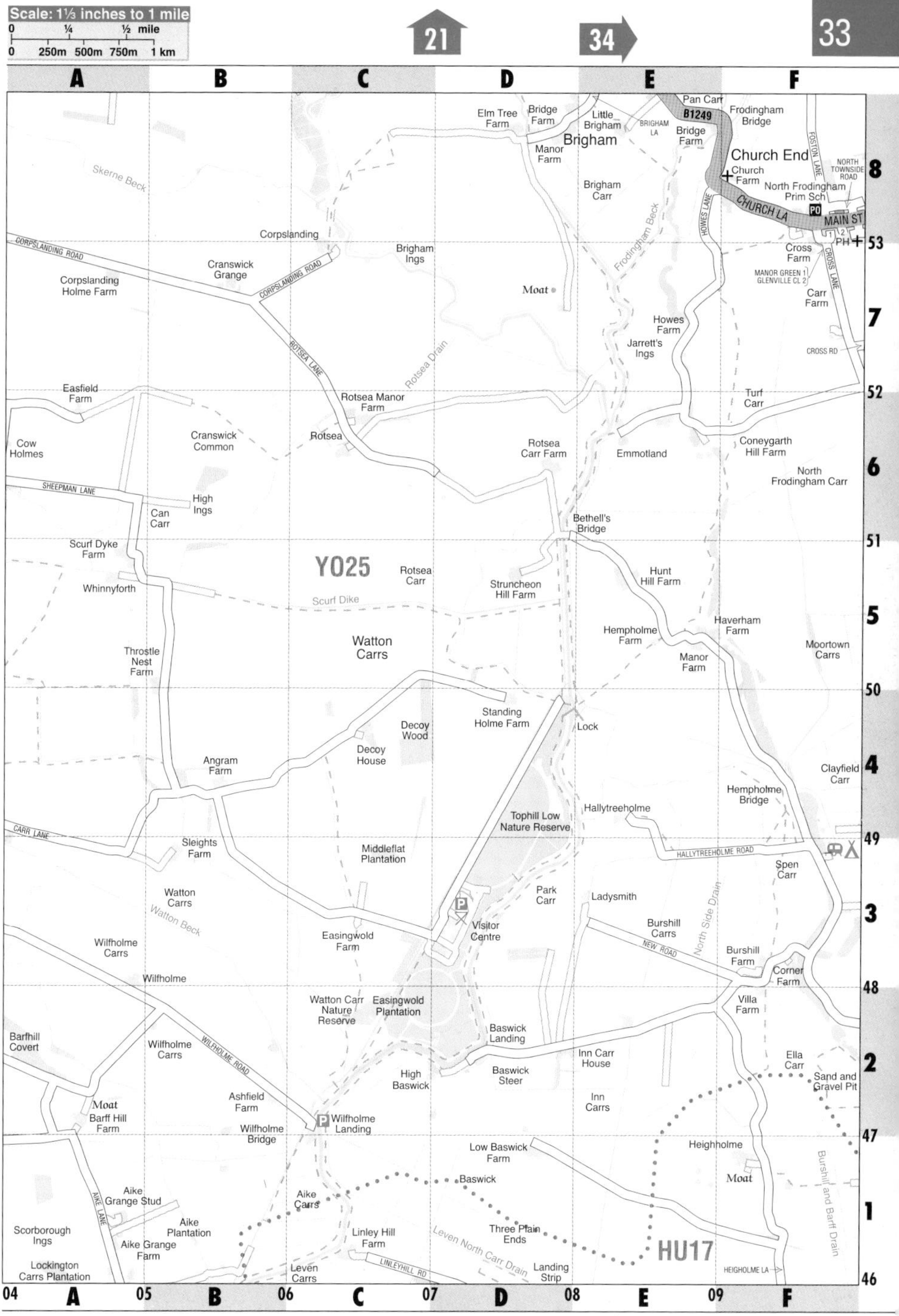
Scale: 1⅓ inches to 1 mile
0 ¼ ½ mile
0 250m 500m 750m 1 km
A
B
C
D
E
F
Pan Carr
B1249
Frodingham Bridge
Elm Tree Farm
Bridge Farm
Little Brigham
BRIGHAM LA
Bridge Farm
Brigham
Manor Farm
Church End
FOSTON LANE
NORTH TOWNSIDE ROAD
Church Farm
North Frodingham Prim Sch
8
Skerne Beck
Brigham Carr
HOWES LANE
CHURCH LA
PO
MAIN ST
Frodingham Beck
PH
53
CORPSLANDING ROAD
Corpslanding
Brigham Ings
Cross Farm
Cranswick Grange
CORPSLANDING ROAD
MANOR GREEN 1
GLENVILLE CL 2
CROSS LANE
Corpslanding Holme Farm
Moat
Carr Farm
7
Howes Farm
Jarrett's Ings
ROTSEA LANE
Rotsea Drain
CROSS RD
Easfield Farm
Rotsea Manor Farm
Turf Carr
52
Cow Holmes
Cranswick Common
Rotsea
Rotsea Carr Farm
Emmotland
Coneygarth Hill Farm
6
North Frodingham Carr
SHEEPMAN LANE
High Ings
Can Carr
Bethell's Bridge
Scurf Dyke Farm
51
YO25
Rotsea Carr
Hunt Hill Farm
Whinnyforth
Struncheon Hill Farm
Scurf Dike
Hempholme Farm
Haverham Farm
5
Watton Carrs
Throstle Nest Farm
Manor Farm
Moortown Carrs
50
Standing Holme Farm
Decoy Wood
Lock
Decoy House
Angram Farm
4
Clayfield Carr
Hempholme Bridge
Hallytreeholme
Tophill Low Nature Reserve
CARR LANE
Sleights Farm
49
Middleflat Plantation
HALLYTREEHOLME ROAD
Spen Carr
Watton Carrs
Park Carr
Ladysmith
Watton Beck
3
P
Visitor Centre
Burshill Carrs
North Side Drain
Easingwold Farm
NEW ROAD
Wilfholme Carrs
Burshill Farm
Corner Farm
Wilfholme
48
Watton Carr Nature Reserve
Easingwold Plantation
Villa Farm
Barfhill Covert
Baswick Landing
Wilfholme Carrs
WILFHOLME ROAD
Inn Carr House
Ella Carr
2
Baswick Steer
High Baswick
Sand and Gravel Pit
Ashfield Farm
Moat
Barff Hill Farm
Inn Carrs
P
Wilfholme Landing
Wilfholme Bridge
47
Low Baswick Farm
Heighholme
Burshill and Barff Drain
Aike
Baswick
Moat
Aike Grange Stud
AIKE LANE
Aike Carrs
1
Aike Plantation
Three Plain Ends
Scorborough Ings
Linley Hill Farm
Leven North Carr Drain
Aike Grange Farm
HU17
Lockington Carrs Plantation
Leven Carrs
LINLEYHILL RD
Landing Strip
HEIGHOLME LA
46
04
05
06
07
08
09

44
34

33
22

Scale: 1⅓ inches to 1 mile
0 ¼ ½ mile
0 250m 500m 750m 1 km

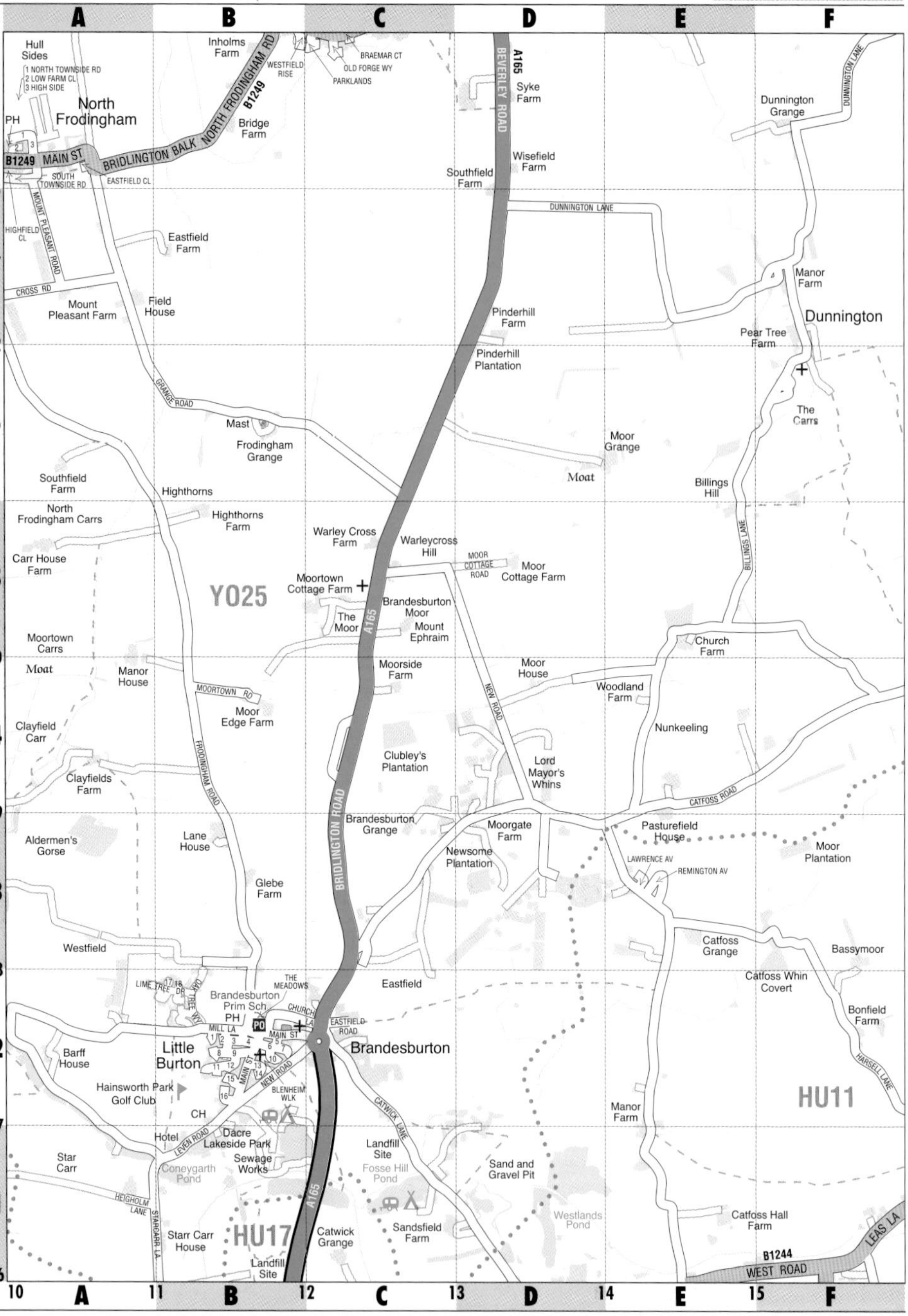

B2
1 PARK AVE
2 ALTOFT CL
3 LITTLE BURTON
4 CHARTER'S LA
5 CROSS HL
6 BOARDMAN LA
7 BOARDMAN PK
8 MAPLE WK
9 ST QUINTIN PK
10 ALDERMANS WY
11 HYMERS CL
12 REEDSWAY
13 STOCKWELL LA
14 BARLEY GARTH
15 THE POPLARS
16 ELMFIELD DR
17 CHERRY TREE CL
18 WILLOW CL

33
45

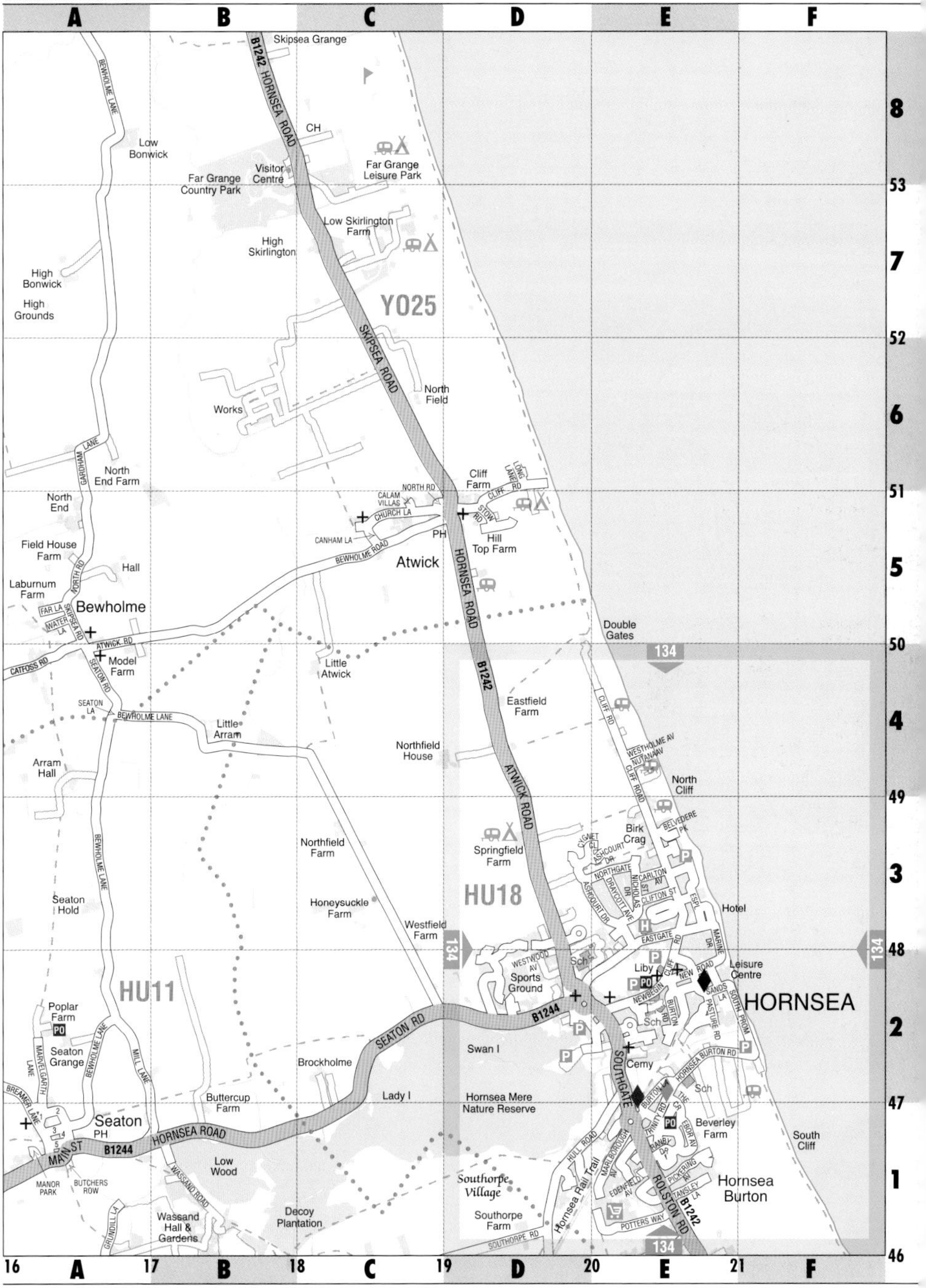

For full street detail of the highlighted area see page 134.

A1
1 COMMON LA
2 NICHOLSON LA
3 BACK LA
4 WITTYS PADDOCK
5 MIDDLE LA

132

C7
1 THE CRESENT
2 LILAC AVE
3 PLEASANT AVE
4 BEECH AVE
5 CHERRY TREE DR
6 CUNDALL DR
7 THE WILLOWS
8 OAK AVE
9 THE CLOSE
10 ELM AVE

D8
1 MAIN ST
2 FERRY FARM CL
3 MAYPOLE GR
4 ST MATTHEW'S CT

133

Scale: 1⅓ inches to 1 mile
0 ¼ ½ mile
0 250m 500m 750m 1 km

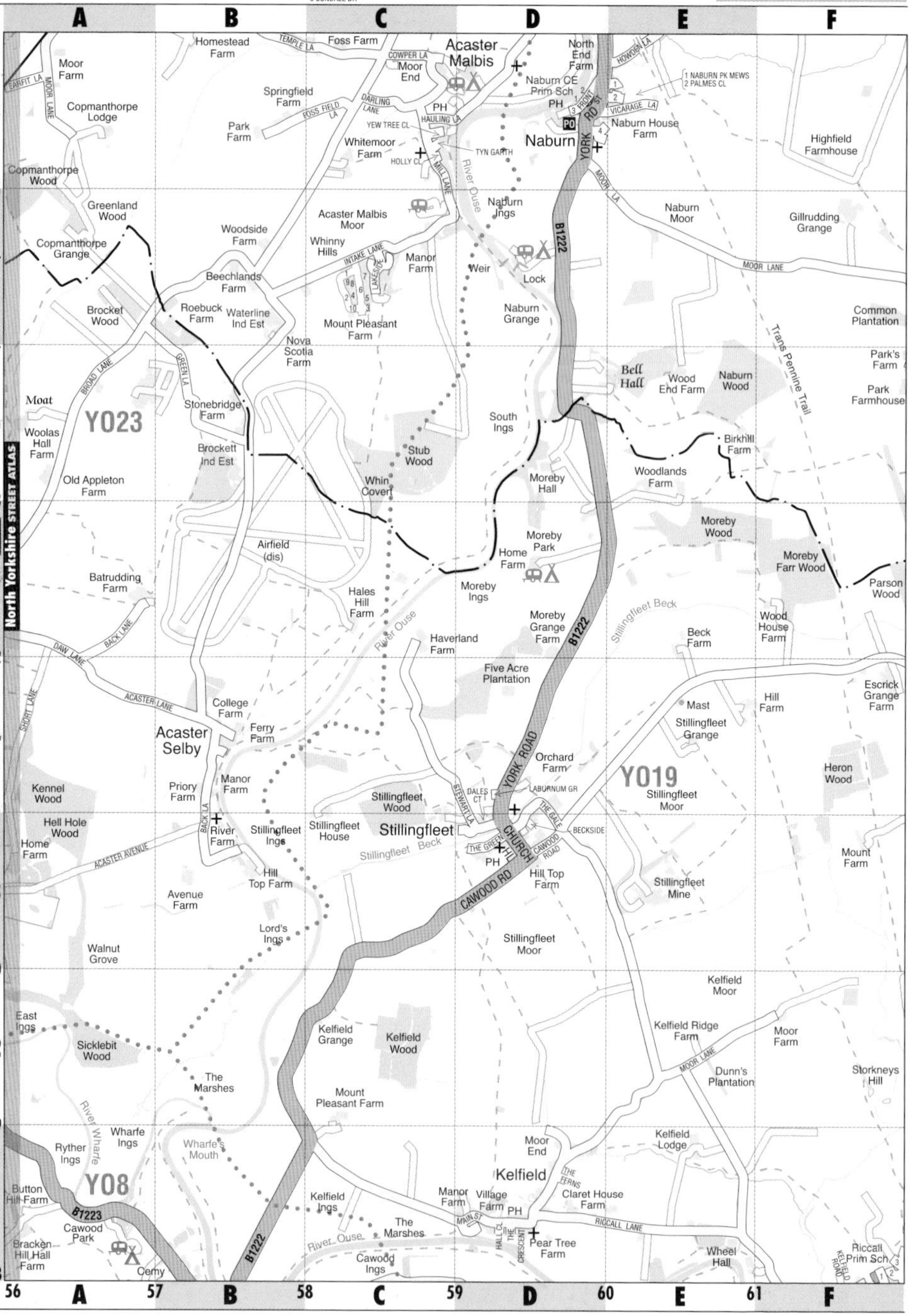

48

F1
1 COPPERGATE
2 ELMS CL
3 NORTHFIELD LA

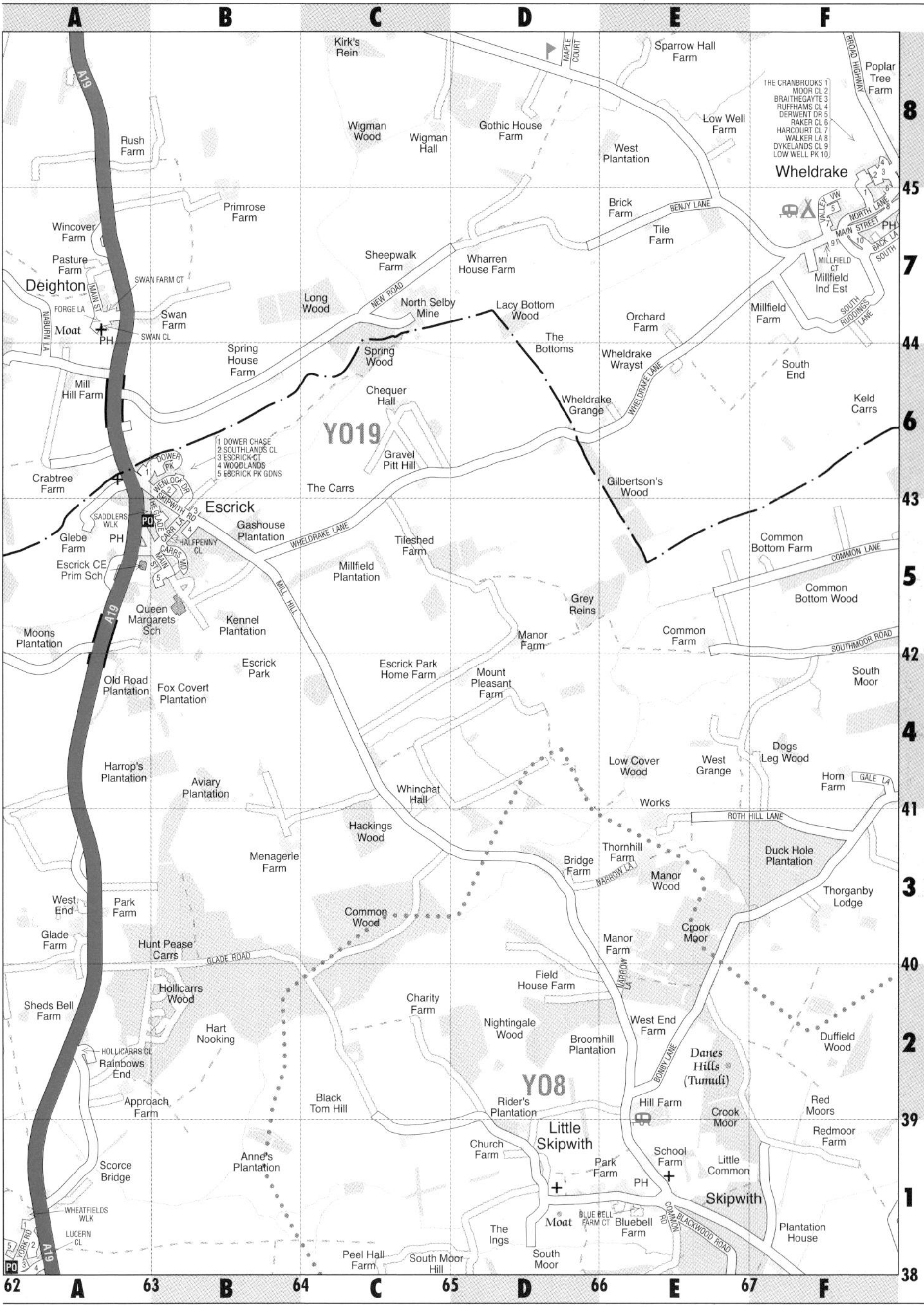
A B C D E F
8 7 6 5 4 3 2 1
45 44 43 42 41 40 39 38
62 63 64 65 66 67
A19
Kirk's Rein
MAPLE COURT
Sparrow Hall Farm
BROAD HIGHWAY
Poplar Tree Farm
THE CRANBROOKS 1
MOOR CL 2
BRAITHEGAYTE 3
RUFFHAMS CL 4
DERWENT DR 5
RAKER CL 6
HARCOURT CL 7
WALKER LA 8
DYKELANDS CL 9
LOW WELL PK 10
Rush Farm
Wigman Wood
Wigman Hall
Gothic House Farm
Low Well Farm
West Plantation
Wheldrake
Primrose Farm
Brick Farm
BENJY LANE
Tile Farm
VALLEY VW
NORTH LANE
MAIN STREET
BACK LA SOUTH
PH
Wincover Farm
Pasture Farm
Deighton
SWAN FARM CT
MAIN ST
FORGE LA
NABURN LA
Moat
PH
SWAN CL
Swan Farm
Sheepwalk Farm
Wharren House Farm
NEW ROAD
Long Wood
North Selby Mine
Lacy Bottom Wood
Orchard Farm
Millfield Farm
MILLFIELD CT
Millfield Ind Est
SOUTH RUDDINGS LANE
Spring House Farm
Spring Wood
The Bottoms
Wheldrake Wrayst
South End
Mill Hill Farm
Chequer Hall
Wheldrake Grange
WHELDRAKE LANE
Keld Carrs
YO19
1 DOWER CHASE
2 SOUTHLANDS CL
3 ESCRICK CT
4 WOODLANDS
5 ESCRICK PK GDNS
DOWER PK
Gravel Pitt Hill
Crabtree Farm
WENLOCK DR
SKIPWITH RD
Gilbertson's Wood
The Carrs
Escrick
SADDLERS WLK
THE GLADE
CARR LA
PO
Gashouse Plantation
Glebe Farm
PH
HALFPENNY CL
WHELDRAKE LANE
Tileshed Farm
Common Bottom Farm
COMMON LANE
Escrick CE Prim Sch
CARRS MD
MAIN ST
Millfield Plantation
Common Bottom Wood
MILL HILL
Queen Margarets Sch
Grey Reins
Moons Plantation
Kennel Plantation
Manor Farm
Common Farm
SOUTHMOOR ROAD
Escrick Park
Escrick Park Home Farm
Mount Pleasant Farm
South Moor
Old Road Plantation
Fox Covert Plantation
Dogs Leg Wood
Harrop's Plantation
Low Cover Wood
West Grange
Horn Farm
GALE LA
Aviary Plantation
Whinchat Hall
Works
ROTH HILL LANE
Hackings Wood
Thornhill Farm
Duck Hole Plantation
Menagerie Farm
Bridge Farm
NARROW LA
Manor Wood
Thorganby Lodge
West End
Park Farm
Common Wood
Crook Moor
Glade Farm
Hunt Pease Carrs
Manor Farm
GLADE ROAD
Field House Farm
NARROW LA
Hollicarrs Wood
Charity Farm
Sheds Bell Farm
Hart Nooking
Nightingale Wood
Broomhill Plantation
West End Farm
Duffield Wood
HOLLICARRS CL
Rainbows End
BONBY LANE
Danes Hills (Tumuli)
YO8
Approach Farm
Black Tom Hill
Rider's Plantation
Hill Farm
Red Moors
Crook Moor
Little Skipwith
Redmoor Farm
Church Farm
School Farm
Little Common
Scorce Bridge
Anne's Plantation
Park Farm
PH
Skipwith
WHEATFIELDS WLK
LUCERN CL
YORK RD
Moat
BLUE BELL FARM CT
Bluebell Farm
COMMON RD
BLACKWOOD ROAD
Plantation House
The Ings
Peel Hall Farm
South Moor Hill
South Moor
PO

37
27

Scale: 1⅓ inches to 1 mile
0 ¼ ½ mile
0 250m 500m 750m 1 km

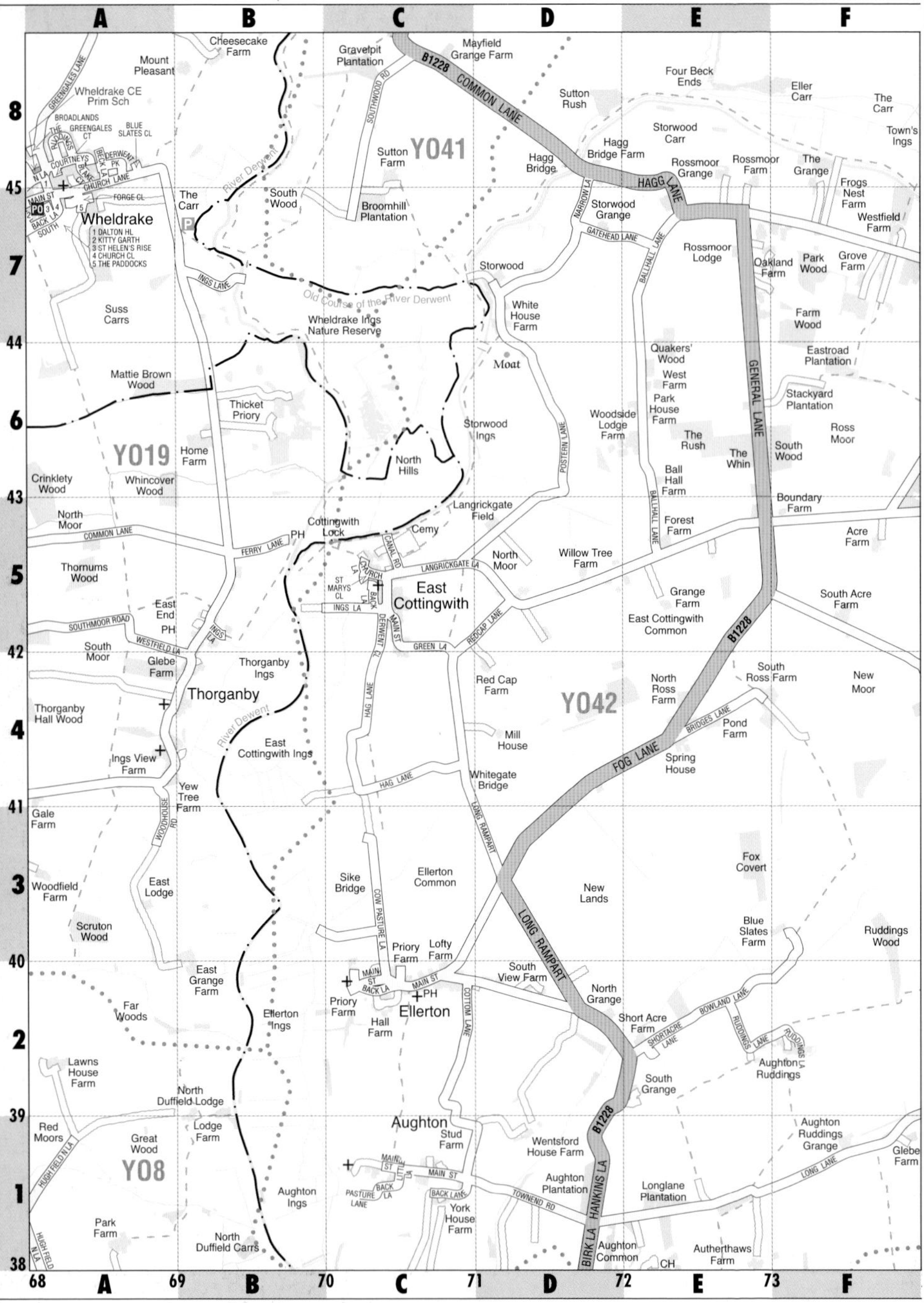

37
50

Scale: 1⅓ inches to 1 mile
0 ¼ ½ mile
0 250m 500m 750m 1 km

28
40

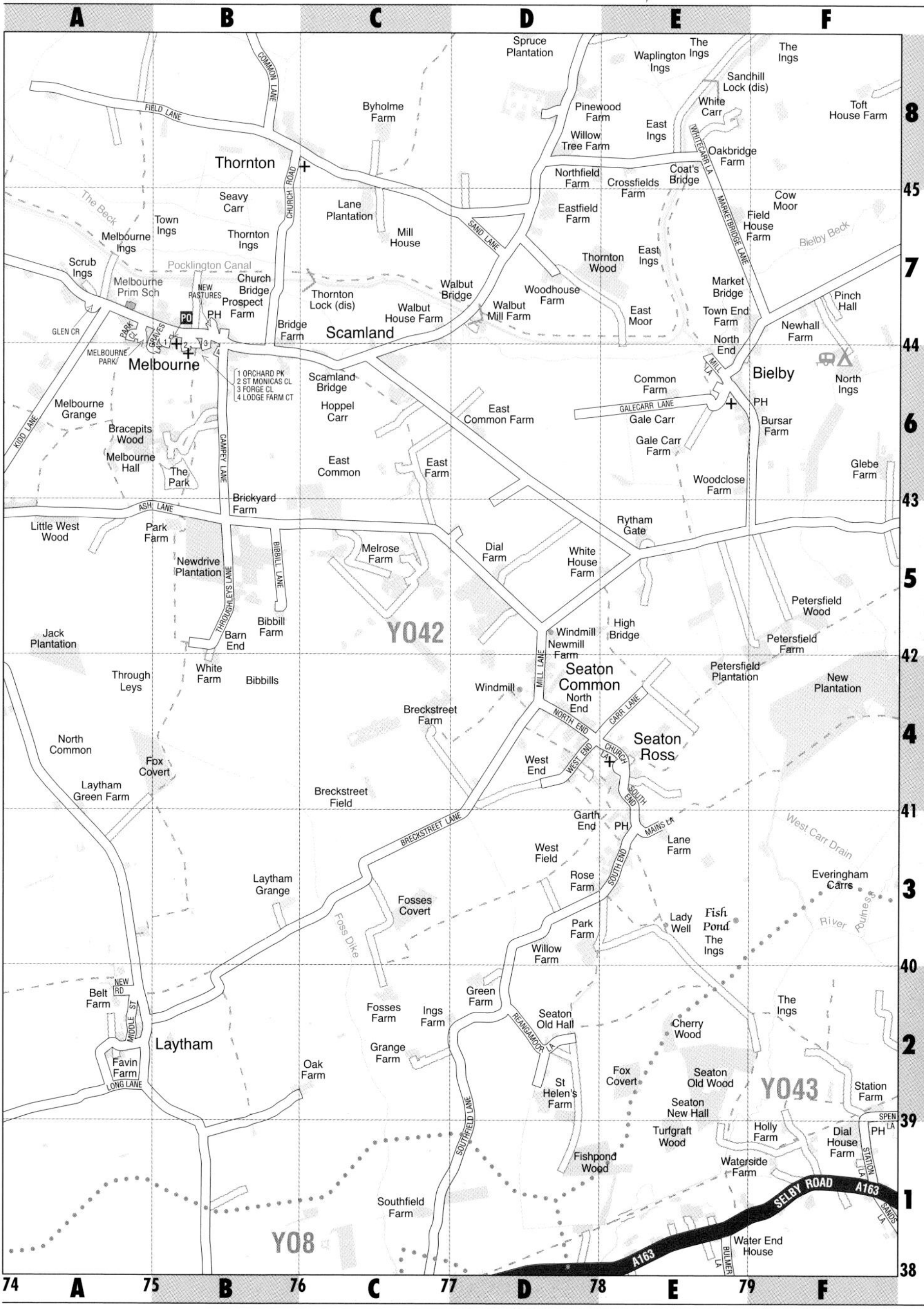

51
40

39
29

Scale: 1⅓ inches to 1 mile
0 ¼ ½ mile
0 250m 500m 750m 1 km

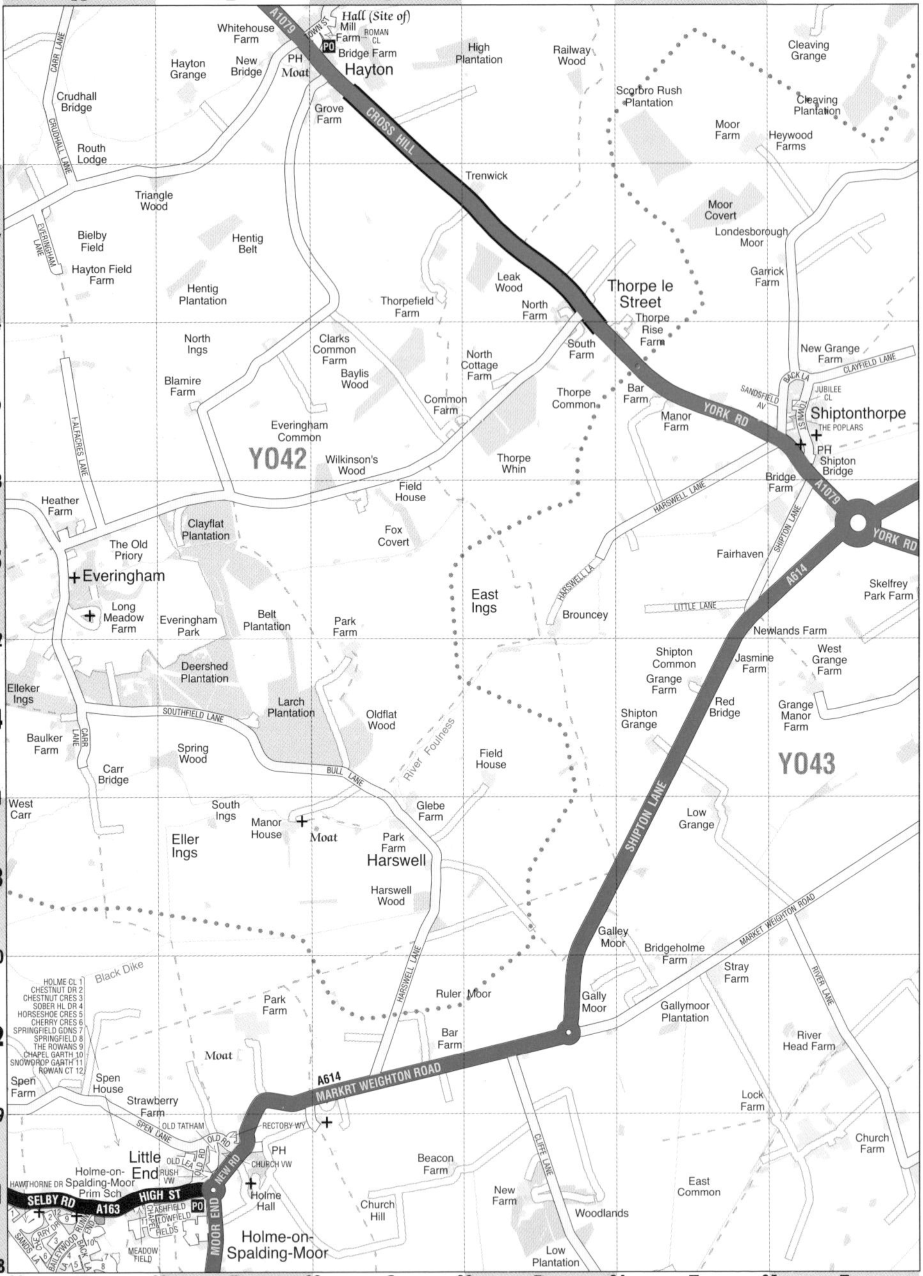

A B C D E F

39
52

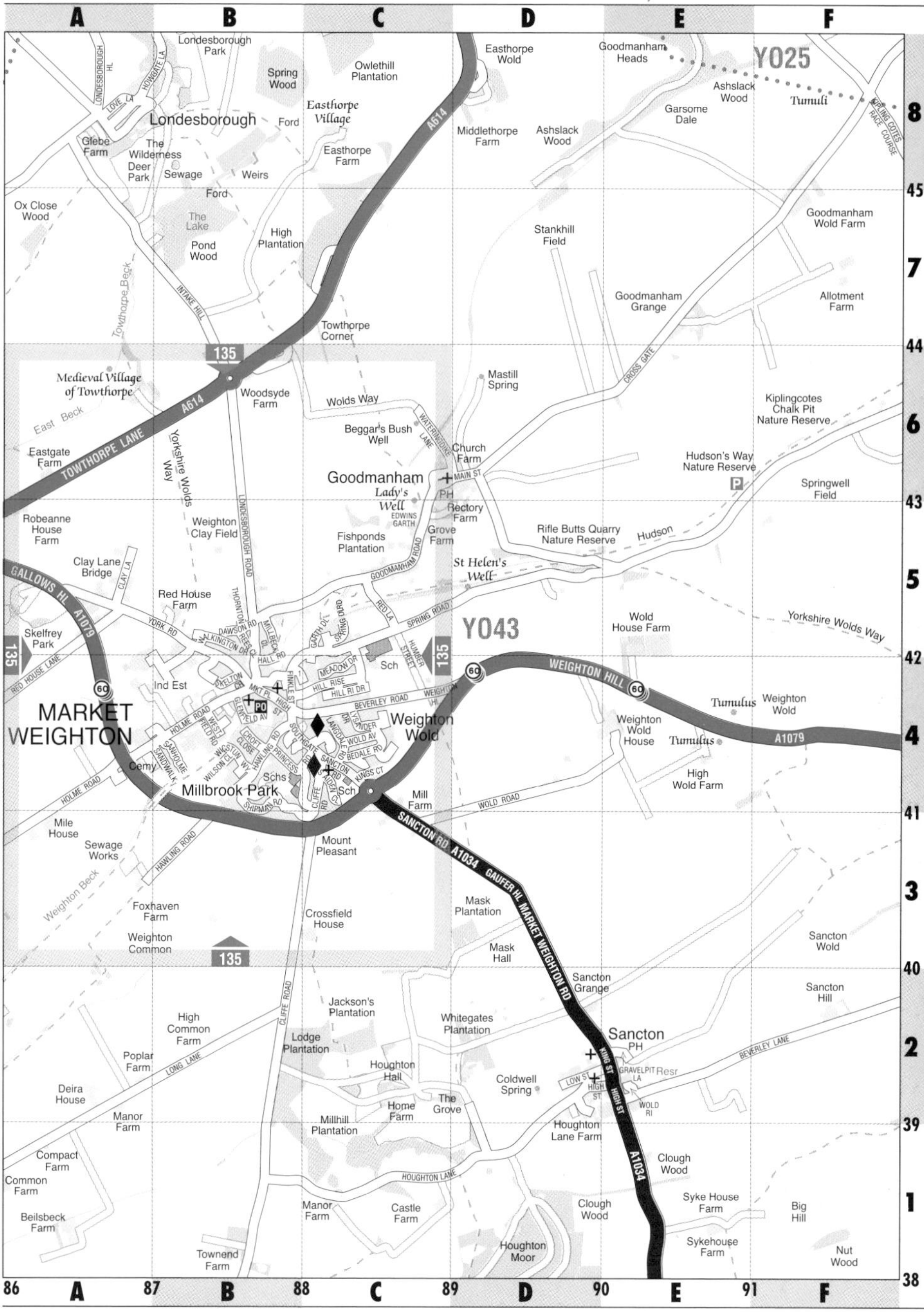

For full street detail of the highlighted area see page 135.

41
31

Scale: 1⅓ inches to 1 mile
0 ¼ ½ mile
0 250m 500m 750m 1 km

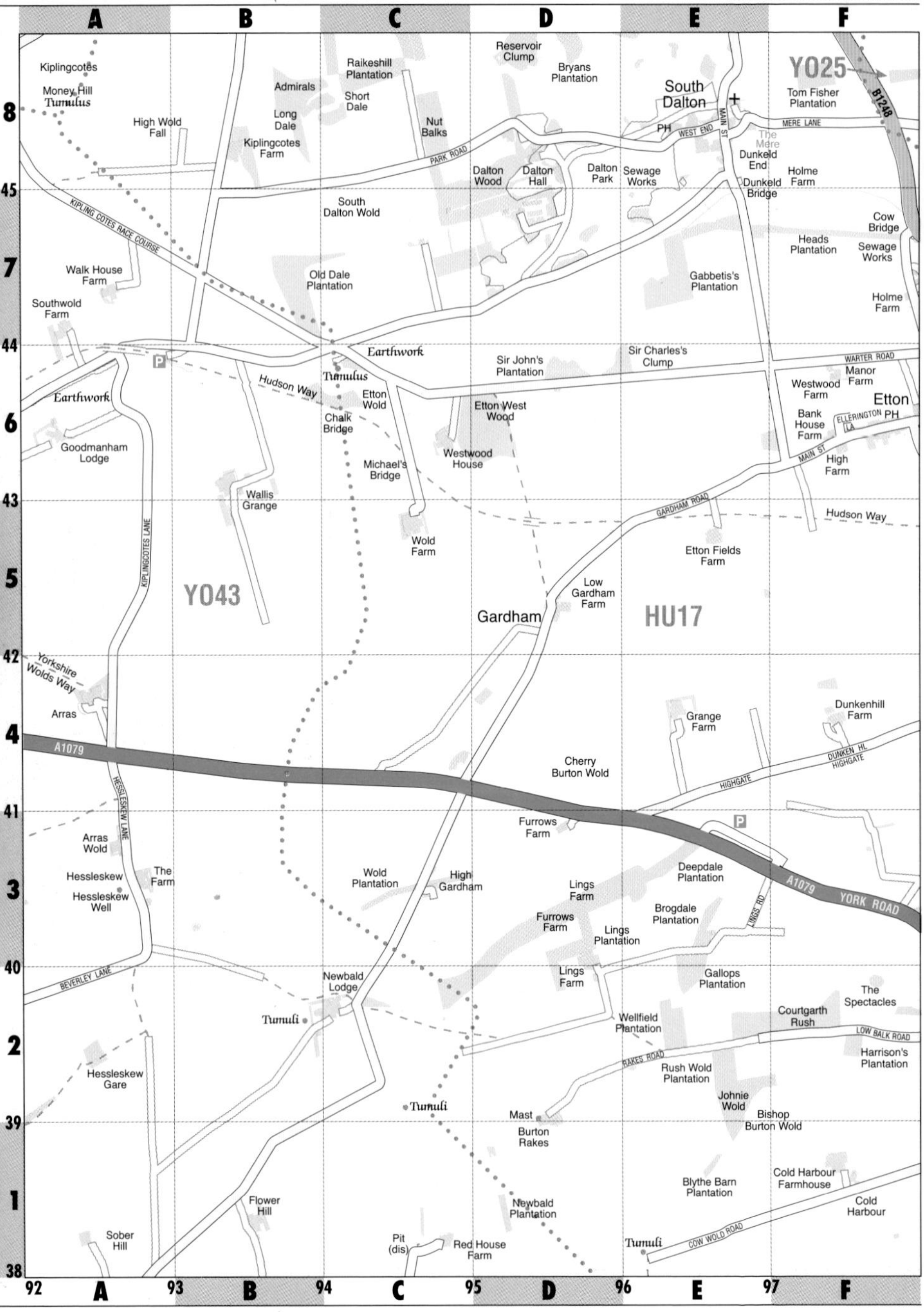

41
54

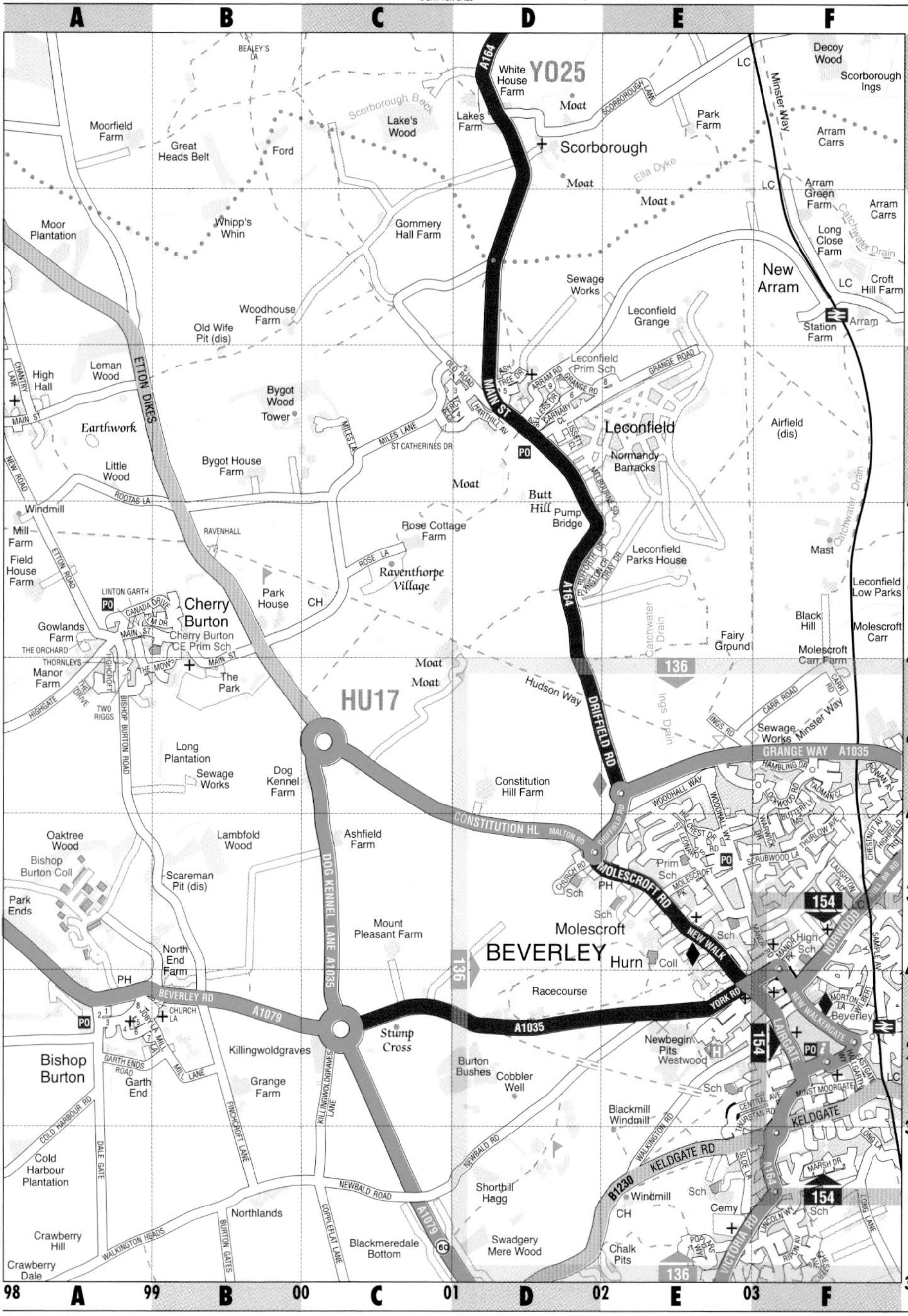
A B C D E F
YO25
HU17
White House Farm
Lakes Farm
Lake's Wood
Scorborough Beck
Scorborough
Scorborough Lane
Moat
Park Farm
Decoy Wood
Scorborough Ings
Minster Way
Arram Carrs
Arram Green Farm
Long Close Farm
Catchwater Drain
Croft Hill Farm
New Arram
Arram
Station Farm
LC
Moorfield Farm
Great Heads Belt
Ford
Ella Dyke
Moor Plantation
Whipp's Whin
Gommery Hall Farm
Sewage Works
Leconfield Grange
Woodhouse Farm
Old Wife Pit (dis)
High Hall
Leman Wood
Etton Dikes
Bygot Wood
Tower
Earthwork
Main St
Miles Lane
St Catherines Dr
Leconfield Prim Sch
Grange Road
Leconfield
Normandy Barracks
Airfield (dis)
Little Wood
Bygot House Farm
Rootas La
Butt Hill
Pump Bridge
Melbourne Rd
Windmill
Mill Farm
Field House Farm
Etton Road
Ravenhall
Rose Cottage Farm
Rose La
Raventhorpe Village
Leconfield Parks House
Mast
Leconfield Low Parks
A164
Cherry Burton
Cherry Burton CE Prim Sch
Linton Garth
Canada Drive
Park House
CH
Gowlands Farm
The Orchard
Thornleys
Manor Farm
Highcroft
The Drive
Highgate
Two Riggs
The Park
Black Hill
Molescroft Carr
Molescroft Carr Farm
Fairy Ground
Catchwater Drain
136
Hudson Way
Driffield Rd
Ings Drain
Ings Rd
Carr Road
Sewage Works
Minster Way
Grange Way A1035
Long Plantation
Sewage Works
Dog Kennel Farm
Constitution Hill Farm
Woodhall Way
Oaktree Wood
Lambfold Wood
Ashfield Farm
Constitution Hl
Malton Rd
Bishop Burton Coll
Scareman Pit (dis)
Dog Kennel Lane A1035
Church Rd
Molescroft Rd
Prim Sch
Sch
PH
Park Ends
Mount Pleasant Farm
Molescroft
New Walk
Norwood
154
High Sch
North End Farm
BEVERLEY
Hurn
Coll
Racecourse
York Rd
Lairgate
New Walkergate
Beverley
Beverley Rd A1079
Church La
Stump Cross
A1035
Newbegin Pits Westwood
Bishop Burton
Killingwoldgraves
Garth Ends Road
Garth End
Mill Lane
Grange Farm
Burton Bushes
Cobbler Well
Minst Moorgate
Keldgate
Blackmill Windmill
Cold Harbour Rd
Cold Harbour Plantation
Dale Gate
Finchcroft Lane
Killingwoldgraves Lane
Newbald Rd
Keldgate Rd
B1230
Walkington Rd
Newbald Road
Shorthill Hagg
Windmill
CH
Sch
Cemy
Marsh Dr
Crawberry Hill
Northlands
Walkington Heads
Burton Gates
Coppleflat Lane
Blackmeredale Bottom
A1079
Swadgery Mere Wood
Chalk Pits
Victoria Rd
Lincoln Wy
Long Lane
Crawberry Dale
98 99 00 01 02 03
38 39 40 41 42 43 44 45
1 2 3 4 5 6 7 8

Scale: 1⅓ inches to 1 mile
0 ¼ ½ mile
0 250m 500m 750m 1 km

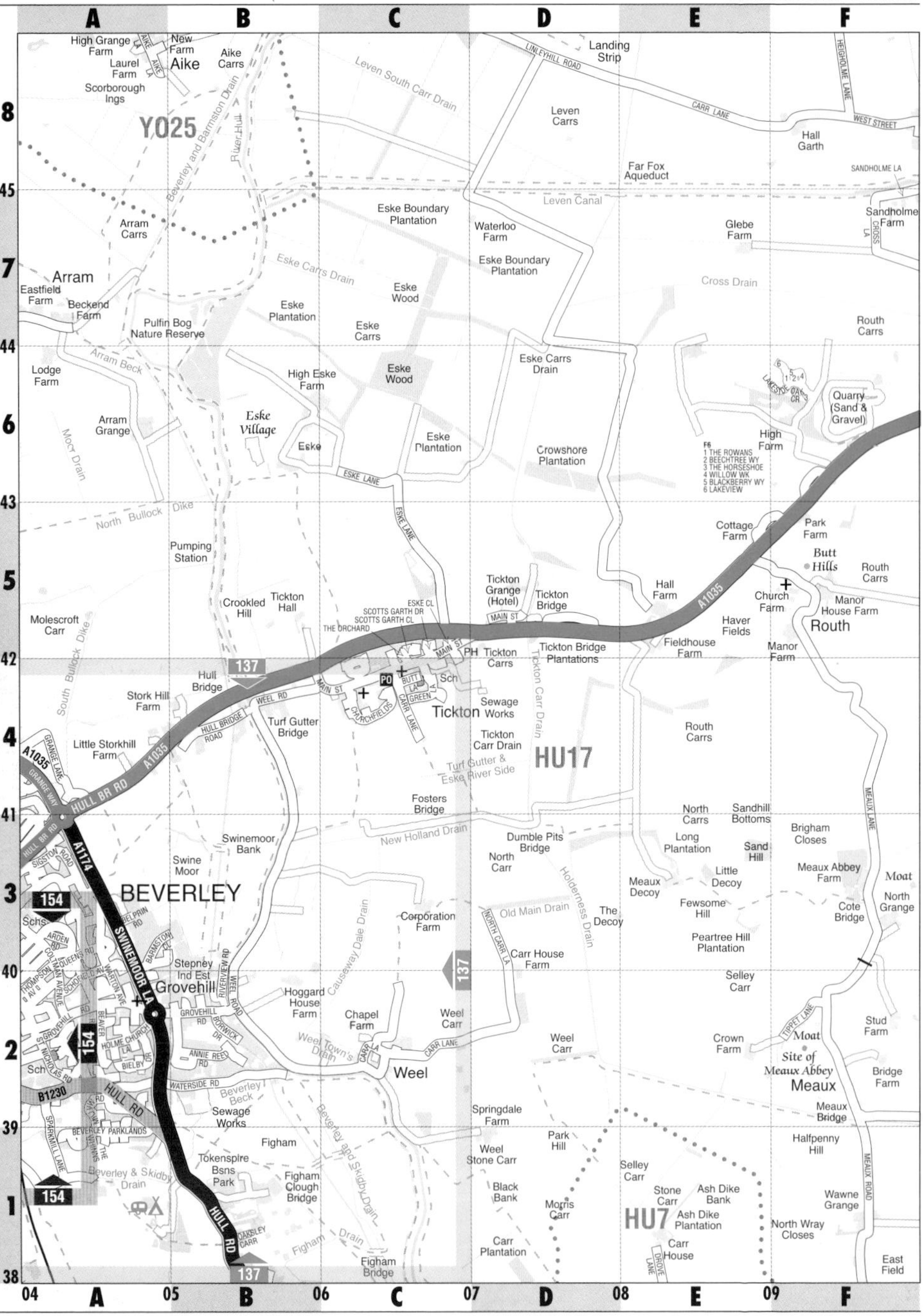
A
B
C
D
E
F
8
45
7
44
6
43
5
42
4
41
3
40
2
39
1
38
04
05
06
07
08
09
High Grange Farm
Laurel Farm
New Farm
Aike
Aike Carrs
Scorborough Ings
YO25
Beverley and Barmston Drain
River Hull
Leven South Carr Drain
LINLEYHILL ROAD
Landing Strip
Leven Carrs
CARR LANE
HEIGHOLME LANE
WEST STREET
Hall Garth
SANDHOLME LA
Far Fox Aqueduct
Leven Canal
Sandholme Farm
CROSS LA
Eske Boundary Plantation
Waterloo Farm
Eske Boundary Plantation
Glebe Farm
Arram Carrs
Arram
Eastfield Farm
Beckend Farm
Eske Carrs Drain
Eske Wood
Cross Drain
Pulfin Bog Nature Reserve
Eske Plantation
Eske Carrs
Routh Carrs
Arram Beck
Lodge Farm
High Eske Farm
Eske Wood
Eske Carrs Drain
Quarry (Sand & Gravel)
Arram Grange
Moor Drain
Eske Village
Eske
Eske Plantation
Crowshore Plantation
High Farm
F6
1 THE ROWANS
2 BEECHTREE WY
3 THE HORSESHOE
4 WILLOW WK
5 BLACKBERRY WY
6 LAKEVIEW
ESKE LANE
North Bullock Dike
Cottage Farm
Park Farm
Pumping Station
Butt Hills
Routh Carrs
Tickton Grange (Hotel)
Tickton Bridge
Hall Farm
Church Farm
Manor House Farm
Crookled Hill
Tickton Hall
Molescroft Carr
ESKE CL
SCOTTS GARTH DR
SCOTTS GARTH CL
THE ORCHARD
MAIN ST
A1035
Haver Fields
Routh
Fieldhouse Farm
Manor Farm
PH
Tickton Carrs
Tickton Bridge Plantations
137
Hull Bridge
South Bullock Dike
Stork Hill Farm
WEEL RD
MAIN ST
PO
BUTT LA
GREEN LA
Sch
CHURCHFIELDS
CARR LANE
Tickton
Sewage Works
Tickton Carr Drain
HULL BRIDGE ROAD
Turf Gutter Bridge
Routh Carrs
GRANGE LANE
A1035
Little Storkhill Farm
Tickton Carr Drain
HU17
GRANGE WAY
HULL BR RD
Turf Gutter & Eske River Side
MEAUX LANE
Fosters Bridge
North Carrs
Sandhill Bottoms
HULL BR RD
A1174
New Holland Drain
Swinemoor Bank
Dumble Pits Bridge
Long Plantation
Brigham Closes
SIGSTON RD
Swine Moor
North Carr
Sand Hill
Little Decoy
Meaux Abbey Farm
Moat
154
BEVERLEY
Meaux Decoy
Holderness Drain
North Grange
Fewsome Hill
Schs
Causeway Dale Drain
Old Main Drain
The Decoy
Cote Bridge
BELPRIN RD
ARDEN RD
Corporation Farm
Peartree Hill Plantation
SWINEMOOR LA
BARMSTON CL
NORTH CARR LA
Carr House Farm
THOMPSON AV
COLTMAN AVENUE
QUEENS RD
SCHOFIELD AV
Stepney Ind Est
Grovehill
RIVERVIEW RD
WEEL ROAD
137
Selley Carr
Hoggard House Farm
Chapel Farm
Weel Carr
GROVEHILL RD
BORWICK DR
TIPPET LANE
Moat
Stud Farm
Weel Carr
Crown Farm
ST NICHOLAS RD
HOLME CHURCH LA
BEAVER RD
BIELBY DR
ANNIE REED RD
Weel Town's Drain
CARR LA
CARR LANE
Site of Meaux Abbey
Sch
154
Weel
Meaux
Bridge Farm
WATERSIDE RD
Beverley Beck
B1230
HULL RD
Sewage Works
Springdale Farm
Meaux Bridge
BEVERLEY PARKLANDS
Figham
Halfpenny Hill
SPARKMILL LANE
Park Hill
Weel Stone Carr
Tokenspire Bsns Park
Beverley and Skidby Drain
Selley Carr
Beverley & Skidby Drain
Figham Clough Bridge
Black Bank
Stone Carr
Ash Dike Bank
Wawne Grange
MEAUX ROAD
154
Morris Carr
HU7
Ash Dike Plantation
North Wray Closes
HULL RD
OAKSLEY CARR
Figham Drain
Carr Plantation
Carr House
DROVE LANE
137
Figham Bridge
East Field

For full street detail of the highlighted area see page 154.

For full street detail of the highlighted area see page 137.

Scale: 1⅓ inches to 1 mile
0 ¼ ½ mile
0 250m 500m 750m 1 km

A8
1 KINGFISHER CL
2 MALLARD AVE
3 THE VINEYARDS
4 THE CLOSE
5 APPLE TREE GARTH
6 WESTLANDS WY

34
46

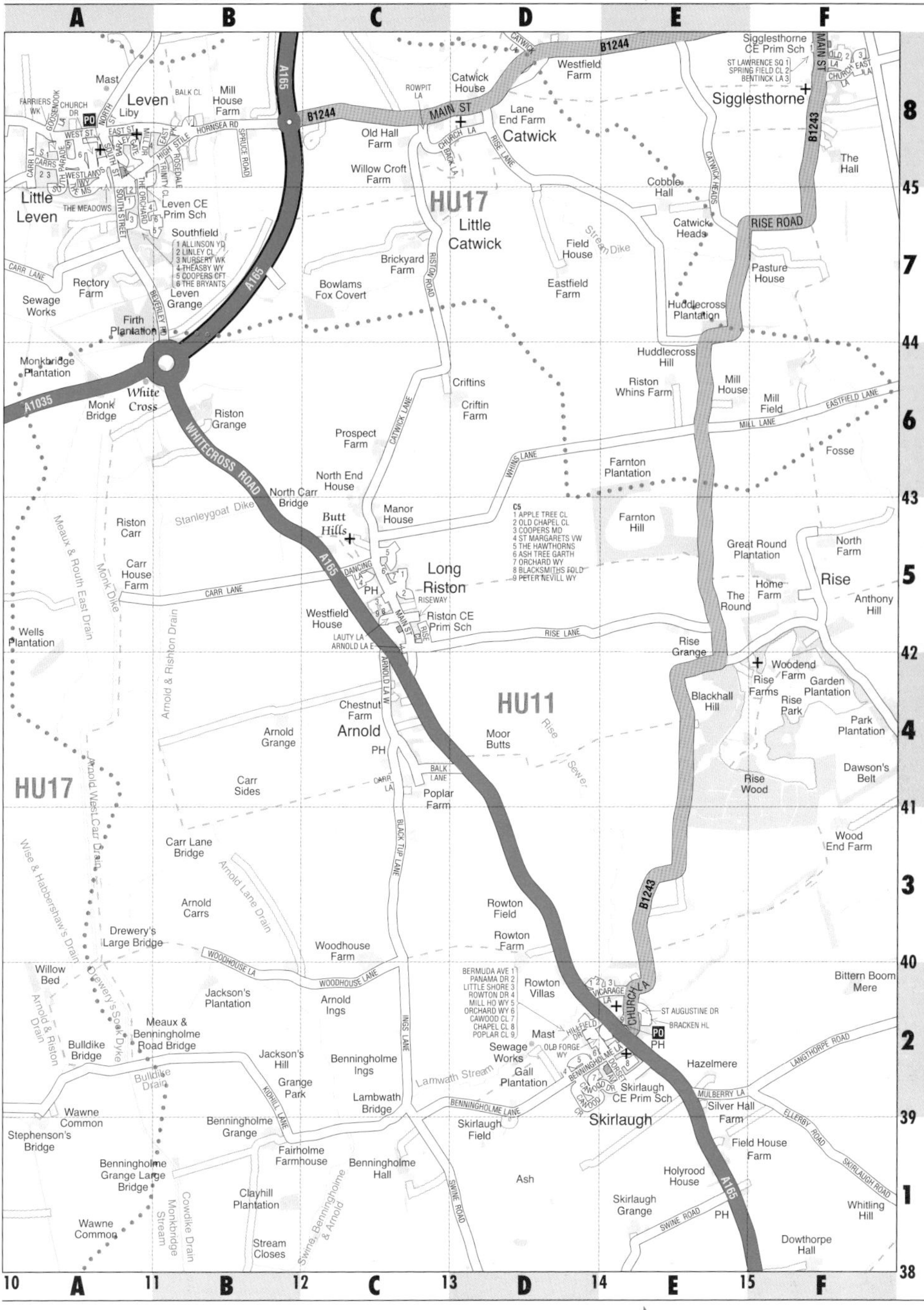

Scale: 1⅓ inches to 1 mile
0 ¼ ½ mile
0 250m 500m 750m 1 km

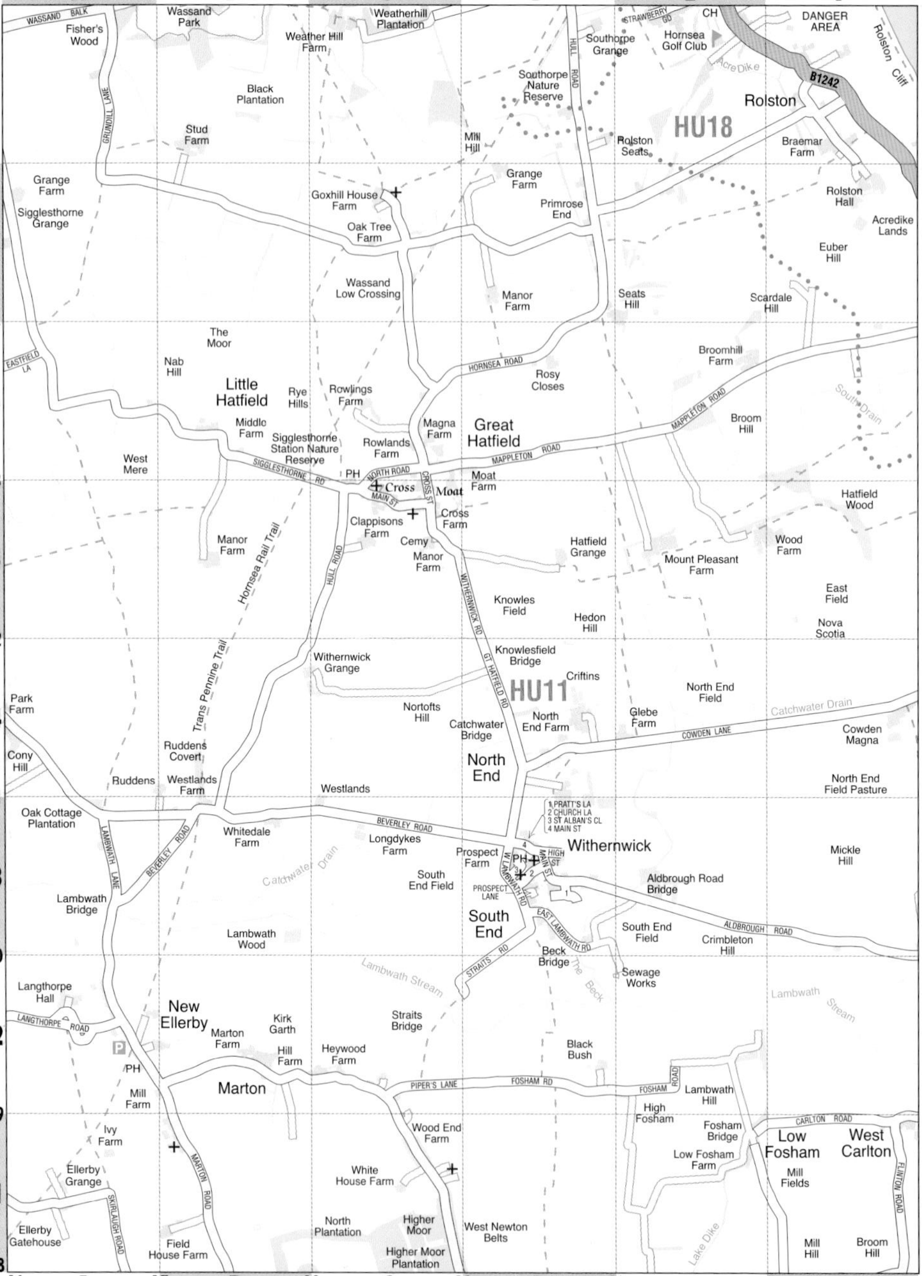

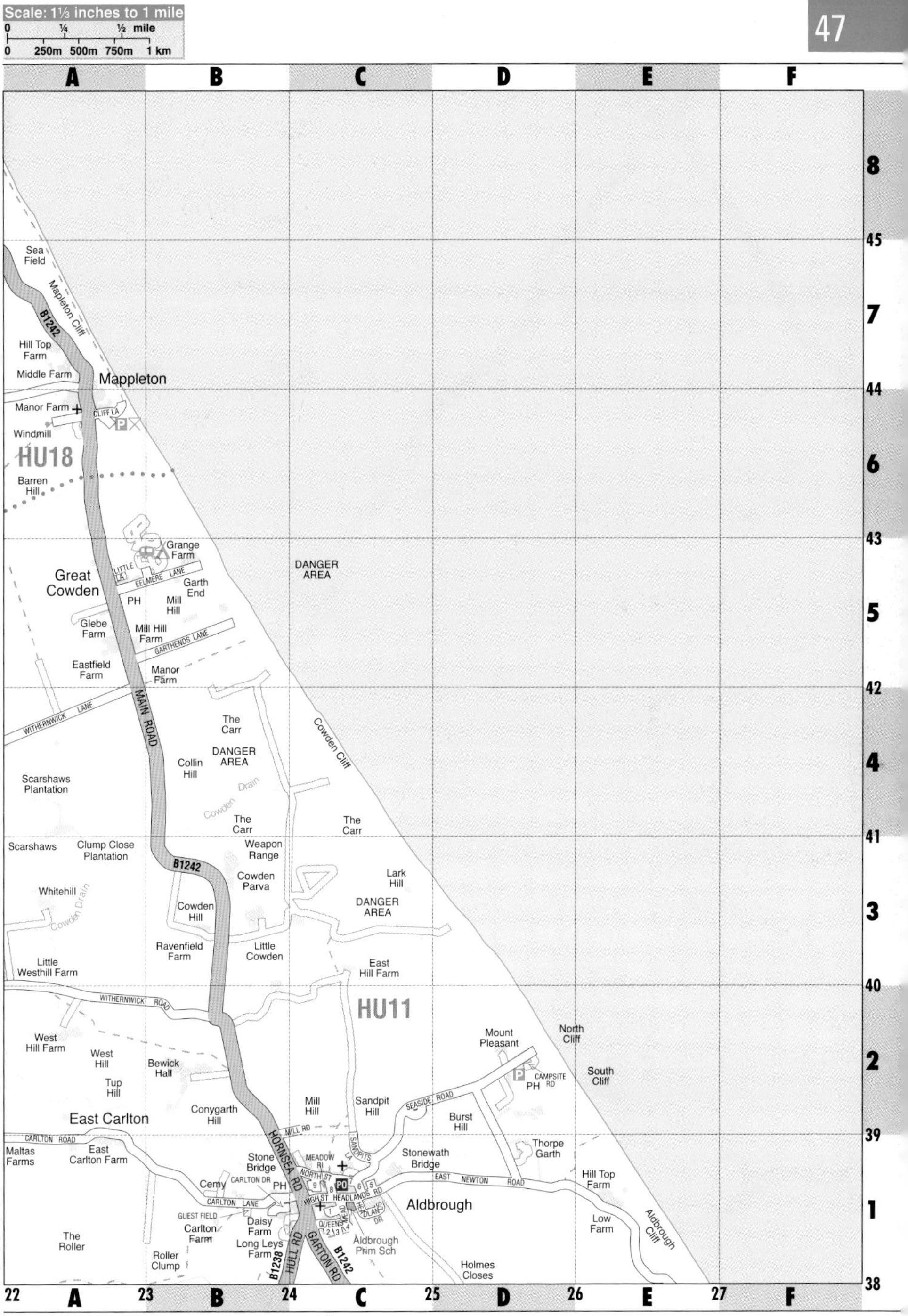
Scale: 1⅓ inches to 1 mile
0 ¼ ½ mile
0 250m 500m 750m 1 km
A B C D E F
8 7 6 5 4 3 2 1
45 44 43 42 41 40 39 38
22 23 24 25 26 27
Sea Field
Mapleton Cliff
B1242
Hill Top Farm
Middle Farm
Mappleton
Manor Farm
CLIFF LA
Windmill
HU18
Barren Hill
Grange Farm
Great Cowden
LITTLE LA
EELMERE LANE
Garth End
PH
Mill Hill
Glebe Farm
Mill Hill Farm
GARTHENDS LANE
Eastfield Farm
Manor Farm
DANGER AREA
WITHERNWICK LANE
MAIN ROAD
The Carr
Cowden Cliff
Collin Hill
Scarshaws Plantation
Cowden Drain
The Carr
Scarshaws
Clump Close Plantation
Weapon Range
Cowden Parva
Lark Hill
Whitehill
Cowden Hill
Ravenfield Farm
Little Cowden
Little Westhill Farm
East Hill Farm
WITHERNWICK ROAD
HU11
Mount Pleasant
North Cliff
West Hill Farm
West Hill
Bewick Hall
CAMPSITE RD
South Cliff
Tup Hill
Conygarth Hill
Mill Hill
Sandpit Hill
SEASIDE ROAD
Burst Hill
East Carlton
MILL RD
Thorpe Garth
CARLTON ROAD
Maltas Farms
East Carlton Farm
Stone Bridge
MEADOW RI
SANDPITS LA
Stonewath Bridge
Cemy
CARLTON DR
HORNSEA RD
NORTH ST
PO
EAST NEWTON ROAD
Hill Top Farm
CARLTON LANE
HIGH ST
HEADLANDS RD
HEADLANDS DR
Aldbrough
GUEST FIELD
Daisy Farm
QUEENS
Low Farm
Aldbrough Cliff
Carlton Farm
Long Leys Farm
Aldbrough Prim Sch
The Roller
Roller Clump
B1238
HULL RD
GARTON RD
Holmes Closes

C1
1 ELM GROVE
2 CEDAR GROVE
3 WILLOW GROVE
4 ASH GROVE
5 WENTWORTH GROVE
6 NOTTINGHAM RD
7 CHURCH ST
8 CROSS ST
9 CASTLE PARK

59

B8
1 SHERBURN ST
2 MARKET PL
3 CARDINALS CL
4 OLD BOYS SCHOOL LA
5 GOLD THREAD LA
6 KING ST
7 WOLSEY GRANGE
8 RYTHERGATE

D6
1 GREENWAYS DR
2 GREEN WAYS CT
3 MOORFIELDS
4 HILL TOP RD
5 CHURCH WK
6 GARTH CL
7 GEORGE ST
8 CHURCH HL
9 WOODALL CT
10 GRANGE GARTH
11 KINGSTHORPE PK

36

F8
1 ASH GR
2 HAWTHORNS
3 CHURCH ST
4 HALL FARM CL
5 VIKING DR
6 THE CRESCENT
7 NORSEMAN CL
8 WEST CT
9 KELFIELD RD
10 CHURCH CL

Scale: 1⅓ inches to 1 mile
0 ¼ ½ mile
0 250m 500m 750m 1 km

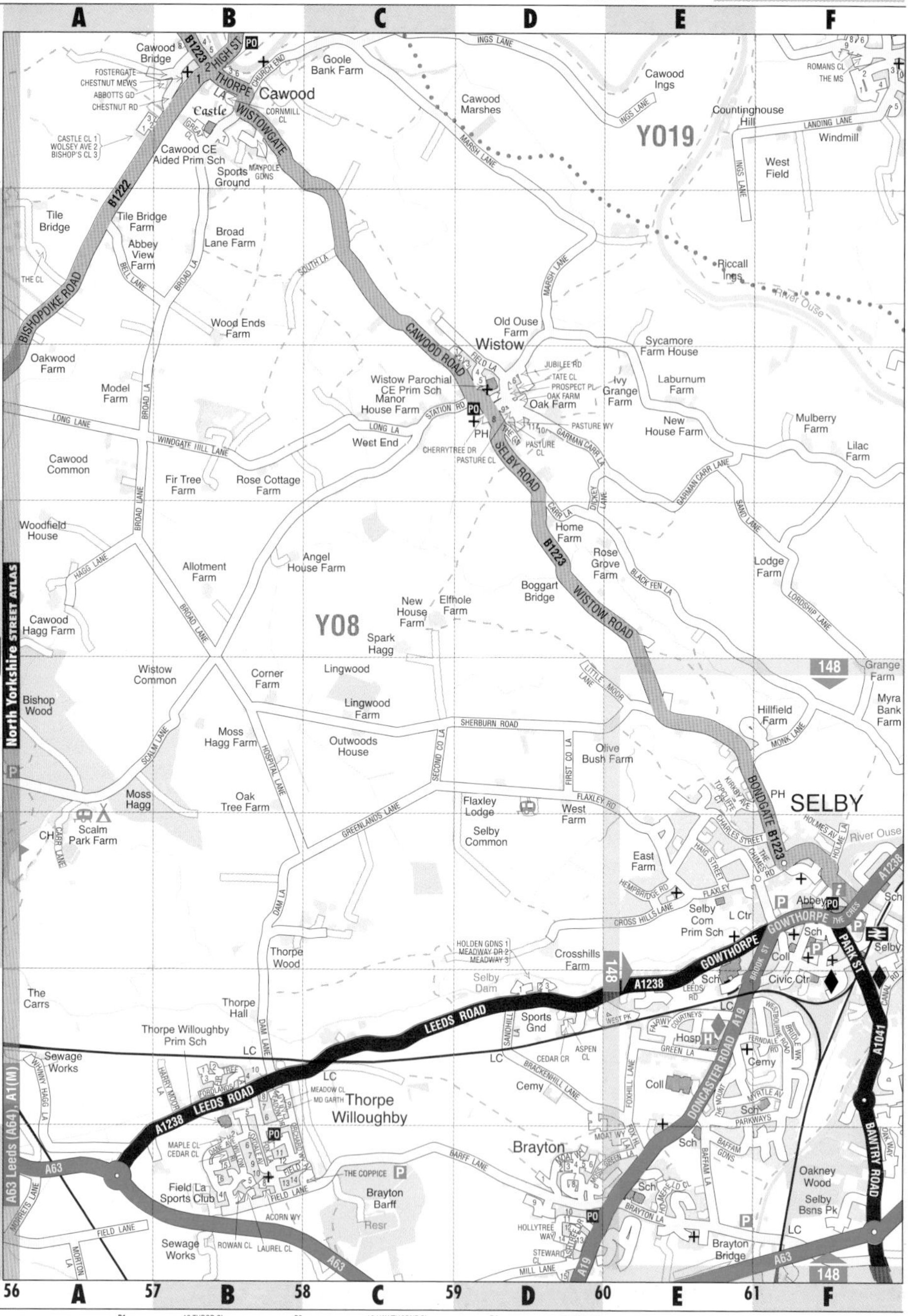

B1
1 SANDWAY DR
2 LIMETREE CL
3 LABURNUM CL
4 BIRCH CL
5 OAK DR
6 SAXON CL
7 NORMAN CL
8 BRAMBLES
9 LINDEN WAY
10 TUDOR CL
11 SANDWAY CL
12 SANDWAY AVE
13 WOOD LA
14 WOOD CL
15 BEECHFIELD CL
16 ALMOND CL

B2
1 FIR TREE WY
2 PINE TREE CL
3 THE FIR TREES
4 FIR TREE CL
5 LONDESBOROUGH GR
6 BARFF GR
7 FRANCIS CT
8 HOLLY GR
9 LINDEN WY
10 HAWTHORNE CL

D1
1 EVERGREEN WY
2 CONIFERS CL
3 GREENACRES GR
4 GREENACRES DR
5 SANDIACRES
6 GREENFIELD DR
7 GREENACRES CRES
8 GREENACRES CL
9 ST WILFRID'S CRES
10 BARFF CL
11 THE POPLARS
12 MAPLE GR
13 CHERRY TREE CL
14 WILLOW BANK
15 MILLCROFT

62

Scale: 1⅓ inches to 1 mile
0 ¼ ½ mile
0 250m 500m 750m 1 km

A8
1 MANOR GARTH
2 BACK LA
3 SILVER ST
4 NOVA SCOTIA WY
5 DANES CT
6 KING RUDDING CL
7 BECKWITH HALL DR

37
50

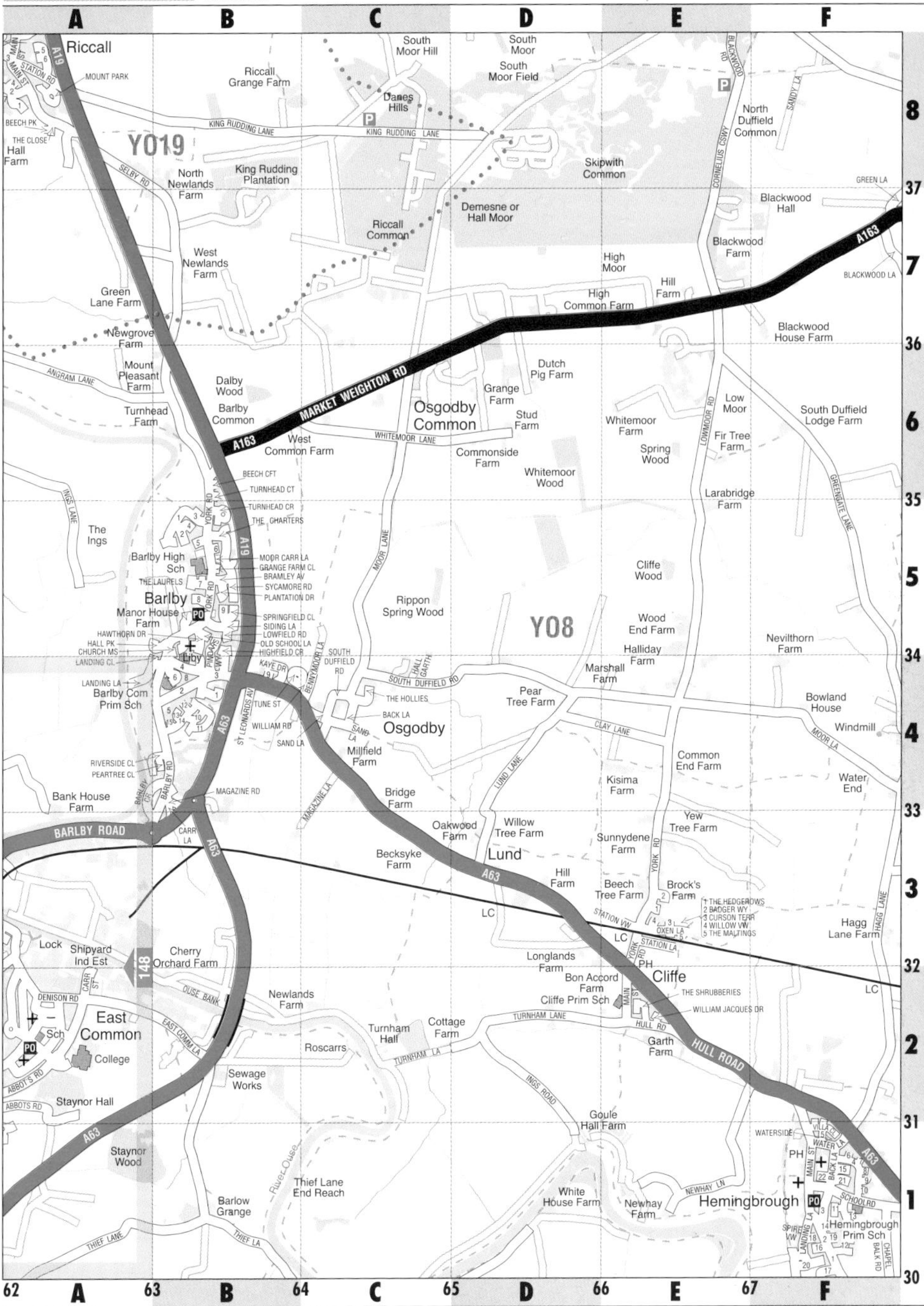

B4
1 GEORGE TERR
2 BARLBY BY-PASS
3 HIGHFIELD VW
4 HOWDEN RD
5 LORDSHIP LA
6 ACORN CL
7 CHERRY TREE WK
8 WILFREDS GR
9 THOMPSON CL
10 MAPLE TREE AVE
11 WOODLANDS VIEW
12 CHERRY TREE CT
13 WOODLANDS CT
14 WOODLANDS DR
15 WOODLANDS CL

B5
1 RIVER VW
2 RIVER CL
3 NORTHFIELD
4 DERWENT DR
5 KINGS CL
6 MOOR LA
7 GROVE PK
8 GLEBE GARTH
9 SPRINGFIELD DR

63
50

F1
1 BARMBY FERRY RD
2 MILL LA
3 GARTHENDS LA
4 CHESTNUT GARTH
5 MANOR CL
6 CHESTNUT RISE
7 CHESTNUT CFT
8 CHESTNUT DR
9 CHESTNUT CT
10 CHESTNUT AVE
11 FERRY CL
12 ST MARY'S AVE
13 CARR CL
14 MILL GARTH
15 THE CLOISTERS
16 SOUTHLANDS
17 MILLFIELD RD
18 DURHAM CL
19 NURSERY CL
20 ORCHARD END
21 OAKFIELD LA
22 CHURCH VW

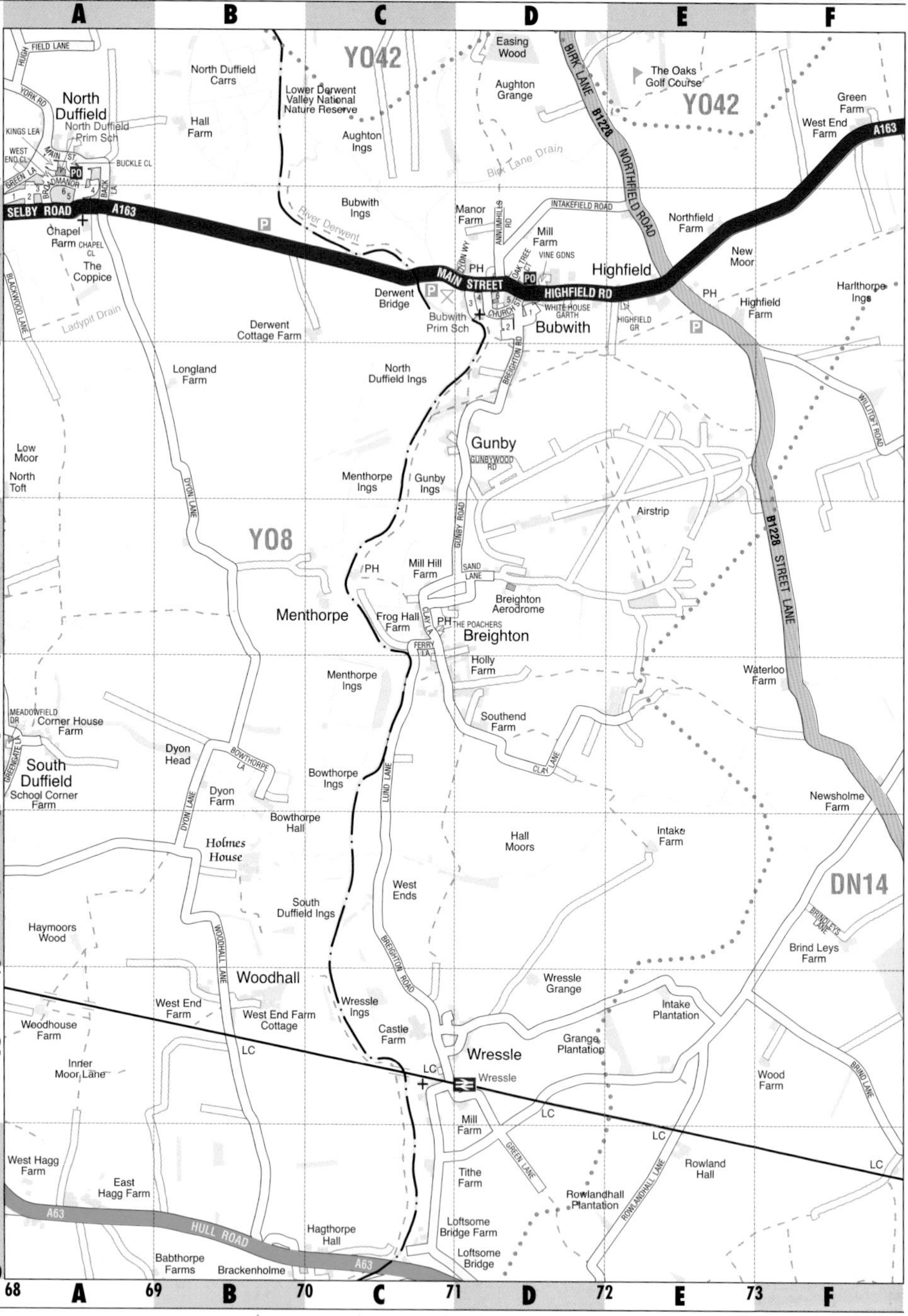
A
B
C
D
E
F
8
37
7
36
6
35
5
34
4
33
3
32
2
31
1
30
68
69
70
71
72
73
FIELD LANE
HIGH
YORK RD
North Duffield
North Duffield Prim Sch
KINGS LEA
WEST END CL
GREEN LA
MAIN ST
BROADMANOR
PO
BUCKLE CL
BACK LA
SELBY ROAD
A163
Chapel Farm
CHAPEL CL
The Coppice
BLACKWOOD LANE
Ladypit Drain
North Duffield Carrs
Hall Farm
Y042
Lower Derwent Valley National Nature Reserve
Aughton Ings
Bubwith Ings
River Derwent
Easing Wood
Aughton Grange
Birk Lane Drain
BIRK LANE
B1228
NORTHFIELD ROAD
The Oaks Golf Course
Green Farm
West End Farm
Manor Farm
ANNUMHILLS RD
INTAKEFIELD ROAD
Mill Farm
VINE GDNS
OAK TREE CT
PH
MAIN STREET
HIGHFIELD RD
Highfield
Northfield Farm
New Moor
Derwent Bridge
Bubwith Prim Sch
CHURCH ST
WHITE HOUSE GARTH
Bubwith
HIGHFIELD GR
Highfield Farm
Harlthorpe Ings
Derwent Cottage Farm
Longland Farm
North Duffield Ings
BREIGHTON RD
WILLITOFT ROAD
Low Moor
North Toft
Gunby
GUNBYWOOD RD
Menthorpe Ings
Gunby Ings
Airstrip
DYON LANE
Y08
GUNBY ROAD
B1228
STREET LANE
PH
Mill Hill Farm
SAND LANE
Breighton Aerodrome
Menthorpe
Frog Hall Farm
CLAY LA
PH
THE POACHERS
Breighton
FERRY LA
Holly Farm
Menthorpe Ings
Waterloo Farm
MEADOWFIELD DR
Corner House Farm
GREENGATE LA
South Duffield
School Corner Farm
Dyon Head
BOWTHORPE LA
Dyon Farm
Bowthorpe Ings
LUND LANE
Southend Farm
CLAY LANE
Newsholme Farm
Bowthorpe Hall
Holmes House
Hall Moors
Intake Farm
DYON LANE
West Ends
DN14
South Duffield Ings
Haymoors Wood
WOODHALL LANE
BREIGHTON ROAD
BRINDLEYS LANE
Brind Leys Farm
Woodhall
Wressle Grange
West End Farm
West End Farm Cottage
Wressle Ings
Intake Plantation
Woodhouse Farm
Castle Farm
Grange Plantation
LC
Wressle
Inner Moor Lane
LC
Wressle
Wood Farm
BRIND LANE
LC
Mill Farm
LC
GREEN LANE
West Hagg Farm
Tithe Farm
Rowland Hall
LC
ROWLANDHALL LANE
East Hagg Farm
Rowlandhall Plantation
A63
HULL ROAD
Hagthorpe Hall
Loftsome Bridge Farm
Babthorpe Farms
Brackenholme
A63
Loftsome Bridge

Scale: 1⅓ inches to 1 mile
0 ¼ ½ mile
0 250m 500m 750m 1 km

39 52

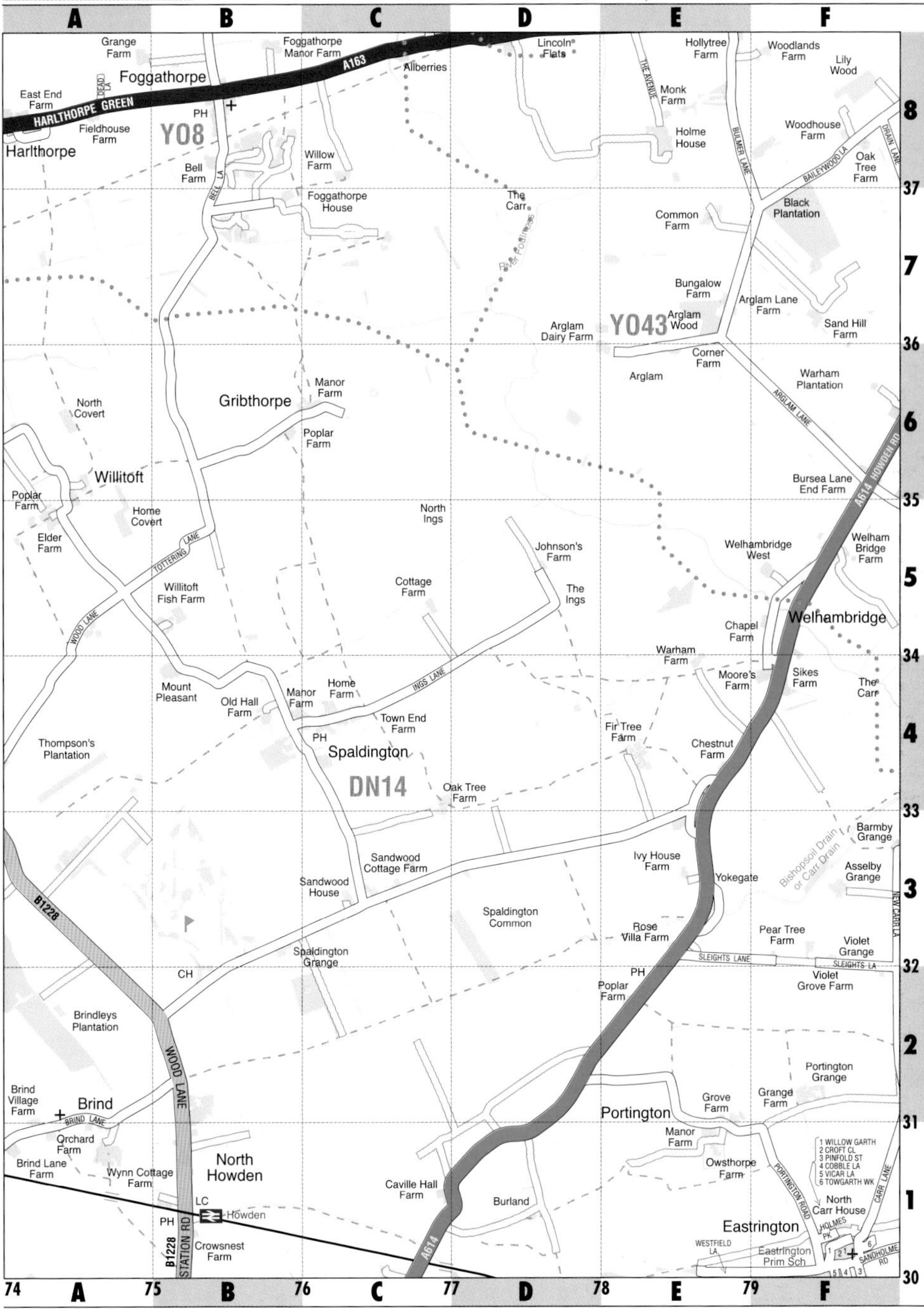

65 52

51
40

Scale: 1⅓ inches to 1 mile
0 ¼ ½ mile
0 250m 500m 750m 1 km

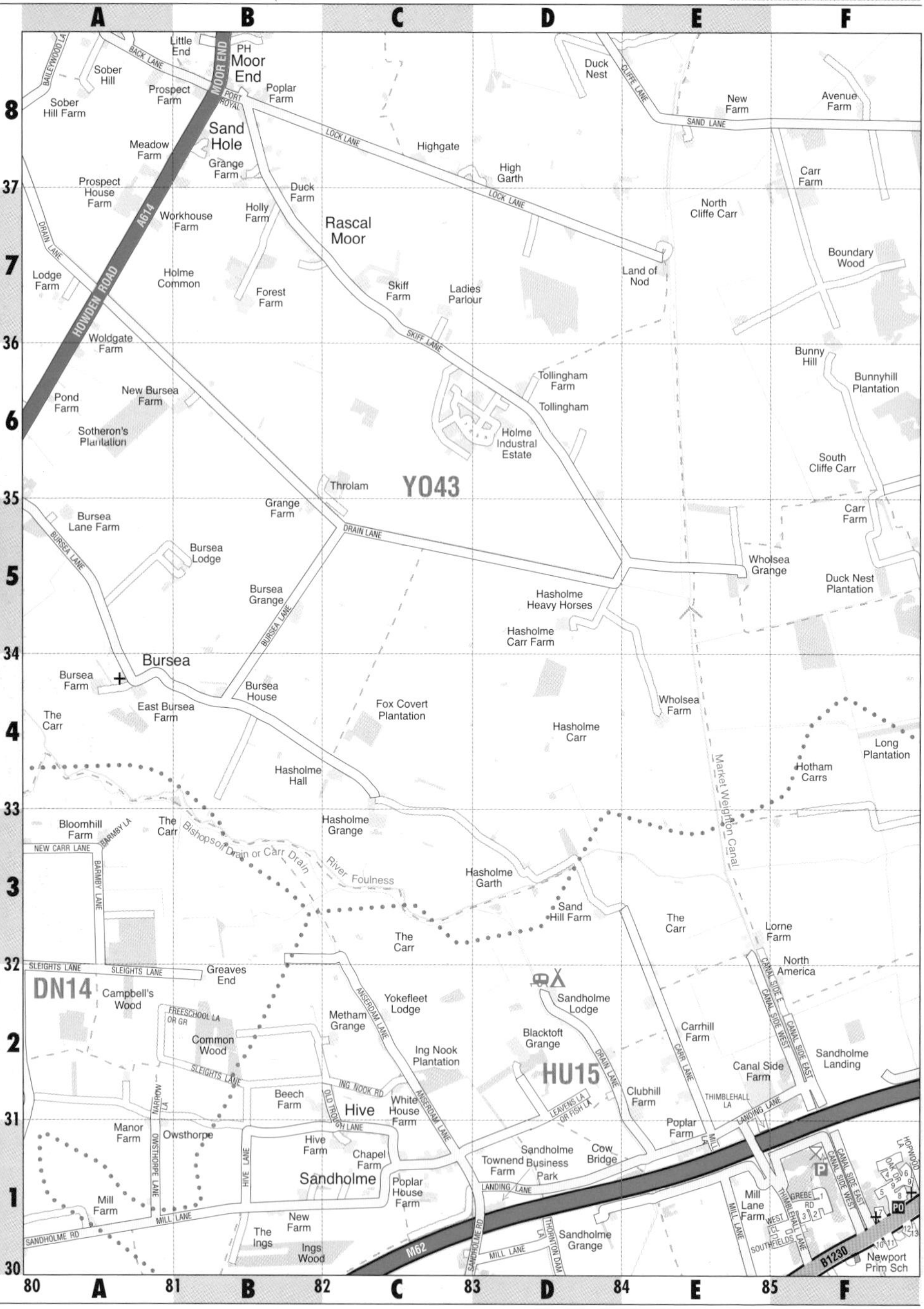

F1
1 TEAL RD
2 GADWALL CL
3 POCHARD CL
4 BRIAR CL
5 HAWTHORN CL
6 THE SPINNEY
7 OCEAN DR
8 BLACKTHORN CL
9 MEADOW LA
10 TURKS HEAD GDNS
11 VILLAGE FARM CL
12 NETTLE HILL
13 MEADOW CT

51
66

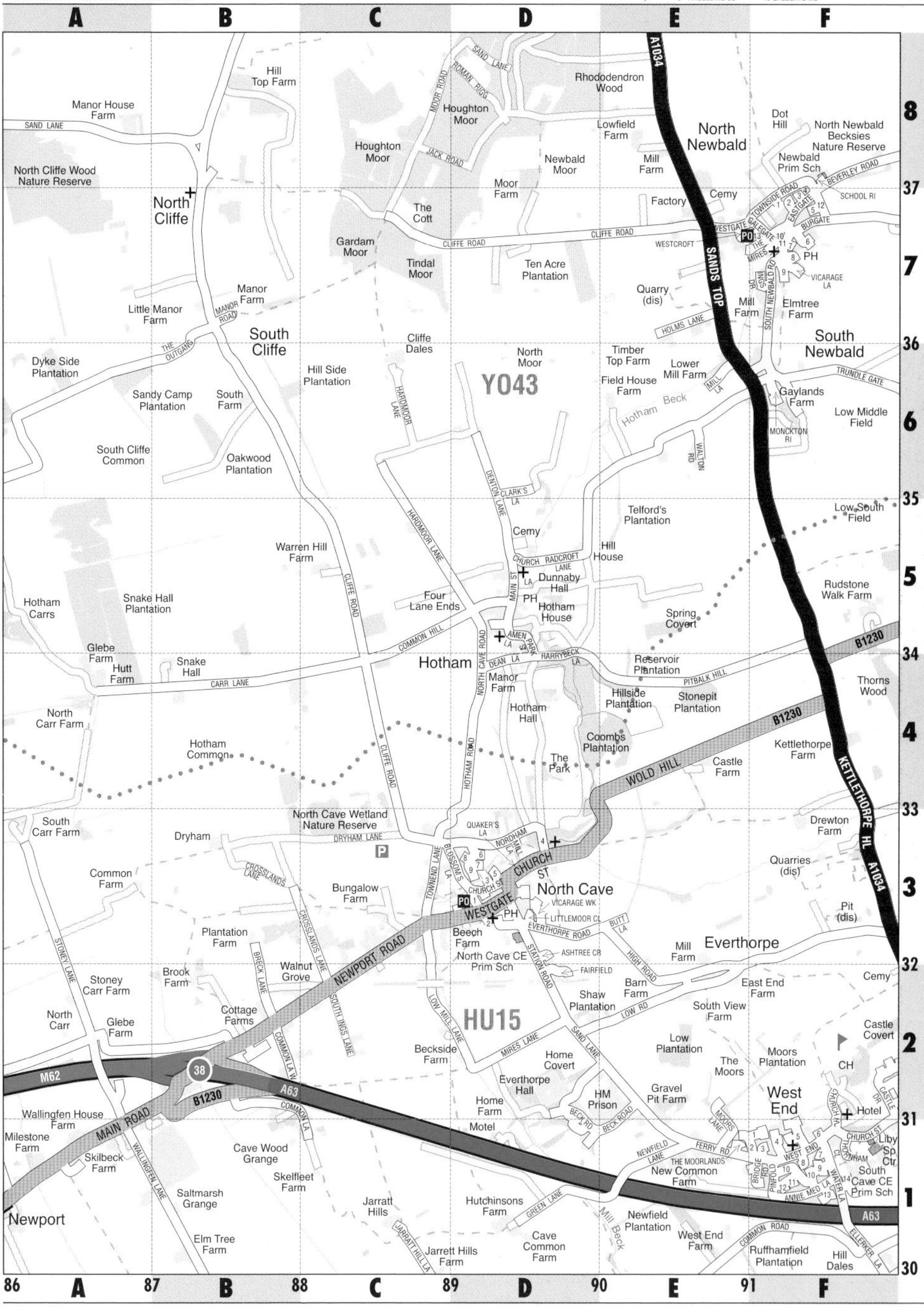
A
B
C
D
E
F
8
37
7
36
6
35
5
34
4
33
3
32
2
31
1
30
86
87
88
89
90
91
Hill Top Farm
Manor House Farm
SAND LANE
North Cliffe Wood Nature Reserve
North Cliffe
Houghton Moor
Gardam Moor
The Cott
Tindal Moor
Rhododendron Wood
Lowfield Farm
Newbald Moor
Moor Farm
Mill Farm
Factory
North Newbald
Dot Hill
North Newbald Becksies Nature Reserve
Newbald Prim Sch
Cemy
CLIFFE ROAD
Ten Acre Plantation
Quarry (dis)
SANDS TOP
A1034
Mill Farm
Elmtree Farm
South Newbald
Manor Farm
Little Manor Farm
South Cliffe
Dyke Side Plantation
Sandy Camp Plantation
South Farm
Hill Side Plantation
Cliffe Dales
North Moor
YO43
Timber Top Farm
Field House Farm
Lower Mill Farm
Hotham Beck
Gaylands Farm
Low Middle Field
South Cliffe Common
Oakwood Plantation
Telford's Plantation
Low South Field
Warren Hill Farm
Cemy
Hill House
Dunnaby Hall
Hotham House
Hotham Carrs
Snake Hall Plantation
Four Lane Ends
Spring Covert
Rudstone Walk Farm
Glebe Farm
Hutt Farm
Snake Hall
CARR LANE
COMMON HILL
Hotham
Manor Farm
Reservoir Plantation
Hillside Plantation
Stonepit Plantation
B1230
Thorns Wood
North Carr Farm
Hotham Common
Hotham Hall
Coombs Plantation
The Park
WOLD HILL
Castle Farm
Kettlethorpe Farm
KETTLETHORPE HL
South Carr Farm
Dryham
North Cave Wetland Nature Reserve
DRYHAM LANE
Drewton Farm
Common Farm
Bungalow Farm
North Cave
Quarries (dis)
Pit (dis)
Plantation Farm
Beech Farm
North Cave CE Prim Sch
Mill Farm
Everthorpe
Brook Farm
Walnut Grove
NEWPORT ROAD
Shaw Plantation
Barn Farm
East End Farm
Cemy
Stoney Carr Farm
North Carr
Glebe Farm
Cottage Farms
HU15
South View Farm
Low Plantation
Castle Covert
Beckside Farm
Home Covert
Moors Plantation
The Moors
M62
38
A63
B1230
Everthorpe Hall
HM Prison
Gravel Pit Farm
West End
Hotel
Wallingfen House Farm
MAIN ROAD
Milestone Farm
Home Farm
Motel
Skilbeck Farm
Cave Wood Grange
Skelfleet Farm
New Common Farm
South Cave CE Prim Sch
Saltmarsh Grange
Jarratt Hills
Hutchinsons Farm
Newfield Plantation
Newport
Elm Tree Farm
Jarratt Hills Farm
Cave Common Farm
Mill Beck
West End Farm
Ruffhamfield Plantation
Hill Dales

53
42

Scale: 1⅓ inches to 1 mile
0 ¼ ½ mile
0 250m 500m 750m 1 km

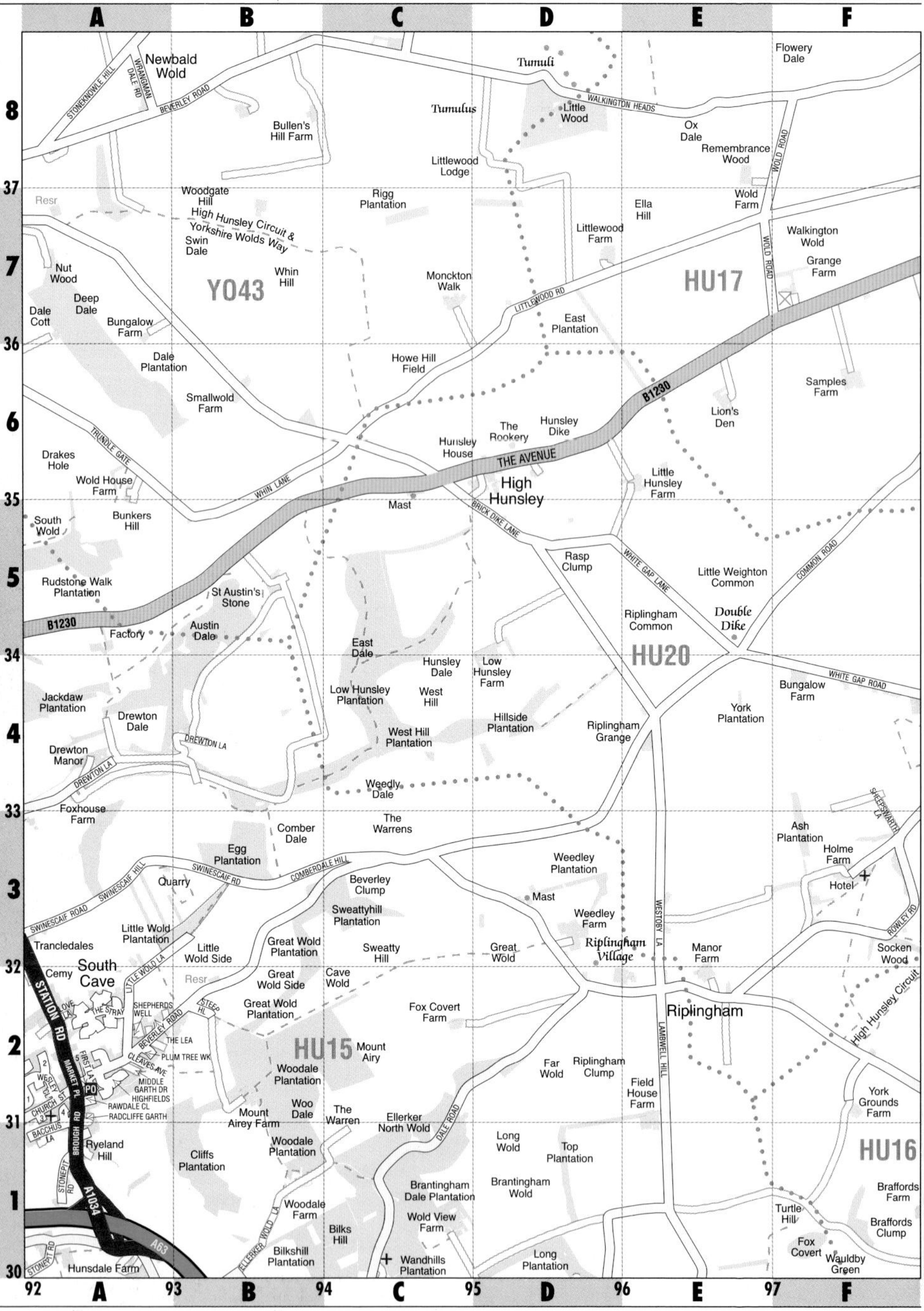

A2
1 CASTLE RISE
2 THE PARKLANDS
3 WOLD VW
4 SOUTHCOTE CL
5 TRINITY FOLD

53
68

B7
1 LAWSON CL
2 FERGUSON RD
3 ALL HALLOWS RD
4 WEST MILL RISE
5 TAYLORS CL

B8
1 WESTFIELD GARTH
2 MIDDLEHOWE GN
3 BIRCH LEA
4 SAUNDERS CFT

C8
1 AUTHERD GARTH
2 WAUDBY CL
3 MEADOW WY
4 SHERWOOD CL

D8
1 SPEEDWELL LA
2 THE HAVEN
3 HAYWARD CL
4 NIGHTINGALE CL
5 HUZZARD CL
6 ORIEL CL
7 ASH DENE
8 MEGSON WAY

43 136 56

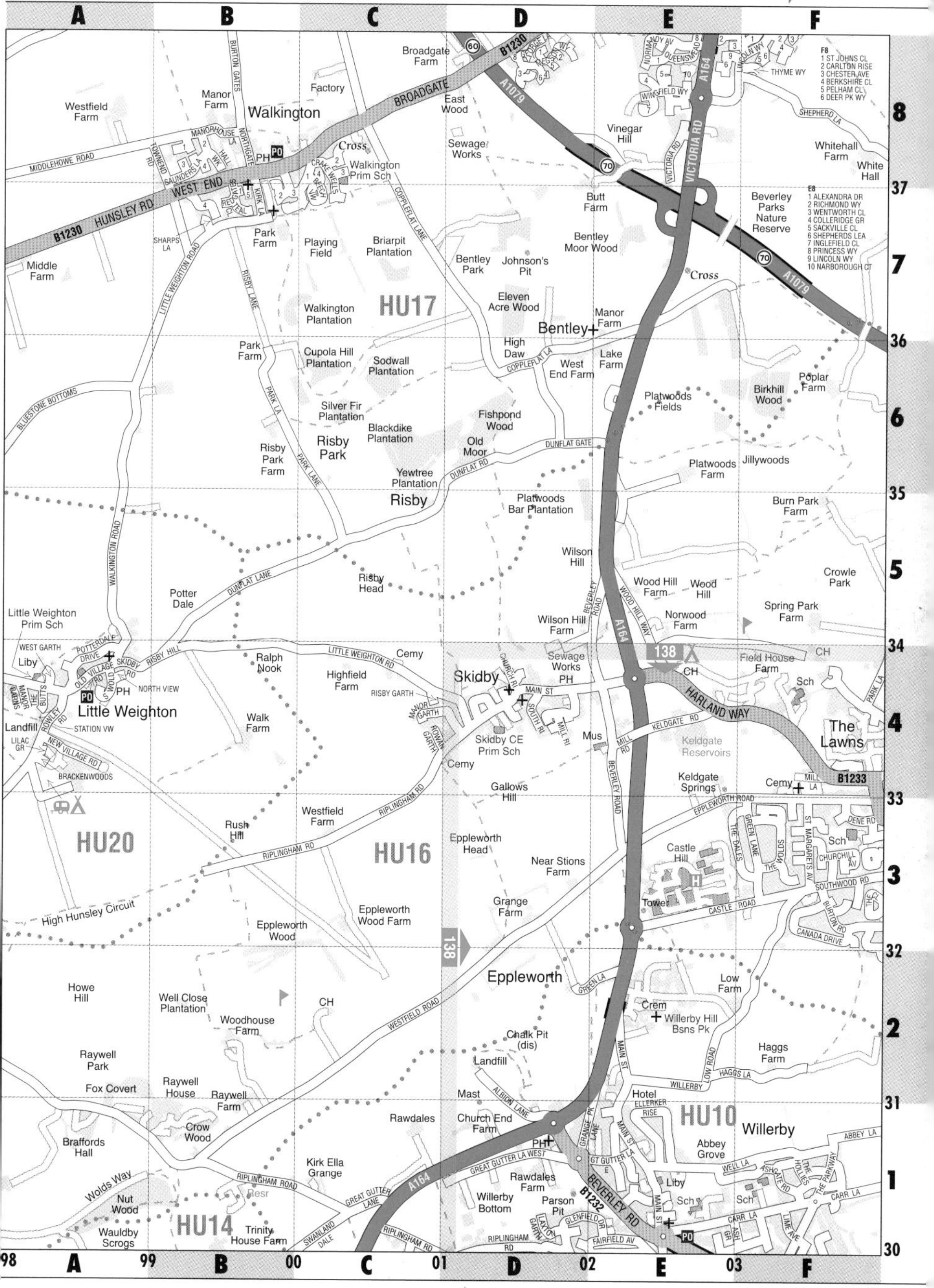

69 139 143
For full street detail of the highlighted area see page 138.

F6
1 ARNCLIFFE CL
2 KETTLEWELL CL
3 WYTHERSTONE CL
4 KILKOY DR
5 SEDBURY CL
6 TRENT PK
7 KINGSBURY WY
8 RAINSWOOD CL
9 FRENSHAM CL
10 RAUCEBY CL
11 GRANTHAM AVE
12 EMBERTON PK
13 THURLSTONE CL

137

14 GREYGARTH CL
15 KINDERSCOUT CL
16 SAPPERTON CL
17 HYKEHAM CL
18 SEDGEBROOK GR
19 QUARRINGTON GR
20 WOOLSTHORPE GR

55

21 SLEIGHTHOLME CL
22 BRECON DR
23 SALCEY CL
24 BRANDON WY
25 LANGLEY PK
26 EMBERTON PK
27 BLACKWATER WY
28 FINDON CL
29 SALTWELL PK
30 KELBERDALE CL
31 NOSELEY WY
32 HIGHGROVE WY
33 CHURCH RD
34 PENNYHOLME CL

44

Scale: 1⅓ inches to 1 mile
0 ¼ ½ mile
0 250m 500m 750m 1 km

For full street detail of the highlighted area see pages 139 and 140.

144

E5
1 BROADWATERS
2 FARTHING DR
3 FLORIN DR
4 BUDWORTH PK
5 CHANCEWATERS
6 CLEARWATERS
7 SOVEREIGN WY
8 CHEVENING PK
9 ALDENHAM PK

138

10 ELVASTON PK
11 CLOVER BANK VW
12 CONNAUGHT RD
13 LINN PK
14 HAUGH PK
15 POOLS BROOK PK
16 HORNSCROFT PK
17 ALTHORPE RD
18 SHINEWATER PK
19 LOSELEY PK
20 GILDERIDGE PK
21 MARKEATON PK
22 HALL LEYS PK
23 RIVELIN PK
24 HALECROFT PK
25 WOODHEYS PK
F5
1 BROOKFIELD CL
2 GRIMSCOTT CL
3 CAMBEAK CL

145

4 DULVERTON CL
5 ASHWORTHY CL
6 COOKBURY CL
7 PADSTOW CL
8 MALPAS CL
9 PENROSE CL
10 KINGSCOTT CL
11 TOWAN CL
12 CAMELFORD CL
13 BLISLAND CL
14 CHERITON CL
15 HARLEQUIN DR
16 FOXGLOVE CL
17 JASMINE GR
18 BEAMSLEY WY
19 MASPIN CL
20 BOSTON CT
21 EVERSFIELD CL
22 KEYNES PK
23 LAVENDER CL
24 FERRY MDW PK
25 KNOLE PK
26 SHILLING CL
27 HARTSHOLME PK
28 TATTON PK
29 MARBURY PK
30 BRADGATE PK
31 TEMPLEWATERS
32 PARCEVALL DR

Scale: 1⅓ inches to 1 mile

0 ¼ ½ mile

0 250m 500m 750m 1 km

A6
1 HARLECH CL
2 LEITHOLM CL
3 BORTHWICK CL
4 SNOWHILL CL
5 RISHWORTH CL
6 RANNOCH CL
7 APPIN CL
8 MOORFOOT CL
9 RANGELEY CL
10 HELVELLYN CL
11 GRASSINGTON CL
12 WHERNSIDE CL
13 WHITEHOPE CL
14 BLACKHOPE CL
15 PYKESTONE CL
16 DALKEITH CL
17 LADYSIDE CL
18 PENDLE CL
19 SADDLEWORTH CL

45

58

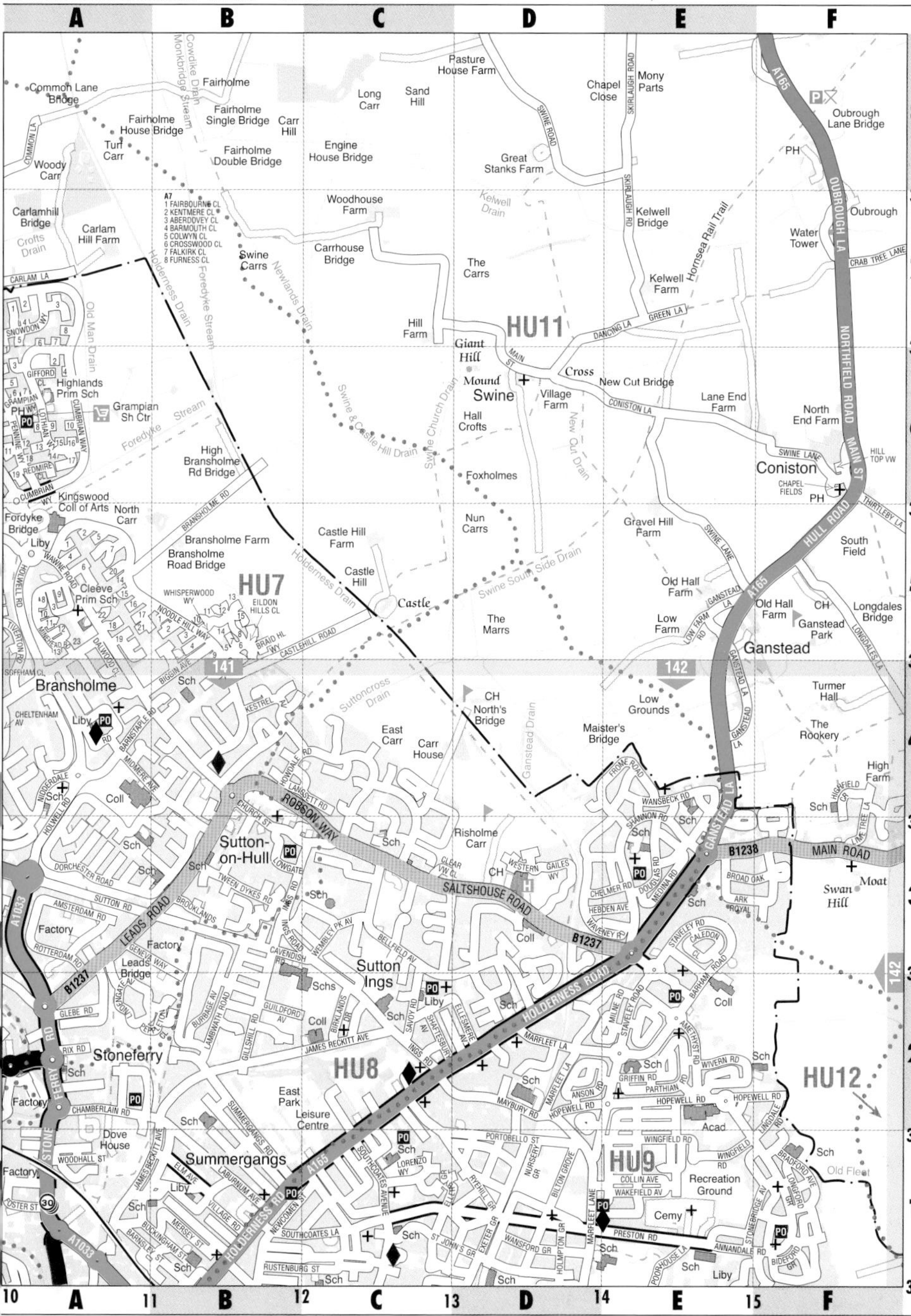

A5
1 ABINGDON GARTH
2 BINBROOK GARTH
3 PORLOCK DR
4 RINGSTEAD GARTH
5 COSFORD GARTH
6 HAYDOCK GARTH
7 DIGBY GARTH
8 ALLERFORD DR
9 LYNMOUTH CL
10 BOSSINGTON CL
11 PITSFOLD CL
12 CLEEVE DR
13 MYLOR CL
14 FINNINGLEY GARTH
15 GATWICK GARTH
16 HUCKNALL GARTH
17 INNSWORTH GARTH
18 YATESBURY GARTH
19 SWINDERBY GARTH
20 ENSTONE GARTH
21 ST BENEDICT CL
22 ZEALS GARTH
23 ST AMBROSE CT

146

B5
1 JASON GARTH
2 KINLOSS GARTH
3 LEEMING GARTH
4 MANSTON GARTH
5 DRUMMOND CT
6 LEADHILLS WY
7 WASELEY HL WY
8 MAIDEN CT
9 NEATSHEAD GARTH

58

10 BRIARWOOD CL
11 HEATHERWOOD CL
12 EASTER WOOD CL
13 CREDENHILL CL
14 THISTLEWOOD CT
15 HONLEY WOOD CL

147

For full street detail of the highlighted area see pages 141 and 142.

57
46

Scale: 1⅓ inches to 1 mile
0 ¼ ½ mile
0 250m 500m 750m 1 km

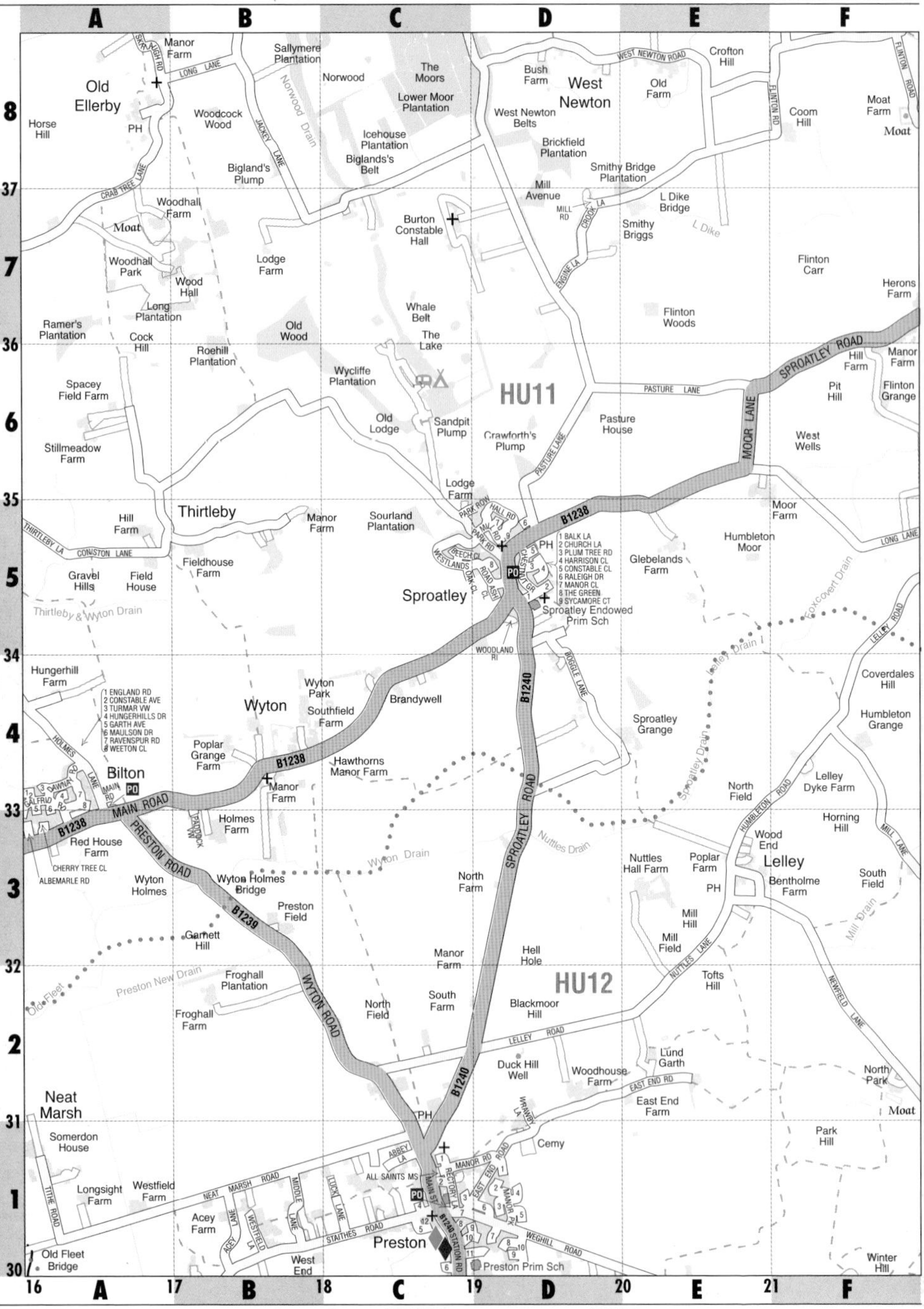

142
72

C1
1 NESS LA
2 KIRK RD
3 THORNTON GR
4 PINFOLD CT
5 VILLAGE FARM RD
6 HELMS AVE
7 SCHOOL RD
8 SYCAMORE CL
9 BROCKLE BANK CT
10 OAK TREE EST
11 ELDON DR
12 CHAPEL CL

D1
1 HIGHFIELD RISE
2 GARBUTT CL
3 GRASSAM CL
4 ELLIS CL
5 HUNTER CL
6 PEACE WK
7 RANDS EST
8 WATKINSON CL
9 BARTLETT CL
10 ADDISON RD

Scale: 1⅓ inches to 1 mile
0 ¼ ½ mile
0 250m 500m 750m 1 km

47 60

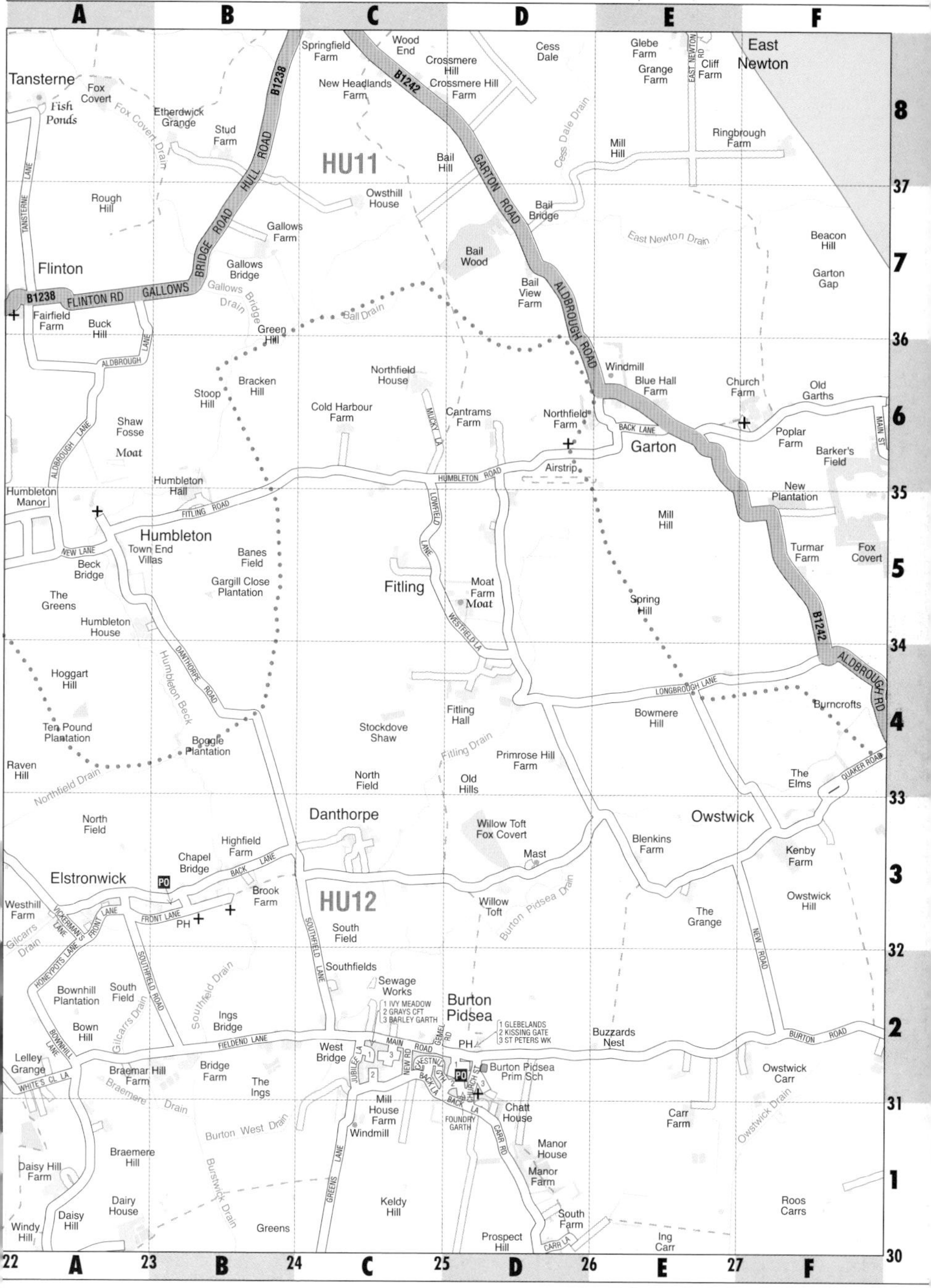

73 60

59

Scale: 1⅓ inches to 1 mile

A B C D E F
8
37
7
36
6
35
5
34
4
33
3
32
2
31
1
30
28 29 30 31 32 33
Great Parks
The Mount Moat
Moat Farm
Sewage Works
Grimston Garth
Grimston Park
Bracken Hill
HU11
Norwood Plantation
Admiral Storr's Tower
Glebe Farm
Tunstall Pastures
TOWER ROAD
Mayfield Farm
Mount Farm
Hilston
Pit (dis)
HOGSEA LANE
QUAKER RD
Gills Mere
Monkwith
B1242
ALDBROUGH ROAD
The Furze
Roos Furze
East Furze
North End Farm
Mill Hill
PASTURES LANE
RECTORY LA
West Furze
Glebe Farm
HU12
FURZE ROAD
Church Farm
Westhill Farm
Manor Farm
Furze Farm
Town Farm
MAIN ST
SEASIDE LANE
Tunstall
Kiln House
Elmtree Farm
Carr Farm
PH
Kiln Well
KILNHOUSE LA
Cliff Farm
BURTON ROAD
Poplar Farm
ROSTUN ROAD
NORTH END RD
North End Villas
North End
East Field
Tunstall Hall
Sewage Works
PINFOLD LA
Hill Top Farm
Cote Farm
Roos CE Prim Sch
1 HINCH GARTH
2 BEECHWOOD VWS
3 PILMAR LA
4 BECKSIDE MANOR
Round Close Plantation
SOUTHFIELD LANE
GREENACRES PK
Tunstall Drain
MAIN ST
PILMAR LANE
B1242
INGLEPOOL CORNER
RECTORY RD
PO
Roos
Cherry Hill
Tedder Hill
HU19
Redhouse Farm
PH
EASTFIELD EST
WITHERNSEA RD
HODGSON LA
Broom Hill
CHESTNUT GARTH
SOUTH PK
SOUTH END RD
ELM GARTH
Thirtle Bridge
LAMB LA
THIRTLE BR LA
Renish
Burnham Carrs
Butcher Bridge

59

74

A8
1 DEER PK CT
2 PRIORY PARK GR
3 PRIORY PARK CL
4 CHURCH LA
5 OLD VICARAGE LA
6 ORCHARD CL
7 THE MEADOWS
8 HILLCREST
9 HILLSIDE CL
10 CHESTNUT GREEN
11 PREBENDAL CL

A7
1 PINE TREE LA
2 ROSE LEA CL
3 HILLAM HALL VW
4 HILLAM HALL LA
5 HILLAM HALL CL
6 BEDFORDS FOLD

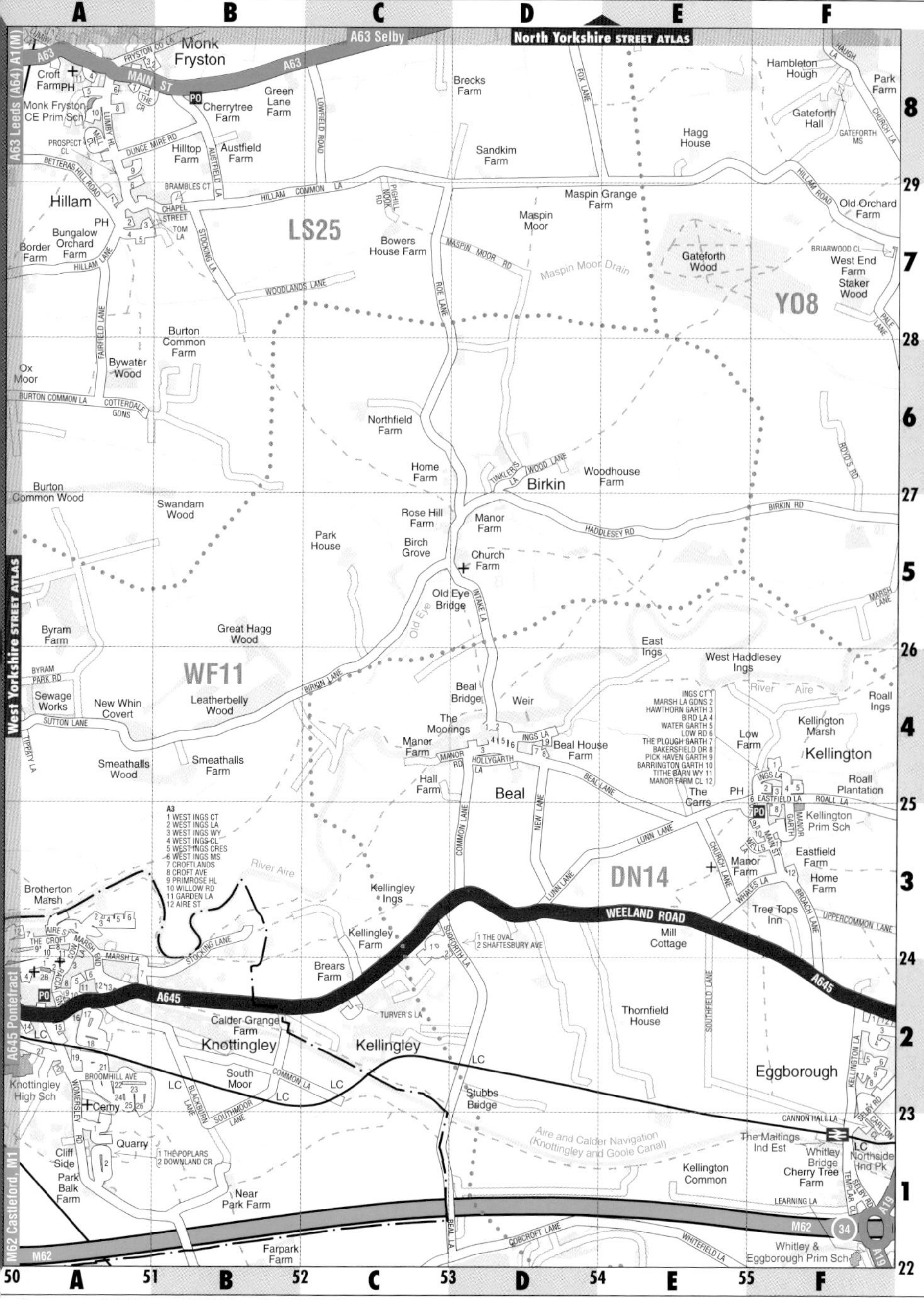
A
B
C
D
E
F
North Yorkshire STREET ATLAS
A63 Selby
A63 Leeds (A64) A1(M)
Monk Fryston
Croft Farm
PH
Monk Fryston CE Prim Sch
MAIN ST
PO
Cherrytree Farm
Green Lane Farm
Brecks Farm
LOWFIELD ROAD
FOX LANE
Hambleton Hough
Park Farm
HAUGH LA
Gateforth Hall
GATEFORTH MS
CHURCH LA
Hagg House
Sandkim Farm
PROSPECT CL
DUNCE MIRE RD
Hilltop Farm
Austfield Farm
AUSTFIELD LA
BETTERAS HILL ROAD
BRAMBLES CT
HILLAM COMMON LA
PIGHILL NOOK RD
Maspin Grange Farm
HILLAM ROAD
Old Orchard Farm
8
29
Hillam
PH
CHAPEL STREET
TOM LA
LS25
Bowers House Farm
MASPIN MOOR RD
Maspin Moor
Maspin Moor Drain
Gateforth Wood
BRIARWOOD CL
West End Farm
Staker Wood
Y08
PALE LANE
7
Border Farm
Bungalow Orchard Farm
HILLAM LANE
STOCKING LA
WOODLANDS LANE
ROE LANE
FAIRFIELD LANE
Burton Common Farm
28
Ox Moor
Bywater Wood
BURTON COMMON LA
COTTERDALE GDNS
Northfield Farm
ROYD'S RD
6
Home Farm
TINKLER'S LA
WOOD LANE
Birkin
Woodhouse Farm
Burton Common Wood
Swandam Wood
27
Rose Hill Farm
Manor Farm
BIRKIN RD
HADDLESEY RD
Park House
Birch Grove
Church Farm
5
Old Eye Bridge
Old Eye
INTAKE LA
MARSH LANE
Byram Farm
Great Hagg Wood
East Ings
26
West Haddlesey Ings
BYRAM PARK RD
WF11
BIRKIN LANE
Beal Bridge
Weir
River Aire
Roall Ings
Sewage Works
New Whin Covert
Leatherbelly Wood
The Moorings
INGS CT 1
MARSH LA GDNS 2
HAWTHORN GARTH 3
BIRD LA 4
WATER GARTH 5
LOW RD 6
THE PLOUGH GARTH 7
BAKERSFIELD DR 8
PICK HAVEN GARTH 9
BARRINGTON GARTH 10
TITHE BARN WY 11
MANOR FARM CL 12
Kellington Marsh
4
SUTTON LANE
TIPPATY LA
Manor Farm
MANOR RD
INGS LA
Beal House Farm
Low Farm
Kellington
Smeathalls Wood
Smeathalls Farm
HOLLYGARTH LA
BEAL LANE
Roall Plantation
Hall Farm
Beal
The Carrs
PH
EASTFIELD LA
ROALL LA
25
COMMON LANE
NEW LANE
PO
Kellington Prim Sch
MANOR GARTH
A3
1 WEST INGS CT
2 WEST INGS LA
3 WEST INGS WY
4 WEST INGS CL
5 WEST INGS CRES
6 WEST INGS MS
7 CROFTLANDS
8 CROFT AVE
9 PRIMROSE HL
10 WILLOW RD
11 GARDEN LA
12 AIRE ST
LUNN LANE
CHURCH LANE
WELLS
MAIN ST
Eastfield Farm
River Aire
DN14
Manor Farm
Home Farm
3
Brotherton Marsh
Kellingley Ings
LUNN LANE
WHALES LA
BROACH LANE
WEELAND ROAD
Tree Tops Inn
UPPERCOMMON LANE
AIRE ST
THE CROFT
MARSH END
Kellingley Farm
STOCKING LANE
SUDFORTH LA
1 THE OVAL
2 SHAFTESBURY AVE
Mill Cottage
SOUTHFIELD LANE
24
MARSH LA
Brears Farm
A645
A645 Pontefract
PO
A645
TURVER'S LA
Thornfield House
Calder Grange Farm
2
Knottingley
Kellingley
LC
KELLINGTON LA
BROOMHILL AVE
COMMON LA
LC
LC
Eggborough
Knottingley High Sch
WOMERSLEY RD
Cemy
BLACKBURN LANE
South Moor
SOUTHMOOR LANE
LC
Stubbs Bridge
SELBY RD
CARLTON CL
23
CANNON HALL LA
Quarry
1 THE POPLARS
2 DOWNLAND CR
Aire and Calder Navigation (Knottingley and Goole Canal)
The Maltings Ind Est
Whitley Bridge
LC
Northside Ind Pk
Cliff Side
Park Balk Farm
Kellington Common
Cherry Tree Farm
1
M62 Castleford, M1
Near Park Farm
LEARNING LA
TEMPLAR CL
A19
BEAL LA
COBCROFT LANE
M62
34
M62
Farpark Farm
WHITEFIELD LA
Whitley & Eggborough Prim Sch
A19
22
West Yorkshire STREET ATLAS
50
51
52
53
54
55
A
B
C
D
E
F

A2
1 PRIMROSE VALE
2 TITHE BARN RD
3 SUNNY BANK
4 ST BOTOLPHS CL
5 FOUNDRY LA
6 FERNLEY GREEN CL
7 TRUNDLES LA
8 GRENLEY ST
9 LAMB INN RD
10 EAST VW
11 RACCA AVE
12 HARKER ST
13 LOW GN
14 MIDDLE LA
15 GILLANN ST
16 WEELAND CT
17 SPRINGFIELDS AVE
18 SPRINGFIELDS
19 BROOMHILL GR
20 QUARRY AVE
21 BROOMHILL WK
22 BROOMHILL PL
23 BROOMHILL CL
24 BROOMHILL SQ
25 BROOMHILL CR
26 BROOMHILL DR
27 SPAWD BONE LA

28 Knottingley CE J&I Sch

D4
1 GARTH MILL
2 MARSH LA
3 MAIN ST
4 RIVERDALE
5 CRAVEN GARTH
6 BROAD LA
7 VILLAGE FARM CT
8 GABLES CL
9 VILLAGE FARM CL

F2
1 WESTFIELD RD
2 WESTFIELD CL
3 WESTFIELD AVE
4 WESTFIELD GR
5 TABARD HAMLET
6 TABARD RD
7 THE TABARDS
8 THE HAMLET
9 KELLINGTON CT

61
48
148

Scale: 1⅓ inches to 1 mile
0 ¼ ½ mile
0 250m 500m 750m 1 km

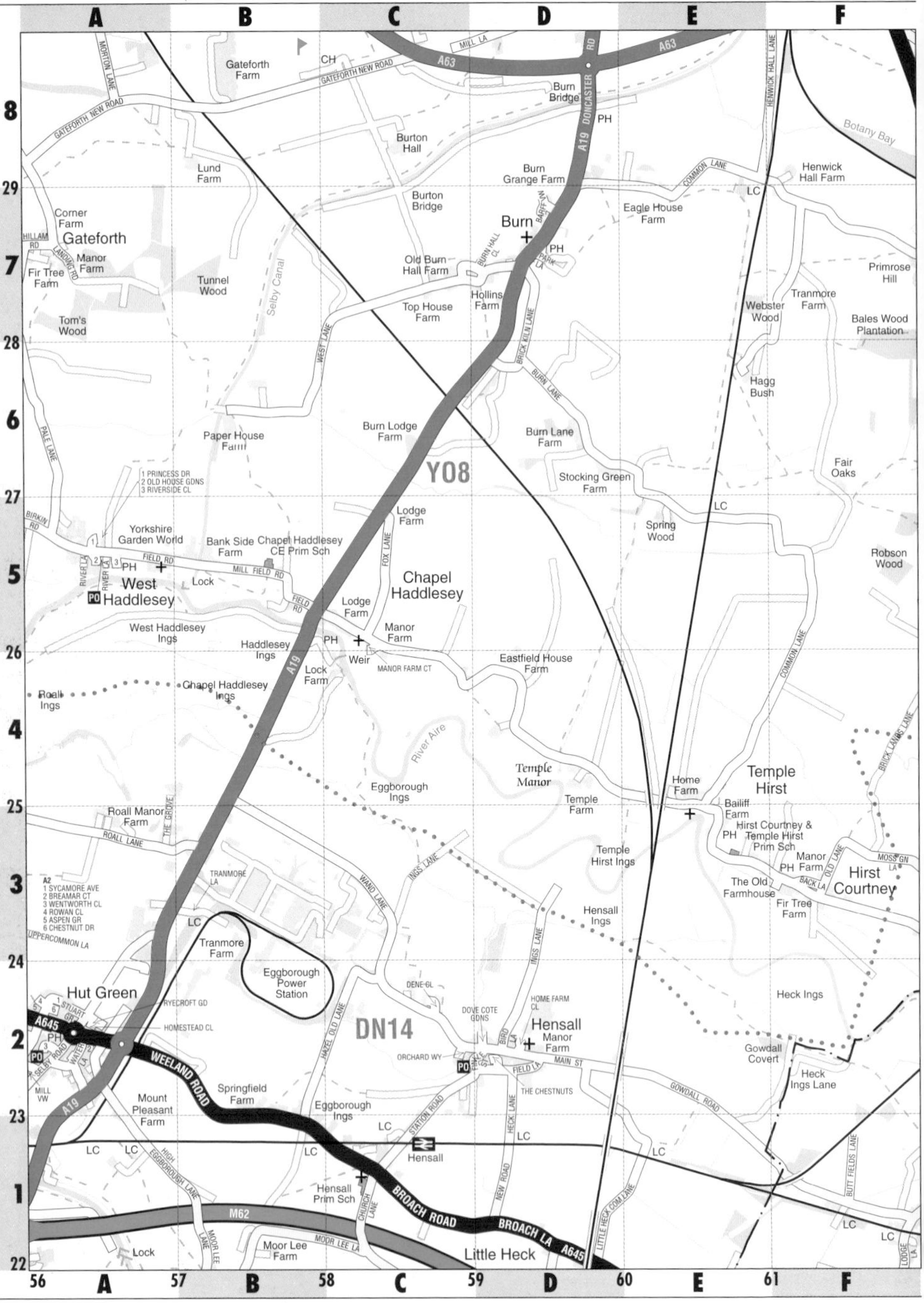

61
77

Scale: 1⅓ inches to 1 mile
0 ¼ ½ mile
0 250m 500m 750m 1 km

49
64

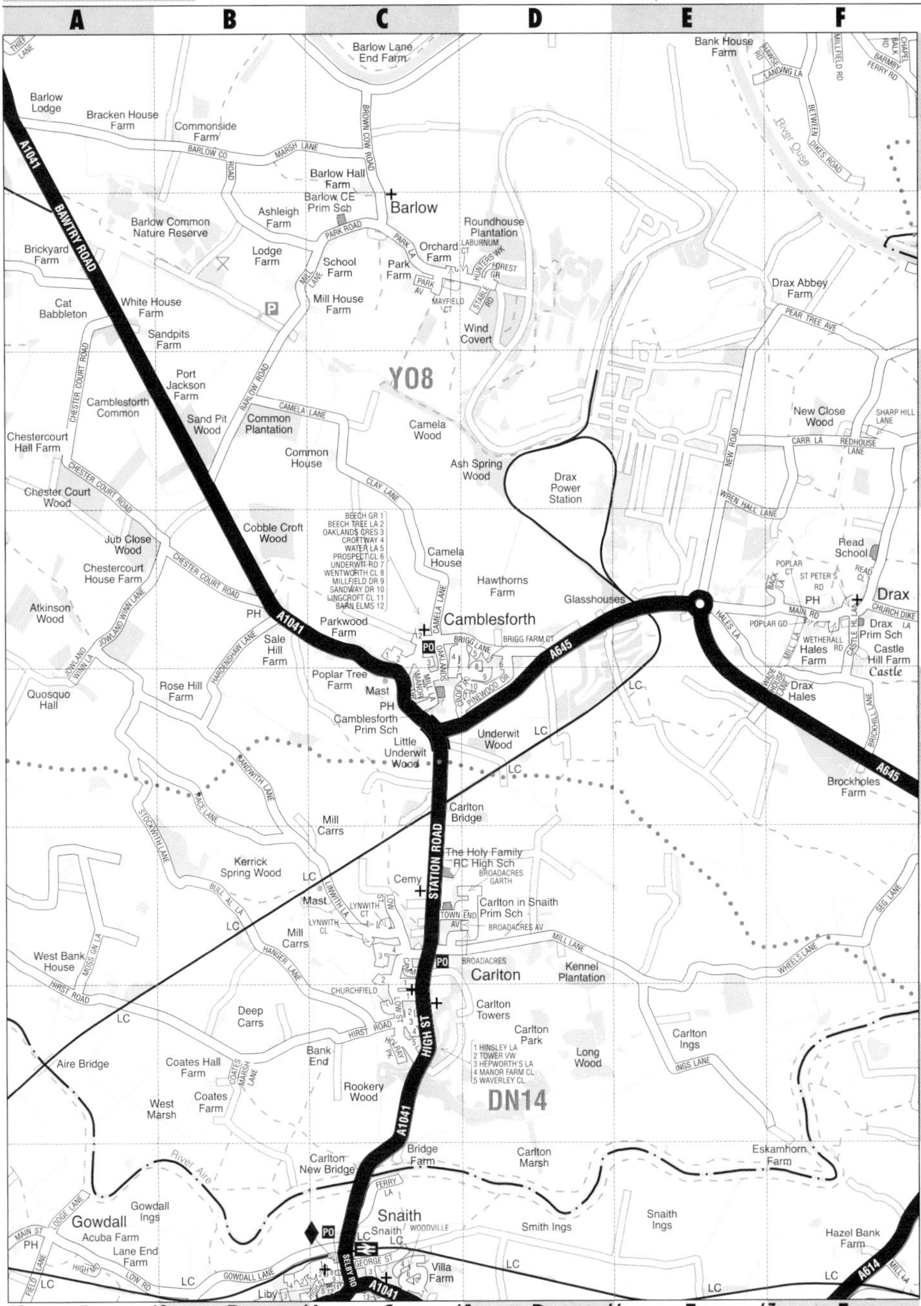

B1
1 PRIORY WAY
2 DAWNAY GARTH
3 MARINA AVE
4 YARBURGH CL

C1
1 PRIORY LA
2 CHURCH LA
3 BUTTLE LA
4 VILLA FIELDS
5 LODGE GDNS
6 SAFFRON DR
7 LABURNUM CL
8 BUTTER MKT
9 MARKET PL
10 JASMINE CL
11 CADMAN LA
12 WEST VW
13 ORCHARD CL

78
64

C1
1 CHURCH LA
2 THE PASTURES
3 THE MEADOWS
4 ALMOND TREE AVE

63
50

Scale: 1⅓ inches to 1 mile
0 ¼ ½ mile
0 250m 500m 750m 1 km

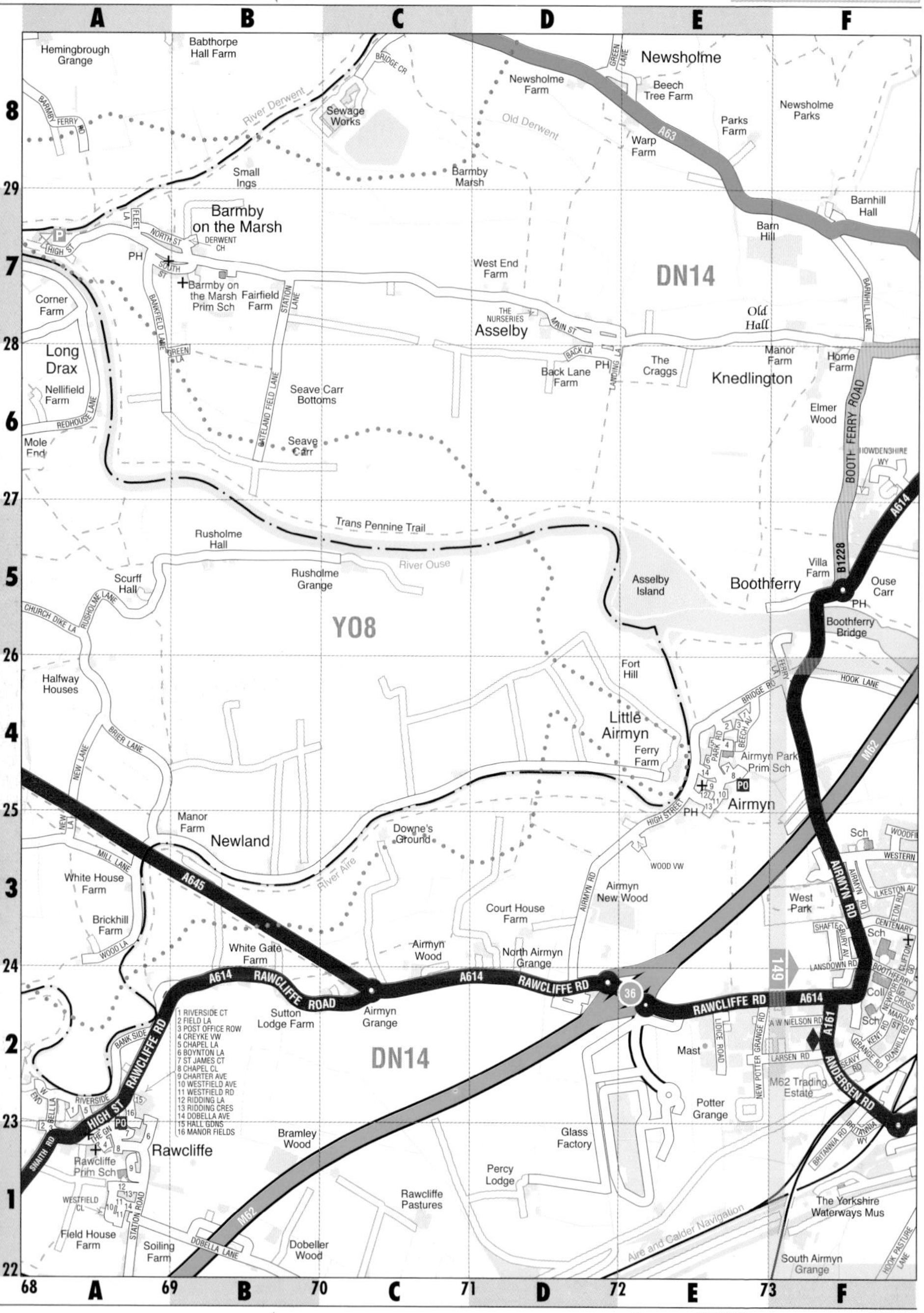

63
79

E4
1 BEECH GR
2 CHESTNUT AVE
3 BEECH AVE
4 PERCY DR
5 HALL CL
6 PARK CL
7 COURTS CL
8 WOODLAND WY
9 ST DAVID'S VW
10 PARSONS CL
11 PARSON'S WK
12 CHURCH VW
13 THE CROSSINGS
14 THE PADDOCK

For full
highlig

A B C D E F

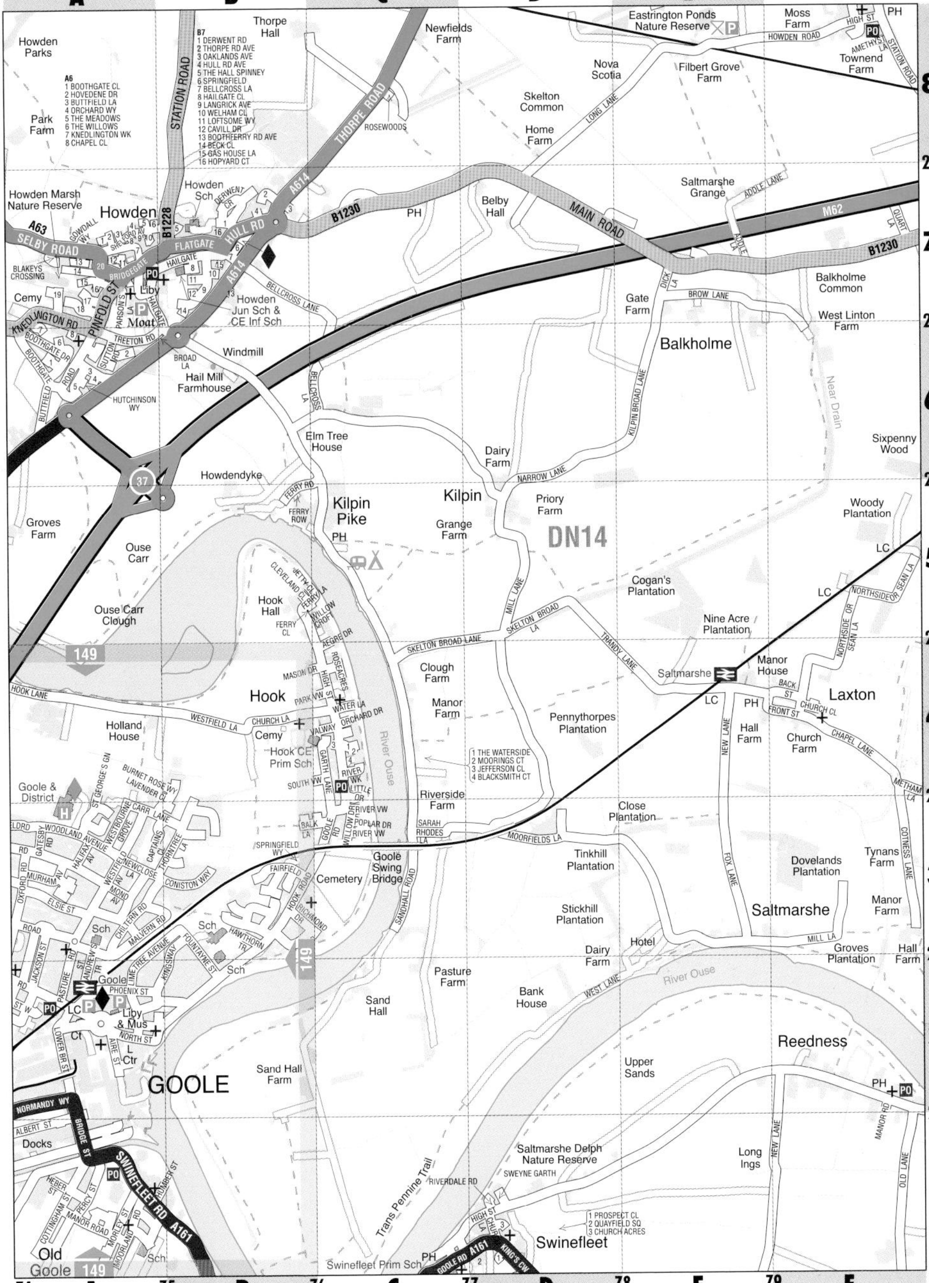

74 A 75 B 76 C 77 D 78 E 79 F
29 8 7 28 6 27 5 26 4 25 3 24 2 23 1 22

65
52

D8
1 SANDHOLME CL
2 THE PEPPERCORNS
3 VICTORIA DR
4 ST STEPHEN'S CRES
5 HANSARD CRES
6 HANSARD DR
7 WILLOW GN
8 CHAPEL MEADOWS
9 BISHOP CT
10 MANOR DR
11 CHAPEL GARTH
12 WESTBROOK RD
13 THE PADDOCK
14 SYCAMORE CL
15 CHESTNUT DR
16 CHERRY CT
17 LABURNUM WK
18 CLAYTONS FOLD
19 LINDEN CL
20 THE ACORNS

Scale: 1⅓ inches to 1 mile
0 ¼ ½ mile
0 250m 500m 750m 1 km

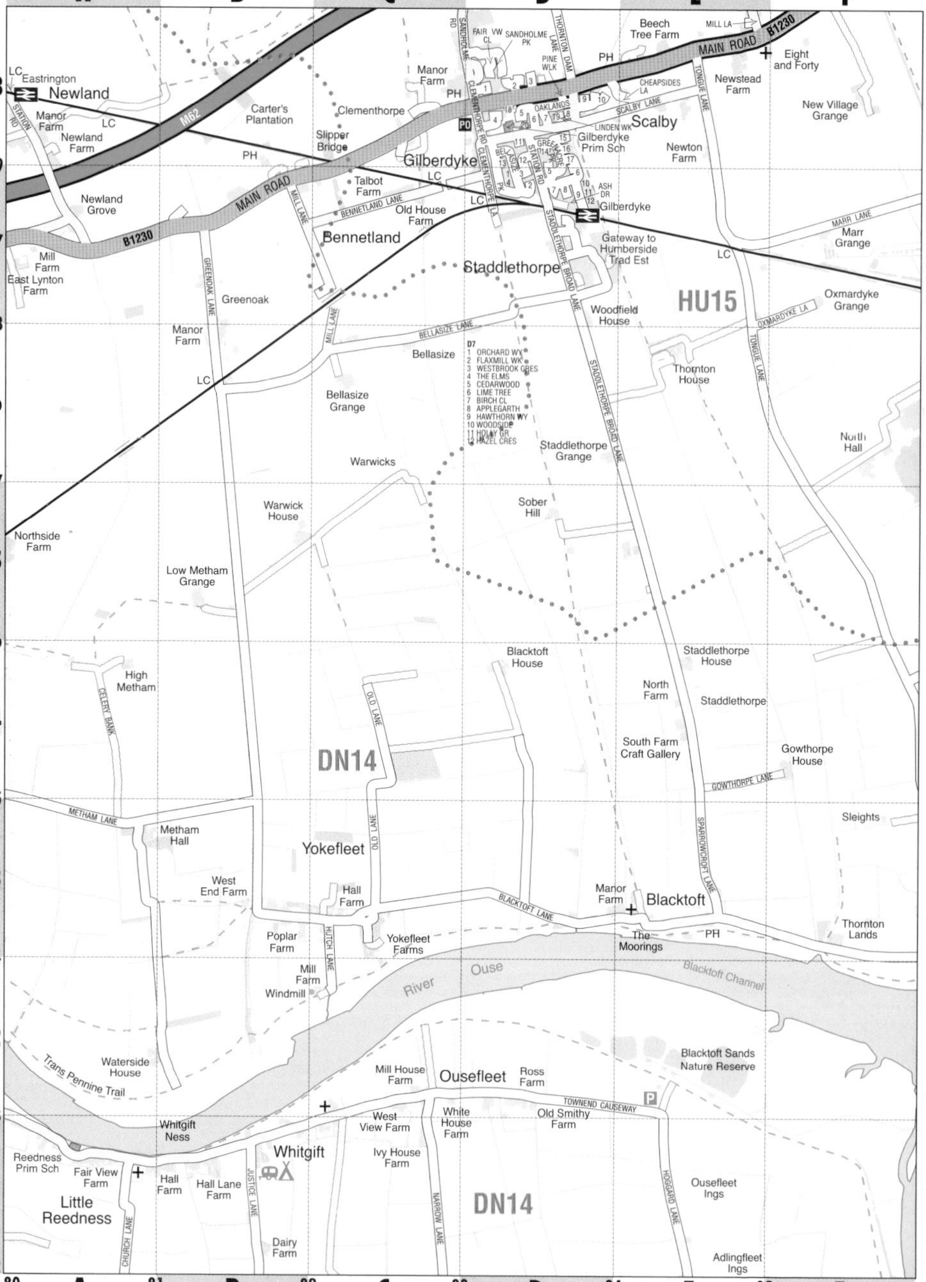

65
81

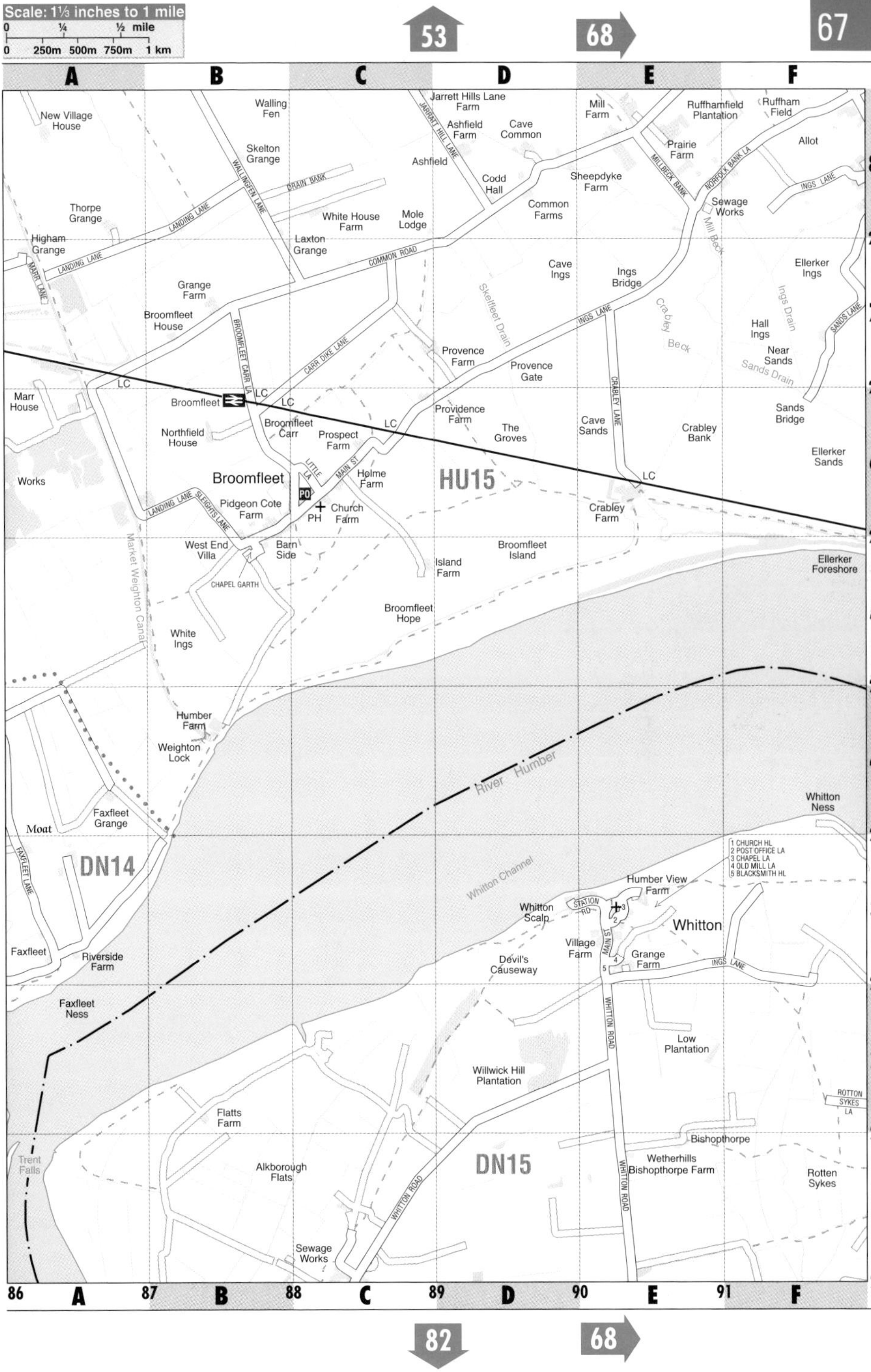
Scale: 1⅓ inches to 1 mile
0 ¼ ½ mile
0 250m 500m 750m 1 km
53
68
A B C D E F
Walling Fen
New Village House
Skelton Grange
Jarrett Hills Lane Farm
Ashfield Farm
Cave Common
Ashfield
Mill Farm
Ruffhamfield Plantation
Ruffham Field
Prairie Farm
Allot
Codd Hall
Sheepdyke Farm
Sewage Works
Thorpe Grange
White House Farm
Mole Lodge
Common Farms
Higham Grange
Laxton Grange
Cave Ings
Ings Bridge
Ellerker Ings
Grange Farm
Broomfleet House
Hall Ings
Near Sands
Provence Farm
Provence Gate
Marr House
Broomfleet
Northfield House
Broomfleet Carr
Prospect Farm
Providence Farm
The Groves
Cave Sands
Crabley Bank
Sands Bridge
Ellerker Sands
Works
Holme Farm
HU15
Pidgeon Cote Farm
Church Farm
PH
PO
Crabley Farm
West End Villa
Barn Side
Broomfleet Island
Island Farm
Ellerker Foreshore
Broomfleet Hope
White Ings
Humber Farm
Weighton Lock
River Humber
Whitton Ness
Faxfleet Grange
Moat
DN14
1 CHURCH HL
2 POST OFFICE LA
3 CHAPEL LA
4 OLD MILL LA
5 BLACKSMITH HL
Humber View Farm
Whitton Channel
Whitton Scalp
Whitton
Village Farm
Grange Farm
Faxfleet
Riverside Farm
Devil's Causeway
Faxfleet Ness
Low Plantation
Willwick Hill Plantation
Flatts Farm
Bishopthorpe
Trent Falls
Alkborough Flats
DN15
Wetherhills Bishopthorpe Farm
Rotten Sykes
Sewage Works
LANDING LANE
MARR LANE
WALLINGFEN LANE
DRAIN BANK
COMMON ROAD
JARRATT HILL LANE
MILLBECK BANK
NORFOLK BANK LA
INGS LANE
SANDS LANE
CARR DIKE LANE
BROOMFLEET CARR LA
INGS LANE
CRABLEY LANE
LITTLE LA
MAIN ST
SLEIGHTS LANE
CHAPEL GARTH
STATION RD
WHITTON ROAD
ROTTON SYKES LA
Skelfleet Drain
Mill Beck
Crabley Beck
Ings Drain
Sands Drain
Market Weighton Canal
LC
8 29 7 28 6 27 5 26 4 25 3 24 2 23 1 22
86 87 88 89 90 91
82
68

C7
1 SPINDLEWOOD
2 STOCKBRIDGE PK
3 CHURCH LA
4 CHURCH VIEW
5 DORSEY WY
6 THORNHAM'S WY

D5
1 BROADACRE PK
2 MEDLAR DR
3 BROADLEY CROFT
4 ASPEN WLK
5 FAIRFIELD VIEW
6 WISKE AVE

67

7 LOXLEY WY
8 MEDEN AVE
9 DEARNE CT
10 AIRE CL
11 FIR CL
12 WILLOW DR
13 MILLIAS CL
14 MYRTLE WY
15 MOOR RD
16 ALDER CL
17 CALTHWAITE DR
18 LANGTHWAITE CL
19 COLTMAN CL
20 RUSKIN WY

54

21 HAREWOOD CREST
22 PICKERING GR
23 PICKERING GR
24 MILLIAS CL
25 CONSTABLE WY
26 ELLOUGHTONTHORPE WY
27 HUSTHWAITE RD
28 ROBIN CL
29 SWALE RD
30 STUBBS CL
31 RYE CRES
32 TRENT WLK
33 EVERTHORPE CL

Scale: 1⅓ inches to 1 mile
0 ¼ ½ mile
0 250m 500m 750m 1 km

B1
1 ORCHARD DR
2 HIGH BURGAGE
3 BACK LA
4 BRAMBLE LA

67

83

C6
1 DROVERS RISE
2 VICARAGE GDNS
3 CHAPEL MEWS
4 PINE WK
5 HOBSON RD
6 HARLAND RD
7 LARCHMONT CL
8 WOODLANDS LA
9 PLOVER DR
10 THORNTON
11 FRYSTON
12 LASTINGHAM
13 CHANTRYS DR
14 RANSOME WAY
15 ELM AVE
16 LAMBERT AVE
17 WOODLAND AVE
18 SPRINGFIELD AVE
19 ATKINSON DR
20 ST PAULINUS CRES
21 COVINGTON
22 LOWERDALE
23 LINTON
24 CARLTON
25 INGLETON RD
26 ROMBALDS CFT
27 PINEFIELD PL
28 WINTRINGHAM

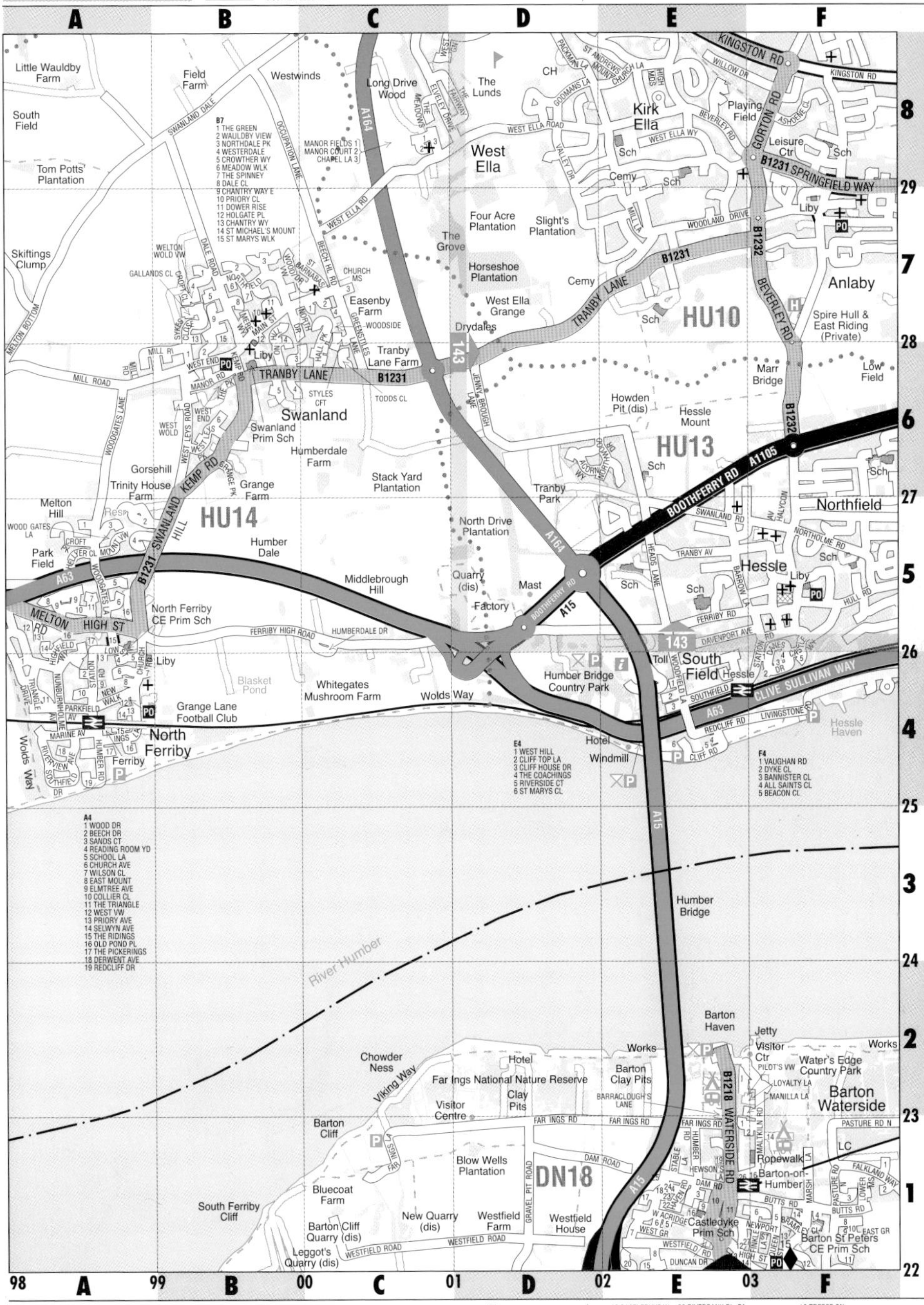
A
B
C
D
E
F
Little Wauldby Farm
Field Farm
Westwinds
Long Drive Wood
The Lunds
CH
Kirk Ella
KINGSTON RD
WILLOW DR
Playing Field
GORTON RD
Leisure Ctr
Sch
South Field
Tom Potts' Plantation
SWANLAND DALE
OCCUPATION LANE
B7
1 THE GREEN
2 WAULDBY VIEW
3 NORTHDALE PK
4 WESTERDALE
5 CROWTHER WY
6 MEADOW WLK
7 THE SPINNEY
8 DALE CL
9 CHANTRY WAY E
10 PRIORY CL
11 DOWER RISE
12 HOLGATE PL
13 CHANTRY WY
14 ST MICHAEL'S MOUNT
15 ST MARYS WLK
MANOR FIELDS 1
MANOR COURT 2
CHAPEL LA 3
A164
West Ella
WEST ELLA ROAD
WEST ELLA WY
BEVERLEY RD
B1231 SPRINGFIELD WAY
Cemy
Sch
Liby
PO
WOODLAND DRIVE
WEST ELLA RD
Four Acre Plantation
Slight's Plantation
The Grove
Skiftings Clump
WELTON WOLD VW
DALE ROAD
BEECH HL RD
CHURCH MS
GALLANDS CL
Horseshoe Plantation
B1231
TRANBY LANE
Cemy
Anlaby
B1232
BEVERLEY RD
Easenby Farm
West Ella Grange
HU10
Spire Hull & East Riding (Private)
MELTON BOTTOM
WOODSIDE
Drydales
Sch
28
MILL RI
WEST END
PO
Liby
TRANBY LANE
Tranby Lane Farm
B1231
143
MILL ROAD
MANOR RD
STYLES CFT
TODDS CL
Marr Bridge
Low Field
Howden Pit (dis)
Hessle Mount
WOODGATES LANE
WEST WOLD
WEST LEYS ROAD
Swanland
Swanland Prim Sch
JENNY BROUGH LANE
HU13
Humberdale Farm
Sch
BOOTHFERRY RD A1105
Sch
Gorsehill
Trinity House Farm
KEMP RD
Grange Farm
Stack Yard Plantation
Tranby Park
Northfield
Melton Hill
HU14
SWANLAND RD
HALCYON AV
WOOD GATES LA
Resr
North Drive Plantation
NORTHOLME RD
Park Field
CROFT
B1231 SWANLAND HILL
Humber Dale
A164
TRANBY AV
Sch
HEADS LANE
BARROW LA
Hessle
Liby
A63
Middlebrough Hill
Quarry (dis)
Mast
Sch
Sch
PO
HULL RD
MELTON RD
HIGH ST
North Ferriby CE Prim Sch
Factory
BOOTHFERRY RD
A15
FERRIBY RD
FERRIBY HIGH ROAD
HUMBERDALE DR
143
DAVENPORT AVE
Liby
Toll
South Field
Hessle
Blasket Pond
Humber Bridge Country Park
Whitegates Mushroom Farm
Wolds Way
SOUTHFIELD
CLIVE SULLIVAN WAY
A63
Grange Lane Football Club
PO
PARKFIELD AV
MARINE AV
North Ferriby
Ferriby
Wolds Way
Hotel
Windmill
REDCLIFF RD
LIVINGSTONE RD
Hessle Haven
CLIFF RD
E4
1 WEST HILL
2 CLIFF TOP LA
3 CLIFF HOUSE DR
4 THE COACHINGS
5 RIVERSIDE CT
6 ST MARYS CL
F4
1 VAUGHAN RD
2 DYKE CL
3 BANNISTER CL
4 ALL SAINTS CL
5 BEACON CL
A4
1 WOOD DR
2 BEECH DR
3 SANDS CT
4 READING ROOM YD
5 SCHOOL LA
6 CHURCH AVE
7 WILSON CL
8 EAST MOUNT
9 ELMTREE AVE
10 COLLIER CL
11 THE TRIANGLE
12 WEST VW
13 PRIORY AVE
14 SELWYN AVE
15 THE RIDINGS
16 OLD POND PL
17 THE PICKERINGS
18 DERWENT AVE
19 REDCLIFF DR
A15
Humber Bridge
River Humber
Barton Haven
Jetty
Works
Works
Chowder Ness
Visitor Ctr
Water's Edge Country Park
Hotel
Barton Clay Pits
Far Ings National Nature Reserve
Viking Way
Clay Pits
B1218 WATERSIDE RD
Barton Waterside
Visitor Centre
BARRACLOUGH'S LANE
FAR INGS RD
PASTURE RD N
Barton Cliff
LC
Blow Wells Plantation
DAM ROAD
Ropewalk
DN18
Barton-on-Humber
Bluecoat Farm
South Ferriby Cliff
New Quarry (dis)
Westfield Farm
Westfield House
Castledyke Prim Sch
Barton Cliff Quarry (dis)
Leggot's Quarry (dis)
WESTFIELD ROAD
Barton St Peters CE Prim Sch
PO
8
29
7
28
6
27
5
26
4
25
3
24
2
23
1
22
98
99
00
01
02
03

139 143 140

For full street detail of the highlighted area see page 155.

Scale: 1⅓ inches to 1 mile
0 ¼ ½ mile
0 250m 500m 750m 1 km

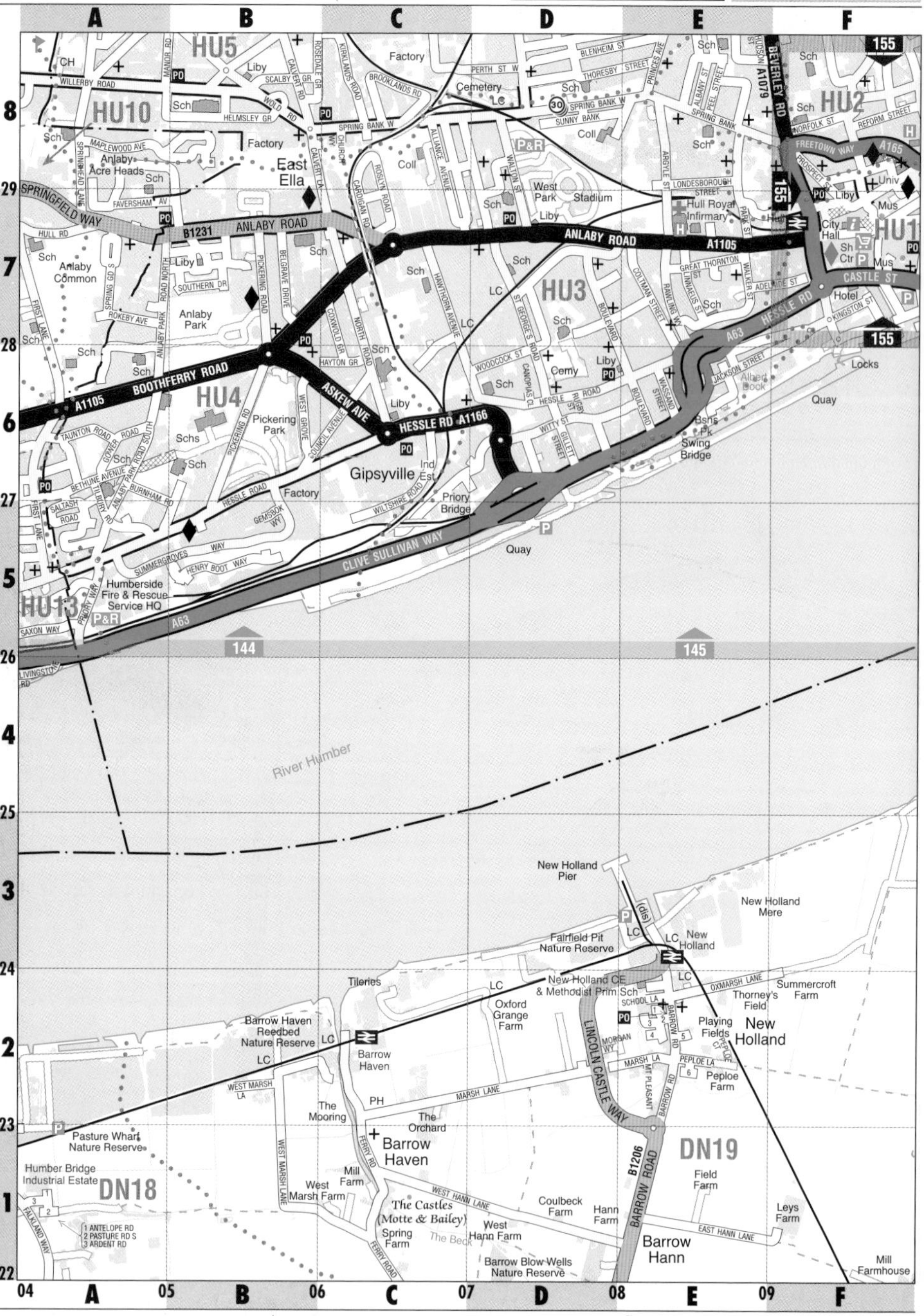
A B C D E F
HU5
HU10
HU2
HU1
HU3
HU4
HU13
DN18
DN19
CH
WILLERBY ROAD
HELMSLEY GR
MAPLEWOOD AVE
Anlaby Acre Heads
SPRINGFIELD WAY
FAVERSHAM AV
HULL RD
Anlaby Common
SPRING GD S
ROKEBY AVE
FIRST LANE
ANLABY PARK
ROAD NORTH
Liby
SOUTHERN DR
Anlaby Park
B1231
ANLABY ROAD
East Ella
Factory
SCALBY GR
WOLD RD
CALVERT RD
CALVERT LA
ROSEDALE GR
KIRKLANDS ROAD
BROOKLANDS RD
SPRING BANK W
CHURCH
Coll
ROSLYN ROAD
CARDIGAN RD
ALLIANCE AVENUE
PERTH ST W
Cemetery
LC
BLENHEIM ST
THORESBY STREET
PRINCES AVE
SPRING BANK W
SUNNY BANK
P&R
WALTON ST
West Park
Stadium
ALBANY ST
PEEL STREET
SPRING BANK
ARGYLE ST
LONDESBOROUGH STREET
Hull Royal Infirmary
PARK ST
BEVERLEY RD
HUDSON ST
A1079
155
NORFOLK ST
REFORM STREET
FREETOWN WAY
A165
PROSPECT ST
Univ
City Hall
Mus
Sh Ctr
CASTLE ST
Hotel
KINGSTON ST
ADELAIDE ST
GREAT THORNTON ST
LINNAEUS ST
WALKER ST
A1105
HESSLE RD
A63
JACKSON STREET
Albert Dock
Locks
Quay
Bsns Pk
Swing Bridge
WASSAND STREET
BOULEVARD
COLTMAN STREET
RAWLING WY
ST GEORGE'S ROAD
CANOPAS CL
WOODCOCK ST
HESSLE ROAD
RUGBY ST
WITTY ST
GILLETT STREET
Cemy
HAWTHORN AVENUE
NORTH ROAD
COXWOLD GR
HAYTON GR
PICKERING ROAD
BELGRAVE DRIVE
BOOTHFERRY ROAD
ASKEW AVE
WEST GROVE
COUNCIL AVENUE
Pickering Park
HESSLE RD A1166
Gipsyville
Ind Est
WILTSHIRE ROAD
Priory Bridge
TAUNTON ROAD
GOZNER ROAD
ANLABY PARK ROAD SOUTH
BETHUNE AVENUE
TILBURY RD
BURNHAM RD
SALTASH ROAD
HESSLE ROAD
GEMSBOK WY
SUMMERGROVES WAY
HENRY BOOT WAY
CLIVE SULLIVAN WAY
Humberside Fire & Rescue Service HQ
PRIORY WAY
SAXON WAY
LIVINGSTONE RD
144
145
River Humber
New Holland Pier
(dis)
New Holland Mere
Fairfield Pit Nature Reserve
New Holland
New Holland CE & Methodist Prim Sch
OXMARSH LANE
Thorney's Field
Summercroft Farm
SCHOOL LA
BARROW RD
Playing Fields
PEPLOE CT
MORGAN WAY
MARSH LA
PEPLOE LA
Peploe Farm
MT PLEASANT
LINCOLN CASTLE WAY
Tileries
Oxford Grange Farm
Barrow Haven Reedbed Nature Reserve
Barrow Haven
WEST MARSH LA
MARSH LANE
PH
The Mooring
The Orchard
Pasture Wharf Nature Reserve
Humber Bridge Industrial Estate
WEST MARSH LANE
FERRY RD
Mill Farm
West Marsh Farm
WEST HANN LANE
The Castles (Motte & Bailey)
Spring Farm
The Beck
West Hann Farm
FERRY ROAD
Barrow Blow Wells Nature Reserve
Coulbeck Farm
Hann Farm
B1206
BARROW ROAD
Barrow Hann
Field Farm
EAST HANN LANE
Leys Farm
Mill Farmhouse
FALKLAND WAY
1 ANTELOPE RD
2 PASTURE RD S
3 ARDENT RD
04 05 06 07 08 09
22 23 24 25 26 27 28 29
1 2 3 4 5 6 7 8

E2
1 WENTWORTH CRES
2 WESTBURN AVE
3 FULFORD CRES
4 GLENEAGLES CRES
5 ALBERT ST
6 PEPLOE CRES

69 85

For full street detail of the highlighted area see pages 144 and 145.

Scale: 1⅓ inches to 1 mile
0 ¼ ½ mile
0 250m 500m 750m 1 km

141
72
142

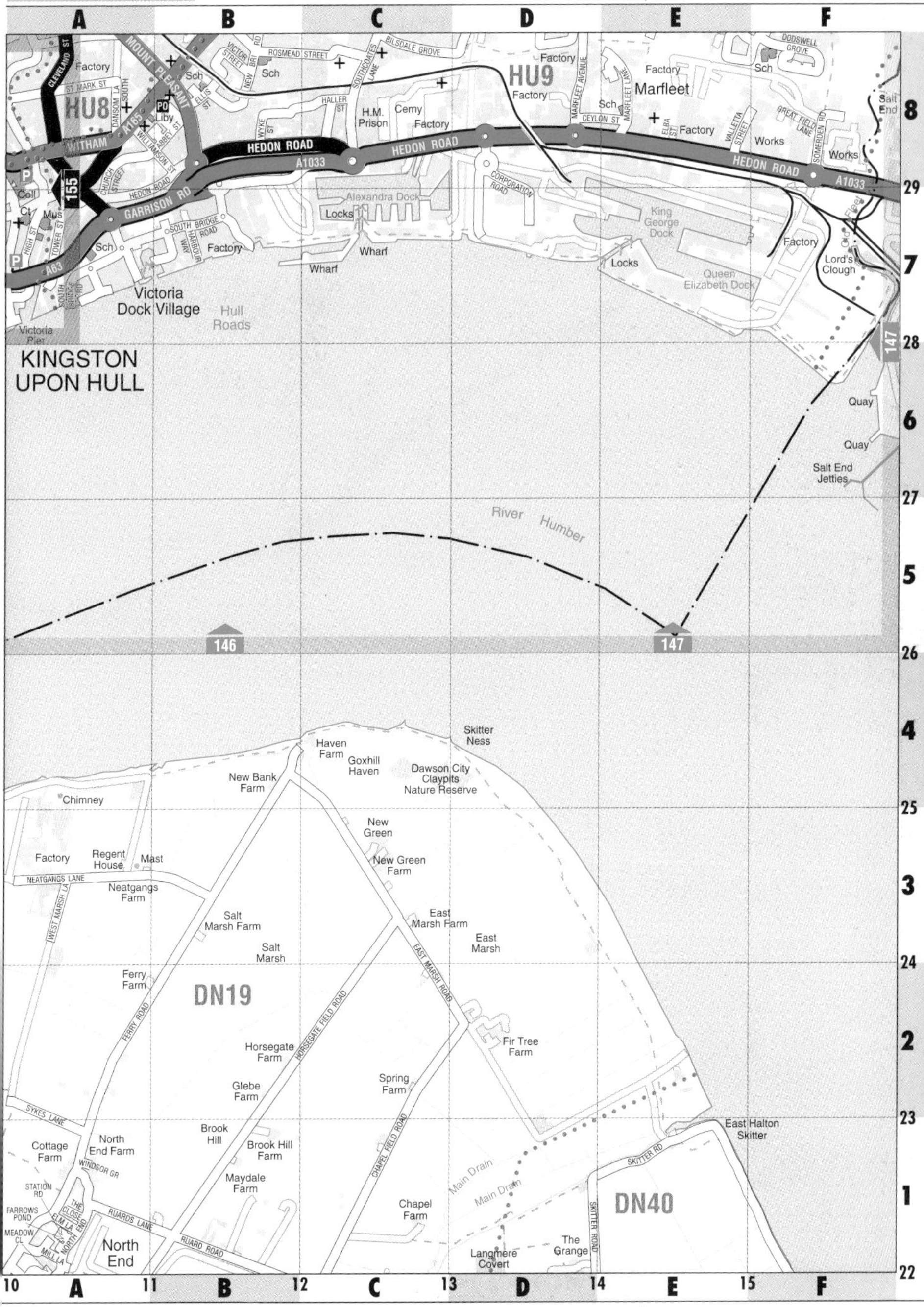
A
B
C
D
E
F
HU8
HU9
Factory
Sch
Marfleet
Salt End
CLEVELAND ST
MOUNT PLEASANT
ST MARK ST
WITHAM
A165
PO
Liby
HEDON ROAD
A1033
GARRISON RD
155
Coll
Mus
Ct
HIGH ST
TOWER ST
A63
SOUTH BRIDGE ROAD
HARBOUR WAY
Victoria Dock Village
Hull Roads
Victoria Pier
KINGSTON UPON HULL
ROSMEAD STREET
BILSDALE GROVE
SOUTHCOATES LANE
HALLER ST
H.M. Prison
Cemy
Alexandra Dock
Locks
Wharf
CORPORATION ROAD
MARFLEET AVENUE
MARFLEET LANE
CEYLON ST
ELBA ST
VALLETTA STREET
GREAT FIELD LANE
SOMERDEN RD
DODSWELL GROVE
Works
King George Dock
Queen Elizabeth Dock
Lord's Clough
Quay
Salt End Jetties
River Humber
146
147
8
29
7
28
6
27
5
26
4
25
3
24
2
23
1
22
Skitter Ness
Haven Farm
Goxhill Haven
Dawson City Claypits Nature Reserve
New Bank Farm
Chimney
New Green
New Green Farm
Factory
Regent House
Mast
NEATGANGS LANE
Neatgangs Farm
WEST MARSH LA
Salt Marsh Farm
Salt Marsh
East Marsh Farm
East Marsh
EAST MARSH ROAD
Ferry Farm
FERRY ROAD
DN19
HORSEGATE FIELD ROAD
Horsegate Farm
Fir Tree Farm
Glebe Farm
Spring Farm
SYKES LANE
Brook Hill
Brook Hill Farm
North End Farm
Cottage Farm
WINDSOR GR
STATION RD
FARROWS POND
MEADOW CL
THE CLOSE
ELM LA
MILL LA
NORTH END
RUARDS LANE
RUARD ROAD
North End
Maydale Farm
CHAPEL FIELD ROAD
Chapel Farm
Main Drain
Langmere Covert
The Grange
SKITTER ROAD
SKITTER RD
East Halton Skitter
DN40
10
11
12
13
14
15

For full street detail of the highlighted area see pages 146 and 147.

86
72

147

C7
1 PRINCES AVE
2 BELLS RD
3 ANDREW LA
4 COLEMANS RD
5 SHIELDS RD
6 ROBSON WY
7 BEECH AVE
8 CEDAR CT
9 OAK GR
10 POPLAR GR
11 FOTHERBIE GARTH
12 HALES CRES
13 WESTLANDS CL
14 CLOEBERRY WY
15 GREEN RD
16 BIRCH TREE DR
17 DRAPER'S LA
18 WARN AVE
19 KETWELL LA
20 WAYFBAIN LA
21 CHURCH GARTH
22 SPENCER CL
23 LAMBERT PK RD
24 HAVEN STAITHES
25 WESTWICK
26 WOODMARKETGATE
27 IVESON CL
28 GEORGE ST
29 KING'S PL
30 ST AUGUSTINE'S GARTH
31 MARKET PL
32 DRAPER'S LA
33 DISTAFF LA
34 ST MEWS
35 RICHARDSON RD
36 MARKET HILL
37 MARKET HILL CT
38 VICAR LA
39 AUGUSTINE'S MS
40 ST AUGUSTINE'S CT

58

Scale: 1⅓ inches to 1 mile
0 ¼ ½ mile
0 250m 500m 750m 1 km

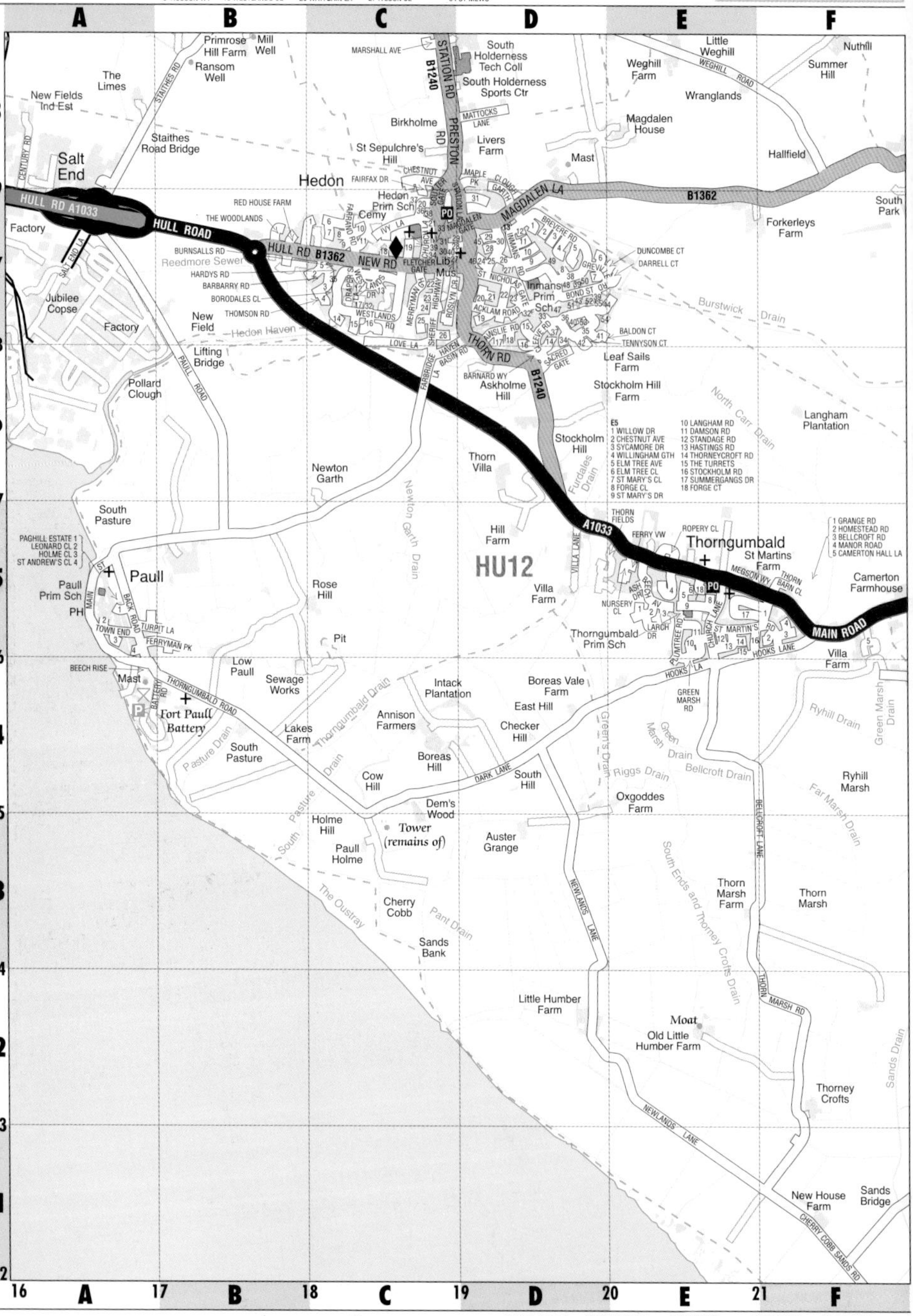

71

D7
1 ALBINA GARTH
2 HAVEN GARTH
3 GUY GARTH
4 POULTNEY GARTH
5 CONSTABLE GARTH
6 BETHELL CT
7 VILLIERS CT
8 MAGDALEN CT
9 ALURED GARTH

87

10 HOLCROFT GARTH
11 FLEET GARTH
12 BECK GARTH
13 THIRTY ACRE LA
14 WYNTRYNGHAM CL
15 WATERLAND CL
16 CHAYTOR CL
17 ANDERSONS CL
18 MANDERVILLE CL
19 HILDYARD CL
20 ADELIZA GARTH
21 APPLE GARTH
22 CHARLES ST
23 STOCKHOLM PK
24 ST ANTHONY'S DR
25 ST ANTHONY'S PK
26 FEWSON GARTH
27 NEVILLE GARTH
28 CHAPELRY GARTH
29 ALISON GARTH
30 WATSON DR
31 CHERRY TREE LA
32 BERKELEY DR
33 HARRINGTON CT
34 GARVEY WY
35 CROMWELL RD
36 GIBSON LA
37 STEPHENSON CL
38 ST MARY'S DR
39 ST MICHAEL'S DR
40 ELWYN WY
41 BALLDON CT
42 DANN CT
43 HAYMER DR
44 TAILLER RD
45 THE MOAT
46 BURGESS SQ
47 MARSHALL WY
48 BENNINGTON CL
49 TYRELL OAKS
50 JUBILEE CL
51 BONFREY WY
52 SHAPE CL
53 REVENSER CT
54 KNOWLE WY
55 KELD CL

Scale: 1⅓ inches to 1 mile
0 ¼ ½ mile
0 250m 500m 750m 1 km

A6
1 ELM TREE FARM RD
2 NORTH RISE
3 NETTLETON GARTH
4 BURNHAM AVE
5 RAINES CLOSE
6 CHESTNUT CL
7 STATION RD

59
74

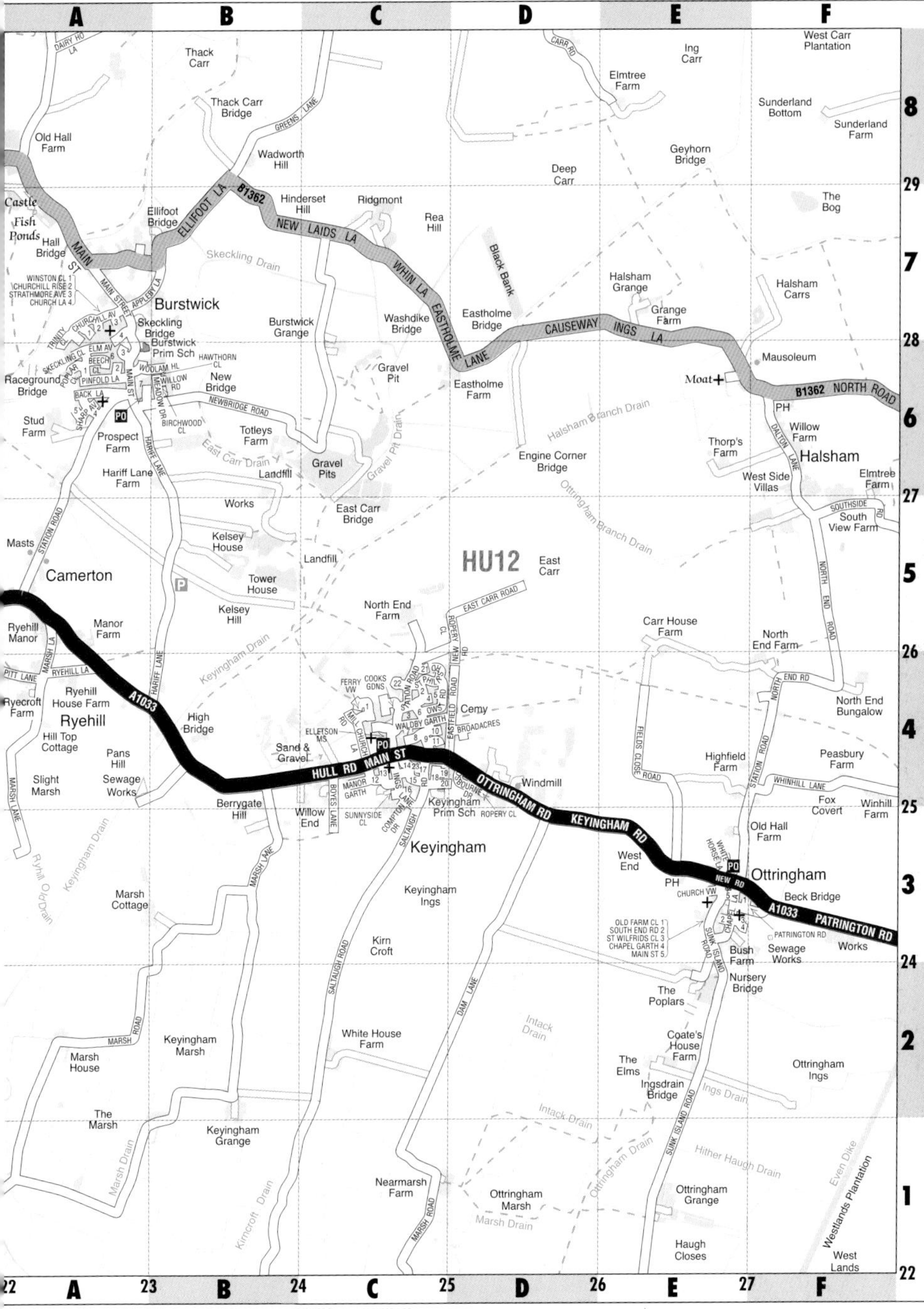

C4
1 EBOR MANOR
2 ALBEMARLE RD
3 KELSEY DR
4 LANGDALE DR
5 ETHERINGTON CL
6 SEYMOUR RD
7 ELM TREE CL
8 WESTERDALE CL
9 MARRITT WY
10 MAUDE CL
11 OMBLER CL
12 MAISTER RD
13 CHAPEL LA
14 BECK LA
15 SCHOOL LA
16 KIRNCROFT CL
17 JELLISON WK
18 GRIFFITHS WY
19 MELVILLE CL
20 RUSSELL DR
21 CABRY DR
22 NORTH FIELD
23 GREENACRE

88
74

F7
1 HUBERT ST
2 CAMMIDGE ST
3 GEORGE ST
4 ALMA ST
5 WALTER ST
6 EDWARD ST

Scale: 1⅓ inches to 1 mile
0 ¼ ½ mile
0 250m 500m 750m 1 km

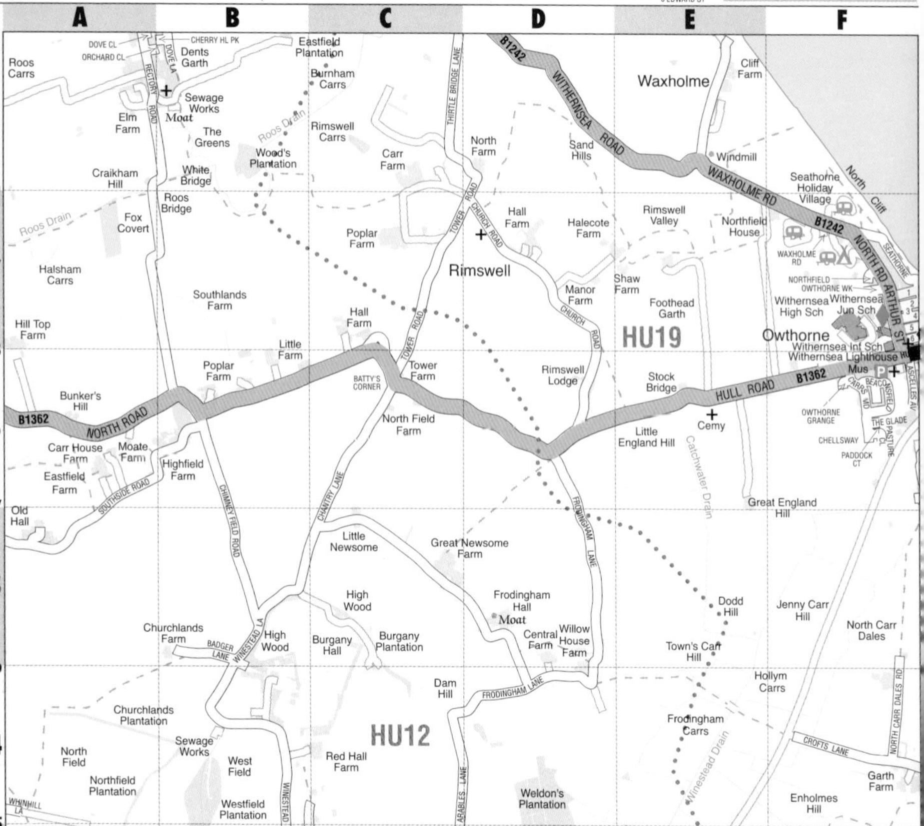

D1
1 HUNTER CL
2 GUARDIANS RD
3 FRANCIS WY
4 WESTGATE MANOR
5 PUMP ROW
6 NORTHSIDE CT
7 CHURCH VW
8 TITHE BARN LA
9 TITHE BARN CL
10 CLARKS LA
11 BEECH DR
12 THE CLOSE
13 THE CRESCENT
14 ST PATRICK'S GN
15 SAFFRON GARTH
16 CROMWELL CL
17 RUSTON TERR
18 RUSTON CT

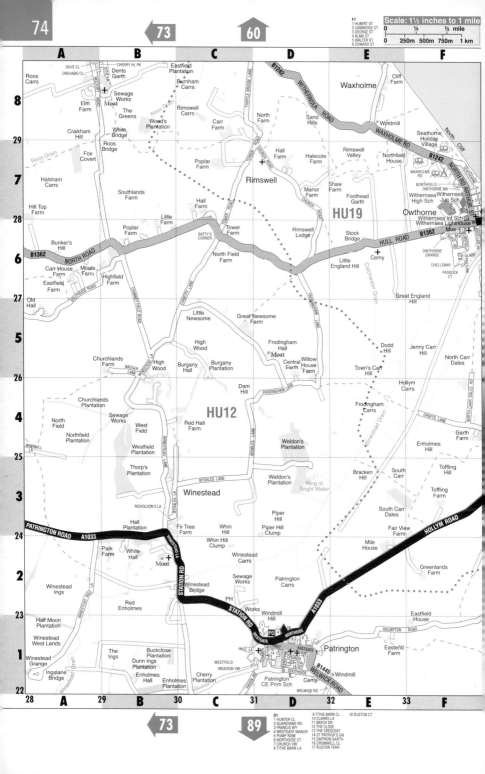

Scale: 1⅓ inches to 1 mile

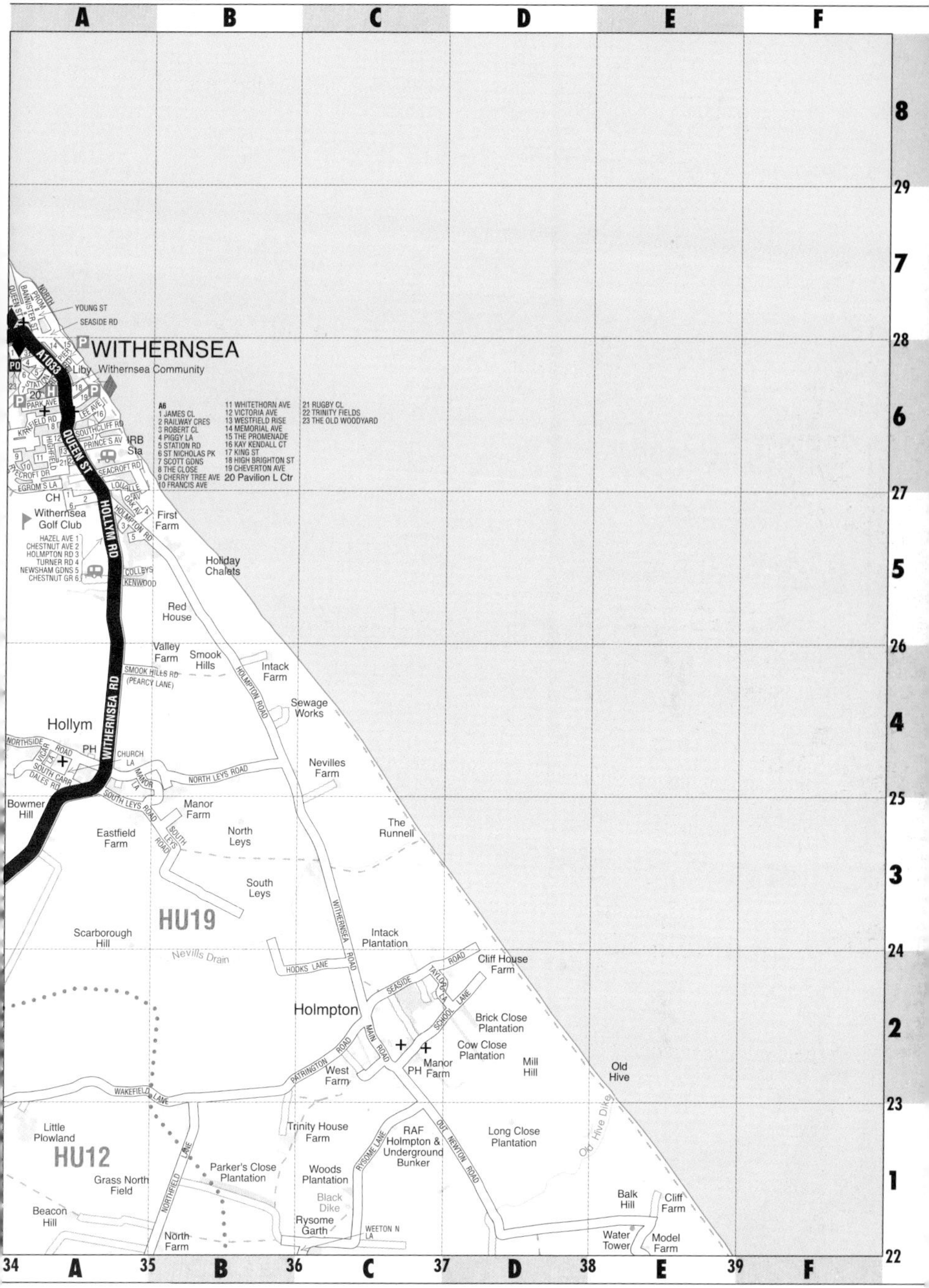
A
B
C
D
E
F
8
29
7
28
6
27
5
26
4
25
3
24
2
23
1
22
34
35
36
37
38
39
WITHERNSEA
Withernsea Community
Liby
IRB
Sta
YOUNG ST
SEASIDE RD
QUEEN ST
HOLLYM RD
A1033
WITHERNSEA RD
A6
1 JAMES CL
2 RAILWAY CRES
3 ROBERT CL
4 PIGGY LA
5 STATION RD
6 ST NICHOLAS PK
7 SCOTT GDNS
8 THE CLOSE
9 CHERRY TREE AVE
10 FRANCIS AVE
11 WHITETHORN AVE
12 VICTORIA AVE
13 WESTFIELD RISE
14 MEMORIAL AVE
15 THE PROMENADE
16 KAY KENDALL CT
17 KING ST
18 HIGH BRIGHTON ST
19 CHEVERTON AVE
20 Pavilion L Ctr
21 RUGBY CL
22 TRINITY FIELDS
23 THE OLD WOODYARD
Withernsea Golf Club
HAZEL AVE 1
CHESTNUT AVE 2
HOLMPTON RD 3
TURNER RD 4
NEWSHAM GDNS 5
CHESTNUT GR 6
CH
First Farm
Holiday Chalets
Red House
Valley Farm
Smook Hills
SMOOK HILLS RD
(PEARCY LANE)
Intack Farm
HOLMPTON ROAD
Sewage Works
Hollym
PH
CHURCH LA
NORTH LEYS ROAD
Nevilles Farm
Bowmer Hill
Manor Farm
SOUTH LEYS ROAD
Eastfield Farm
North Leys
The Runnell
South Leys
HU19
Scarborough Hill
Nevills Drain
Intack Plantation
HOOKS LANE
WITHERNSEA ROAD
Cliff House Farm
SEASIDE ROAD
Holmpton
Brick Close Plantation
Cow Close Plantation
MAIN ROAD
SCHOOL LANE
PATRINGTON ROAD
West Farm
PH
Manor Farm
Mill Hill
Old Hive
WAKEFIELD LANE
Little Plowland
HU12
Trinity House Farm
RAF Holmpton & Underground Bunker
RYSOME LANE
OUT NEWTON ROAD
Long Close Plantation
Old Hive Dike
Grass North Field
Parker's Close Plantation
Woods Plantation
NORTHFIELD LANE
Black Dike
Beacon Hill
Rysome Garth
WEETON N LA
Balk Hill
Cliff Farm
Water Tower
Model Farm
North Farm

90

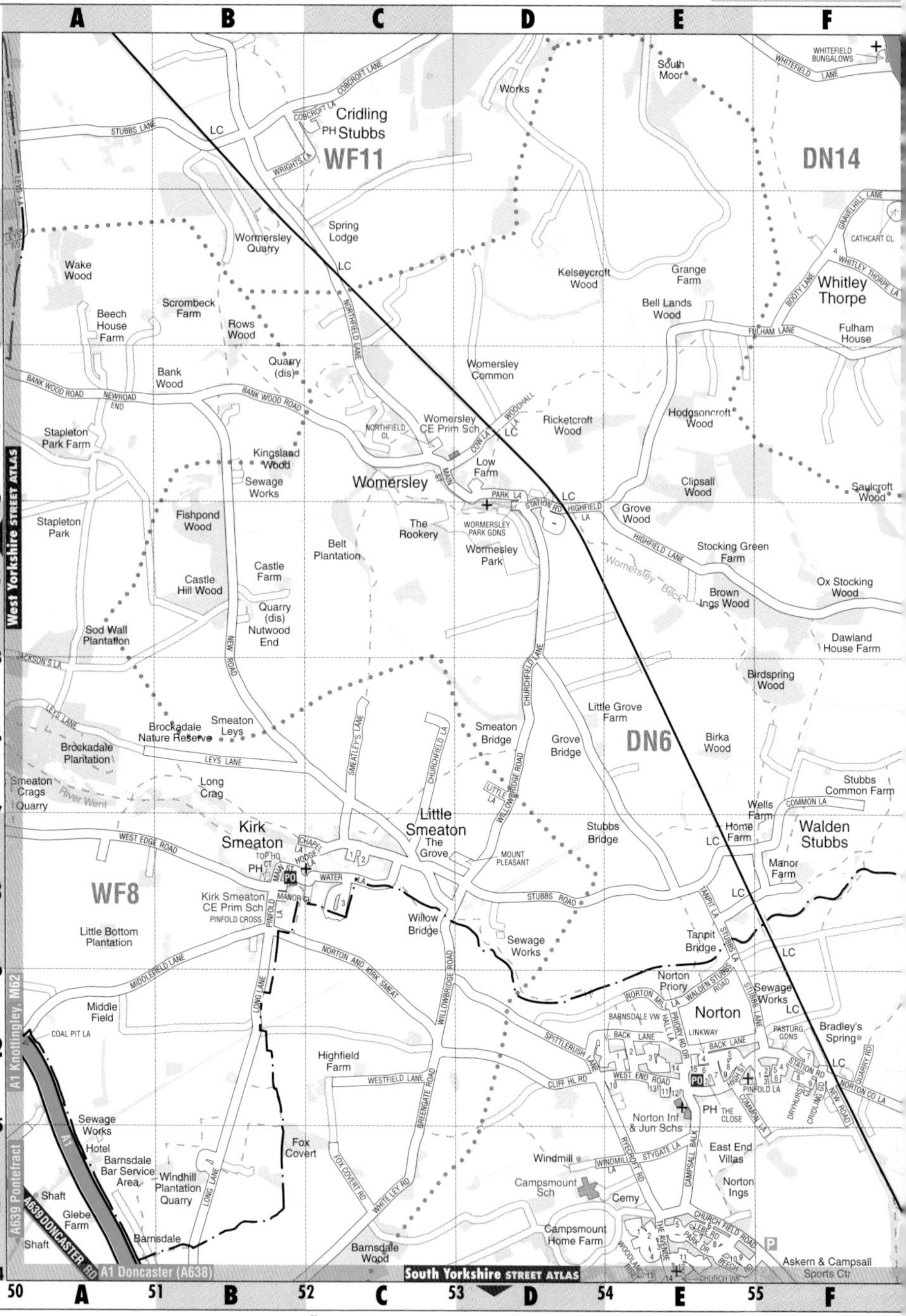

C3
1 WENTDALE
2 STAN VALLEY
3 SPRINGFIELD CRES

E1
1 TENNYSON AVE
2 SHAKESPEARE AVE
3 BYRON AVE
4 WORDSWORTH AVE
5 WELLINGTONIA DR
6 LANGLEYS RD
7 EAST VW
8 GRANGE RD
9 WILLOW RD
10 VAUGHAN RD
11 CAMPSALL PK RD
12 CAMPSALL HALL RD
13 SHERWOOD CL
14 HIGH ST

E2
1 BROC-O-BANK
2 NEWTHORPE RD
3 FORRESTER'S CL
4 TRAFFORD RD
5 ARUNDEL RD
6 ADELAIDE RD
7 HEADINGLEY RD
8 ORCHARD DR
9 ORCHARD CL
10 RYECROFT AVE
11 FIR TREE DR
12 MANOR CL
13 WINDMILL MD
14 KIPLIN DR
15 LANGOLD DR

F2
1 LYNDHURST DR
2 LYNDHURST CL
3 LYNDHURST RISE
4 ASHBURNHAM CL
5 ASHBURNHAM WK
6 DENVER RD
7 MANOR GARTH
8 SWAN SYKE DR
9 DRYHURST CL

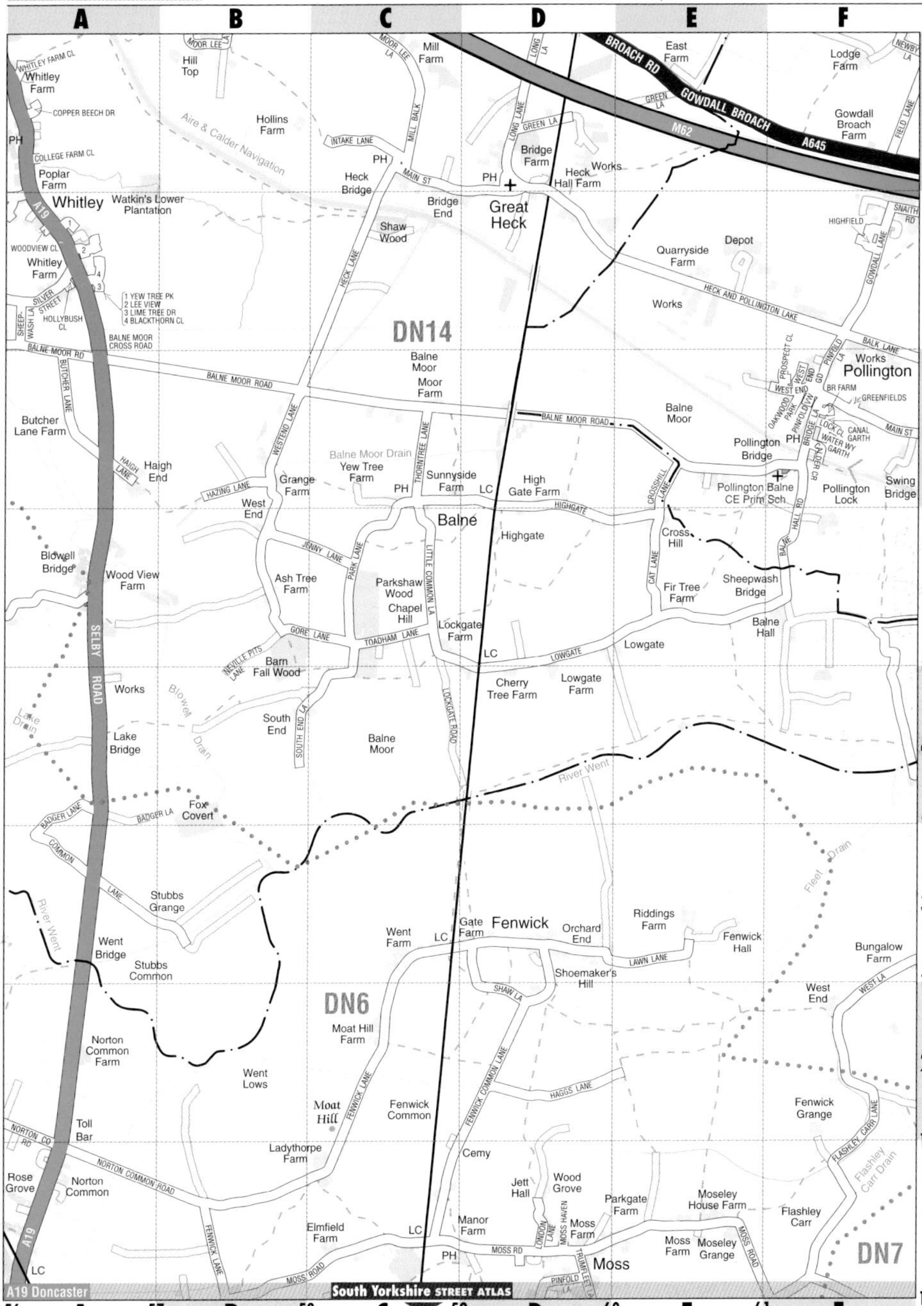
A B C D E F
8 7 6 5 4 3 2 1
21 20 19 18 17 16 15 14
56 57 58 59 60 61
Whitley Farm
WHITLEY FARM CL
COPPER BEECH DR
COLLEGE FARM CL
Poplar Farm
Whitley
Watkin's Lower Plantation
WOODVIEW CL
Whitley Farm
1 YEW TREE PK
2 LEE VIEW
3 LIME TREE DR
4 BLACKTHORN CL
SILVER STREET
SHEEP-WASH LA
HOLLYBUSH CL
BALNE MOOR CROSS ROAD
BALNE MOOR RD
BUTCHER LANE
Butcher Lane Farm
HAIGH LANE
Haigh End
MOOR LEE LA
Hill Top
Hollins Farm
Aire & Calder Navigation
INTAKE LANE
MILL BALK
Mill Farm
Heck Bridge
MAIN ST
Bridge End
Great Heck
Shaw Wood
HECK LANE
LONG LANE
GREEN LA
Bridge Farm
Heck Hall Farm
Works
BROACH RD
GOWDALL BROACH
East Farm
Lodge Farm
NEWBY LA
Gowdall Broach Farm
FIELD LANE
M62
A645
SNAITH RD
HIGHFIELD
GOWDALL LANE
Depot
Quarryside Farm
HECK AND POLLINGTON LANE
Works
DN14
Balne Moor
Moor Farm
BALNE MOOR ROAD
BALK LANE
Works
Pollington
PROSPECT CL
WEST END
PINFOLD LA
BR FARM
GREENFIELDS
OAKWOOD PARK
PINFOLD VW
BRIDGE LA
LOCK CL
WATER WY
GARTH
CANAL GARTH
MAIN ST
Balne Moor
Pollington Bridge
CALDER GR
Pollington Balne CE Prim Sch
Pollington Lock
Swing Bridge
Balne Moor Drain
Yew Tree Farm
THORNTREE LANE
WESTEND LANE
Grange Farm
HAZING LANE
West End
Sunnyside Farm
High Gate Farm
CROSSHILL LANE
HIGHGATE
Balne
Highgate
Cross Hill
BALNE HALL RD
JENNY LANE
PARK LANE
LITTLE COMMON LA
Ash Tree Farm
Parkshaw Wood
Chapel Hill
CAT LANE
Fir Tree Farm
Sheepwash Bridge
Blowell Bridge
Wood View Farm
SELBY ROAD
GORE LANE
TOADHAM LANE
Lockgate Farm
Balne Hall
LOWGATE
Lowgate
NEVILLE PITS LANE
Barn Fall Wood
Works
Blowell Drain
Cherry Tree Farm
Lowgate Farm
Lake Drain
South End
SOUTH END LA
LOCKGATE ROAD
Lake Bridge
Balne Moor
River Went
BADGER LANE
BADGER LA
Fox Covert
COMMON LANE
Stubbs Grange
Fleet Drain
River Went
Went Bridge
Went Farm
Gate Farm
Fenwick
Orchard End
Riddings Farm
Fenwick Hall
LAWN LANE
Bungalow Farm
Stubbs Common
SHAW LA
Shoemaker's Hill
West End
WEST LA
DN6
Moat Hill Farm
Norton Common Farm
FENWICK COMMON LANE
Went Lows
HAGGS LANE
Moat Hill
FENWICK LANE
Fenwick Common
Fenwick Grange
Toll Bar
NORTON CO RD
NORTON COMMON ROAD
Ladythorpe Farm
Cemy
FLASHLEY CARR LANE
Flashley Carr Drain
Rose Grove
Norton Common
Jett Hall
Wood Grove
Parkgate Farm
Moseley House Farm
Flashley Carr
Elmfield Farm
Manor Farm
LONDON LANE
MOSS HAVEN
Moss Farm
MOSS RD
Moss Farm
Moseley Grange
MOSS ROAD
DN7
A19
LC
PH
MOSS ROAD
TRUMFLEET LA
PINFOLD
Moss
A19 Doncaster
South Yorkshire STREET ATLAS

C8
1 ROLAND SIMPSON CL
2 THE CHASE
3 BEAN GDNS
4 SOUTH PARKWAY
5 PARK GDNS
6 OAKDALE CL
7 HALL CL
8 COURT GDNS
9 THE PARKWAY
10 MITTEN AVE
11 WALNUT CRES
12 SYCAMORE CL

Scale: 1⅓ inches to 1 mile
0 ¼ ½ mile
0 250m 500m 750m 1 km

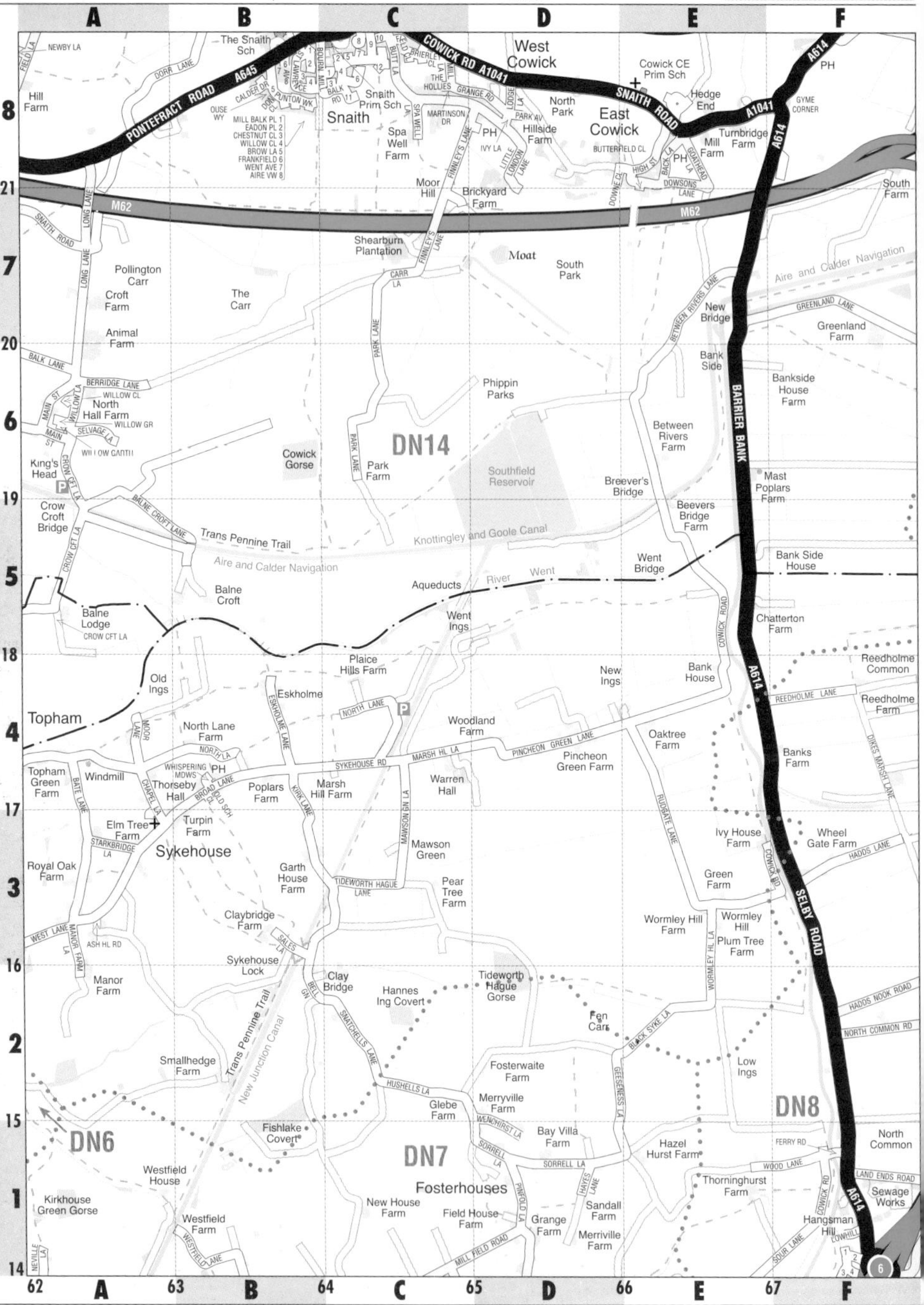

F1
1 QUAYSIDE 1
2 WATERSIDE RD
3 WATERSIDE
4 QUAY RD

Scale: 1⅓ inches to 1 mile

0 ¼ ½ mile

0 250m 500m 750m 1 km

64 80 149

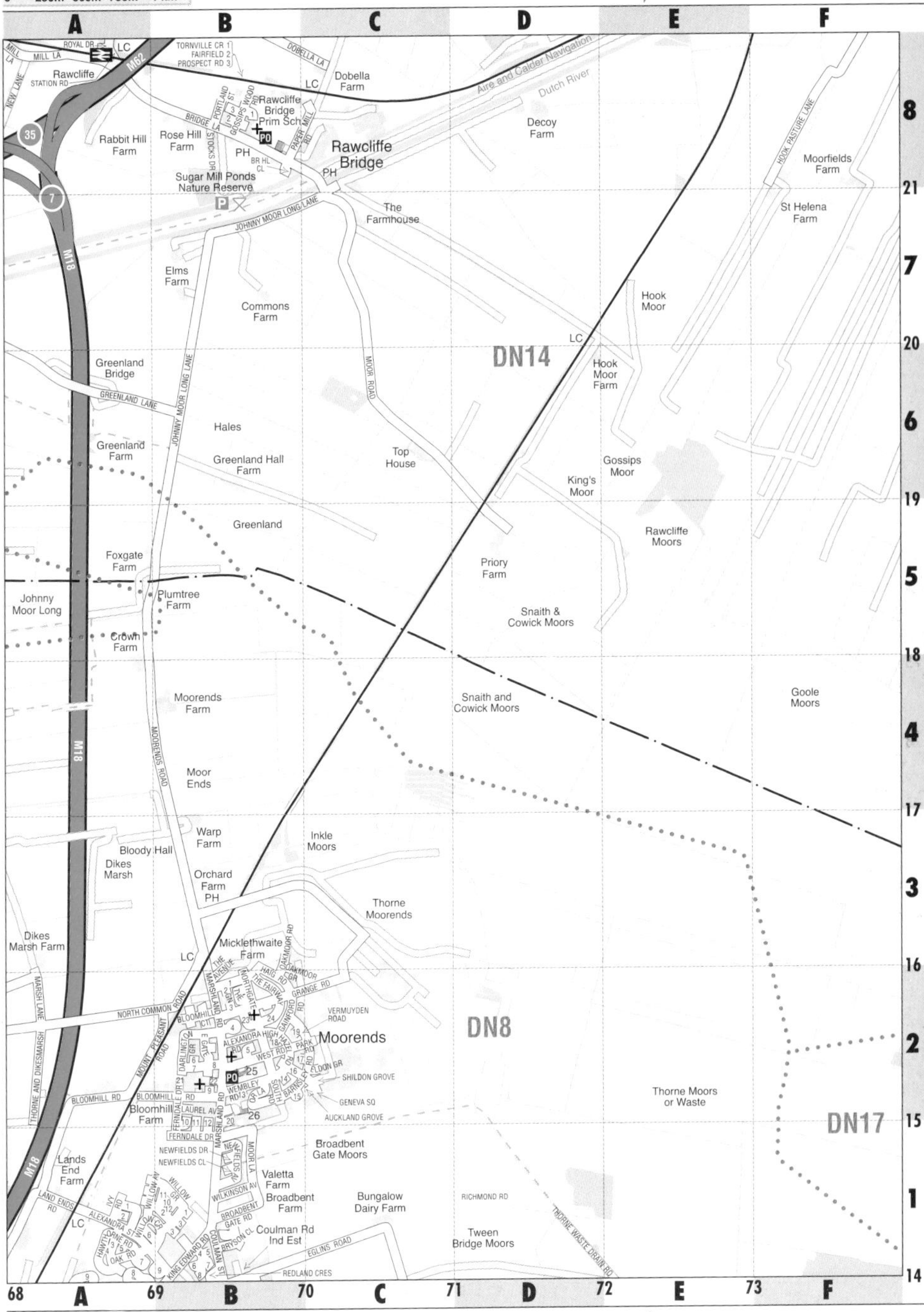

A1
1 WALNUT RD
2 BIRCHWOOD CL
3 CHERRY TREE DR
4 HAWTHORNE AVE
5 HAWTHORNE GR
6 WILLOW RD
7 OAK CR
8 CORONA DR
9 HIGHFIELD CRES

B1
1 MAPLE RD
2 CEDAR RD
3 WILLOW GR
4 KINGS CT RD
5 JAMES CT
6 EDWARD CT
7 CHARLES CT
8 HENRY CT
9 KING EDWARD CRES
10 HOLLY WK
11 HOLLY RD
12 MAPLE RD

B2
1 MICKLETHWAITE RD
2 MICKLETHWAITE GR
3 GRANGE GR
4 BLOOMHILL CL
5 THE HERMITAGE
6 ALDER GR
7 BELVEDERE DR
8 NEWHOLME DR
9 BLOOM HL GR
10 ROWAN CL
11 LABURNUM AVE
12 MULBERRY AVE
13 DUNELM CRES
14 KENTS GDNS
15 SILKSTONE OVAL
16 LOCARNO RD
17 WINDLESTONE SQ
18 GAINFORD SQ
19 THRISLINGTON SQ
20 KINGSMEAD
21 MOUNT PLEASANT RD
22 MOORSIDE CT
23 GARDEN RD
24 RICHMOND RD
25 West Rd Prim Sch
26 Thorne Moorends Marshlands Prim Sch

93 80

149 79 65

Scale: 1⅓ inches to 1 mile

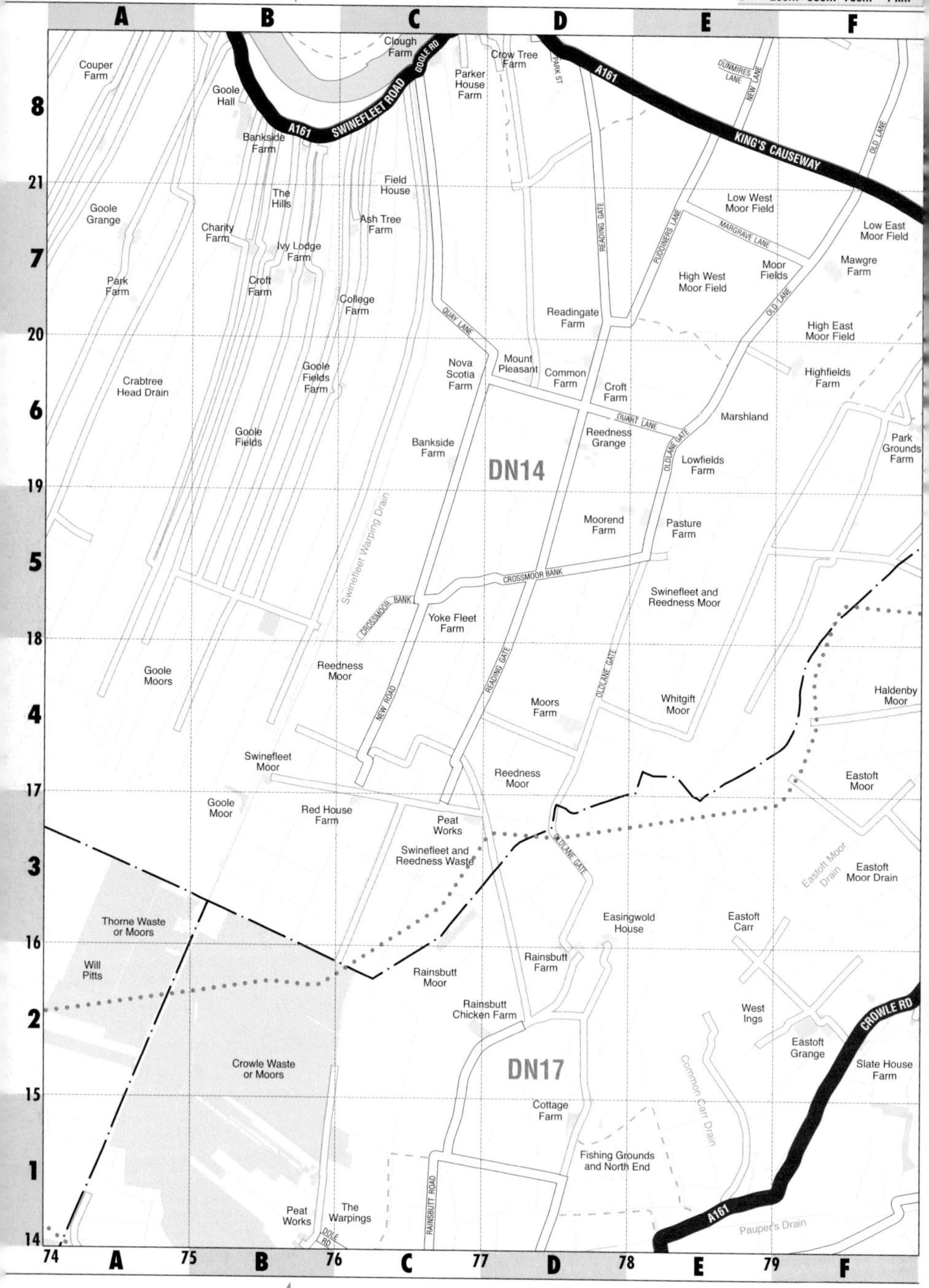

Couper Farm
Goole Hall
Clough Farm
Crow Tree Farm
Parker House Farm
A161
SWINEFLEET ROAD
GOOLE RD
PARK ST
DUNMIRES LANE
NEW LANE
KING'S CAUSEWAY
OLD LANE
Bankside Farm
Field House
The Hills
Goole Grange
Charity Farm
Ash Tree Farm
Ivy Lodge Farm
Low West Moor Field
MARGRAVE LANE
Low East Moor Field
Moor Fields
Mawgre Farm
High West Moor Field
PUDDINERS LANE
READING GATE
Park Farm
Croft Farm
College Farm
Readingate Farm
High East Moor Field
QUAY LANE
Crabtree Head Drain
Goole Fields Farm
Nova Scotia Farm
Mount Pleasant
Common Farm
Croft Farm
Highfields Farm
Marshland
QUART LANE
Goole Fields
Bankside Farm
Reedness Grange
OLDLANE GATE
Lowfields Farm
Park Grounds Farm
DN14
Swinefleet Warping Drain
Moorend Farm
Pasture Farm
CROSSMOOR BANK
Swinefleet and Reedness Moor
Yoke Fleet Farm
Goole Moors
Reedness Moor
NEW ROAD
Moors Farm
Whitgift Moor
Haldenby Moor
Swinefleet Moor
Reedness Moor
Eastoft Moor
Goole Moor
Red House Farm
Peat Works
Swinefleet and Reedness Waste
Eastoft Moor Drain
Eastoft Moor Drain
Thorne Waste or Moors
Easingwold House
Eastoft Carr
Will Pitts
Rainsbutt Farm
Rainsbutt Moor
Rainsbutt Chicken Farm
West Ings
CROWLE RD
Eastoft Grange
Slate House Farm
Crowle Waste or Moors
DN17
Common Carr Drain
Cottage Farm
Fishing Grounds and North End
RAINSBUTT ROAD
Peat Works
The Warpings
DOLE RD
Pauper's Drain

79 94

Scale: 1⅓ inches to 1 mile
0 ¼ ½ mile
0 250m 500m 750m 1 km

66
82

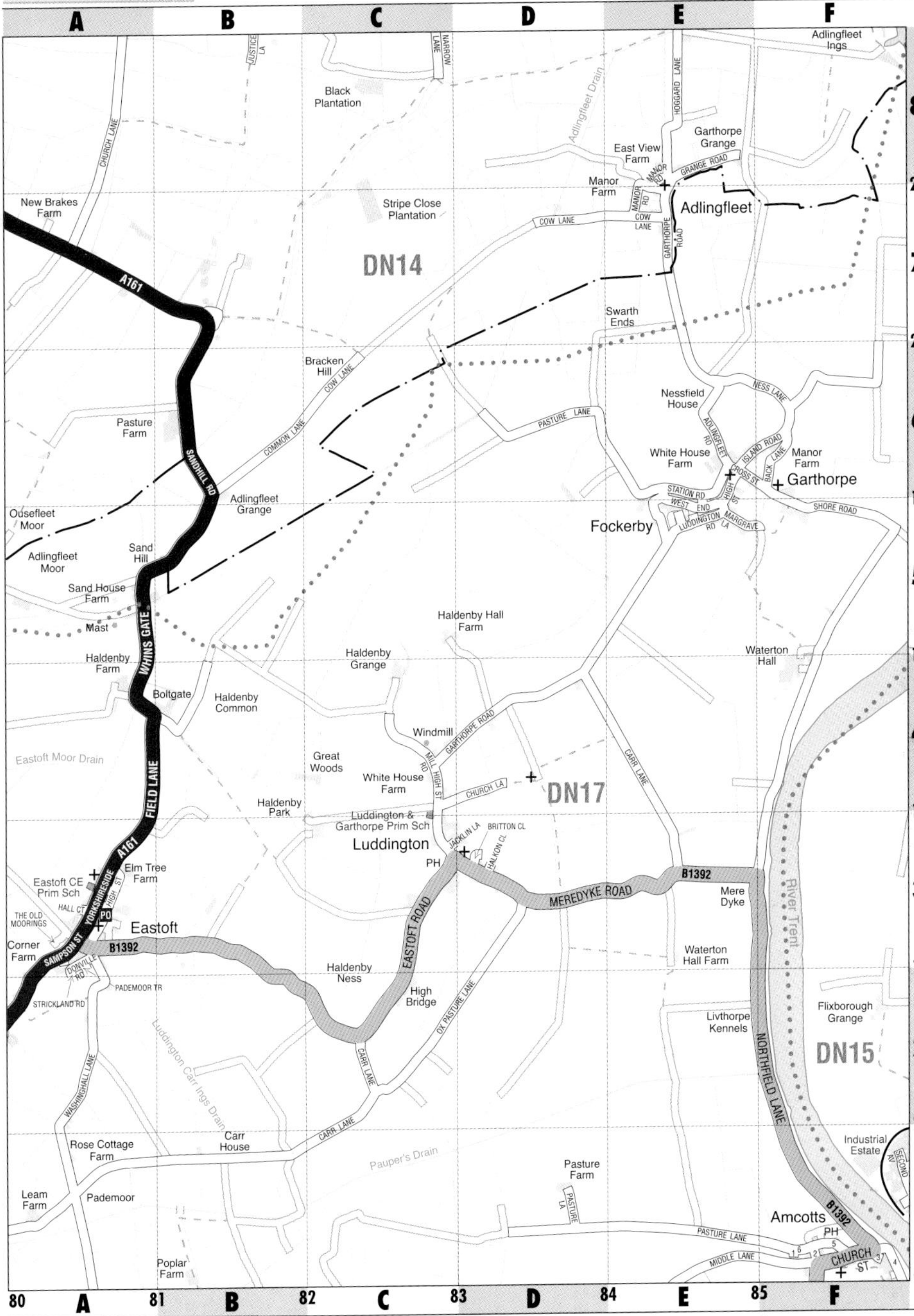

95
82

F1
1 BELTHORN RD
2 CHAPEL ST
3 CROSS LA
4 TRENT SIDE
5 DARK LA
6 MANOR HOUSE LA

81
67

Scale: 1⅓ inches to 1 mile
0 ¼ ½ mile
0 250m 500m 750m 1 km

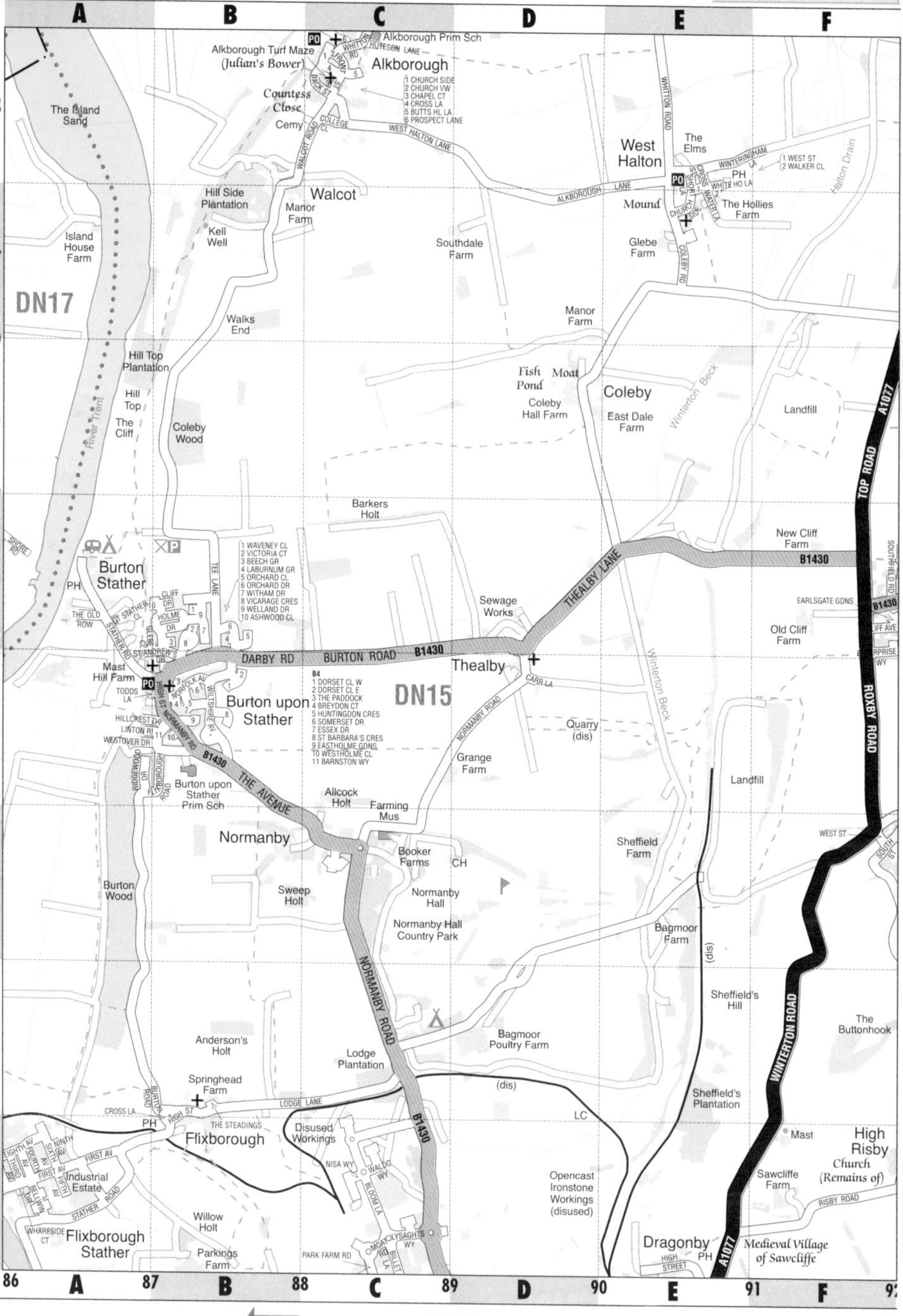
A B C D E F
8
21
7
20
6
19
5
18
4
17
3
16
2
15
1
14
86 87 88 89 90 91 92
Alkborough Turf Maze
(Julian's Bower)
Alkborough
Alkborough Prim Sch
HUTESON LANE
WHITTON RD
BACK ST
1 CHURCH SIDE
2 CHURCH VW
3 CHAPEL CT
4 CROSS LA
5 BUTTS HL LA
6 PROSPECT LANE
Countess Close
Cemy
COLLEGE CL
WALCOT ROAD
WEST HALTON LANE
The Island Sand
Hill Side Plantation
Walcot
Manor Farm
Kell Well
Island House Farm
DN17
Southdale Farm
Walks End
Hill Top Plantation
Hill Top
The Cliff
River Trent
Coleby Wood
West Halton
The Elms
WHITTON ROAD
WINTERINGHAM LA
1 WEST ST
2 WALKER CL
PH
WHITE HO LA
ALKBOROUGH LANE
Mound
CHURCH SIDE
The Hollies Farm
Glebe Farm
COLEBY RD
Halton Drain
Manor Farm
Fish Pond
Moat
Coleby
Coleby Hall Farm
East Dale Farm
Winterton Beck
Landfill
A1077
TOP ROAD
Barkers Holt
New Cliff Farm
B1430
SOUTHFIELD RD
EARLSGATE GDNS
SHORE RD
Burton Stather
PH
THE OLD ROW
TEE LANE
1 WAVENEY CL
2 VICTORIA CT
3 BEECH GR
4 LABURNUM GR
5 ORCHARD CL
6 ORCHARD DR
7 WITHAM DR
8 VICARAGE CRES
9 WELLAND DR
10 ASHWOOD CL
CLIFF DR
HOLME DR
ST ANDREW'S DR
STATHER RD
Sewage Works
THEALBY LANE
Old Cliff Farm
Mast Hill Farm
DARBY RD
BURTON ROAD
Thealby
CARR LA
TODDS LA
HILLCREST DR
LINTON RI
WESTOVER DR
NORFOLK AV
WILTSHIRE AV
HIGH ST
NORMANBY RD
Burton upon Stather
B4
1 DORSET CL W
2 DORSET CL E
3 THE PADDOCK
4 BREYDON CT
5 HUNTINGDON CRES
6 SOMERSET DR
7 ESSEX DR
8 ST BARBARA'S CRES
9 EASTHOLME GDNS
10 WESTHOLME CL
11 BARNSTON WY
DN15
NORMANBY ROAD
Quarry (dis)
ROXBY ROAD
RIDGEWOOD DR
FLIXBOROUGH ROAD
Burton upon Stather Prim Sch
THE AVENUE
Grange Farm
Landfill
Allcock Holt
Farming Mus
Normanby
Booker Farms
CH
Sheffield Farm
WEST ST
SOUTH ST
Burton Wood
Sweep Holt
Normanby Hall
Normanby Hall Country Park
Bagmoor Farm
(dis)
Sheffield's Hill
WINTERTON ROAD
Anderson's Holt
Lodge Plantation
Bagmoor Poultry Farm
The Buttonhook
Springhead Farm
(dis)
LODGE LANE
BURTON ROAD
CROSS LA
PH
HIGH ST
THE STEADINGS
Flixborough
LC
Sheffield's Plantation
Disused Workings
Mast
High Risby
Church (Remains of)
EIGHTY AV
SIXTH AV
NINTH AV
FOURTH AV
FIRST AV
THIRD AV
FIFTH AV
BELLWIN DR
Industrial Estate
STATHER ROAD
NISA WY
WALDO WY
BLOOM LA
Opencast Ironstone Workings (disused)
Sawcliffe Farm
RISBY ROAD
WHARFSIDE CT
Flixborough Stather
Willow Holt
Parkings Farm
PARK FARM RD
MOAT RD
OLYSAGHTS WY
BILLET LA
Dragonby
HIGH STREET
PH
Medieval Village of Sawcliffe

81
96

Scale: 1⅓ inches to 1 mile

0 ¼ ½ mile

0 250m 500m 750m 1 km

A5
1 FARNDALE WY
2 NORTHLANDS AVE
3 FOWLER CT
4 BOYNTON CRES
5 HILLSMERE GR
6 BOSTON CL
7 WATERLOW DR
8 PLYMOUTH CL
9 LEEK HILL
10 WESTWINDS RD
11 MALKINSON CL
12 HAWTHORNE CL
13 BLANKNEY CT
14 MARKET ST
15 QUEEN ST
16 CHURCH SIDE
17 SAFFRE CL

68
84

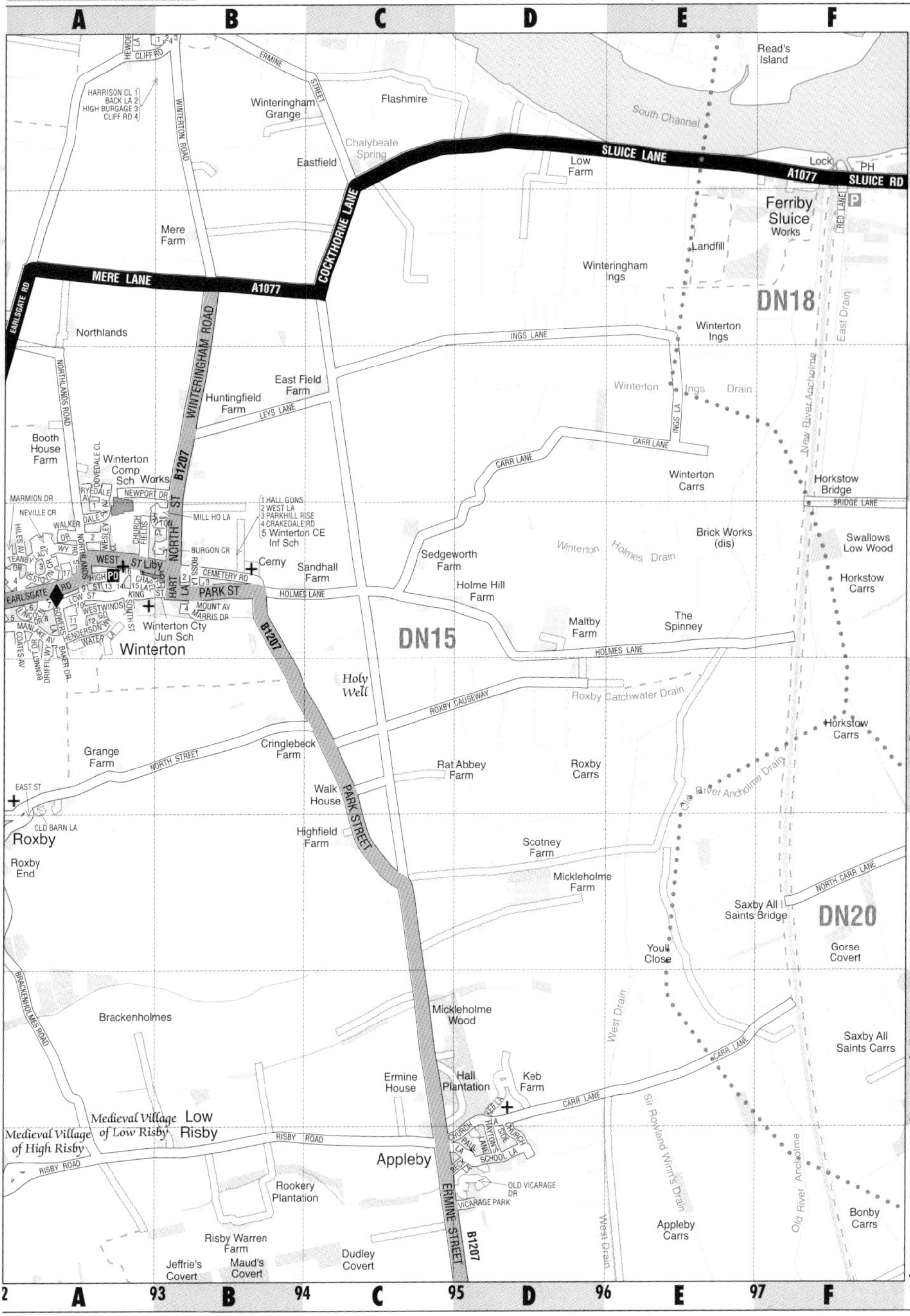

97
84

A7
1 BEAULAH VILLAS
2 BEAULAHLAND
3 SKINNERS LA
4 QUEEN ELIZABETH AVE
5 OLD POST OFFICE LA

83

E8
1 SUNNYBANK
2 TOFTS RD
3 BRADWELL CL
4 MILSON CL
5 PELHAM CL
6 MASONS CT
7 NICHOLAS CT
8 GEORGINA CT
9 GODDARD CL
10 HARROWDYKE
11 BERETUN GN
12 GRANGE AVE
13 MOUNT AVE

69

14 BEACON AVE
15 PARKDALE
16 ELMDALE
17 WELTON CL
18 STEVENSON'S WY
19 HARVEST AVE
20 SHARPE CL
21 MALKIN RD
22 HESSLE VW
23 HUMBER VW
24 RIVERBANK RISE
25 FURNISS CT
26 HERON WY
27 CURLEW CT
28 EIDER CL
29 MALLARD WY

Scale: 1⅓ inches to 1 mile
0 ¼ ½ mile
0 250m 500m 750m 1 km

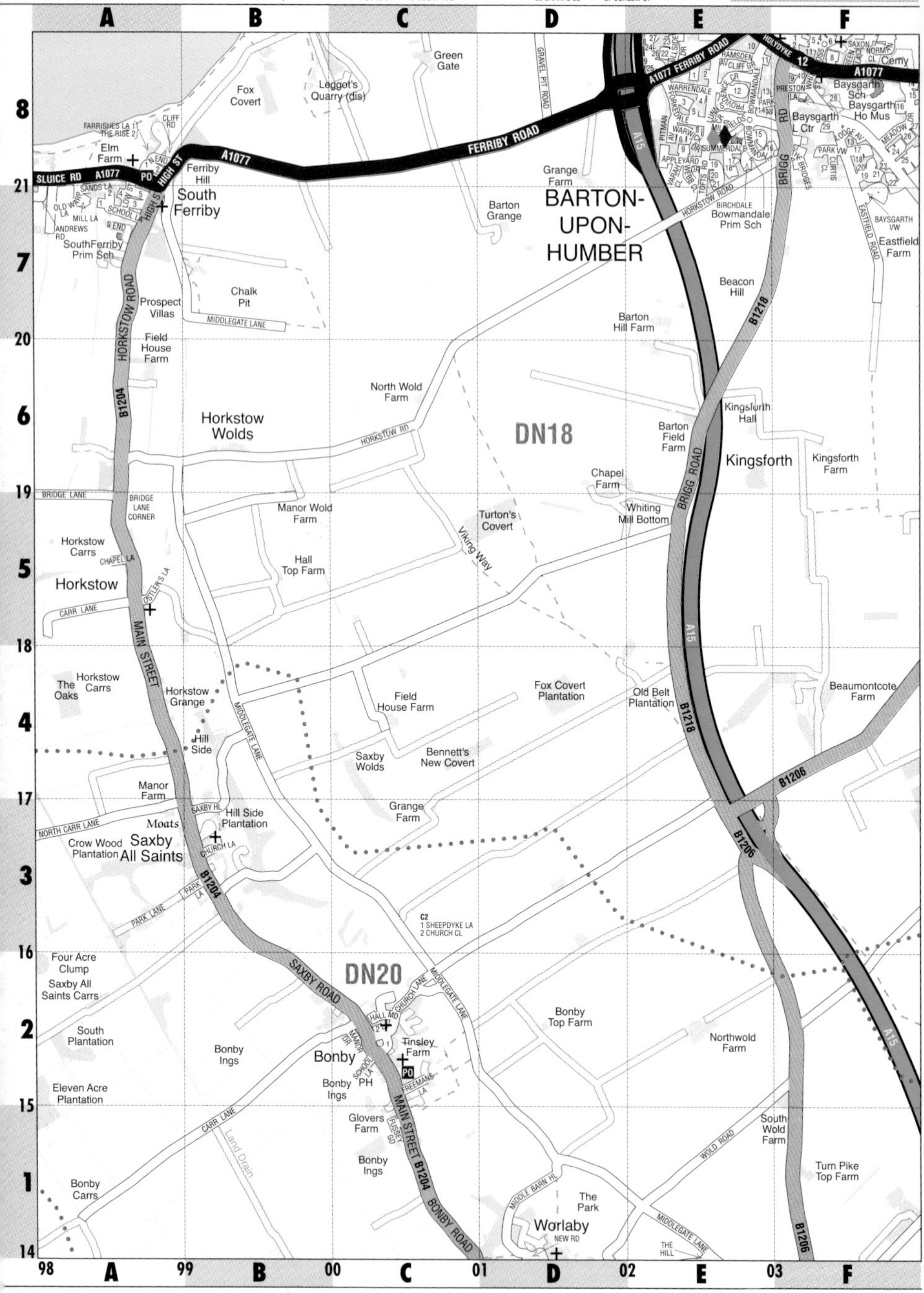

83
98

F8
1 KING ST
2 GEORGE ST
3 PRIESTGATE
4 BURGATE
5 ST MARY'S LA
6 BECK HILL
7 EAST ACRIDGE
8 CHURCH VW
9 CASTLE CT
10 CASTLEDYKE S
11 MARKET PL
12 MARKET LA
13 ORCHARD CL
14 STEPHEN CRES
15 HIGHFIELD CRES
16 NICOLSON DR
17 HAWTHORN GATE
18 RAVENDALE
19 QUEEN ELIZABETH WY
20 PRINCE CHARLES DR
21 PRINCE PHILIP DR
22 PRINCESS DR
23 MILLBROOK WY
24 LINCOLN DR
25 FAIRFIELD DR
26 RIVER VW
27 KINGSTON VW
28 NIGHTINGALE CL
29 STOWGARTH

Scale: 1⅓ inches to 1 mile
0 ¼ ½ mile
0 250m 500m 750m 1 km

C8
1 HARVEST RISE
2 THE BRAMBLES
3 ROWAN CL
4 HEDGEROW CL
5 SCHOFIELD CL
6 HAWTHORN RISE
7 MILLFIELDS WY
8 PADDOCK RISE
9 MIDDLEGATE CL
10 HIGHFIELDS
11 GLEN HALL RISE

70

86

D8
1 JOHN HARRISON'S CL
2 WILLOW GDNS
3 CROSS ST
4 CHURCHSIDE
5 BECK LA
6 GLANFORD GR
7 BARRICK CL
8 THE SPINNEY
9 THORNGARTH LA

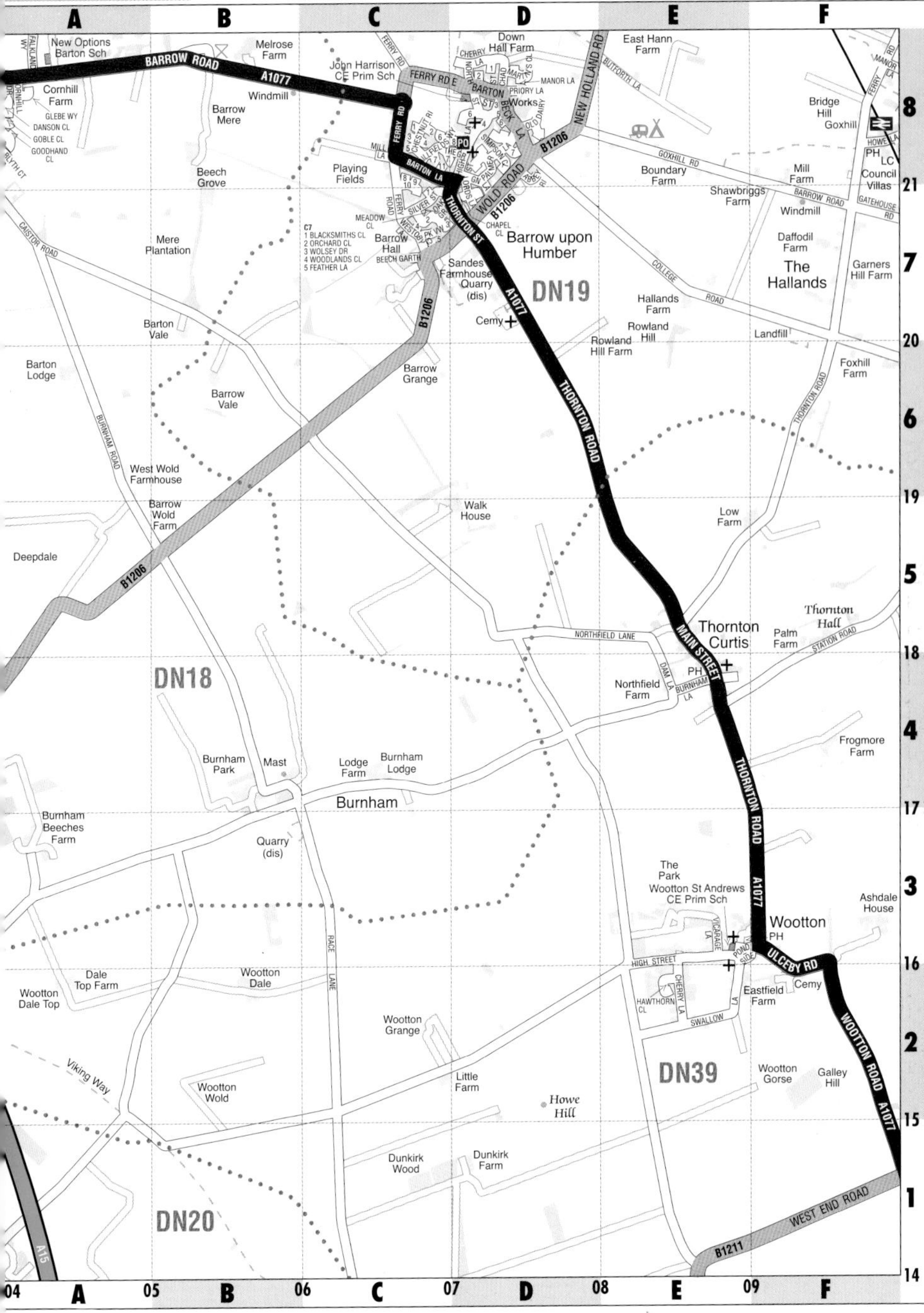

A B C D E F
8 21 7 20 6 19 5 18 4 17 3 16 2 15 1 14
04 05 06 07 08 09
BARROW ROAD
A1077
New Options Barton Sch
Melrose Farm
John Harrison CE Prim Sch
FERRY RD E
Down Hall Farm
East Hann Farm
Cornhill Farm
GLEBE WY
DANSON CL
GOBLE CL
GOODHAND CL
Windmill
Barrow Mere
MANOR LA
PRIORY LA
Works
NEW HOLLAND RD
BUTFORTH LA
Bridge Hill
Goxhill
FERRY RD
MANOR LA
Beech Grove
Playing Fields
FERRY RD
BARTON LA
B1206
WOLD ROAD
GOXHILL RD
Boundary Farm
Mill Farm
PH
LC
Council Villas
Shawbriggs Farm
BARROW ROAD
Windmill
GATEHOUSE RD
CAISTOR ROAD
Mere Plantation
C7
1 BLACKSMITHS CL
2 ORCHARD CL
3 WOLSEY DR
4 WOODLANDS CL
5 FEATHER LA
MEADOW CL
Barrow Hall
BEECH GARTH
THORNTON ST
CHAPEL CL
Barrow upon Humber
Daffodil Farm
The Hallands
Garners Hill Farm
Sandes Farmhouse
Quarry (dis)
DN19
COLLEGE ROAD
Hallands Farm
Barton Vale
Cemy
Rowland Hill
Landfill
Rowland Hill Farm
Barton Lodge
Barrow Grange
Foxhill Farm
Barrow Vale
THORNTON ROAD
BURNHAM ROAD
West Wold Farmhouse
Barrow Wold Farm
Walk House
Low Farm
Deepdale
B1206
NORTHFIELD LANE
Thornton Curtis
Thornton Hall
Palm Farm
STATION ROAD
MAIN STREET
PH
DN18
Northfield Farm
DAM LA
BURNHAM LA
Burnham Park
Mast
Lodge Farm
Burnham Lodge
Frogmore Farm
Burnham
Burnham Beeches Farm
Quarry (dis)
The Park
Wootton St Andrews CE Prim Sch
Ashdale House
Wootton
PH
VICARAGE LA
POND SIDE
HIGH STREET
ULCEBY RD
Cemy
RACE LANE
Dale Top Farm
Wootton Dale
Wootton Dale Top
HAWTHORN CL
CHERRY LA
SWALLOW LA
Eastfield Farm
Wootton Grange
DN39
Wootton Gorse
Galley Hill
WOOTTON ROAD
Viking Way
Wootton Wold
Little Farm
Howe Hill
Dunkirk Wood
Dunkirk Farm
DN20
A15
B1211
WEST END ROAD

99

86

A8
1 STOTHARDS LA
2 GREENGATE LA
3 PIDGEON COTE LA
4 WESTFIELD RD
5 CHURCH ST
6 CHESTNUT WY
7 ROWEN CT
8 JASMINE CT
9 THE BRIDLES
10 BRIAR CT
11 ROSBROOK WY
12 ST JOHNS CL

85
71

Scale: 1⅓ inches to 1 mile
0 ¼ ½ mile
0 250m 500m 750m 1 km

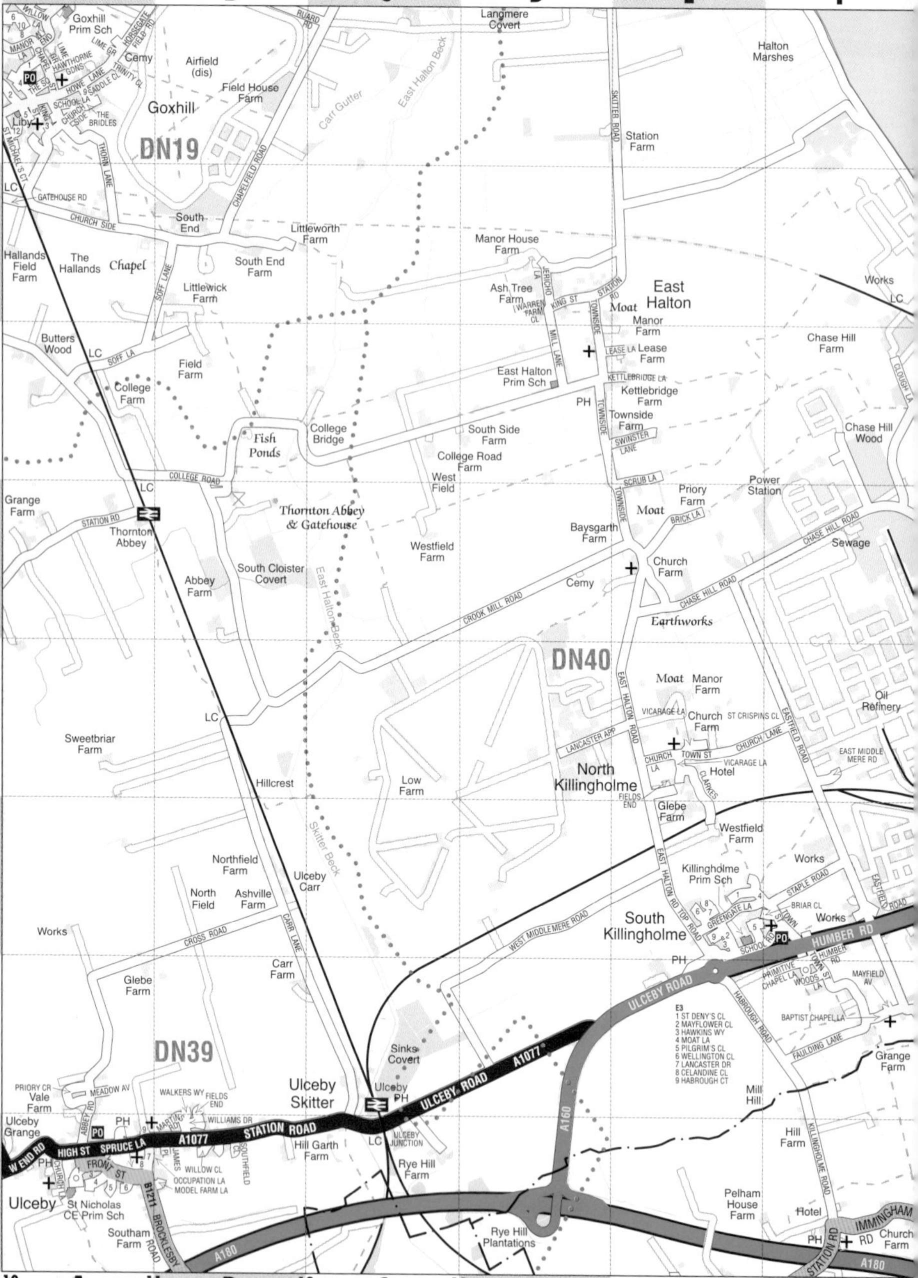

A1
1 HALLCROFT
2 STEPHEN CL
3 FORGE CR
4 MOUNT ROYALE CL
5 PITMOOR LA
6 NELTHORPE CL
7 CORONATION RD
8 PARKS CL
9 ADVENT CT

85
100

Scale: 1⅓ inches to 1 mile
0 ¼ ½ mile
0 250m 500m 750m 1 km

72
88

B1
1 MAIDEN CL
2 VIKING CL
3 MILLHOUSE RISE
4 CLEVELAND CL
5 HAZEL CFT
6 LYDIA CT
7 JACKSON MEWS
8 ST ANDREWS WY
9 HELEN CR
10 ANCHOLME AVE
11 STEEPING DR
12 HOLLINGSWORTH AVE
13 LANSDOWN RD
14 BALFOUR PL
15 STAINTON DR
16 AINSWORTH RD
17 HOLBECK PL
18 LEYDEN CL
19 CHILTON CL
20 BRADFORD RD
21 BLOSSOM WY
22 HIGHFIELD AVE
23 LINDUM AVE
24 MACKENZIE PL
25 CLARENCE CL
26 BOWMAN WY
27 HAMISH WK
28 KINLOCH WY
29 JAMES WY
30 KISHORN CT
31 HIGHLAND TARN
32 OBAN CT
33 PADDOCK CT
34 VALDA VALE
35 CALDER CL
36 AIRE CL
37 Allerton Prim Sch

C1
1 ALLERTON DR
2 SPINNEY CL
3 BEECHWOOD AVE
4 MUIRFIELD CFT
5 BERWICK CT
6 MAYFLOWER AVE
7 ROUNDWAY
8 JAPONICA HILL
9 MAGNOLIA RISE
10 CUSHMAN CR
11 ORKNEY PL
12 DEANE RD
13 EATON RD
14 SACKVILLE CL
15 SACKVILLE RD
16 COLLIER RD
17 BREWSTER AVE
18 CRAIK HILL AVE
19 PAM CL

101

C2
1 COPSE CL
2 CEDAR DR
3 MAPLE GR
4 ROSE GDNS
5 ASH TREE CL
6 HOYLAKE DR
7 SUNNINGDALE DR
8 BIRKDALE DR
9 WILLOW TREE CL
10 PELHAM RD

88

D2
1 HAWTHORN AVE
2 LARCH CL
3 TRENCHARD CL

87
73

Scale: 1⅓ inches to 1 mile
0 ¼ ½ mile
0 250m 500m 750m 1 km

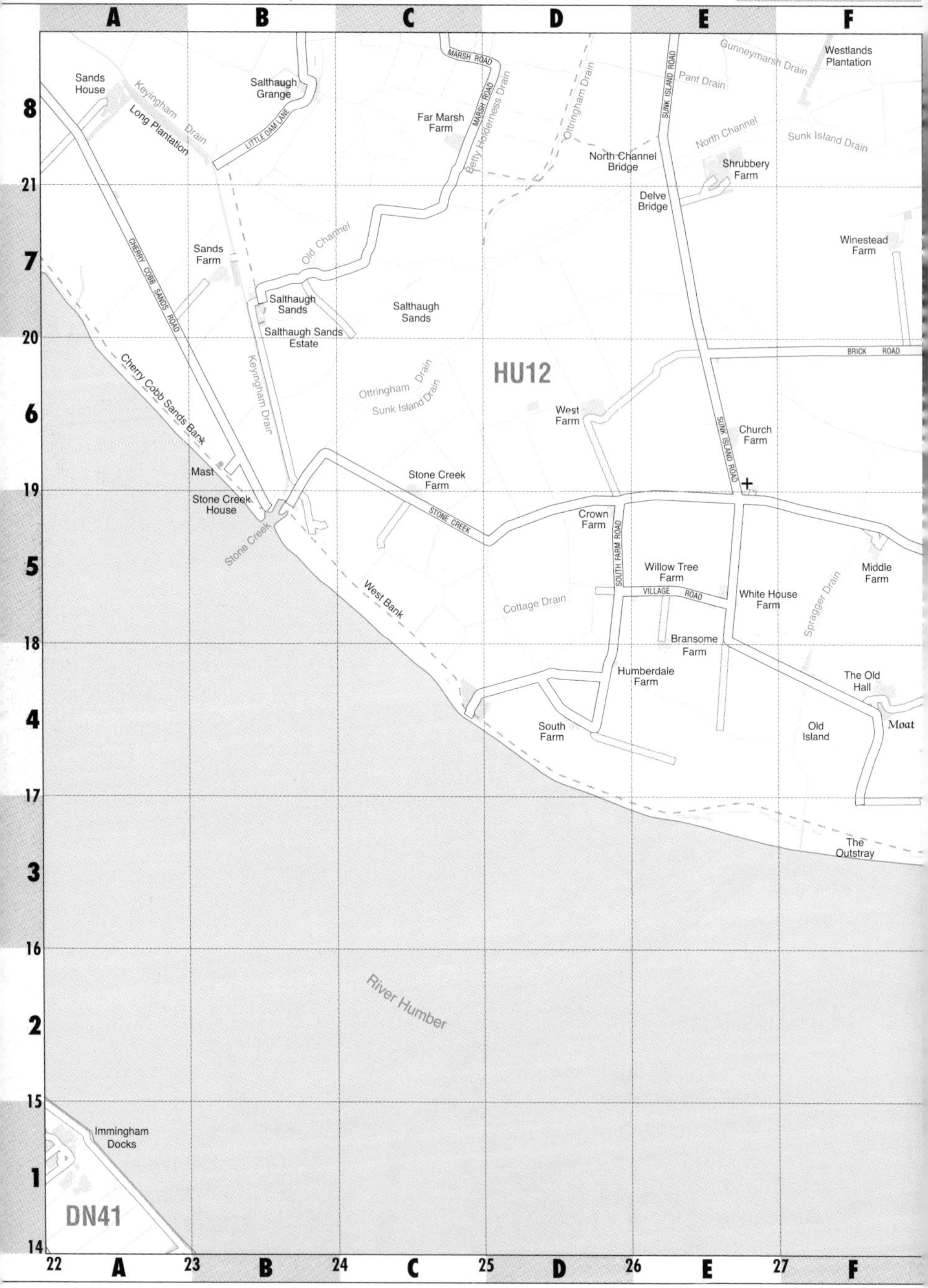

87
102

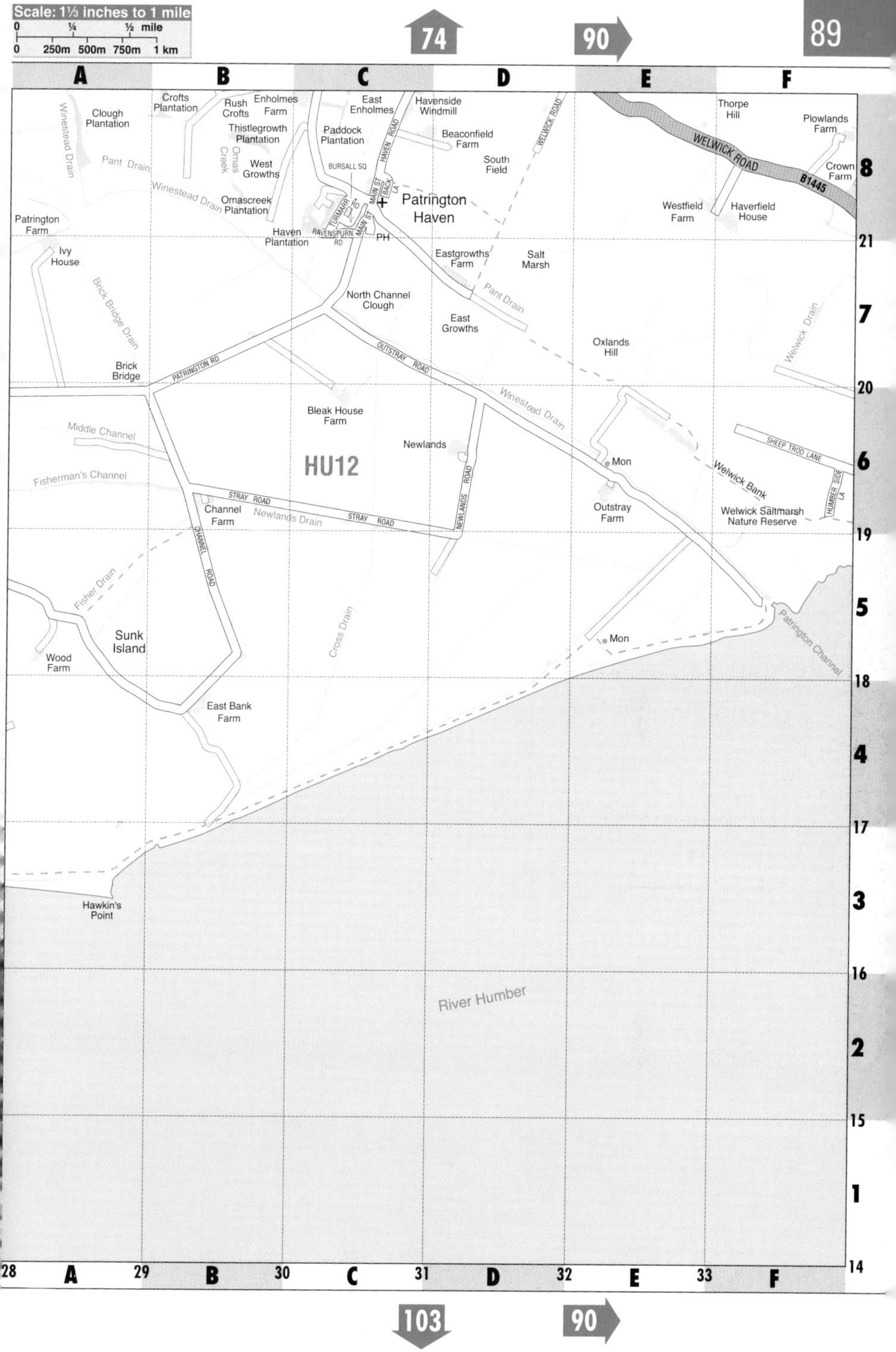
Scale: 1⅓ inches to 1 mile
74
90
A B C D E F
Clough Plantation
Crofts Plantation
Rush Crofts
Enholmes Farm
East Enholmes
Havenside Windmill
Thistlegrowth Plantation
Paddock Plantation
Beaconfield Farm
West Growths
Omascreek Plantation
South Field
Winestead Drain
Pant Drain
Omas Creek
Patrington Haven
Patrington Farm
Haven Plantation
PH
Ivy House
Eastgrowths Farm
Salt Marsh
Thorpe Hill
Plowlands Farm
WELWICK ROAD
B1445
Crown Farm
Westfield Farm
Haverfield House
Brick Bridge Drain
North Channel Clough
East Growths
Oxlands Hill
Welwick Drain
Brick Bridge
PATRINGTON RD
OUTSTRAY ROAD
Bleak House Farm
Newlands
Middle Channel
Fisherman's Channel
HU12
Mon
SHEEP TROD LANE
Welwick Bank
HUMBER SIDE LA
Channel Farm
STRAY ROAD
Newlands Drain
NEWLANDS ROAD
Outstray Farm
Welwick Saltmarsh Nature Reserve
Fisher Drain
CHANNEL ROAD
Cross Drain
Sunk Island
Wood Farm
Patrington Channel
East Bank Farm
Hawkin's Point
River Humber
28 29 30 31 32 33
14 15 16 17 18 19 20 21
1 2 3 4 5 6 7 8
103
90

89
75

Scale: 1⅓ inches to 1 mile
0 ¼ ½ mile
0 250m 500m 750m 1 km

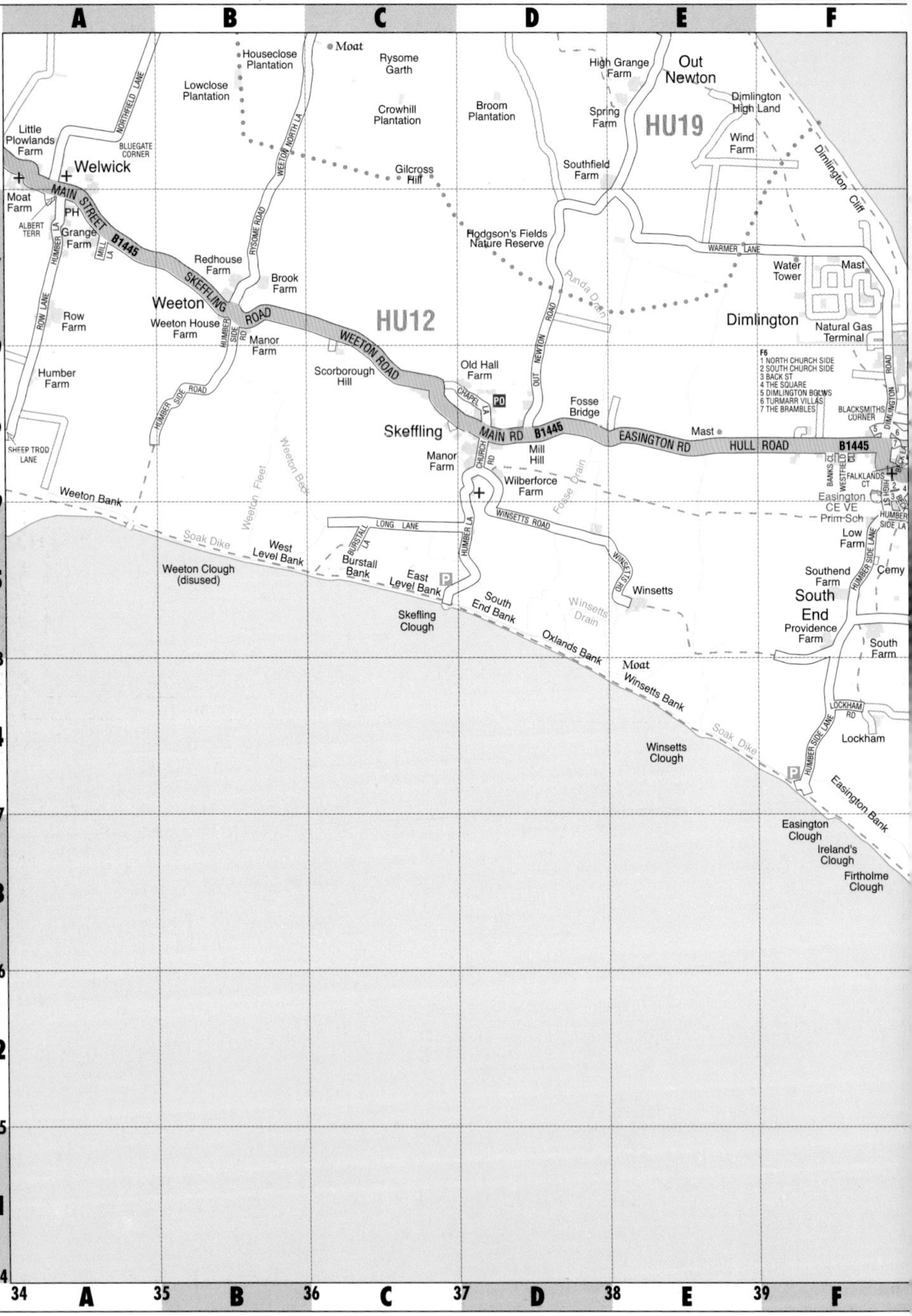

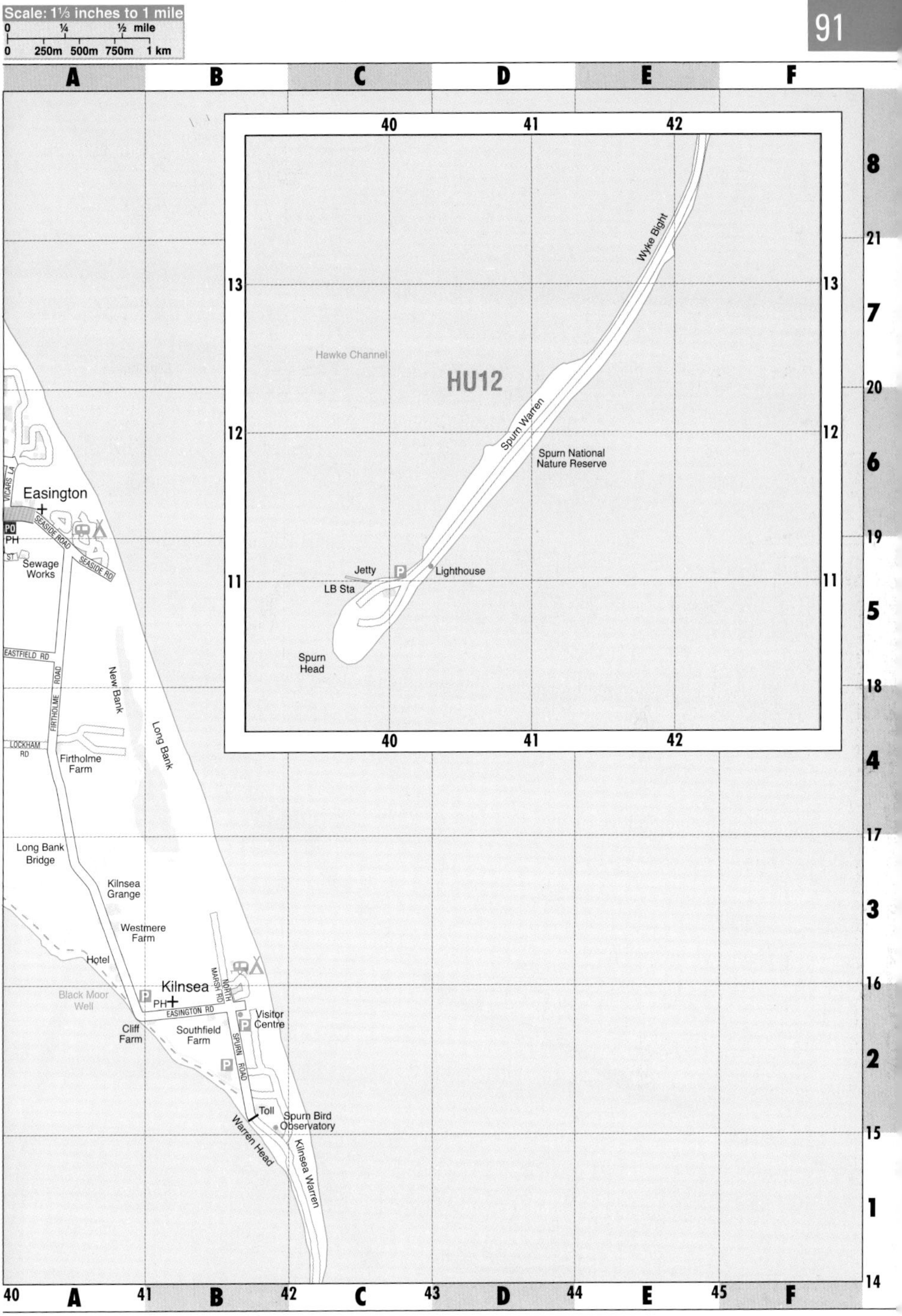
Scale: 1⅓ inches to 1 mile
0 ¼ ½ mile
0 250m 500m 750m 1 km
A B C D E F
8 7 6 5 4 3 2 1
21 20 19 18 17 16 15 14
40 41 42
13 12 11
Hawke Channel
HU12
Wyke Bight
Spurn Warren
Spurn National Nature Reserve
Jetty
Lighthouse
LB Sta
Spurn Head
Easington
VICARS LA
PO
PH
ST
SEASIDE ROAD
SEASIDE RD
Sewage Works
EASTFIELD RD
FIRTHOLME ROAD
New Bank
Long Bank
LOCKHAM RD
Firtholme Farm
Long Bank Bridge
Kilnsea Grange
Westmere Farm
Hotel
Black Moor Well
Kilnsea
PH
EASINGTON RD
NORTH MARSH RD
Visitor Centre
Cliff Farm
Southfield Farm
SPURN ROAD
Toll
Spurn Bird Observatory
Warren Head
Kilnsea Warren
40 41 42 43 44 45

C6
1 SILVER ST
2 NEW GREEN
3 THORNE RD
4 BREEZEMOUNT CT
5 KENNETH AVE
6 ASHFIELD GR
7 BEECH CRES
8 NUTFIELDS GR
9 DR ANDERSON AVE
10 CROSSWAYS
11 HOLME GDNS
12 BOOTHAM RD
13 DUKE ST
14 KINGSWAY
15 STANLEY GDNS
16 STANLEY RD
17 THOMAS RD
18 TURNBERRY MS

78

E4
1 AMBROSE AVE
2 BRABBS AVE
3 WESTFIELD VILLAS
4 WESTFIELD RD
5 SPRINGFIELD AVE
6 LEYLAND AVE
7 BROCKENHURST RD
8 MANOR GDNS
9 OLD EPWORTH RD (WEST)

Scale: 1⅓ inches to 1 mile
0 ¼ ½ mile
0 250m 500m 750m 1 km

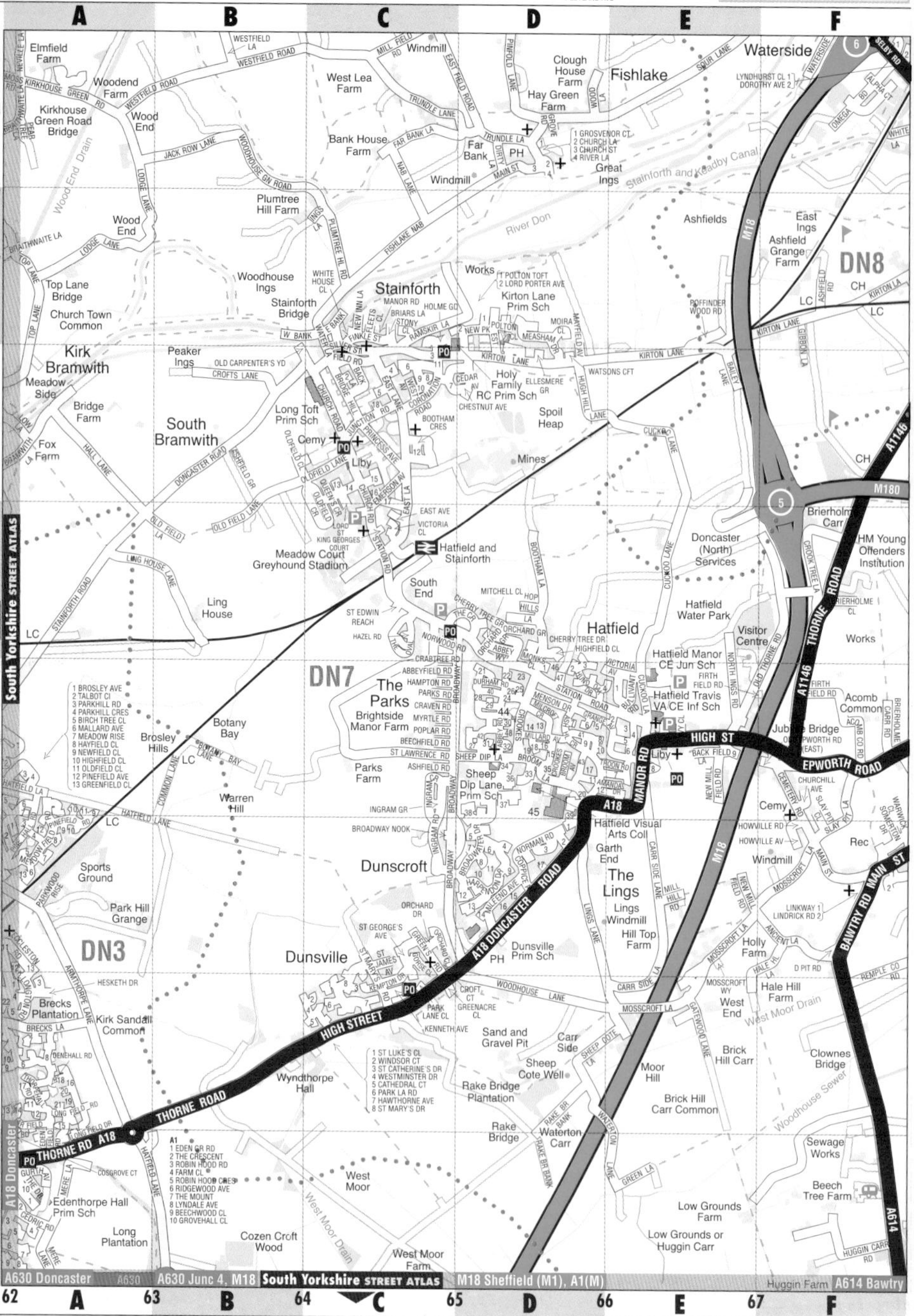

A2
1 TYNEDALE CT
2 GRANGE PK
3 TARLETON CL
4 HAREWOOD AVE
5 CURZEN CRES
6 ELIZABETH AVE
7 REDHALL CL
8 NEWHALL RD
9 DERWENT DR
10 WINDERMERE CRES
11 EDEN FIELD RD
12 HARVEST CL
13 EDENCROFT DR
14 FAR FIELD CL
15 MEADOW CFT
16 FOTHERGILL DR
17 FERNHALL CL
18 HOLMSHAW CL
19 HAMPSON GDNS
20 HURLSTONE CL
21 MEADOW WLK
22 EDGE GN

A3
1 THE SPINNEY
2 ST ANDREW'S WY
3 LIMEDALE VW
4 PINEFIELD AVE
5 MILL FIELD CT
6 GREENFIELD CL
7 HEATHFIELD CL
8 WHEATFIELD CL
9 LOWFIELD CL
10 THOROLD PL
11 SUTTON RD
12 LONGTON RD

D3
1 COPPICE LA
2 DANUM RD
3 NORMAN DR
4 ASTON GN
5 BRETTON CL
6 HARPENDON DR
7 WIDFORD GN
8 AMWELL GN
9 BARNET GN
10 AYOTS GN
11 SHENLEY CL
12 HARPENDEN CL
13 HODDESDON CRES
14 NASEBY CL
15 BLENHEIM CL
16 BOSWORTH CL
17 BEECHWOOD CT

D4
1 BOOTHAM CL
2 NETTLEHOLME
3 HOMESTEAD GARTH
4 BRACKEN HEEN CL
5 GRANGE CL
6 LINDEN CL
7 KING'S CL
8 PARKSTONE GR
9 TOLLESBY LA
10 ST ANDREWS GR
11 COOKRIDGE DR
12 PARKWAYS
13 MILCROFT CRES
14 THOMPSON NOOK
15 ROSEBERRY AVE
16 THOMPSON DR
17 NUNTHORPE CL
18 MILLARD NOOK
19 WHITE HO CL
20 ASH HL RD
21 CANTERBURY RD
22 GLENCOE CL
23 PRESCOTT GR
24 INVERNESS RD
25 BALMORAL RD
26 BRAMAR RD
27 ST EDWINS CL
28 YORK RD
29 WINCHESTER RD
30 ABBEY GN
31 WARREN CL
32 ABBEY GDNS
33 OAKLAND AVE
34 BROADWATER DR
35 LODGE CT
36 LEVERSTOCK GN
37 KINSBOURNE GN
38 BROADLANDS CL
39 COPPICE GR
40 LICHFIELD RD
41 CLEVELAND WY
42 WARRENNE RD
43 MARTON GR
44 Crookesbroom Prim Sch
45 Chase Sch
46 STATION CT
47 PUDDING & DIP LA
48 ABBEY GR

Scale: 1⅓ inches to 1 mile
0 ¼ ½ mile
0 250m 500m 750m 1 km

A8
1 CASSON'S RD
2 HIGHFIELD CRES
3 MARSDEN GR
4 LIME TREE GR
5 UPR KENYON ST
6 LWR KENYON ST
7 BELLWOOD CRES
8 BROOKFIELD CL
9 FOSTER RD
10 DURHAM AVE
11 GODFREY RD
12 BOATING DYKE WY
13 CAPSTAN WY
14 ASHBURNHAM RD
15 BROWNS LA
16 QUEEN ST
17 QUEEN'S CT
18 CHAPEL LA
19 BELLE VUE TERR
20 THE GREEN
21 HORSE FAIR GN
22 FAIRTREE WK
23 MIDDLEBROOK LA
24 SILVER ST
25 PINFOLD LA
26 DUNSTAN DR
27 CLIFTON CT
28 KENYON CL
29 WINDLASS CL
30 DUNSTAN DR
31 ANCHOR CL
32 MILLCROFT CL
33 STATION CT
34 DUNSTAN WLK

79

B8
1 INGLENOOK DR
2 REDLAND CRES
3 ALBERT ST
4 COULMAN RD
5 COULMAN ST
6 LOCKWOOD CL
7 TENNYSON AVE
8 CHURCH CL
9 HAYNES GN
10 HOUPS RD
11 LITTLEWOOD RD
12 COVENTRY RD
13 TITHE BARN LA
14 DANUM CL
15 HAYNES GDNS
16 TRAVIS CL
17 TRAVIS GR
18 TRAVIS AVE
19 ALWYN RD

94

A B C D E F
8 13 7 12 6 11 5 10 4 09 3 08 2 07 1 06
68 69 70 71 72 73
Thorne North
Thorne
Thorne King Edward Prim Sch
Coulman Road Ind Est
Tween Bridge Moors
Trinity Academy
Holme Farm
South Moors or Sand Moors
Doncaster Coll
Willows Farm
Moorhouse
MOOR OWNERS ROAD
THORNE WASTE DRAIN RD
Thorne Lock
Canal Side
Tithe Farm
Cemy
Brooke Prim Sch
Four Winds Farm
Whitaker's Plantations
Nun Moors
Moors Farm
Nun Moors
HATFIELD RD
FIELD SIDE
Thorne South
Moor's Bridge
LC
Orchard Farm
Stainforth & Keadby Canal
Wyke End House
HIGH BRIDGE ROAD
Maud's Bridge
Wike Well End
Wykewell Bridge
Burgar Common
Buildings Farm
CLAY BANK ROAD
HATFIELD ROAD
TUDWORTH RD
A614
Bradholme
DOUBLE BRIDGES ROAD
Old Laithe Farm
GREEN BANK
DN8
Sandhill Farm
A18
HIGH LEVELS BANK
Levels Farm
Grove House
Sand Hill
Tudworth Hall Farm
Grove House Farm
Red House
High Levels
Tithe Farm
PH
Hains Farm
Drain House
M180
Tudworth Hill
Dale Mount
Hatfield Chase
CROW TREE BANK
Bank House Farm
Ferne Carrs
Crow Tree Farm
PH
Black Bull Farm
SANDTOFT ROAD
Cherry Tree Farm
Stoupersgate Farm
Woodhouse Farm
Elder House
Plains House Farm
STONE HL
Bull Moors
Elder Glen Farm
BULL MOOR ROAD
CROSS RD
Stone Hill
Hatfield Woodhouse Prim Sch
Hatfield Woodhouse
Brier Hills
Low Levels
LOW LEVELS BANK
PLAINS LANE
MOOR LANE
Brier Hills Farm
Bull Moor Drain
Hollin Bridge Farm
HOLLIN BR LA
STAINFORTH MOOR ROAD
Works
Hollin Bridge
Goodcop Farm
1 LAUROLD AVE
2 REMPLE LA
3 REMPLE AVE
TURF MOOR RD
Wks
Moor Farm
DN7
Park Farm
MOOR DIKE ROAD
Lindholme Grange
White Bridge Farm
Hatfield Moors
Roe Carr
Woodhouse Grange
West Carr
Don Farm
LINDHOLME BANK ROAD
DN9
West Carr
Hatfield Moor Drain
Hatfield Moors
Roe Carr
Lindholme Lake
H M Prison Moorland
Lindholme Hall
Hatfield Moors
West Carr Houses
VULCAN WY
IDLE BANK

A7
1 ASHFIELD AVE
2 CANAL VW
3 CHEVIOT CL
4 MALVERN CL
5 QUANTOCK CL
6 MARINA VW
7 WENDAN RD
8 WEST CT
9 PICKERING GR
10 PARK VIEW
11 PARK CRES
12 SOUTH WOOD DR
13 ASH TREE RD
14 Green Top Prim Sch
15 CANALSIDE

B7
1 HAYNES GR
2 HAYNES CL
3 CHESTNUT AVE
4 ELM TREE GR
5 PEEL HL RD
6 WIKE GATE GR
7 WIKE GATE CL
8 PEEL CASTLE RD
9 MARLBOROUGH RD
10 MILLER CL
11 OLDFIELD RD
12 FENLAND RD
13 ST MICHAEL'S CL
14 SOUTHFIELD CL
15 AXHOLME GN
16 ST GEORGES RD
17 SWANLAND CL
18 MOWBRAY RD
19 ST GEORGES CL
20 PASHLEY RD
21 BEECH TREE AVE
22 THE CROFT
23 SWANLAND CT
24 OLD NURSERY YD
25 MEDLAR CT

104
94

D8
1 COX LA
2 CRANIDGE CL
3 JUSTICE HALL LA
4 BOWLING GN LA
5 CHAPEL ST
6 PRINTING OFFICE LA
7 LOW CROSS ST
8 CROSS SLACK
9 KESTEVEN GR

93

D7
1 VICAR'S WK
2 CHANCERY LA
3 WEST TERRACE ST
4 HIGH ST
5 MARKET CT
6 THE PADDOCKS
7 QUEENS DR
8 SOUTHFIELD RD
9 CROWLAND RD
10 LABURNUM GR
11 MULBERRY DR
12 ST JAMES CL
13 LINCOLN CL
14 WOLDS CL
15 REGENT DR

80

16 SAFFRON WAY
17 CHERRY TREE GDNS
18 MAPLE AVE
19 WINDSOR LA
20 ELIZABETH CL
21 CHESTNUT AVE

Scale: 1⅓ inches to 1 mile
0 ¼ ½ mile
0 250m 500m 750m 1 km

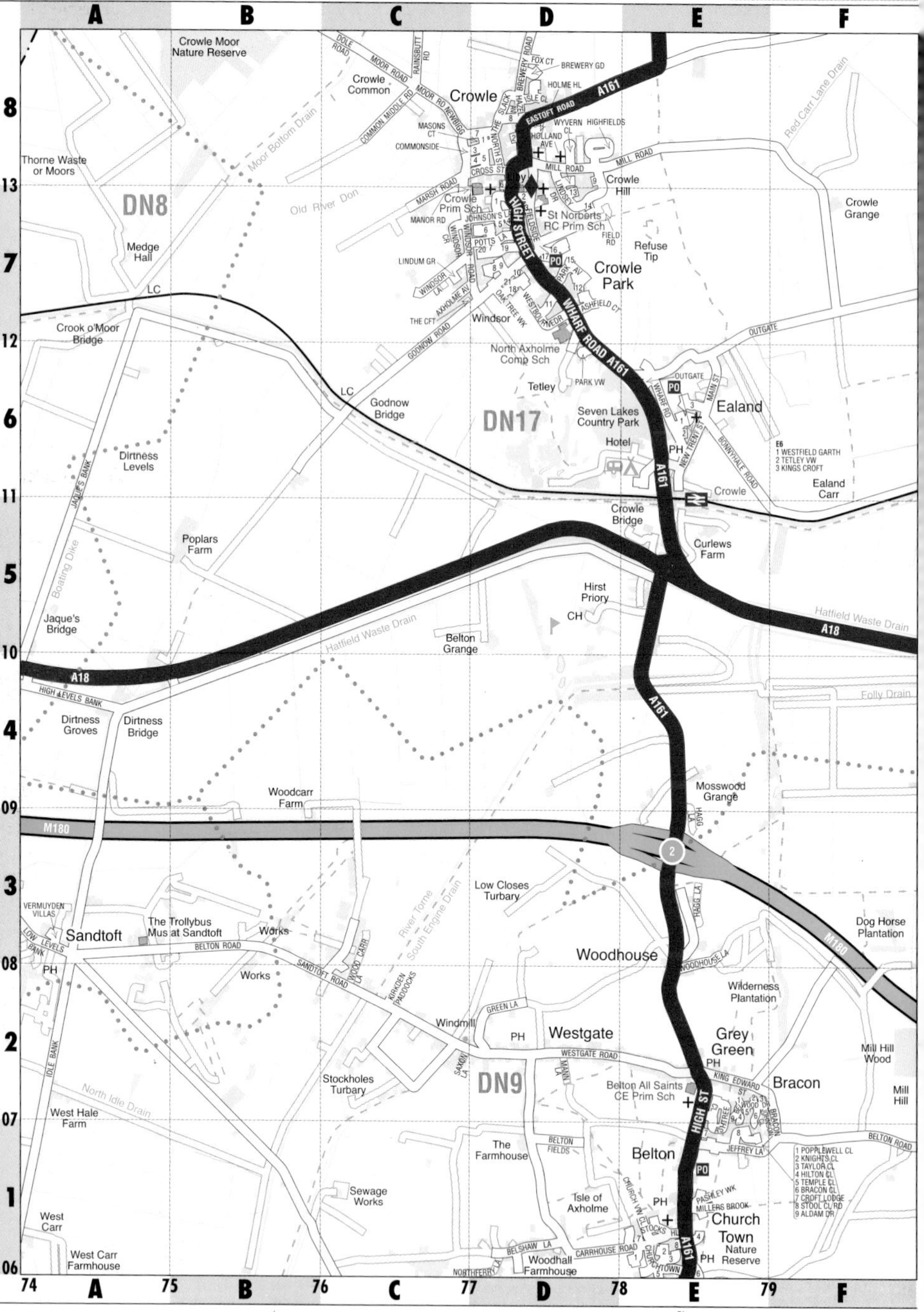

93
105

E1
1 SOUTHFIELD CL
2 KEEPER'S WY
3 POACHER'S CFT
4 MEADOWBANK
5 CHERRY GR
6 BELGRAVE CL
7 LABURNUM DR
8 ORCHARD GR

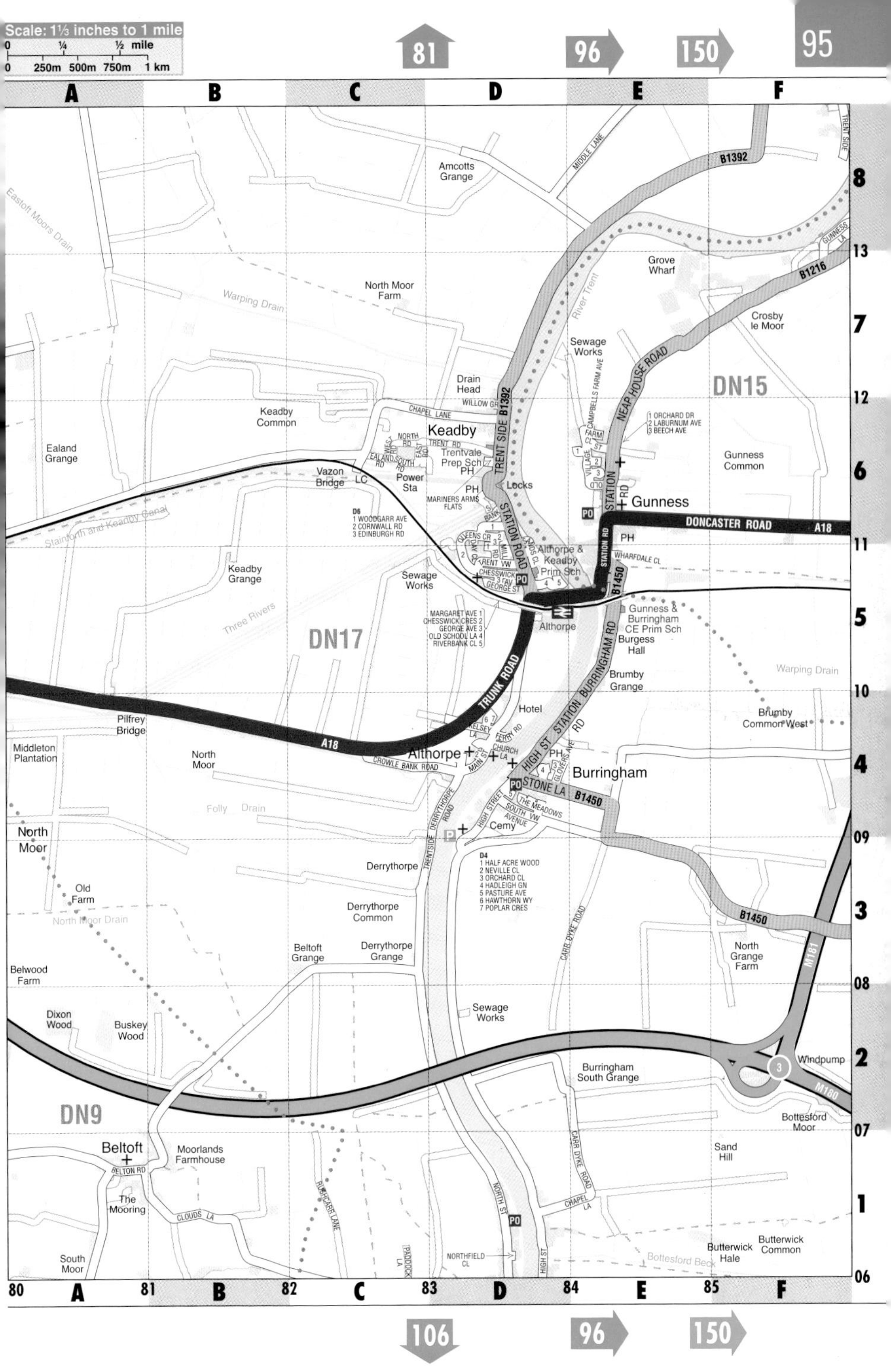
Scale: 1⅓ inches to 1 mile
0 ¼ ½ mile
0 250m 500m 750m 1 km
81
96
150
A B C D E F
8 13 7 12 6 11 5 10 4 09 3 08 2 07 1 06
80 81 82 83 84 85
Amcotts Grange
North Moor Farm
Eastoft Moors Drain
Warping Drain
Keadby Common
Keadby
Ealand Grange
Vazon Bridge
LC
Power Sta
Trentvale Prep Sch
Drain Head
Locks
Grove Wharf
Crosby le Moor
Sewage Works
DN15
Gunness Common
Gunness
DOUCASTER ROAD
A18
B1392
B1216
B1450
NEAP HOUSE ROAD
1 ORCHARD DR
2 LABURNUM AVE
3 BEECH AVE
D6
1 WOODGARR AVE
2 CORNWALL RD
3 EDINBURGH RD
Stainforth and Keadby Canal
Keadby Grange
Three Rivers
DN17
Sewage Works
MARGARET AVE 1
CHESSWICK CRES 2
GEORGE AVE 3
OLD SCHOOL LA 4
RIVERBANK CL 5
Althorpe & Keadby Prim Sch
Althorpe
Gunness & Burringham CE Prim Sch
Burgess Hall
Brumby Grange
Warping Drain
Brumby Common West
TRUNK ROAD
A18
Pilfrey Bridge
Middleton Plantation
North Moor
Hotel
Althorpe
CROWLE BANK ROAD
Burringham
STONE LA
Folly Drain
North Moor
Old Farm
North Moor Drain
Derrythorpe
Derrythorpe Common
Cemy
D4
1 HALF ACRE WOOD
2 NEVILLE CL
3 ORCHARD CL
4 HADLEIGH GN
5 PASTURE AVE
6 HAWTHORN WY
7 POPLAR CRES
CARR DYKE ROAD
North Grange Farm
M181
Belwood Farm
Beltoft Grange
Derrythorpe Grange
Dixon Wood
Buskey Wood
Sewage Works
Windpump
Burringham South Grange
M180
DN9
Bottesford Moor
Beltoft
Moorlands Farmhouse
BELTON RD
The Mooring
CLOUDS LA
Sand Hill
South Moor
NORTHFIELD CL
Butterwick Hale
Butterwick Common
Bottesford Beck
106
96
150

B7
1 PRIMROSE WY
2 POPPY CL
3 WOODALE CL
4 BETONY CL
5 COLTSFOOT CL
6 FLETCHER CL
7 BLACKTHORN CL
8 AVENSWOOD LA
9 ST MARY'S CT
10 HERON CL
11 PIPPIN CT
12 RUSSET CL
13 SEDGEWOOD WY
14 LUNEBURG PL
15 AVE ROUEN
16 AVE LOURDES
17 AVE FONTENAY
18 WILLOWMEAD CL

95

E2
1 CHERRY MOUNT
2 ROWAN CRES
3 CHARTERHOUSE DR
4 ROSSALL CL
5 OUNDLE CL
6 MILL HL DR

82

7 QUEENSWOOD RD
8 CHELTENHAM CL
9 OAKLEIGH
10 RICHMOND DR
11 MILL CFT
12 BURNET DR
13 HOLLY CL
14 PLANTAIN CL
15 PIMPERNEL WY
16 JONQUIL AVE
17 CHAMOMILE CL
18 TAMARISK WY
19 LAUREL WY
20 WILKINSON WY
21 JOHNSON DR
22 OAKWELL CT
23 IVY HO CT
24 HONEYSUCKLE CT
25 GRANGE LANE S
26 TIMBERLAND
27 NUTWELL CT

Scale: 1⅓ inches to 1 mile
0 ¼ ½ mile
0 250m 500m 750m 1 km

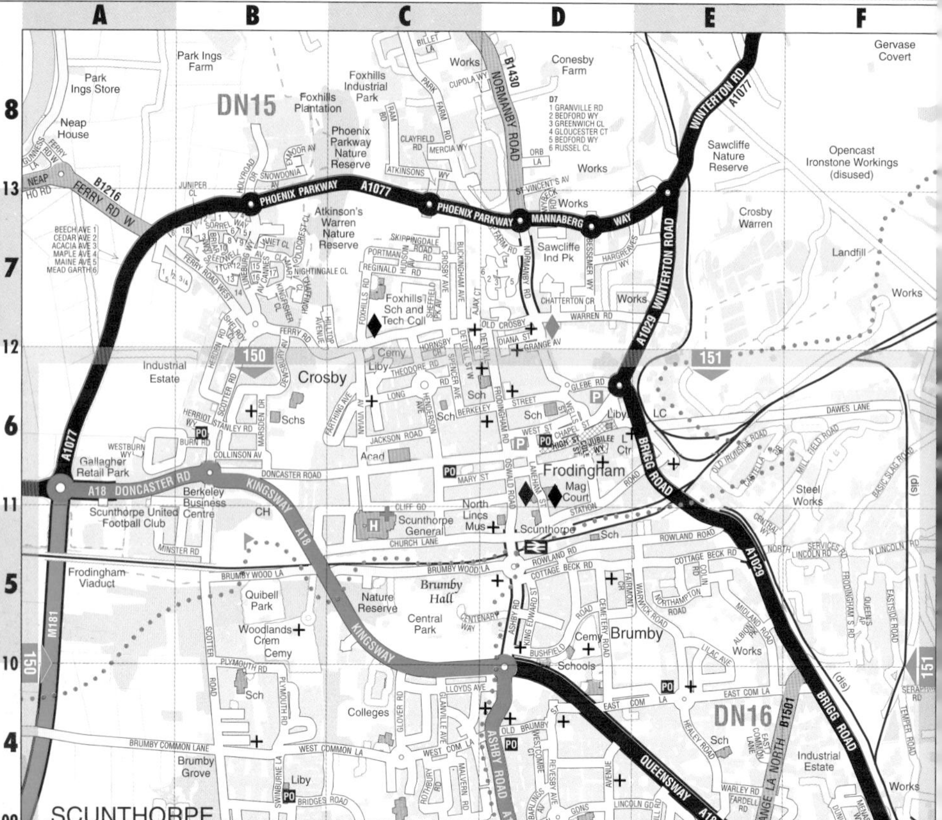

C2
1 SALMONBY RD
2 WALESBY RD
3 DRAGONBY RD
4 FOTHERBY RD
5 VANCOUVER CRES
6 OTTAWA RD
7 ALBERTA CRES
8 LOVELL RD
9 STAINTON DR
10 CRESTA DR
11 DOLMAN CRES
12 HARROW GDNS
13 KEDDINGTON RD
14 PRINCESS ALEXANDRA CO
15 SANDRINGHAM CRES
16 MESSINGHAM RD
17 AUSTIN CRES
18 KIRMAN CRES
19 THORNHILL CRES
20 SOUTH RI CRES
21 BRANKWELL CRES
22 HILLFOOT DR
23 THE OVAL
24 WADDINGTON DR
25 HAMMERTON RD
26 HEADINGLEY AVE
27 EDGBASTON AVE
28 JESMOND AVE
29 FENNERS AVE

E2
28 WOODCROSS AVE
29 BOYDS CT
30 TIMBERLAND
31 ST JAMES PL
32 GORSE CL
33 KIMBERLEY CT

F2
1 HEATHER GR
2 SILVERBELL CL

For full street detail of the highlighted area see pages 150 and 151.

95

107

D1
1 TYDEMAN CL
2 HOLSTEIN DR
3 HALES CL
4 HALLBROOK CT
5 LAXTON GR
6 TALISMAN DR
7 LAMBOURNE RI
8 BRAMLEY CRES
9 RIBSTON CL
10 CONFERENCE CT
11 WORCESTER CL
12 RILESTON PL
13 MALLING WK
14 MERRYWEATHER CT
15 STURMER CT
16 PIPPIN DR
17 WREN CL
18 MARTIN CL
19 FIELDFARE CL
20 HAZEL GR
21 MESSINGHAM RD
22 ALEXANDRIA DR
23 ARMERIA DR
24 ACORN WY
25 MONTBRETIA DR
26 DUNNOCK CL

D2
1 OAKWOOD RI
2 CROSSBECK RD
3 MAGDALEN CL
4 BRUNEL CL
5 GIRTON CL
6 NUFFIELD CL
7 MOUNTBATTEN CL
8 ST CATHERINES CRES
9 CAVENDISH RD
10 TRINITY RD
11 DOWNING CRES
12 NEWNHAM CRES
13 PEMBROKE AVE
14 THORNHOLME DR
15 WAYSIDE CL
16 KNIGHT'S CT
17 TEMPLAR CT
18 EMMANUEL DR
19 CHURCH LA
20 OLD SCHOOL LA
21 REPTON DR
22 SILVER BIRCH RI
23 BEECHES AVE
24 COPPER BEECH WK
25 ROSEWOOD WY
26 CAMPBELL AVE
27 HORNBEAM AVE
28 FIR CL
29 PETERHOUSE CT

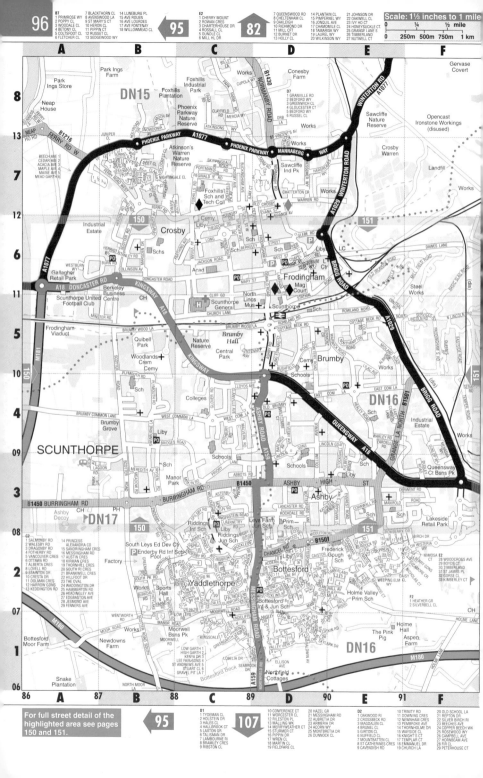

Scale: 1⅓ inches to 1 mile
¼ ½ mile
250m 500m 750m 1 km

83
98

D4
1 HERON HOLT
2 WESTMINSTER RD
3 THE BLACKTHORNS
4 WESTWOOD
5 TRINITY CT
6 YARBOROUGH CRES

E4
1 BADGER WY
2 RUE DE NOZAY
3 BEECHWOOD CRES
4 PINETREE CL
5 CHESTNUT GR
6 SCHOOL HOUSES
7 HUNTS CL
8 EASTWOOD DR
9 ST BERNARD'S CL
10 AIREDALE CL
11 LABRADOR DR
12 BEAGLE CL
13 DANE CL

108
98

97
84

F7
1 WOODLAND DR
2 DOLL LA
3 DUNNS PADDOCK
4 MALTKILN LA

Scale: 1⅓ inches to 1 mile
0 ¼ ½ mile
0 250m 500m 750m 1 km

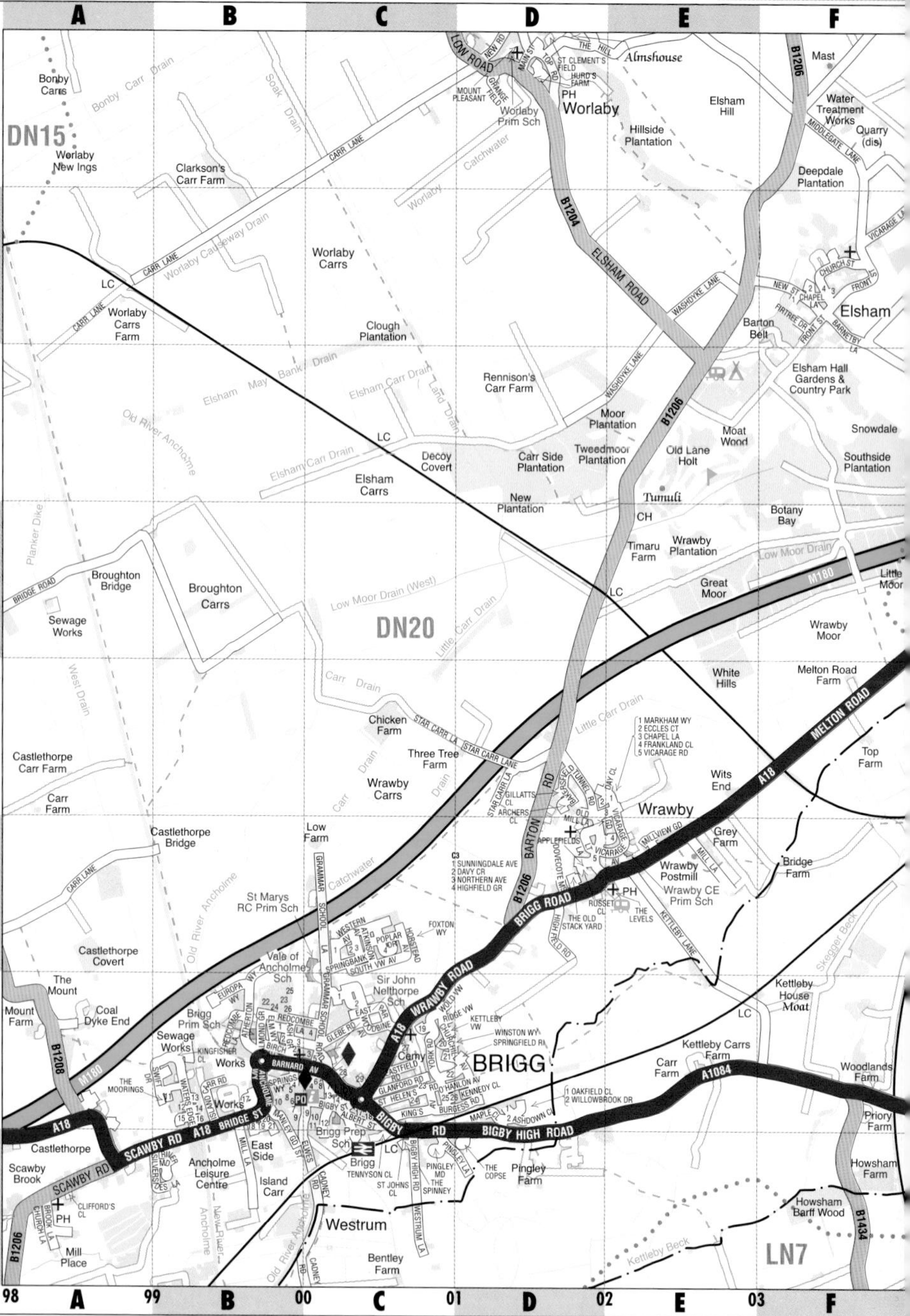

B2
1 CHERRY TREE AVE
2 KINGSWAY
3 COLTON ST
4 CARY LA
5 MARKET LA
6 EXCHANGE PL
7 ANCHORAGE ST
8 MARKET PL
9 PARADISE PL
10 BRIDGE ST
11 RIVERSIDE
12 TEAL CL
13 THE NARROW BOATS
14 MILLERS QUAY
15 MILL CL
16 ANCHORS WY
17 KILN LA
18 WEST TERR
19 ENGINE ST
20 FORRESTER ST
21 JAMES ST
22 FOXGLOVE CL
23 POPPYFIELD WY
24 BRAMBLE WY
25 BLUEBELL GR
26 CLOVER CT
27 LINDUM CRES

97
109

C2
1 PRESTON DR
2 HAWTHORN AVE
3 MAGRATH CT
4 DIXON CL
5 WESLEY RD
6 OLD COURTS RD
7 GRAMMAR SCHOOL RD S
8 WRAWBY ST
9 ELWES ST
10 THE BOTTLINGS
11 ANCHOLME GDNS
12 ST CLARES WK
13 CROSS ST
14 GARDEN ST
15 QUEEN ST
16 BIGBY RD
17 PRINCES ST
18 NEW ST
19 HOLME CL
20 WELLBECK CL
21 CHAPEL WY
22 ST JAMES RD
23 GLANFORD RD
24 HEDGEROW LA
25 YARBOROUGH RD
26 SPRINGFIELD RD
27 NICOLGATE LA
28 DUDLEY RD
29 HEALTH PL

Scale: 1⅓ inches to 1 mile
0 ¼ ½ mile
0 250m 500m 750m 1 km

85
100

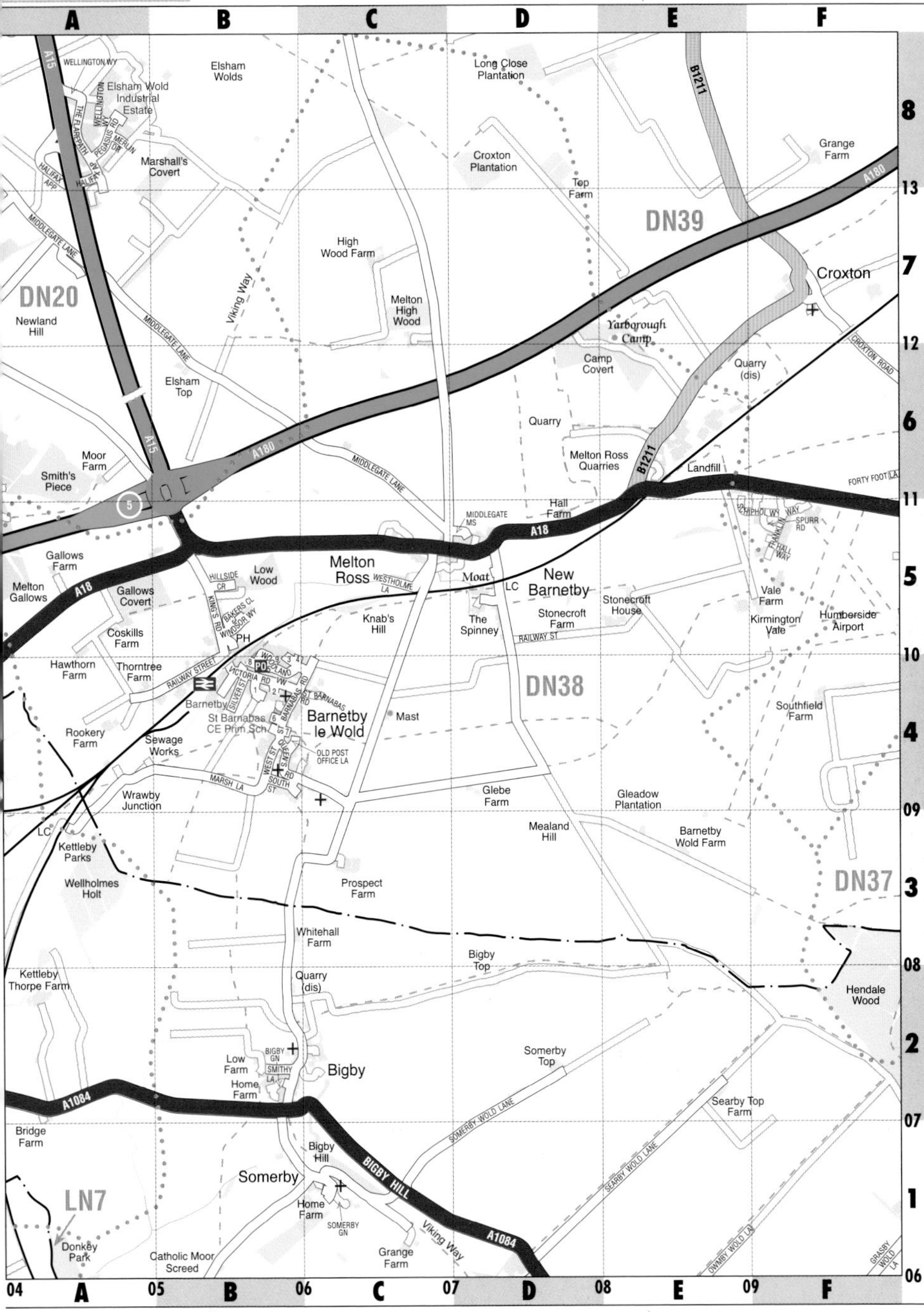

99
86

Scale: 1⅓ inches to 1 mile

99
111

Scale: 1⅓ inches to 1 mile
0 ¼ ½ mile
0 250m 500m 750m 1 km

B8
1 KISHORN CT
2 KINLOCH WY
3 PERTH WY
4 TUMMEL CT
5 OBAN CT

C8
1 GUERNSEY GR
2 ALDERNEY WY
3 ORKNEY PL
4 SHETLAND WY
5 FAIRISLE RISE

87
102

F5
1 APPLE TREE CT
2 MALLARD CL
3 SWALLOW DR
4 WREN CL
5 CARLTON RD
6 IVY FARM CT
7 PINNEY'S CT
8 MAPLE GR
9 FORD'S AVE
10 MCVEIGH CT
11 BEVERLEY CT
12 WESTWOOD RD
13 ASHLEIGH CT
14 FORSYTHIA AVE
15 BLUEBELL CT
16 SALADINE CT
17 CORNFLOWER CL
18 ROOKERY RD
19 PRIMROSE CL
20 POPPY MS

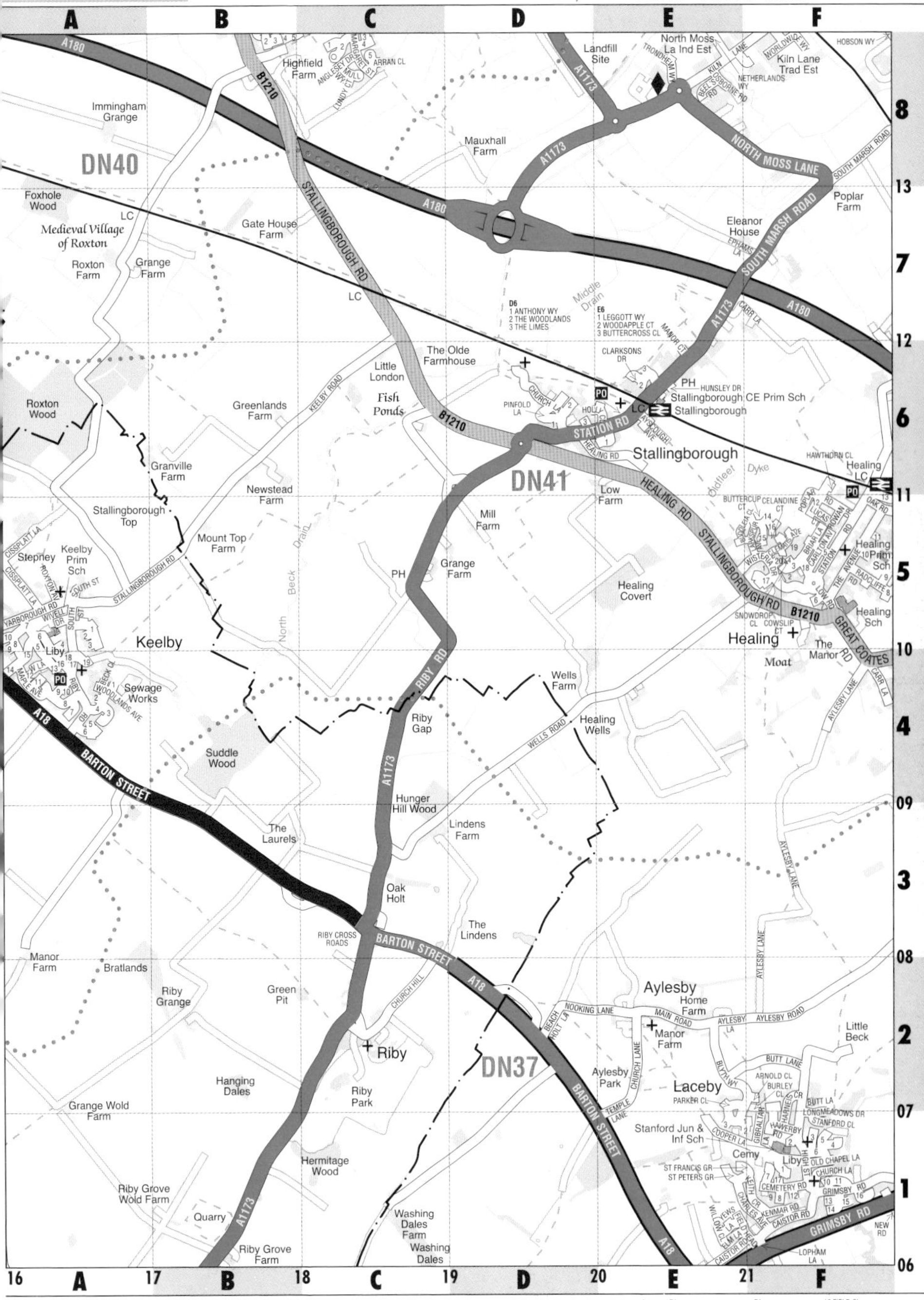

A4
1 MIDFIELD WY
2 ROWAN CL
3 RAITHBY AVE
4 SUDDLE WY
5 THORNTON GDNS
6 COTHAM GDNS
7 LONGMEADOW RI
8 MILSON RD
9 CADDLE RD
10 KAREN AVE
11 MULBERRY CL
12 MAPLE CL
13 HALLS LA
14 MILL LA
15 PELHAM CRES
16 ST MARTIN'S PL
17 ST BARTHOLOMEW'S CL
18 KING ST
19 CHURCH LA

A5
1 EASTFIELD RD
2 TOMLINE RD
3 WINDSOR CL
4 MANOR CL
5 VICTORIA RD
6 MANOR ST
7 BROADWAY
8 ST ANNE'S RD
9 WEST VIEW CL
10 CHURCHILL AVE

112
102

E1
1 LEALAND CL
2 LAURIDSON CL
3 MARSHALL CL

F1
1 THE MEAD
2 BUTTERFIELD CL
3 SEED CL LA
4 PHILLIPS LA
5 AUSTIN GARTH
6 NEW CHAPEL LA
7 CEMETERY CRES
8 KNIGHTS CL
9 ST MARGARET'S CL
10 FIELD CL
11 SPRING LA
12 ALTOFT CL
13 WHITGIFT CL
14 GRANGE AVE
15 TREVOR CL
16 GEORGE BUTLER CL
17 BROOKS CL

C4
1 SERVICE RD 22
2 SERVICE RD 23
3 SERVICE RD 4
4 SERVICE RD 5
5 SERVICE RD 25
6 HEMSWELL DR
7 SCOTT CL
8 SERVICE RD 6
9 SERVICE RD 7
10 SERVICE RD 17
11 SERVICE RD 18
12 SERVICE RD 1
13 SERVICE RD 19
14 SERVICE RD 20
15 SERVICE RD 2
16 BINBROOK WY
17 SERVICE RD 3
18 SERVICE RD 16
19 SERVICE RD 15
20 BARMOUTH DR
21 MATLOCK DR

101
88

Scale: 1⅓ inches to 1 mile
0 ¼ ½ mile
0 250m 500m 750m 1 km

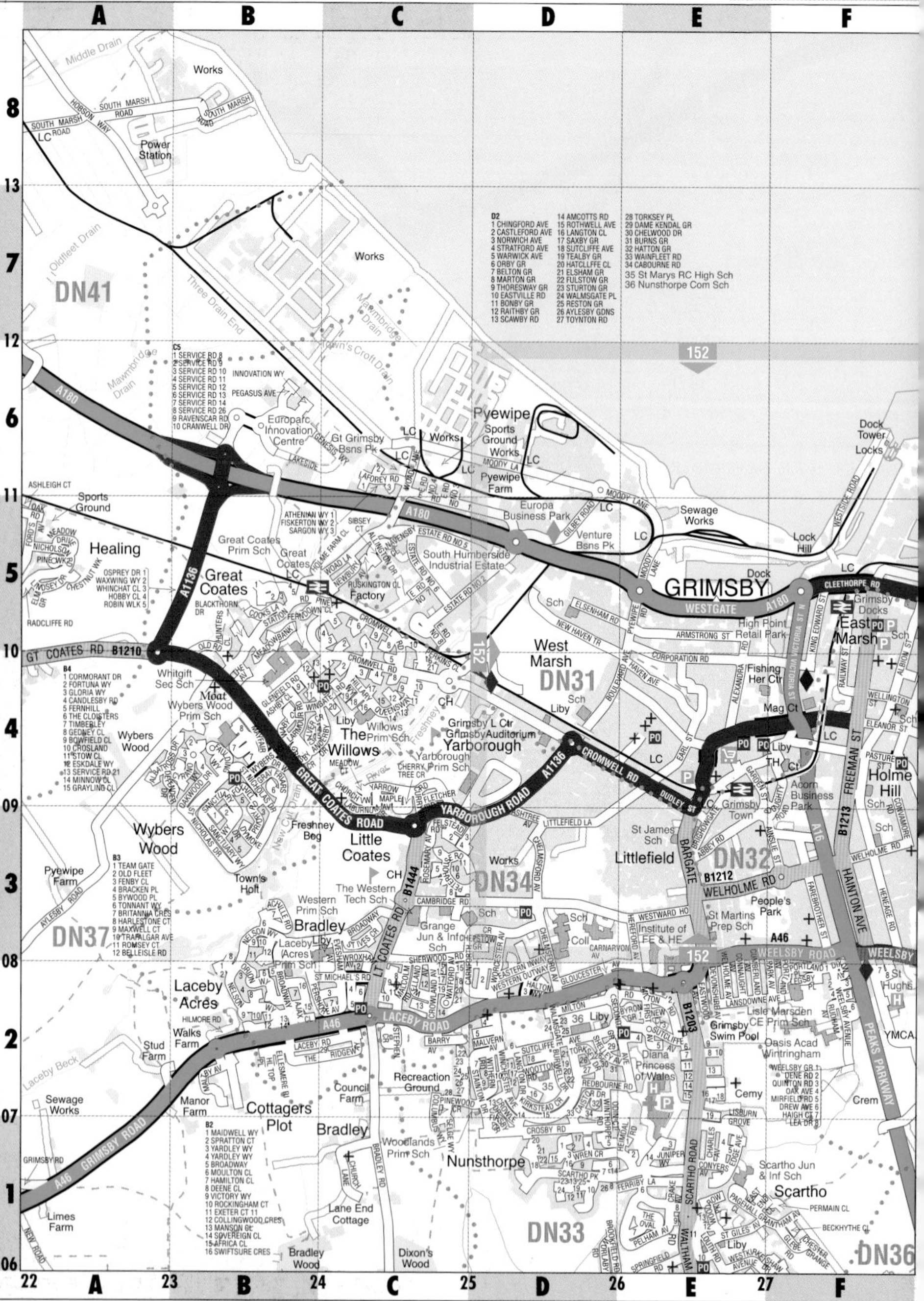

C2
1 BLAYDON GR
2 NEWBURY GR
3 WINCHCOMBE AVE
4 LONGFIELD RD
5 SELBOURNE RD
6 CLARENDON RD
7 THORNTON GR
8 WELLBECK RD
9 WELBECK PL
10 BROCKLESBY RD
11 BROCKLESBY PL
12 WILLOUGHBY GR
13 REVESBY AVE
14 TATTERSHALL AVE
15 WINSLOW GR
16 BARDNEY GDNS
17 GOXHILL GDNS
18 WICKENBY CL
19 WIRRAL AVE
20 FISKERTON CL
21 HIBALDSTOW CL
22 ALDER VW
23 DOLBY VALE
24 BREMERHAVEN WY
25 BEECHWOOD AVE
26 WYMARK VW
27 DALE VW
28 TALLERT WY
29 THE CROSS WAY

101

D1
1 BELGRAVE RD
2 FULHAM PK
3 MARYLEBONE WK
4 UTGARD WY
5 ASGARD WY
6 HAMPSTEAD PK
7 FINSBURY DR
8 EASON RD
9 WALLIS CT
10 FENWICK RD
11 BRAY CL
12 ALDRED GDN
13 LANCASTER CT
14 WATERLOO DR
15 HYDE PARK CL
16 BUCKINGHAM GDN
17 BUCKINGHAM GR
18 CASPIAN CR
19 VINCENT RD
20 MACARTHY CL
21 STOCKHAM CT
22 PAYNTER WLK
23 WALSH GDN
24 PATCHETT CL
25 GILL CT
26 NEWMARCH CT

113

C3
1 TOOTHILL RD
2 TOOTHILL GDNS
3 BARONESS RD
4 BARONESS CT
5 FOXGLOVE GDNS
6 ST CATHERINES CT
7 DOWNING CL
8 MAGDALENE RD
9 GIRTON RD
10 SELWYN CT
11 HOMERTON PL

E1
1 BROCK CL
2 BALDER CT
3 LAUREL CL
4 ANTRIM WY
5 ULSTER AVE
6 FAUCONBERG AVE
7 SOPHIA AVE
8 PELHAM AVE
9 PELHAM PL
10 PINFOLD LA
11 GATE LA
12 CHURCH LA
13 SUNNY CR
14 FORSYTHIA DR

E2
1 NEW CL
2 LEIGHTON GR
3 WALTON GR
4 KINGSLEY
5 CORNWELL CL
6 ST MARTIN'S CRES
7 FRUSHER AVE
8 HOMEFIELD AVE
9 RUPERT RD
10 ROOKERY AVE
11 WESTFIELD AVE
12 LIMETREE AVE
13 ST HELENS AVE
14 BEECH AVE
15 SYCAMORE AVE
16 MILLFIELD AVE
17 LYNDHURST AVE
18 MELBOURNE AVE
19 CRAGSTON AVE

Scale: 1⅓ inches to 1 mile
0 ¼ ½ mile
0 250m 500m 750m 1 km

89

For full street detail of the highlighted area see pages 152 and 153.

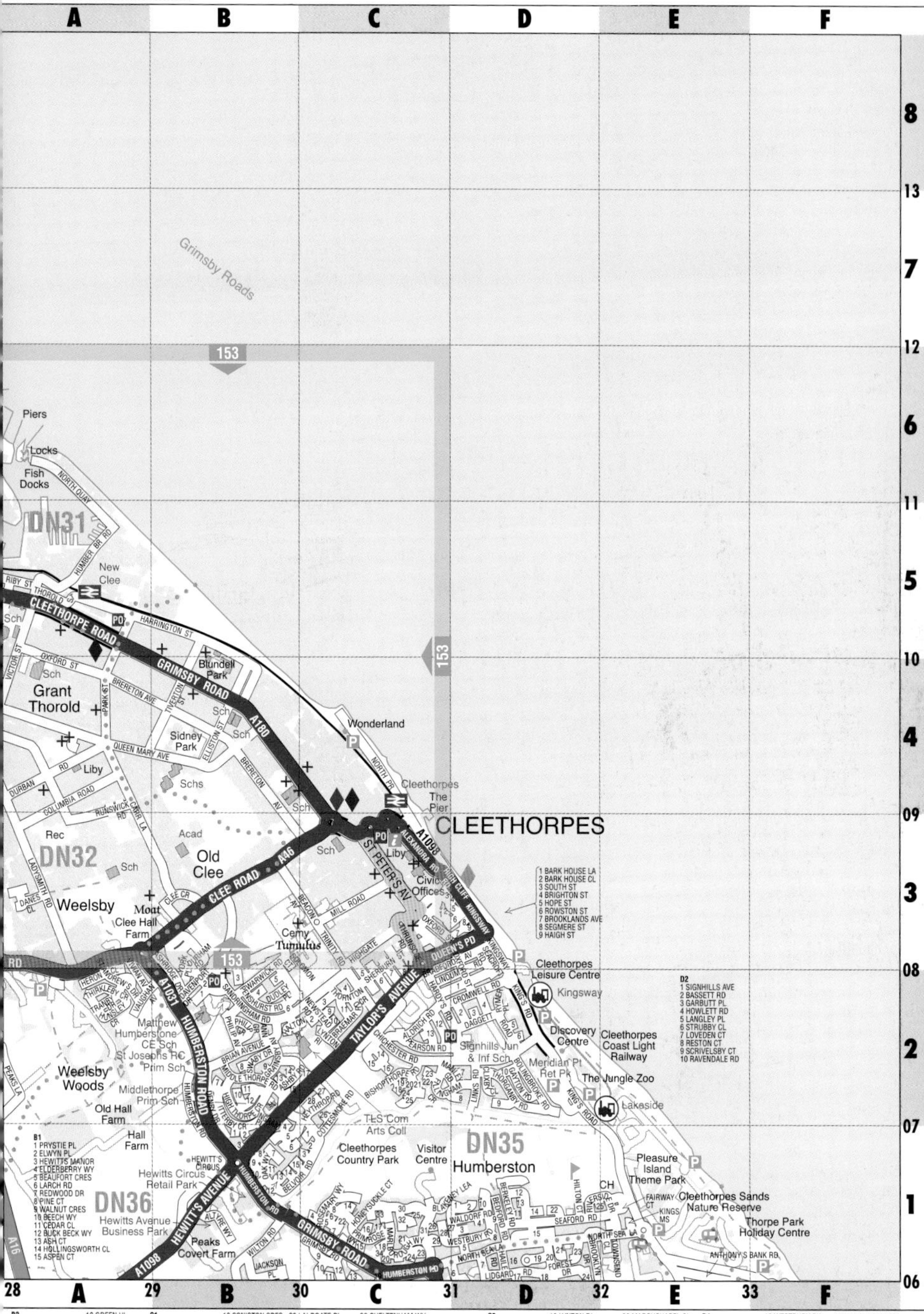

114

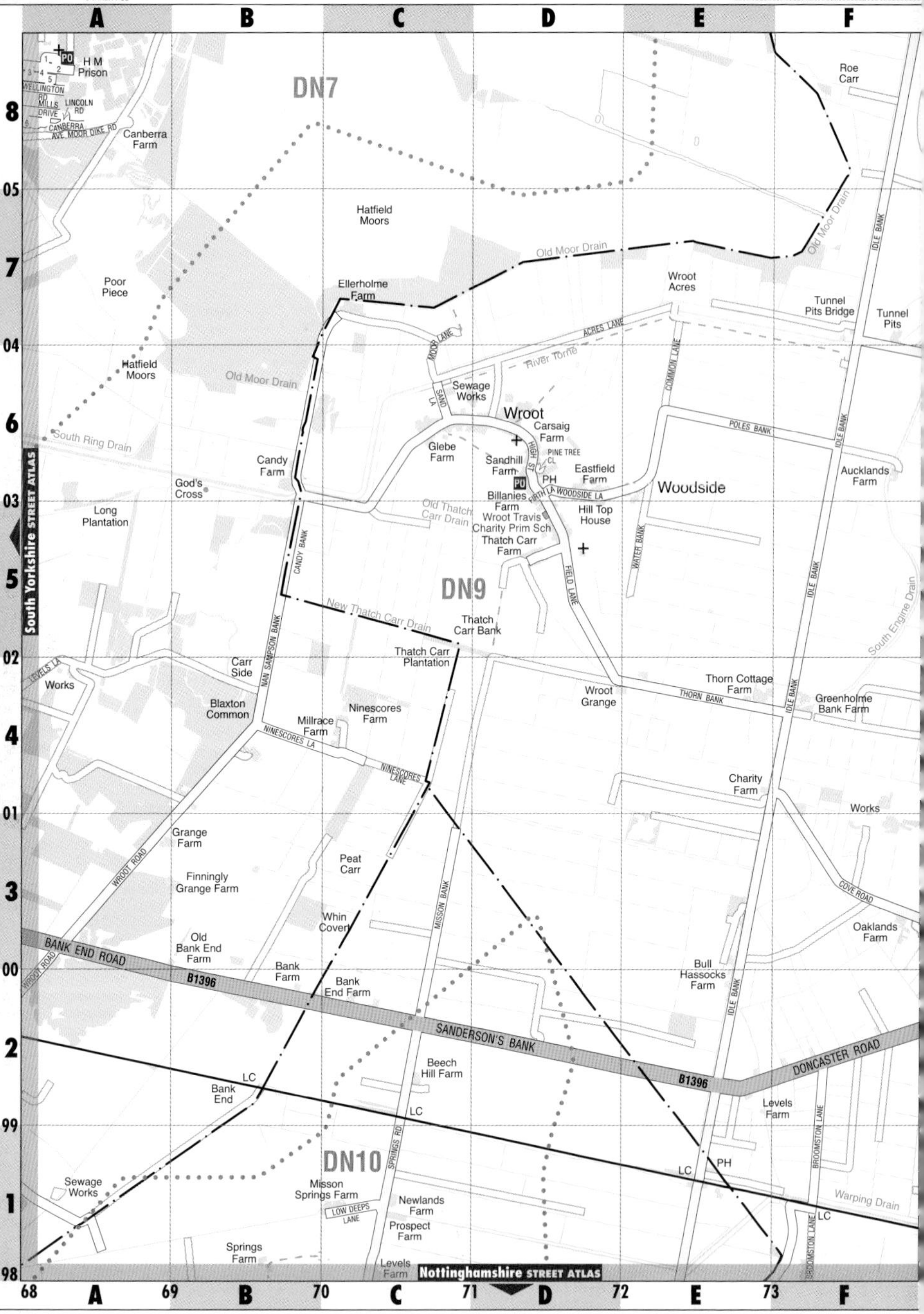
A
B
C
D
E
F
8
05
7
04
6
03
5
02
4
01
3
00
2
99
1
98
68
69
70
71
72
73
H M Prison
PO
WELLINGTON RD
MILLS DRIVE
LINCOLN RD
CANBERRA AVE
MOOR DIKE RD
Canberra Farm
DN7
Roe Carr
Hatfield Moors
Old Moor Drain
Poor Piece
Ellerholme Farm
Wroot Acres
Tunnel Pits Bridge
Tunnel Pits
IDLE BANK
MOOR LANE
ACRES LANE
River Torne
COMMON LANE
Hatfield Moors
Old Moor Drain
Sewage Works
SAND LA
Wroot
Carsaig Farm
POLES BANK
South Ring Drain
Glebe Farm
Sandhill Farm
PINE TREE CL
HIGH ST
Candy Farm
God's Cross
PH
Eastfield Farm
Woodside
Auklands Farm
Billanies Farm
FIRTH LA
WOODSIDE LA
Long Plantation
Old Thatch Carr Drain
Wroot Travis Charity Prim Sch
Hill Top House
Thatch Carr Farm
CANDY BANK
WATER BANK
DN9
FIELD LANE
IDLE BANK
New Thatch Carr Drain
Thatch Carr Bank
South Engine Drain
NAN SAMPSON BANK
Thatch Carr Plantation
LEVELS LA
Works
Carr Side
Thorn Cottage Farm
Wroot Grange
THORN BANK
Greenholme Bank Farm
Blaxton Common
Ninescores Farm
Millrace Farm
NINESCORES LA
NINESCORES LANE
Charity Farm
Works
Grange Farm
WROOT ROAD
Peat Carr
Finningly Grange Farm
MISSON BANK
COVE ROAD
Whin Covert
Oaklands Farm
Old Bank End Farm
BANK END ROAD
WROOT ROAD
B1396
Bank Farm
Bank End Farm
Bull Hassocks Farm
SANDERSON'S BANK
B1396
DONCASTER ROAD
Beech Hill Farm
LC
Bank End
LC
Levels Farm
BROOMSTON LANE
DN10
SPRINGS RD
PH
LC
Sewage Works
Misson Springs Farm
Newlands Farm
Warping Drain
LOW DEEPS LANE
LC
Prospect Farm
Springs Farm
Levels Farm
BROOMSTON LANE
South Yorkshire STREET ATLAS
Nottinghamshire STREET ATLAS

Scale: 1⅓ inches to 1 mile
0 ¼ ½ mile
0 250m 500m 750m 1 km

D6
1 MANLEY CT
2 STANFIELD RD
3 MORFIELD GR
4 SOUTHFIELD DR
5 GUISEFIELD RD
6 BIRCHFIELD RD
7 THE LIDGETT
8 MASSEY CL
9 TREE CL
10 CORONATION CRES
11 AXHOLME DR
12 WHITEHOUSE WY
13 WATERHALL
14 FIELD REEVES WK
15 BROCK CL
16 SELBY CL

94

E6
1 CASTLE DR
2 VINEGARTH
3 WESLEY CL
4 CHURCH ST
5 MARKET PL
6 CHAPEL ST
7 MANOR CT RD
8 FAIRFIELD CFT
9 ROOKERY CFT
10 PINFOLD
11 NEWLAND VW
12 MOORLAND WY
13 QUEEN ST

106

14 POPPLEWELL TERR
15 REAPER'S RISE
16 CHERRY ORCHARD
17 SOUTH FURLONG CFT
18 FERN CFT
19 WOODLAND WY
20 MOWBRAY CT
21 LINDSEY CT
22 HOLLINGSWORTH LA

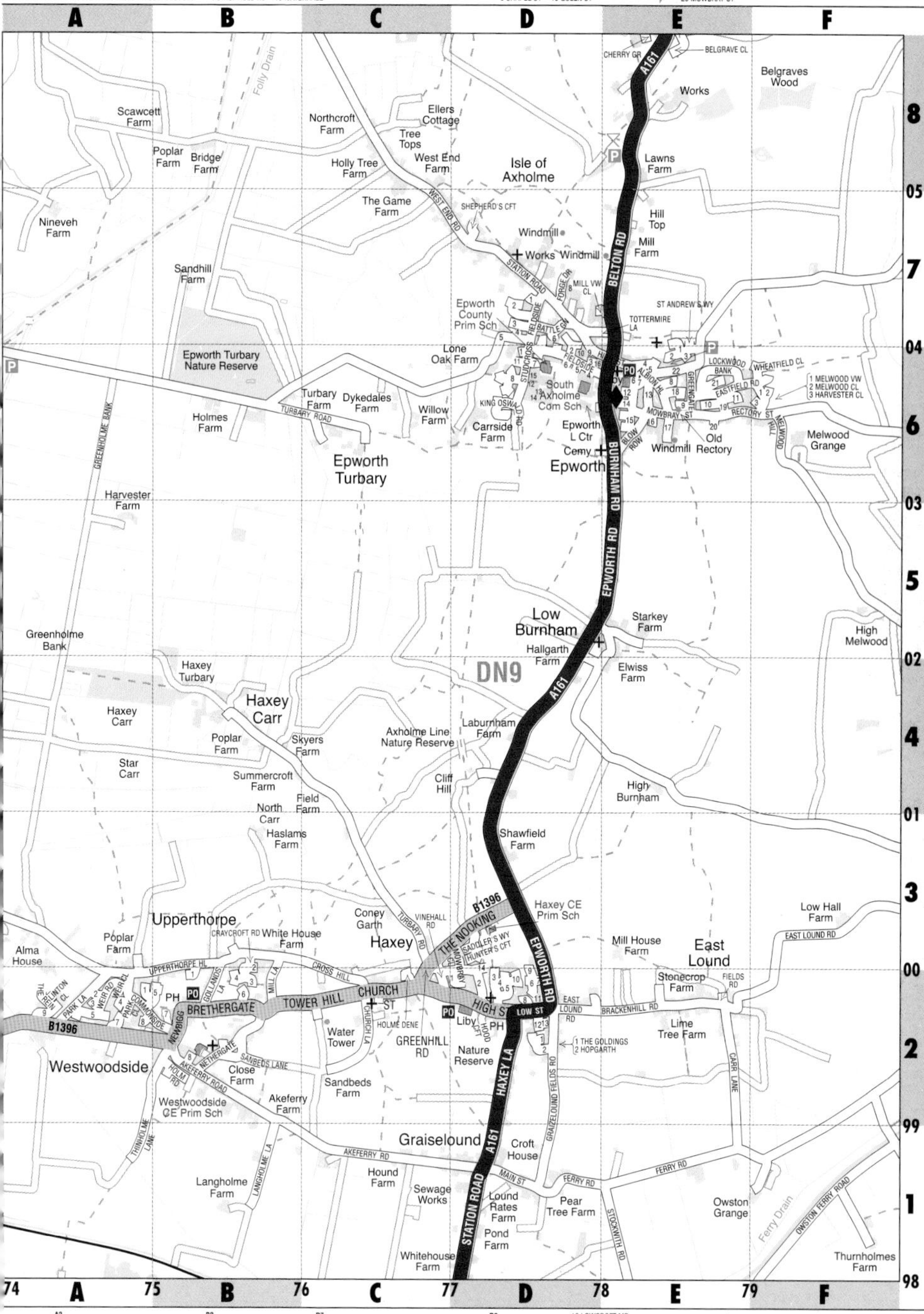

A2
1 THE ROWANS
2 AXHOLME RD
3 COLLEYWELL CL
4 PARK DR
5 THE MEADOWS
6 MOORLANDS
7 DREWRY LA
8 WEAVERS CFT
9 WESTMORELAND CL

B2
1 TAVELLA CT
2 HIGHFIELD CRES
3 WESTLAND RD
4 CHAPEL CL
5 THE BIRCHES
6 CRACKLE HILL
7 GRANGE CT
8 SCHOOL CFT

D7
1 FERNBANK
2 FIELDS CL
3 ORCHARD CFT
4 SWALLOW CT
5 CARRSIDE
6 NICHOLSON WY
7 PADDOCK CL
8 BLACKSMITH CL

116

D2
1 HALLCROFT RD
2 MARLBOROUGH AVE
3 LOWCROFT AVE
4 LOWCROFT CL
5 ASH TREE DR
6 REAPER'S WY
7 GRANARY CFT
8 HAXEY GRANGE
9 HAYFIELD CL
10 LOWCROFT MD
11 BURRELLS CL
12 CHATSWOTH WY
13 FARRRIERS FOLD
14 BLACKMOOR RD

106

105
95

D8
1 THE CROFT
2 FARM LA
3 PARKLANDS

Scale: 1⅓ inches to 1 mile
0 ¼ ½ mile
0 250m 500m 750m 1 km

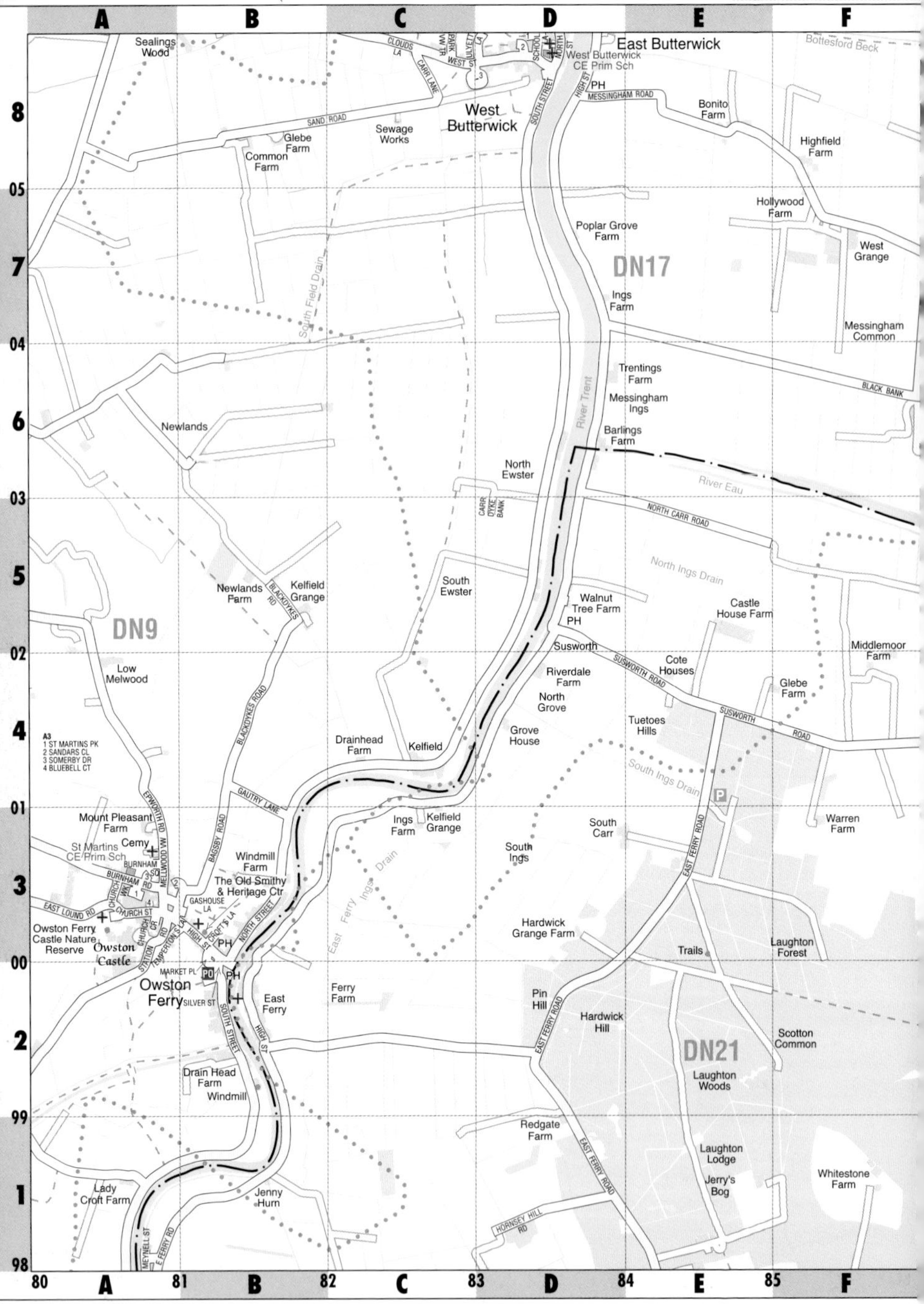

105
117

Scale: 1⅓ inches to 1 mile

96
108

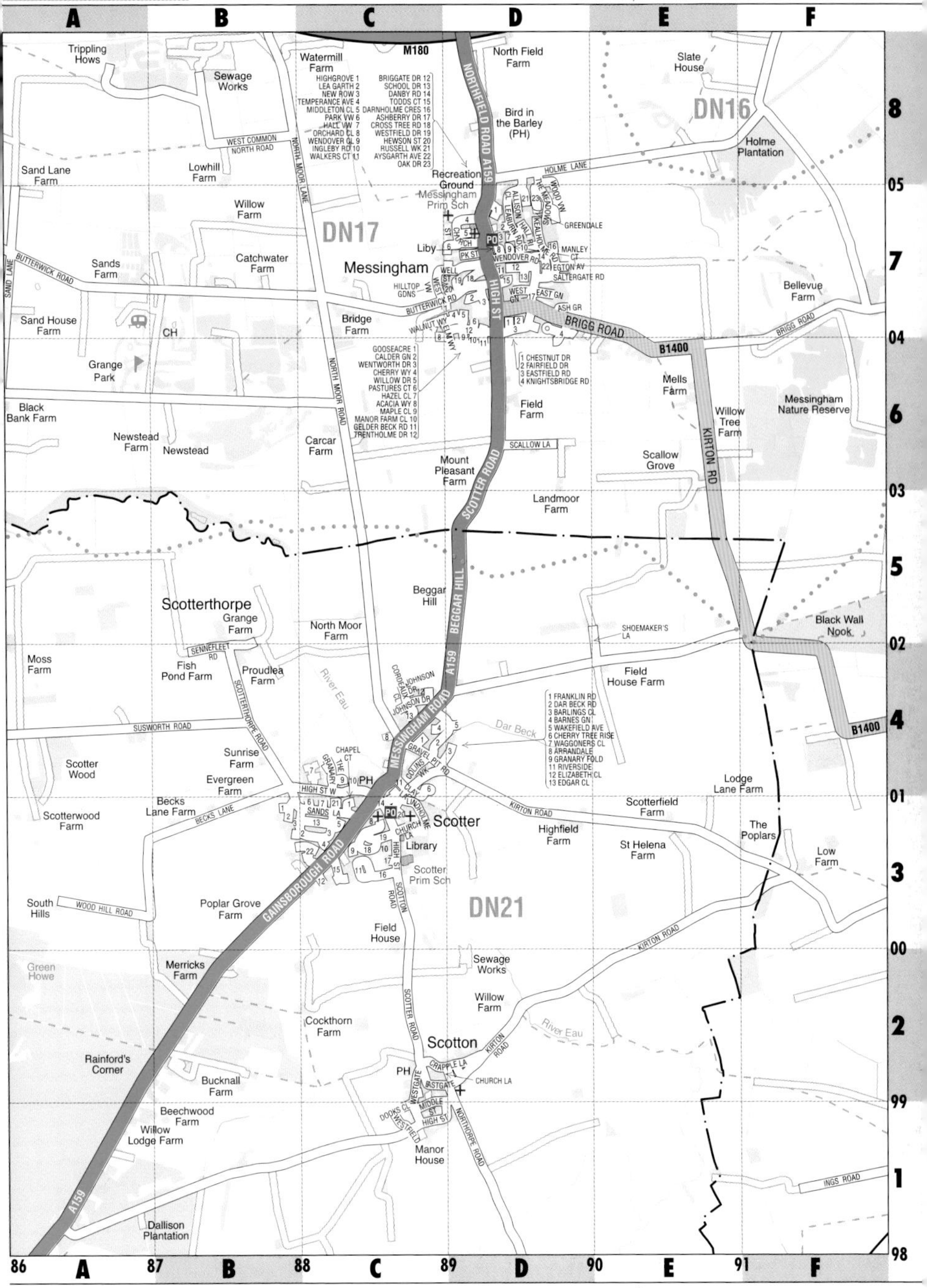
M180
Tripping Hows
Sewage Works
Watermill Farm
North Field Farm
Slate House
DN16
Bird in the Barley (PH)
NORTHFIELD ROAD A159
HIGHGROVE 1
LEA GARTH 2
NEW ROW 3
TEMPERANCE AVE 4
MIDDLETON CL 5
PARK VW 6
HALL VW 7
ORCHARD CL 8
WENDOVER CL 9
INGLEBY RD 10
WALKERS CT 11
BRIGGATE DR 12
SCHOOL DR 13
DANBY RD 14
TODDS CT 15
DARNHOLME CRES 16
ASHBERRY DR 17
CROSS TREE RD 18
WESTFIELD DR 19
HEWSON ST 20
RUSSELL WK 21
AYSGARTH AVE 22
OAK DR 23
Holme Plantation
WEST COMMON
NORTH ROAD
HOLME LANE
Sand Lane Farm
Lowhill Farm
Recreation Ground
Messingham Prim Sch
Willow Farm
DN17
GREENDALE
MANLEY CT
EGTON AV
SALTERGATE RD
Catchwater Farm
Sands Farm
Liby
Messingham
BUTTERWICK ROAD
SAND LANE
HILLTOP GDNS
HIGH ST
WEST GN
EAST GN
ASH GR
Bellevue Farm
Sand House Farm
CH
Bridge Farm
BUTTERWICK RD
WALNUT WY
BRIGG ROAD
B1400
Grange Park
GOOSEACRE 1
CALDER GN 2
WENTWORTH DR 3
CHERRY WY 4
WILLOW DR 5
PASTURES CT 6
HAZEL CL 7
ACACIA WY 8
MAPLE CL 9
MANOR FARM CL 10
GELDER BECK RD 11
TRENTHOLME DR 12
1 CHESTNUT DR
2 FAIRFIELD DR
3 EASTFIELD RD
4 KNIGHTSBRIDGE RD
Mells Farm
Black Bank Farm
NORTH MOOR ROAD
Field Farm
Willow Tree Farm
Messingham Nature Reserve
Newstead Farm
Newstead
Carcar Farm
SCALLOW LA
KIRTON RD
Mount Pleasant Farm
Scallow Grove
SCOTTER ROAD
Landmoor Farm
Beggar Hill
BEGGAR HILL
Scotterthorpe
Grange Farm
North Moor Farm
SHOEMAKER'S LA
Black Wall Nook
SENNEFLEET RD
Moss Farm
Fish Pond Farm
Proudlea Farm
River Eau
CORDEAUX CL
JOHNSON DR
Field House Farm
MESSINGHAM ROAD
SUSWORTH ROAD
SCOTTERTHORPE ROAD
Dar Beck
1 FRANKLIN RD
2 DAR BECK RD
3 BARLINGS CL
4 BARNES GN
5 WAKEFIELD AVE
6 CHERRY TREE RISE
7 WAGGONERS CL
8 ARRANDALE
9 GRANARY FOLD
11 RIVERSIDE
12 ELIZABETH CL
13 EDGAR CL
Scotter Wood
Sunrise Farm
CHAPEL CT
THE GRANARY
GRAVEL PIT RD
COLINS WK
PH
Evergreen Farm
Lodge Lane Farm
Becks Lane Farm
HIGH ST W
SANDS LA
CLAY LA
LINDHOLME
KIRTON ROAD
Scotterfield Farm
Scotterwood Farm
BECKS LANE
Scotter
CHURCH LA
Library
Highfield Farm
The Poplars
St Helena Farm
Low Farm
Scotter Prim Sch
South Hills
WOOD HILL ROAD
GAINSBOROUGH ROAD
Poplar Grove Farm
SCOTTON ROAD
DN21
Field House
Green Howe
Merricks Farm
Sewage Works
KIRTON ROAD
Willow Farm
SCOTTER ROAD
Cockthorn Farm
River Eau
Scotton
Rainford's Corner
KIRTON ROAD
CRAPPLE LA
CHURCH LA
Bucknall Farm
PH
WESTGATE
EASTGATE
Beechwood Farm
DOOKS CL
MIDDLE ST
HIGH ST
WESTFIELD
NORTHORPE ROAD
Willow Lodge Farm
Manor House
INGS ROAD
A159
Dallison Plantation

B3
1 BELLBUTTS VW
2 LARK RISE
3 ASH GR

C3
1 POPLAR GR
2 ROOKLANDS
3 BEECHWOOD DR
4 CHESTNUT CL
5 PINETREE AVE
6 BRAMLEY GR
7 CEDAR CL
8 ORCHARD AVE
9 ST PETER'S GR
10 CECIL CL
11 MILL CRES
12 SOUTHCLIFFE RD
13 WAKERLEY RD
14 HOBB LA
15 CHARLES AVE
16 WESTCLIFFE RD
17 REVILL CL
18 ASTLEY CRES
19 ST PETER'S RD
20 THE GREEN
21 CROWN GDNS
22 THE ROOKERY

118
108

107
97

F5
1 DICKINSON CL
2 COCKETTS LA
3 BARNSIDE
4 OLD SCHOOL DR
5 MEADOW CT
6 ST ALBANS CL
7 CHAPEL CT
8 SARGENT'S WY
9 BELLS DR

Scale: 1⅓ inches to 1 mile
0 ¼ ½ mile
0 250m 500m 750m 1 km

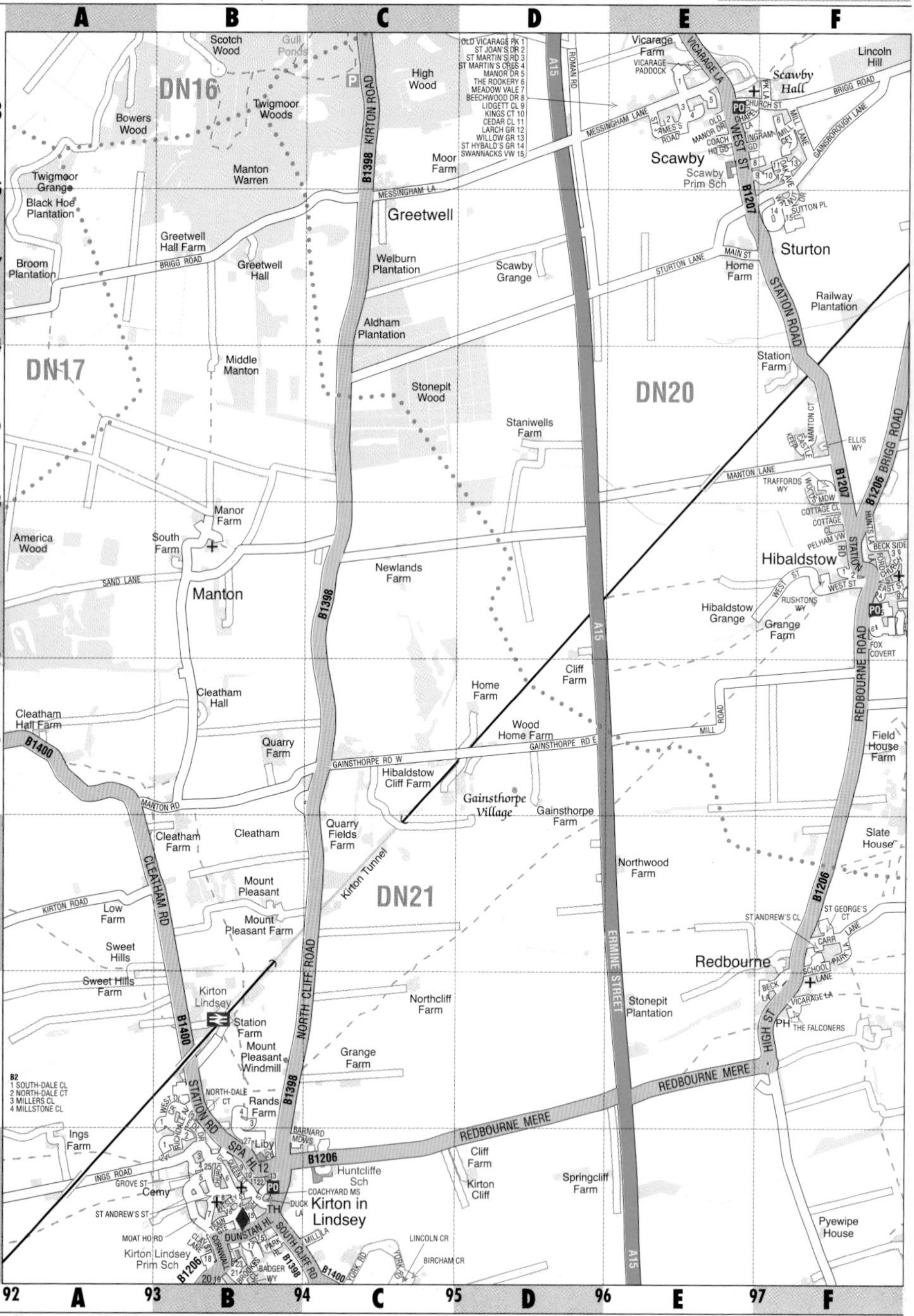

B1
1 HIGHFIELD DR
2 ORCHARD CL
3 WHITEWELL CL
4 DARWIN ST
5 TURNER ST
6 MARCH ST
7 CORNWALL ST
8 OLD SCHOOL YD
9 SUNNY HILL
10 UNICORN ROW
11GEORGE ST
12 KING EDWARD ST
13 SYLVESTER ST
14 WRAY ST
15 EAST CROSS ST
16 WEST CROSS ST
17 DUNSTAN VILLAS
18 LOWFIELD CL
19 GRAYINGHAM RD
20 GAINSBOROUGH RD
21 FAIRFIELDS
22 MARKET PL
23 ENDELL DR
24 LANES END
25 TORKSEY ST
26 KING EDWARD ST
27 WINDMILL WY

107
119

Scale: 1⅓ inches to 1 mile
0 ¼ ½ mile
0 250m 500m 750m 1 km

98
110

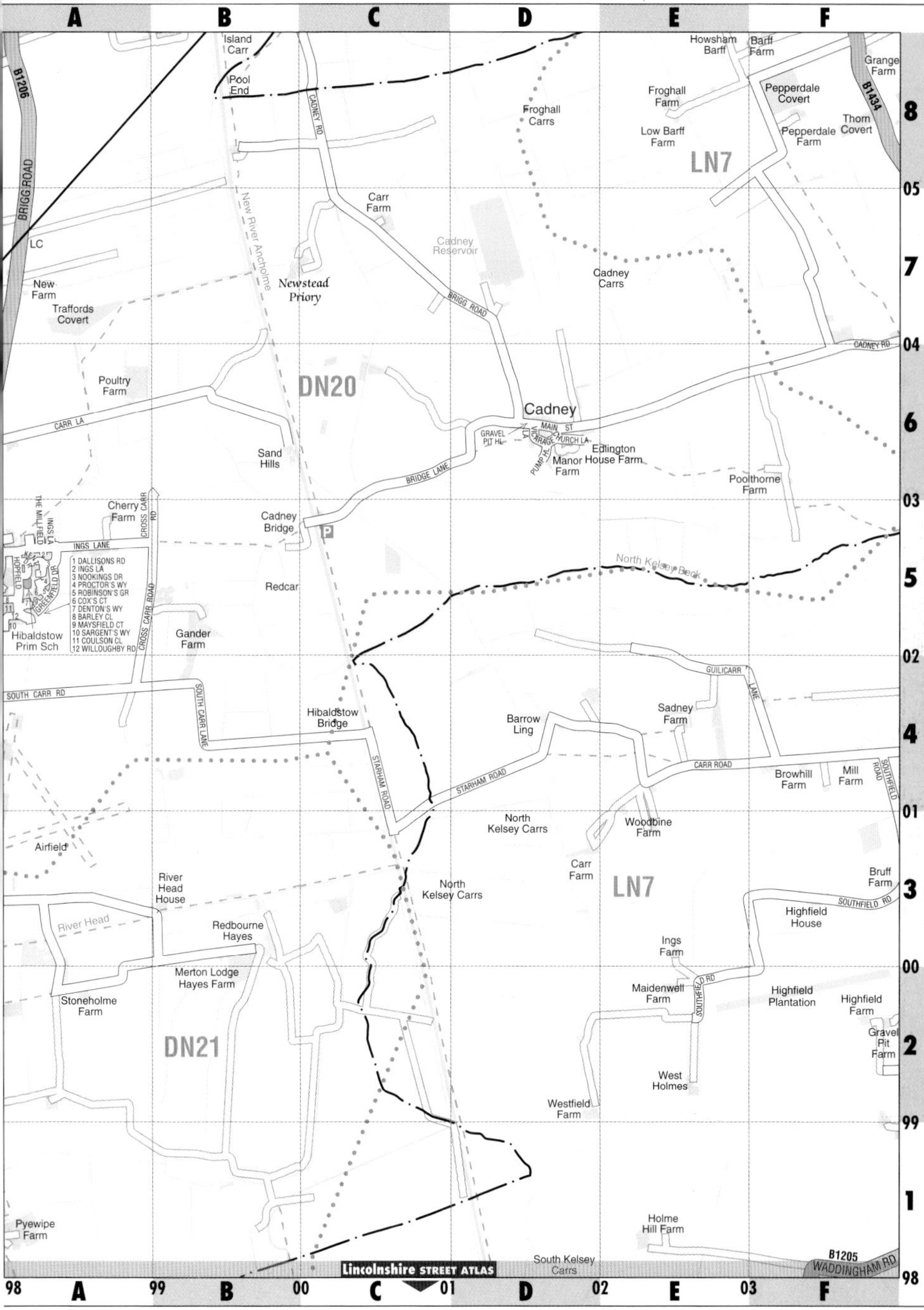

110

109
99

Scale: 1⅓ inches to 1 mile
0 ¼ ½ mile
0 250m 500m 750m 1 km

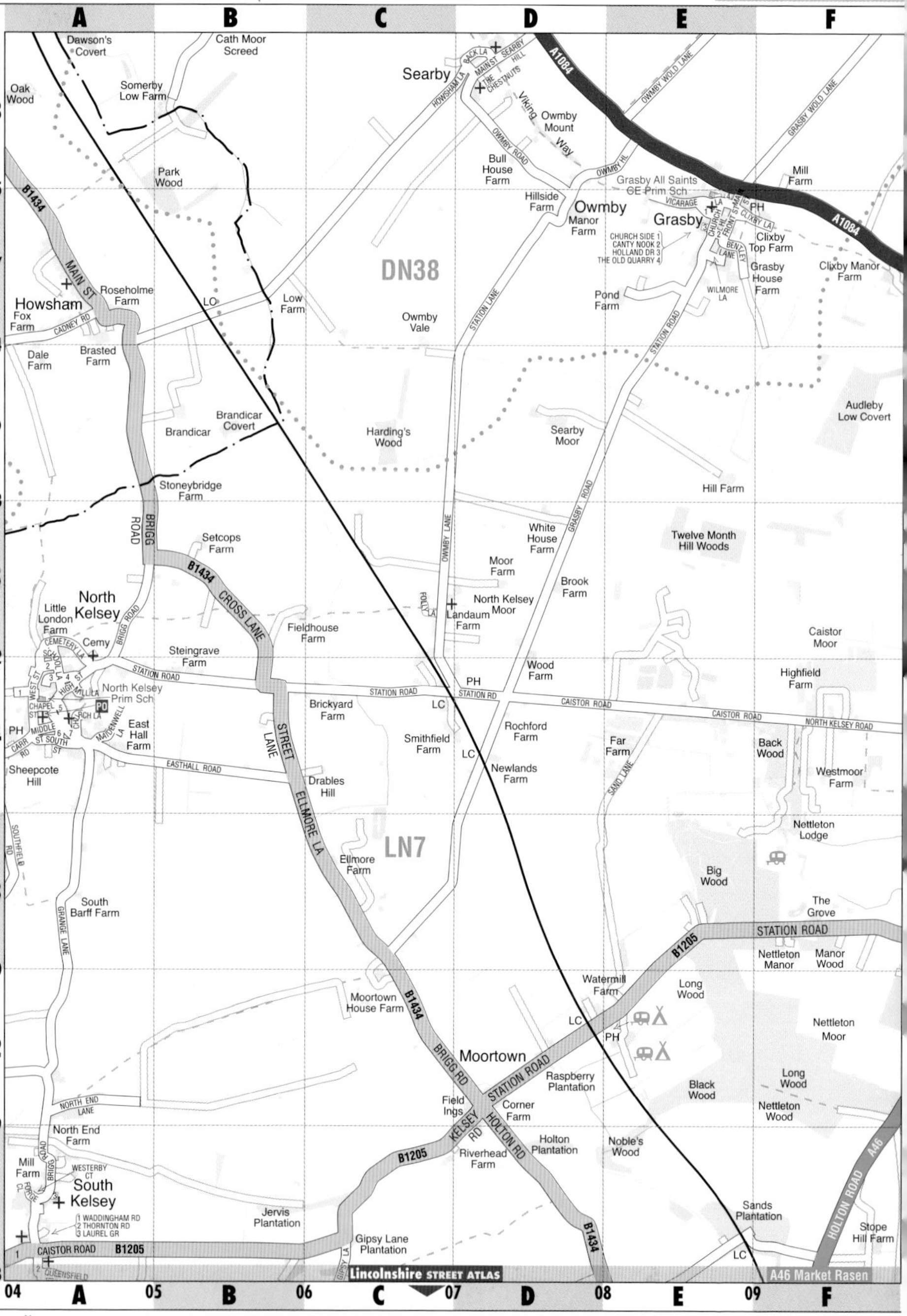

109

A4
1 OCCUPATION LA
2 LINDUM WK
3 PATRICKS CL
4 OLD SCHOOL LA
5 HALLS LA
6 GREEN LA
7 CHURCH ST

100
112

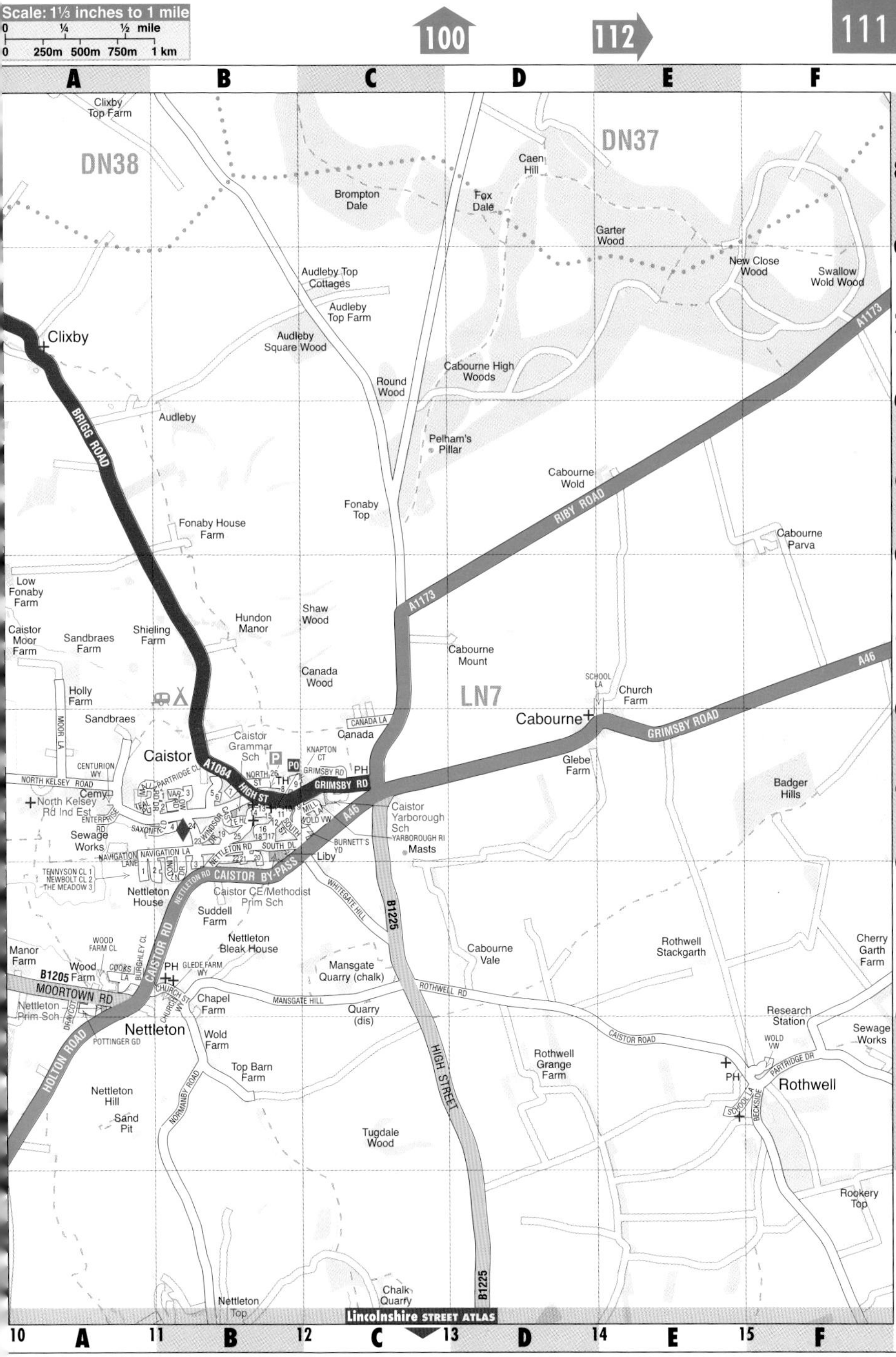

B4
1 PHEASANT CT
2 PLOVER SQ
3 AYSCOUGH GR
4 SAXON WY
5 KEYWORTH DR
6 HANSARD CRES
7 CHERRY HOLT
8 GEORGE MEWS
9 THE ROPEWALK
10 BUTTER MKT
11 MARKET PL
12 PLOUGH HL
13 CHAPEL ST
14 CHURCH ST
15 BANK LA
16 FOUNTAIN ST
17 HORSE MKT
18 WESTBROOKE GR
19 CHICHESTER DR
20 WESTWOLD RD
21 RISEDALE
22 RAWLINSON AVE
23 MILLFIELDS
24 HERSEY RD
25 CROMWELL VW
26 WATERHILLS CT

112

111
101

Scale: 1⅓ inches to 1 mile
0 ¼ ½ mile
0 250m 500m 750m 1 km

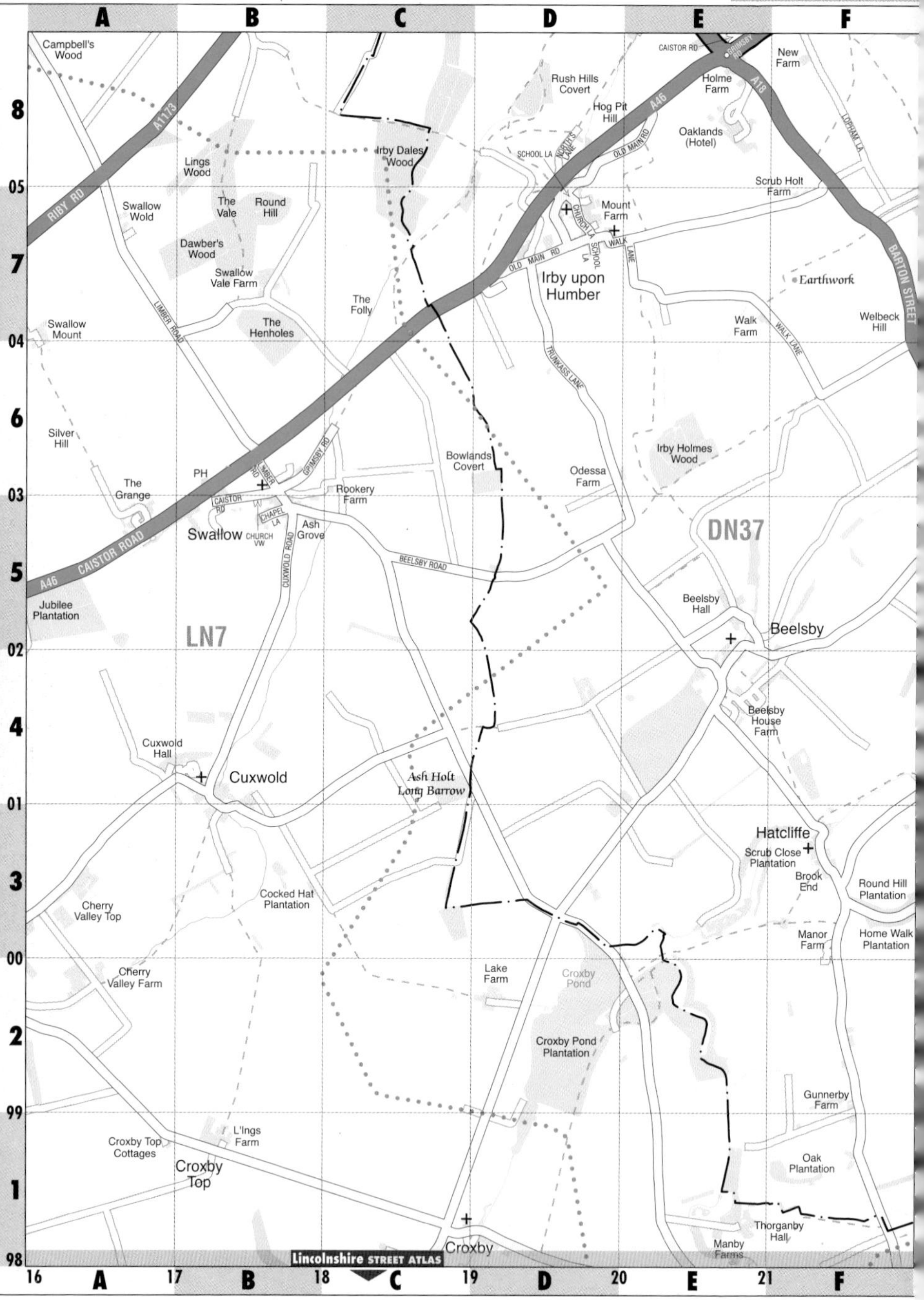

111

D7
1 CARDINAL CT
2 CORAL DR
3 PEACE HAVEN
4 LUDGATE CL
5 ALBERTINE CT
6 FOUNTAIN CL
7 SWEET BRIAR CL
8 FRANCES CT
9 WRAY CL

102 114

E8
1 LARDEN AVE
2 ALLESTREE DR
3 BARBARA CL
4 FLEETWOOD CL
5 RIVAN AVE
6 RIVAN GR
7 ADELPHI DR
8 WOOD CL
9 HEATHERDALE CL
10 ORCHARD CFT
11 HILARY RD
12 EASTBOURNE WY
13 BEATTY AVE
14 CROXBY GR
15 WESTBOURNE GR
16 SPURN AVE
17 LINWOOD AVE
18 DOVEDALE DR
19 TAUNTON WY
20 BRACKEN PK
21 TONBRIDGE WLK
22 WICKLOW AVE
23 GRAMPIAN WY
24 LANCING WY
25 SOUTHWOLD CRES
26 CHILTERN WY
27 DERRY WY
28 THE COPSE
29 HAWTHORNE AVE
30 LINDSEY RISE
31 COLLEGE AVE
32 COLLEGE GDNS

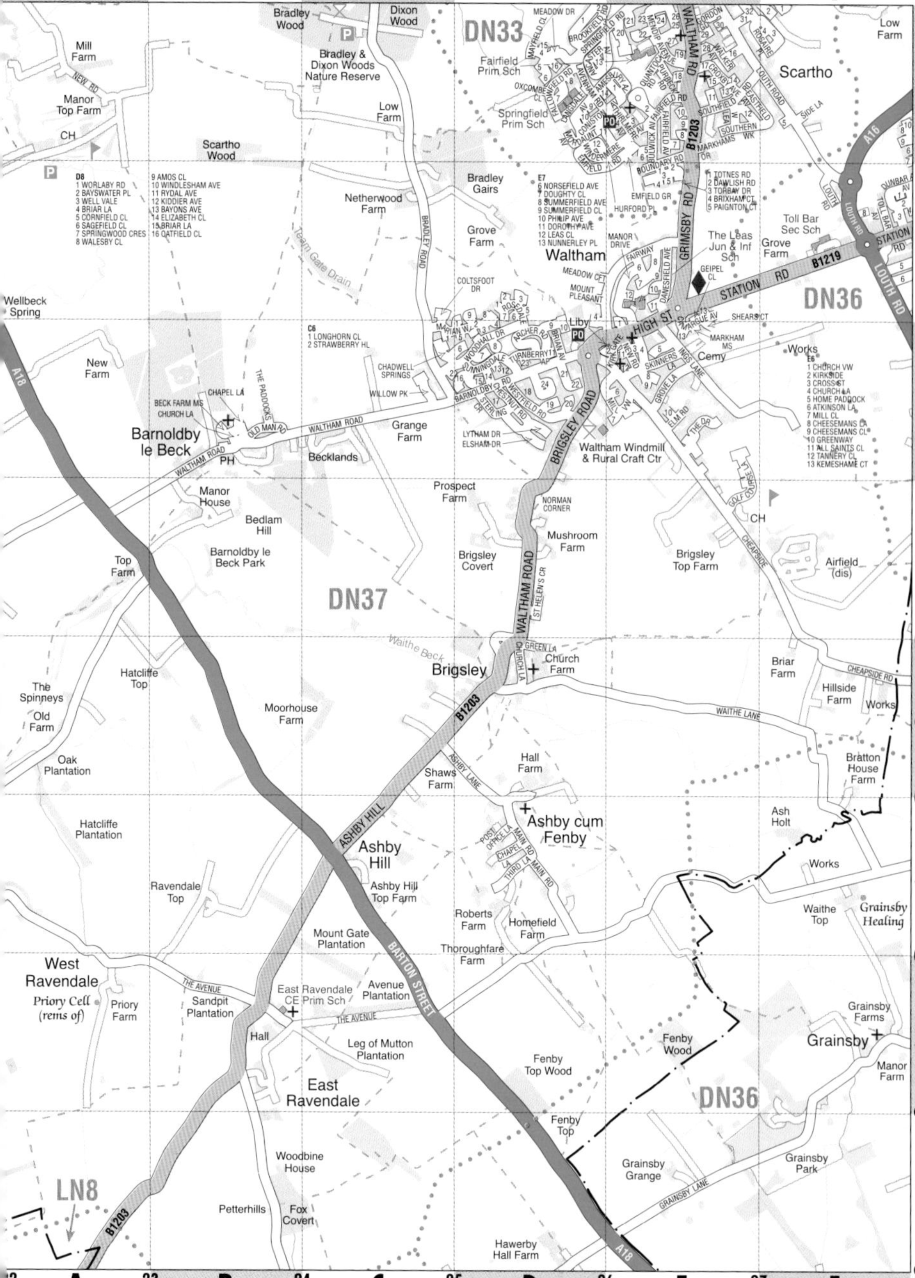

120

D6
1 DRURY CL
2 WHEATFIELD DR
3 BARKWORTH CT
4 HARVEST CRES
5 OLD FARM CT
6 ALDERLEY EDGE
7 ASHBOURNE
8 LINDRICK WK
9 NEVILLE TURNER WY
10 ORCHARD CT
11 PEAR TREE CL
12 SUNNINGDALE
13 CARNOUSTIE
14 BIRKDALE
15 GLENEAGLES
16 MUIRFIELD
17 CHESTNUT CL
18 MAYFAIR CRES
19 CHILTERN DR
20 COTSWOLD DR
21 LABURNHAM AVE
22 LABURNHAM CL
23 ASCOT RD
24 SALISBURY AVE

114

F7
1 DURSLEY AVE
2 CONISBOROUGH AVE
3 PEMBERTON DR
4 LINDISFARNE AVE
6 HAWTHORNE AVE
7 MAPLE GR
8 SIMPSON'S FOLD CT

F8
1 SHAW DR
2 WESTKIRKE AVE
3 KENSINGTON PL
4 CHRISTINE PL
5 BRAETON LA
6 JOSEPH OGLE CL
7 MARTIN WY
8 HUNTSMANS CH
9 ELLEN WY
10 LAVENDER GR

A7
1 SHAFTESBURY MEWS
2 CHANDLERS CL
3 DRURY LA
4 ADELPHI CT
5 DUNBAR AVE
6 ALDWYCH CFT
7 BARBICAN WY
8 PICCADILLY
9 DOMINION CL
10 WYNDHAM RD
11 FARMHOUSE MEWS
12 SAVOY CT
13 GREENLANDS AVE
14 THE ORCHARD
15 KAYMILE CL
16 RUTLAND DR
17 CHARLES AVE
18 MARGARET PL
19 WADDINGHAM PL
20 GRANGE FARM LA

113

103

D8
1 STANILAND WY
2 CHIPPENDALE CL
3 SHERATON DR
4 WOODFIELD CL
5 EASTFIELD
6 ROWAN DR
7 BURCOM AVE
8 COULAM PL
9 CHAPMAN CRES
10 ASHWOOD DR
11 ANDREW RD
12 VISCOUNT WY
13 HUMBERSTON AVE
14 SINDERSON RD
15 AMELIA CT
16 TUDOR CL
17 CHERRY CL
18 TAWNY OWL CL

Scale: 1⅓ inches to 1 mile
0 ¼ ½ mile
0 250m 500m 750m 1 km

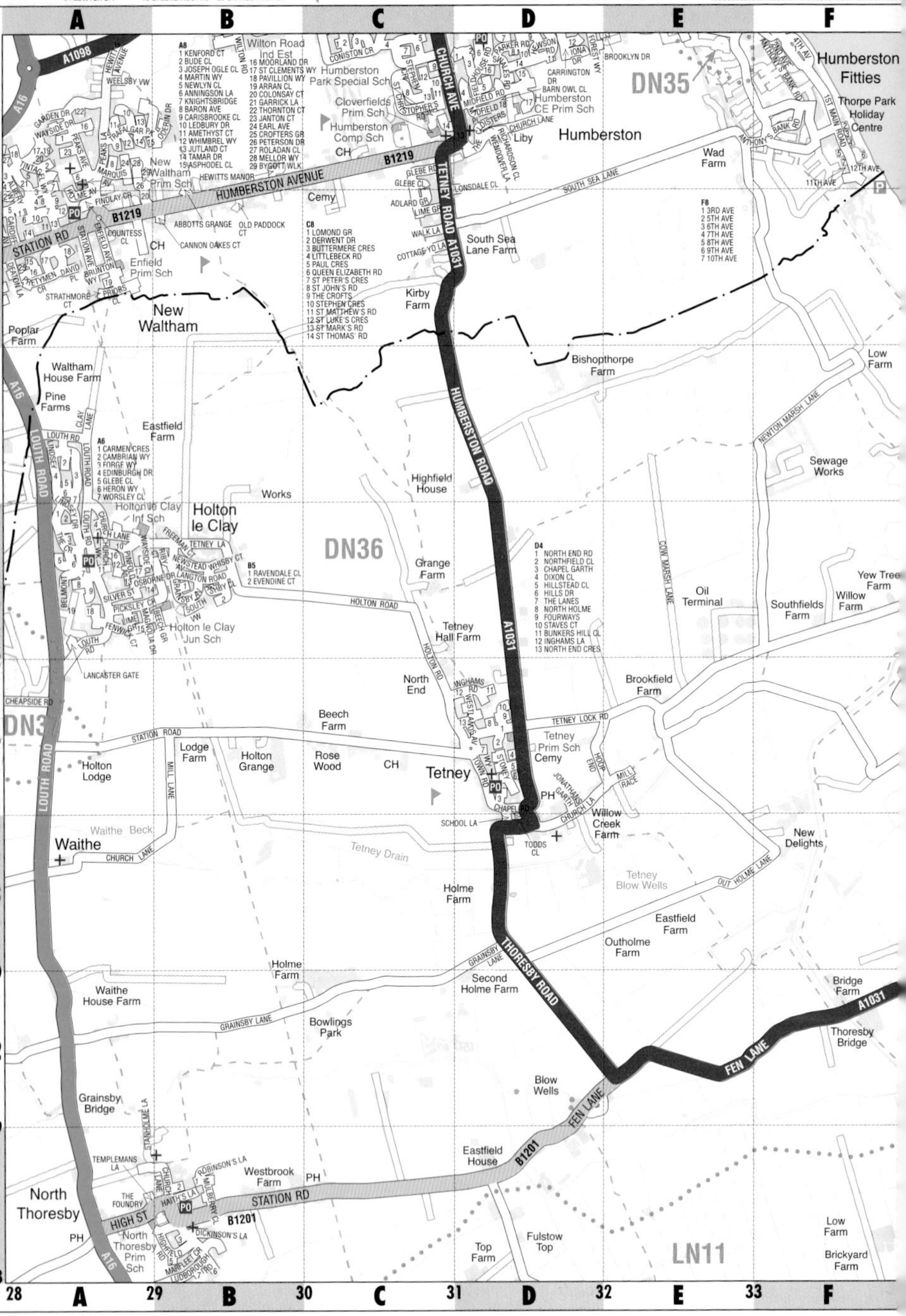

A5
1 PELHAM RD
2 YARBOROUGH CL
3 HAYS CL
4 EASTFIELD RISE
5 BEAUMONDE
6 WOLD VW
7 HOLTON MT
8 HOLTON CT
9 MOUNT PLEASANT
10 ST PETER'S CL
11 PEPPERCORN WK
12 CAMPIONS CL
13 GARTHWAY
14 PINFOLD GDNS
15 SOUTHFIELD RD
16 SARGE CL
17 NURSERY GDNS
18 BEVERLEY CL
19 NICKERSON WY

B1
1 PLUMTREE LA
2 OLD PLUMTREE LA
3 BORMAN'S LA
4 SMITH FIELD
5 HIGHFIELD CL
6 CAMPIONS' LA
7 MUMBY CL

113

121

Scale: 1⅓ inches to 1 mile
0 ¼ ½ mile
0 250m 500m 750m 1 km

A
B
C
D
E
F
8
05
7
04
6
03
5
02
4
01
3
00
2
99
1
98
34
35
36
37
38
39
Tetney High Sands
Tetney Haven
Northcoates Point
NEWTON MARSH LA
Braybrook Farm
NEWTON MARSH LANE
Stonebridge Farm
EARLE'S RD
SEAWALL LA
SANDY CL
FITTIES LA
MARSH FEN WK
DYKE ROAD
SEA LANE
SAMPHIRE CL
North Coates Airfield
Horse Shoe Point
THE WHARF
Tetney Lock
PH
NORTH COATES ROAD
DN36
Tuttle Farm
Grange Farm
LOCK ROAD
Low Farm
Grainthorpe Haven
SEA LANE
North Cotes
North Cotes CE (Con) Prim Sch
SHEEP MARSH LANE
FLEETWAY
INGS LANE
Poplar Farm
Keyholme Farm
The Fitties
MABLETHORPE RD A1031
THORESBY ROAD
DUCKTHORPE LA
COWPER CL
NORTHWAY
NORTH LANE
Marshchapel
HILLGARTH
VICTORIA CL
PH
PLUM TREE DR
DUCKTHORPE LANE
Marshchapel Prim Sch
STANBY CL
MILL LA
MILL CL
HARPHAM ROAD
LITTLEFIELD LANE
PO
KEYHOLME LANE
Sea Bank Farm
Evergreen Farm
Sea Farm
Holme Farm
LOW ROAD
CHURCH LANE
Eskham
New Farm
WEST END LA
West End
Louth Canal
LN11
LN11
COAL SHORE LA
Heelgate Farm
LAND DIKE
Low Farm
LOW GATE
Marshchapel Ings
A1031
Beacon Hill
Ivy House
GRAINS GATE
Lincolnshire STREET ATLAS
A1031 Mablethorpe (A1104)
Lincolnshire STREET ATLAS

105

Scale: 1⅓ inches to 1 mile
0 ¼ ½ mile
0 250m 500m 750m 1 km

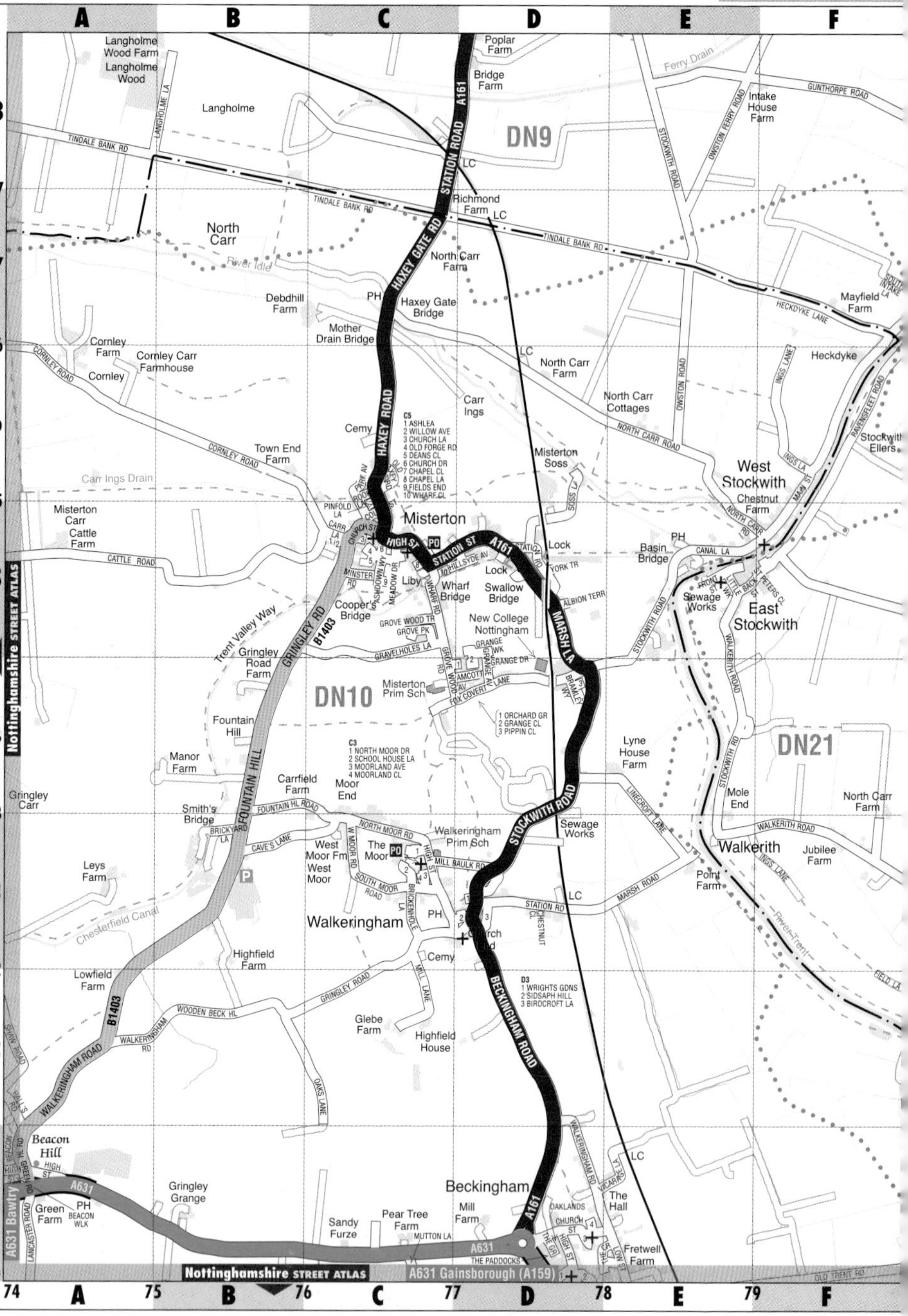

D1
1 RAVENCROFT LA
2 THE LIMES
3 RECTORY GDNS
4 CHURCH VW

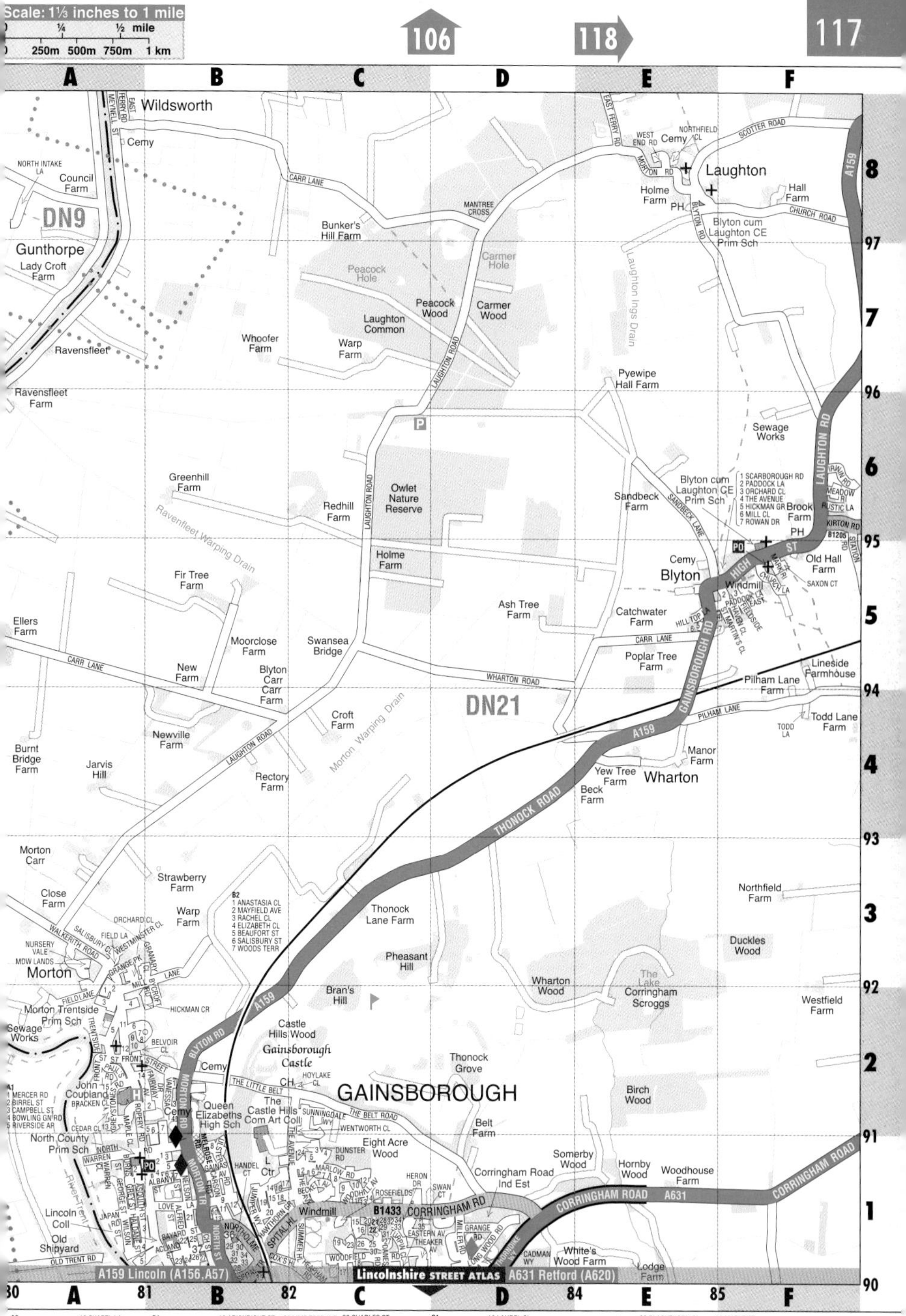

A2
1 SOUTHLANDS AVE
2 SOUTHLANDS GDNS
3 SOUTHLANDS DR
4 MORTON CL
5 CROOKED BILLET ST
6 NORTH ST
7 CROSS ST
8 SOUTH ST
9 WEST ST
10 CHAPEL LA
11 WALKERITH RD
12 DOG AND DUCK LA
13 WILLOW CL
14 WOODLAND AVE
15 HORSLEY RD

B1
1 HOTSPUR RD
2 NOEL ST
3 MOWBRAY ST
4 CURZON ST
5 MELROSE RD
6 HENLEY CT
7 ROWSTON CL
8 OLD SHOWFIELDS
9 CONNAUGHT RD
10 ARKWRIGHT ST
11 EDWARD RD
12 ARTHUR RD
13 CROMFORD ST
14 BEECH AVE
15 CHESTNUT AVE
16 BIRCH GR
17 ASH GR
18 LABURNUM AVE
19 ACACIA AVE
20 LIME TREE AVE
21 GARFIELD ST
22 LINCOLN ST
23 BALFOUR ST
24 CECIL ST
25 FORSTER ST
26 FAWCETT ST
27 SCOTT ST
28 DRILL HALL LA
29 CARLISLE ST
30 CHARLES ST
31 TOWER ST
32 TENNYSON ST
33 RECTORY AVE
34 JUBILEE CRES
35 CROSS ST
36 Handel House Prep Sch
37 Parish Church Prim Sch

C1
1 HAWTON CL
2 STIRLING CL
3 MILTON RD
4 ARUNDEL CL
5 MILTON CL
6 DUNBAR CL
7 PENDEEN CL
8 IONA CL
9 SYCAMORE DR
10 LAUREL CL
11 LARCH CT
12 HARROW CL
13 ASPEN CT
14 OAK TREE AVE
15 REDMAN CL
16 BRAMLEY CT
17 NEWLANDS
18 CHERRY TREE RD
19 FIELDING WY

118

20 BLACKTHORN CL
21 BIRCHWOOD VW
22 THE ALDERS
23 HIGHFIELD CL
24 THE AVENUE
25 BIRCHWOOD VW
26 THE HOLT
27 COUPLAND CL
28 THE SPINNEY
29 FOSSEWAY
30 MAPLE CT
31 HEATHER CL
32 FALCON GR
33 KESTREL AVE
34 LING DR
35 PEACOCK PL

117
107

Scale: 1⅓ inches to 1 mile

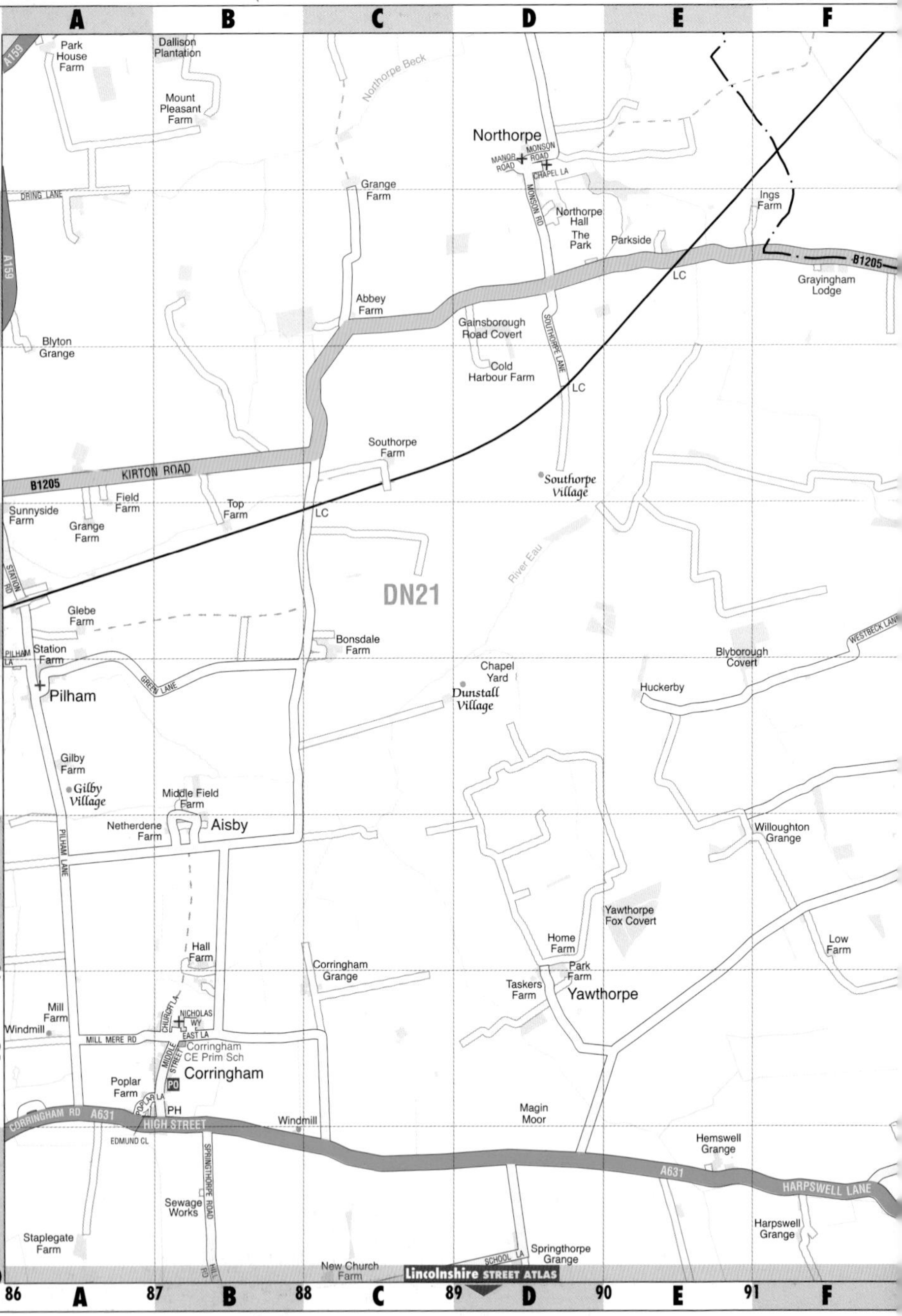
A
B
C
D
E
F
Park House Farm
Dallison Plantation
Mount Pleasant Farm
Northorpe Beck
Northorpe
MANOR ROAD
MONSON ROAD
CHAPEL LA
DRING LANE
Grange Farm
Ings Farm
MONSON RD
Northorpe Hall
The Park
Parkside
A159
B1205
LC
Grayingham Lodge
Abbey Farm
Gainsborough Road Covert
SOUTHORPE LANE
Blyton Grange
Cold Harbour Farm
Southorpe Farm
KIRTON ROAD
Southorpe Village
Field Farm
Top Farm
Sunnyside Farm
Grange Farm
River Eau
STATION RD
DN21
Glebe Farm
Bonsdale Farm
PILHAM LA
Station Farm
Blyborough Covert
WESTBECK LANE
Chapel Yard
GREEN LANE
Pilham
Huckerby
Dunstall Village
Gilby Farm
Gilby Village
Middle Field Farm
Netherdene Farm
Aisby
Willoughton Grange
PILHAM LANE
Yawthorpe Fox Covert
Low Farm
Hall Farm
Home Farm
Corringham Grange
Park Farm
Taskers Farm
Yawthorpe
Mill Farm
CHURCH LA
NICHOLAS WY
Windmill
MILL MERE RD
EAST LA
Corringham CE Prim Sch
MIDDLE STREET
Corringham
Poplar Farm
PO
POPLAR LA
PH
Magin Moor
CORRINGHAM RD
A631
HIGH STREET
Windmill
EDMUND CL
Hemswell Grange
SPRINGTHORPE ROAD
HARPSWELL LANE
Sewage Works
Harpswell Grange
Staplegate Farm
HILL RD
New Church Farm
SCHOOL LA
Springthorpe Grange
Lincolnshire STREET ATLAS
8
97
7
96
6
95
5
94
4
93
3
92
2
91
1
90
86
87
88
89
90
91

117

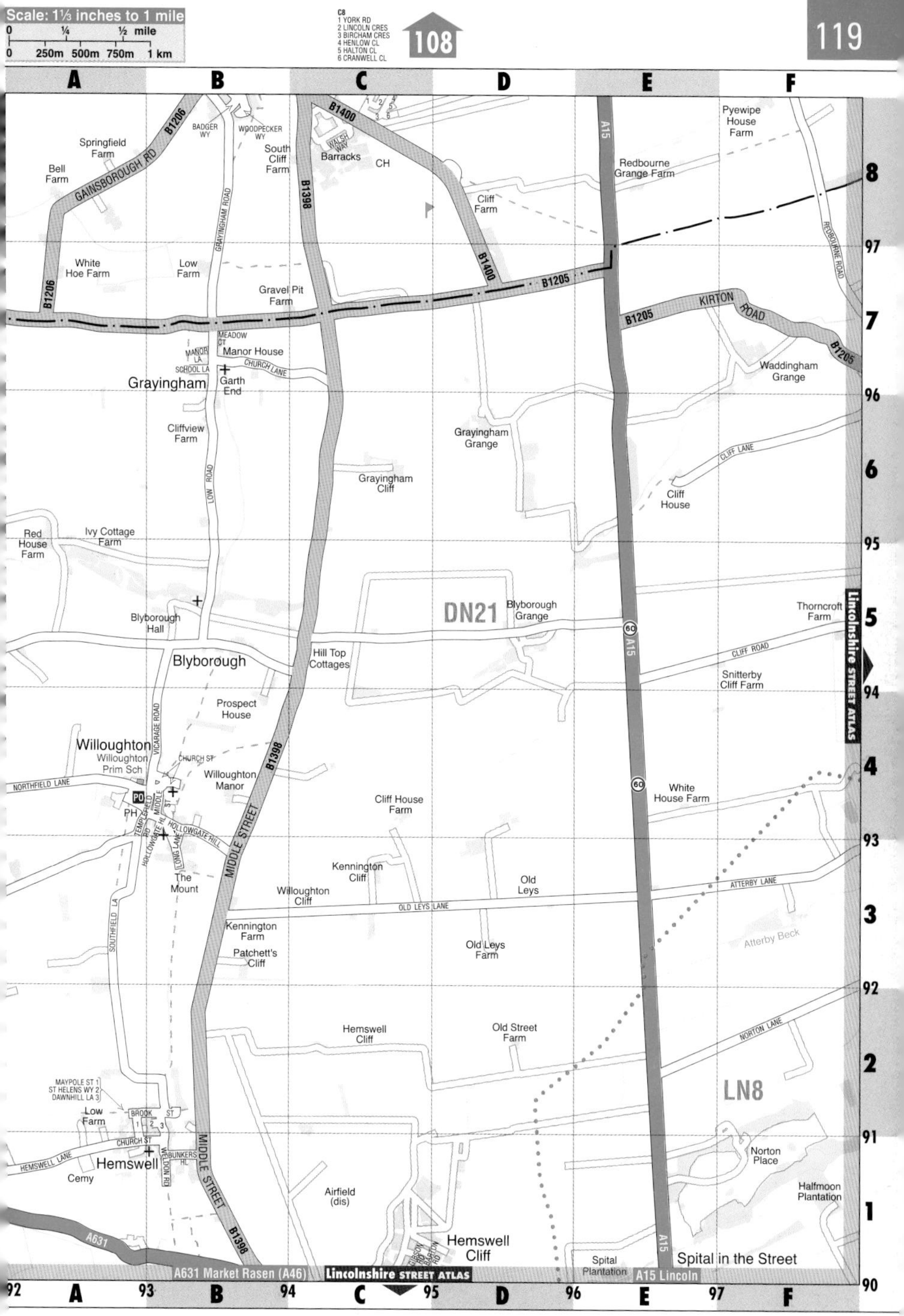
Scale: 1⅓ inches to 1 mile
0 ¼ ½ mile
0 250m 500m 750m 1 km
C8
1 YORK RD
2 LINCOLN CRES
3 BIRCHAM CRES
4 HENLOW CL
5 HALTON CL
6 CRANWELL CL
108
A B C D E F
8 97 7 96 6 95 5 94 4 93 3 92 2 91 1 90
92 93 94 95 96 97
Springfield Farm
Bell Farm
GAINSBOROUGH RD
B1206
BADGER WY
WOODPECKER WY
South Cliff Farm
GRAYINGHAM ROAD
B1398
B1400
WALSH WAY
Barracks
CH
Pyewipe House Farm
Redbourne Grange Farm
Cliff Farm
A15
REDBOURNE ROAD
White Hoe Farm
Low Farm
Gravel Pit Farm
B1205
KIRTON ROAD
MEADOW CT
MANOR LA
Manor House
SCHOOL LA
CHURCH LANE
Grayingham
Garth End
Waddingham Grange
Cliffview Farm
Grayingham Grange
CLIFF LANE
LOW ROAD
Grayingham Cliff
Cliff House
Red House Farm
Ivy Cottage Farm
DN21
Blyborough Grange
Thorncroft Farm
Blyborough Hall
60
Hill Top Cottages
CLIFF ROAD
Blyborough
Snitterby Cliff Farm
Prospect House
VICARAGE ROAD
Willoughton
Willoughton Prim Sch
CHURCH ST
Willoughton Manor
NORTHFIELD LANE
PO
PH
TEMPLEFIELD RD
MIDDLE ST
HOLLOWGATE HILL
LONG LANE
Cliff House Farm
White House Farm
Kennington Cliff
The Mount
Willoughton Cliff
Old Leys
ATTERBY LANE
MIDDLE STREET
OLD LEYS LANE
SOUTHFIELD LA
Kennington Farm
Patchett's Cliff
Old Leys Farm
Atterby Beck
Hemswell Cliff
Old Street Farm
NORTON LANE
LN8
MAYPOLE ST 1
ST HELENS WY 2
DAWNHILL LA 3
Low Farm
BROOK ST
CHURCH ST
BUNKERS HL
WELDON RD
HEMSWELL LANE
Hemswell
Cemy
Norton Place
Airfield (dis)
Halfmoon Plantation
A631
Hemswell Cliff
GIBSON RD
BARTON RD
Spital Plantation
Spital in the Street
A631 Market Rasen (A46)
Lincolnshire STREET ATLAS
A15 Lincoln

113

Scale: 1⅓ inches to 1 mile
0 ¼ ½ mile
0 250m 500m 750m 1 km

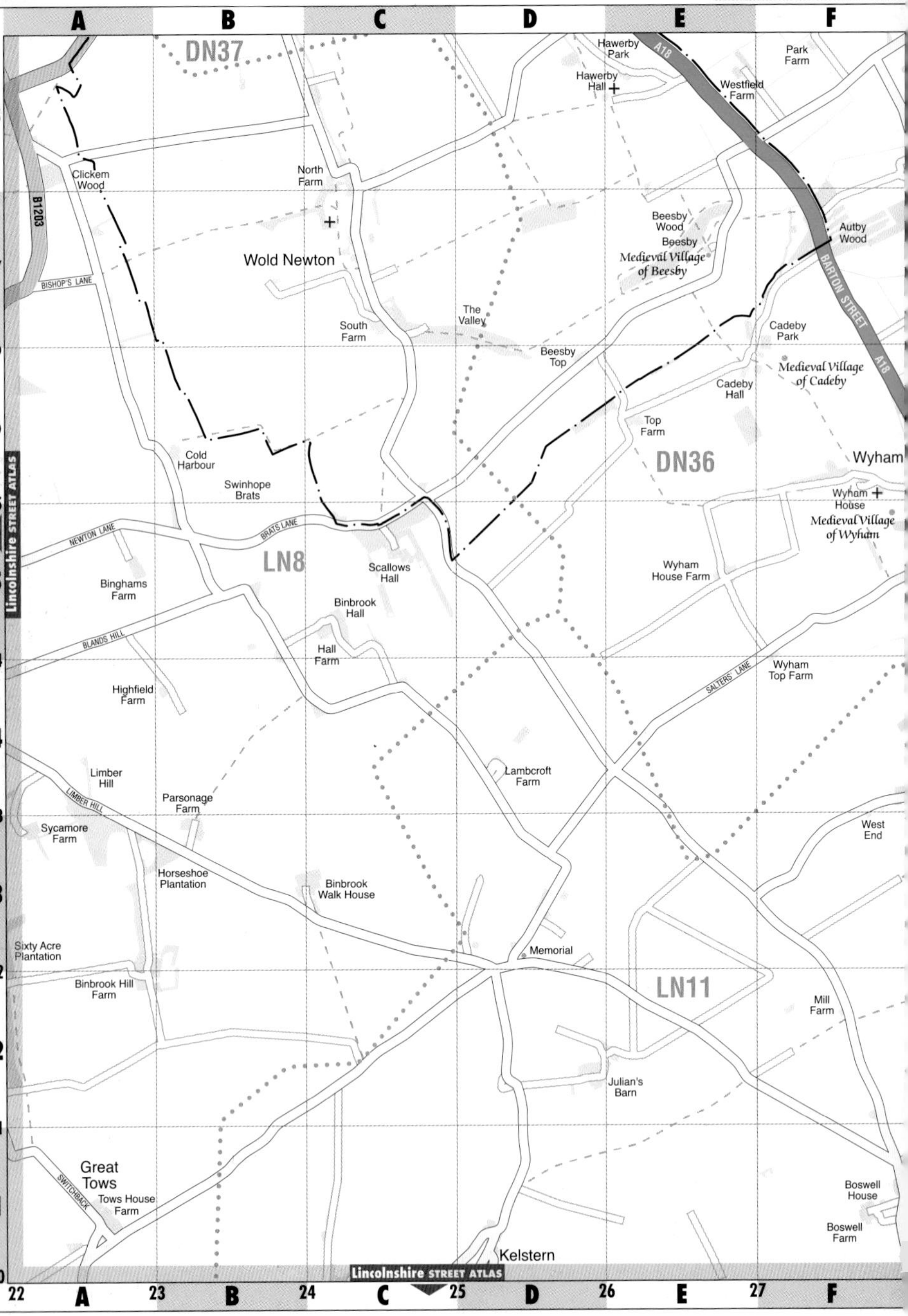
A
B
C
D
E
F
8
97
7
96
6
95
5
94
4
93
3
92
2
91
1
90
22
23
24
25
26
27
DN37
Hawerby Park
Hawerby Hall
A18
Park Farm
Westfield Farm
Clickem Wood
North Farm
B1203
Beesby Wood
Beesby
Medieval Village of Beesby
Autby Wood
Wold Newton
BISHOP'S LANE
BARTON STREET
South Farm
The Valley
Cadeby Park
Beesby Top
Medieval Village of Cadeby
Cadeby Hall
Top Farm
Cold Harbour
DN36
Wyham
Swinhope Brats
Wyham House
Medieval Village of Wyham
NEWTON LANE
BRATS LANE
LN8
Scallows Hall
Wyham House Farm
Binghams Farm
Binbrook Hall
BLANDS HILL
Hall Farm
Wyham Top Farm
SALTERS' LANE
Highfield Farm
Lambcroft Farm
Limber Hill
LIMBER HILL
Parsonage Farm
Sycamore Farm
West End
Horseshoe Plantation
Binbrook Walk House
Sixty Acre Plantation
Memorial
Binbrook Hill Farm
LN11
Mill Farm
Julian's Barn
Great Tows
SWITCHBACK
Tows House Farm
Boswell House
Boswell Farm
Kelstern
Lincolnshire STREET ATLAS

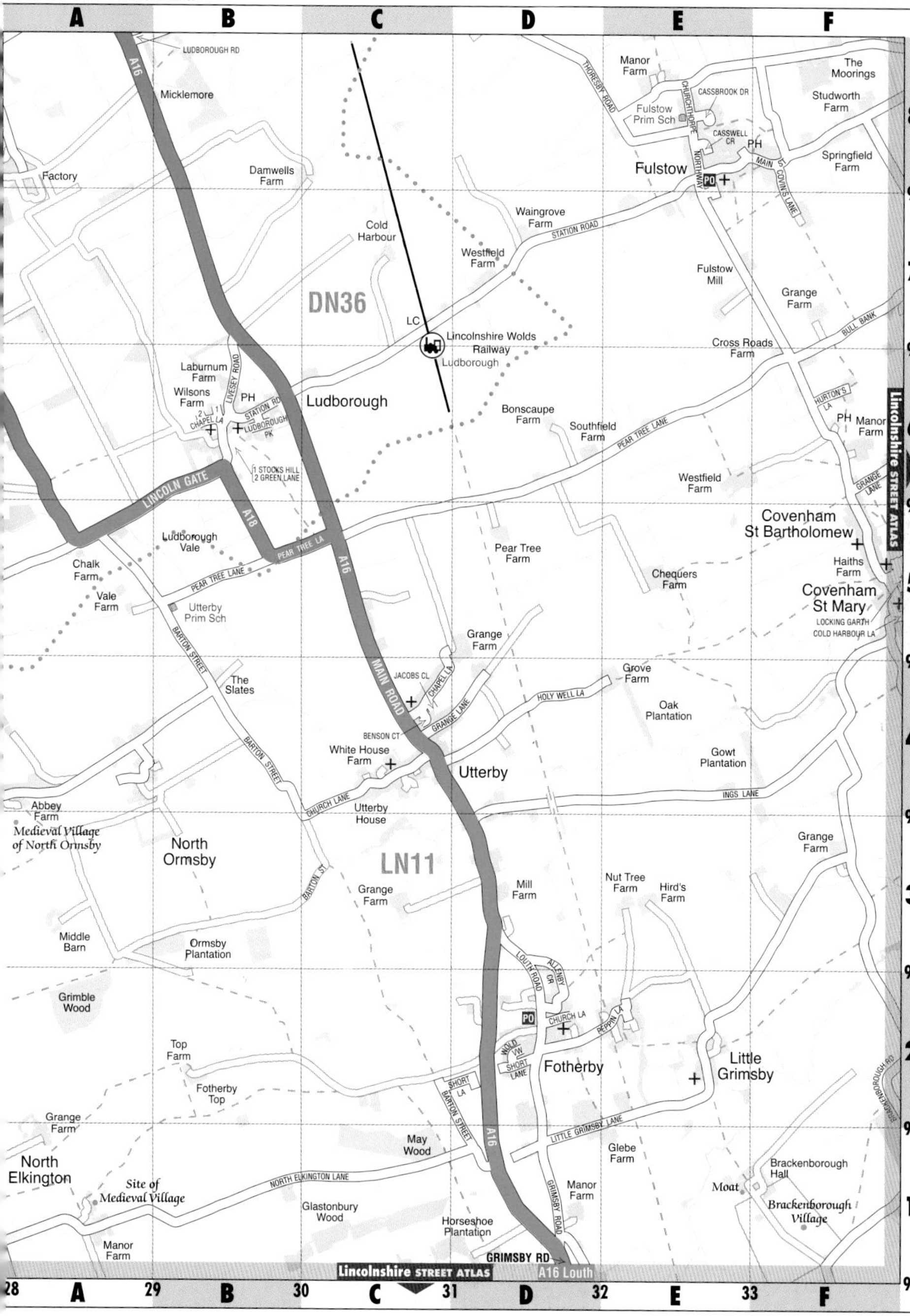
A B C D E F
8 97 7 96 6 95 5 94 4 93 3 92 2 91 1 90
28 29 30 31 32 33
LUDBOROUGH RD
A16
Micklemore
Factory
Damwells Farm
Cold Harbour
DN36
LC
Lincolnshire Wolds Railway
Ludborough
Manor Farm
THORESBY ROAD
CHURCHTHORPE
CASSBROOK DR
Fulstow Prim Sch
CASSWELL CR
PH
MAIN ST
COVINS LANE
NORTHWAY
Fulstow
PO
The Moorings
Studworth Farm
Springfield Farm
Waingrove Farm
STATION ROAD
Westfield Farm
Fulstow Mill
Grange Farm
Cross Roads Farm
BULL BANK
Laburnum Farm
LIVESEY ROAD
Wilsons Farm
PH
STATION RD
CHAPEL LA
LUDBOROUGH PK
1 STOCKS HILL
2 GREEN LANE
Ludborough
Bonscaupe Farm
Southfield Farm
PEAR TREE LANE
HURTON'S LA
PH
Manor Farm
LINCOLN GATE
A18
Westfield Farm
GRANGE LANE
Covenham St Bartholomew
Ludborough Vale
PEAR TREE LA
Pear Tree Farm
Chequers Farm
Haiths Farm
Chalk Farm
PEAR TREE LANE
Vale Farm
Utterby Prim Sch
Covenham St Mary
LOCKING GARTH
COLD HARBOUR LA
Grange Farm
BARTON STREET
The Slates
JACOBS CL
CHAPEL LA
MAIN ROAD
Grove Farm
HOLY WELL LA
Oak Plantation
GRANGE LANE
BENSON CT
White House Farm
Utterby
Gowt Plantation
BARTON STREET
Abbey Farm
Medieval Village of North Ormsby
CHURCH LANE
Utterby House
INGS LANE
North Ormsby
LN11
Grange Farm
BARTON ST
Grange Farm
Mill Farm
Nut Tree Farm
Hird's Farm
Middle Barn
Ormsby Plantation
LOUTH ROAD
ALLENBY CR
Grimble Wood
PO
CHURCH LA
PEPPIN LA
Top Farm
WOLD VW
SHORT LANE
Fotherby
Little Grimsby
BRACKENBOROUGH RD
Fotherby Top
SHORT LA
BARTON STREET
A16
LITTLE GRIMSBY LANE
Grange Farm
May Wood
Glebe Farm
North Elkington
Site of Medieval Village
NORTH ELKINGTON LANE
Manor Farm
GRIMSBY ROAD
Brackenborough Hall
Moat
Brackenborough Village
Glastonbury Wood
Horseshoe Plantation
Manor Farm
GRIMSBY RD
A16 Louth

10
4

D6
1 TRENTHAM MEWS
2 PINFOLD WY NORTH
3 PINFOLD CT
4 PINFOLD CL
5 CHATSWORTH CL
6 SANDRINGHAM CL
7 THORESBY MEWS
8 BALMORAL CL

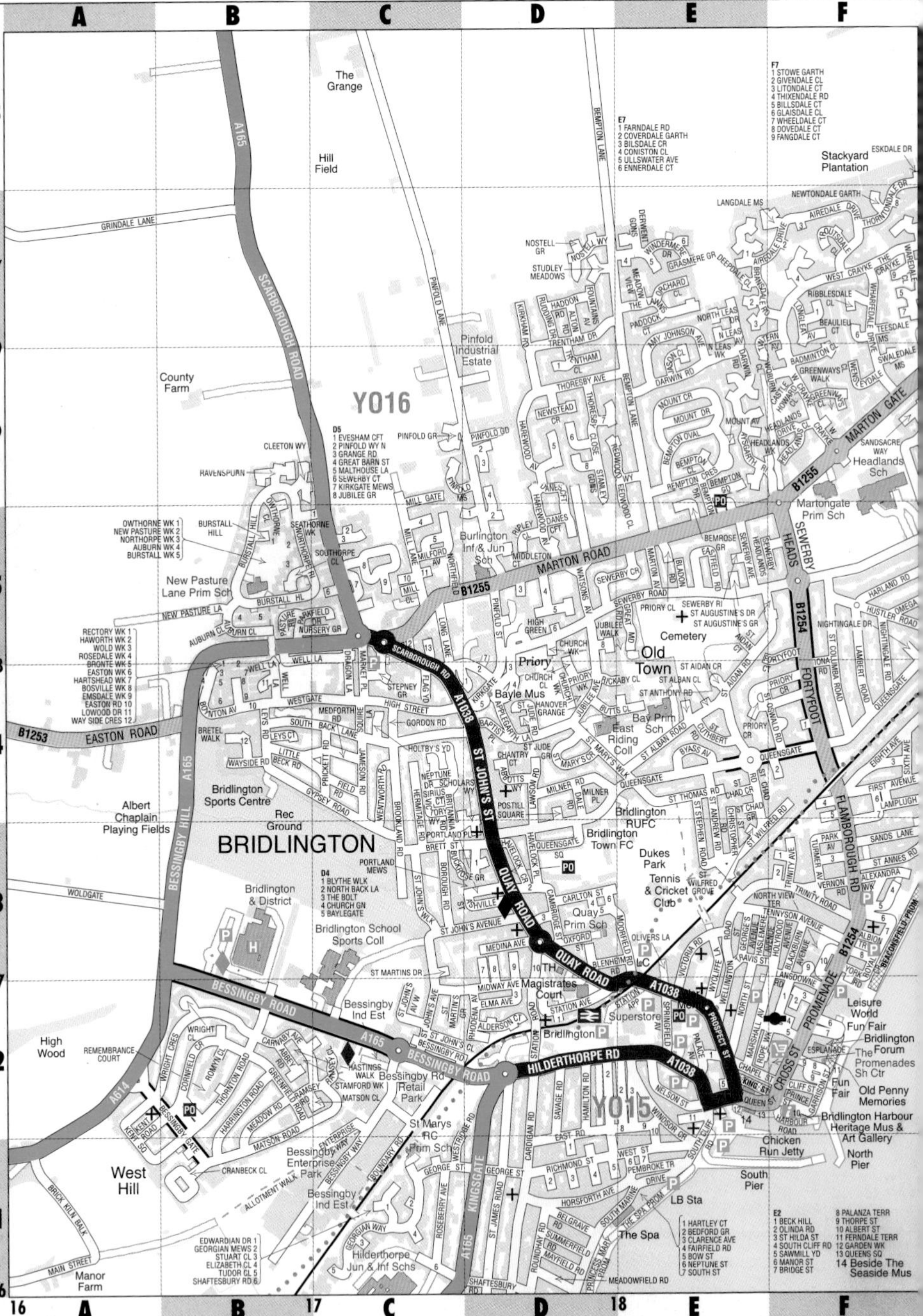

C5
1 SEATHORNE RD
2 WYKENHAM CL
3 ELLERBURN DR
4 MILLFIELD RD
5 MILFORD CRES
6 NEW PASTURE CL
7 SCARBOROUGH RD
8 SCARBOROUGH CRES
9 THE HOLLOWS
10 MILL CT
11 MILLBANK
12 SHORT LA
13 STEPNEY AVE

D2
1 ADMIRALS MEWS
2 NEW BURLINGTON RD
3 ELMA VILLAS

10

D3
1 BURLINGTON GDNS
2 HAVELOCK ST
3 SWINDON ST
4 GILBERT ST
5 THOMPSON ST
6 HILL ST
7 MELBOURNE AVE
8 WESTBOURNE AVE
9 ASHBOURNE AVE
10 STATION AVE

11

F2
1 CLARENCE RD
2 WESTMORLAND GR
3 WESTMORLAND AVE
4 PRINCESS ST
5 PRINCESS TERR
6 FORT TERR
7 REGENT TERR
8 MARLBOROUGH TERR
9 THE CRESCENT
10 BRITANNIA CT
11 ROYAL PRINCE'S PAR

F3
1 TRINITY GR
2 TRINITY MEWS
3 SWANLAND AVE
4 ALEXANDRA CT
5 ALEXANDRA DR
6 GLADSTONE TERR
7 BRIGHT CR
8 CARLISLE RD
9 LANSDOWNE CRES
10 PROVIDENCE PL

F4
1 FORTYFOOT GR
2 PARK VW
3 SEVENTH AVE
4 EDGECLIFFE VILLAS
5 CANTON VILLAS
6 LAMPLUGH SQ
7 LAMPLUGH LA

A7
1 NIDDERDALE CL
2 CALDERDALE CL
3 YORDAS CT
4 CARROWAY CL
5 LYTH CL
6 MARTON CT
7 COTTERDALE CL

20
20

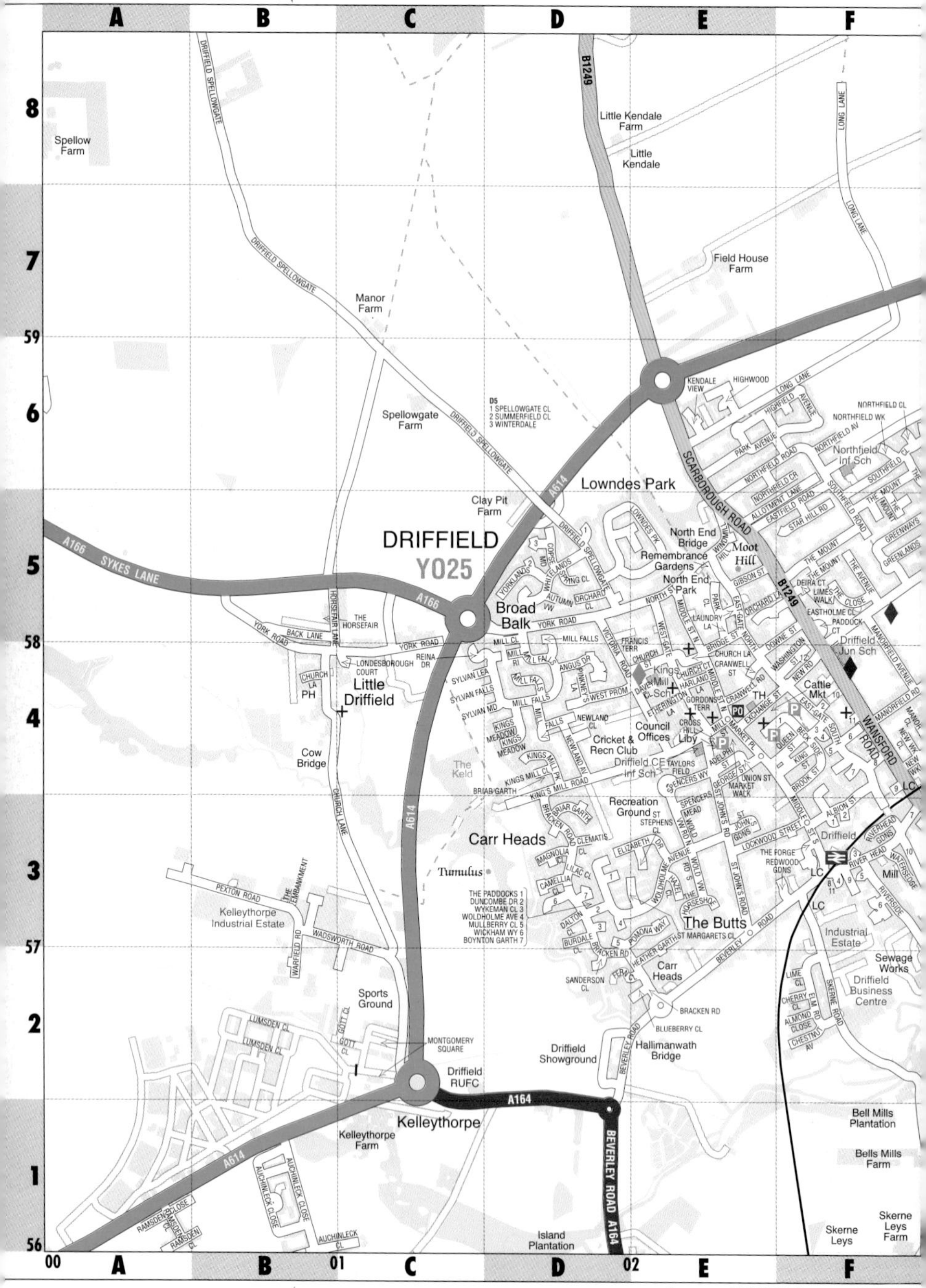

F3
1 ST JOHN'S WK
2 ST JOHN'S PL
3 RIVER HEAD DR
4 GEORGIAN MEWS
5 RIVERSIDE MEWS
6 RIVERSIDE CL
7 ANDERSON ST
8 WOODLANDS
9 THE BEECHLANDS
10 BEECHWOOD LA
11 WOOD GN

F4
1 PROVIDENCE PL
2 JEVANS CT
3 GALLOWAY LA
4 GALLOWAY CT
5 BRIDGE LA
6 DUNN'S LA
7 NAYFIELD CL
8 HARPER ST
9 FAWCETT GDNS
10 EASTERFIELD CT
11 LANGLEY GARTH
12 FLETCHERS CT

20
20

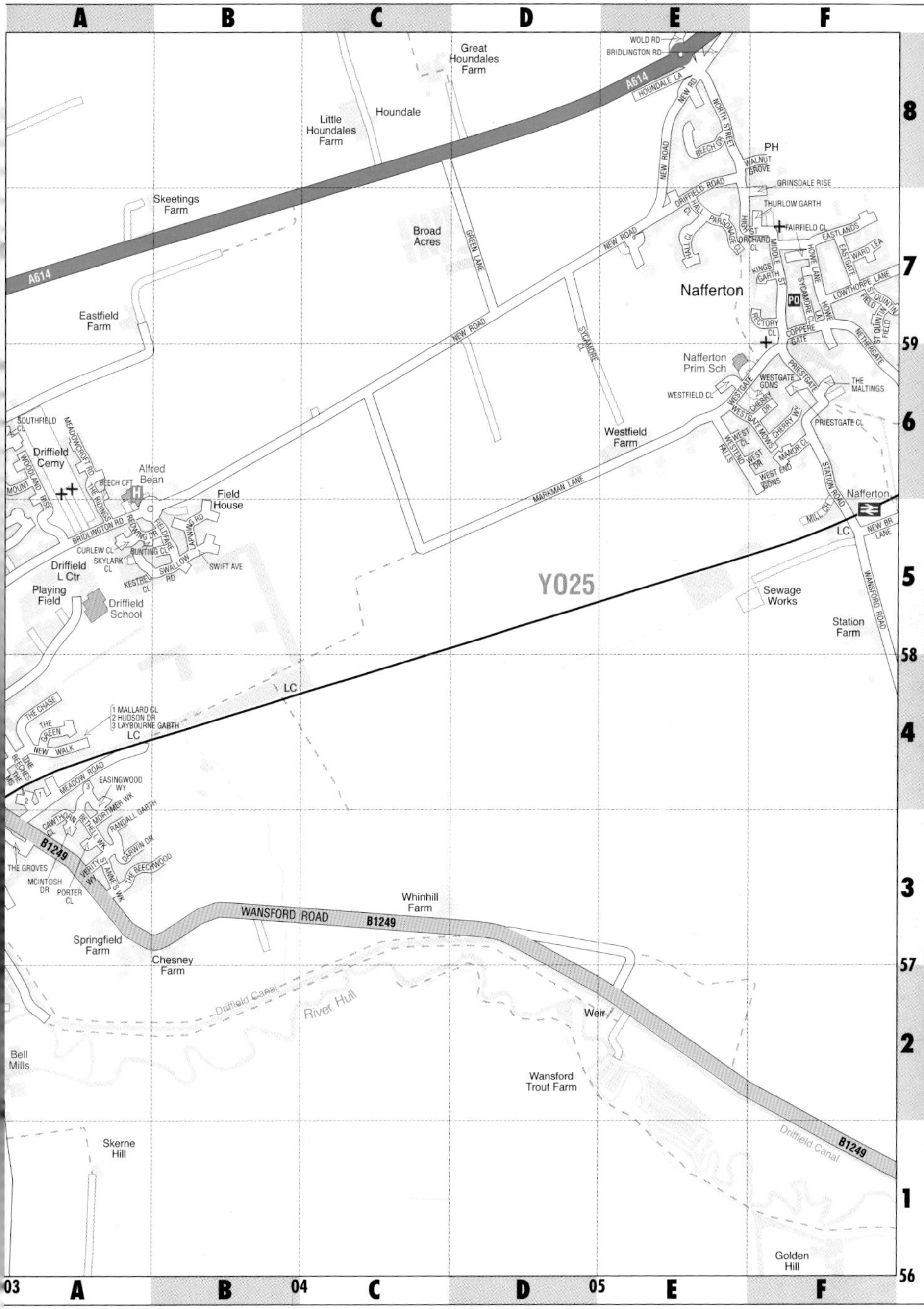

20
21
21
A
B
C
D
E
F
Great Houndales Farm
Houndale
Little Houndales Farm
A614
WOLD RD
BRIDLINGTON RD
HOUNDALE LA
NEW RD
NORTH STREET
BEECH GR
NEW ROAD
PH
WALNUT GROVE
GRINSDALE RISE
THURLOW GARTH
DRIFFIELD ROAD
HALL CL
PARSONAGE CL
HIGH ST
ORCHARD CL
FAIRFIELD CL
EASTLANDS
EASTGATE
WARD LEA
HOWE LANE
MIDDLE ST
KINGS GARTH
SYCAMORE CL
LOWTHORPE LANE
ST QUINTIN FIELD
HOWE LA
Nafferton
PO
RECTORY CL
COPPERE GATE
NETHERGATE
Skeetings Farm
Broad Acres
GREEN LANE
NEW ROAD
Eastfield Farm
NEW ROAD
SYCAMORE CL
Nafferton Prim Sch
WESTGATE
WESTGATE GDNS
PRIESTGATE
THE MALTINGS
WESTFIELD CL
CHERRY DR
WESTGATE MDWS
CHERRY WK
PRIESTGATE CL
SOUTHFIELD CL
MEADOWCROFT RD
Driffield Cemy
WOODLAND RISE
MOUNT
THE RIDINGS
BEECH CFT
Alfred Bean
H
Field House
Westfield Farm
WEST CL
WESTEND FALLS
WEST DR
MANOR CL
WEST END GDNS
STATION ROAD
Nafferton
MARKMAN LANE
MILL CL
LC
NEW BR LANE
BRIDLINGTON RD
REDWING DR
FIELDFARE
LAPWING RD
CURLEW CL
BUNTING CL
SKYLARK CL
SWALLOW RD
SWIFT AVE
KESTREL CL
Driffield L Ctr
Playing Field
Driffield School
YO25
Sewage Works
WANSFORD ROAD
Station Farm
THE CHASE
THE GREEN
NEW WALK
1 MALLARD CL
2 HUDSON DR
3 LAYBOURNE GARTH
LC
LC
THE BEECHES
MEADOW ROAD
EASINGWOOD WY
MORTIMER WK
RANDALL GARTH
CAWTHORN CL
BETHELL WK
DARWIN DR
B1249
THE GROVES
MCINTOSH DR
PORTER CL
VERITY WY
ST ANNE'S WK
THE BEECHWOOD
Whinhill Farm
WANSFORD ROAD
B1249
Springfield Farm
Chesney Farm
Driffield Canal
River Hull
Weir
Bell Mills
Wansford Trout Farm
Skerne Hill
Driffield Canal
B1249
Golden Hill
8
7
59
6
5
58
4
3
57
2
1
56
03
04
05
20
21
21

12
13

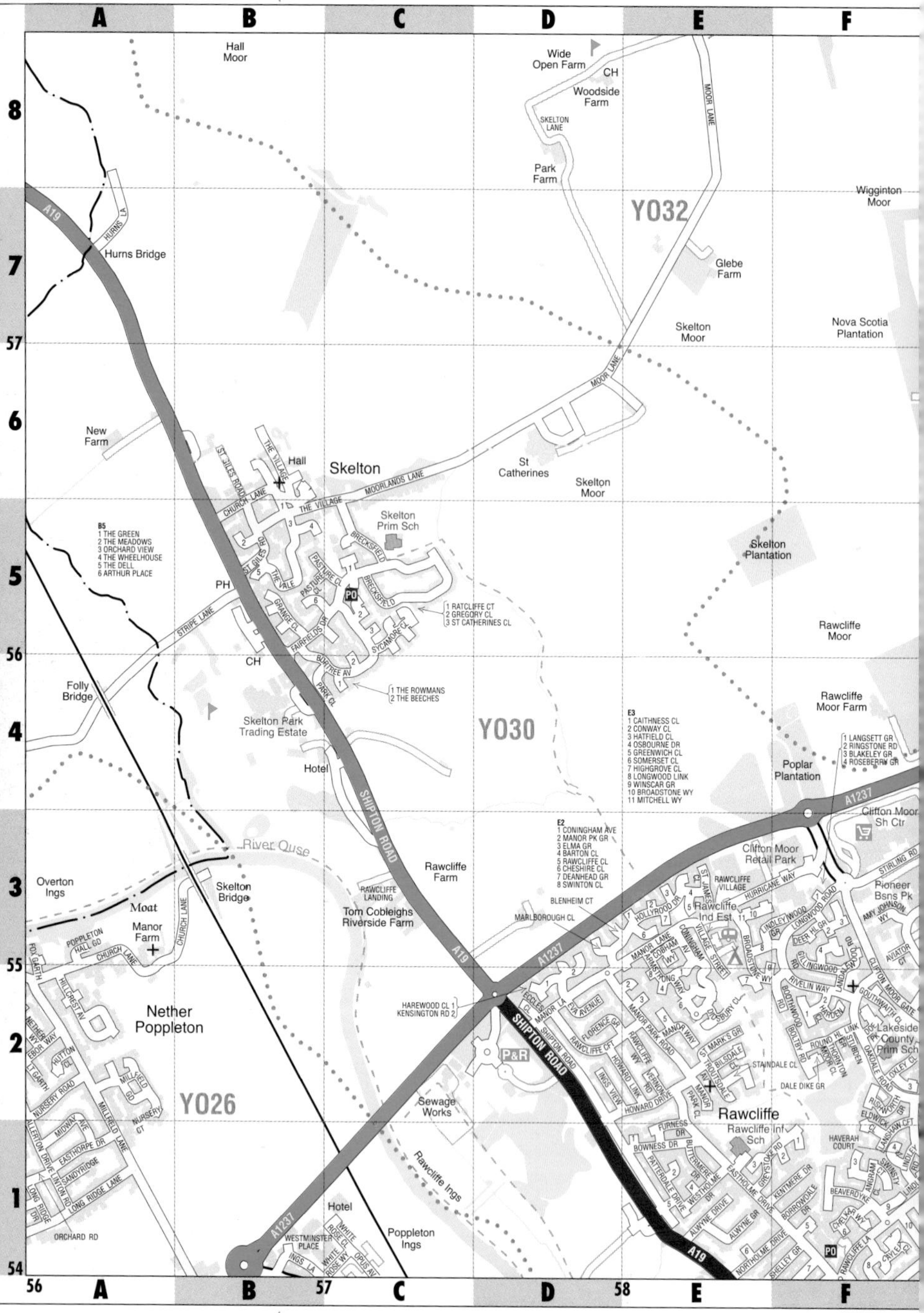

12
129

E1
1 CONISTON CL
2 WASDALE CL
3 GARBURN GR
4 SCAFELL CL
5 LOWESWATER RD
6 FYLINGDALES AVE

F1
1 EMBLETON DR
2 COLEDALE CL
3 LEIGHTON CFT
4 BARMBY CL
5 GRASMERE GR
6 BARDEN CT
7 SOUTHOLME DR
8 MILTON CARR
9 FEWSTON DR
10 REIGHTON DR

F2
1 MOREHALL CL
2 WHARNSCLIFFE DR
3 RYBURN CL

C7
1 PLOUGHLANDS
2 THE GREENWAY
3 FOXCROFT

C8
1 DEALTRY AVE
2 ARENHALL CL
3 MINSTER CL
4 UPPERCROFT
5 BECKS CL
6 THE CHESTNUTS
7 COPWOOD GR
8 HESLIN CL
9 RUDDINGS CL
10 HUNTERS CL
11 CORNWOOD WY

13

D8
1 MEADOW LN
2 CHERRY ORCHARD
3 ORCHARD PADDOCK
4 CHERRY PADDOCK

128

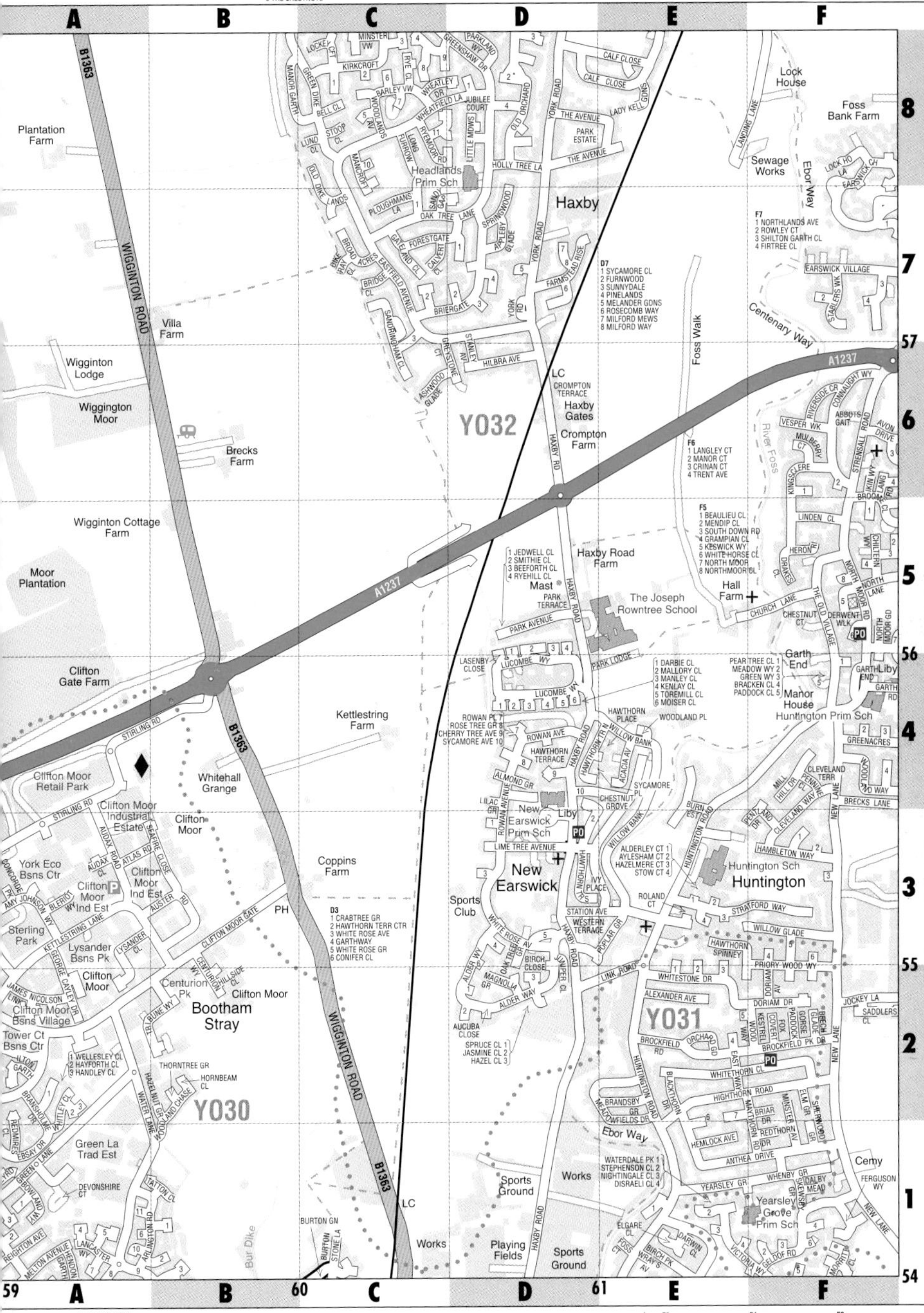

A1
1 CALDBECK CL
2 STONELANDS CT
3 BELMONT CL
4 HASTINGS CL
5 HARROW GLADE
6 WIMPOLE CL
7 HALIFAX CT
8 WATER LA
9 TAMWORTH RD
10 LUNDY CLOSE
11 PENTIRE CLOSE

B1
1 HERDWICK CL
2 HEADLEY CL
3 MINCHIN CL

130

128

E2
1 SCAWTON AVE
2 GORMIRE AVE
3 ROLSTON AVE
4 HEATHER CFT
5 BADGER PADDOCK
6 PINEWOOD GR
7 THORNFIELD DR

F1
1 DICKENS CL
2 HOMESTEAD CL
3 CARRNOCK CT
4 ANDREW DR
5 MONKTON RD
6 THERESA CL

F3
1 CHEVIOT CL
2 CAMBRIAN CL
3 KENDREW CL
4 MERLIN COVERT
5 FIRWOOD WHIN
6 OAK GLADE

127 14 14

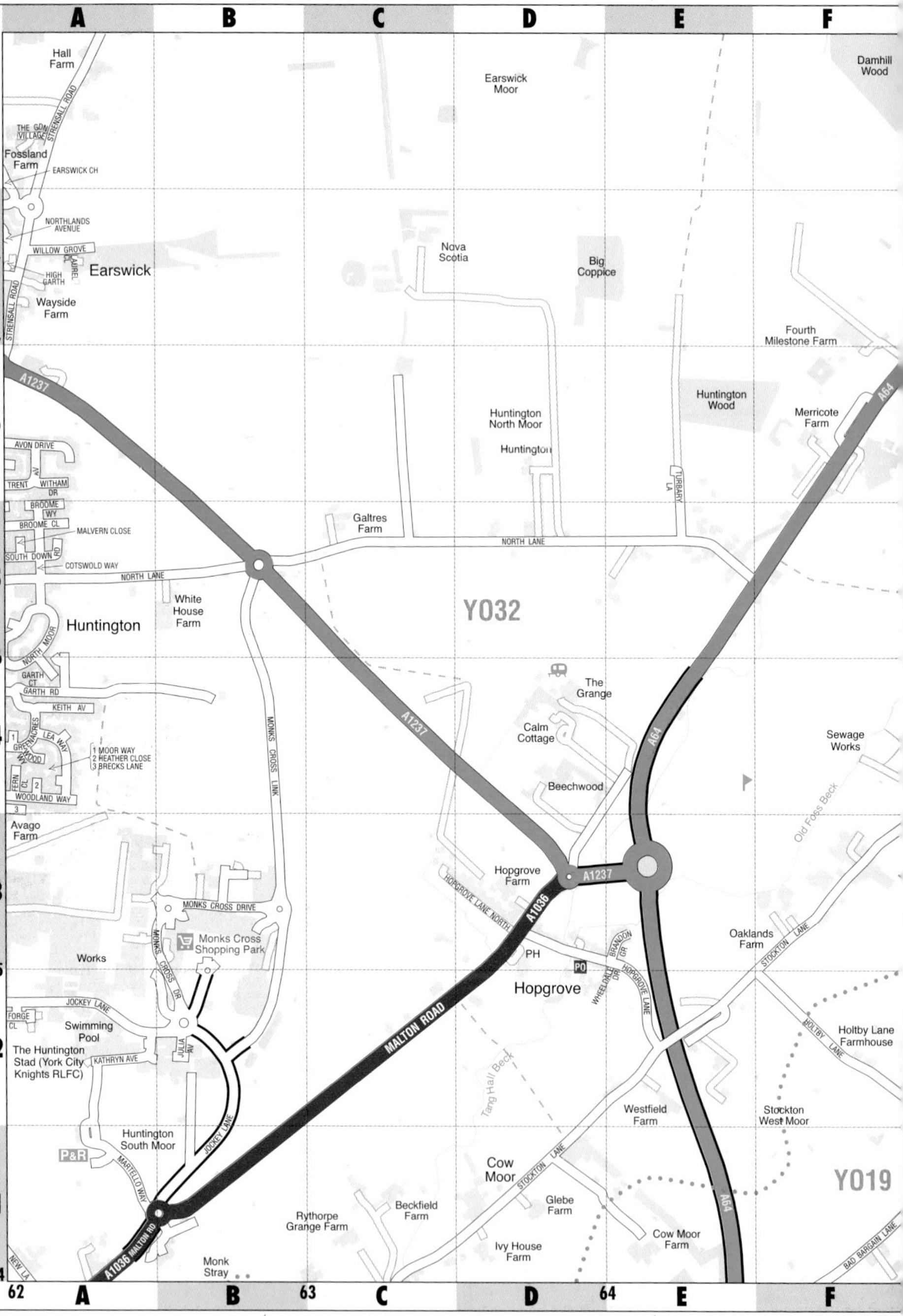

A B C D E F
8 7 6 5 4 3 2 1
57 56 55 54
62 63 64
Hall Farm
STRENSALL ROAD
THE GDN VILLAGE
Fossland Farm
EARSWICK CH
NORTHLANDS AVENUE
WILLOW GROVE
LAUREL CL
HIGH GARTH
Earswick
Wayside Farm
Earswick Moor
Damhill Wood
Nova Scotia
Big Coppice
Fourth Milestone Farm
A1237
Huntington Wood
Merricote Farm
A64
Huntington North Moor
Huntington
AVON DRIVE
TRENT AV
WITHAM DR
BROOME WY
BROOME CL
MALVERN CLOSE
SOUTH DOWN RD
COTSWOLD WAY
TURBARY LA
Galtres Farm
NORTH LANE
White House Farm
YO32
Huntington
NORTH MOOR
GARTH CT
GARTH RD
KEITH AV
The Grange
MONKS CROSS LINK
Calm Cottage
GREENACRES
LEA WAY
1 MOOR WAY
2 HEATHER CLOSE
3 BRECKS LANE
Sewage Works
FERN CL
WOODLAND WAY
Beechwood
Old Foss Beck
Avago Farm
Hopgrove Farm
HOPGROVE LANE NORTH
A1036
MONKS CROSS DRIVE
Monks Cross Shopping Park
Oaklands Farm
STOCKTON LANE
BRANDON GR
Works
PH
PO
WHEELDALE DR
HOPGROVE LANE
Hopgrove
JOCKEY LANE
FORGE CL
Swimming Pool
MONKS CROSS DR
JULIA AV
MALTON ROAD
HOLTBY LANE
Holtby Lane Farmhouse
The Huntington Stad (York City Knights RLFC)
KATHRYN AVE
Tang Hall Beck
Westfield Farm
Stockton West Moor
Huntington South Moor
P&R
JOCKEY LANE
MARTELLO WAY
Cow Moor
YO19
Beckfield Farm
Glebe Farm
Rythorpe Grange Farm
Cow Moor Farm
NEW LA
A1036 MALTON RD
Monk Stray
Ivy House Farm
BAD BARGAIN LANE

127 131 14

24 | 126 | 130

D6
1 REGENTS MS
2 MARQUIS CT
3 DUKES CT

F5
1 CHUDLEIGH RD
2 BROMLEY ST
3 ALBANY ST
4 WALWORTH ST N
5 HANOVER ST E
6 UPR HANOVER ST
7 HANOVER ST W
8 STAMFORD ST W
9 WALWORTH ST S
10 STAMFORD ST E
11 KINGSLAND TERR
12 BRUNNEL CT
13 ST BARNABAS CT
14 REGENTS CT
15 VICTORIA CT
16 CARLISLE ST
17 CARLETON ST

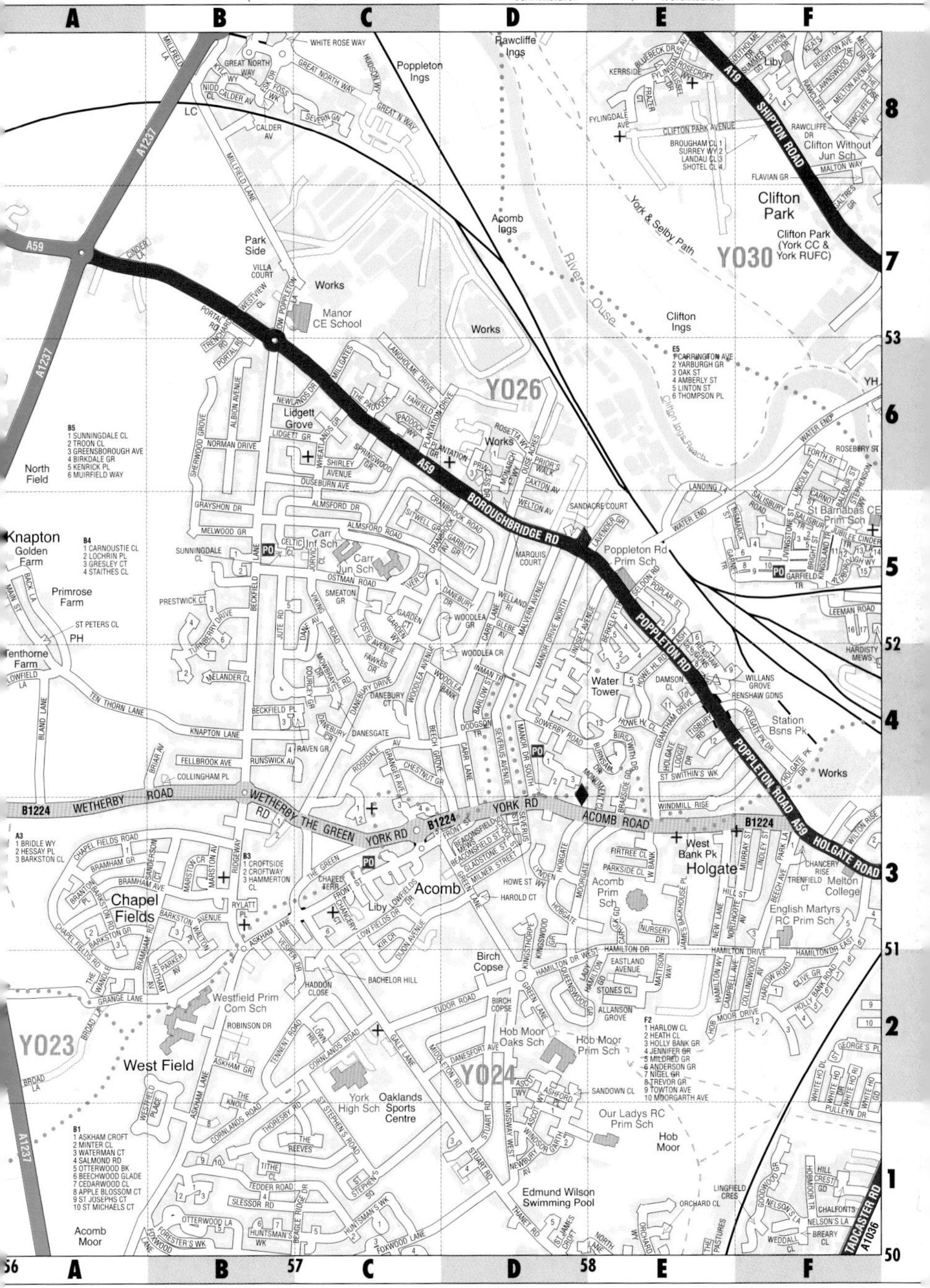

C1
1 THORNWOOD COVERT
2 MAPLEWOOD PADDOCK
3 FOXWOOD LANE
4 HERMAN WALK
5 FIR HEATH CL

C3
1 KIRK VIEW
2 CHURCH MEWS
3 ELMTREE GDNS
4 OAK RISE
5 CROSS ST
6 GALE FARM CT

D1
1 WOODFORD PL
2 KEMPTON CL
3 CLAY PL
4 CHESNEY FIELDS
5 ST JAMES PLACE

D4
1 PATELY PL
2 HEBDON RISE
3 BAILDON CL

E4
1 WINCHESTER GR
2 GARLAND ST
3 WINCHESTER AVE
4 CHATSWORTH TERR
5 DILYS GR
6 PEPPERCORN CL
7 BONINGTON CT
8 RENSHAW GDNS
9 HILLARY GARTH
10 SEGRAVE WK
11 MANTHORPE WK
12 CHELWOOD WK
13 BOUTHWAITE DR

F3
1 FALCONER ST
2 ENFIELD CRES
3 BARRETT AVE
4 BARBARA GR
5 CAROLINE CL
6 ROBIN GR

24 | 132 | 130

A8
1 LINDEN GROVE
2 MARTEN CLOSE
3 RAINSBOROUGH WAY
4 LOCKYER CL

A7
1 BELCOMBE WAY
2 HUDSON CRESCENT
3 CLIFTON PLACE
4 PINFOLD COURT

129

C7
1 UPR NEWBOROUGH ST
2 ALLAN ST
3 MURROUGH WILSON PL
4 FEVERSHAM CRES
5 HILLSBOROUGH TERR
6 HUDSON ST

127

E8
1 KIRKHAM AVE
2 THE CROSSWAY
3 LILLING AVE
4 PINSENT CT

E5
1 HAWTHORN ST
2 EMMERSON ST
3 FLEMING AVE
4 SCROPE AVE

F8
1 ALBERT CL
2 VICTORIA WY
3 MORRITT CL
4 FOSTON GR
5 THORNFIELD AVE
6 LABURNUM GARTH

For full street detail of the highlighted area see page 156

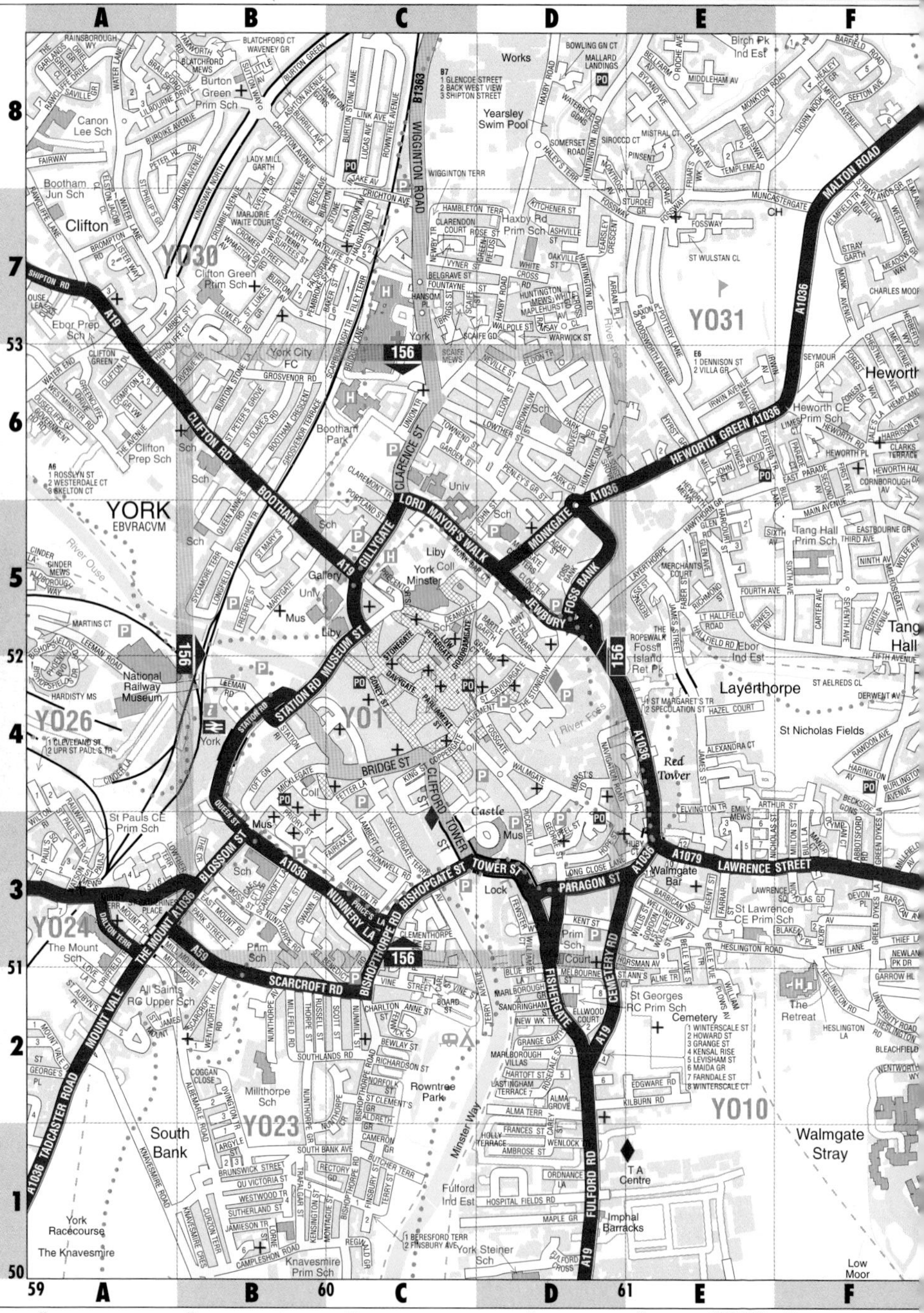

A B C D E F

A2
1 TOWTON AVE
2 TRENTHOLME DR
3 MOORGARTH AVE
4 WHITE HO GDNS

A3
1 ENFIELD CRES
2 WATSON TERR
3 CECILIA PL
4 CAMBRIDGE ST
5 OXFORD ST
6 MOUNT EPHRAIM
7 HOLGATE BR GDNS

129

B1
1 WINDSOR ST
2 HUBERT ST
3 RUBY ST
4 COUNT DE BURGH TERR
5 BALMORAL TERR
6 LICHFIELD CT

133

B2
1 TELFORD TERR
2 PHILADELPHIA TERR
3 ADELAIDE ST

E3
1 BRINKWORTH TERR
2 THOMAS ST
3 HILDA ST
4 GRANVILLE TERR
5 LANSDOWNE TERR
6 HERBERT ST
7 CHAUCER ST
8 DAYSFOOT CT
9 APOLLO ST
10 THE TANNERY
11 LAWRENCE CT
12 LEAKE ST

F3
1 ST NICHOLAS PL
2 ARNSIDE PL

A5
1 MELROSE CL
2 APPLEBY PL
3 INGLETON WK
4 WOODHOUSE GR
5 HORNBY CT

128

26

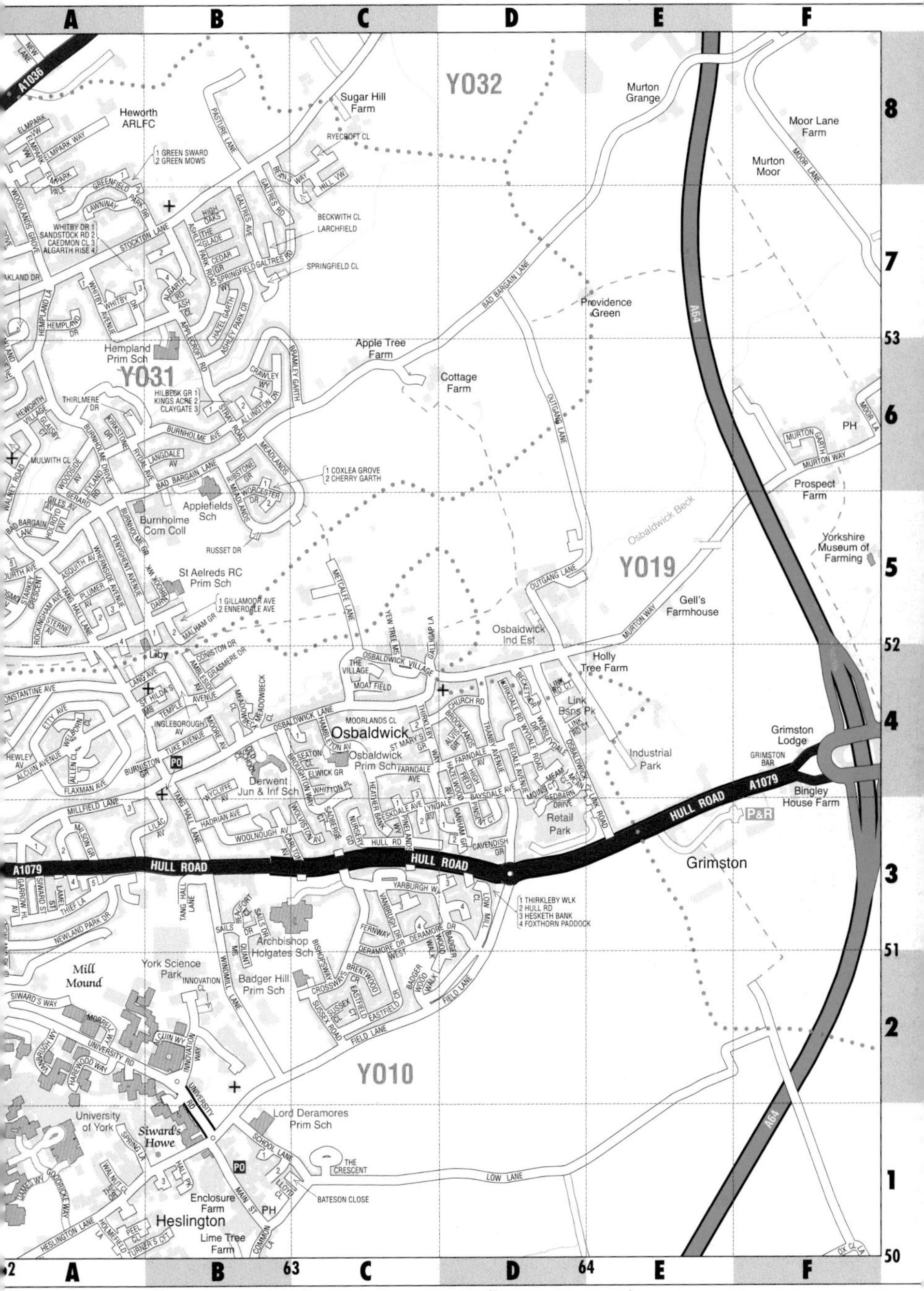

A3
1 HEATHFIELD RD
2 OWSTON AVE
3 WAYNEFLEET GR
4 CYCLE ST
5 NORMAN ST

B1
1 ENCLOSURE GDNS
2 HESLINGTON CT
3 HOLBURNS CFT

C3
1 SHALLOWDALE GR
2 BRACKEN HILL
3 KIMBERLOWS WOOD HILL
4 PINEWOOD HILL

C4
1 VICARAGE GDNS
2 ST THOMAS'S CL
3 GIVENDALE GR

26

26

24
129

C8
1 HINTON AVE
2 LYDHAM CT
3 MARTIN CHEESEMAN CT
4 CRANFIELD PL
5 DOHERTHY WLK
6 BURGESS WLK

D8
1 FARMLANDS RD
2 DRINGFIELD CL
3 HERDSMAN RD
4 SANDCROFT CL
5 DEEPDALE

E8
1 TURNMIRE RD
2 SOUTHFIELD CRES
3 MEADOW CT
4 THE PASTURES
5 ST HELEN'S RD
6 RAILWAY VW

F8
1 KENSINGTON CT
2 REGENCY MEWS
3 CALCARIA CT

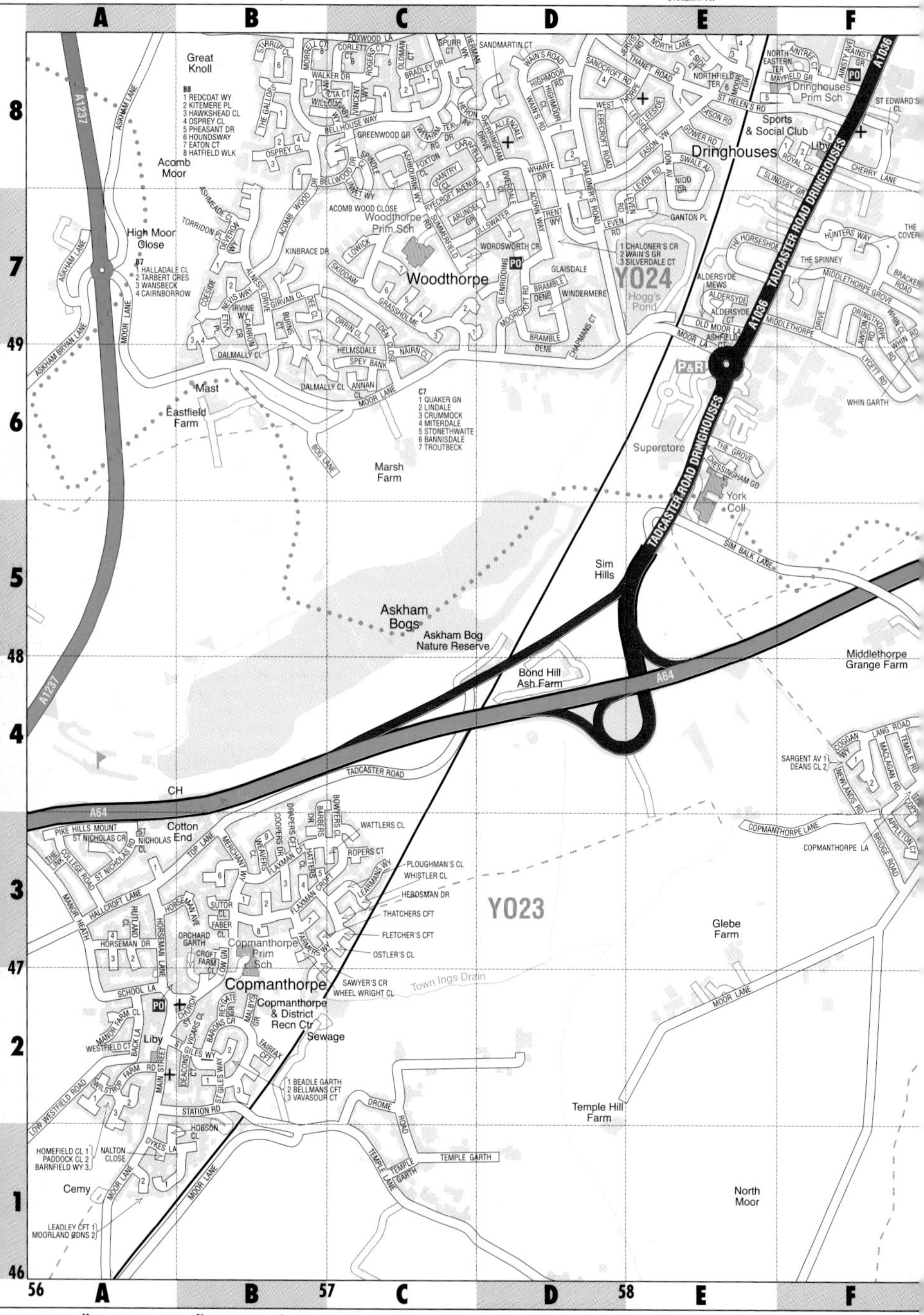

A3
1 LARKFIELD CL
2 HORSEMAN CL
3 LYNWOOD AVE
4 LYNWOOD VW

B3
1 SADDLERS CL
2 FARRIERS CFT
3 WAGGONERS DR
4 POTTERS DR
5 WAINERS CL
6 MILLERS CFT
7 LORINERS DR
8 GARDENERS CL
9 WEAVERS PK

24
36

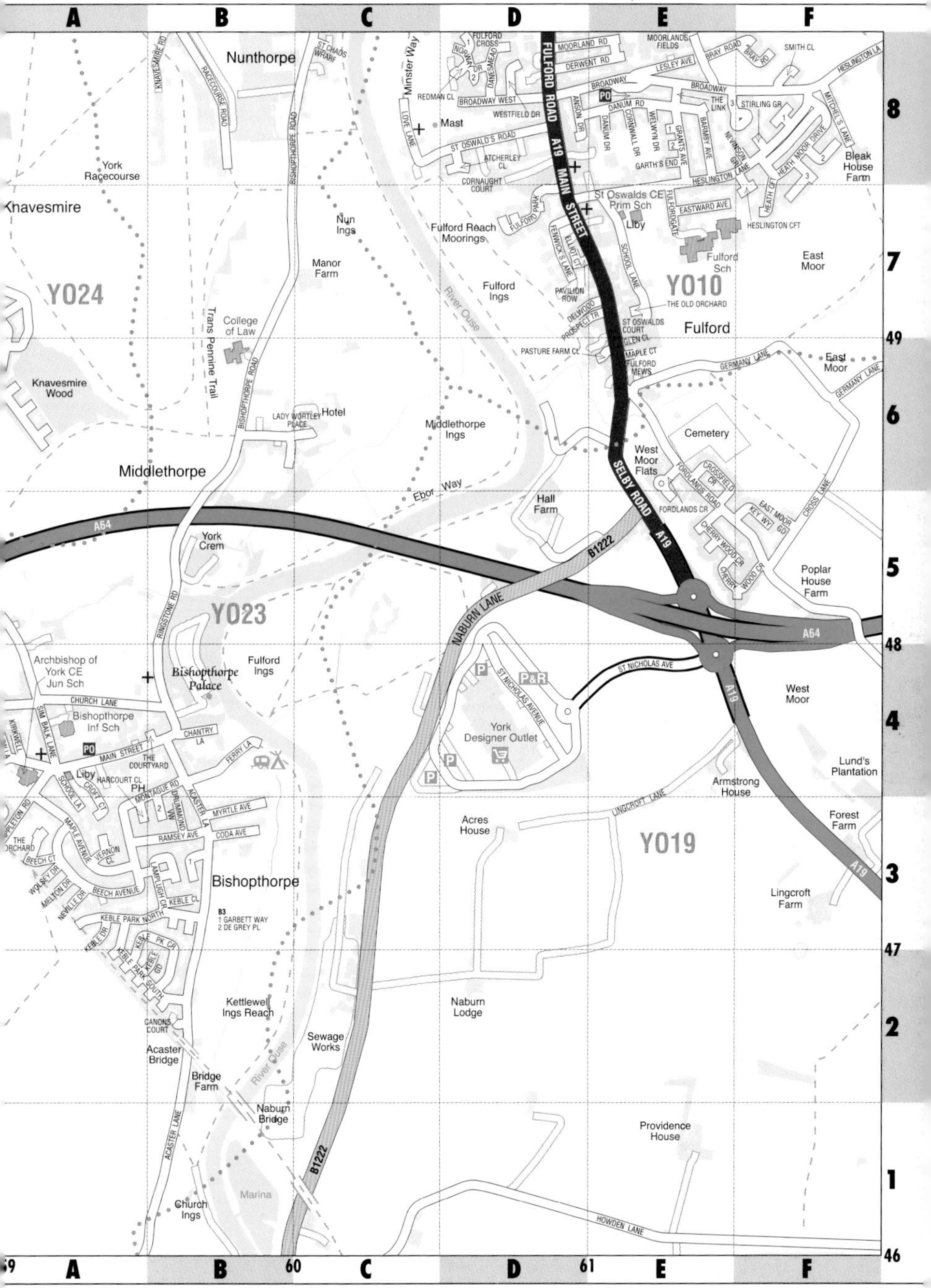
A B C D E F
8 7 49 6 5 48 4 3 47 2 1 46
59 60 61
Nunthorpe
ST CHADS WHARF
KNAVESMIRE RD
RACECOURSE ROAD
BISHOPTHORPE ROAD
Minster Way
LOVE LANE
Mast
REDMAN CL
FULFORD CROSS
NORWAY DR
DANESMEAD
BROADWAY WEST
WESTFIELD DR
ST OSWALD'S ROAD
ATCHERLEY CL
CORNAUGHT COURT
FULFORD ROAD
A19
MAIN STREET
MOORLAND RD
DERWENT RD
MOORLANDS FIELDS
LESLEY AVE
BROADWAY
PO
DANUM RD
ANSON DR
CORNWALL DR
WELWYN DR
GRANTS AVE
BARMBY AVE
GARTH'S END
THE LINK
STIRLING GR
NEVINSON GR
HESLINGTON LANE
BRAY ROAD
BRAY RD
SMITH CL
HESLINGTON LA
MITCHEL'S LANE
HEATH MOOR DRIVE
HEATH CFT
Bleak House Farm
York Racecourse
Knavesmire
St Oswalds CE Prim Sch
Liby
FULFORD PARK
EASTWARD AVE
FULFORDGATE
HESLINGTON CFT
Nun Ings
Fulford Reach Moorings
FENWICK'S LANE
ELLIOT CT
SCHOOL LANE
Fulford Sch
East Moor
Manor Farm
YO24
Fulford Ings
River Ouse
PAVILION ROW
DELWOOD
PROSPECT TR
ST OSWALDS COURT
GLEN CL
YO10
THE OLD ORCHARD
Fulford
Trans Pennine Trail
College of Law
PASTURE FARM CL
MAPLE CT
FULFORD MEWS
GERMANY LANE
East Moor
Knavesmire Wood
LADY WORTLEY PLACE
Hotel
Middlethorpe Ings
Cemetery
West Moor Flats
SELBY ROAD
FORDLANDS ROAD
CROSSFIELD CR
FORDLANDS CR
EAST MOOR GD
KEY WY
CROSS LANE
Middlethorpe
Ebor Way
Hall Farm
CHERRY WOOD CR
A64
York Crem
B1222
Poplar House Farm
YO23
RINGSTONE RD
NABURN LANE
Archbishop of York CE Jun Sch
Fulford Ings
Bishopthorpe Palace
ST NICHOLAS AVE
ST NICHOLAS AVENUE
P&R
West Moor
CHURCH LANE
Bishopthorpe Inf Sch
SIM BALK LANE
KIRKWELL
CHANTRY LA
MAIN STREET
THE COURTYARD
FERRY LA
York Designer Outlet
Lund's Plantation
Liby
HARCOURT CL
PH
SCHOOL LA
CROFT CT
MONTAGUE RD
DRUMMOND VW
ACASTER LA
MYRTLE AVE
Armstrong House
LINGCROFT LANE
Acres House
Forest Farm
YO19
RAMSEY AVE
CODA AVE
APPLETON RD
THE ORCHARD
MAPLE AVENUE
VERNON CL
BEECH CT
WOLSEY DR
MELTON DR
NEVILLE DR
BEECH AVENUE
LAMPLUGH CR
KEBLE CL
Bishopthorpe
KEBLE PARK NORTH
B3
1 GARBETT WAY
2 DE GREY PL
KEBLE DR
KEBLE PK CR
KEBLE GD
KEBLE PARK SOUTH
Lingcroft Farm
Kettlewell Ings Reach
Naburn Lodge
CANONS COURT
Acaster Bridge
Sewage Works
Bridge Farm
Naburn Bridge
ACASTER LANE
Providence House
Marina
Church Ings
HOWDEN LANE

35
35

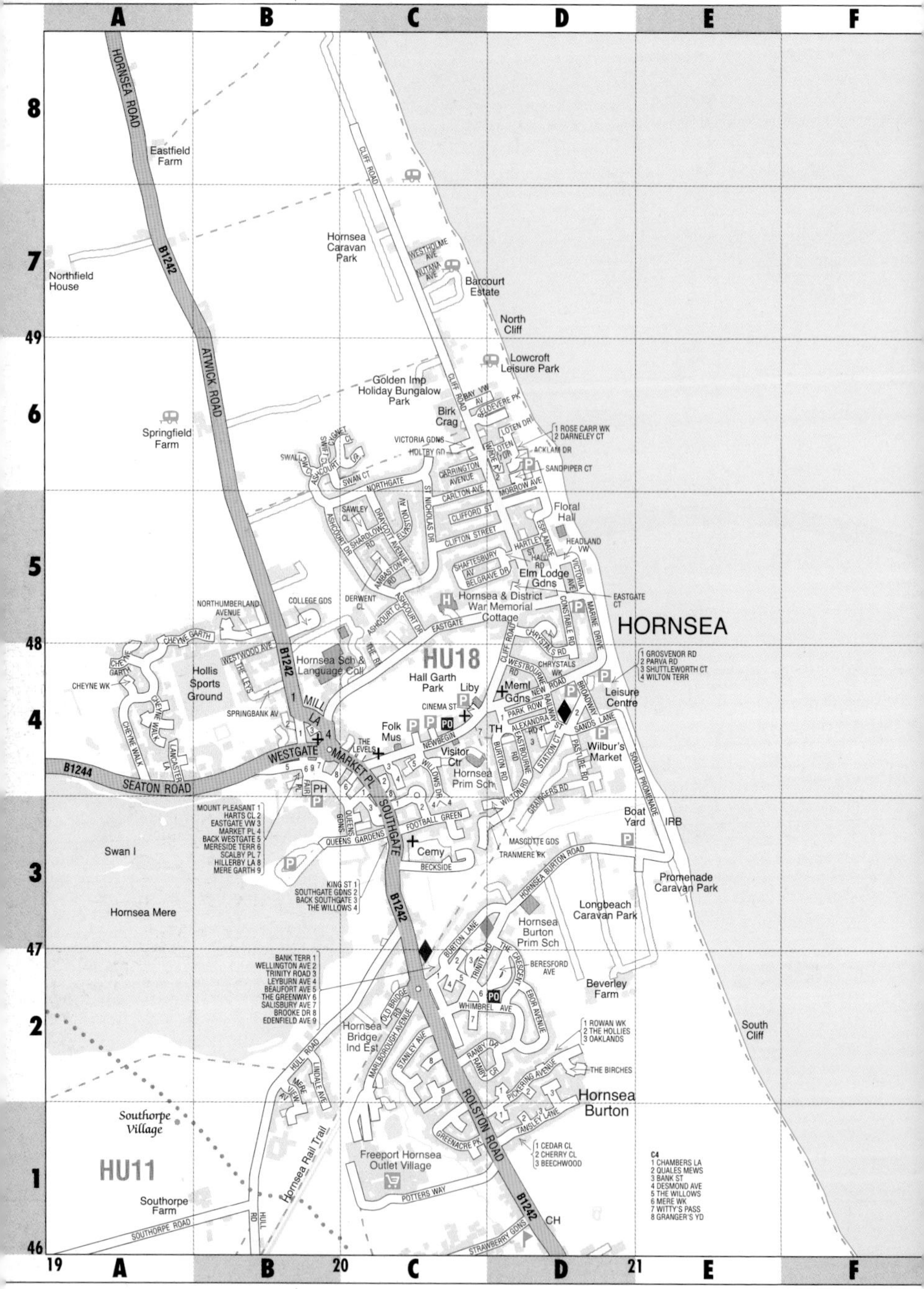
HORNSEA
HU18
HU11
HORNSEA ROAD
ATWICK ROAD
B1242
B1244
SEATON ROAD
WESTGATE
MARKET PL
SOUTHGATE
ROLSTON ROAD
CLIFF ROAD
EASTGATE
NORTHGATE
MARINE DRIVE
SOUTH PROMENADE
HORNSEA BURTON ROAD
HULL ROAD
SOUTHORPE ROAD
POTTERS WAY
Hornsea Rail Trail
Eastfield Farm
Northfield House
Springfield Farm
Hornsea Caravan Park
Barcourt Estate
North Cliff
Lowcroft Leisure Park
Golden Imp Holiday Bungalow Park
Birk Crag
Floral Hall
Elm Lodge Gdns
Hornsea & District War Memorial Cottage
Hollis Sports Ground
Hornsea Sch & Language Coll
Hall Garth Park
Liby
Meml Gdns
Leisure Centre
Folk Mus
Visitor Ctr
Hornsea Prim Sch
Wilbur's Market
Boat Yard
IRB
Swan I
Hornsea Mere
Cemy
Promenade Caravan Park
Longbeach Caravan Park
Hornsea Burton Prim Sch
Beverley Farm
South Cliff
Hornsea Bridge Ind Est
Hornsea Burton
Southorpe Village
Southorpe Farm
Freeport Hornsea Outlet Village
MOUNT PLEASANT 1
HARTS CL 2
EASTGATE VW 3
MARKET PL 4
BACK WESTGATE 5
MERESIDE TERR 6
SCALBY PL 7
HILLERBY LA 8
MERE GARTH 9
KING ST 1
SOUTHGATE GDNS 2
BACK SOUTHGATE 3
THE WILLOWS 4
BANK TERR 1
WELLINGTON AVE 2
TRINITY ROAD 3
LEYBURN AVE 4
BEAUFORT AVE 5
THE GREENWAY 6
SALISBURY AVE 7
BROOKE DR 8
EDENFIELD AVE 9
1 ROSE CARR WK
2 DARNELEY CT
1 GROSVENOR RD
2 PARVA RD
3 SHUTTLEWORTH CT
4 WILTON TERR
1 ROWAN WK
2 THE HOLLIES
3 OAKLANDS
1 CEDAR CL
2 CHERRY CL
3 BEECHWOOD
C4
1 CHAMBERS LA
2 QUALES MEWS
3 BANK ST
4 DESMOND AVE
5 THE WILLOWS
6 MERE WK
7 WITTY'S PASS
8 GRANGER'S YD
A
B
C
D
E
F
8
7
49
6
5
48
4
3
47
2
1
46
19
20
21

35
46

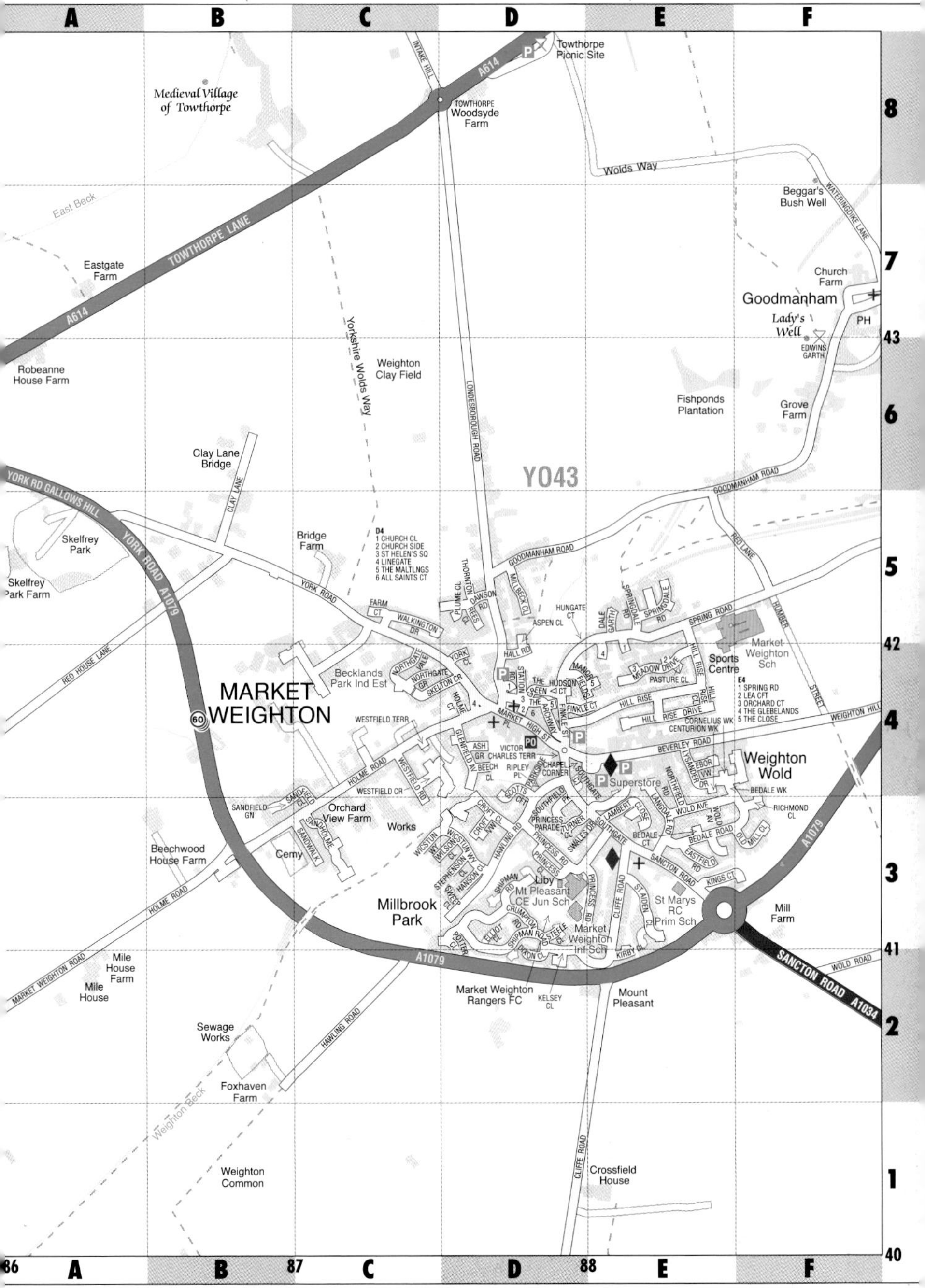
40
41
41
A
B
C
D
E
F
Towthorpe Picnic Site
Medieval Village of Towthorpe
TOWTHORPE Woodsyde Farm
INTAKE HILL
A614
Wolds Way
Beggar's Bush Well
WATERINGDIKE LANE
East Beck
TOWTHORPE LANE
Eastgate Farm
Church Farm
Goodmanham
Lady's Well
PH
EDWINS GARTH
Robeanne House Farm
Weighton Clay Field
Yorkshire Wolds Way
LONDESBOROUGH ROAD
Fishponds Plantation
Grove Farm
Clay Lane Bridge
CLAY LANE
YO43
GOODMANHAM ROAD
YORK RD GALLOWS HILL
YORK ROAD
A1079
Skelfrey Park
Skelfrey Park Farm
Bridge Farm
D4
1 CHURCH CL
2 CHURCH SIDE
3 ST HELEN'S SQ
4 LINEGATE
5 THE MALTLNGS
6 ALL SAINTS CT
RED LANE
SPRING ROAD
Market Weighton Sch
Sports Centre
HUMBER STREET
E4
1 SPRING RD
2 LEA CFT
3 ORCHARD CT
4 THE GLEBELANDS
5 THE CLOSE
RED HOUSE LANE
Becklands Park Ind Est
MARKET WEIGHTON
WESTFIELD TERR
WEIGHTON HILL
BEVERLEY ROAD
Weighton Wold
Superstore
BEDALE WK
RICHMOND CL
SANDFIELD GN
Orchard View Farm
Works
HOLME ROAD
Beechwood House Farm
Cemy
Millbrook Park
Liby
Mt Pleasant CE Jun Sch
St Marys RC Prim Sch
Market Weighton Inf Sch
Mill Farm
SANCTON ROAD A1034
WOLD ROAD
MARKET WEIGHTON ROAD
Mile House Farm
Mile House
Market Weighton Rangers FC
KELSEY CL
Mount Pleasant
HAWLING ROAD
Sewage Works
Foxhaven Farm
Weighton Beck
CLIFFE ROAD
Weighton Common
Crossfield House
8
7
43
6
5
42
4
3
41
2
1
40
86
87
88

43
43

D6
1 WOODHALL DR
2 MOLESCROFT W CL
3 MOLESCROFT AVE
4 MOLESCROFT PK
5 MOLESCROFT GDNS

F7
1 WOODCOATES CL
2 MEADOW BANK
3 BEECH TREE CL
4 BRAMBLE GARTH
5 WILLOW TREE GARTH

43
55

E1
1 LEATHLEY CL
2 CAVENDISH DR
3 BERKELEY DR
4 HEREFORD CL
5 WINCHESTER AVE
6 OXFORD CL
7 ST ALBANS CL
8 CATHEDRAL CL
9 WELTON CL

For full street detail of the highlighted area see page 154.

A6
1 SOUTHFIELD DR
2 SIGSTON RD
3 EASTFIELD CL
4 SYMMONS CL

44
44

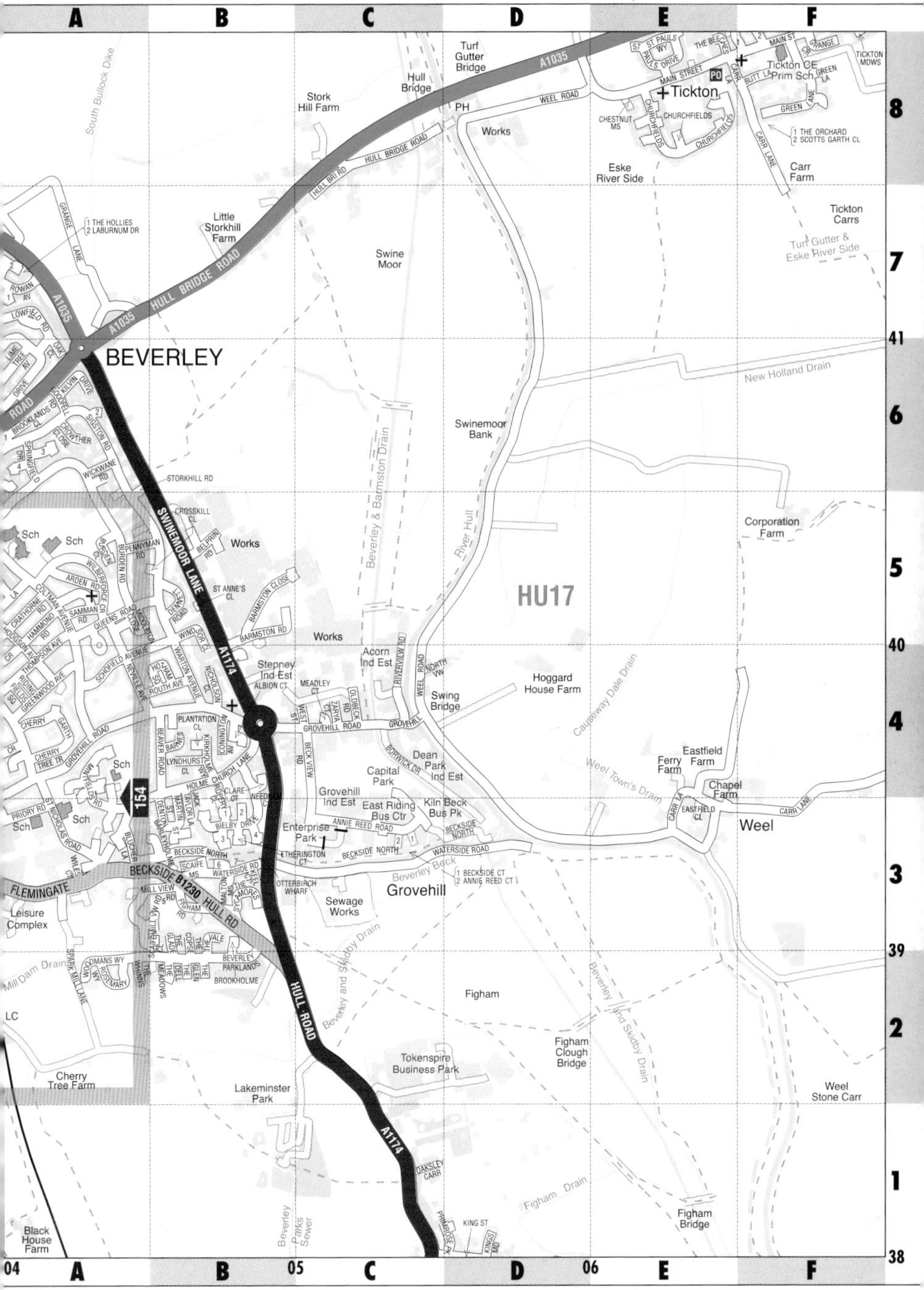

B3
1 TATTERSALL DR
2 HOLGATE CL
3 GILLYON CL
4 AKESTER CL
5 MILL VIEW PL
6 BARKERS MILL
7 MARIN CT

56
44

55
55

A
B
C
D
E
F
8
7
33
6
5
32
4
3
31
2
1
30
01
02
03
Pit (dis)
Sewage Works
CH
Field House Farm
Skidby
CAROLINES PL
PH
Eastfield Farm
CHURCH RI
CHAPEL CL
MAIN STREET
DAVID'S CL
Townend Farm
Skidby Hill Farm
A164
WOOD HILL WAY
B1233
HARLAND WAY
Cottingham High Sch
BADGERS WOOD
PARK LANE
LITTLE WEIGHTON RD
ORCHARD RD
ST MICHAEL'S CL
SOUTH RI
MILL RI
APPLE CFT
TRINITY GARTH
RIPLINGHAM RD
Skidby CE Prim Sch
CHERRY TREES
FORGE PL
MILL ROAD
KELDGATE ROAD
BEVERLEY ROAD
The Lawns
FERENS GD
Skidby Windmill & Museum of East Riding Rural Life
Cemy
Keldgate Reservoirs
HU16
E6
1 NEWBALD WY
2 WELTON AVE
3 SWANLAND WY
4 ELLOUGHTON GR
5 BRANTINGHAM CL
6 GOODMANHAM WY
THE WOODLANDS
MILL LANE
Cemetery
WEST END RD
Gallows Hill
Keldgate
Keldgate Springs
EPPLEWORTH ROAD
THE DALES
SANCTON CL
THE WOLDS
STEWART GARTH
RYDAL GR
THE RIDINGS
PARKSIDE CL
DENE ROAD
WESTFIELD RD
Epplewort Head
LUND AV
ST MARGARETS CL
MAYLAND DR
BONDYKE CL
ST MARGARET'S AVE
Westfield Prim Sch
WESTFIELD CL
WESTFIELD RD
GREEN LANE
Castle Hill
HUME CR
CASTLE GN
BECK RD
ARRAS DR
DRIFFIELD CL
CAVE CR
SPENCER CL
WINSTON DR
CHURCHILL AV
WOODSTOCK CL
SOUTHWOOD AVE
SOUTHWOOD ROAD
Near Stions Farm
Far Stions Farm
P
H
GREENDALE CT
HOLLY DR
BIRDSALL CL
ETTON CL
Grange Farm
Quarry (dis)
Tower
CASTLE ROAD
CANADA DRIVE
QUEBEC DR
ST LAWRENCE AV
BURTON RD
MURRAY CR
MEADOW WY
SOUTHWOOD GD
THE CLOSE
East Cottage Farm
White House Farm
WESTFIELD ROAD
TRAVIS RD
AWMAND GREEN
Plattwood Farm
BELTHAM GN
Hindhouse Farm
Eppleworth
Stackyard Farm
Willerby Hill Farm
F5
1 TOWNSHEND DR
2 INVEREWE WY
3 CHELSEA CT
4 MONTREAL CRES
5 SOUTH FIELD CT
6 OTTAWA CL
7 WOLFE CL
8 MONTCALM WK
9 MAPLELEAF CT
10 MONKTON CL
11 RAMSDEN PL
GREEN LA
Green Lane Farm
Willerby Hl Bsns Pk
Haltenprice Crem
Low Farm
WILLERBY LOW ROAD
MAIN STREET
Chalk Pit (dis)
Haggs Farm
Landfill
HAGGS LANE
HAGGS LA
Haggs House Farm
Hotel
Mast
ALBION LANE
WHITE HOUSE CL
OAK HL
EDEN RI
ELLERKER RISE
HU10
DERRYMORE ROAD
THE REDWOODS
ABBEY LANE
Church End Farm
PH
Church Farm
B1232
GRANGE PARK LANE
YORK WAY
VICTORIA AV
WELL LA
FISHER CL
Bellfield Farm
Abbey Grove
GREAT GUTTER LANE WEST
Rawdales Farm
GREAT GUTTER LA
VIKING CL
ST STEPHEN'S CL
BEECHFIELD DR
WELL LANE
ASHGATE RD
GLOUCESTER RD
THE HOLLIES
SOUTHGATE CL
WHEATCROFT AV
THE PARKWAY
SWADDALE AV
BRIMINGTON RD
BESSACARR AV
Hotel
BELLFIELD DR
Liby
Willerby Bottom
ASHWORTH DR
Parson Pit
BEVERLEY ROAD
Factory
JOHN GRAY CT
Wolfreton Lower Sch
Carr Lane Inf Sch
NORTHSTEAD CL
Carr Lane Prim Sch
LADYSMITH RD
THE CLOSE
WILLINGHAM WY
GLENFIELD DR
OAKLANDS DR
KINGSLEY DR
PO
REGENT CL
LAYTON GARTH
CHILTON RI
ANNANDALE RD
GLENDALE CL
TUDOR CT
CARR LANE
THE OCTAGON
ASH GROVE
WILLOW CT
LIME AVENUE
BIRCH DR
WOLFRETON LANE
APPLETREE MS
KINGSTON
B1232 RD
FERNDALE AV
LILAC AVE
HAWTHORNE AVENUE
OVERTON AV
PRUNUS AV
RIPLINGHAM ROAD
THE GLEN
FAIRFIELD AVE
Willerby

55
143

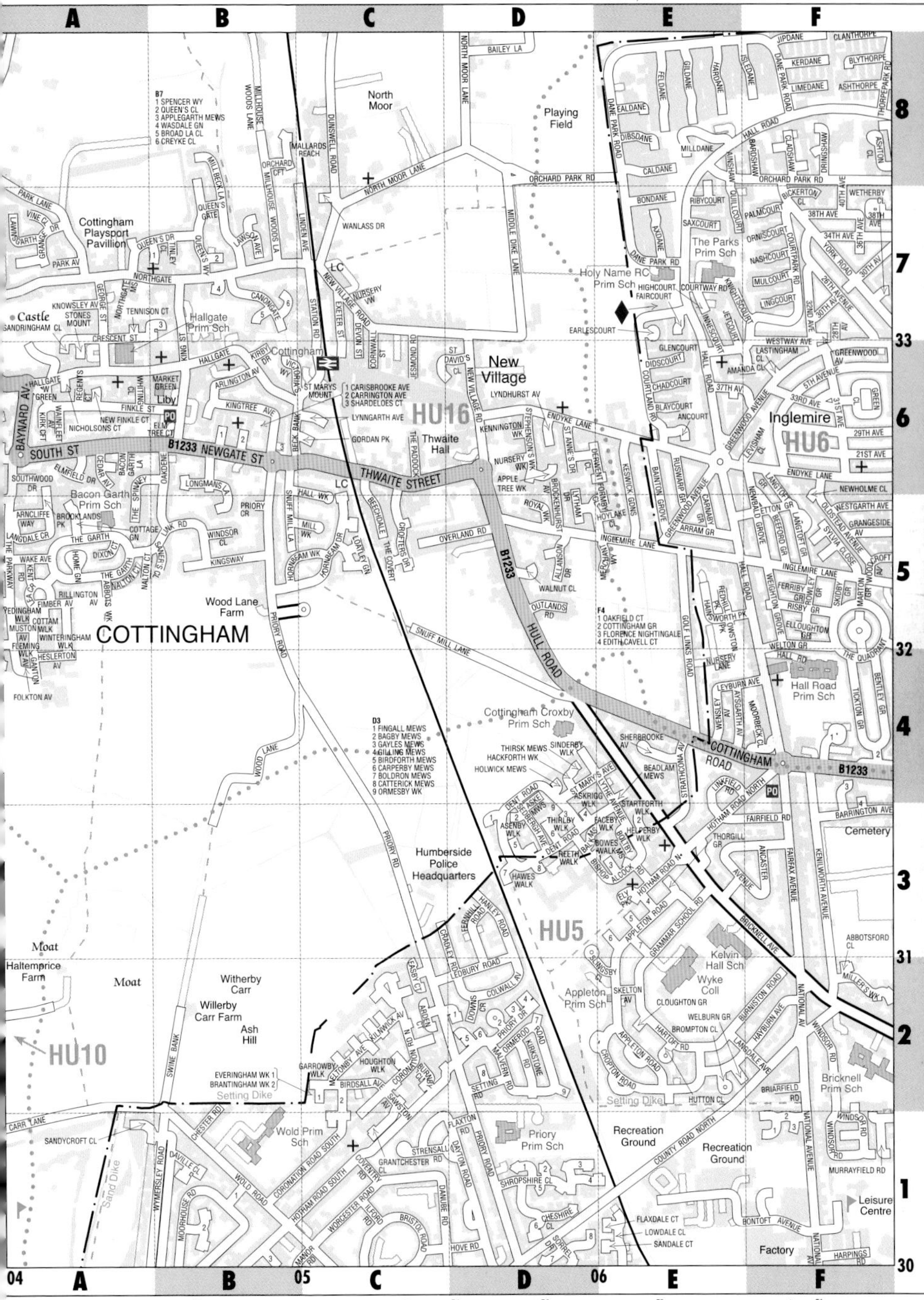

B1
1 MOORHOUSE RD
2 WILLERBY CARR CL
3 HUNSLEY AVE

D1
1 WORCESTERSHIRE CL
2 HERTFORDSHIRE CL
3 YORKSHIRE CL
4 ERNEST KIRKWOOD CL
5 SUSSEX CL
6 WARWICKSHIRE CL
7 HEATHER CL
8 CELANDINE CL

D2
1 ST FRANCIS CT
2 ST THOMAS'S GRANGE
3 ST JUDE'S CT
4 ST EDMUND'S CT
5 ST OSWALD CT
6 ST HEDDA'S CT
7 ORMEROD CRES
8 SETTING CRES
9 MALVERN CRES

E3
1 MARSKE WK
2 BURRILL MEWS
3 CALDBERG MEWS
4 SALTON AVE
5 EBBERSTON GR
6 CASTLETON AVE
7 KNAPTON AVE

F1
1 WOOLSHEDS CL
2 WISES FARM RD
3 HAVERFLATS CL

139

56

C8
1 FLAG WK
2 LARARD AVE

C7
1 BEECHCLIFFE AVE
2 CULLINGWORTH AVE
3 DENHOLME AVE
4 STEETON AVE
5 SILSDEN AVE

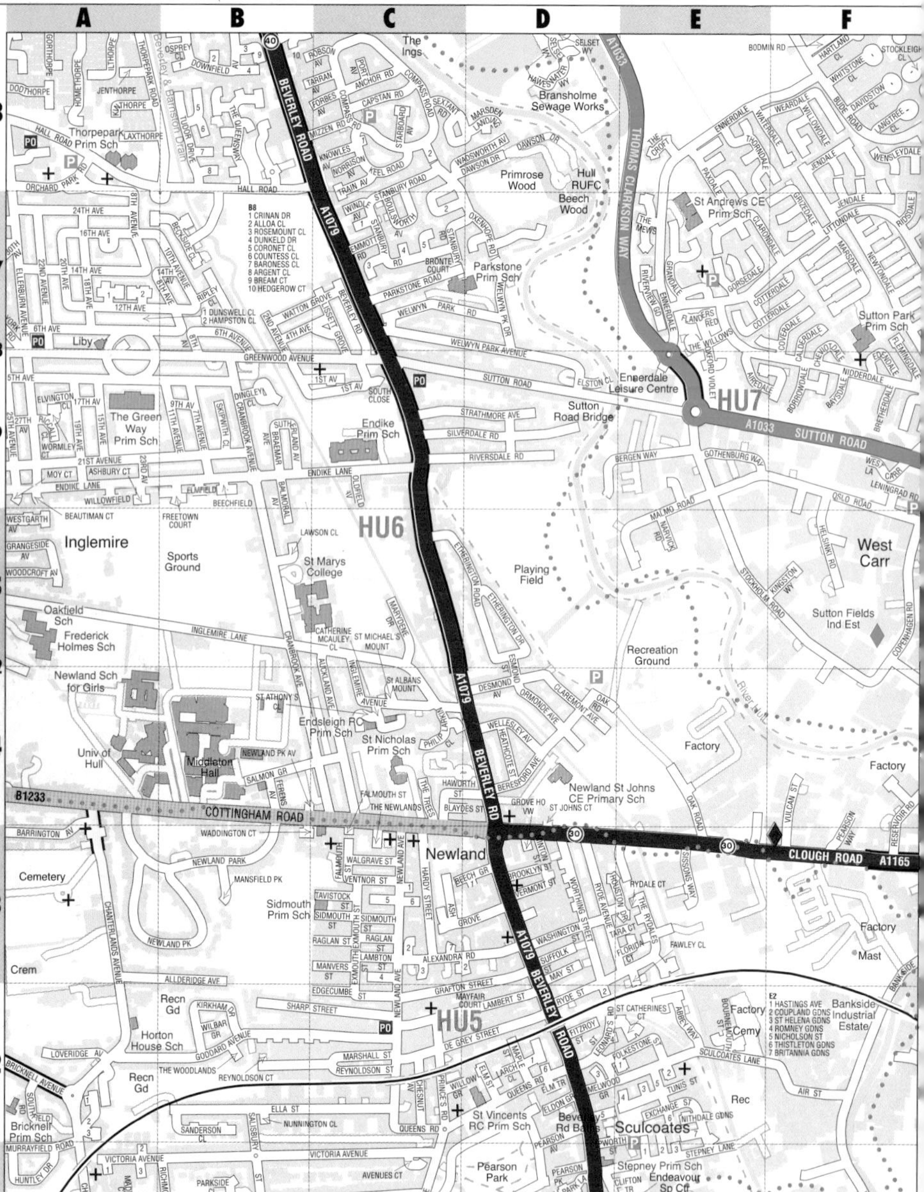

A1
1 VICTORIA GDNS
2 REGINA CRES
3 WHITEHALL GDNS
4 MADISON GDNS

A2
1 ERNEST HL CT
2 RAINHILL RD
3 RAINHILL CT

139

C3
1 NEWLAND GR
2 GOULDESBOROUGH CT
3 ST MONICA'S CT
4 MELBOURNE ST
5 TORRINGTON ST
6 WALTER'S TERR
7 THEARNE CL

145

D1
1 CAVE TERR
2 HUDSON GDNS
3 BARROW CT
4 BROMPTON CT
5 FRIARY CT
6 HAMPSTEAD CT
7 KNIGHTSBRIDGE CT

D2
1 BEACONSFIELD ST
2 SELSEY CL
3 BADEN CL
4 CROMER ST
5 ADDERBURY GR
6 BEACONSFIELD ST

D3
1 STRATHEARN ST
2 ST AUGUSTINE'S CT

E1
1 FENCHURCH ST
2 FARRINGDON ST
3 CLOVELLY GDNS
4 HADLEIGH CL
5 SCOTNEY CL
6 STAFFORD ST

155

B7
1 PEVENSEY CL
2 PEACEHAVEN CL

57

D8
1 GOLDCREST CL
2 CORMORANT CL
3 LOWLAND CL
4 HOUSEMARTIN DR

142

F5
1 HAMMERSMITH RD
2 SHOREDITCH CL
3 TOTTENHAM CL
4 WILLESDEN CL

155

B1
1 CUDWORTH GR
2 OAKWELL GR
3 WOMBWELL GR
4 ALSTON AVE

C1
1 DEARNE GR
2 AVON ST
3 DUNELM CL
4 BRANDON CT
5 BUCKINGHAM ST

146

D1
1 JAMES NIVEN CT
2 FERENS CT

142

E1
1 ROTHESAY CL
2 ESKDALE AVE

F1
1 EDGEWARE AVE
2 NORTH COUNTRY CT
3 TRINITY GR
4 WADHAM GR
5 MERTON GR

F2
1 FITLING GR
2 ELLERBY GR
3 NORTHORPE GR
4 ELLERBY GR

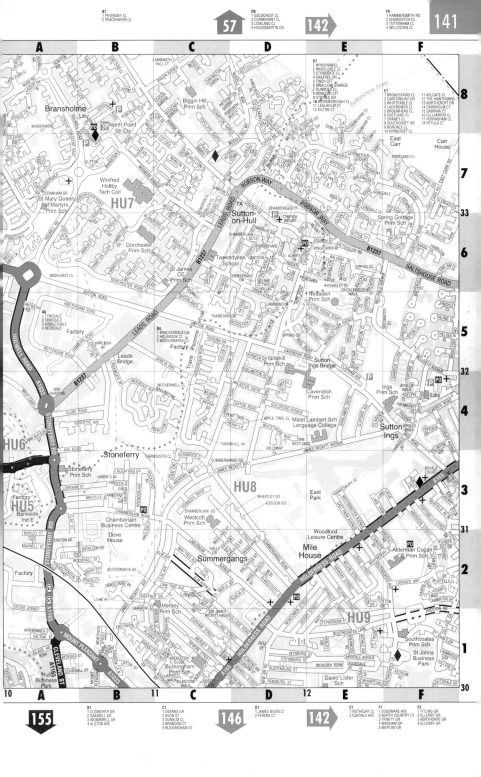

A5
1 PETERSHAM CL
2 TWICKENHAM CL
3 CHISWICK CL
4 WIMBLEDON CL
5 BELLFIELD AVE
6 HAUXWELL GR
7 PINDERFIELD CL
8 GUY'S CRES
9 ALDER HEY DR

B5
1 ALWOODLEY CL
2 ATLANTA CT
3 GANTON CT
4 BELTON CL
5 HARLESTON CL

141

C5
1 DUNMOW CL
2 SHORWELL CL
3 ROOKLEY CL
4 COLDSTREAM CL
5 DRAYTON CL
6 FOYNES GN

57

C6
1 BICKLEIGH GR
2 HARLOW CL
3 ST MARGARETS CT
4 PARKHURST CL

58

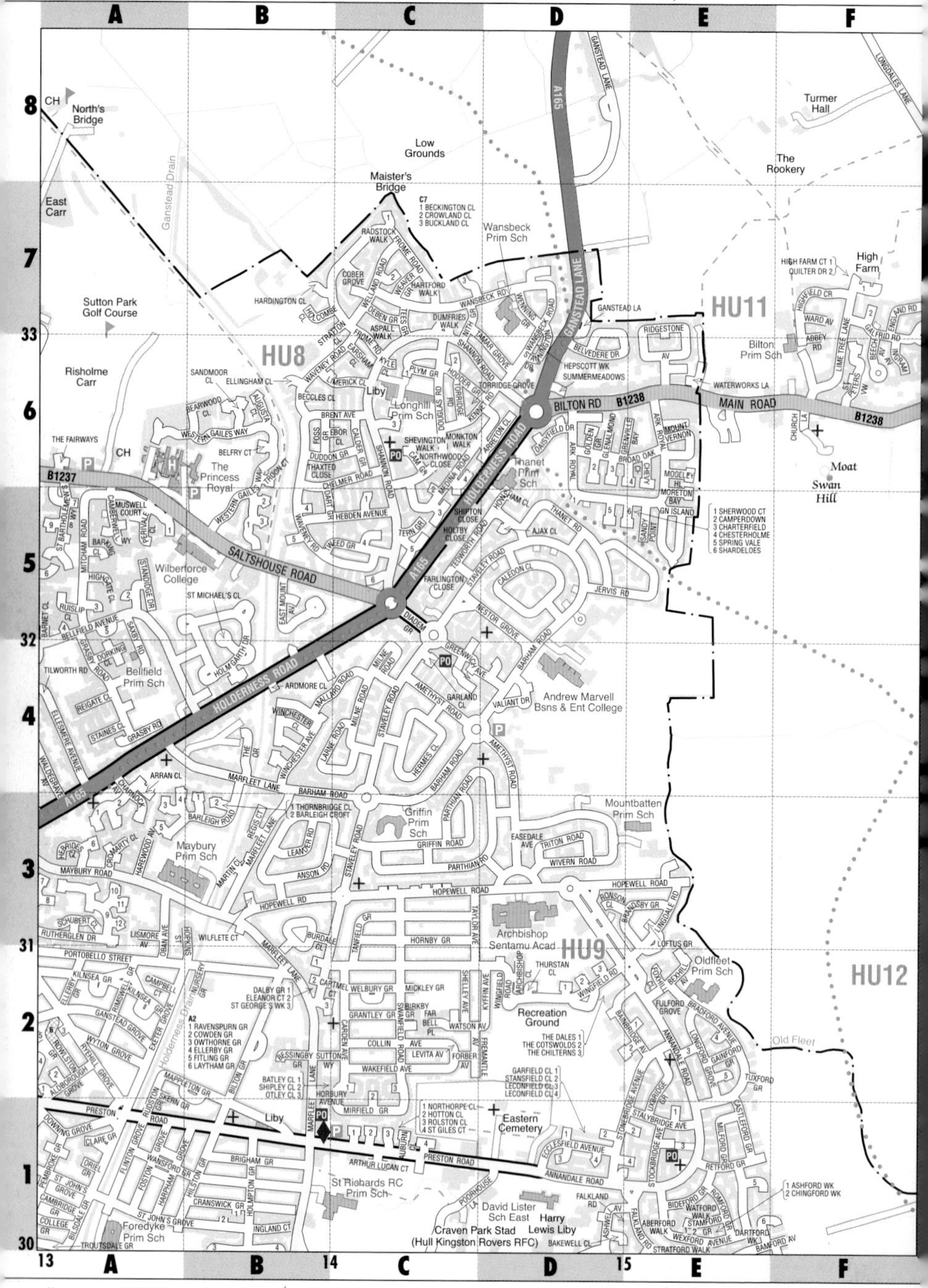

A3
1 FAROES CL
2 SPERRIN CL
3 BROUGHTON CL
4 BROADLAND DR
5 BEAULIEU CT
6 RONALDSWAY CL
7 MAJESTIC CT
8 THE BROADWAY
9 BROADWAY DR
10 GOLDEN CT
11 ZEIGFIELD CT
12 IMPERIAL CT

B1
1 ULROME CT
2 ATWICK CT
3 ENDEAVOUR CRES
4 BEWHOLME GR

141

147

58

E1
1 STEMBRIDGE CL
2 CORBRIDGE CL
3 ELMBRIDGE PAR
4 WADEBRIDGE GR
5 CHELMSFORD CL
6 CRAYFORD CL

E2
1 FELBRIDGE CL
2 TONBRIDGE GR
3 SLEAFORD AVE
4 STAPLEFORD CL
5 TWYFORD CL

69
138
144

E7
1 CROMWELL CT
2 WOODHILL CL
3 NORWOOD CL
4 WAULDBY CL
5 WEETON WY

E8
1 COLLYNSON CL
2 SETTERWOOD GARTH
3 OAKDALE AVE

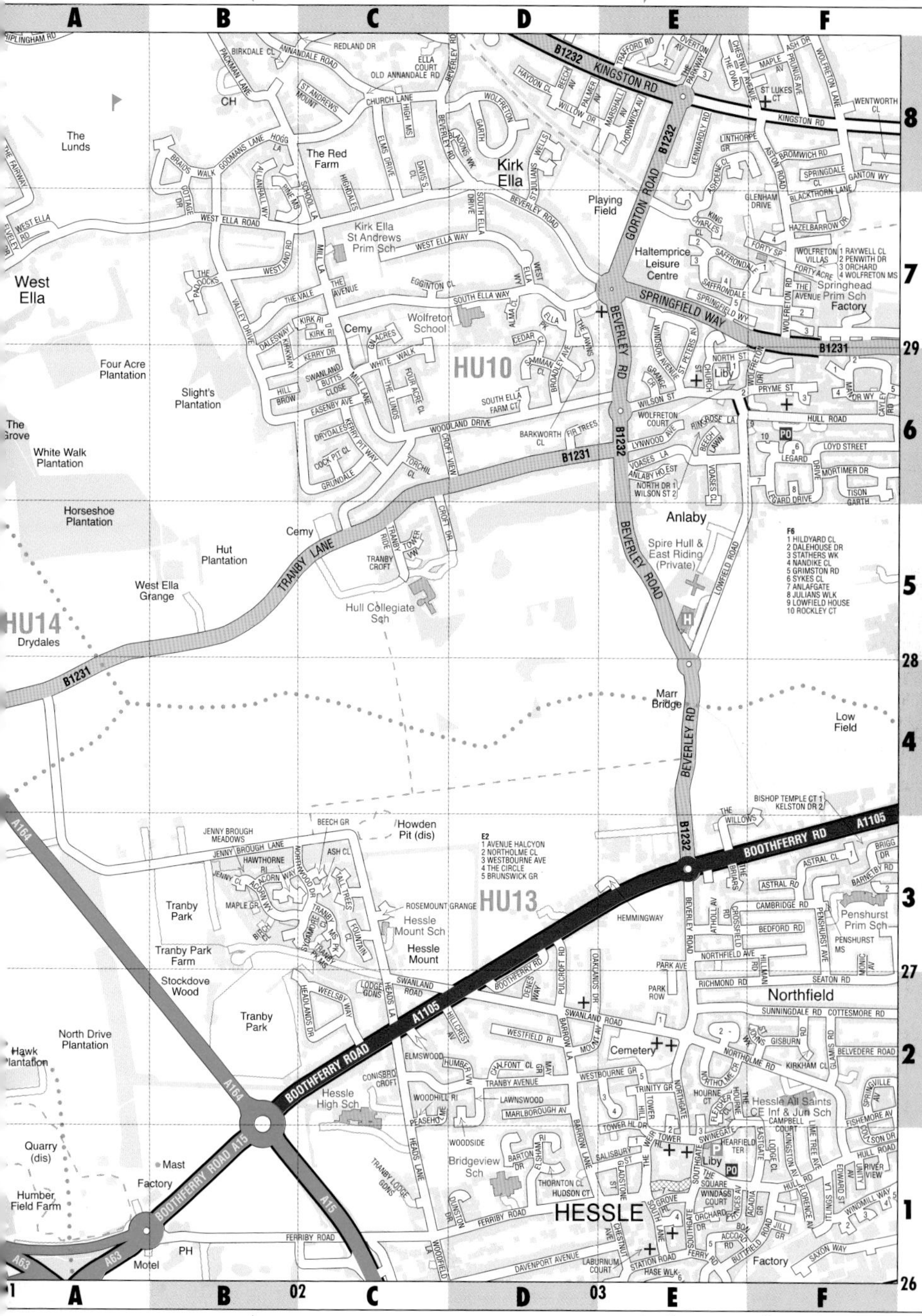

69
69
144

E1
1 SPIRE VW
2 TOWER HILL MEWS
3 VICARAGE LA
4 CLOWES CT
5 FISHWICK AVE
6 CHAMPNEYS CL
7 PRESTONGATE

F1
1 MARGARET GR
2 BISHOP BLUNT CL
3 BISHOP KEMPTHORNE CL
4 BISHOP GURDON CL
5 CANON TARDREW CL

A3
1 BARNETBY RD
2 KELSTON DR
3 YARMOUTH AVE
4 WINTHORPE RD
5 BROCKLESBY CL
6 CORRAN GARTH
7 CHURCH FIELD

B7
1 LANGFORD WK
2 HOLLYTREE AVE
3 LABURNUM DR
4 ROSEWOOD CL

143

139

D8
1 LOCKTON GR
2 HACKNESS GR
3 BARGATE GR
4 SNAINTON GR
5 SORREL DR

E6
1 AIRMYN AVE
2 ST MARTINS AVE
3 BUTTERMERE CL

F6
1 HAWTHORN CT

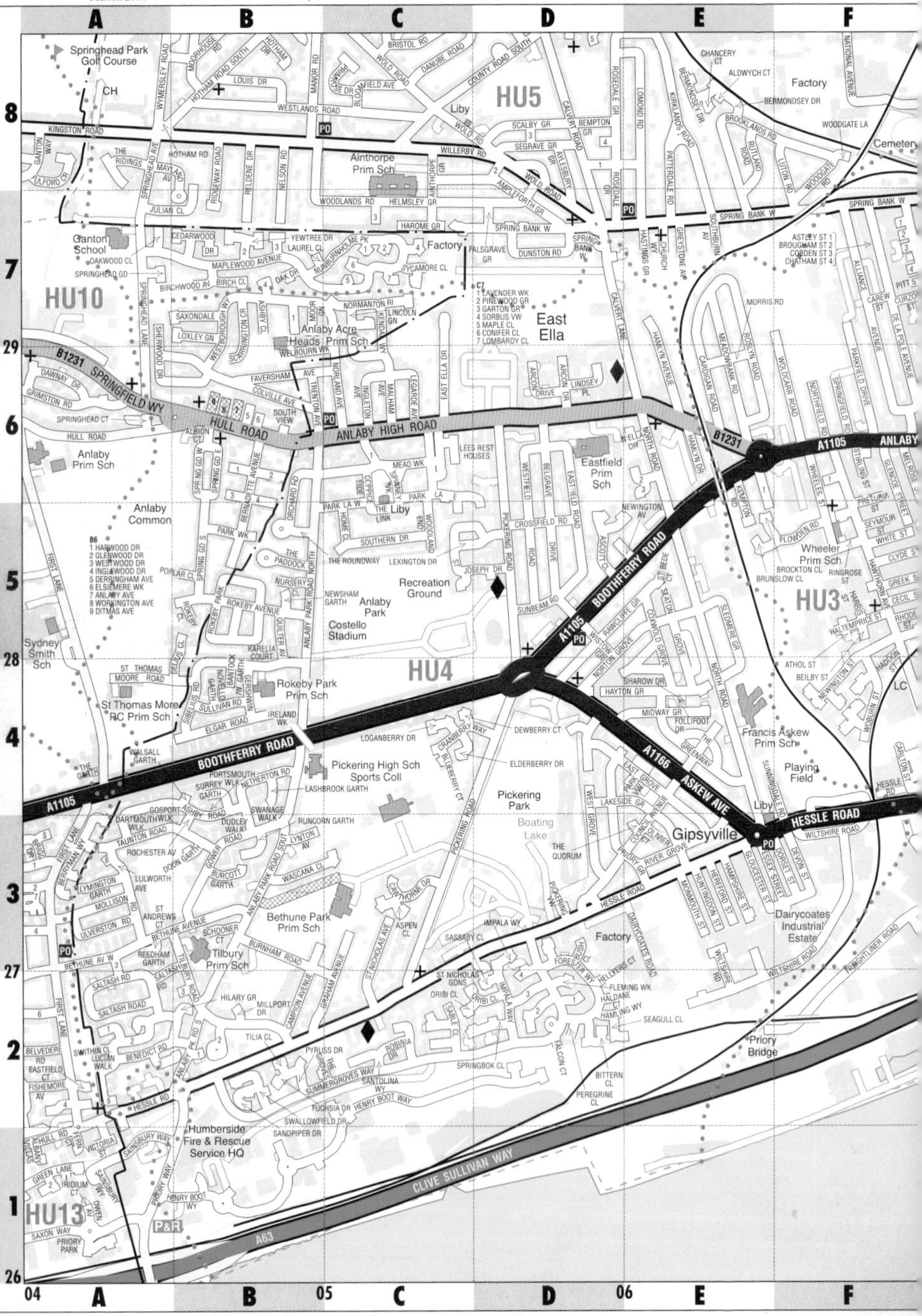

A1
1 BISHOP COCKIN CL
2 CHAPEL CL

143

A2
1 VALENTINE CL
2 BENEDICT CL
3 VINCENT CL
4 NEWLYN CL
5 CRISPIN CL
6 COTTESMORE RD

B2
1 AVONDALE
2 WOOLWICH DR
3 DATCHET GARTH

C6
1 THE GREENWAY

70

D2
1 KIPLING WK
2 WHEATFIELD CL
3 GEMSBOK WY
4 PRIORY FARM DR

For full street detail of the highlighted area see page 155.

A6
1 GRANVILLE ST
2 SANDRINGHAM ST
3 COULTAS CT
4 ACLAND ST
5 LONSDALE ST
6 CARNEGIE ST

B8
1 ROXBURGH ST
2 RICHMOND ST
3 LANARK ST

C6
1 KINGS LEIGH
2 KING'S CROSS CL
3 THORN LEIGH

D8
1 BERKELEY ST
2 CROMWELL CL
3 BROWNING CL
4 LEONARD ST
5 TRAFALGAR ST
6 SHAKESPEARE CL

140 146

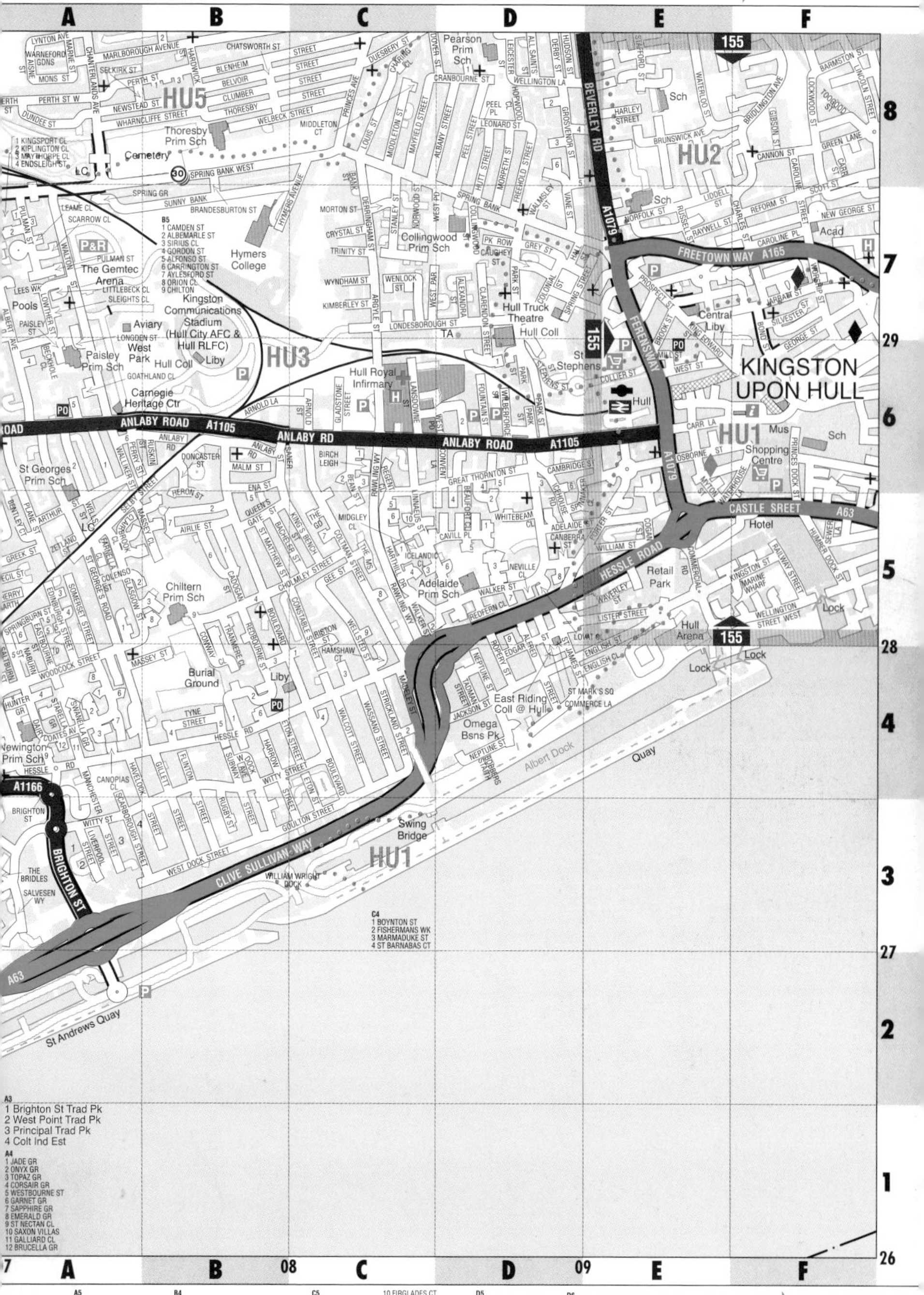

A5
1 CORDELLA CL
2 DORADO CL
3 SANDLEMERE CL
4 DARRISMERE VILLAS
5 BRIXHAM CT
6 OTTERBURN ST

B4
1 DIVISION RD
2 SEFTON ST
3 NEWTON ST
4 RIBBLE ST
5 DEE ST
6 ROSAMOND ST

70

C5
1 LYRIC CL
2 THORNWICK CL
3 BARBERRY CT
4 WINSHIP CL
5 EVER THORPE CL
6 TICHBOURNE CL
7 WESLEY CT
8 BEECH CL
9 CAROL DICKSON CT
10 FIRGLADES CT

D5
1 BRISBANE ST
2 HAZEL GR
3 FIRETHORN CL
4 NEWPORT CL
5 PEACH TREE CT
6 ELDERWOOD CT
7 QUANTOCK CL
8 BATHURST ST
9 MECHANIC LA

D6
1 BLOOMSBURY CT
2 ARLINGTON ST
3 ALMOND GR
4 BLACKTHORN CT
5 SORBUS CT
6 ST LUKE'S ST

146

B7
1 PEMBERTON ST
2 BLYTH ST
3 NAYLOR'S ROW
4 WILSON ST
5 EAST ST
6 ALMA ST

C7
1 PELHAM DR
2 EDWARD COLLINS SQ
3 ROSEY ROW
4 ALDERSON MEWS
5 BROADLEY CL
6 DENMARK CT
7 EMILY ST

141

C8
1 NORNABELL ST
2 VICTOR ST
3 BALFOUR ST
4 ST QUINTINS CL
5 BRODSWORTH ST

D7
1 BUTTERCUP CL
2 PENISTONE CT
3 BEAUMONT CT
4 BRUMBY'S TERR
5 EMPRINGHAM ST
6 CRAVEN CT

E8
1 DOVEDALE GR
2 DEEPDALE GR
3 MIDDLEHAM CL
4 BYLAND CT

A B C D E F

8 7 29 6 5 28 4 3 27 2 1 26

10 A B 11 C D 12 E F

For full street detail of the highlighted area see page 155.

145

71

142
72

A
B
C
D
E
F
ENDEAVOUR CR
BEWHOLME GR
MARFLEET LA
POORHOUSE LA
BYWELL WLK
ASHWELL AV
BOTHWELL GR
AVENUE
HEMSWELL
FALKLAND ROAD
DODSWELL GROVE
STOCKWELL GR
Stockwell Prim Sch
1 SOUTHWELL AVE
2 BAMFORD AVE
3 SALTFORD AVE
4 HALLIWELL CL
Holderness Drain
Factory
BURMA DRIVE
MARFLEET AVENUE
MARFLEET LANE
ACASTA WAY
GREAT FIELD LA
Factory
Marfleet
Marfleet Prim Sch
Factory
LITTLEFAIR ROAD
CYPRUS ST
FRODSHAM ST
DELHI ST
EGYPT ST
CHURCH LANE
CEYLON ST
GREAT FIELD LANE
VALLETTA STREET
SOMERDEN ROAD
Factory
ELBA ST
A1033
Works
NORTHERN GATEWAY
HU9
HEDON ROAD
TOWER HO LA
Works
CORPORATION ROAD
KING GEORGE DOCK
A1033
HULL RD
Old Fleet
King George Dock
HU12
CORPORATION RD
Lord's Clough
Factory
Lock
Lock
Lock
Queen Elizabeth Dock
Salt End
Quay
Quay
Salt End
River Humber
Salt End Jetties No 1
Salt End Jetties No 3
8
7
29
6
5
28
4
3
27
2
1
26
3
14
15

71
72

C5
1 YORK ST
2 HARPER ST
3 DOUGLAS ST
4 RAINCLIFFE ST
5 LONDESBOROUGH ST
6 HILDA ST
7 PORTHOLME CRES
8 SOUTH PAR
9 TURNERS SQ
10 AUDUS ST
11 MARKET PL
12 NEW CHURCH TERR
13 Market Cross Shop Ctr
14 MARKET LA

48

D5
1 MICKLEGATE
2 WREN LA
3 CHURCH HL
4 CHURCH LA
5 CORUNNA CT
6 CHURCH AVE
7 GANT WK
8 ABBEY PL

49 49

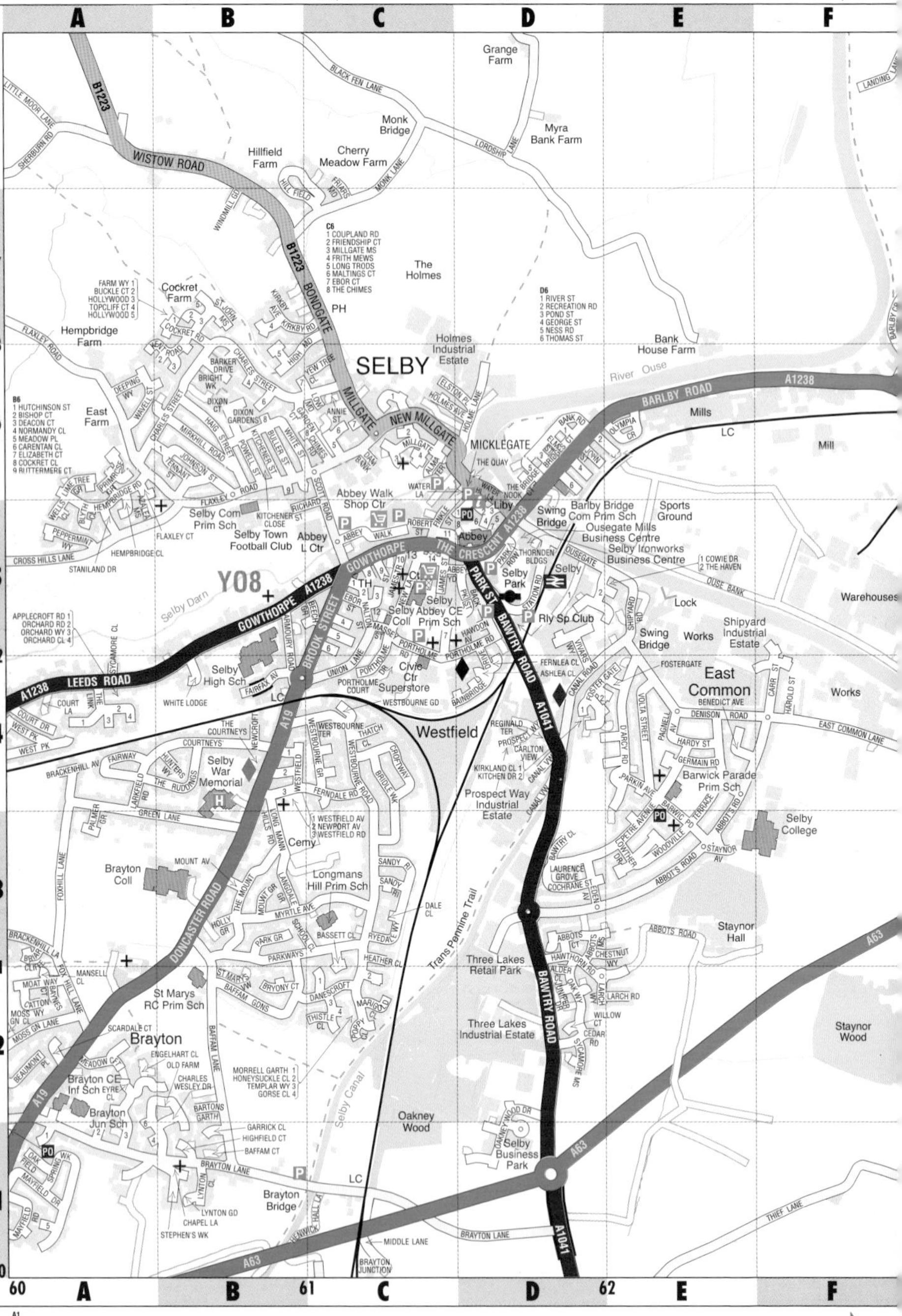

A1
1 MANOR FARM CL
2 HOLMEFIELD CT
3 HOLMEFIELD CL
4 CHILVERS CT
5 MAYFIELD DR
6 MIDDLEBROOK GDNS

62 63 49

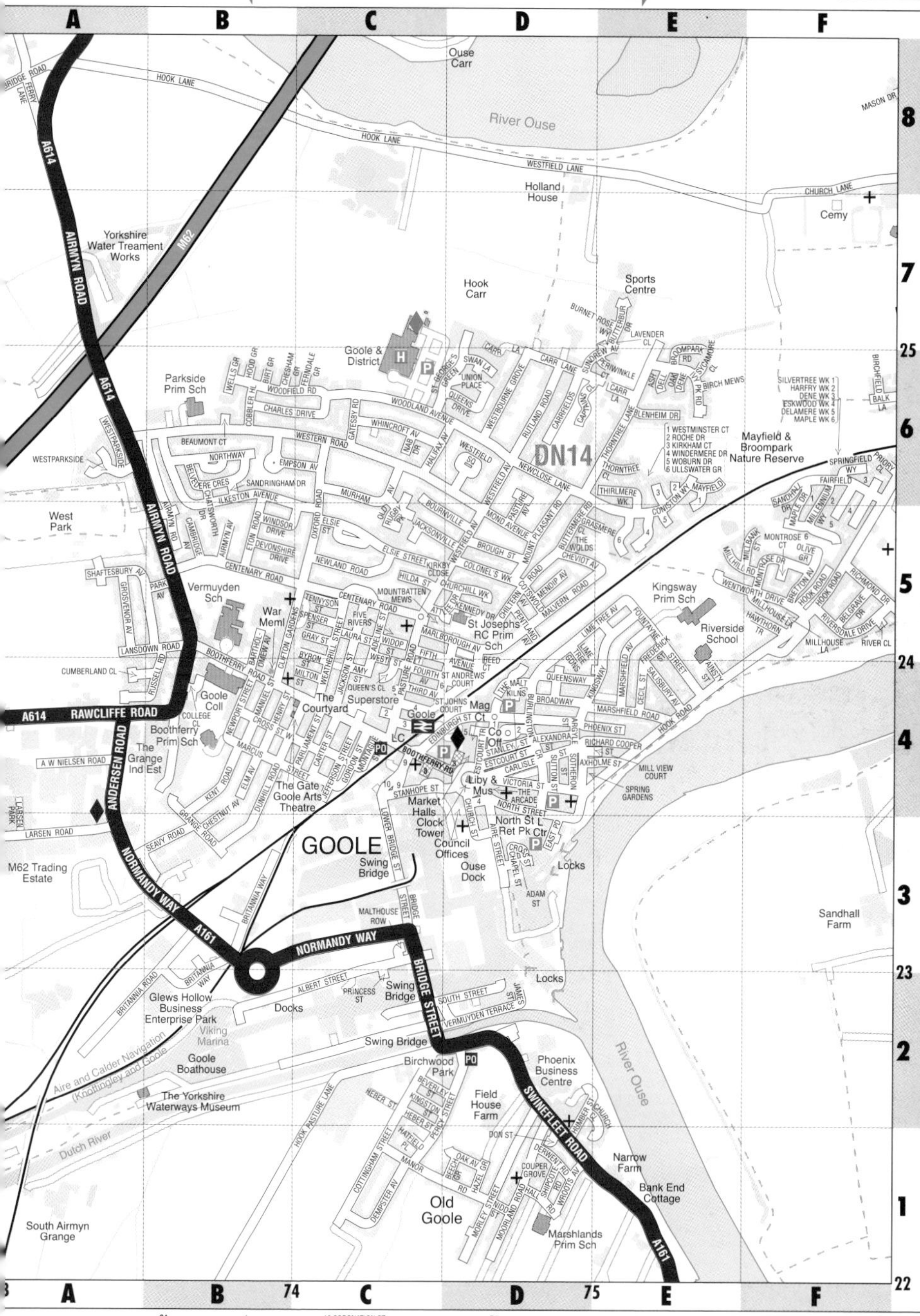

C4
1 CROSS GORDON ST
2 RED LION ST
3 FIRST AVE
4 SECOND AVE
5 WILSON ST
6 ST ANDREW'S TERR
7 POOL CT
8 BELGRAVIA
9 MARINERS ST

10 CORONATION ST

D4
1 GOVERNMENT ST
2 EASTGATE
3 PARADISE PL
4 CALDER ST
5 WESLEY SQ

95
96

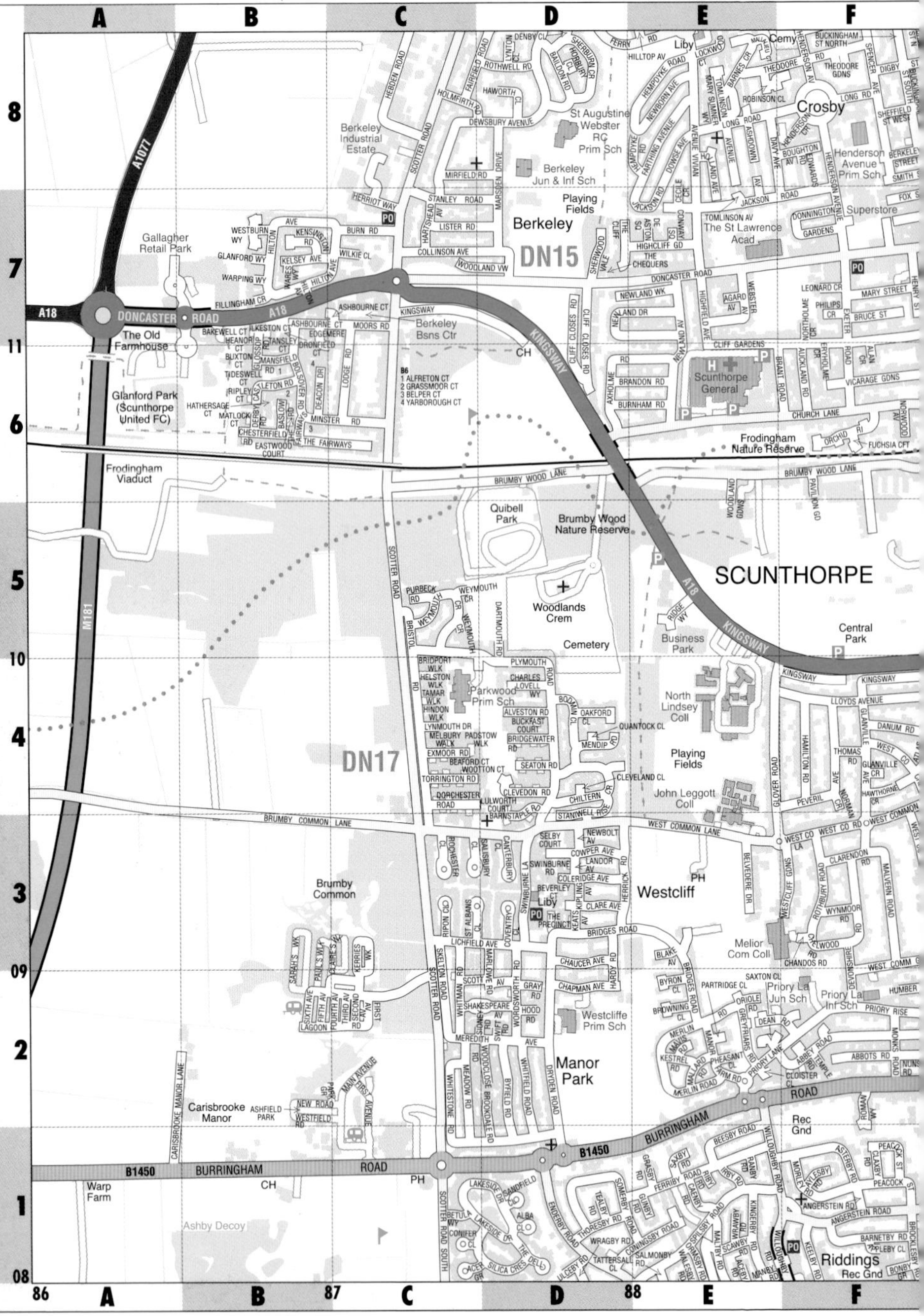
A
B
C
D
E
F
8
7
11
6
5
10
4
3
09
2
1
08
86
87
88
SCUNTHORPE
DN15
DN17
Berkeley
Crosby
Westcliff
Manor Park
Riddings
Brumby Common
Carisbrooke Manor
Warp Farm
Ashby Decoy
Gallagher Retail Park
The Old Farmhouse
Glanford Park (Scunthorpe United FC)
Frodingham Viaduct
Berkeley Industrial Estate
Berkeley Bsns Ctr
St Augustine Webster RC Prim Sch
Berkeley Jun & Inf Sch
Playing Fields
Henderson Avenue Prim Sch
Superstore
The St Lawrence Acad
Scunthorpe General
Frodingham Nature Reserve
Quibell Park
Brumby Wood Nature Reserve
Woodlands Crem
Cemetery
Business Park
Central Park
North Lindsey Coll
John Leggott Coll
Parkwood Prim Sch
Melior Com Coll
Priory La Jun Sch
Priory La Inf Sch
Westcliffe Prim Sch
Rec Gnd
Riddings Rec Gnd
Liby
Cemy
A18
A1077
M181
B1450
DONCASTER ROAD
KINGSWAY
DONCASTER ROAD
BRUMBY WOOD LANE
BRUMBY COMMON LANE
WEST COMMON LANE
BURRINGHAM ROAD
SCOTTER ROAD
SCOTTER ROAD SOUTH
SKELTON ROAD
CARISBROOKE MANOR LANE
WILLOUGHBY ROAD
GLOVER ROAD
B6
1 ALFRETON CT
2 GRASSMOOR CT
3 BELPER CT
4 YARBOROUGH CT
HEBDEN ROAD
FAIRFIELD ROAD
ROTHWELL RD
HOLMFIRTH RD
HAWORTH CL
DEWSBURY AVENUE
MIRFIELD RD
MARSDEN DRIVE
STANLEY ROAD
LISTER RD
HARTSHEAD AV
COLLINSON AVE
WOODLAND VW
HERRIOT WAY
WESTBURN WY
KENSINGTON RD
BURN RD
WILKIE CL
HILTON AVE
KELSEY AVE
GLANFORD WY
WARPING WY
FILLINGHAM CR
ASHBOURNE CT
MOORS RD
BAKEWELL CT
ILKESTON CT
HEANOR CT
TANSLEY CT
EDGEMERE
DRONFIELD CT
BUXTON CT
MANSFIELD RD
TIDESWELL CT
RIPLEY CT
HATHERSAGE CT
MATLOCK CT
CHESTERFIELD RD
EASTWOOD COURT
THE FAIRWAYS
MINSTER RD
DEACON DR
LODGE RD
BOLSOVER RD
BASLOW RD
DERBY CT
DENBY CL
SHERBURN CR
BAILDON RD
LYNTON CL
FERRY RD
HILLTOP AV
HEMPDYKE ROAD
NEWBORN AVE
FARTHING AVENUE
DOWSE AVE
JACKSON RD
LOCKWOOD
MARY SUMNER
TOMLINSON AV
BARNES CR
HOLLAND AVE
ASHDOWN
LONG ROAD
ROBINSON CL
THEODORE
THEODORE GDNS
HENDERSON AV
BUCKINGHAM ST NORTH
SPENCER AVE
DIGBY ST
SHEFFIELD ST WEST
BERKELEY STREET
SMITH ST
BOUGHTON AV
EDWARDS
DAVY AVE
DONNINGTON GARDENS
CONWAY SQ
DE ASTON SQ
THE CLIFF
HIGHCLIFF GD
THE CHEQUERS
SHERWOOD VALE
CLIFF CLOSES RD
NEWLAND WK
NEWLAND DR
NEWLAND AV
HIGHFIELD AVE
AGARD AV
WEBSTER
LEONARD CR
MARY STREET
PHILIPS CR
EXETER
BRUCE ST
NORTHOLME
CLIFF GARDENS
AXHOLME
BRANDON RD
BURNHAM RD
BRANT ROAD
AUCKLAND RD
FRYHOLME
ALAN CR
VICARAGE GDNS
CHURCH LANE
NORWOOD AV
ORCHID RI
FUCHSIA CFT
WOODLAND GDNS
PAVILION GD
PURBECK RD
WEYMOUTH CR
BRISTOL RD
DARTMOUTH RD
RIDGE WY
BRIDPORT WLK
HELSTON WLK
TAMAR WLK
HINDON WLK
LYNMOUTH DR
MELBURY WALK
PADSTOW WLK
EXMOOR RD
BEAFORD CT
WOOTTON CT
TORRINGTON RD
DORCHESTER ROAD
LULWORTH COURT
BARNSTAPLE RD
PLYMOUTH ROAD
CHARLES LOVELL WY
ALVESTON RD
BUCKFAST COURT
BRIDGEWATER RD
SEATON RD
CLEVEDON RD
BODMIN CL
OAKFORD CL
QUANTOCK CL
MENDIP RD
CLEVELAND CL
CHILTERN CR
STANWELL RS
KINGSWAY
LLOYDS AVENUE
GLANVILLE AVE
DANUM RD
HAMILTON RD
THOMAS RD
GLANVILLE CR
WEST CO
HAWTHORNE CR
NORMAN CR
PEVERIL RD
WEST COMMON
ROCHESTER CL
SALISBURY CL
CANTERBURY CL
SELBY COURT
NEWBOLT AV
COWPER AVE
LANDOR AV
SWINBURNE RD
SWINBURNE LA
COLERIDGE AVE
BEVERLEY CT
HERRICK RD
KIPLING AV
KEATS AV
CLARE AVE
THE PRECINCT
RIPON CL
ST ALBANS CL
COVENTRY CL
LICHFIELD AVE
BRIDGES ROAD
BELVEDERE DR
WESTCLIFF GDNS
ROTHBURY ROAD
CLARENDON RD
MALVERN ROAD
WYNMOOR RD
CHELWOOD RD
CHANDOS RD
DEVONSHIRE RD
WEST COMM
HUMBER
SARAH'S WK
PAUL'S WK
CLAIRE'S WK
KERRIES WK
SIXTH AVE
FIFTH AV
FOURTH AV
THIRD AV
SECOND RD
FIRST AV
LAGOON
CHAUCER AVE
CHAPMAN AVE
HARDY RD
BLAKE AV
BYRON CL
BROWNING CL
PARTRIDGE CL
SAXTON CL
ORIOLE RD
DEAN RD
PRIORY RISE
MONKS ROAD
ABBOTS RD
NUNS RD
WHITMAN RD
MARLOWE RD
SCOTT AV
GRAY RD
HOOD RD
SHAKESPEARE AV
WORDSWORTH RD
MEREDITH AVE
WHITESTONE RD
MEADOW RD
WOODCLOSE RD
BROOKDALE RD
BYFIELD RD
WHITFIELD ROAD
DRYDEN ROAD
MERLIN ROAD
KESTREL RD
MALLARD RD
PHEASANT CL
MANOR FARM RD
GREYFRIARS RD
PRIORY LANE
CLOISTER CL
ABBEY ROAD
TEMPLE
ASHFIELD PARK
NEW ROAD
WESTFIELD RD
MAIN AVENUE
FIRST AVENUE
PARK GR
LAKESIDE DR
SANDFIELD
ALBA CL
BETULA WY
CONIFER CL
ACER CL
SILICA CRES
THE DELL
ENDERBY ROAD
TEALBY RD
THORESBY RD
SOMERBY ROAD
GRASBY RD
GUNBY RD
SAXBY RD
FERRIBY ROAD
CAENBY RD
RIBY RD
IRBY RD
BEESBY ROAD
RANBY RD
WRAGBY RD
CONINGSBY ROAD
SALMONBY RD
TATTERSALL CL
ULCEBY RD
WALESBY RD
ORMSBY RD
SPILSBY ROAD
MALTBY RD
SCAWBY RD
WRAWBY RD
KINGERBY RD
LACEBY RD
MANBY RD
KEELBY RD
MORLEY RD
AYLESBY RD
ASTERBY RD
CLAXBY RD
PEACOCK ST
PEACOCK
ANGERSTEIN RD
ANGERSTEIN ROAD
BARNETBY RD
APPLEBY CL
BONBY GR
BROCKLESBY RD
ROMAN WAY
CH
PH
PO
P
H

95
96

B7
1 BELGRAVE SQ
2 SOUTHGATE
3 ETHEL CT
4 LESLIE CT
5 KINSLEY WK
6 JUBILEE WY
7 WILSONS CL
8 WALKERS CL
9 GREENS CL
10 MANLEY ST
11 CARLTON ST
12 The Parishes Shop Ctr
13 The Base Youth Arts Ctr

B8
1 NORTH ST
2 CROSS ST

C7
1 DAWES LA

96
97

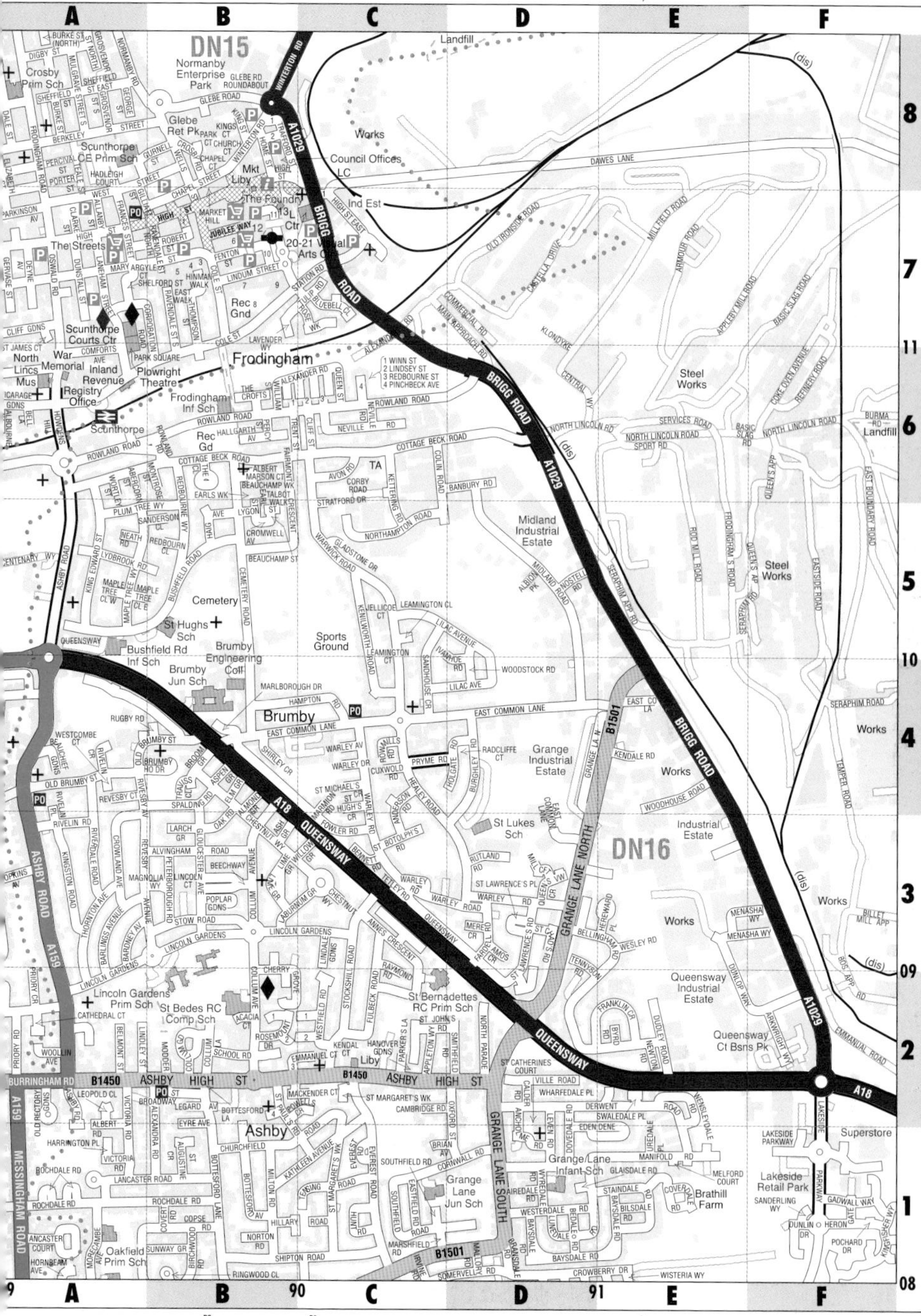

B2
1 ASHBERRY DR
2 ORCHARD CL
3 MACKENDER CT
4 ST PAUL'S GDNS

C2
1 NORTHFIELD CL
2 SPRINGFIELD CL

96
97

102
102

F5
1 FREEMAN WAY
2 THESIGER WK
3 ALBERT PL
4 ALBERT CL
5 COMBER PL

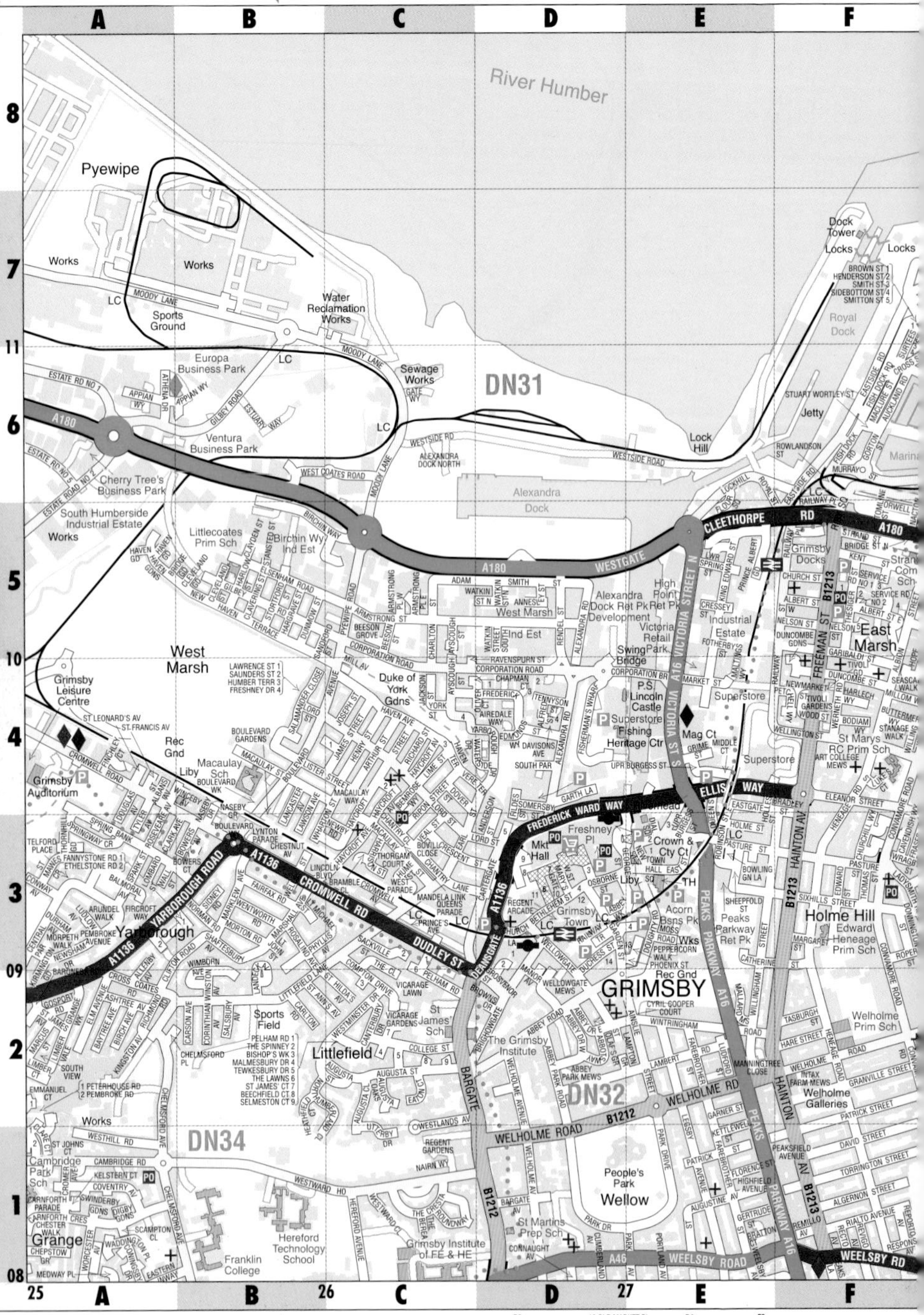

D3
1 DEANSGROVE
2 GROSVENOR CRES
3 E ST MARY'S GATE
4 S ST MARY'S GATE
5 NEW CARTERGATE
6 OLD MARKET PL
7 VICTORIA ST W
8 FLOTTERGATE MALL
9 FRESHNEY PL
10 OLD MARKET PL
11 BULL RING LA
12 ABBEYGATE
13 KEIR HARDIE WK
14 PHYLLIS TAYLOR GDNS

D4
1 RAVENSPURN WY
2 FARNDALE WY
3 WHARFEDALE WY
4 TENNYSON MEWS

E3
1 TOWN HALL ST
2 VICTORIA ST W
3 VICTORIA ST S
4 KEIRHARDIE WK

102
102

A5
SALACON WY
CALVI CT
BRADMAN CT
CASSWELL CL
MUNSTER CT
MANSFIELD CT
7 ACTON CT
8 APPLEBY CT
9 ARNOLD CT
10 WESLEY CT
11 NORFOLK CT
12 SURREY CT
13 SUFFOLK CT
14 SUSSEX CT
15 MARLBOROUGH CL
16 BANBURY CT
17 BELPER CT
18 BEXLEY CT
19 MILFORD CT
20 GUILDFORD ST
21 WORDSWORTH CT
22 WINDSOR CT

103
103

103
103

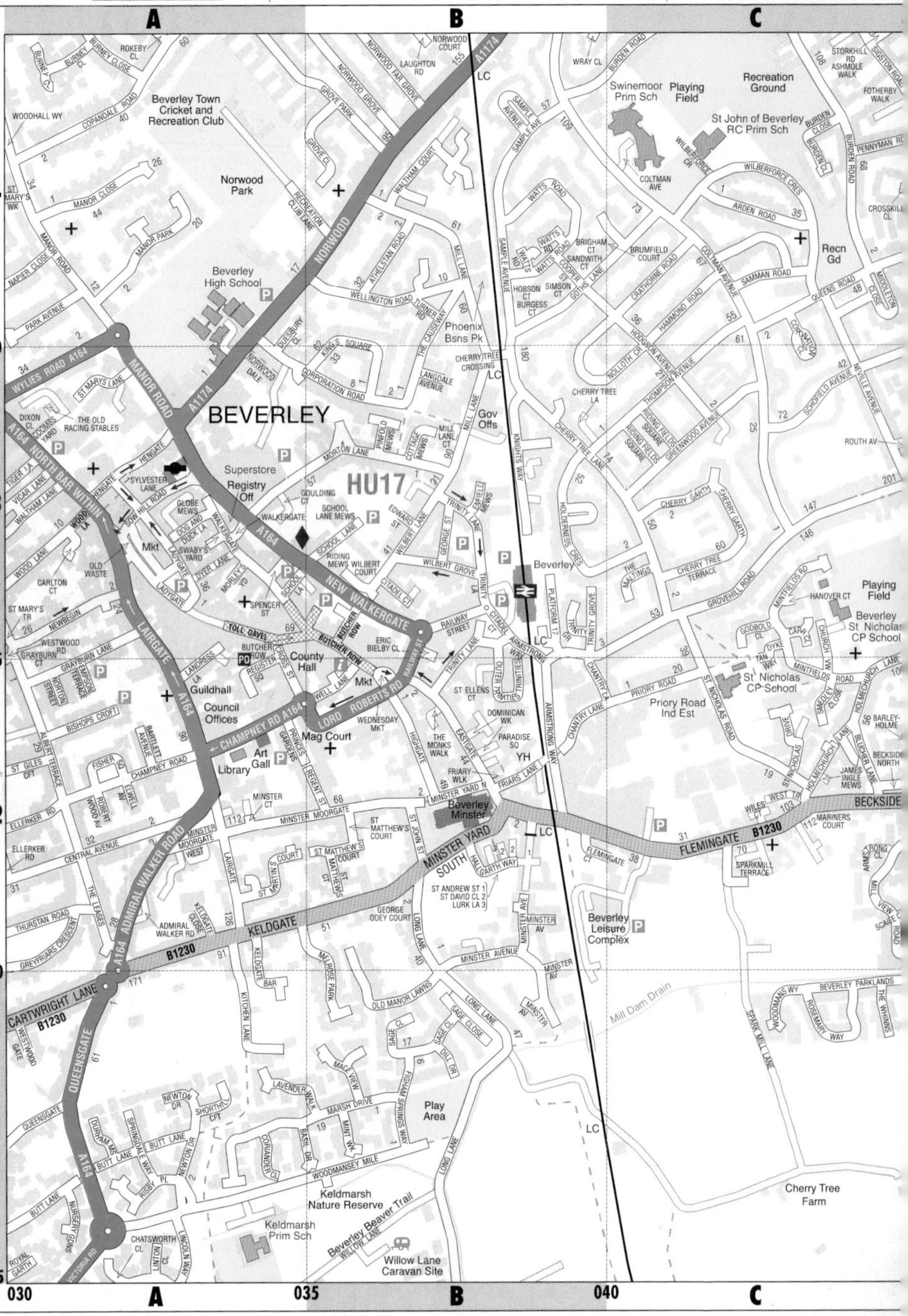
A
B
C
4
400
3
395
2
390
1
385
030
035
040
BEVERLEY
HU17
Beverley Town Cricket and Recreation Club
Norwood Park
Beverley High School
Swinemoor Prim Sch
Playing Field
Recreation Ground
St John of Beverley RC Prim Sch
Recn Gd
Phoenix Bsns Pk
Gov Offs
Superstore
Registry Off
Beverley
Mkt
County Hall
Guildhall
Council Offices
Art Gall
Library
Mag Court
Beverley Minster
Beverley Leisure Complex
Priory Road Ind Est
St Nicholas CP School
Beverley St Nicholas CP School
Playing Field
Play Area
Keldmarsh Nature Reserve
Keldmarsh Prim Sch
Beverley Beaver Trail
Willow Lane Caravan Site
Cherry Tree Farm
Mill Dam Drain
A1174
A164
B1230
NORWOOD
NEW WALKERGATE
LAIRGATE
ADMIRAL WALKER ROAD
QUEENSGATE
KELDGATE
MINSTER YARD SOUTH
FLEMINGATE
BECKSIDE
WYLIES ROAD
NORTH BAR WITHIN
MANOR ROAD
CHAMPNEY RD
LORD ROBERTS RD
CARTWRIGHT LANE
WOODMANSEY MILE
CHERRY TREE LANE
GROVEHILL ROAD
PRIORY ROAD
ARMSTRONG WAY
SAMMAN ROAD
QUEENS ROAD
WILBERFORCE CRES
MILL LANE
LONG LANE
LC
YH

A B C

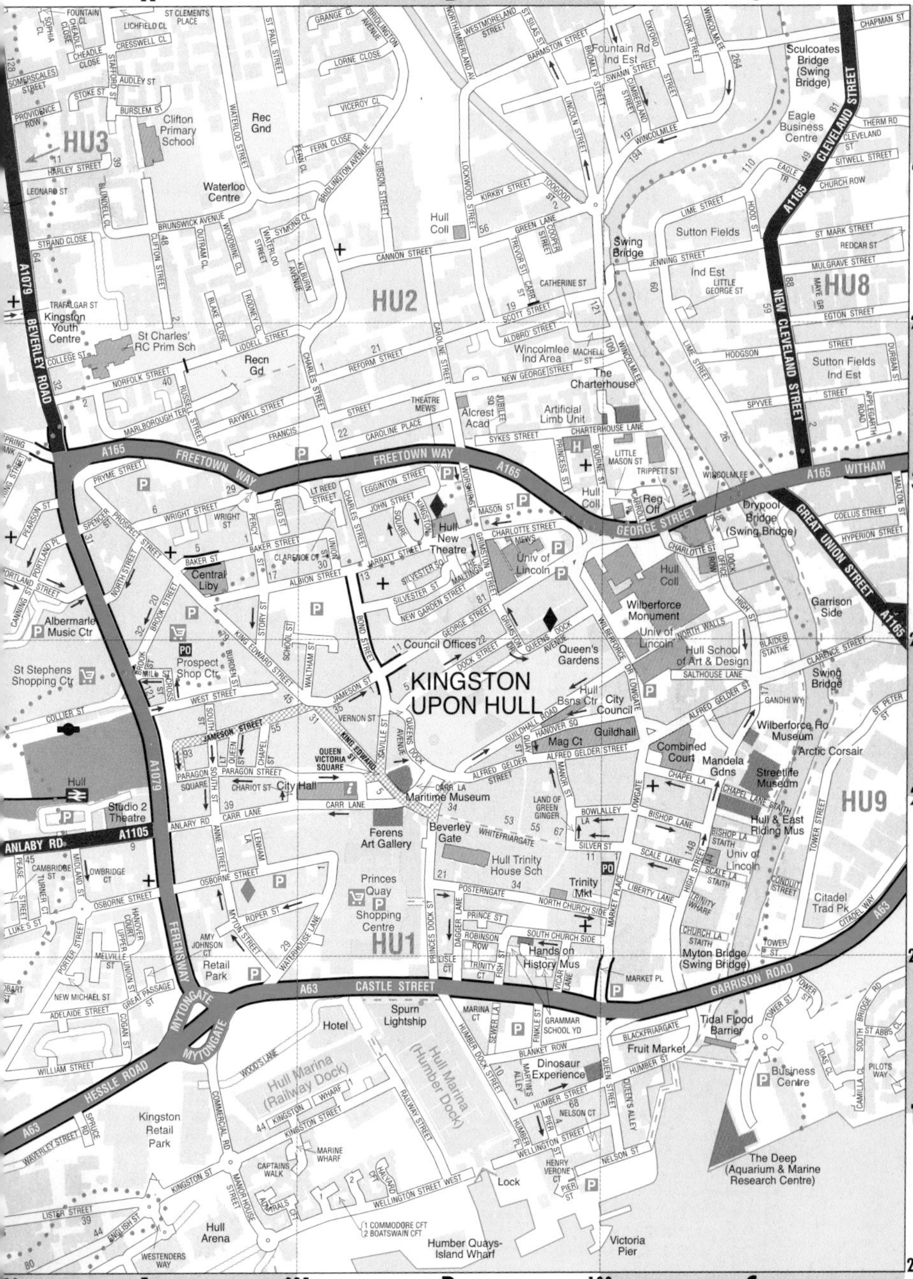
KINGSTON UPON HULL
HU1
HU2
HU3
HU8
HU9
FREETOWN WAY
A165
GEORGE STREET
WITHAM
BEVERLEY ROAD
A1079
NEW CLEVELAND STREET
CLEVELAND STREET
A1165
GREAT UNION STREET
CASTLE STREET
A63
GARRISON ROAD
HESSLE ROAD
MYTONGATE
FERENSWAY
ANLABY RD
A1105
WINCOLMLEE
CHARLES STREET
SPRING BANK
PROSPECT STREET
KING EDWARD STREET
JAMESON STREET
CARR LANE
ALFRED GELDER STREET
LOWGATE
HIGH STREET
QUEEN STREET
HUMBER DOCK STREET
WELLINGTON STREET WEST
KINGSTON STREET
COMMERCIAL RD
WHITEFRIARGATE
POSTERNGATE
MARKET PLACE
Clifton Primary School
Waterloo Centre
Rec Gnd
Kingston Youth Centre
St Charles' RC Prim Sch
Recn Gd
Hull Coll
Wincolmlee Ind Area
The Charterhouse
Artificial Limb Unit
Alcrest Acad
Fountain Rd Ind Est
Swing Bridge
Sutton Fields Ind Est
Sculcoates Bridge (Swing Bridge)
Eagle Business Centre
Drypool Bridge (Swing Bridge)
Hull New Theatre
Univ of Lincoln
Central Liby
Albermarle Music Ctr
St Stephens Shopping Ctr
Prospect Shop Ctr
Council Offices
Queen's Gardens
Wilberforce Monument
Hull School of Art & Design
Garrison Side
Hull Bsns Ctr
City Council
Guildhall
Mag Ct
Combined Court
Mandela Gdns
Wilberforce Ho Museum
Arctic Corsair
Streetlife Museum
Hull & East Riding Mus
Hull
Studio 2 Theatre
City Hall
Maritime Museum
Ferens Art Gallery
Beverley Gate
Hull Trinity House Sch
Princes Quay Shopping Centre
Trinity Mkt
Hands on History Mus
Retail Park
Citadel Trad Pk
Mytton Bridge (Swing Bridge)
Spurn Lightship
Hotel
Hull Marina (Railway Dock)
Hull Marina (Humber Dock)
Fruit Market
Tidal Flood Barrier
Dinosaur Experience
Business Centre
The Deep (Aquarium & Marine Research Centre)
Kingston Retail Park
Hull Arena
Lock
Humber Quays-Island Wharf
Victoria Pier
4
295
3
290
2
285
1
280
90
095
100

A B C

One-way streets

130 130 130

House numbers
1 59
HIGH ST

Scale: 5⅓ inches to 1 mile
0 110 yards 220 yards
0 125 m 250 m

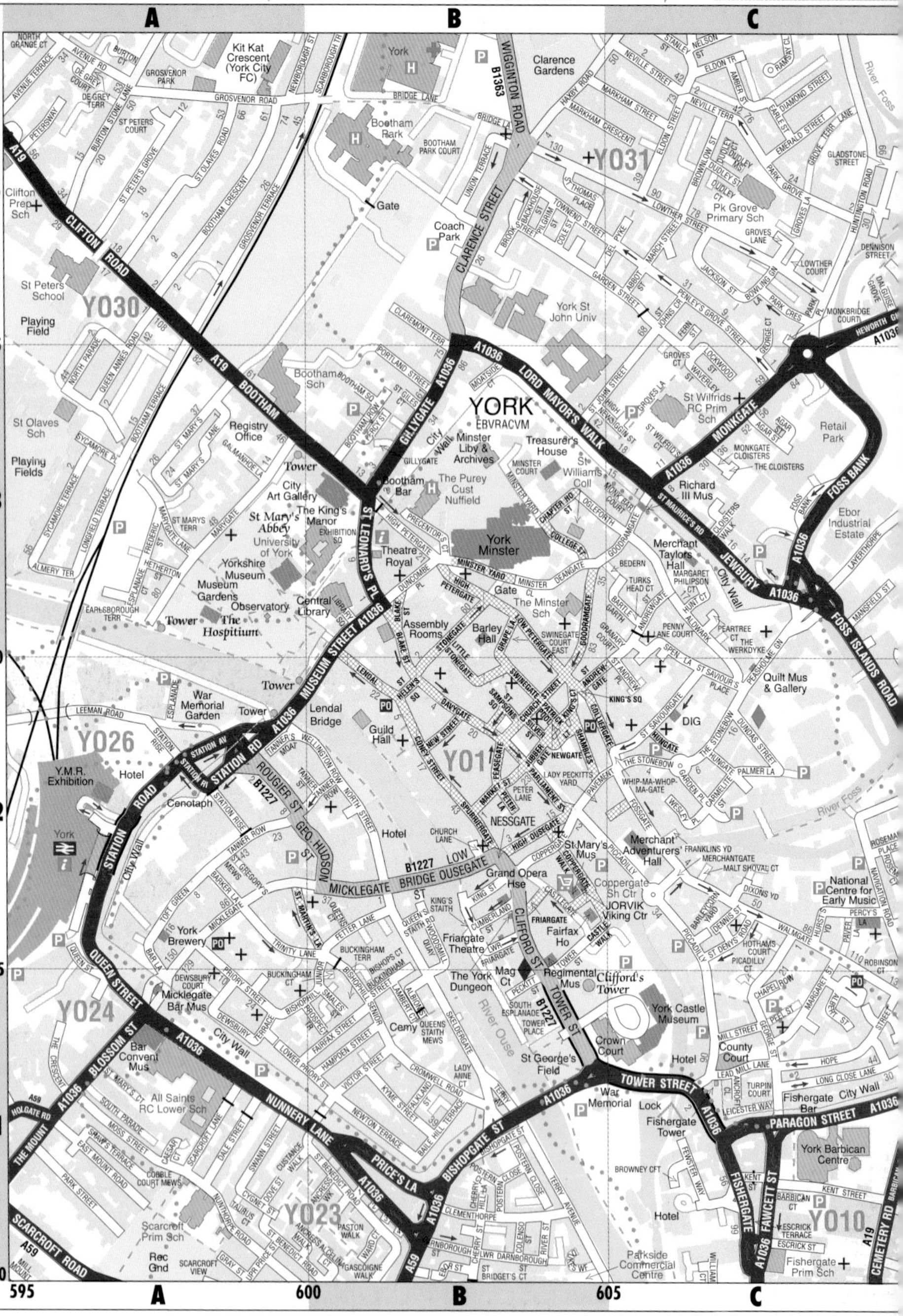

Index

Place name May be abbreviated on the map
Location number Present when a number indicates the place's position in a crowded area of mapping
Locality, town or village Shown when more than one place has the same name
Postcode district District for the indexed place
Page and grid square Page number and grid reference for the standard mapping

Church Rd 6 Beckenham BR2..........53 C6

Cities, towns and villages are listed in CAPITAL LETTERS **Public and commercial buildings** are highlighted in magenta
Places of interest are highlighted in blue with a star★

Abbreviations used in the index

cad	**Academy**	Comm	**Common**	Gd	**Ground**	L	**Leisure**	Prom	**Promenade**
pp	**Approach**	Cott	**Cottage**	Gdn	**Garden**	La	**Lane**	Rd	**Road**
rc	**Arcade**	Cres	**Crescent**	Gn	**Green**	Liby	**Library**	Recn	**Recreation**
ve	**Avenue**	Cswy	**Causeway**	Gr	**Grove**	Mdw	**Meadow**	Ret	**Retail**
glw	**Bungalow**	Ct	**Court**	H	**Hall**	Meml	**Memorial**	Sh	**Shopping**
ldg	**Building**	Ctr	**Centre**	Ho	**House**	Mkt	**Market**	Sq	**Square**
sns, Bus	**Business**	Ctry	**Country**	Hospl	**Hospital**	Mus	**Museum**	St	**Street**
vd	**Boulevard**	Cty	**County**	HQ	**Headquarters**	Orch	**Orchard**	Sta	**Station**
ath	**Cathedral**	Dr	**Drive**	Hts	**Heights**	Pal	**Palace**	Terr	**Terrace**
ir	**Circus**	Dro	**Drove**	Ind	**Industrial**	Par	**Parade**	TH	**Town Hall**
l	**Close**	Ed	**Education**	Inst	**Institute**	Pas	**Passage**	Univ	**University**
nr	**Corner**	Emb	**Embankment**	Int	**International**	Pk	**Park**	Wk, Wlk	**Walk**
oll	**College**	Est	**Estate**	Intc	**Interchange**	Pl	**Place**	Wr	**Water**
om	**Community**	Ex	**Exhibition**	Junc	**Junction**	Prec	**Precinct**	Yd	**Yard**

Index of towns, villages, streets, hospitals, industrial estates, railway stations, schools, shopping centres, universities and places of interest

st Ave HU6 . . . . 140 C6
st Main Rd DN36 . . . . . . .114 F8
nd Ave
Humberston DN36. . . . . . . .114 F8
Kingston upon Hull HU6 . . .140 B7
rd Ave 1 DN36. . . . . .114 F8
h Ave
Humberston DN36. . . . . . . .114 F8
Kingston upon Hull HU6 . . .140 B7
h Ave
2 Humberston Fitties DN36. . . . . .114 F8
Kingston upon Hull HU6 . . .139 F6
h Ave
3 Humberston Fitties DN36. . . . . .114 F8
Kingston upon Hull HU6 . . 140 A7
h Ave
4 Humberston Fitties DN36. . . . . .114 F8
Kingston upon Hull HU6 . . .140 B6
h Ave
5 Humberston Fitties DN36. . . . . .114 F8
Kingston upon Hull HU6 . . 140 A7
h Ave
6 Humberston Fitties DN36. . . . . .114 F8
Kingston upon Hull HU6 . . .140 B6
)th Ave
7 Humberston Fitties DN36. . . . . .114 F8
Kingston upon Hull HU6 . . .140 B7
lth Ave
Humberston Fitties DN36. . . . . .114 F8
Kingston upon Hull HU6 . . .140 B6
2th Ave
Humberston DN36. . . . . . . .114 F8
Kingston upon Hull HU6 . . 140 A7
4th Ave HU6. . . . . 140 A7
5th Ave HU6. . . . . 140 A6
6th Ave HU6. . . . . 140 A7
7th Ave HU6. . . . . 140 A6
8th Ave HU6. . . . . 140 A7
9th Ave HU6. . . . . 140 A6
)-21 Visual Arts Ctr★ DN15 . . . . 151 C7
0th Ave HU6. . . . . 140 A7
1st Ave HU6 . . . . .139 F6
2nd Ave HU6 . . . . 140 A7
3rd Ave HU6. . . . . 140 A6
4th Ave HU6. . . . . 140 A7
25th Ave HU6. . . . . 140 A6
26th Ave HU6. . . . . .139 F7
27th Ave HU6. . . . . 140 A6
28th Ave HU6. . . . . .139 F7
29th Ave HU6. . . . . .139 F6
30th Ave HU6. . . . . .139 F7
31st Ave HU6 . . . . .139 F6
32nd Ave HU6 . . . . .139 F7
33rd Ave HU6. . . . . .139 F6
34th Ave HU6. . . . . .139 F7
36th Ave HU6. . . . . .139 F7
37th Ave HU6. . . . . .139 E6
38th Ave HU6. . . . . .139 F7
40th Ave HU6. . . . . .139 F7

A

Abber La LS24 . . . . .24 A2
Abbey Drive E DN32. . . . . 152 D2
Abbey Drive W DN32. . . . 152 D2
Abbeyfield Rd DN7. . . . . .92 C4
Abbeygate 12 DN31 . . . . . 152 D3
Abbey Gdns 32 DN7 . . . . . . .92 D4
Abbey Gn 30 DN7 . . . . .92 D4
Abbey La
Kingston upon Hull HU10 . .138 E2
Preston HU12 . . . . .58 C1
Abbey L Ctr YO8 . . . . 148 C5
Abbey Park Mews DN32. 152 D2
Abbey Park Rd DN32. . . . 152 D2
Abbey Pl 9 YO8 . . . . 148 D5
Abbey Rd
Bridlington YO16 . . . . .122 B2
Grimsby DN32 . . . . 152 D2
Hatfield DN7 . . . . .92 D4
Kingston upon Hull HU11 . .142 F6
Scunthorpe DN17. . . . . .150 F2
Ulceby DN39 . . . . .86 A1
Abbey Rise DN19 . . . . .85 D8
Abbey St
Kingston upon Hull HU9 . . 146 C7
York YO30 . . . . 130 A7
Abbey Walk Sh Ctr YO8 . 148 C6
Abbey Way
Hatfield DN7 . . . . .92 D5
Sculcoates HU5 . . . . .140 E2
Abbey Wlk
Grimsby DN31 . . . . 152 D3
Selby YO8. . . . . 148 C5
Abbey Yd YO8. . . . . 148 C5
Abbots Cl HU8. . . . . .141 E5
Abbots Ct YO8 . . . . 148 D3
Abbotsford Cl HU5. . . . . . . .139 F3
Abbotsford Rd YO10. . . . . .130 F3
Abbots Gait YO32 . . . . .127 F6
Abbots Rd
Scunthorpe DN17. . . . . .150 F2
Selby YO8. . . . . .148 E3
Abbot's Rd YO8 . . . . .148 E3
Abbot St YO31 . . . . 156 C4
Abbotsway
Grimsby DN32 . . . . 152 D2
York YO31 . . . . .130 E8
Abbots Wlk HU16 . . . . 139 A5
Abbotts Gdns YO8 . . . . .48 A8
Abbotts Grange DN36 . . . .114 B7
Abbotts Mews YO8. . . . . . 148 D3
Abbotts Way YO16 . . . . . . 122 D4
Abelton Gr 33 YO32 . . . . .13 E5
Abercorn St DN16. . . . . . . 151 A6
Aberdeen St HU9 . . . . .141 F3
Aberdovey Cl 3 HU7. . . . . .57 A7
Aberford Wlk HU9 . . . . . . .142 E1
Abingdon Garth 1 HU7 . . .57 A5
Abraxus Ct YO15 . . . . .10 D2
Acacia Ave
Flixborough DN15 . . . . .96 B7
19 Gainsborough DN21. . . .117 B1
York YO32 . . . . .127 E4
Acacia Ct DN16 . . . . .151 B2
Acacia Dr HU8. . . . . 141 D2
Acacia Gr 36 YO32 . . . . .13 E5
Acacia Way DN17 . . . . 107 C6
Acadia Gr HU13. . . . . .143 F1
Acasta Way HU9 . . . . 147 C8
Acaster Ave YO23 . . . . .36 A3
Acaster La
Acaster Malbis YO23 . . . . . .133 B1
Acaster Selby YO23 . . . . .36 A4
ACASTER MALBIS 36 D8
ACASTER SELBY 36 B4
Accommodation Rd YO25 . .8 D6
Acer Gr DN17. . . . . 150 C1
Acey La HU12. . . . . .58 B1
Achille Rd DN34 . . . . .102 B3
ACKLAM 16 E8
Acklam Dr HU18 . . . . 134 D6
Acklam Gr DN32 . . . . .153 B2
Acklam Rd HU12. . . . . .72 D7
Ackworth St HU8 . . . . 141 C1
Acland St
Gainsborough DN21 . . . . . .117 B1
4 Kingston upon Hull HU3. . . . . 145 A6
ACOMB 129 C3
Acomb Comm Rd DN7 . . . .92 F4
Acomb Prim Sch YO24 . . .129 E3
Acomb Rd YO24. . . . . 129 D3
Acom Bsns Pk DN32 . . . . .152 E3
Acomb Wood Cl YO24 . . . 132 C7
Acomb Wood Dr YO24. . . .132 B7
Acorn Cl
6 Barlby YO8 . . . . .49 B4
Bridlington YO16 . . . . .123 B7
Acorn Gr HU8 . . . . .141 E7
Acorn Ind Est
Beverley HU17. . . . . 137 C4
Kingston Upon Hull HU9 . . .146 B7
Acorns The 20 HU15. . . . . . .66 D8
Acorn Way
24 Bottesford DN16 . . . . . . .96 D1
Gateforth YO8 . . . . .48 B1
Hessle HU13 . . . . .143 B3
York YO24 . . . . 132 D7
Acredykes 7 YO15. . . . . .4 D3
Acres La
Scrayingham YO41. . . . . .16 B8
Wroot DN9. . . . . 104 D7
Acton Cl HU8 . . . . .141 F5
Acton Ct 7 DN32. . . . . . . 153 A5
Adam Smith St DN31. . . . 152 C5
Adam St DN14 . . . . 149 D3
Adderbury Gr 5 HU5 . . . 140 D2
Addison Gdns HU8. . . . . . 141 D3
Addison Rd 10 HU12 . . . . . .58 D1
Addlekeld YO42 . . . . .30 A5
Addle La DN14. . . . . .65 E7
Adelaide Prim Sch HU3 . 145 D5
Adelaide Rd 6 DN6. . . . . . . .76 E2
Adelaide St
Kingston upon Hull HU1 . . 155 A1
3 York YO23 . . . . .130 B2
Adeline St DN14 . . . . 149 C5
Adeliza Garth 20 HU12 . . . .72 D7
Adelphi Cl HU8 . . . . .141 F4
Adelphi Ct 4 DN36 . . . . . 114 A7
Adelphi Dr 7 DN33 . . . . . .113 E8
Adelphi St YO25 . . . . .124 E4
Adlard Gr DN36. . . . . 114 C7
ADLINGFLEET 81 E7
Adlingfleet Rd DN17 . . . . . .81 E6
Adlington Cl 8 YO32. . . . . .14 A7
Admirals Croft HU1 . . . . . 155 A1
Admirals Mews 1 YO15. 122 D2
Admiral Walker Rd HU17 . . . . 154 A2
Advent Ct 9 DN39. . . . . . . .86 A1
Aegre Dr DN14 . . . . .65 C4
Africa Cl 15 DN34. . . . . . . .102 B2
Agard Ave DN15 . . . . .150 E7
Agar St YO31 . . . . 156 C3
AIKE. 44 A8
Aike La YO25 . . . . .33 A1
Ainshaw HU6 . . . . .139 E8
Ainslie Rd HU12 . . . . .72 D7
Ainslie St DN32. . . . . .152 E2
Ainsty Ave YO24 . . . . .132 F8
Ainsty Gr YO24. . . . . .132 F8
Ainsty St DN14. . . . . .149 E4
Ainsty View YO17. . . . . .16 E8
Ainsworth Rd 16 DN40 . . . .87 B1
Ainthorpe Gr HU5. . . . . . . 144 C7
Ainthorpe Prim Sch HU5 144 C8
Aintree Cl HU17 . . . . .136 E6
Aintree Ct YO24. . . . . .132 F8
Aire Cl
10 Brough HU15 . . . . .68 D5
36 Immingham DN40 . . . . . . .87 B1
Airedale HU7 . . . . .140 E6
Airedale Cl 10 DN20. . . . . . . .97 E4
Airedale Dr YO16 . . . . .122 F7
Airedale Rd DN16. . . . . . . 151 D1
Airedale Way DN31 . . . . . 152 D4
Aire St
Goole DN14 . . . . 149 D3
Knottingley WF11. . . . . .61 A3
12 Knottingley WF11. . . . . . .61 A3
Airfield Ind Est YO41 . . . . . .26 F3
Airlie St HU3 . . . . .145 B5
AIRMYN 64 E4
Airmyn Ave
Goole DN14 . . . . .149 B5
1 Kingston upon Hull HU3. . . . . .144 E6
Airmyn Park Prim Sch DN14 . . . . .64 E4
Airmyn Rd
Airmyn DN14 . . . . .64 D3
Goole DN14 . . . . .149 B5
Air St HU5. . . . . .140 F2
AISBY 118 B3
Aisne St HU5 . . . . 145 A8
Ajax Cl
Grimsby DN34 . . . . .102 B2
Kingston upon Hull HU9 . . 142 D5
Ajax Ct DN15 . . . . .96 C7
Akeferry Rd
Haxey DN9. . . . . 105 C1

Akeferry Rd *continued*
Westwoodside DN9 105 B2
Akester Cl 4 HU17 137 B3
Alan Cres DN15 150 F6
Alaska St HU8 141 B1
Alba Cl DN17 150 D1
Albany St
Gainsborough DN21 117 B1
Kingston upon Hull HU3 145 D8
3 York YO26 129 F5
Albany Villas HU13 144 A1
Albatross Dr DN37 102 A4
Albemarle Cl 5 HU15 68 B5
Albemarle Rd
Bilton HU11 58 A3
2 Keyingham HU12 73 C4
York YO23 130 B2
Albemarle St 2 HU3 145 B5
Albermarle Music Ctr* HU2 155 A2
Alberta Cres 7 DN17 96 C2
Albert Ave HU3 145 A7
Albert Avenue Pools HU3 145 A7
Albert Cl
4 Grimsby DN32 152 F5
1 York YO32 130 F8
Albertine Ct 5 DN37 113 D7
Albert Marson Ct DN16 151 B6
Albert Pl 3 DN32 152 F5
Albert Rd
Cleethorpes DN35 153 F2
Scunthorpe DN16 151 A1
Albert St
10 Bridlington YO15 122 E2
Brigg DN20 98 C2
Goole DN14 149 C2
5 New Holland DN19 70 E2
3 Thorne/Moorends DN8 93 B8
York YO10 156 C1
Albert Street E DN32 152 F5
Albert Street W DN32 152 F5
Albert Terr
Beverley HU17 154 A2
Kingston upon Hull HU7 141 D6
Welwick HU12 90 A7
Albery Way DN36 114 A8
Albina Garth 1 HU12 72 D7
Albion Ave YO26 129 B6
Albion Ct
Beverley HU17 137 B4
Kingston upon Hull HU4 144 B6
Albion Hill DN9 105 E6
Albion La HU10 138 A3
Albion Pk DN16 151 D5
Albion St
Great Driffield YO25 124 F3
Grimsby DN32 152 F4
Kingston upon Hull HU1 155 A3
York YO1 156 B1
Albion Terr
Bridlington YO15 122 F3
Misterton DN10 116 D5
Albourne Ave DN15 151 A6
Albright Cl 31 YO42 29 A3
Alcelina Ct YO23 156 B1
Alcrest Acad HU2 155 B3
Alcuin Ave YO10 131 A4
Alcuin Way YO10 131 B2
Aldam Dr DN9 94 F1
Aldborough Gr HU9 142 A2
Aldborough Way YO26 129 F5
Aldbro' St HU2 155 B3
ALDBROUGH 47 C1
Aldbrough La HU11 59 A6
Aldbrough Prim Sch HU11 47 C1
Aldbrough Rd
East Garton HU11 59 D7
Withernwick HU11 46 E3
Alden Cl DN40 87 C1
Aldenham Pk HU7 56 E5
Alder Cl
16 Brough HU15 68 D5
Selby YO8 148 D2
Alder Gr 6 DN8 79 B2
Alder Hey Dr 9 HU9 142 A5
Alderley Ct YO32 127 E3
Alderley Edge 6 DN37 113 D6
Alderman Cogan CE Prim Sch 16 HU9 141 F2
Aldermans Way 10 YO25 34 B2
Alderney Way 2 DN40 101 C8
Alderson Ct YO16 122 D2
Alderson Mews 5 HU9 146 C7
Alders The 22 DN21 117 C1
Aldersyde YO24 132 E7
Aldersyde Ct YO24 132 E7
Aldersyde Mews YO24 132 E7
Alder View 22 DN33 102 C2
Alder Way YO32 127 D2
Aldreth Gr YO23 130 C2
Aldrich Rd DN35 103 C2
Aldwark YO1 156 C3
Aldwych Croft 6 DN36 114 A7
Aldwych Ct HU5 144 E8
Alexander Ave YO31 127 E2
Alexander Rd DN16 151 B6
Alexandra Ct
4 Bridlington YO15 122 F3
York YO10 130 E1
Alexandra Dock N DN31 152 C6
Alexandra Dock Ret Pk DN31 152 D5
Alexandra Dr
1 Beverley HU17 55 E8
5 Bridlington YO15 122 F3
Alexandra Prom YO15 123 A3
Alexandra Rd
Cleethorpes DN35 153 F2
Grimsby DN31 152 D4
Hornsea HU18 134 D4
Kingston upon Hull HU5 140 C3
Scunthorpe DN16 151 B2
Strensall YO32 14 A6
Thorne/Moorends DN8 79 B2
Alexandra Road N DN40 87 D3
Alexandra Road S DN40 87 D2
Alexandra St
Goole DN14 149 D4
Kingston upon Hull HU3 145 D7
Thorne DN8 79 A1
Alexandra Wlk YO15 122 F3
Alfonso St 5 HU3 145 B5
Alfred Bean Hospl YO25 125 A6
Alfred Gelder St HU1 155 B2
Alfred St
Gainsborough DN21 117 B1
Grimsby DN31 152 D4
Kingston upon Hull HU3 145 D5
Alfreton Ct 1 DN15 150 B6
Alfriston Cl HU7 141 B6
Algarth Rd
Pocklington YO42 29 A4
York YO31 131 B7
Algarth Rise
Pocklington YO42 28 F4
York YO31 131 B7
Algernon St DN32 152 F1
Alison Garth 23 HU12 72 D7
ALKBOROUGH 82 C8
Alkborough Flats* DN15 67 B1
Alkborough La DN15 82 D7
Alkborough Prim Sch DN15 82 C8
Alkborough Turf Maze (Julian Bower)* DN15 82 B8
Allanby St DN15 151 A7
Allanhall Way HU10 143 B8
Allanson Dr HU16 139 D5
Allanson Gr YO24 129 E2
Allan St 2 YO30 130 C7
Allderidge Ave HU5 140 B3
Allenby Ave DN34 152 A2
Allenby Cres LN11 121 D3
Allen Cl YO10 131 A4
Allendale YO24 132 D8
Allerford Dr 8 HU7 57 A5
ALLERTHORPE 28 E2
Allerthorpe Comm Nature Reserve* YO42 28 B2
Allerthorpe Lakeland Pk* YO42 28 E1
Allerton Dr
1 Immingham DN40 87 C1
22 Poppleton YO26 12 F1
Allerton Prim Sch 37 DN40 87 B1
Allestree Dr 2 DN33 113 E8
All Hallows Rd 3 HU17 55 B7
Alliance Ave HU3 144 F7
Alliance La HU3 144 F7
Allington Dr
Great Coates DN31 102 C5
York YO31 131 B6
Allinson Yd HU17 45 A7
Allison Cl DN17 107 D7
Allison La
14 Flamborough YO15 5 A2
Ulrome YO25 22 F4
Alloa Cl 2 HU6 140 B8
Allotment La YO25 124 E5
Allotment Wlk YO16 122 B1
All Saints Cl
4 Kingston upon Hull HU13 69 F4
11 Waltham DN37 113 E6
All Saints Ct 6 YO43 135 D4
All Saints Mews HU12 58 C1
All Saints RC Lower Sch YO23 156 A1
All Saints RC Upper School YO29 130 B2
All Saints' St HU3 145 D8
Alma Cl HU10 143 D7
Alma Gr YO10 130 D2
Alma St
6 Kingston upon Hull HU9 146 B7
4 Withernsea HU19 74 F7
Alma Terr
Selby YO8 148 C6
York YO10 130 D2
Almery Terr YO30 156 A3
Almond Cl
Great Driffield YO25 124 F2
Hambleton YO8 48 B1
Almond Gr
Brigg DN20 98 B2
3 Kingston upon Hull HU3 145 D6
Scunthorpe DN16 151 B4
York YO32 127 D4
Almond Tree Ave DN14 63 C3
Almsford Dr YO26 129 C5
Almsford Rd YO26 129 C5
Alness Dr YO24 132 B7
Alne Terr YO10 130 E2
Alpha Ave HU17 136 D6
Alpha Ct DN8 92 F8
Alsenham Pk 9 HU7 56 E5
Alston Ave 4 HU8 141 B1
ALTHORPE 95 D4
Althorpe & Keadby Prim Sch DN17 95 D5
Althorpe Park 17 HU7 56 E5
Althorpe Sta DN17 95 D5
Altoft Cl
2 Brandesburton YO25 34 B2
12 Laceby DN37 101 F1
Alton Park Mews YO25 22 C1
Alton Rd YO16 122 D7
Altyre Way DN36 103 B1
Alured Garth 9 HU12 72 D7
Alveston Rd DN17 150 D4
Alvingham Ave 25 DN35 103 C2
Alvingham Rd DN16 151 B3
Alvin Wlk 9 YO41 27 B2
Alvis Gr YO10 131 D4
Alwoodley Cl 1 HU8 142 B5
Alwyne Dr YO30 126 E1
Alwyne Gr YO30 126 E1
Alwyn Rd 19 DN8 93 B8
Amanda Cl HU6 139 E6
Amanda Dr DN7 92 D4
Ambaston Rd HU18 134 C5
Amber Ct YO31 156 C4
Amberley Cl HU7 141 B6
Amberly St 4 YO26 129 E5
Amber St YO31 156 C4
Ambler's La YO30 12 F7
Ambleside Ave YO10 131 B4
Ambrey Cl 16 YO14 2 F8
Ambrose Ave 1 DN7 92 E4
Ambrose St YO10 130 D1
Amcott Ave DN10 116 D4
AMCOTTS 81 F1
Amcotts Rd 14 DN33 102 D1
Amelia Ct 15 DN36 114 D8
Amen La YO43 53 D5
Amesbury Ave DN33 113 D8
Amethyst Ct 11 DN36 114 A8
Amethyst La DN14 65 F8
Amethyst Rd HU9 142 C4
Amos Cl 9 DN33 113 D8
Amos Cres DN16 151 D3
Ampleforth Gr HU5 144 D8
Amsterdam Rd HU7 141 A5
Amwell Gn 8 DN7 92 D3
Amy Johnson Ave YO16 122 E6
Amy Johnson Ct HU1 155 A1
Amy Johnson Way YO30 127 A3
Amy St DN14 149 C4
Anastasia Cl 1 DN21 117 B2
Ancaster Ave
Grimsby DN33 113 D8
Kingston upon Hull HU5 139 F3
Ancaster Ct DN16 151 A1
Ancholme Ave 10 DN40 87 B1
Ancholme Gdns 11 DN20 98 C2
Ancholme L Ctr DN20 98 B1
Ancholme Rd DN16 151 D2
Ancholme Way DN20 98 B2
Anchorage St 7 DN20 98 B2
Anchor Cl 31 DN8 93 A8
Anchor Rd
Kingston upon Hull HU6 140 C8
Scunthorpe DN16 97 A3
Anchors Way 16 DN20 98 B2
Ancient La DN7 92 F3
Ancourt HU6 139 E6
Ancress Wlk YO23 156 A1
Ancroft Cl YO1 156 C1
Anderby Dr DN37 102 B4
Anderson Gr 6 YO24 129 F2
Anderson Rd
Goole DN14 149 A4
Scunthorpe DN16 151 C3
Andersons Cl 17 HU12 72 D7
Anderson St
7 Great Driffield YO25 124 F3
Grimsby DN31 152 D3
Andrew Dr 4 YO32 127 F1
Andrew La 3 HU12 72 C7
Andrew Marvell Bsns & Ent Coll HU9 142 D4
Andrew Paddock DN20 108 F5
Andrew Rd 11 DN36 114 D8
Andrew's Ct 15 YO42 28 F4
Andrews Rd DN18 84 A7
Andrews Way 8 DN40 87 B1
Angerstein Rd DN17 150 F1
Anglesey Dr DN40 101 C8
ANGRAM 24 C3
Angram Cl YO30 126 F1
Angram La YO8 49 A6
Angram Rd YO26 24 A5
Angus Dr YO25 124 D4
ANLABY 143 E5
Anlaby Acre Head Prim Sch HU4 144 B7
Anlaby Ave 7 HU4 144 B6
Anlaby High Rd HU4 144 C6
Anlaby House Est HU10 143 E6
Anlaby Park Road N HU4 144 B5
Anlaby Park Road S HU4 144 B2
Anlaby Prim Sch HU10 144 A6
Anlaby Rd HU3 155 A2
Anlafgate 7 HU10 143 F6
Anlary Rd HU1 155 A2
Annan Cl YO24 132 C6
Annandale Rd
Kingston upon Hull HU9 142 E2
Willerby HU10 138 B1
Annerley Dr YO16 123 A7
Annes Cres DN16 151 C3
Annesley St DN31 152 D5
Anne St
Kingston upon Hull HU1 155 A2
Anne St *continued*
York YO23 130 C2
Ann Gr DN35 103 B2
Annie Med La HU15 53 F1
Annie Reed Rd HU17 137 C3
Annie Road Ct HU17 137 C3
Annie St YO8 148 C6
Anningson La 6 DN36 114 A8
Annumhills Rd YO8 50 D7
Ann Watson St HU7 141 A4
Anserdam La HU15 52 C2
Anson Dr YO10 133 D8
Anson Rd HU9 142 B3
Antelope Rd DN18 70 A1
Anthea Dr YO31 127 E1
Antholme Cl HU7 141 C6
Anthony's Bank Rd DN35 103 E1
Anthony Way 1 DN41 101 D6
Antrim Way 4 DN33 102 E1
Antwerp Rd HU7 141 A5
Anvil Wlk DN15 82 F3
Apollo St 9 YO10 130 E3
Apollo Wlk HU8 141 F4
Apperston Ct 21 YO42 29 A4
Appian Way DN31 152 A6
Appin Cl 7 HU7 57 A6
Apple Blossom Ct 8 YO24 129 B1
APPLEBY 83 C1
Appleby Cl DN17 150 F1
Appleby Ct 8 DN32 153 A5
Appleby Gdns DN20 97 D4
Appleby Glade YO32 127 D7
Appleby La
Broughton DN20 97 D4
Burstwick HU12 73 A7
Appleby Mill Rd DN16 151 E7
Appleby Pl 2 YO31 131 A5
Apple Croft HU16 138 B8
Applecroft Rd
Selby YO8 148 A4
York YO31 131 B7
Appledore Cl HU9 146 C6
Applefields DN20 98 D3
Applefields Sch YO31 131 B5
Applegarth 8 HU15 66 D7
Apple Garth
21 Hedon HU12 72 D7
15 Poppleton YO26 12 F1
Applegarth Cl DN35 153 D1
Applegarth La
Bainton YO25 31 E7
Bridlington YO16 122 D4
Applegarth Mews 3 HU16 139 B7
Applegarth Rd HU8 155 C3
Appleton Ct YO23 132 F3
Appleton Gdns 8 HU15 53 F1
Appleton Prim Sch HU5 139 E2
Appleton Rd
Bishopthorpe YO23 133 A3
Kingston upon Hull HU5 139 E3
Appleton Way DN16 151 C2
Apple Tree Cl
Kingston upon Hull HU8 141 D4
1 Long Riston/Arnold HU11 45 C5
Apple Tree Ct 1 DN41 101 F5
Apple Tree Garth 5 HU17 45 A8
Appletree Mews HU10 138 C1
Apple Tree Wlk HU16 139 D6
Appleyard Dr DN18 84 E8
Arables La HU12 74 C4
Arcade The DN14 149 D4
Archbishop Cl HU9 142 D2
Archbishop Holgates Sch YO10 131 B3
Archbishop of York CE Jun Sch YO23 133 A4
Archbishop Sentamu Acad HU9 142 D3
Archer Rd DN37 113 D6
Archers Cl DN20 98 D4
Archibald Cl 16 YO42 28 F4
Archway The YO43 135 D4
Arcon Dr HU4 144 D6
Arctic Corsair* HU1 155 C2
Arden Ct HU5 139 C2
Arden Rd HU17 154 C4
Ardent Rd DN18 70 A1
Arden Village 21 DN35 103 C1
Ardmore Cl HU9 142 B4
Arenhall Cl 2 YO32 127 C8
Argam Dikes*
Grindale YO25 3 B2
Rudston YO25 10 A7
Argam La YO25 2 F1
Argent Cl 8 HU6 140 B8
Arglam La YO43 51 F6
Argyle Ct DN15 151 A7
Argyle St
Goole DN14 149 D4
Kingston upon Hull HU3 145 C7
York YO23 130 B1
Ariston St DN32 153 B3
Arkley Cl 18 HU15 68 C5
Ark Royal HU11 142 E6
Arkwright St 10 DN21 117 B1
Arkwright Way DN16 151 F2
Arlington Ave HU16 139 B6
Arlington Rd YO30 127 A1
Arlington St 2 HU3 145 D6
Armeria Dr 23 DN17 96 D1
Armour Rd DN16 151 E7
Armoury Rd YO8 148 B5
Armstrong Cl HU17 154 C2
Armstrong Place E DN31 152 C5
Armstrong Place W DN31 152 C
Armstrong St DN31 152 C
Armstrong Way
Beverley HU17 154 B
Rawcliffe YO32 126 E
Armthorpe La DN3 92 A
Arncliffe Cl 1 HU7 56 F
Arncliffe Way HU16 139 A
ARNOLD 45 C
Arnold Cl DN37 101 F
Arnold Ct 9 DN32 153 A
Arnold La HU3 145 B
Arnold Lane E HU11 45 C
Arnold Lane W HU11 45 C
Arnold St HU3 145 B
Arnside Pl 2 YO10 130 F
ARRAM 44 A
Arram Gr HU6 139 E
Arram Rd HU17 43 D
Arram Sta HU17 43 F
Arran Cl
Immingham DN40 101 C
Kingston upon Hull HU9 142 A
19 New Waltham DN36 114 A
Arrandale DN21 107 C
Arran Pl YO31 130 D
Arras Dr HU16 138 E
Arreton Cl HU8 142 D
Art College Mews DN32 152 F
Arthur Lucan Ct HU9 142 C
Arthur Pl 6 YO30 126 B
Arthur Rd 12 DN21 117 B
Arthur St
Grimsby DN31 152 C
Kingston upon Hull HU3 145 A
Withernsea HU19 74 F
York YO10 130 D
Arundel Cl
4 Gainsborough DN21 117 C
Kingston upon Hull HU9 146 C
Arundel Gr YO24 132 C
Arundel Pl DN35 153 E
Arundel Rd 5 DN6 76 E
Arundel Wlk DN34 152 A
Ascot Rd
23 Waltham DN37 113 D
Wigginton YO32 13 D
Ascott Cl
Beverley HU17 136 E
Kingston upon Hull HU4 144 D
Ascot Way YO24 129 D
Asenby Wlk HU5 139 D
Asgard Way 5 DN33 102 D
Ash Ave HU15 68 C
Ashberry Dr
Messingham DN17 107 D
1 Scunthorpe DN16 151 B
Ashbourne 7 DN37 113 D
Ashbourne Ct DN15 150 E
Ashbourne Way YO24 132 C
Ashburnham Cl 4 DN6 76 F
Ashburnham Rd 14 DN8 93 A
Ashburnham Wlk 5 DN6 76 F
Ashbury Ct HU6 140 A
ASHBY 151 B
Ashby Cl
Grimsby DN37 102 B
Holton le Clay DN36 114 B
Kingston upon Hull HU4 144 B
ASHBY CUM FENBY 113 D
Ashby High St DN16 151 A
ASHBY HILL 113 C
Ashby Hill DN37 113 C
Ashby La DN37 113 C
Ashby Rd
Cleethorpes DN35 103 B
Kingston upon Hull HU4 144 B
Scunthorpe DN16 151 A
Ash Cl
Hessle HU13 143 C
Newton on Derwent YO41 27 E
Sproatley HU11 58 D
York YO31 131 B
Ashcombe Rd HU7 56 E
Ashcourt Cl HU18 134 C
Ashcourt Dr HU18 134 B
Ash Ct 13 DN35 103 B
Ashdale Pk 14 HU14 69 A
Ashdale Rd 19 YO19 26 F
Ash Dell DN14 149 E
Ash Dene 7 HU17 55 D
Ashdene Cl HU10 143 E
Ashdown Ave DN15 150 E
Ashdown Cl DN20 98 D
Ashdown Way
Gringley on the Hill DN10 116 A
Misterton DN10 116 C
Ash Dr
Kingston upon Hull HU10 143 F
Scalby HU15 66 D
Thorngumbald HU12 72 E
Ashendon Dr HU8 141 A
Ashfield YO43 40 A
Ashfield Ave 1 DN8 93 A
Ashfield Ct
Crowle DN17 94 D
York YO24 132 E
Ashfield Gr 6 DN7 92 C
Ashfield Pk DN17 150 E
Ashfield Rd
Hatfield DN7 92 C
Thorne DN8 92 F
Ashford Pl YO24 129 D
Ashford Wlk HU9 142 E
Ashgate Rd HU10 138 E

sh Gr
4 Aldbrough HU11 47 C1
Brigg DN20 98 B2
17 Gainsborough DN21 117 B1
Hutton Cranswick YO25 32 E6
Market Weighton YO43 135 D4
Messingham DN17 107 D7
Newland HU5 140 C3
1 Riccall YO19 48 F8
3 Scotter DN21 107 B3
Scunthorpe DN16 151 B3
Willerby HU10 138 D1
sh Hill Cres DN7 92 D4
sh Hill Rd
20 Hatfield DN7 92 D4
Sykehouse DN14 78 A3
sh Holt Long Barrow*
DN37 112 D4
sh La
8 Haxby YO32 13 E5
Melbourne YO42 39 A5
shlea 1 DN10 116 C5
shlea Cl YO8 148 D4
shleigh Ct 13 DN41 101 F5
shleigh Dr 6 YO25 22 D1
shley Park Cres YO31 131 B6
shley Park Rd YO31 131 B7
shmeade Cl YO24 132 B8
shmole Wlk HU17 154 C4
shridge Dr DN32 153 B1
sh St YO26 129 E4
shthorpe HU6 139 F8
shton Ave YO30 130 B8
shton Cl HU6 139 F8
shtree Ave DN34 152 A2
shtree Cl DN9 94 E1
sh Tree Cl 5 DN40 87 C2
shtree Cres HU15 53 D3
shtree Dr YO8 48 D1
sh Tree Dr
5 Haxey DN9 105 D2
Leconfield HU17 43 D6
sh Tree Garth 6 HU11 45 C5
sh Tree Rd 13 DN8 93 A7
shville St
Bridlington YO16 122 D3
York YO31 130 D7
shwell Ave HU9 142 D1
shwood Cl
21 Brough HU15 68 C5
Burton Stather DN15 82 B5
shwood Dr 17 DN36 103 D1
shwood Glade YO32 127 C6
shworth Dr HU10 138 B1
shworthy Cl 5 HU7 56 F5
ske Mews HU5 139 D3
skern & Campsall Sports
Ctr DN6 76 F1
skew Ave HU4 144 E4
Askham Bog Nature
Reserve* TO23 132 C5
ASKHAM BRYAN 24 F3
Askham Bryan Coll YO23 24 F2
Askham Bryan La YO23 132 A6
Askham Croft 1 YO24 129 B1
Askham Fields La YO23 24 F2
Askham Gr YO24 129 B2
Askham La
Askham Bryan YO24 132 A8
Woodthorpe YO23 132 A7
York YO24 129 B1
ASKHAM RICHARD 24 D3
Askrigg Wlk HU5 139 D4
Aspall Wlk HU8 142 C7
Aspen Cl
3 Dunnington YO19 26 F7
Gipsyville HU4 144 C3
Market Weighton YO43 135 D5
Selby YO8 48 D2
Aspen Ct
15 Cleethorpes DN35 103 B1
13 Gainsborough DN21 117 C1
Aspen Gr DN16 151 B4
Aspen Wlk 4 HU15 68 D5
Asphodel Cl 15 DN36 114 B8
Asquith Ave YO31 131 A5
Asquith St DN21 117 A1
ASSELBY 64 D7
Asterby Rd DN17 150 F1
Astley Cres 18 DN21 107 C3
Astley St HU3 144 F7
Aston Gn 4 DN7 92 D3
Aston Hall Dr 11 HU14 69 A5
Aston Rd HU10 143 F8
Astoria Cres HU8 141 F4
Astral Cl
Northfield HU13 143 F3
Sutton-on-Hull HU7 141 D7
Astral Gdns HU7 141 C7
Astral Rd HU13 143 F3
Astral Way HU7 141 C7
Atcherley Cl YO10 133 D8
Athelstan Rd HU17 154 B4
Athena Dr DN31 152 A6
Athenian Way DN37 102 C6
Atherton Way DN20 98 B2
Atholl Ave HU13 143 E3
Athol St HU3 144 F4
Atkinson Ave DN20 98 C3
Atkinson Dr 19 HU15 68 C6
Atkinson La 6 DN37 113 E6
Atkinson's Warren Nature
Reserve* DN15 96 B7
Atkinsons Way DN15 96 C8
Atlanta Ct 2 HU8 142 B5
Atlas Rd
Scunthorpe DN17 150 F4
York YO30 127 A3
Atterby La LN8 119 F3
Atterwith La YO26 24 A7
Attlee Dr DN14 149 C5
ATWICK 35 C5
Atwick Ct 2 HU9 142 B1
Atwick Rd
Bewholme YO25 35 A4
Hornsea HU18 134 B6
Atwood Cl 4 DN40 87 B2
Aubretia Dr 22 DN17 96 D1
Auburn Cl
Bridlington YO16 122 B5
Kingston upon Hull HU9 142 C1
Auburn Wlk YO16 122 B5
Auchinleck Cl YO25 124 B1
Auckland Ave HU6 140 C5
Auckland Gr DN8 79 C2
Auckland Rd
Grimsby DN31 152 F6
Scunthorpe DN15 150 F6
Aucuba Cl YO32 127 D2
Audax Cl YO30 127 A3
Audax Rd YO30 127 A3
Audern Rd DN16 96 D2
Audley St HU2 155 A4
Audus St 10 YO8 148 C5
AUGHTON 38 C1
Augusta Cl
Grimsby DN34 152 C2
Kingston upon Hull HU8 142 B6
Augusta Oaks DN34 152 C2
Augusta St DN34 152 B2
Augustine's Mews 39
HU12 72 C7
Augustus Dr 13 HU15 68 C5
Auster Rd YO30 127 B3
Austfield La LS25 61 B8
Austin Cres 17 DN17 96 C2
Austin Garth 1 DN37 101 F1
Autherd Garth 1 HU17 55 C8
Autumn View YO25 124 D5
Avebue The DN37 113 B2
Avenswood La 8 DN15 96 B7
Avenue Cannes DN15 96 B7
Avenue Clamart DN15 96 B7
Avenue Fontenay 17
DN15 96 B7
Avenue Halycon 1
HU13 143 E2
Avenue Lourdes 16 DN15 96 B7
Avenue Nozay DN20 97 E4
Avenue Rd YO30 156 A4
Avenue Rouen 15 DN15 96 B7
Avenues Ct HU5 140 C1
Avenue Terr YO30 156 A4
Avenue The
Blyton DN21 117 E5
Burton upon Stather DN15 82 B4
Campsall DN6 76 E1
East Ravendale DN37 113 C2
19 Gainsborough DN21 117 B1
Great Driffield YO25 124 F5
Grimsby DN37 102 B4
Haxby YO32 127 D8
Healing DN41 101 F5
Holme-on-Spalding-Moor
YO43 51 E8
Kirk Ella HU10 143 C7
Nun Monkton YO26 12 A4
11 Pocklington YO42 29 A4
Rowley HU20 54 D6
Rufforth YO23 24 C6
Sutton-on-Hull HU7 141 E6
Thorne/Moorends DN8 79 B3
Watton YO25 32 D4
5 Wigginton YO32 13 E5
York YO30 130 A6
Avenue Vivian DN15 150 E8
Aviator Ct YO30 126 F3
Avocet Way YO15 11 B4
Avondale 1 HU4 144 B2
Avon Dr YO32 127 F6
Avon Rd DN16 151 C6
Avon St 2 HU8 141 C1
Awmand Gn HU16 138 F5
Awnhams La
Bishop Wilton YO42 16 D2
North Cave HU15 53 E4
AW Nielsen Rd DN14 149 A4
Axdane HU6 139 E7
Axholme Ave DN17 94 C7
Axholme Ct HU9 146 B5
Axholme Dr 11 DN9 105 D6
Axholme Gn 15 DN8 93 B7
Axholme Line Nature
Reserve* DN9 105 C4
Axholme Rd
Scunthorpe DN15 150 D6
2 Westwoodside DN9 105 A2
Axholme St DN14 149 E4
Axminster Cl HU7 141 A8
Aylesbury Gr HU5 144 D8
AYLESBY 101 E2
Aylesby Gdns 26 DN33 102 D2
Aylesby La DN37 101 F2
Aylesby Rd
Aylesby DN37 101 E2
Scunthorpe DN17 150 F1
Aylesford St 7 HU3 145 B5
Aylesham Ct YO32 127 E3
Ayots Gn 10 DN7 92 D3
Ayscough Ave DN41 101 E6
Ayscough Gr 3 LN7 111 B4
Ayscough St DN31 152 C4
Aysgarth Ave
Kingston upon Hull HU6 139 E4
Messingham DN17 107 D7
Aysgarth Rise YO16 122 E6
Azalea Mews YO8 148 A5

B

Babington Row HU9 146 C8
Bacchus La HU15 54 A1
Bacheler St HU3 145 B5
Bachelor Hill YO24 129 C2
Backcarr La YO25 21 C5
Back Field La DN7 92 E4
Backhouse St YO31 156 B4
Back La
Acaster Selby YO23 36 B3
Allerthorpe YO42 28 E2
Appleton Roebuck YO23 36 A5
Asselby DN14 64 D6
Barlby with Osgodby YO8 49 C4
Bilbrough YO23 24 D1
Burstwick HU12 73 A6
Burton Agnes YO25 10 A2
Burton Pidsea HU12 59 C2
Catwick HU17 45 C8
Copmanthorpe YO23 132 A2
Cottingwith YO42 38 C5
Drax YO8 63 F5
Driffield YO25 124 B5
East Garton HU11 59 E6
Ellerton YO42 38 C1
Elstronwick HU12 59 B3
Fangfoss YO41 28 C8
Garthorpe & Fockerby DN17 81 F6
11 Haxby YO32 13 D5
Hayton YO42 29 C1
Hemingbrough YO8 49 F1
Hirst Courtney YO8 62 F3
Holme-on-Spalding-Moor
YO43 40 A1
Holtby YO19 26 E8
Kilham YO25 9 B3
Luttons YO17 7 B8
Newton-on-Ouse YO30 12 B6
North Duffield YO8 50 A7
Norton DN6 76 E2
Nunburnholme YO42 29 F3
Patrington Haven HU12 89 C8
2 Riccall YO19 49 A8
Searby cum Owmby DN38 110 D8
3 Seaton HU11 35 A1
Shiptonthorpe YO43 40 F6
Snaith & Cowick DN14 78 E8
Stainforth DN7 92 C6
Wilberfoss YO41 27 F5
3 Winteringham DN15 68 B1
Wold Newton YO25 2 A4
York YO26 129 A5
Back Lane S YO19 37 F7
Back O' Newton YO41 27 E3
Back Park St YO8 148 D5
Back Rd HU12 72 A5
Back Side YO17 6 B5
Back Southgate HU18 134 C3
Back St
Alkborough DN15 82 C8
Bainton YO25 31 E7
Burton Fleming YO25 2 E3
3 Easington HU12 90 F6
East/West Stockwith
DN21 116 E5
Fridaythorpe YO25 18 B6
Langtoft YO25 8 D5
Laxton DN14 65 F4
Skerne & Wansford YO25 21 A2
Skipsea YO25 23 A2
Wold Newton YO25 2 A4
Back Westgate HU18 134 B4
Back West View 2 YO30 130 B7
Bacon Garth La HU16 139 A5
Bacon Garth Prim Sch
HU16 139 A5
Bad Bargain La YO31 131 A5
Baden Cl 3 HU5 140 D2
Bader Way DN21 119 B8
Badger Hill Prim Sch
YO10 131 B2
Badger La
Halsham HU12 74 B5
Walden Stubbs DN6 77 A3
Badger Paddock 5
YO31 127 E2
Badgers Wood HU16 138 F8
Badger Way
1 Broughton DN20 97 E4
Cliffe YO8 49 E3
Kirton in Lindsey DN21 108 B1
Badger Wood Wlk YO10 131 D3
Badminton Cl YO16 122 F6
Baffam Ct YO8 148 B1
Baffam Gdns YO8 148 B2
Baffam La YO8 148 B2
Bagby Mews 2 HU5 139 D3
Baggaby Hill YO42 29 E4
Bagsby Rd DN9 106 B3
Baildon Cl 3 YO26 129 D4
Baildon Rd DN15 150 D8
Baile Hill Terr YO1 156 B1
Bailey La
Hatfield DN8 92 E6
Kingston upon Hull HU16 139 D8
Warter YO42 30 B5
Baileywood La YO43 51 F8
Bainbridge Ave HU9 142 D2
Bainbridge Dr YO8 148 C4
BAINTON 31 E7
Bainton Cl HU17 136 D5
Bainton Gr HU6 139 E6
Bainton Rd YO25 19 E2
Bakehouse La 5 YO25 9 C3
Baker Dr DN15 83 A5
Bakers Cl DN38 99 B5
Bakersfield DN20 98 D4
Bakersfield Dr DN14 61 F3
Baker St
Kingston upon Hull HU2 155 A3
York YO30 130 C7
Bakewell Cl HU9 142 D1
Bakewell Ct DN15 150 B7
Balder Ct 2 DN33 102 E1
Baldwin Ave DN16 96 D1
Balfour Pl 14 DN40 87 B1
Balfour St
23 Gainsborough DN21 117 B1
3 Kingston upon Hull
HU9 146 C8
York YO26 129 F5
Balfour Way YO32 14 A6
Balham Ave HU8 141 E6
Balk Cl HU17 45 B8
BALKHOLME 65 E6
Balk La
Hook DN14 149 F6
Pollington DN14 77 F7
Riston HU11 45 C4
Sproatley HU11 58 D5
Balk Mews HU5 139 D3
Balk The
Bishop Wilton YO41 16 C2
Millington YO42 29 C7
Pocklington YO42 29 A3
Ballantyne Cl HU7 141 C4
Balldon Ct HU12 72 D7
Ballhall La YO42 38 E6
Balliol Dr DN16 96 D2
Balmoral Ave
Grimsby DN34 152 A3
Kingston upon Hull HU6 140 B6
Balmoral Cl 8 YO16 122 D6
Balmoral Dr HU17 136 E1
Balmoral Rd
2 Cleethorpes DN35 103 B2
25 Hatfield DN7 92 D4
Balmoral Terr 5 YO23 130 B1
BALNE 77 C5
Balne Croft La DN14 78 A6
Balne Hall Rd DN14 77 F5
Balne Moor Rd DN14 77 B6
Bamford Ave HU9 142 E1
Banbury Ct 16 DN32 153 A5
Banbury Rd DN16 151 D6
Bank End Rd DN9 104 A3
Bankfield La DN14 64 A7
Bank La 15 LN7 111 B4
Bank Rd YO8 148 D6
Banks Cl HU12 90 F6
Bank Side
Kingston upon Hull HU5 140 F2
Rawcliffe DN14 64 A2
Bankside 3 YO26 12 F1
Bankside Ind Est HU5 140 F7
Bank St
3 Hornsea HU18 134 C4
Kingston upon Hull HU3 145 C7
Bank Terr HU18 134 C2
Bank Wood Rd WF8 76 A6
Bannisdale 6 YO24 132 C7
Bannister Cl 3 HU13 69 F4
Bannister Dr HU9 146 C7
Bannister St HU19 75 A7
Bantock Garth HU4 144 B4
Baptist Chapel La DN40 86 F2
Baptist Pl YO16 122 D4
Barbara Cl 3 DN33 113 E8
Barbara Gr 4 YO24 129 F3
Barbarry Rd HU12 72 B7
Barberry Ct
24 Brough HU15 68 C5
3 Kingston upon Hull
HU3 145 C5
Barbers Dr YO23 132 B4
Barbican Ct YO10 156 C1
Barbican Mews YO10 130 E3
Barbican Rd YO10 156 C1
Barbican Way 7 DN36 114 A7
Barbriggs La YO25 22 E2
Bar Convent Mus*
YO24 156 A1
Barcroft St DN35 153 B4
Barden Ct 6 YO30 126 F1
Bardney Ave DN16 151 A3
Bardney Gdns 16 DN34 102 C2
Bardney Rd 14 YO14 2 F8
Bardshaw HU6 139 F8
Barff Cl 10 YO8 48 D1
Barff Gr 6 YO8 48 B2
Barff La YO8 48 C1
Barff View YO8 62 D7
Barfhill Cswy YO25 32 F2
Barfield Rd YO31 130 F8
Barf La YO41 16 D4
Bargate DN34 152 C2
Bargate Ave DN32 152 D1
Bargate Gr 3 HU5 144 D8
Barham Rd HU9 142 B4
Barker Dr YO8 148 B6
Barker La YO1 156 A2
Barkers Mill 6 HU17 137 B3
Barkhouse La DN35 153 F1
Bark House La DN35 153 F1
Barkhouse Wood La
WF11 61 D6
Barking Cl HU8 142 A5
Bark St DN35 153 F1
Barkston Ave YO26 129 B3
Barkston Cl 3 YO26 129 A3
Barkston Gr YO26 129 A3
Barkston Rd YO26 129 A3
Barkworth Cl HU10 143 D6
Barkworth Ct 3 DN37 113 D6
Bar La YO1 156 A2
BARLBY 49 B5
Barlby Bridge Com Prim Sch
YO8 148 D6
Barlby Bridge Prim Sch
YO8 148 D5
Barlby By-pass 2 YO8 49 B4
Barlby Com Prim Sch
YO8 49 B4
Barlby Cres YO8 148 F7
Barlby High Sch YO8 49 B5
Barlby Rd YO8 148 E6
Barleigh Croft HU9 142 B3
Barleigh Rd HU9 142 B3
Barley Cl DN20 109 A5
Barleycorn Yd YO1 156 C2
Barley Garth
14 Brandesburton YO25 34 B2
Burton Pidsea HU12 59 C2
Barley Gate HU17 45 A8
Barley Hall* YO1 156 B3
Barleyholme HU17 154 C2
Barley Rise
Bridlington YO16 123 A6
Strensall YO32 14 A6
Barley View YO32 127 C8
Barlings Ave DN16 151 A3
Barlings Cl DN21 107 D4
BARLOW 63 C7
Barlow CE Prim Sch YO8 63 C7
Barlow Comm Nature
Reserve* YO8 63 B7
Barlow Comm Rd YO8 63 B8
Barlow Rd YO8 63 B6
Barlow St YO26 129 D4
Barmby Ave YO10 133 E8
Barmby Cl 4 YO30 126 F1
Barmby Ferry Rd 1 YO8 49 F1
Barmby La DN14 52 A3
BARMBY MOOR 28 E3
Barmby Moor CE Prim Sch
YO42 28 D4
BARMBY ON THE
MARSH 64 B7
Barmby on the Marsh Prim
Sch DN14 64 B7
Barmby Rd YO42 28 E4
Barmouth Cl 4 HU7 57 A7
Barmouth Dr 20 DN37 102 C4
BARMSTON 23 A6
Barmston Cl HU17 137 B5
Barmston La HU17 56 C8
Barmston Rd HU17 137 B5
Barmston St HU2 155 B4
Barnard Ave DN20 98 B2
Barnard Mdws DN21 108 B1
Barnards Dr 9 HU15 53 F1
Barnard Way HU12 72 D6
Barn Elms YO8 63 C5
Barnes Cl HU17 137 B4
Barnes Cres DN15 150 E8
Barnes Gn DN21 107 C4
Barnes Way HU7 56 E5
Barnetby La DN20 98 F7
BARNETBY LE WOLD 99 C4
Barnetby Rd
1 Kingston upon Hull
HU13 144 A3
Scunthorpe DN17 150 F1
Barnetby Sta DN38 99 B4
Barnet Cl HU8 142 A5
Barnet Dr DN36 114 B8
Barnet Gn 9 DN7 92 D3
Barnett Pl DN35 153 B3
Barnfield Way YO23 132 A2
Barnhill La DN14 64 F7
BARNOLDBY LE BECK 113 B6
Barnoldby Rd DN37 113 D6
Barn Owl Cl DN36 114 D8
Barnsdale View DN6 76 E2
Barnside DN20 108 F5
Barnsley Rd DN8 79 B2
Barnsley St HU8 141 B1
Barnstaple Rd
Kingston upon Hull HU7 141 B7
Scunthorpe DN17 150 D3
Barnston Way 11 DN15 82 B4
Baron Ave 8 DN36 114 A8
Baroness Cl 7 HU6 140 B8
Baroness Ct 4 DN34 102 C3
Baroness Rd DN34 152 A3
Barons Cres YO23 132 B2
Baronwood Cres 7 YO25 22 D1
Barra Cl HU8 141 F6
Barraclough's La DN18 69 E2
Barrett Ave 8 YO24 129 F3
Barrick Cl 7 DN19 85 D8
Barrier Bank DN14 78 E6
Barrington Ave HU5 139 F3
Barrington Garth DN14 61 F3
Barr La YO32 14 D4
Barrow Blow Wells Nature
Reserve* DN19 70 D1
Barrowby Cl 9 DN20 97 E3
Barrow Ct 3 HU3 140 D1
BARROW HANN 70 E1
BARROW HAVEN 70 C1
Barrow Haven Reedbed
Nature Reserve* DN18 70 B2
Barrow Haven Sta DN19 70 C2
Barrow La HU13 143 D2

Barrow Rd
Barrow upon Humber DN19 70 E1
Barton-upon-Humber DN18 85 A8
New Holland DN19 70 E2
The Hallands DN18 85 F7
BARROW UPON HUMBER 85 D7
Barry Ave DN34 102 C2
Barstow Ave YO10 130 F3
Bartholomew Ave DN14 149 B5
Bartindale Rd YO14 3 A5
Bartle Garth YO1 156 C3
Bartlett Ave HU17 154 A2
Bartlett Cl 9 HU12 58 D1
Barton Dr HU13 143 D1
Barton La DN19 85 C8
Barton-on-Humber Sta DN18 69 F1
Barton Rd
Caenby Corner Estate DN21 119 C1
Wrawby DN20 98 D3
Barton St Peters CE Prim Sch DN18 69 F1
Bartons Garth YO8 148 B2
Barton St
Barrow upon Humber DN19 85 D8
Irby DN37 112 F7
Keelby DN41 101 A4
Wyham cum Cadeby DN36 120 F7
BARTON-UPON-HUMBER 84 D7
BARTON WATERSIDE 69 F2
Bartrams HU15 68 D6
Barwick Parade Prim Sch YO8 148 E4
Barwic Par YO8 148 E4
Base Youth Arts Ctr The DN15 151 B7
Basic Slag Rd DN16 151 E6
Basil Dr HU17 154 A1
Baslow Rd DN15 150 B6
Bassett Cl
1 Broughton DN20 97 E3
Selby YO8 148 C3
Bassett Rd 2 DN35 103 D2
Bate La DN14 78 A4
Bateson Cl YO10 131 C1
Bath St DN32 153 A5
Bathurst St 8 HU3 145 D5
Batley Cl HU9 142 C2
Battersea Cl HU8 141 F5
Battery Rd HU12 72 A4
Battery St DN40 87 C1
Battleflats Way YO41 15 D2
Battle Gn DN9 105 D7
Batty La 7 DN14 65 A7
Bawtry Cl YO8 148 D3
Bawtry Rd
Hatfield DN7 92 F3
Selby YO8 148 D3
Baxter Gate HU12 72 D7
Bayard St DN21 117 B1
Baylegate 6 YO16 122 D4
Bayle Mus* YO16 122 D4
Baynard Ave HU16 139 A6
Baynes Ct YO8 148 A2
Bayons Ave 13 DN33 113 D8
Bay Prim Sch YO16 122 E4
Baysdale HU7 140 F6
Baysdale Ave YO10 131 D3
Baysdale Rd DN16 151 D1
Baysgarth House Mus* DN18 84 F8
Baysgarth L Ctr DN18 84 F8
Baysgarth Sch DN18 84 F8
Baysgarth View DN18 84 F7
Bayswater Ct HU8 141 E5
Bayswater Pl 2 DN33 113 D8
Baytree Ave DN34 152 A2
Bay View Ave HU18 134 C6
Beach Holt La DN37 101 D2
Beacon Ave
14 Barton-upon-Humber DN18 84 E8
Cleethorpes DN35 153 D2
Beacon Cl 5 HU13 69 F4
Beacon Ct DN32 153 D2
Beacon Hill* DN10 116 A1
Beacon Hill Rd DN10 116 A1
Beacon La YO25 21 B8
Beacon Rd
Bridlington YO16 123 A6
Millington YO42 17 B1
Beaconsfield HU19 74 F6
Beaconsfield Mews YO24 129 D3
Beaconsfield Prom YO15 122 F3
Beaconsfield St
1 Kingston upon Hull HU5 140 D2
6 Sculcoates HU5 140 D2
York YO24 129 D3
Beaconthorpe Rd DN35 153 E3
Beacon View YO43 40 B1
Beadlam Mews HU5 139 E4
Beadle Garth YO23 132 B2
Beaford Ct DN17 150 C4
Beagle Cl 12 DN20 97 E4
Beagle Croft YO41 15 C1
Beagle Ridge Dr YO24 129 C1
Beagle Spinney YO41 15 C1
BEAL 61 D4
Bealey's La YO25 32 B1
Beal La
Beal DN14 61 D4
Cridling Stubbs WF11 61 C1
Beamsley Way 18 HU7 56 F5
Bean Gdns 3 DN14 78 C8
Beanland La YO32 14 D2
Bean St HU3 145 C6
Bean's Way YO31 131 B8
Bearwood Cl HU9 142 B6
Beatty Ave 13 DN33 113 E8
Beauchamp St DN16 151 B5
Beauchamp Wlk DN16 151 B6
Beauchief Gdns DN16 151 A4
Beaufort Ave HU18 134 C2
Beaufort Cl
Kingston upon Hull HU3 145 D6
York YO10 131 B3
Beaufort Cres 5 DN35 103 B1
Beaufort St 5 DN21 117 B2
Beaulahland 2 DN18 84 A7
Beaulah Villas 1 DN18 84 A7
Beaulieu Cl 1 YO32 127 F5
Beaulieu Ct
Bridlington YO16 122 F7
5 Kingston upon Hull HU9 142 A3
Beaumonde 5 DN36 114 A5
Beaumont Ct
Goole DN14 149 B6
3 Kingston upon Hull HU9 146 D7
Beaumont Pl YO8 148 A2
Beautiman Ct HU6 140 A5
Beaverdyke YO30 126 F1
Beaver Rd HU17 137 B4
Beccles Cl HU8 142 B6
Beck Bank HU16 139 C6
Beck Cl
6 Elvington YO41 27 B2
14 Howden DN14 65 B7
Keelby DN41 101 A4
Beckdale 4 HU7 141 A6
Beckett Ave DN21 117 C1
Beckett Dr YO10 131 D4
Beck Farm Mews DN37 113 B6
Beckfield La YO26 129 B5
Beckfield Pl YO26 129 B4
Beck Garth 12 HU12 72 D7
Beck Hill
6 Barton-upon-Humber DN18 84 F8
1 Bridlington YO15 122 E2
Beckhole Cl HU3 145 A6
Beckhythe Cl DN33 102 F1
BECKINGHAM 116 D1
Beckingham Rd DN10 116 D2
Beckington Cl 1 HU8 142 C7
Beck La
Appleby DN15 83 D1
5 Barrow upon Humber DN19 85 D8
Broughton DN20 97 E3
Easington HU12 90 F6
Redbourne DN21 108 F2
Scunthorpe DN16 96 D2
Wheldrake YO19 38 A8
Becklands Park Ind Est YO43 135 C4
Beck Rd
Cottingham HU16 138 E6
North Cave HU15 53 D2
Willerby HU10 138 D1
Beck Row YO41 16 D5
Becks Cl 5 YO32 127 C8
Beckside
Beverley HU17 154 C2
4 Brough HU15 68 D6
7 Elvington YO41 27 B2
Hornsea HU18 134 C3
Rothwell LN7 111 F2
Stillingfleet YO19 36 D3
Wilberfoss YO41 27 F6
Beck Side
Barmby Moor YO42 28 D3
Great Driffield YO25 124 F4
Hibaldstow DN20 108 F5
Beckside Cl
4 Humberston DN35 103 C1
Kingston upon Hull HU6 140 B7
Beckside Ct HU17 137 C3
Beckside Gdns YO10 130 F4
Beckside Manor HU12 60 B1
Beckside N HU17 154 C2
Becks La DN21 107 A3
Beck St HU12 90 F6
Beck View 14 YO42 29 A3
Beck View Rd HU17 137 C4
Beckwith Cl YO31 131 C7
Beckwith Hall Dr 7 YO19 49 A8
Beck Wlk 7 DN35 103 C1
Bedale Ave
Kingston upon Hull HU9 141 E1
York YO10 131 D4
Bedale Ct YO43 135 E3
Bedale Mews 31 HU15 68 C5
Bedale Pl 28 DN35 103 C2
Bedale Rd
Market Weighton YO43 135 E3
Scunthorpe DN16 151 D1
Bedale Wlk YO43 135 F4
Bede Ave YO30 130 B7
Bedern YO1 156 C3
Bedford Gr YO15 122 D1
Bedford Rd
Humberston DN35 103 D1
Kingston upon Hull HU13 143 F3
Bedfords Fold 6 LS25 61 A7
Bedford St
Grimsby DN32 153 A5
Kingston upon Hull HU8 141 A1
Bedford Way 2 DN15 96 D7
Beech Ave
3 Airmyn DN14 64 E4
Beverley HU17 136 F6
Bishopthorpe YO23 133 A3
3 Flamborough YO15 5 A2
Flixborough DN15 96 A7
14 Gainsborough DN21 117 B1
14 Grimsby DN33 102 E2
Gunness DN15 95 E6
Kingston upon Hull HU8 141 C2
4 Naburn YO23 36 C7
7 Preston HU12 72 C7
York YO24 129 F3
Beech Cl
4 Broughton DN20 97 D3
Burstwick HU12 73 A6
2 Elvington YO41 27 B2
Garton-on-the-Wolds YO25 19 F6
Kilham YO25 9 B3
8 Kingston upon Hull HU3 145 C5
Market Weighton YO43 135 D4
Sproatley HU11 58 C5
Beechcliffe Ave 1 HU6 140 C7
Beech Cres 7 DN7 92 C6
Beech Croft
Barlby with Osgodby YO8 49 B6
Driffield YO25 125 A5
Beech Ct
Bishopthorpe YO23 133 A3
6 Pocklington YO42 29 A4
Beechdale HU16 139 C5
Beech Dr
Bridlington YO16 123 A6
2 North Ferriby HU14 69 A4
11 Patrington HU12 74 D1
Beeches Ave 23 DN16 96 D2
Beeches The
Great Driffield YO25 125 A4
Pocklington YO42 29 A4
Skelton YO30 126 C4
Tickton HU17 137 E8
26 Upper Poppleton YO26 12 F1
Beechfield
Kingston upon Hull HU6 140 B6
Newton-on-Ouse YO30 12 B6
Beechfield Cl 15 YO8 48 B1
Beechfield Ct DN34 152 C2
Beechfield Dr HU10 138 C2
Beechfield Rd DN7 92 C4
Beech Garth DN19 85 C7
Beech Glade YO31 127 F2
Beech Gr
1 Airmyn DN14 64 E4
Burton upon Stather DN15 82 B5
Camblesforth YO8 63 C5
2 Flamborough YO15 5 A2
Goole DN14 149 D1
Holton le Clay DN36 114 B5
Nafferton YO25 125 E8
Newland HU5 140 C3
Northfield HU13 143 C3
Selby YO8 148 C5
1 Swanland HU14 69 C7
York YO26 129 C4
Beech Hill Rd HU14 69 C7
Beechlands 9 YO25 124 F3
Beechlands The 9 YO25 124 F3
Beech Lawn HU10 143 E6
Beech Pk YO19 49 A8
Beech Pl 5 YO32 14 A6
Beech Rd
Brough HU15 68 C6
Campsall DN6 76 E1
Beech Rise HU12 72 A4
Beech Tree Ave 21 DN8 93 B7
Beech Tree Cl 3 HU17 136 F7
Beech Tree La YO8 63 C5
Beechtree Way 2 HU17 44 F6
Beech View
Hutton Cranswick YO25 32 E6
Walkington HU17 55 C8
Beechway DN16 151 B3
Beech Way
10 Cleethorpes DN36 103 B1
25 Upper Poppleton YO26 12 F1
Beechwood HU18 134 D1
Beechwood Ave
25 Grimsby DN33 102 C2
3 Immingham DN40 87 C1
Beechwood Cl 9 DN3 92 A1
Beechwood Cres 3 DN20 97 E4
Beechwood Ct 17 DN7 92 D3
Beechwood Dr
Scawby DN20 108 E8
3 Scotter DN21 107 C3
Beechwood Glade 6 YO24 129 B1
Beechwood La 10 YO25 124 F2
Beechwood The YO25 125 A3
Beechwood Views HU12 60 B1
BEEFORD 22 C1
Beeford CE Prim Sch YO25 22 C1
Beeford Gr HU6 139 F5
Beeford Rd YO25 22 F1
Beeforth Cl YO32 127 D5
Beeley Rd DN32 153 C2
BEELSBY 112 F5
Beelsby Rd LN7 112 C5
Beel's Rd DN41 101 E8
Beesby Dr 22 DN35 103 C2
Beesby Medieval Village* DN36 120 E7
Beesby Rd DN17 150 E1
Beeson Gr DN31 152 C5
Beeson St DN31 152 C5
Beggar Hill DN21 107 D5
Beilby St HU3 144 F4
Belcombe Way 1 YO30 130 A7
Beldevere Pk HU18 134 C6
Belfry Ct HU8 142 B6
Belgrave Cl
6 Belton DN9 94 E1
Belton DN9 105 E8
Belgrave Dr
Goole DN14 149 F5
Hornsea HU18 134 C5
Kingston upon Hull HU4 144 D5
7 North Cave HU15 53 D3
Belgrave Rd
Bridlington YO15 122 D1
1 Grimsby DN33 102 D1
Belgrave Sq 1 DN15 151 B7
Belgrave St YO31 130 C7
Belgravia 8 DN14 149 C4
Bellamy Ct HU9 146 C7
Bellasize La DN14 66 C6
Bellasize Pk HU15 66 D8
Bellbutts View 1 DN21 107 B3
Bell Cl
Haxby YO32 127 C8
Kingston upon Hull HU7 141 D5
Bellcroft La HU12 72 E4
Bellcroft Rd HU12 72 F5
Bellcross La 7 DN14 65 B7
Belleisle Rd 12 DN34 102 B3
Bellerby Way YO42 28 F3
Belle Vue St YO10 130 E3
Belle Vue Terr
19 Thorne/Moorends DN8 93 A8
York YO10 130 E3
Bellfarm Ave YO31 130 E8
Bellfield Ave 5 HU8 142 A5
Bellfield Dr HU10 138 D1
Bellfield Prim Sch HU8 142 A4
Bell Gn DN14 78 B2
Bellground La YO30 12 D4
Bell Hall* YO19 36 E6
Bellhouse Way YO24 132 B8
Bellingham Rd DN16 151 D3
Bell La
Cawood YO8 48 A7
Foggathorpe YO8 51 B7
Rawcliffe DN14 64 A2
Scunthorpe DN15 151 A6
Bellmans Croft YO23 132 B2
Bell Mills YO25 125 A2
Bells Dr 9 DN20 108 F5
Bells Rd 2 HU12 72 B7
Bellwin Dr DN15 82 A1
Bellwood Cres 7 DN8 93 A8
Bellwood Dr YO24 132 B8
Belmont DN36 114 A5
Belmont Cl
13 Cleethorpes DN35 103 B2
3 York YO30 127 A1
Belmont St
Kingston upon Hull HU9 146 D8
Scunthorpe DN16 151 A2
Belper Ct
17 Cleethorpes DN31 153 A5
3 Scunthorpe DN15 150 B6
Belprin Rd HU17 137 B5
Belshaw La DN9 94 D1
Beltham Gn HU16 138 F4
Belthorn Rd 1 DN17 81 F1
Belthorpe La YO42 16 E1
BELTOFT 95 A1
BELTON 94 E1
Belton All Saints CE Prim Sch DN9 94 E2
Belton Cl 4 HU8 142 B5
Belton Fields DN9 94 D1
Belton Gr 7 DN33 102 D2
Belton Rd
Belton DN9 95 A1
Epworth DN9 105 E7
Sandtoft DN8 94 B3
Belt Rd The DN21 117 C2
Belvedere Cl YO15 11 B4
Belvedere Cres DN14 149 B6
Belvedere Dr
Kingston upon Hull HU11 142 D6
Scunthorpe DN17 150 E3
7 Thorne/Moorends DN8 79 B2
Belvedere Gr YO15 11 B4
Belvedere Par YO15 11 B4
Belvedere Rd
Bridlington YO15 11 B4
Kingston upon Hull HU13 143 F2
Belvoir Ave 8 YO41 27 B2
Belvoir Cl DN21 117 A2
Belvoir Rd DN35 103 B1
Belvoir St HU5 145 C8
Belwood Dr DN9 94 E2
BEMPTON 4 D4
Bempton Cl YO16 122 E6
Bempton Cliffs Nature Reserve* YO15 4 D5
Bempton Cres YO16 122 E6
Bempton Dr YO16 122 E6
Bempton Gdns YO16 122 E6
Bempton Gr
Grimsby DN32 153 A1
Kingston upon Hull HU5 144 D8
Bempton La
Bempton YO16 4 B1
Bridlington YO16 122 D8
Bempton Oval YO16 122 E6
Bempton Prim Sch YO15 4 C
Bempton Sta YO16 4 C
Bemrose Gr YO16 122 E
Bemrose Way DN31 152 C
Bence The YO42 17 C
Benedict Ave YO8 148 E
Benedict Cl 2 HU4 144 A
Benedict Rd HU4 144 A
BENINGBROUGH 12 D
Beningbrough Hall & Gdns* YO30 12 B
Beningbrough La YO30 12 D
Benjy La YO19 37 E
BENNETLAND 66 C
Bennetland La HU15 66 C
Bennett Dr DN15 83 A
Bennett Rd
Cleethorpes DN35 153 D
Scunthorpe DN16 151 C
Benningholme La HU11 45 D
Bennington Cl 48 HU12 72 D
Bennymoor La YO8 49 C
Benson Ct LN11 121 C
Bentinck La HU11 45 F
BENTLEY 55 D
Bentley Ct HU3 145 A
Bentley Gr HU6 139 F
Bentley La DN38 110 E
Bentley St DN35 153 E
Berea The DN34 152 C
Beresford Ave
Hornsea HU18 134 D
Kingston upon Hull HU6 140 D
Beresford Terr YO23 130 C
Beretun Gn 11 DN18 84 E
Bergen Way HU7 140 D
BERKELEY 150 D
Berkeley Bsns Ctr DN15 150 C
Berkeley Dr
3 Beverley HU17 136 E
32 Hedon HU12 72 D
Berkeley Ind Est DN15 150 C
Berkeley Jun & Inf Sch DN15 150 D
Berkeley Rd DN35 103 D
Berkeley St
1 Kingston upon Hull HU3 145 D
Scunthorpe DN15 150 F
Berkeley Terr YO26 129 E
Berkshire Cl 4 HU17 55 F
Berkshire St HU8 141 C
Bermondsey Dr HU5 144 E
Bermuda Ave HU11 45 D
Bernadette Ave HU4 144 B
Berners Rd 15 DN35 103 D
Berridge La DN14 78 A
Berriman's La YO25 9 B
Berryman Way HU13 144 A
Berwick Ct 5 DN40 87 C
Beside the Seaside Mus* 14 YO16 122 E
Bessacarr Ave HU10 138 F
Bessemer Way DN15 96 D
BESSINGBY 10 F
Bessingby Gate YO16 122 A
Bessingby Gr HU9 142 B
Bessingby Hill YO16 122 B
Bessingby Rd YO16 122 C
Bessingby Road Ret Pk YO16 122 C
Bessingby Way YO16 122 C
Bestall Rd DN32 153 C
BESWICK 32 D
Beswick Hall* YO25 32 D
Beswick Heads YO25 32 C
Beswick Rd YO25 32 E
Beswick & Walton CE Prim Sch YO25 32 D
Bethell Ct 6 HU12 72 D
Bethell Wlk YO25 125 A
Bethlehem St DN32 152 D
Bethune Ave HU4 144 A
Bethune Avenue W HU13 144 A
Bethune Park Prim Sch HU4 144 C
Betony Cl 4 DN15 96 B
Betteras Hill Rd LS25 61 A
Betula Ct HU8 141 E
Betula Way DN17 150 C
Between Dikes Rd YO8 63 F
Between Rivers La DN14 78 E
BEVERLEY 154 A
Beverley Balk YO41 15 B
Beverley Boys Gram Sch HU17 136 D
Beverley Cl 18 DN36 114 A
Beverley Cres DN32 153 A1
Beverley Ct
11 Healing DN41 101 F
Scunthorpe DN17 150 D
Beverley Dr HU17 136 D
Beverley High Sch HU17 154 A
Beverley La YO43 41 E
Beverley L Complex HU17 154 C
Beverley Minst* HU17 154 B
Beverley Minst CE Prim Sch HU17 136 D
Beverley Parklands HU17 154 C1
Beverley Parks Nature Reserve* HU17 55 F
Beverley Racecourse HU17 136 B
Beverley Rd
Beeford YO25 22 D1

Beverley Rd *continued*
Bishop Burton HU17 43 B2
Great Driffield YO25 124 E2
Hutton Cranswick YO25 20 E1
Kingston upon Hull HU3 155 A4
Kirkburn YO25 124 D1
Leven HU17 45 A7
Market Weighton YO43 135 E4
Middleton YO25 31 D4
Newbald YO43 53 F8
Northfield HU13 143 E3
Skidby HU16 138 C7
South Cave HU15 54 A2
Watton YO25 32 D5
Withernwick HU11 46 A3
Beverley Rd Baths HU5 140 D2
Beverley St DN14 149 C2
Beverley Sta HU17 154 B3
BEWHOLME 35 A5
Bewholme Gr
4 Kingston upon Hull HU9 142 B1
Kingston upon Hull HU9 147 B8
Bewholme La
Bewholme YO25 35 A8
Seaton HU11 35 A2
Skipsea YO25 23 A1
Bewholme Rd YO25 35 C5
Bewlay St YO23 130 C2
Bexhill Ave HU9 142 E2
Bexley Ct 18 DN31 153 A5
Bibbill La YO42 39 B5
Bibury Cl HU8 141 B2
Bickerton Cl HU6 139 F7
Bickleigh Gr 1 HU8 142 C6
Bideford Gr HU9 142 E1
BIELBY 39 F6
Bielby Dr HU17 137 B3
BIGBY 99 C2
Bigby Gn DN38 99 B2
Bigby Gr DN17 96 C2
Bigby High Rd DN20 98 C1
Bigby Hill DN38 99 C1
Bigby Rd 16 DN20 98 C2
Bigby St DN20 98 C2
Biggin Ave HU7 141 C8
Biggin Hill Prim Sch HU7 141 C8
BILBROUGH 24 D1
Billet La DN15 96 C8
Billet Mill App DN16 151 F3
Billet Mill App Rd DN16 97 A5
Billet Mill Rd DN16 151 E5
Billinghay Ct 16 DN35 103 C2
Billings La YO25 34 E5
Billsdale Ct 5 YO16 122 F7
Bilsdale Cl YO30 126 E2
Bilsdale Cres 3 YO16 122 E7
Bilsdale Gr HU9 146 F8
Bilsdale Rd DN16 151 E1
BILTON 58 A4
Bilton Gr HU9 142 B2
Bilton Prim Sch HU11 142 E6
Bilton Rd HU11 142 D6
Binbrook Garth 2 HU7 57 A5
Binbrook Way 16 DN37 102 C4
Bircham Cres 3 DN21 119 C8
Birch Ave
Brigg DN20 98 B2
Grimsby DN34 152 A2
Birch Cl
Beverley HU17 136 F6
5 Bridlington YO16 123 A6
22 Brough HU15 68 C5
East Ella HU5 144 B7
7 Gilberdyke HU15 66 D7
Northfield HU13 143 B3
4 Thorpe Willoughby YO8 48 B1
York YO32 127 D3
Birch Copse YO24 129 D2
Birch Croft HU15 68 C6
Birchdale DN18 84 E7
Birch Dr
Bottesford DN16 96 F2
Kingston upon Hull HU10 138 E1
Birches The
5 Haxey DN9 105 B2
Hornsea HU18 134 D2
Birchfield DN14 149 F6
Birchfield Rd 6 DN9 105 D6
Birch Gdns DN18 69 E1
Birch Gr 16 DN21 117 B1
Birchin Way DN31 152 B5
Birchin Way Ind Est DN31 152 B5
Birch La 18 YO32 13 E5
Birch Lea 3 HU17 55 B8
Birch Leigh HU3 145 C6
Birch Mews DN14 149 E6
Birch Park Ind Est YO31 130 E8
Birch Pk YO31 127 E1
Birch Tree Cl DN3 92 A4
Birch Tree Dr 16 HU12 72 C7
Birch Way 4 DN38 99 B4
Birchwood Ave HU5 144 B7
Birchwood Cl
Burstwick HU12 73 B6
2 Thorne/Moorends DN8 79 A1
Birchwood Pk DN14 149 C2
Birchwood Rd DN16 151 B1
Birchwood View 21 DN21 117 C1
Birdcroft La 3 DN10 116 D3
Birdforth Mews 5 HU5 139 D3
Bird La
Hensall DN14 62 D2
Kellington DN14 61 F4
Birdsall Ave HU5 139 C2
Birdsall Cl HU16 138 E5
Birkby Gr HU9 142 C2
Birkdale 14 DN37 113 D6
Birkdale Cl HU10 143 B8
Birkdale Dr 8 DN40 87 C2
Birkdale Gr 4 YO26 129 B5
Birkdale Rd DN17 96 B2
Birkdale Way HU9 146 D8
Birker La
Newton on Derwent YO41 27 D4
Wilberfoss YO41 27 F6
BIRKIN 61 D6
Birkin La WF11 61 B4
Birkin Rd YO8 61 F5
Birk La YO8 50 D8
Birklands Dr HU8 141 E4
Birnam Ct HU6 140 B8
Birrel St 2 DN21 117 A1
Birstwith Dr YO26 129 E4
Birt Gr DN14 149 B6
Bishop Alcock Rd HU5 139 D3
Bishop Blunt Cl 2 HU13 143 F1
BISHOP BURTON 43 A2
Bishop Burton Coll HU17 43 A3
Bishop Burton Coll (Main Campus) DN20 97 E3
Bishop Burton Rd HU17 43 A4
Bishop Cockin Cl 1 HU4 144 A1
Bishop Ct
9 Gilberdyke HU15 66 D8
2 Selby YO8 148 B6
Bishopdike Rd YO8 48 A6
Bishopgate St YO23 156 B1
Bishop Gurdon Cl 4 HU13 143 F1
Bishophill Jun YO1 156 A1
Bishophill Senior YO1 156 B1
Bishop Kempthorne Cl 3 HU13 143 F1
Bishop La HU1 155 C2
Bishop La Staith HU1 155 C2
Bishop's Cl YO8 48 A8
Bishops Croft HU17 154 A2
Bishops Ct YO1 156 B1
Bishopsfields Dr YO26 130 A5
Bishop's La LN8 120 A7
Bishopsway YO10 131 C3
Bishop's Wlk DN34 152 C2
Bishop Temple Ct HU13 143 F3
BISHOPTHORPE 133 B3
Bishopthorpe Inf Sch YO23 133 A4
Bishopthorpe Palace* YO23 133 B4
Bishopthorpe Rd
Bishopthorpe YO23 133 B5
Cleethorpes DN35 103 C2
BISHOP WILTON 16 F2
Bishop Wilton CE Prim Sch YO42 16 F2
Bisley Gr HU7 141 A7
Bismarck St YO26 129 E5
Bittern Cl
24 Barton Waterside DN18 69 E1
Kingston upon Hull HU4 144 D2
Black Bank DN17 106 F6
Blackberry Way 5 HU17 44 F6
Blackburn Ave
Bridlington YO15 122 F3
Brough HU15 68 C5
Blackburn La WF11 61 B2
Black Dike La YO26 24 F8
Blackdykes Rd DN9 106 B4
Black Fen La YO8 148 C8
Blackfriargate HU1 155 C1
Blackhope Cl 16 HU7 57 A6
Blacklee Cl 3 YO32 14 B8
Blackmoor Rd 14 DN9 105 D2
Blacksmith Ct DN14 65 C4
Blacksmith Hill DN15 67 E3
Blacksmiths Cl
1 Barrow upon Humber DN19 85 C7
5 Elvington YO41 27 C2
Blacksmiths Cnr HU12 90 F6
Blacksmiths Fold 8 HU11 45 C5
Black Syke La DN14 78 E2
Blackthorn Cl
20 Gainsborough DN21 117 C1
8 Newport HU15 52 F1
7 Scunthorpe DN15 96 B7
Whitley DN14 77 A7
Blackthorn Ct 4 HU3 145 D6
Blackthorn Dr
Healing DN37 102 B5
York YO31 127 E2
Blackthorn La HU10 143 F7
Blackthorns The 3 DN20 97 D4
BLACKTOFT 66 E3
Blacktoft La DN14 66 D3
Black Tup La HU11 45 C3
Blackwater Way 27 HU7 56 F6
Blackwood La YO8 49 F7
Blackwood Rd YO8 49 E8
Bladon Rd YO16 122 E5
Bladons Wlk HU10 143 C8
Blaides Staithe HU1 155 C2
Blake Ave DN17 150 E3
Blake Cl HU2 155 A4
Blake Ct YO19 38 A8
Blakeley Gr YO30 126 F3
Blakeney Lea DN35 103 C1
Blakeney Pl YO10 130 F3
Blake St YO1 156 B3
Blakeys Crossing DN14 65 A7
Blandford Cl HU7 141 B6
Bland La YO26 129 A4
Blands Hill LN8 120 A5
Blanket Row HU1 155 B1
Blankney Ct 13 DN15 83 A5
Blanshards La 1 HU15 53 D3
Blatchford YO30 130 B8
Blatchford Mews YO30 130 B8
Blaycourt HU6 139 E6
Blaydes St HU6 140 C4
Blaydon Gr 1 DN34 102 C2
Bleaberry La YO41 16 B5
Bleachfield YO10 130 F2
Blenheilm Rd YO42 28 E3
Blenheim Cl 15 DN7 92 D3
Blenheim Ct
Rawcliffe YO30 126 D3
Scunthorpe DN16 96 D1
Blenheim Dr DN14 149 E6
Blenheim Pl 4 DN35 103 C2
Blenheim Rd
Beverley HU17 136 E1
Bridlington YO16 122 E3
5 Moorland Prison DN7 104 A8
Blenheim St HU5 145 C8
Blenheim Wlk YO25 34 B2
Blenkin St HU9 146 B7
Bleriot Way YO30 127 A3
Blisland Cl 13 HU7 56 F5
Bloomfield Ave HU5 144 C8
Bloomhill Cl 4 DN8 79 B2
Bloomhill Ct DN8 79 B2
Bloom Hill Gr 16 DN8 79 B2
Bloomhill Rd DN8 79 A2
Bloom La DN15 82 C1
Bloom Mill App DN16 97 A4
Bloomsbury Ct 1 HU3 145 D6
Bloomsbury Gdn 16 DN33 102 D1
Blossom Gr HU8 141 D8
Blossom's La HU15 53 C3
Blossom St YO24 156 A1
Blossom Way 21 DN40 87 B1
Blow Row DN9 105 E6
Blucher La HU17 154 C2
Bluebeck Dr YO30 129 E8
Bluebell Cl DN15 151 C7
Bluebell Ct
15 Healing DN41 101 F5
4 Owston Ferry DN9 106 A3
Blue Bell Farm Ct YO8 37 E1
Bluebell Gr 27 DN20 98 B2
Bluebell Grove 27 DN20 98 B2
Blueberry Cl YO25 124 E2
Blueberry Ct HU4 144 C4
Blue Bridge La YO10 130 D2
Blue Coat YO19 26 D7
Blue Slates Cl YO19 38 A8
Bluestone Bottoms HU17 55 A6
Bluestone Cl DN32 153 A4
Bluestone La DN40 87 B1
Blundell Ave DN35 153 C4
Blundell Cl HU2 155 A4
Blundell Pk (Grimsby Town FC) DN35 153 C5
BLYBOROUGH 119 B5
Blyth Cl YO8 148 A5
Blyth Ct DN18 85 A8
Blythe Wlk 1 YO16 122 D4
Blythorpe HU6 139 F8
Blyth St 2 HU9 146 B7
Blyth Way DN37 101 E2
BLYTON 117 E5
Blyton cum Laughton CE Prim Sch (Blyton Site) DN21 117 F6
Blyton cum Laughton CE Prim Sch (Laughton Site) DN21 117 F8
Blyton Rd
Gainsborough DN21 117 B2
Laughton DN21 117 E8
Boardman La 6 YO25 34 B2
Boardman Pk 7 YO25 34 B2
Board St YO23 130 C2
Boatcliffe Rd YO14 3 D7
Boating Dyke Way 12 DN8 93 A8
Boatswain Croft HU1 155 B1
Bobbers Staith HU3 145 D4
Bodiam Way DN32 152 F4
Bodmin Cl DN17 150 D4
Bodmin Rd HU7 140 E8
Boggle La HU11 58 D5
Bog La YO24 132 B6
Bolam La YO15 4 C2
Boldron Mews 7 HU5 139 D3
Bolingbroke Rd
Cleethorpes DN35 103 D2
Scunthorpe DN17 96 C2
Bolsover Rd DN15 150 B6
Boltby Mews HU5 139 E3
Boltby Rd YO30 126 F2
BOLTON 28 D7
Bolton La
Bishop Wilton YO42 16 E1
Wilberfoss YO41 28 A5
Bolt The 3 YO16 122 D4
Bon Accord Rd HU13 143 E1
BONBY 84 C2
Bonby Gr
11 Grimsby DN33 102 D2
Scunthorpe DN17 150 F1
Bonby La YO8 37 E2
Bonby Rd DN20 84 C1
Bondane HU6 139 E7
Bondgate YO8 148 B7
Bond St
Hedon HU12 72 D7
Kingston upon Hull HU1 155 B3
Bondyke Cl HU16 138 E6
Bonfrey Way 51 HU12 72 D7
Bonington Ct 7 YO26 129 E4
Bonnyhale Rd DN17 94 E6
Bontoft Ave HU5 139 E1
Bootham YO30 156 A3
Bootham Bar* YO31 156 B3
Bootham Cl 1 DN7 92 D4
Bootham Cres
Stainforth DN7 92 C6
York YO30 156 A4
Bootham Jun Sch YO30 130 A7
Bootham Park Ct YO31 156 B4
Bootham Park Hospl YO31 156 B4
Bootham Rd 12 DN7 92 C6
Bootham Row YO30 156 B3
Bootham Sch YO30 156 A3
Bootham Sq YO30 156 B3
BOOTHAM STRAY 127 B2
Bootham Terr YO30 156 A3
BOOTHFERRY 64 E5
Boothferry Prim Sch DN14 149 B4
Boothferry Rd HU13 143 B2
Booth Ferry Rd DN14 64 F6
Boothferry Road Ave 13 DN14 65 B7
Boothgate DN14 65 A6
Boothgate Cl DN14 65 A6
Boothgate Dr DN14 65 A6
Booth Nooking La DN15 68 A3
Boothwood Rd YO30 126 E2
Booty La DN14 76 F7
Bore Tree Baulk YO19 26 D6
Borman's La 3 DN36 114 B1
Borodales Cl HU12 72 C7
Boroughbridge Rd YO26 129 D5
Borough Rd YO16 122 C3
Borrowdale HU7 140 F6
Borrowdale Dr YO30 126 F1
Borthwick Cl 3 HU7 57 A6
Borwick Dr HU17 137 C4
Bos Appraoch Rd DN16 151 F3
BOSSALL 15 D7
Bossington Cl 10 HU7 57 A5
Boston Cl 6 DN15 83 A5
Boston Ct 20 HU7 56 F5
Bosville Wlk YO16 122 B4
Bosworth Cl 16 DN7 92 D3
Botany Bay DN3 92 B4
Botany Bay La DN3 92 B4
Bothwell Gr HU9 147 D8
BOTTESFORD 96 D2
Bottesford Ave DN16 151 B1
Bottesford Inf Sch DN16 96 D2
Bottesford Jun Sch DN16 96 D2
Bottesford La DN16 151 B1
Bottesford Sports Hall DN17 96 B2
Bottlings The 10 DN20 98 C2
Boughton Ave DN15 150 F8
Boulevard HU3 145 B5
Boulevard Ave DN31 152 B4
Boulevard Gdns DN31 152 B4
Boulevard Way DN31 152 B3
Boulevard Wlk DN31 152 B4
Boulsworth Ave HU6 140 C7
Boulton Gr HU9 141 E2
Boundary Rd
Bridlington YO15 122 C1
Grimsby DN33 113 E7
Bournemouth St HU5 140 E2
Bourne St HU2 155 B3
Bourn Mill Balk Rd DN14 78 B8
Bournville DN14 149 C5
Bouthwaite Dr 13 YO26 129 E4
Bovill Cl DN31 152 C3
Bowers Ave DN31 152 B3
Bowers Ct DN31 152 B3
Bowes Ave YO31 130 E5
Bowes Wlk HU5 139 E3
Bowfield Cl 9 DN37 102 B4
Bowlalley La HU1 155 B2
Bowland La YO42 38 E2
Bowland Way YO30 127 A1
Bowling Green Ct YO31 130 D8
Bowling Green La
4 Crowle DN17 94 D8
Grimsby DN32 152 E3
9 Hunmanby YO14 2 F8
York YO31 156 C4
Bowling Green Rd 4 DN21 117 A1
Bowling La DN35 153 E2
Bowmandale DN18 84 E8
Bowmandale Prim Sch DN18 84 E7
Bowman Way 26 DN40 87 B1
Bowmont Way HU17 56 F6
Bowness Dr YO30 126 E1
Bownhill La HU12 59 A2
Bow Rd HU15 68 F6
Bow St YO15 122 D1
Bowthorpe La YO8 50 B4
Bowyers Cl YO23 132 C4
Boyds Ct 29 DN16 96 E2
Boyes La HU12 73 C4
BOYNTON 10 D7
Boynton Ave YO16 122 B4
Boynton Cres 4 DN15 83 A5
Boynton Garth
Driffield YO25 124 D3
Driffield YO25 124 D3
Boynton La DN14 64 A1
Boynton Prim Sch YO16 10 E7
Boynton St 1 HU3 145 C4
Brabbs Ave 2 DN7 92 E4
Brackenborough Rd LN11 121 F2
Bracken Cl
Gainsborough DN21 117 A2
York YO32 127 F4
Brackendale Cl 1 HU7 141 B4
Bracken Heen Cl 4 DN7 92 D4
Bracken Hill
Skirlaugh HU11 45 E2
2 York YO10 131 C3
Brackenhill Ave YO8 148 A4
Brackenhill La YO8 148 A3
Brackenhill Rd DN9 105 E2
Brackenhills YO26 12 F1
Brackenholmes Rd DN15 83 A2
Bracken La YO25 32 A5
Bracken Pk 20 DN33 113 E8
Bracken Pl 4 DN37 102 B3
Bracken Rd
Great Driffield YO25 124 D3
York YO24 132 F7
Brackenwoods HU20 55 A4
Brackley Cl HU8 141 B2
BRACON 94 F2
Bracon DN9 94 F2
Bracon Cl DN9 94 E2
Bradford Ave
Cleethorpes DN35 103 C2
Kingston upon Hull HU9 142 E2
Bradford Rd 20 DN40 87 B1
Bradgate Pk 30 HU7 56 F5
BRADLEY
Grimsby 102 B3
Nunsthorpe 102 C1
Bradley Cres YO23 24 D6
Bradley & Dixon Woods Nature Reserve* DN37 113 C8
Bradley Dr YO24 132 C8
Bradley La YO23 24 C5
Bradley Rd DN37 102 C1
Bradley St DN32 152 E4
Bradman Ct 3 DN32 153 A5
Bradwell Cl 3 DN18 84 E8
Braemar Ave HU6 140 B6
Braemar Ct YO25 34 C8
Braemar Rd DN35 103 C2
Braeside Gdns YO24 129 E3
Braeton La 5 DN33 113 F8
Braid Hill Way HU7 57 B5
Braids Wlk HU10 143 B8
Brailsford Cres YO30 130 A8
Braithegayte YO19 37 F8
Braithwaite La DN7 92 A7
Bramar Rd 26 DN7 92 D4
Bramble Cl DN31 152 C3
Bramble Dene YO24 132 D7
Bramble Garth 4 HU17 136 F7
Bramble Hill HU17 136 E1
Bramble La 4 DN15 68 B1
Brambles 6 YO8 48 B1
Brambles Ct LS25 61 B7
Brambles The
2 Barrow upon Humber DN19 85 C8
7 Easington HU12 90 F6
Bramble Way
24 Brigg DN20 98 B2
15 Humberston DN35 103 C1
Bramhall St DN35 153 C3
Bramham Ave YO26 129 A3
Bramham Gr YO26 129 A3
Bramham Rd YO26 129 A2
Bramley Ave YO8 49 B5
Bramley Cl DN18 69 F1
Bramley Cres 8 DN16 96 D1
Bramley Ct 16 DN21 117 C1
Bramley Garth YO31 131 B6
Bramley Gr 6 DN21 107 C3
Bramley Way DN10 116 D4
Brampton Way DN35 103 B2
Bramwith La DN7 92 A6
BRANDESBURTON 34 C2
Brandesburton Prim Sch YO25 34 B2
Brandesburton St HU3 145 B7
Brandon Ct 4 HU8 141 C1
Brandon Gr YO32 128 E3
Brandon Rd DN15 150 D6
Brandon Way 24 HU7 56 F6
Brandsby Gr
Kingston upon Hull HU9 142 E3
York YO31 127 E2
Brankwell Cres 21 DN17 96 C2
Bransdale Gr HU9 146 F8
Bransdale Rd
Bridlington YO16 122 E7
Scunthorpe DN16 151 D1
BRANSHOLME 141 A8
Bransholme Dr YO30 127 A2
Bransholme Rd HU7 57 B5
BRANTINGHAM 68 C8
Brantingham Cl 5 HU16 138 E6
Brantingham Rd HU15 68 C7
Brantingham Wlk HU5 139 C2
Branton Pl YO26 129 A3
Brant Rd DN15 150 E6
Brats La LN8 120 B5
Bratt La YO42 29 E3
Bratton Ct DN32 152 E1
Bravener Ct YO30 12 B6
Bray Cl 11 DN33 102 D1

Bray Gate YO42 16 E2
Bray Rd YO10 133 F8
BRAYTON 148 A2
Brayton CE Inf Sch YO8 148 A2
Brayton Coll YO8 148 A3
Brayton Junc YO8 148 C1
Brayton Jun Sch YO8 148 A2
Brayton La YO8 148 B1
Brazil St HU9 146 C8
Breamar Ct 2 DN14 62 A2
Bream Ct 9 HU6 140 B8
Breamer La HU11 35 A2
Breary Cl YO24 129 F1
Breck La HU15 53 B3
Brecksfield YO30 126 C5
Brecks La
Kirk Sandall DN3 92 A2
Strensall YO32 14 B7
York YO32 127 F4
Breckstreet La YO42 39 C3
Brecon Dr 22 HU7 56 F6
Brecon St HU8 141 B1
Breeze La YO25 22 D1
Breezemount Ct 4 DN7 92 C6
BREIGHTON 50 D5
Breighton Aerodrome* YO8 50 D5
Breighton Rd
Bubwith YO8 50 D6
Wressle YO8 50 C3
Bremerhaven Way 24 DN33 102 C2
Brendon Ave HU8 141 B3
Brent Ave HU8 142 B6
Brentwood Cl HU15 68 B6
Brentwood Cres YO10 131 C2
Brereton Ave DN35 153 C4
Brereton Cl HU17 136 E6
Bretel Wlk YO16 122 B4
Bretherdale HU7 140 F6
Brethergate DN9 105 B2
Bretton Ave DN14 149 F5
Bretton Cl 5 DN7 92 D3
Brett St YO16 122 C3
Brevere Rd HU12 72 D7
Brewery Gdns DN17 94 D8
Brewery Rd DN17 94 D8
Brewster Ave 17 DN40 87 C1
Breydon Ct 4 DN15 82 B4
Brian Ave
Cleethorpes DN35 103 B2
Scunthorpe DN16 151 C1
Waltham DN37 113 D6
Briar Ave YO26 129 B4
Briar Cl
4 Newport HU15 52 F1
South Killingholme DN40 86 F3
Briar Cliffe YO8 148 A3
Briar Ct 10 DN19 86 A8
Briar Dr YO31 127 F2
Briarfield Rd HU5 139 F2
Briar Garth
Driffield YO25 124 D4
Great Driffield YO25 124 D3
Briar La
4 Grimsby DN33 113 D8
Healing DN41 101 F5
15 Scartho DN33 113 D8
Briarsfield YO42 28 D4
Briars La DN7 92 C7
Briars The HU13 143 E3
Briar Way DN15 96 B7
Briarwood Cl
10 Bransholme HU7 57 B5
Gateforth YO8 61 F7
Brick Dike La HU20 54 C5
Brickenhole La DN10 116 C3
Brickhill La YO8 63 F4
Brick Kiln Balk YO16 122 A1
Brick Kiln La YO8 62 D6
Brick La DN40 86 E5
Brick Lands La DN14 62 F4
Bricknell Ave HU5 139 E3
Bricknell Prim Sch HU5 139 F2
Brick Rd HU12 88 F6
Brickyard DN37 100 D3
Brickyard La
Melton HU14 68 F4
Walkeringham DN10 116 B3
Wrawby DN20 98 C3
Bridge Cl
Haxby YO32 127 C7
Kingston upon Hull HU9 146 D6
Bridge Cres YO8 64 C8
Bridge Ct YO8 148 D6
Bridge Farm DN14 77 F6
Bridgegate DN14 65 A7
Bridgegate Dr HU9 146 C6
Bridge Gdns DN31 152 A5
Bridge Hill DN7 92 C6
Bridge Hill Cl DN14 79 B8
Bridge La
Cadney DN20 109 C6
5 Great Driffield YO25 124 F4
Horkstow DN18 83 F5
Pollington DN14 77 F6
Rawcliffe DN14 79 B8
York YO30 156 B4
Bridge Rd
Airmyn DN14 149 A8
Bishopthorpe YO23 132 F3
Broughton DN20 97 F5
South Cave HU15 53 F1
Bridges Ct YO8 148 D6
Bridges La YO42 38 E4
Bridges Rd DN17 150 E3
Bridge St
7 Bridlington YO15 122 E2
10 Brigg DN20 98 B2
Goole DN14 149 C3
Great Driffield YO25 124 E4
Pocklington YO42 29 A4
Thorne/Moorends DN8 93 A8
York YO1 156 B2
Bridges The DN18 84 F8
Bridge Street North DN31 152 F5
Bridgeview Sch HU13 143 D1
Bridgewater Rd DN17 150 D4
Bridles The
9 Goxhill DN19 86 A8
Kingston upon Hull HU3 144 F2
Bridle Way 1 YO26 129 A3
Bridle Wlk YO8 148 C4
BRIDLINGTON 122 B3
Bridlington Ave HU2 155 B4
Bridlington Balk YO25 34 A8
Bridlington Bay Rd YO15 10 E4
Bridlington & District Hospl YO16 122 B3
Bridlington Forum YO15 122 F2
Bridlington Harbour Heritage Mus & Art Gallery* YO15 122 F2
Bridlington Leisure World YO15 122 F2
Bridlington Rd
Barmston YO25 22 F6
Brandesburton YO25 34 C3
Flamborough YO15 4 F1
Hunmanby YO14 3 A7
Sledmere YO25 7 C4
1 Stamford Bridge YO41 15 D2
Ulrome YO25 23 A2
Wold Newton YO25 2 A4
Bridlington Sch Sports Coll YO16 122 C3
Bridlington Sports Ctr YO16 122 B4
Bridlington St YO14 2 F8
Bridlington Sta YO15 122 D2
Bridport Cl HU7 141 C7
Bridport Wlk DN17 150 C4
Briergate YO32 127 C7
Brierholme Carr Rd DN7 92 F5
Brierholme Cl DN7 92 F5
Brierholme Ings Rd DN7 92 F5
Brier La YO8 64 A4
Brierley Cl
10 Howden DN14 65 A7
Snaith DN14 78 C8
BRIGG 98 D2
Briggate Dr DN17 107 D7
Brigg Dr HU13 143 F3
Brigg Farm Ct YO8 63 D5
Brigg La YO8 63 D5
Brigg Prep Sch DN20 98 C1
Brigg Prim Sch DN20 98 B2
Brigg Rd
Barton-upon-Humber DN18 84 E5
Broughton DN20 97 F3
Cadney DN20 109 C7
Grasby LN7 111 A6
Hibaldstow DN21 108 F6
Messingham DN17 107 D7
North Kelsey LN7 110 A5
Scunthorpe DN15 151 C7
South Kelsey LN7 110 A1
Wrawby DN20 98 D3
Briggs St YO31 130 C7
Brigg Sta DN20 98 C1
BRIGHAM 33 E8
Brigham Ct HU17 154 B4
Brigham Gr HU9 142 B1
Brigham La
Brigham YO25 33 E8
Foston YO25 21 E1
Brighowgate DN34 152 D2
Bright Cres 7 YO15 122 F3
Brighton St HU3 145 A3
Brighton Street Trading Pk 1 HU3 145 A3
Bright St
Kingston upon Hull HU8 146 B8
York YO26 129 F5
Bright Wlk YO8 148 B6
BRIGSLEY 113 D4
Brigsley Rd DN37 113 D6
Brimington Rd HU10 138 F2
Brimley HU17 136 C5
Brimley Gn HU17 136 C5
BRIND 51 A2
Brind La DN14 50 F2
Brindlegate 4 YO42 29 A4
Brindleys La DN14 50 F3
Brindley St HU9 141 E2
Brinkworth Rush YO41 27 A2
Brinkworth Terr 1 YO10 130 E3
Brisbane St HU3 145 D5
Bristol Rd
Kingston upon Hull HU5 144 C8
Scunthorpe DN17 150 C5
Britannia Cres 7 DN34 102 B3
Britannia Ct 10 YO16 122 F2
Britannia Gdns 7 HU5 140 E2
Britannia Rd
Bridlington YO16 122 C4
Goole DN14 149 A2
Britannia Way DN14 149 B3
Britton Cl DN17 81 D3
Brixham Ct
5 Kingston upon Hull HU3 145 A5
Waltham DN33 113 E7
Brixton Cl HU8 141 E5
Broach La
Heck DN14 62 D1
Kellington DN14 61 F3
Broach Rd
Heck DN14 77 D8
Hensall DN14 62 C1
Broadacre Pk 1 HU15 68 D5
Broadacre Prim Sch HU7 56 F6
Broadacres
Carlton DN14 63 D3
Keyingham HU12 73 D4
Broad Acres YO32 127 C7
Broadacres Ave DN14 63 D3
Broadacres Garth DN14 63 D3
BROAD BALK 124 D6
Broad Balk YO17 6 A5
Broadbent Gate Rd DN8 79 B1
Broadgate HU17 136 B1
Broad Highway YO19 37 F8
Broad La
Appleton Roebuck YO23 36 A6
6 Beal DN14 61 D4
Catton YO41 27 C7
Cawood YO8 48 A6
Howden DN14 65 B6
Rufforth YO23 129 A2
Sykehouse DN14 78 B4
Upper Poppleton YO26 12 D2
Wistow YO8 48 A5
Broad La Cl 5 HU16 139 B7
Broadland Dr 4 HU9 142 A3
Broadlands YO19 38 A8
Broadlands Cl 38 DN7 92 D4
Broadley Ave HU10 143 D6
Broadley Cl 6 HU9 146 C7
Broadley Croft 3 HU15 68 D5
Broadley Way HU15 68 D5
Broadmanor
North Duffield YO8 50 A7
Pocklington YO42 29 A3
Broad Manor YO42 29 A3
Broad Oak HU11 142 D6
Broad Oak La 18 YO32 13 E5
Broadstairs Cl 1 HU8 141 E7
Broadstone Cl HU7 141 C6
Broadstone Way
10 Rawcliffe YO30 126 E3
York YO30 126 E3
Broadwater Dr 34 DN7 92 D4
Broadwaters 1 HU7 56 E5
Broadway
Goole DN14 149 D4
5 Grimsby DN34 102 B2
Hatfield DN7 92 C3
Hornsea HU18 134 D4
7 Keelby DN41 101 A5
Scunthorpe DN16 151 A2
York YO10 133 E8
Broadway Dr 9 HU9 142 A3
Broadway Gr 3 YO10 133 E8
Broadway Nook DN7 92 C3
Broadway The 8 HU9 142 A3
Broadway W YO10 133 D8
Brockadale Nature Reserve* WF8 76 B4
Brock Cl
15 Epworth DN9 105 D6
1 Grimsby DN33 102 E1
Brockenhurst Ave HU16 139 D6
Brockenhurst Rd 7 DN7 92 E4
Brockett Ind Est YO23 36 B6
BROCKFIELD 14 E2
Brockfield Park Dr YO31 127 F2
Brockfield Rd YO31 127 E2
Brockle Bank Ct 9 HU12 58 C1
BROCKLESBY 100 E6
Brocklesby Ave DN40 87 B1
Brocklesby Cl 5 HU13 144 A3
Brocklesby Junc DN39 100 B8
Brocklesby Park Prim Sch DN37 100 E4
Brocklesby Pl 11 DN34 102 C2
Brocklesby Rd
10 Grimsby DN34 102 C2
Scunthorpe DN17 150 F1
Ulceby DN41 100 B8
Brockley Cl HU8 141 E6
Brockton Cl HU3 144 F5
Broc-o-Bank 1 DN6 76 E2
Brodsworth St 5 HU9 146 C8
Bromley St
Kingston upon Hull HU2 155 B4
2 York YO26 129 F5
Brompton Cl HU5 139 E2
Brompton Ct 4 HU3 140 D1
Brompton Rd YO30 130 A7
Bromwich Rd HU10 143 F8
Bronte Ct HU6 140 C7
Bronte Wlk YO16 122 B4
Bronzegarth DN32 153 B1
Brookdale Rd DN17 150 D2
Brooke Dr HU18 134 C2
Brooke Prim Sch DN8 93 B7
Brookes Cl DN21 108 B1
Brooke St DN8 93 A8
Brookfield Cl
Carnaby YO16 10 E4
1 Kingston upon Hull HU7 56 F5
8 Thorne/Moorends DN8 93 A8
Brookfield Rd DN33 102 D1
Brookholme HU17 137 B3
Brook La DN20 98 A1
Brookland Rd YO16 122 C4
Brooklands
2 Broughton DN20 97 E3
Kingston upon Hull HU7 141 C5
York YO10 131 D4
Brooklands Ave
Broughton DN20 97 D4
Cleethorpes DN35 103 D3
Brooklands Cl HU17 137 A6
Brooklands Pk HU16 139 A5
Brooklands Rd HU5 144 E8
Brooklyn Dr DN36 114 D8
Brooklyn St HU5 140 D3
Brooks Cl 17 DN37 101 F1
Brookside 2 HU15 68 D6
Brookside Cl YO42 28 D3
Brook St
Great Driffield YO25 124 F4
Hemswell DN21 119 A2
Kingston upon Hull HU2 155 A3
Selby YO8 148 C4
York YO31 156 B4
Broome Cl YO32 127 F5
Broome Way YO32 128 A5
Broomfield Way YO25 23 A6
BROOMFLEET 67 B6
Broomfleet Carr La HU15 67 B7
Broomfleet Sta HU15 67 B6
Broom Gr DN16 151 B4
Broomhead Cl 5 HU8 141 E7
Broomhill Cl 23 WF11 61 A2
Broomhill Cres 25 WF11 61 A2
Broomhill Dr 26 WF11 61 A2
Broomhill Gr 19 WF11 61 A2
Broomhill Pl 22 WF11 61 A2
Broomhill Sq 24 WF11 61 A2
Broomhill Wlk 21 WF11 61 A2
Broompark Rd DN14 149 E6
Broomston La DN9 104 F1
Brosley Ave DN3 92 A4
BROUGH 68 C5
Brougham Cl YO30 129 F8
Brougham St HU3 144 F7
Brough Prim Sch HU15 68 C6
Brough Rd HU15 54 A1
Brough Sh Pl 32 HU15 68 C5
Brough St DN14 149 D5
Brough Sta HU15 68 B5
BROUGHTON 97 E4
Broughton Cl 3 HU9 142 A3
Broughton Inf Sch DN20 97 E3
Broughton Jun Sch DN20 97 E3
Broughton Way YO10 131 B4
Brow La
Kilpin DN14 65 E7
Snaith DN14 78 B8
Brown Cow Rd YO8 63 C8
Browney Croft YO10 156 C1
Browning Cl
3 Kingston upon Hull HU3 145 D8
Scunthorpe DN17 150 E2
Browning Rd 20 YO42 29 A3
Brownlow St YO31 156 C4
Brown Moor 22 YO41 15 D2
Brownmoor La YO32 13 B8
Browns La 15 DN8 93 A8
Browns Orch DN32 152 D2
Brown St DN31 152 F7
Bruce Cl 6 DN20 97 D3
Brucella Gr 12 HU3 145 A4
Bruce St DN15 150 F7
BRUMBY 151 B4
Brumby Comm La DN17 150 C3
Brumby Engineering College DN16 151 B5
Brumby House Dr DN16 151 A4
Brumby Jun Sch DN16 151 B4
Brumby's Terr 4 HU9 146 D7
Brumby Wood La DN17 150 D6
Brumby Wood Nature Reserve* DN17 150 D5
Brumfield Ct HU17 154 C4
Brunel Cl
Grimsby DN32 152 F1
4 Scunthorpe DN16 96 D2
Brunel Ct 12 YO26 129 F5
Brunslow Cl HU3 144 E5
Brunswick Ave HU2 155 A4
Brunswick Cl 2 YO32 14 C8
Brunswick Gr 5 HU13 143 E2
Brunswick St YO23 130 B1
Brunton Way DN36 114 A7
Bryan Mere 3 HU17 43 A2
Bryants The HU17 45 A7
Bryony Ct YO8 148 B2
Bryson Cl DN8 79 B1
BUBWITH 50 D7
Bubwith Prim Sch YO8 50 D7
Buccaneer Ct YO41 27 A3
Buccaneer Way 16 HU15 68 C5
Buck Beck Way 12 DN36 103 B1
Buckfast Ct DN17 150 D4
Buckingham Ave DN15 96 C7
Buckingham Ct YO1 156 A1
Buckingham Gr 17 DN33 102 D1
Buckingham Prim Sch HU8 141 C1
Buckingham St
5 Kingston upon Hull HU8 141 C1
York YO1 156 B1
Buckingham Street N DN15 150 F8
Buckingham Street S DN15 150 F8
Buckingham Terr YO1 156 B2
Buck Inn Yd 35 YO42 29 A3
Buckland Cl 3 HU8 142 C7
Buckle Cl YO8 50 A
Buckle Ct YO8 148 B
Buckrose Gr YO16 122 C
BUCKTON 4 C
Buckton Gate YO15 4 C
Buddleia Cl DN41 101 F
Bude Cl 2 DN36 114 A
Bude Park Prim Sch HU7 56 F
Bude Rd HU7 140 F
Budworth Pk 4 HU7 56 E
BUGTHORPE 16 D
Bugthorpe CE Prim Sch YO41 16 D
Bugthorpe La YO41 16 D
Bugthorpe Lane Town E YO41 16 E
Bull Alley La DN14 63 B
Bull Balk YO41 27 E
Bull Bank LN11 121 F
Buller St
Grimsby DN32 153 A
Selby YO8 148 B
Bullfinch La 5 DN35 103 C
Bullivant Rd DN7 92 E
Bull La
Everingham YO42 40 C
Huby YO32 13 B
York YO10 130 F
Bull Moor La YO60 15 A
Bull Moor Rd DN7 93 A
Bull Pasture 14 HU15 53 F
Bull Ring La 11 DN31 152 D
Bulmer La YO43 51 E
Bulwick Ave DN33 113 E
Bunkers Hill DN21 119 B
Bunkers Hill Cl 11 DN36 114 D
Bunting Cl YO25 125 A
Burbage Ave HU8 141 C
Burcom Ave 7 DN36 114 D
Burcott Garth HU4 144 B
Burdale Cl
Great Driffield YO25 124 D
Kingston upon Hull HU9 142 B
Burden Cl HU17 154 C
Burden Rd HU17 154 C
Burden St HU1 155 A
Burdike Ave YO30 130 A
Burdock Rd DN16 96 E
Burgar Rd DN8 93 A
Burgate
4 Barton-upon-Humber DN18 84 F
North Newbald YO43 53 F
Burgess Ct HU17 154 B
Burgess Rd DN20 98 C
Burgess Sq 46 HU12 72 D
Burgess Wlk YO24 132 C8
Burghley Cl LN7 111 A
Burghley Rd DN16 151 D4
Burgon Cres DN15 83 B5
Burke St DN15 151 A8
Burke Street N DN15 151 A8
Burlands La YO26 24 F
Burleigh St HU8 146 C8
Burley Ave 18 DN35 103 C2
Burley Cl DN37 101 F2
Burlington Ave YO10 130 F4
Burlington Cres DN14 149 D4
Burlington Gdns YO16 122 D3
Burlington Inf Sch YO16 122 D5
Burlington Jun Sch YO16 122 C5
Burlington Rd HU8 141 D5
Burlyn Rd 3 YO14 3 A8
Burma Dr HU9 147 B8
Burma Rd DN16 151 F6
BURN 62 D7
Burnaby Cl HU17 136 E6
Burnbutts La YO25 32 C7
BURNBY 29 D1
Burnby Cl HU5 139 C2
Burnby Hall Gdns* YO42 29 A3
Burnby La YO42 29 A3
Burn Est YO32 127 E4
Burnet Dr 12 DN16 96 E2
Burnet Rose Way DN14 149 E7
Burnett's Yd LN7 111 C4
Burney Cl HU17 154 A4
Burn Hall Cl YO8 62 D7
BURNHAM 85 C3
Burnham Ave 4 HU12 73 A6
Burnham La DN39 85 E4
Burnham Rd
Barton-upon-Humber DN18 85 A6
Epworth DN9 105 E6
Kingston upon Hull HU4 144 B3
Owston Ferry DN9 106 A3
Scunthorpe DN15 150 D6
Burnham Reach 26 DN35 103 C1
Burnham Sq DN9 106 A3
Burnholme Ave YO31 131 B6
Burnholme Com Coll YO31 131 A5
Burnholme Dr YO31 131 A6
Burnholme Gr YO31 131 A5
Burniston Gr YO10 131 A4
Burniston Rd HU5 139 E2
Burn La YO8 62 D6
Burn Rd DN15 150 C7
Burnsall Dr YO26 129 E4
Burnsalls Rd HU12 72 C7
Burns Cl 2 YO42 28 F4
Burns Ct YO24 132 B7
Burns Gr 31 DN33 102 D2
Burnside DN20 97 D3
Burns St DN21 117 A1

urrells Cl 11 DN9 ... 105 D2
urrill Ave YO30 ... 130 B8
urrill Dr 13 YO32 ... 13 D5
urrill La HU15 ... 68 B8
urrill Mews 2 HU5 ... 139 E3
URRINGHAM ... 95 E4
urringham Rd DN17 ... 150 B1
urrs The HU15 ... 68 B5
ursall Sq HU12 ... 89 C8
ursar Prim Sch DN35 ... 153 E2
ursar St DN35 ... 153 E2
URSEA ... 52 A4
ursea La YO43 ... 52 A5
urslem St HU2 ... 155 A4
urstall Hill YO16 ... 122 B5
urstall La HU12 ... 90 C5
urstall Wlk YO16 ... 122 B5
URSTWICK ... 73 B7
urstwick Prim Sch HU12 73 B6
URTON AGNES ... 10 A1
urton Agnes Balk YO25 ... 9 F5
urton Agnes CE Prim Sch
YO25 ... 10 A1
urton Agnes Hall & Gdns*
YO25 ... 10 A2
urton Ave YO30 ... 130 B7
urton Comm La LS25 ... 61 A6
urton Constable Hall*
HU11 ... 58 C7
urton Ct YO30 ... 156 A4
urton Fields Cl 12 YO41 ... 15 D2
urton Fields Rd 4 YO41 ... 15 D2
URTON FLEMING ... 2 E3
urton Fleming Rd
Rudston YO25 ... 9 F8
Wold Newton YO25 ... 2 B3
urton Gates HU17 ... 55 B8
urton Gn YO30 ... 130 B8
urton Green Prim Sch
YO30 ... 130 B8
urton La HU18 ... 134 C2
URTON PIDSEA ... 59 D2
urton Pidsea Prim Sch
HU12 ... 59 D2
urton Rd
Beverley HU17 ... 136 C6
Flixborough DN15 ... 82 B2
Hornsea HU18 ... 134 D4
Kilham YO25 ... 9 C3
Kingston upon Hull HU16 ... 138 F5
Roos HU12 ... 59 F2
URTON STATHER ... 82 A5
urton Stone La YO30 ... 156 A4
URTON UPON STATHER ... 82 B4
urton upon Stather Prim
Sch DN15 ... 82 B4
urtree Ave YO30 ... 126 B4
urwell Dr DN33 ... 102 D2
ush Cl HU4 ... 144 D3
ushey Pk HU7 ... 56 F5
ushfield Rd DN16 ... 151 B5
ushfield Road Inf Sch
DN16 ... 151 A5
utcher La DN14 ... 77 A6
utcher Row
Beverley HU17 ... 154 A3
Seaton HU11 ... 35 A1
utcher's La
Burton Fleming YO25 ... 2 E3
Withernwick HU11 ... 46 D3
utchers Row HU11 ... 35 A1
utcher Terr YO23 ... 130 C1
utforth La DN19 ... 85 E8
utler Pl DN35 ... 153 B3
utlers La 23 YO15 ... 5 A2
utacre La YO23 ... 24 D2
utt Balk YO25 ... 9 E1
utterbur Dr DN14 ... 149 E7
UTTERCRAMBE ... 15 E5
uttercrambe Rd
Gate Helmsley YO41 ... 15 C3
Sand Hutton YO41 ... 15 C5
uttercross Cl 3 DN41 ... 101 E6
uttercup Cl 1 HU9 ... 146 D7
utterfield Cl
2 Laceby DN37 ... 101 F1
Snaith DN14 ... 78 D8
utterfly La YO16 ... 10 F5
utterfly Mdws HU17 ... 136 E6
uttermere Cl 3 HU4 ... 144 E6
uttermere Cres 3
DN36 ... 114 C8
uttermere Ct 9 YO8 ... 148 B6
uttermere Dr YO30 ... 126 E1
uttermere Rd DN14 ... 149 D5
uttermere Way DN32 ... 152 F4
utter Mkt
10 Caistor LN7 ... 111 B4
8 Snaith DN14 ... 63 C1
utters Cl 20 YO32 ... 13 D5
UTTERWICK ... 1 B2
utterwick Cl 23 DN35 ... 103 C2
utterwick Rd
Foxholes YO17 ... 1 B1
Langtoft YO25 ... 8 C7
Messingham DN17 ... 107 A7
uttfield La DN14 ... 65 A6
uttfield Rd
Howden DN14 ... 65 A6
Kingston upon Hull HU13 ... 143 E1
utt Fields La DN14 ... 62 F1
utt Hedge YO26 ... 24 A5
utt Hill 22 YO32 ... 13 D5
utt La
Beverley HU17 ... 154 A1
Laceby DN37 ... 101 F2
Laceby DN37 ... 101 F2
North Cave HU15 ... 53 E3

Butt La *continued*
Nunburnholme YO42 ... 29 E3
Snaith DN14 ... 78 C8
Thwing YO25 ... 9 A8
Tickton HU17 ... 137 F8
Warter YO42 ... 30 A5
Wold Newton YO25 ... 2 A3
Buttle La 3 DN14 ... 63 C1
Butts Cl
Bridlington YO16 ... 122 D4
19 Stamford Bridge YO41 ... 15 D2
Butts Hill YO14 ... 3 C6
Butts Hill La DN15 ... 82 C8
Butts La YO25 ... 19 E2
Butts Rd DN18 ... 69 F1
BUTTS THE ... 124 E3
Butts The HU20 ... 55 A4
Buxton Ct DN15 ... 150 B6
Byass Ave YO16 ... 122 E4
Bycroft Rd DN21 ... 117 B3
Bydales La HU12 ... 74 B3
Byedales 4 YO15 ... 4 D3
Byfield Rd DN17 ... 150 D2
Bygot Cl 1 HU17 ... 43 D6
Bygott Wlk 29 DN36 ... 114 A8
Byland Ave YO31 ... 130 E8
Byland Ct 4 HU9 ... 146 E8
Byram Park Rd WF11 ... 61 A4
Byrd Rd DN16 ... 151 E2
Byron Ave 3 DN6 ... 76 E1
Byron Cl DN17 ... 150 E2
Byron Dr YO30 ... 129 F8
Byron Gr DN33 ... 102 E2
Byron St
Goole DN14 ... 149 C5
Kingston upon Hull HU8 ... 141 D2
Bywell Wlk HU9 ... 147 D8
Bywood Pl 5 DN37 ... 102 B3

C

CABOURNE ... 111 D4
Cabourne Rd 34 DN33 ... 102 D2
Cabry Dr 21 HU12 ... 73 C4
Caddle Rd 9 DN41 ... 101 A4
Cadeby Medieval Village*
DN36 ... 120 F6
Cadeleigh Cl HU7 ... 141 A8
Cadman Rd YO16 ... 123 A7
CADNEY ... 109 D6
Cadney Rd
Bigby DN20 ... 98 C1
Cadney DN20 ... 109 C8
Cadogan St HU3 ... 145 B5
Caedmon Cl YO31 ... 131 A7
Caenby Rd
14 Cleethorpes DN35 ... 103 C2
Scunthorpe DN17 ... 150 E1
Caesar Ct YO24 ... 156 A1
Cairnborrow 4 YO24 ... 132 B7
CAISTOR ... 111 B4
Caistor Ave DN16 ... 96 D2
Caistor By-pass LN7 ... 111 B3
Caistor CE/Methodist Prim
Sch LN7 ... 111 B4
Caistor Dr DN33 ... 102 D2
Caistor Grammar School
LN7 ... 111 B4
Caistor Rd
Barton-upon-Humber
DN18 ... 85 A7
Laceby DN37 ... 112 E8
Nettleton LN7 ... 111 A3
North Kelsey LN7 ... 110 D4
Rothwell LN7 ... 111 E2
South Kelsey LN7 ... 110 A1
Swallow LN7 ... 112 A5
Caistor Yarborough Sch
LN7 ... 111 C4
Caithness Cl 1 YO30 ... 126 E3
Calais Croft 7 HU17 ... 43 A2
Calam Villas YO25 ... 35 C5
Calcaria Ct 3 YO24 ... 132 F8
Caldane HU6 ... 139 E8
Caldbeck Cl 1 YO30 ... 127 A1
Caldberg Mews 3 HU5 ... 139 E3
Calder Ave YO26 ... 129 B8
Calder Cl 35 DN40 ... 87 B1
Calder Cres DN14 ... 77 F6
Calderdale HU7 ... 140 F6
Calderdale Cl 2 YO16 ... 123 A7
Calder Dr DN14 ... 78 B8
Calder Gn DN17 ... 107 D7
Calder Gr HU8 ... 142 C6
Calder Rd DN16 ... 151 D2
Calder Sq HU15 ... 68 D5
Calder St 4 DN14 ... 149 D4
Caledon Cl HU9 ... 142 D5
Caledonia Pk HU9 ... 146 B5
Calf Cl YO32 ... 127 D8
Callas 6 HU17 ... 43 A2
Calthwaite Dr 17 HU15 ... 68 D5
Calver Cres DN37 ... 102 B4
Calvert Cl YO32 ... 127 C7
Calvert La HU4 ... 144 D7
Calvert Rd HU5 ... 144 D8
Calvi Ct 2 DN32 ... 153 A5
Camargue Ave DN37 ... 113 E7
Cambeak Cl 3 HU7 ... 56 F5
Camberwell Way HU8 ... 142 A5
CAMBLESFORTH ... 63 D5
Camblesforth Prim Sch
YO8 ... 63 C4
Camborne Gr HU8 ... 141 B3
Cambrian Cl 2 YO32 ... 127 F3
Cambrian Way 2 DN36 ... 114 A6

Cambridge Ave
Goole DN14 ... 149 B5
Scunthorpe DN16 ... 96 D2
Cambridge Gr HU9 ... 141 F1
Cambridge Park Sch
DN34 ... 152 A1
Cambridge Rd
Grimsby DN34 ... 152 A1
Kingston upon Hull HU13 ... 143 F3
Scunthorpe DN16 ... 151 C2
Cambridge St
Bridlington YO16 ... 122 D3
Cleethorpes DN35 ... 153 F2
Kingston upon Hull HU1 ... 155 A2
4 York YO24 ... 130 A3
Camden St 1 HU3 ... 145 B5
Camela La YO8 ... 63 B6
Camelford Cl 12 HU7 ... 56 F5
Camellia Cl YO25 ... 124 D3
Cameron Gr YO23 ... 130 C1
CAMERTON ... 73 A5
Camerton Gr HU9 ... 141 F2
Camerton Hall La HU12 ... 72 F5
Cam Gr HU8 ... 142 C6
Camilla Cl HU9 ... 155 C1
Cammidge St 2 HU19 ... 74 F7
Camm La DN14 ... 63 C3
Campbell Ave
26 Scunthorpe DN16 ... 96 D2
York YO24 ... 129 E2
Campbell Ct HU9 ... 142 A2
Campbells Farm Ave
DN15 ... 95 E6
Campbell St 3 DN21 ... 117 A1
Campden Cres DN35 ... 153 D3
Camperdown HU11 ... 142 D6
Campey La YO42 ... 39 B6
Campion Ave HU4 ... 144 B2
Campions Cl 12 DN36 ... 114 A5
Campions' La 6 DN36 ... 114 B1
Campleshon Rd YO23 ... 130 B1
Campsall Balk DN6 ... 76 E1
Campsall Hall Rd 12 DN6 ... 76 E1
Campsall Park Rd 11 DN6 76 E1
Campsite Rd HU11 ... 47 D2
Campsmount Sch DN6 ... 76 D1
Canada Dr
Cherry Burton HU17 ... 43 A5
Kingston upon Hull HU16 ... 138 E5
Canada La LN7 ... 111 C4
Canal Garth DN14 ... 77 F6
Canal La
Barmby Moor YO42 ... 28 F3
West Stockwith DN10 ... 116 E5
Canal Rd
Cottingwith YO42 ... 38 C5
Selby YO8 ... 148 D4
CANAL SIDE ... 93 A7
Canalside 15 DN8 ... 93 A7
Canal Side E HU15 ... 52 E3
Canal Side W HU15 ... 52 E2
Canal View
Selby YO8 ... 148 D3
2 Thorne/Moorends DN8 ... 93 A7
Canberra Ave DN7 ... 104 A8
Canberra St HU3 ... 145 D5
Candlesby Rd 4 DN37 ... 102 B4
Candy Bank DN9 ... 104 B5
Canham Gr YO10 ... 131 D3
Canham La YO25 ... 35 C5
Cannaught Road 12 HU7 ... 56 E5
Canning St HU1 ... 155 A2
Cannon Hall La DN14 ... 61 F1
Cannon Oakes Ct DN36 ... 114 B7
Cannon St HU2 ... 155 B4
Canongate HU16 ... 139 B7
Canon Lee Sch YO30 ... 130 A8
Canon Peter Hall CE Prim
Sch DN40 ... 87 C1
Canons Ct YO23 ... 133 B2
Canon Tardrew Cl 5
HU13 ... 143 F1
Canopias Cl HU3 ... 145 A4
Canterbury Cl
Beverley HU17 ... 136 D1
9 Haxby YO32 ... 13 D5
Scunthorpe DN17 ... 150 D3
Canterbury Dr
Grimsby DN34 ... 152 C2
2 Kingston upon Hull
HU8 ... 141 E7
Canterbury Rd 21 DN7 ... 92 D4
Canton Villas 5 YO15 ... 122 F4
Canty Nook DN38 ... 110 E7
Capital Park HU17 ... 137 C4
Capstan Rd HU6 ... 140 C8
Capstan Way 13 DN8 ... 93 A8
Captains Cl DN14 ... 149 D6
Captains Wlk HU1 ... 155 A1
Carden Ave HU9 ... 142 C2
Cardiff Ave DN36 ... 114 A7
Cardigan Rd
Bridlington YO15 ... 122 D1
Kingston upon Hull HU3 ... 144 E6
Cardinal Ct 1 DN37 ... 113 D7
Cardinals Cl 3 YO8 ... 48 B8
Carentan Cl 6 YO8 ... 148 B6
Carew St HU3 ... 144 F7
Carey St YO10 ... 130 D1
Carisbrooke Ave HU16 ... 139 B6
Carisbrooke Cl 9 DN36 ... 114 A8
Carisbrooke Manor La
DN17 ... 150 A1
Carlam La HU7 ... 57 A7
Carleton St 17 YO26 ... 129 F5
Carlisle Rd 8 YO15 ... 122 F3
Carlisle St
29 Gainsborough DN21 ... 117 B1

Carlisle St *continued*
Goole DN14 ... 149 D4
16 York YO26 ... 129 F5
Carl St YO23 ... 130 C2
CARLTON ... 63 D3
Carlton Ave
Healing DN41 ... 101 F5
Hornsea HU18 ... 134 C5
York YO10 ... 131 B3
Carlton Cl
Eggborough DN14 ... 61 F1
22 Humberston DN35 ... 103 D1
Carlton Ct HU17 ... 154 A3
Carlton Dr HU11 ... 47 B1
Carlton in Snaith CP Sch
DN14 ... 63 C3
Carlton La HU11 ... 47 B1
Carlton Rd
Aldbrough HU11 ... 46 F1
24 Brough HU15 ... 68 C6
Grimsby DN34 ... 152 B2
5 Healing DN41 ... 101 F5
Sutton upon Derwent YO41 ... 27 C1
Carlton Rise 2 HU17 ... 55 F8
Carlton St
Bridlington YO16 ... 122 D3
Kingston upon Hull HU3 ... 144 F4
11 Scunthorpe DN15 ... 151 B7
Carlton Twrs* DN14 ... 63 D2
Carlton View YO8 ... 148 D4
Carmelite St YO1 ... 156 C2
Carmen Cres 1 DN36 ... 114 A6
Carmires Ave YO32 ... 13 F5
CARNABY ... 10 E4
Carnaby Ave YO16 ... 122 B2
Carnaby Cl HU17 ... 43 D6
Carnaby Gr
Grimsby DN32 ... 153 A1
Kingston upon Hull HU6 ... 139 E5
Carnaby Ind Est YO15 ... 10 E3
Carnegie Heritage
Information Ctr* HU3 ... 145 A6
Carnegie St 6 HU3 ... 145 A6
Carnforth Cres DN34 ... 152 A1
Carnforth Par DN34 ... 152 A1
Carnot St YO26 ... 129 F5
Carnoustie 13 DN37 ... 113 D6
Carnoustie Cl
Kingston upon Hull HU8 ... 141 C3
1 York YO26 ... 129 B4
Carol Dickson Ct 9 HU3 145 C5
Caroline Cl 5 YO24 ... 129 F3
Caroline Pl HU2 ... 155 B3
Carolines Pl HU16 ... 138 B8
Caroline St HU2 ... 155 B4
Carperby Mews 6 HU5 ... 139 D3
Carrbank La YO32 ... 14 D2
Carr Cl
Beverley HU17 ... 154 C3
13 Hemingbrough YO8 ... 49 F1
Carr Dike La HU15 ... 67 C7
Carr Dyke Bank DN17 ... 106 D5
Carr Dyke Rd DN17 ... 95 D3
Carrfield YO24 ... 132 C8
Carrfields DN14 ... 149 D6
CARR HEADS ... 124 D3
Carrhouse Rd DN9 ... 94 D1
Carrick Gdns YO24 ... 129 E3
Carr Inf Sch YO26 ... 129 C5
Carrington Ave
Hornsea HU18 ... 134 C6
Kingston upon Hull HU16 ... 139 B6
1 York YO26 ... 129 E5
Carrington Dr 20 DN36 ... 103 D1
Carrington St 6 HU3 ... 145 B5
Carr Jun Sch YO26 ... 129 C5
Carr La
Appleby DN15 ... 83 D2
Barlow YO8 ... 63 C7
Blyton DN21 ... 117 A5
Bonby DN20 ... 84 B1
Bridlington YO16 ... 123 A8
Broughton DN20 ... 97 F3
Burton Pidsea HU12 ... 59 D1
Burton upon Stather DN15 ... 82 D4
Eastrington DN14 ... 51 F1
Escrick YO19 ... 37 B5
Everingham YO42 ... 40 A4
Garthorpe & Fockerby DN17 81 E4
Goole DN14 ... 149 D6
Grimsby DN32 ... 153 B3
Haxey DN9 ... 105 E2
Healing DN41 ... 101 F4
Hibaldstow DN20 ... 109 A6
Horkstow DN18 ... 84 A5
Hotham YO43 ... 53 A4
Kingston upon Hull HU1 ... 155 A2
Leven HU17 ... 44 E8
Long Drax YO8 ... 63 F6
Luddington & Haldenby
DN17 ... 81 C1
Misterton DN10 ... 116 C5
Nafferton YO25 ... 21 C4
Newport HU15 ... 52 E2
Newton on Derwent YO41 ... 27 F4
Pocklington YO42 ... 40 A8
Redbourne DN21 ... 108 F3
Riston HU11 ... 45 B5
Seaton Ross YO42 ... 39 E4
Snaith & Cowick DN14 ... 78 C7
Stallingborough DN41 ... 101 E7
Tickton HU17 ... 137 E3
Ulceby DN39 ... 86 B3
Watton YO25 ... 33 A4
West Butterwick DN17 ... 106 C8
Wildsworth DN21 ... 117 C8
Winterton DN15 ... 83 D6
Wistow YO8 ... 48 A3

Carr La *continued*
Worlaby DN20 ... 98 A7
York YO26 ... 129 D5
Carr Lane Inf Sch HU10 ... 138 E1
Carr Lane Prim Sch
HU10 ... 138 E1
Carnock Ct 3 YO32 ... 127 F1
Carroll Pl HU1 ... 155 C3
Carron Cres YO24 ... 132 B7
Carroway Cl 4 YO16 ... 123 A7
Carr Rd
Burton Pidsea HU12 ... 59 D1
Molescroft HU17 ... 136 E8
North Kelsey LN7 ... 109 E4
Carrside 5 DN9 ... 105 D7
Carr Side La DN7 ... 92 E2
Carrs Mdw
Escrick YO19 ... 37 B5
Withernsea HU19 ... 74 F6
Carr St
Kingston Upon Hull HU2 ... 155 B4
Selby YO8 ... 148 F4
Carson Ave DN34 ... 152 B2
Carson Rd DN21 ... 117 B1
Carter Ave YO31 ... 130 F5
Carter Dr HU17 ... 136 E7
Cartergate DN31 ... 152 D3
Carter La YO15 ... 5 A2
Carter St DN14 ... 149 C4
Cartledge Ave DN32 ... 153 B2
Cartmel Ct HU9 ... 142 B2
Cartmel Gr DN32 ... 153 B2
Cartwright La HU17 ... 154 A1
Carver Rd DN40 ... 87 C1
Cary La 4 DN20 ... 98 B2
Caspian Cres 18 DN33 ... 102 D1
Cassbrook Dr LN11 ... 121 E8
Casson's Rd 1 DN8 ... 93 A8
Casswell Cl 4 DN32 ... 153 A5
Casswell Cres LN11 ... 121 E8
Castella Dr DN15 ... 151 D7
Castle Cl
Cawood YO8 ... 48 A8
1 Haxby YO32 ... 13 D5
3 Leconfield HU17 ... 43 D6
Castle Cres 16 YO15 ... 5 A2
Castle Ct 9 DN18 ... 84 F8
Castle Dr
1 Epworth DN9 ... 105 E6
South Cave HU15 ... 53 F2
Castledyke Prim Sch
DN18 ... 69 E1
Castledyke S 10 DN18 ... 84 F8
Castledyke W 10 DN18 ... 69 E1
Castleford Ave 2 DN34 ... 102 D2
Castleford Gr HU9 ... 142 E2
Castlegate YO1 ... 156 B2
Castle Gn HU16 ... 138 E6
Castle Hill
Caistor LN7 ... 111 B4
8 Hunmanby YO14 ... 2 F8
Castle Hill Hospl HU16 ... 138 D5
Castle Hill La YO8 ... 63 F5
Castlehill Rd HU7 ... 141 D8
Castle Hills Community Art
Coll The DN21 ... 117 B1
Castle Howard Cl YO16 ... 122 F6
Castle Keep DN20 ... 108 F6
Castle Pk 9 HU11 ... 47 C1
Castle Rd HU16 ... 138 D5
Castle Rise 1 HU15 ... 54 A2
Castle St
Grimsby DN32 ... 153 A4
Kingston upon Hull HU1 ... 155 A1
Castleton Ave 6 HU5 ... 139 E3
Castleton Rd DN15 ... 150 B6
Castle View YO25 ... 23 A1
Castle Way HU13 ... 69 F4
Castle Wlk YO1 ... 156 C2
Catford Cl HU8 ... 141 E5
Catfoss Rd YO25 ... 35 A4
Cathcart Cl DN14 ... 76 F7
Cathedral Cl 8 HU17 ... 136 E1
Cathedral Ct
Hatfield DN7 ... 92 C2
Scunthorpe DN16 ... 151 A2
Catherine Gr 6 DN20 ... 97 E3
Catherine McAuley Cl
HU6 ... 140 C5
Catherine St
13 Barton-upon-Humber
DN18 ... 69 F1
Grimsby DN32 ... 152 E3
Kingston upon Hull HU2 ... 155 B4
Catkin Rd DN16 ... 96 D1
Cat La
Balne DN14 ... 77 E5
Bilbrough YO23 ... 24 D1
Catterick Mews 8 HU5 ... 139 D3
Catterton La LS24 ... 24 A1
Cattistock Rd 27 DN35 ... 103 C2
Cattle Rd DN10 ... 116 A5
Catton La YO42 ... 28 F4
Catton Way YO8 ... 148 A2
CATWICK ... 45 D8
Catwick Heads HU11 ... 45 E8
Catwick La
Brandesburton YO25 ... 34 C2
Catwick HU11 ... 45 D8
Caughey St HU3 ... 145 D7
Causeway Ings La HU12 ... 73 E7
Causewy The HU17 ... 154 B3
Cave Cres HU16 ... 138 E5
Cavendish Cl 14 DN35 ... 103 D1
Cavendish Dr 2 HU17 ... 136 E1

Cavendish Gr YO10 . . . . . . 131 D3
Cavendish Pk 8 HU15 . . . . 68 C5
Cavendish Prim Sch
HU8 . . . . 141 E4
Cavendish Rd
Kingston upon Hull HU8 . . 141 D5
9 Scunthorpe DN16 . . . . 96 D2
Cavendish Sq HU3 . . . . . . 140 D1
Cavendish Way DN32 . . . . . 152 F3
Cave Rd HU15 . . . . 68 B6
Cave's La DN10 . . . . 116 B3
Cave St HU5 . . . . 140 D1
Cave Terr 1 HU5 . . . . 140 D1
Cavill Dr 12 DN14 . . . . 65 B7
Cavill Pl HU3 . . . . 145 D5
CAWKELD 32 B5
CAWOOD 48 B8
Cawood CE Aided Prim Sch
YO8 . . . . 48 B8
Cawood Cl HU11 . . . . 45 D2
Cawood Cres HU11 . . . . 45 D2
Cawood Dr HU11 . . . . 45 D2
Cawood Rd
Stillingfleet YO19 . . . . 36 D3
Wistow YO8 . . . . 48 C7
Cawthorn Cl YO25 . . . . . . 125 A3
Cawthorne Dr HU4 . . . . . . 144 C3
Caxton Ave YO26 . . . . 129 D6
Cayley Cl YO30 . . . . 126 F1
Cayley Rd HU10 . . . . 143 F6
Cayton Rd HU8 . . . . 141 D4
Cecil Cl 10 DN21 . . . . 107 C3
Cecile Cres DN15 . . . . 150 E7
Cecilia Pl 3 YO24 . . . . . . 130 A3
Cecil Rd 7 YO14 . . . . 3 A8
Cecil St
24 Gainsborough DN21 . . . . 117 B1
Goole DN14 . . . . 149 E4
Kingston upon Hull HU3 . . . 144 F5
Cedar Ave
Flixborough DN15 . . . . 96 A7
Kingston upon Hull HU16 . 139 A6
Stainforth DN7 . . . . 92 D6
Cedar Cl
11 Cleethorpes DN35 . . . . . 103 B1
Gainsborough DN21 . . . . . 117 A2
Hambleton YO8 . . . . 48 B1
Hornsea HU18 . . . . 134 D1
Kingston upon Hull HU10 . 143 D7
Scawby DN20 . . . . 108 F8
7 Scotter DN21 . . . . 107 C3
Wawne HU7 . . . . 56 F8
Cedar Cres YO8 . . . . 48 D2
Cedar Ct
Bridlington YO16 . . . . 123 A8
8 Hedon HU12 . . . . 72 C7
Cedar Dr 2 DN40 . . . . 87 C2
Cedar Glade YO19 . . . . 26 E7
Cedar Gr
2 Aldbrough HU11 . . . . 47 C1
Stainforth DN7 . . . . 92 D6
York YO31 . . . . 131 B7
Cedar Gr The HU17 . . . . . 136 C6
Cedar Rd
Selby YO8 . . . . 148 D2
2 Thorne/Moorends DN8 . . . 79 B1
Cedarwood 5 HU15 . . . . . . 66 D7
Cedarwood Cl 7 YO24 . . . 129 B1
Cedarwood Dr HU5 . . . . . . 144 B7
Cedric Rd DN3 . . . . 92 A1
Celandine Cl
8 Kingston upon Hull
HU5 . . . . 139 D1
8 South Killingholme DN40 86 E3
Celery Bank DN14 . . . . 66 A4
Celtic Cl YO26 . . . . 129 B5
Cemetery Cres 7 DN37 . . 101 F1
Cemetery La
North Kelsey LN7 . . . . 110 A5
Pocklington YO42 . . . . 29 A3
Cemetery Rd
Hatfield DN7 . . . . 92 F4
Laceby DN37 . . . . 101 F1
Scunthorpe DN16 . . . . 151 B5
Winterton DN15 . . . . 83 B5
York YO10 . . . . 156 C1
Centenary Rd DN14 . . . . . . 149 B5
Centenary Way DN17 . . . . 151 A5
Central Ave
Beverley HU17 . . . . 154 A2
Ulrome YO25 . . . . 23 B3
Central Parade DN34 . . . . 152 A3
Central Promenade
DN35 . . . . 153 F2
Central St HU2 . . . . 140 F1
Central Way DN16 . . . . 151 D6
Centurion Pk YO30 . . . . . . 127 B2
Centurion Way
Brough HU15 . . . . 68 C5
Caistor LN7 . . . . 111 A4
Clifton YO30 . . . . 127 B3
Centurion Wlk YO43 . . . . . 135 E4
Century Rd HU12 . . . . 72 A8
Ceylon St HU9 . . . . 147 C7
Chadcourt HU6 . . . . 139 E6
Chadwell Springs DN37 . 113 C6
Chaffinch Cl DN15 . . . . 96 B7
Chaffinch Dr 14 DN35 . . . 103 C1
Chaldon Cl 4 YO32 . . . . 14 A6
Chalfont Cl HU13 . . . . 143 D2
Chalfonts YO24 . . . . 129 F1
Chaloner's Cres YO24 . . . 132 D7
Chaloner's Rd YO24 . . . . . 132 D8
Chamberlain Bsns Pk
HU8 . . . . 141 B3
Chamberlain Cl HU7 . . . . 141 D6
Chamberlain Ct HU7 . . . . 141 D7
Chamberlain Gdns HU8 . 141 C3
Chamberlain Rd HU8 . . . . . 141 B3
Chamberlain St HU7 . . . . 141 D6
Chambers La 1 HU18 . . . 134 C4
Chamomile Cl 17 DN16 . . . . 96 E2
Champney Rd HU17 . . . . . 154 A2
Chancel Rd DN16 . . . . 96 D2
Chancel Wlk 8 DN20 . . . . . 97 E3
Chancery Ct
Kingston upon Hull HU5 . . . 144 E8
York YO24 . . . . 129 C3
Chancery La 2 DN17 . . . . . 94 D7
Chancery Rise YO24 . . . . . 129 F3
Chancewaters 5 HU7 . . . . . 56 E5
Chandlers Cl 2 DN36 . . . . 114 A7
Chandlers Ct HU9 . . . . 146 C6
Chandos Rd DN17 . . . . 150 F3
Channel Rd HU12 . . . . 89 B6
Chanterlands Ave HU5 . . 140 A1
Chantreys Dr 13 HU15 . . . . 68 C6
Chantry Ave 14 YO26 . . . . . 12 F1
Chantry Cl
Grimsby DN31 . . . . 152 C3
York YO24 . . . . 132 C8
Chantry Ct YO16 . . . . 122 D4
Chantry Gap 11 YO26 . . . . . 12 F1
Chantry Gr 13 YO26 . . . . . . 12 F1
Chantry La
Beverley HU17 . . . . 154 B2
Bishopthorpe YO23 . . . . . . 133 B4
Etton HU17 . . . . 43 A6
Grimsby DN31 . . . . 152 C3
Rimswell HU12 . . . . 74 C5
Chantry Mdws 1 YO25 . . . . 9 C3
Chantry Way 13 HU14 . . . . . 69 B7
Chantry Way E 9 HU14 . . . 69 B7
Chapel Balk Rd YO8 . . . . . . 49 F1
Chapel Cl
Barrow upon Humber
DN19 . . . . 85 D7
27 Flamborough YO15 . . . . . . 5 A2
8 Howden DN14 . . . . 65 A6
2 Kingston upon Hull
HU4 . . . . 144 A1
7 Misterton DN10 . . . . . . 116 C5
North Duffield YO8 . . . . 50 A7
12 Preston HU12 . . . . 58 C1
Rawcliffe DN14 . . . . 64 A1
Skidby HU16 . . . . 138 A8
Skirlaugh HU11 . . . . 45 E2
4 Westwoodside DN9 . . . . 105 B2
Chapel Cnr YO43 . . . . 135 D4
Chapel Ct
Alkborough DN15 . . . . 82 C8
7 Hibaldstow DN20 . . . . . . 108 F5
Scotter DN21 . . . . 107 C4
Scunthorpe DN15 . . . . 151 B8
Chapelfield Rd DN19 . . . . . . 86 B7
CHAPEL Fields 129 B3
Chapel Fields
Coniston HU11 . . . . 57 F6
Holme-on-Spalding-Moor
YO43 . . . . 40 A1
Chapel Fields Rd YO26 . . 129 A3
Chapel Garth
Broomfleet HU15 . . . . 67 B5
11 Gilberdyke HU15 . . . . 66 D8
Holme-on-Spalding-Moor
YO42 . . . . 40 A1
Ottringham HU12 . . . . 73 E3
Skipsea YO25 . . . . 23 A1
3 Tetney DN36 . . . . 114 D4
CHAPEL HADDLESEY 62 C5
Chapel Haddlesey CE Prim
Sch YO8 . . . . 62 B5
Chapel Hill 1 HU15 . . . . . . 68 E6
Chapel Hill Rd YO42 . . . . . . 29 A4
Chapel La
Ashby cum Fenby DN37 . . . 113 D3
Askham Bryan YO23 . . . . 24 F3
Barmston YO25 . . . . 23 A6
Barnoldby le Beck DN37 . . . 113 B6
14 Barton-upon-Humber
DN18 . . . . 69 E1
Brayton YO8 . . . . 148 B1
Broughton DN20 . . . . 97 E3
Elsham DN20 . . . . 98 F7
10 Gainsborough DN21 . . . 117 A2
Habrough DN40 . . . . 100 E8
Horkstow DN18 . . . . 84 A5
Keadby with Althorpe DN17 . 95 C6
13 Keyingham HU12 . . . . 73 C4
Kilham YO25 . . . . 9 B3
Kingston upon Hull HU1 . . 155 C2
Langtoft YO25 . . . . 8 D5
Laxton DN14 . . . . 65 F4
Little Smeaton WF8 . . . . 76 B3
Ludborough DN36 . . . . 121 B6
Middleton YO25 . . . . 31 C4
8 Misterton DN10 . . . . 116 C5
Northorpe DN21 . . . . 118 D8
Ottringham HU12 . . . . 73 E3
Rawcliffe DN14 . . . . 64 A2
Reighton YO14 . . . . 3 E5
8 Riccall YO19 . . . . 37 A1
Scawby DN20 . . . . 108 E8
Skeffling HU12 . . . . 90 C6
Swallow LN7 . . . . 112 B5
Sykehouse DN14 . . . . 78 A4
18 Thorne/Moorends DN8 . . . 93 A8
Utterby LN11 . . . . 121 C4
Wansford YO25 . . . . 21 C3
1 Wawne HU7 . . . . 56 E7
West/East Butterwick
DN17 . . . . 95 D1
West Ella HU10 . . . . 69 C8
Chapel La *continued*
Whitton DN15 . . . . 67 E3
Winterton DN15 . . . . 83 A5
Wrawby DN20 . . . . 98 D4
Chapel Lane Staith HU1 . 155 C2
Chapel Mdws 8 HU15 . . . . 66 D8
Chapel Mews 3 HU15 . . . . 68 C6
Chapel Rd
Broughton DN20 . . . . 97 E3
Habrough DN40 . . . . 100 E8
Tetney DN36 . . . . 114 D4
Chapel Row YO10 . . . . 156 C1
Chapelry Garth 28 HU12 . . 72 D7
Chapel St
2 Amcotts DN17 . . . . 81 F1
Barmby Moor YO42 . . . . 28 D3
Bridlington YO15 . . . . 122 E2
13 Caistor LN7 . . . . 111 B4
5 Crowle DN17 . . . . 94 D8
6 Epworth DN9 . . . . 105 E6
6 Flamborough YO15 . . . . 5 A2
Goole DN14 . . . . 149 D3
Goxhill DN19 . . . . 86 A8
Hillam LS25 . . . . 61 B7
Kingston upon Hull HU1 . . 155 A2
Lockington YO25 . . . . 32 B2
North Kelsey LN7 . . . . 110 A4
Scunthorpe DN15 . . . . 151 B7
Chapel Terr YO24 . . . . 129 C3
Chapel Way 21 DN20 . . . . . . 98 C2
Chapel Wlk 4 YO19 . . . . 37 A1
Chapman Ave DN17 . . . . . 150 D2
Chapman Cl 1 YO32 . . . . . . 14 C8
Chapman Ct DN31 . . . . . . 152 D4
Chapman Gr DN35 . . . . . . 153 F1
Chapman Rd DN35 . . . . . . 153 D3
Chapmans Ct YO24 . . . . . . 132 D6
Chapman's La YO30 . . . . . . 12 E7
Chapman St HU8 . . . . 155 C4
Chapter House St YO1 . . . 156 B3
Chapter Wk DN20 . . . . 97 E3
Charing Cl HU3 . . . . 145 C8
Chariot St HU1 . . . . 155 A2
Chariot Way 6 YO25 . . . . . . 19 B6
Charles Ave
Grimsby DN33 . . . . 102 E1
Laceby DN37 . . . . 101 E1
17 New Waltham DN36 . . . 114 A7
15 Scotter DN21 . . . . 107 C3
Charles Ct 7 DN8 . . . . 79 B1
Charles Dr DN14 . . . . 149 B6
Charles Hume Ct DN32 . . . 153 B4
Charles Lovell Way
DN17 . . . . 150 D4
Charles Moor YO31 . . . . . . 130 F7
Charles St
Cleethorpes DN35 . . . . 153 F1
30 Gainsborough DN21 . . . . 117 B1
22 Hedon HU12 . . . . 72 D7
Kingston upon Hull HU2 . . . 155 B3
Selby YO8 . . . . 148 B6
Charlestown Way HU9 . . 146 C6
Charles Wesley Dr YO8 . . . 148 B2
Charlotte St Mews HU1 . . 155 B3
Charlotte St HU1 . . . . 155 C3
Charlton St
Grimsby DN31 . . . . 152 C4
York YO23 . . . . 130 C2
Charnock Ave HU9 . . . . . . 142 A4
Charnwood Cl 29 HU7 . . . . 56 F6
Charter Ave DN14 . . . . 64 A1
Charterfield HU11 . . . . 142 D6
Charterhouse Dr 3 DN16 . 96 E2
Charterhouse La HU2 . . . . 155 B3
Charterhouse The*
HU2 . . . . 155 C3
Charter's La 4 YO25 . . . . . . 34 B2
Charters The YO8 . . . . 49 B5
Chase Hill Rd DN40 . . . . . . 86 E5
Chase Sch 45 DN7 . . . . 92 D4
Chase Side Ct YO24 . . . . . 132 E8
Chase The
Driffield YO25 . . . . 125 A4
2 Snaith DN14 . . . . 78 C8
Chatham St HU3 . . . . 144 F7
Chatsworth Cl
Beverley HU17 . . . . 154 A1
5 Bridlington YO16 . . . . . 122 D6
Chatsworth Dr
Goole DN14 . . . . 149 B6
16 Haxby YO32 . . . . 13 F5
Chatsworth Pl 1 DN35 . . . 103 B2
Chatsworth St HU5 . . . . . 145 B8
Chatsworth Terr 4
YO26 . . . . 129 E4
Chatsworth Way 12 DN9 . 105 D2
Chatterton Cres DN15 . . . . 96 D7
Chaucer Ave DN17 . . . . . . 150 D3
Chaucer La YO32 . . . . 14 B8
Chaucer St
Kingston upon Hull HU8 . . 141 C2
7 York YO10 . . . . 130 E3
Chaumont Way 1 YO32 . . . 14 D2
Chaytor Cl 16 HU12 . . . . 72 D6
Cheadle Cl
Kingston upon Hull HU2 . . 155 A4
Sculcoates HU2 . . . . 140 E1
Cheapside
Kingston upon Hull HU8 . . 155 C4
Waltham DN37 . . . . 113 E5
Cheapside Rd DN37 . . . . . 113 F4
Cheapsides La HU15 . . . . . 66 D8
Checker La YO19 . . . . 49 A7
Cheesemans Cl 9 DN37 . 113 E6
Cheesemans La 8 DN37 . 113 E6
Chelkar Way YO30 . . . . 126 F1
Chellsway HU19 . . . . 74 F6
Chelmer Rd HU8 . . . . 142 B5
Chelmsford Ave DN34 . . . 152 A1
Chelmsford Cl 5 HU9 . . . . 142 E1
Chelmsford Pl DN34 . . . . . 152 B2
Chelsea Cl HU8 . . . . 141 F5
Chelsea Ct 3 HU16 . . . . . . 138 F5
Chelsea Wlk 1 DN35 . . . . 103 D1
Cheltenham Ave HU7 . . . 141 A8
Cheltenham Cl 8 DN16 . . . 96 E2
Cheltenham Way 30
DN35 . . . . 103 C1
Chelwood Dr 30 DN33 . . . 102 D2
Chelwood Rd DN17 . . . . . . 150 F3
Chelwood Wlk 12 YO26 . . . 129 E4
Chepstow Gr DN34 . . . . . . 152 A1
Chequers The DN15 . . . . . 150 E7
Cheriton Cl 14 HU7 . . . . . . 56 F5
CHERRY BURTON 43 B5
Cherry Burton CE Prim Sch
HU17 . . . . 43 B5
Cherry Cl
Great Driffield YO25 . . . . . 124 F2
Hornsea HU18 . . . . 134 D1
34 Humberston DN35 . . . . . 103 C1
17 Humberston DN36 . . . . 114 D8
Cherry Cobb Sands Rd
HU12 . . . . 87 F8
Cherry Cres YO43 . . . . 40 A1
Cherry Ct 16 HU15 . . . . 66 D8
Cherry Dale 11 DN35 . . . . . 103 B2
Cherry Dr
Holme-on-Spalding-Moor
YO43 . . . . 40 A1
Nafferton YO25 . . . . 125 F6
Cherry Garth
Beverley HU17 . . . . 154 C3
Kingston upon Hull HU3 . . 145 A5
Lund YO25 . . . . 31 F2
York YO31 . . . . 131 B5
Cherry Gr
5 Belton DN9 . . . . 94 E1
Belton DN9 . . . . 105 E8
16 Poppleton YO26 . . . . 12 F1
Scunthorpe DN16 . . . . 151 B2
Cherry Hill La YO23 . . . . . 156 B1
Cherry Hill Pk HU12 . . . . . . 74 B8
Cherry Holt 7 LN7 . . . . . . 111 B4
Cherry La
Barrow upon Humber
DN19 . . . . 85 D8
Kingston upon Hull HU8 . . 141 C4
Wootton DN39 . . . . 85 E2
York YO24 . . . . 132 F8
Cherry Mount 1 DN16 . . . . 96 E2
Cherry Orch
16 Epworth DN9 . . . . 105 E6
2 Haxby YO32 . . . . 127 D8
Cherry Orchard Mews 12
YO42 . . . . 29 A4
Cherry Paddock
4 Haxby YO32 . . . . 127 D8
Kexby YO41 . . . . 15 C2
Cherry Rd 4 YO14 . . . . 3 A8
Cherry St YO23 . . . . 156 B1
Cherry Tree Ave
1 Brigg DN20 . . . . 98 B2
Kingston upon Hull HU8 . . 141 C2
Newton-on-Ouse YO30 . . . . . 12 B6
9 Withernsea HU19 . . . . 75 A6
York YO32 . . . . 127 D4
Cherry Tree Cl
Bilton HU11 . . . . 58 A3
13 Brayton YO8 . . . . 48 D1
Little Burton YO25 . . . . 34 B2
Cherry Tree Cres DN34 . . 102 C4
Cherry Tree Crossing
HU17 . . . . 154 B3
Cherry Tree Ct 12 YO8 . . . . . 49 B4
Cherrytree Dr YO8 . . . . 48 D6
Cherry Tree Dr
Hatfield DN7 . . . . 92 D5
5 Naburn YO23 . . . . 36 C7
3 Thorne/Moorends DN8 . . . 79 A1
Cherry Tree Gdns 17
DN17 . . . . 94 D7
Cherry Tree Gr DN7 . . . . 92 C5
Cherry Tree La
Beverley HU17 . . . . 154 B3
31 Hedon HU12 . . . . 72 D7
Cherry Tree Rd 18 DN21 . 117 C1
Cherry Tree Rise DN21 . . 107 D4
Cherry Trees HU16 . . . . . . 138 A7
Cherry Tree's Bsns Pk
DN31 . . . . 152 A6
Cherry Tree Terr HU17 . . . 154 C3
Cherry Tree Wlk 7 YO8 . . . 49 B4
Cherry Way
Messingham DN17 . . . . 107 D7
Nafferton YO25 . . . . 125 F6
Cherry Wood Cres YO19 . 133 E5
Chesham Gr DN14 . . . . 149 B6
Cheshire Ave YO32 . . . . 14 A6
Cheshire Cl
Kingston upon Hull HU5 . . 139 D1
6 Rawcliffe YO32 . . . . 126 E2
Chesney Dr DN16 . . . . 96 D2
Chesney Fields 4 YO24 . 129 D1
Chesnut Ave HU5 . . . . 140 C2
Chesnut Way 6 DN19 . . . . . 86 A8
Chessingham Gdns YO24 132 E6
Chessingham Pk YO19 . . . . 26 F6
Chesswick Ave DN17 . . . . . 95 D5
Chesswick Cres DN17 . . . . . 95 D5
Chester Ave HU17 . . . . . . 136 E1
Chester Court Rd YO8 . . . . 63 A6
Chesterfield Rd DN15 . . . . 150 B6
Chester Grange DN33 . . . 102 F1
Chesterholme HU11 . . . . . 142 E6
Chester Pl DN35 . . . . 153 C1
Chester Rd HU5 139
Chester Wlk DN34 152
Chestnut Ave
2 Airmyn DN14 64
Beverley HU17 136
15 Gainsborough DN21 117
Goole DN14 149
Great Driffield YO25 124
Grimsby DN31 152
Hedon HU12 72
10 Hemingbrough YO8 49
Hessle HU13 143
Immingham DN40 87
Kirk Ella HU10 143
Stainforth DN7 92
3 Thorne/Moorends DN8 . . . 93
2 Thorngumbald HU12 72
Withernsea HU19 75
York YO31 130
Chestnut Cl
Beverley HU17 136
Bridlington YO15 123
6 Burstwick HU12 73
4 Scotter DN21 107
Snaith DN14 78
Walkeringham DN10 116
17 Waltham DN37 113
Chestnut Cres YO43 40
Chestnut Croft 7 YO8 49
Chestnut Ct
9 Hemingbrough YO8 49
York YO32 127
Chestnut Dr
15 Gilberdyke HU15 66
8 Hemingbrough YO8 49
Holme-on-Spalding-Moor
YO43 40
Messingham DN17 107
Chestnut Garth
Burton Pidsea HU12 59
4 Hemingbrough YO8 49
Roos HU12 60
Chestnut Gn 10 LS25 61
Chestnut Gr
Acomb YO26 129
8 Barnetby le Beck DN38 . . 99
5 Broughton DN20 97
Huntington YO32 127
Kingston upon Hull HU8 . . . 141
Sproatley HU11 58
Withernsea HU19 75
Chestnut Mews
Cawood YO8 48
Tickton HU17 137
Chestnut Pk YO41 28
Chestnut Rd
Cawood YO8 48
Waltham DN37 113
Chestnut Rise
Barrow upon Humber
DN19 85
6 Hemingbrough YO8 49
Chestnuts The
6 Haxby YO32 127
Hensall DN14 62
Searby DN38 110
Chestnut View YO42 29
Chestnut Way
Scunthorpe DN16 151
Selby YO8 148
Chestnut Wlk DN41 102
Chevering Pk 8 HU7 56
Cheverton Ave 19 HU19 . . . 75
Cheviot Ave DN14 149
Cheviot Cl
3 Thorne/Moorends
DN8 93
1 York YO32 127
Cheviotdale HU7 140
Chevy Chase HU11 142
Cheyne Garth HU18 134
Cheyne Wlk HU18 134
Chichester Dr 19 LN7 111
Chichester Rd DN35 103
Chiltern Cres DN17 150
Chiltern Dr 19 DN37 113
Chiltern Prim Sch HU3 145
Chiltern Rd DN14 149
Chilterns The HU9 142
Chiltern Way
26 Grimsby DN33 113
York YO32 127
Chilton Cl 19 DN40 87
Chilton Rise HU10 138
Chilton St 9 HU3 145
Chilvers Ct 4 YO8 148
Chimes Rd YO8 148
Chimes The 9 YO8 148
Chimney Field Rd HU12 . . . 74
Chingford Ave 1 DN34 . . 102
Chingford Wlk HU9 142
Chippendale Cl 2 DN36 . 114
Chiswick Cl 3 HU8 142
Cholmley St HU3 145
Christine Pl 4 DN33 113
Chrystals Rd HU18 134
Chrystals Wlk HU18 134
Chudleigh Rd 1 YO26 129
Church Acres DN14 65
Church Ave
Humberston DN36 114
6 North Ferriby HU14 69
6 Selby YO8 148
Church Balk
Dunnington YO19 26
Thorne/Moorends DN8 93
Church Cl
Askham Bryan YO23 24

hurch Cl *continued*
Bonby DN20 84 C2
Bridlington YO16 122 D7
4 Bubwith YO8 50 D7
25 Flamborough YO15 5 A2
Goole DN14 149 E2
Grimsby DN32 153 B1
Kingston upon Hull HU7 141 D6
Laxton DN14 65 F4
1 Market Weighton YO43 135 D4
10 Riccall YO19 48 F8
8 Thorne/Moorends DN8 93 B8
5 Wetwang YO25 19 B5
Wheldrake YO19 38 A7
hurch Cres
Owston Ferry DN9 106 A3
4 Wawne HU7 56 E7
hurch Ct
Great Driffield YO25 124 E4
Scunthorpe DN15 151 B8
hurch Dike La YO8 63 F5
hurch Dr
Leven HU17 45 A8
6 Misterton DN10 116 C5
HURCH END 33 F8
hurch End YO8 48 B8
hurch Farm Cl YO23 24 C6
hurch Farm Ct YO25 2 E3
hurchfield DN14 63 C2
hurch Field 7 HU13 144 A3
hurchfield Dr 28 YO32 13 E5
hurchfield La WF8 76 C4
hurchfield Rd DN16 151 B1
hurch Field Rd DN6 76 E1
hurchfields HU17 137 E8
hurch Fields DN15 83 A5
hurch Gate 21 HU12 72 C7
hurch Gn
Beverley HU17 136 B6
5 Bridlington YO16 122 D4
3 Elvington YO41 27 C2
hurch Hill
Grasby DN38 110 E7
10 Hunmanby YO14 2 F8
Reighton YO14 3 C6
Riby DN37 101 B2
3 Selby YO8 148 D5
South Cave HU15 53 F2
Stillingfleet YO19 36 D3
Whitton DN15 67 E3
8 Wistow YO8 48 D6
hurch Hill Rd YO25 31 C4
hurchill Ave
Brigg DN20 98 C2
Burstwick HU12 73 A7
Hatfield DN7 92 F4
Hutton Cranswick YO25 32 E7
10 Keelby DN41 101 A5
Kingston upon Hull HU16 138 F6
hurchill Rise HU12 73 A7
hurchill St HU9 146 D7
hurchill Way DN32 152 F3
hurchill Wlk DN14 149 C5
hurch La
Appleby DN15 83 C1
Atwick YO25 35 C5
Aylesby DN37 101 E2
Barnetby le Beck DN37 113 B6
1 Beeford YO25 22 D1
Beswick YO25 32 B4
Bilton HU11 142 F6
Bishop Burton HU17 43 B2
Bishopthorpe YO23 133 A4
Blyton DN21 117 F5
Bonby DN20 84 C2
Bradley DN37 102 C1
Brandesburton YO25 34 B2
Bridlington YO15 123 B7
Brigsley DN37 113 D4
3 Brough HU15 68 C7
Broughton DN20 97 E3
6 Buckton/Bempton YO15 4 D3
Burstwick HU12 73 A7
Cadney DN20 109 D6
Carlton DN14 63 C3
Carnaby YO16 10 D5
Catton YO41 27 D8
Catwick HU17 45 C8
Corringham DN21 118 B2
Driffield YO25 124 B4
Dunnington YO19 26 E7
4 Elvington YO41 27 C2
Fishlake DN7 92 D8
24 Flamborough YO15 5 A2
Fotherby LN11 121 D2
Fridaythorpe YO25 18 B7
Garton YO25 124 B4
Gateforth YO8 61 F8
Grayingham DN21 119 B7
Great Driffield YO25 124 E4
Great Limber DN37 100 D3
Grimsby DN32 152 D3
12 Grimsby DN33 102 E1
17 Haxby YO32 13 E5
Haxey DN9 105 C2
Hedon HU12 72 C7
Hensall DN14 62 C1
Hollym HU19 75 A4
Holton le Clay DN36 114 A5
Hook DN14 149 F7
Hotham YO43 53 D5
Humberston DN36 114 D8
Hutton Cranswick YO25 32 E8
Immingham DN40 86 E4
Irby DN37 112 D7
Keadby with Althorpe DN17 95 D4
Kellington DN14 61 E3
Keyingham HU12 73 C4

Church La *continued*
2 Kilham YO25 9 C3
Kirk Ella HU10 143 C8
Laceby DN37 101 F1
Langtoft YO25 8 C1
Lockington YO25 32 B1
Luddington & Haldenby DN17 81 D4
Marfleet HU9 147 C8
Marsh Chapel DN36 115 B1
Millington YO42 29 D6
3 Misterton DN10 116 C5
4 Monk Fryston LS25 61 A8
Moor Monkton YO26 12 B2
Nether Poppleton YO26 126 B3
New Earswick YO32 127 F5
4 North Cave HU15 53 D3
North Frodingham YO25 33 F8
North Kelsey LN7 110 A4
North Killingholme DN40 86 E4
North Thoresby DN36 114 B1
Nunburnholme YO42 29 E2
Patrington HU12 74 D1
Poppleton YO26 126 A3
Rudston YO25 9 F6
Saxby All Saints DN20 84 B3
Scawby DN20 98 A1
Scotter DN21 107 C3
Scunthorpe DN15 150 F6
Seaton Ross YO42 39 E4
4 Selby YO8 148 D5
Sigglesthorne HU11 45 F8
Skelton YO30 126 B5
Skirlaugh HU11 45 E2
2 Snaith DN14 63 C1
Sproatley HU11 58 D5
Stallingborough DN41 101 D6
10 Stamford Bridge YO41 15 D2
Strensall YO32 14 A7
Swinefleet DN14 65 D1
Tetney DN36 114 D3
Thorngumbald HU12 72 E5
Thwing YO25 2 A1
Twin Rivers DN14 81 A8
Ulceby DN39 86 A1
Utterby LN11 121 C3
Waithe DN36 114 A3
4 Waltham DN37 113 E6
Watton YO25 32 D4
6 Wawne HU7 56 F7
Wetwang YO25 19 B6
Wheldrake YO19 38 A7
Withernwick HU11 46 D3
York YO1 156 B2
Church Lane Staith HU1 155 C2
Church Mews
Barlby YO8 49 A5
Swanland HU14 69 C7
2 York YO26 129 C3
Church Mount
Kingston upon Hull HU7 141 D6
9 North Newbald YO43 53 F7
Church Rd
Beverley HU17 136 B6
33 Dunswell HU7 56 F6
Laughton DN21 117 F8
North Ferriby HU14 69 A4
Rimswell HU19 74 D7
Skeffling HU12 90 D6
Stainforth DN7 92 C6
Stamford Bridge YO41 15 D2
Thornton YO42 39 B7
Wawne HU7 56 E7
York YO10 131 D4
Church Rise
Holtby YO19 14 F1
Skidby HU16 138 A8
Church Row HU8 155 C4
Churchside 4 DN19 85 D8
Church Side
Alkborough DN15 82 C8
Appleby DN15 83 D2
Goxhill DN19 86 A7
Grasby DN38 110 E7
2 Market Weighton YO43 135 D4
West Halton DN15 82 E7
16 Winterton DN15 83 A5
Church St
7 Aldbrough HU11 47 C1
Amcotts DN17 81 F1
Anlaby HU10 143 E6
Bainton YO25 31 E7
Beckingham DN10 116 D1
6 Brough HU15 68 D6
Bubwith YO8 50 D7
Burton Pidsea HU12 59 D1
14 Caistor LN7 111 B4
Copmanthorpe YO23 132 B2
Dunnington YO19 26 E7
Elsham DN20 98 F7
4 Epworth DN9 105 E6
Fishlake DN7 92 D8
19 Flamborough YO15 5 A2
Gainsborough DN21 117 B1
Goole DN14 149 D4
5 Goxhill DN19 86 A8
Great Driffield YO25 124 D4
Grimsby DN32 152 F5
Haxey DN9 105 C2
Hemswell DN21 119 A1
Hibaldstow DN20 108 F5
Huggate YO42 18 C2
Hutton Cranswick YO25 32 E8
4 Kilham YO25 9 C3
Kingston upon Hull HU7 141 E6
Kirton in Lindsey DN21 108 B1
Messingham DN17 107 D7
Misterton DN10 116 C5

Church St *continued*
Nettleton LN7 111 B3
North Cave HU15 53 D3
North Kelsey LN7 110 A4
Owston Ferry DN9 106 A3
3 Riccall YO19 48 F8
Scawby DN20 108 E8
South Cave HU15 53 F1
Thorne/Moorends DN8 93 A8
Willoughton DN21 119 B4
York YO1 156 B2
Churchthorpe LN11 121 E8
CHURCH TOWN 94 E1
Churchtown DN9 94 E1
Church View
12 Airmyn DN14 64 E4
Alkborough DN15 82 C8
8 Barton-upon-Humber DN18 84 F8
4 Beckingham DN10 116 D1
Beverley HU17 154 C3
4 Brough HU15 68 C7
Eastrington DN14 65 F8
Grimsby DN34 102 C4
22 Hemingbrough YO8 49 F1
Norton DN6 76 E1
Ottringham HU12 73 E3
7 Patrington HU12 74 D1
Swallow LN7 112 B5
1 Waltham DN37 113 E6
Church View Cl DN9 94 E1
Church Way
East Ella HU5 144 E7
Nettleton LN7 111 B3
Church Wlk
Bridlington YO16 122 D5
Holton le Clay DN36 114 A5
Owston Ferry DN9 106 A3
5 Wistow YO8 48 D6
Cinder La
Upper Poppleton YO26 129 A7
York YO26 129 F5
Cinder Mews YO26 130 A5
Cinema St HU18 134 C4
Circle The 4 HU13 143 E2
Cissplatt La DN41 101 A5
Citadel Ct HU17 154 B3
Citadel Trading Pk HU9 155 C2
Citadel Way HU9 155 C2
City Art Gallery* YO30 156 B3
Cladshaw HU6 139 F8
Claire's Wlk DN17 150 C3
Clanthorpe HU6 139 F8
Clapham Ave HU8 141 E5
Clapson's La 19 HU14 69 E1
Clare Ave DN17 150 D3
Clare Ct
Beverley HU17 137 B4
Grimsby DN34 152 A1
Clare Gr HU9 142 A1
Claremont Ave HU6 140 D4
Claremont Rd DN32 153 D2
Claremont Terr YO31 156 B4
Clarence Ave
Bridlington YO15 122 D1
Kingston upon Hull HU8 141 E4
Clarence Cl 25 DN40 87 B1
Clarence Ct HU2 155 A3
Clarence Rd 1 YO16 122 F2
Clarence St
Kingston upon Hull HU9 155 C2
York YO31 156 B4
Clarendon Ct YO31 130 C7
Clarendon Rd
6 Grimsby DN34 102 C2
Scunthorpe DN17 150 F3
Clarendon St HU3 145 D7
Clark Ave DN31 152 A3
Clarke Cres 6 YO15 4 D3
Clarkes Rd DN40 86 E4
Clarke St DN15 151 A7
Clarks La 10 HU12 74 D1
Clark's La YO43 53 D6
Clarksons Dr DN41 101 E6
Clarks Terr YO31 130 F6
Clarondale HU7 140 E7
Clavering St DN31 152 B5
Claxby Rd DN17 150 F1
CLAXTON 15 B7
Clay Bank Rd DN8 93 C6
Clayden St DN31 152 B5
Clayfield Cl 18 YO42 29 A4
Clayfield La
Pocklington YO42 29 A4
Shipton Thorpe YO43 40 F6
Clayfield Rd
Pocklington YO42 29 A3
Scunthorpe DN15 96 C7
Claygate YO31 131 B6
Clay Hill YO41 16 C3
Clay La
Bubwith YO8 50 C5
Camblesforth YO8 63 C6
Cliffe YO8 49 D4
Holton le Clay DN36 114 A6
Kirton in Lindsey DN21 108 B1
Market Weighton YO43 135 B5
Millington YO42 29 C6
Scotter DN21 107 C4
Claymore Cl DN35 153 E2
Claypit La DN14 63 C3
Clay Pl 3 YO24 129 D1
Clay St HU8 141 A3
Claytons Fold 18 HU15 66 D8
Clear View Cl HU8 141 F6
Clearwaters 6 HU7 56 E5
Cleatham Rd DN21 108 A3
Cleaves Ave HU15 54 A2

Clee Cres DN32 153 C1
Cleefields Cl DN32 153 B1
Clee Ness Dr 16 DN36 103 D1
Clee Rd DN35 153 D2
Cleethorpe Rd DN32 153 A5
CLEETHORPES 153 C2
Cleethorpe Sands Nature Reserve* DN35 103 E1
Cleethorpes Coast Light Rly* DN35 103 E2
Cleethorpes Ctry Pk* DN35 103 C1
Cleethorpes Discovery Ctr* DN35 103 D2
Cleethorpes L Ctr DN35 103 D2
Cleethorpes Sta DN35 153 F3
Cleeton La YO25 23 A2
Cleeton Way YO16 122 B6
Cleeve Dr 12 HU7 57 A5
Cleeve Prim Sch HU7 57 A5
Cleeve Rd HU12 72 D6
Clee Village DN32 153 C2
Clematis Ave DN41 101 F5
Clematis Cl YO25 124 D3
Clematis Way DN16 96 E2
Clementhorpe YO23 156 B1
Clementhorpe La HU15 66 D8
Clementhorpe Rd HU15 66 D8
Clement St 4 YO23 156 B1
Clerke St DN35 153 B4
Clevedon Rd DN17 150 D4
Cleveland Cl
Hook DN14 65 B5
4 Immingham DN40 87 B1
Scunthorpe DN17 150 D4
Cleveland Gdns
Grimsby DN31 152 B5
Stockton on the Forest YO32 14 D3
Cleveland St
Grimsby DN31 152 B5
Kingston upon Hull HU8 155 C4
York YO24 130 A4
Cleveland Terr YO32 127 F4
Cleveland Way
41 Hatfield DN7 92 D4
York YO32 127 F3
Cliff Ave DN15 82 F5
Cliff Closes Rd DN15 150 D6
Cliff Dr DN15 82 B5
CLIFFE 49 E2
Cliffe La YO43 52 D8
Cliffe Prim Sch YO8 49 E2
Cliffe Rd
Market Weighton YO43 135 D1
Newbald YO43 53 C7
Cliff Gdns DN15 150 E6
Cliff Gr DN18 84 E8
Cliff Hill Rd DN6 76 D2
Cliff House Dr 3 HU13 69 E4
Cliff La
Bempton YO15 4 D4
Mappleton HU18 47 A6
Waddingham DN21 119 F6
Clifford Ave HU8 141 E4
Clifford's Cl DN20 98 A1
Clifford St
Hornsea HU18 134 C5
York YO1 156 B2
Clifford's Twr* YO1 156 B1
Cliff Rd
Atwick YO25 35 D5
Bridlington YO15 123 B6
Hessle HU13 69 E4
Hornsea HU18 134 C6
Snitterby DN21 119 F5
South Ferriby DN18 84 A8
Winteringham DN15 83 A8
Cliff St
Bridlington YO15 122 F2
Scunthorpe DN16 151 C6
Cliff The DN15 150 D7
Cliff Top La 2 HU13 69 E4
CLIFTON 130 A7
Clifton Ct 27 DN8 93 A8
Clifton Dale YO30 130 A6
Clifton Gdns DN14 149 B4
Clifton Gn YO30 130 A6
Clifton Green Prim Sch YO30 130 B7
Clifton Moor Bsns Village YO30 127 A2
Clifton Moorgate YO30 127 B3
Clifton Moor Gate YO30 127 A2
Clifton Moor Ind Estate YO30 127 A3
Clifton Moor Retail Pk YO30 127 A4
Clifton Moor Sh Ctr YO30 126 F3
Clifton Park Ave YO30 129 E8
Clifton Park (York CC & York RUFC) YO30 129 F7
Clifton Pl 3 YO30 130 A7
Clifton Prep Sch YO30 156 A4
Clifton Prim Sch HU2 155 A4
Clifton Rd
Grimsby DN34 152 A2
York YO30 156 A4
Clifton St
Hornsea HU18 134 C5
Kingston upon Hull HU2 155 A4
Clifton Terr HU5 140 E1
Clifton Without Jun Sch YO30 129 F8
Clive Gr YO24 129 F2
Clive Sullivan Way HU4 144 C1
CLIXBY 111 A7

Clixby Cl DN35 103 D2
Clixby La DN38 110 E7
Clockmill La YO42 29 A4
Cloeberry Way 14 HU12 72 C7
Cloister Cl DN17 150 F2
Cloisters The
6 Grimsby DN37 102 B4
15 Hemingbrough YO8 49 F1
Humberston DN36 114 D8
Wilberfoss YO41 27 F6
York YO31 156 C3
Cloisters Wlk YO31 156 C3
Cloister Wk DN20 97 E3
Close The
9 Acaster Malbis YO32 36 C7
Cawood YO8 48 A7
Goxhill DN19 71 A1
Great Driffield YO25 124 F5
Grimsby DN34 152 C3
Kingston upon Hull HU10 138 F1
4 Leven HU17 45 A8
5 Market Weighton YO43 135 E4
Norton DN6 76 E2
12 Patrington HU12 74 D1
Riccall YO19 49 A8
Scunthorpe DN16 151 B6
Sutton-on-Hull HU7 141 D6
8 Withernsea HU19 75 A6
York YO30 129 F8
Clouds La
Belton DN9 95 B1
West Butterwick DN17 106 C8
Clough Garth HU12 72 D8
Clough La DN40 86 F6
Clough Rd HU5 140 F3
Cloughton Gr HU5 139 E2
Clovelly Gdns 3 HU5 140 E1
Clover Bank View 11 HU6 56 E5
Clover Ct 26 DN20 98 B2
Cloverfields Prim Sch DN36 114 C8
Cloverley Cl YO41 15 C2
Cloverley Rd 6 YO16 123 A6
Clowes Ct 4 HU13 143 E1
Clumber Pl DN35 153 E1
Clumber St HU5 145 C8
Clyde St
Grimsby DN32 152 F4
Kingston upon Hull HU3 144 F5
Clyfton Cres DN40 87 B1
Coach House Garth YO42 28 D3
Coach House Gdns DN20 108 E8
Coachings The 4 HU13 69 E4
Coachyard Mews DN21 108 B1
Coal Pit La WF8 76 A2
Coal Shore La LN11 115 E1
Coastguard Hill YO14 3 E5
Coates Ave DN15 83 A5
Coates Marsh La DN14 63 B2
Cobble Court Mews YO24 156 A1
Cobble La DN14 51 F1
Cobbler Hill DN14 149 B6
Cobcroft La WF11 76 B8
Cobdale La YO42 29 F7
Cobden St HU3 144 F7
Cobden Street North End DN32 152 F4
Cober Gr HU8 142 C7
Cobham Way YO32 126 E3
Cochrane St YO8 148 D3
Cockerell La YO25 22 B4
Cocketts La DN20 108 F5
COCK HILL 12 B2
Cock Pit Cl HU10 143 C6
Cockret Cl 8 YO8 148 B6
Cockret Ct YO8 148 B7
Cockret Rd YO8 148 B7
Cockthorne La DN15 83 C7
Coda Ave YO23 133 B3
Coelus St HU9 155 C3
Coeside YO24 132 B7
Cogan St HU1 155 A1
Coggan Cl YO23 130 B2
Coggan Way YO23 132 F4
Cohort Cl 10 HU15 68 C5
Coke Oven Ave DN16 151 F6
Cold Harbour La LN11 121 F4
Cold Harbour Rd HU17 43 A1
Cold Harbour View 5 HU17 43 A2
Coldstream Cl 4 HU8 142 C5
COLEBY 82 E6
Coleby Rd DN15 82 E7
Coledale Cl 2 YO30 126 F1
Coleford Gr HU7 141 A7
Colemans Rd 4 HU12 72 C7
Colenso St
Kingston upon Hull HU3 145 A5
York YO23 156 B1
Coleridge Ave DN17 150 D3
Coleridge St HU8 141 D2
Cole St
Scunthorpe DN15 151 B6
York YO31 156 B4
Colin Ave DN32 153 B2
Colin Rd DN16 151 C6
Colins Wlk DN21 107 C4
College Ave 31 DN33 113 E8
College Cl
Alkborough DN15 82 C8
Goole DN14 149 B4
College Farm Cl DN14 77 A8
College Gdns
32 Grimsby DN33 113 E8

College Gdns *continued*
Hornsea HU18 ... 134 B5
College Gr HU9 ... 141 F1
College of Law YO23 ... 133 B7
College Rd
Barrow upon Humber DN19 ... 85 E7
Copmanthorpe YO23 ... 132 A3
Thornton Curtis DN39 ... 86 B6
College St
Cleethorpes DN35 ... 153 E2
Grimsby DN34 ... 152 C2
Kingston upon Hull HU3 ... 155 A3
York YO1 ... 156 B3
Colleridge Gr 4 HU17 ... 55 E8
Colleys HU19 ... 75 A5
Colleywell Cl 3 DN9 ... 105 A2
Collier Cl 10 HU14 ... 69 A4
Colliergate YO1 ... 156 B2
Collier Hag La YO23 ... 24 B3
Collier Rd 16 DN40 ... 87 C1
Collier St HU1 ... 155 A2
Collin Ave HU9 ... 142 C2
Collingwood Ave YO24 ... 129 F2
Collingwood Cres 12 DN34 ... 102 B2
Collingwood Prim Sch HU3 ... 145 C7
Collingwood Rd 3 YO15 ... 4 C3
Collingwood St HU3 ... 145 D7
Collinson Ave DN15 ... 150 C7
Collum Ave DN16 ... 151 B3
Collum Gdns DN16 ... 151 B2
Collum La DN16 ... 151 B2
Collynson Cl 1 HU10 ... 143 E8
Colonel's Wlk DN14 ... 149 D5
Colonial St HU2 ... 145 D7
Colonsay Ct 20 DN36 ... 114 A8
Colson Pl DN35 ... 153 B3
Colt Ind Est 4 HU3 ... 145 A3
Coltman Ave HU17 ... 154 C4
Coltman Cl
19 Brough HU15 ... 68 D5
Molescroft HU17 ... 136 F7
Coltman St HU3 ... 145 C5
Colton St
3 Brigg DN20 ... 98 B2
Misterton DN10 ... 116 C5
Coltsfoot Cl 5 DN15 ... 96 B7
Coltsfoot Dr DN37 ... 113 D7
Columbia Rd DN32 ... 153 A3
Columbus Way DN33 ... 102 C2
Colville Ave HU4 ... 144 B6
Colwall Ave HU5 ... 139 D2
Colwyn Cl 5 HU7 ... 57 A7
Comberdale Hil HU15 ... 54 B3
Comber Pl 5 DN32 ... 152 F5
Combe St DN35 ... 153 C4
Comforts Ave DN15 ... 151 A6
Commerce La HU1 ... 145 D4
Commercial Rd
Kingston upon Hull HU1 ... 155 A1
Scunthorpe DN15 ... 151 C7
Commodore Croft HU1 ... 155 B1
Common Croft La YO26 ... 12 E1
Common Hill YO43 ... 53 C5
Common La
Barnby Dun with Kirk Sandall DN3 ... 92 B4
Beal DN14 ... 61 D3
Burn YO8 ... 62 E7
Catton YO41 ... 27 E8
Dunnington YO19 ... 26 F5
Fangfoss YO41 ... 16 B1
Knottingley WF11 ... 61 B1
North Cave HU15 ... 53 B2
Norton DN6 ... 76 E2
1 Seaton HU11 ... 35 A1
Sutton upon Derwent YO41 ... 38 C8
Temple Hirst YO8 ... 62 F4
Thorganby YO19 ... 37 F5
Thornton YO42 ... 39 B8
Twin Rivers DN14 ... 81 B6
Walden Stubbs DN6 ... 76 F4
Warthill YO19 ... 14 F2
Wawne HU7 ... 56 F7
Welton HU15 ... 68 D4
Woodside DN8 ... 104 E6
York YO10 ... 131 B1
Common Lane W HU15 ... 53 B2
Common Middle Rd DN17 ... 94 C8
Common Rd
Broughton DN20 ... 97 E4
Dunnington YO19 ... 26 F7
Rowley HU20 ... 54 F5
Skipwith YO8 ... 37 E1
South Cave HU15 ... 67 C7
Commonside
Crowle DN17 ... 94 C8
Westwoodside DN9 ... 105 A2
Compass Rd HU6 ... 140 C8
Compton Dr
Grimsby DN34 ... 152 C3
Keyingham HU12 ... 73 C3
Compton St YO30 ... 130 A6
Comrie Dr 16 YO42 ... 29 A3
Concast Rd DN16 ... 97 A3
Concorde Pk YO30 ... 127 A3
Conduit St HU9 ... 155 C2
Coneycroft 10 YO19 ... 26 F7
Coneygarth La YO19 ... 26 E5
Coney St YO1 ... 156 B2
Conference Ct 10 DN16 ... 96 D1
Conifer Cl
6 Kingston upon Hull HU5 ... 144 C7
Scunthorpe DN17 ... 150 C1
6 York YO32 ... 127 D3
Conifers Cl 2 YO8 ... 48 D1
Coningham Ave 1 YO30 ... 126 E2
Coningsby Dr DN34 ... 152 A1
Coningsby Rd DN17 ... 150 D1
Conington Ave HU17 ... 137 B4
Conisborough Ave 2 DN36 ... 113 F7
Conisbro Croft HU13 ... 143 C2
CONISTON ... 57 F6
Coniston Ave DN33 ... 113 D8
Coniston Cl
4 Bridlington YO16 ... 122 E7
1 York YO30 ... 126 E1
Coniston Cres 19 DN36 ... 103 C1
Coniston Dr YO10 ... 131 B4
Coniston La
Coniston HU11 ... 58 A5
Swine HU11 ... 57 E6
Coniston Way DN14 ... 149 E5
Connaught Ave DN32 ... 152 D1
Connaught Rd 9 DN21 ... 117 B1
Connaught Way YO32 ... 127 F6
Consort Ct HU9 ... 146 B5
Constable Ave HU11 ... 58 A4
Constable Cl
18 Flamborough YO15 ... 5 A2
Sproatley HU11 ... 58 D5
Constable Garth 5 HU12 ... 72 D7
Constable Rd
Flamborough YO15 ... 5 A2
Hornsea HU18 ... 134 D5
Hunmanby YO14 ... 3 A8
Constable St HU3 ... 145 C5
Constable Way 25 HU15 ... 68 D5
Constantine Ave YO10 ... 131 A4
Constitutional Ave DN35 ... 153 C4
Constitution Hill HU17 ... 136 A6
Convamore Rd DN32 ... 152 F2
Convent Ct HU5 ... 140 D1
Convent La HU3 ... 145 D6
Conway Ave DN34 ... 152 A3
Conway Cl
Kingston upon Hull HU3 ... 145 B5
2 York YO30 ... 126 E3
Conway Sq DN15 ... 150 E7
Conyard Rd DN35 ... 153 E3
Conyers Ave DN33 ... 102 E1
Cookbury Cl 6 HU7 ... 56 F5
Cookridge Dr 11 DN7 ... 92 D4
Cooks Gdns HU12 ... 73 C4
Cooks La
Grimsby DN37 ... 102 B5
Nettleton LN7 ... 111 A3
Coomb Briggs Prim Sch DN40 ... 87 B1
Coombs Yd HU17 ... 154 A3
Cooper La DN37 ... 101 E1
Cooper Rd DN32 ... 153 A3
Coopers Croft HU17 ... 45 A7
Coopers Dr YO23 ... 132 B3
Coopers Mdw 3 HU11 ... 45 C5
Cooper St
Beverley HU17 ... 154 B4
Kingston upon Hull HU2 ... 155 B4
Copandale Rd HU17 ... 154 A4
Copenhagen Rd HU7 ... 140 F5
Cope St DN32 ... 153 A4
COPMANTHORPE ... 132 B2
Copmanthorpe & District Recreation Ctr YO23 ... 132 B2
Copmanthorpe La YO23 ... 132 E3
Copmanthorpe Prim Sch YO23 ... 132 B3
Copmanthorpe Sports Ctr YO23 ... 132 B2
Copper Beech Cl
9 Dunnington YO19 ... 26 E7
6 Swanland HU14 ... 69 B6
Upper Poppleton YO26 ... 24 F8
Copper Beech Dr DN14 ... 77 A8
Copper Beeches The 2 YO19 ... 26 E7
Copper Beech Wlk 24 DN16 ... 96 D2
Coppergate
Nafferton YO25 ... 125 F7
1 Riccall YO19 ... 36 F1
York YO1 ... 156 B2
Coppergate Sh Ctr YO1 ... 156 B2
Coppergate Wlk YO1 ... 156 B2
Coppice Ave DN7 ... 92 D3
Coppice Cl 10 YO32 ... 13 E5
Coppice Gr 39 DN7 ... 92 D3
Coppice La 1 DN7 ... 92 D3
Coppice Side HU4 ... 144 C6
Coppice The
Bishopthorpe YO23 ... 132 F4
Brayton YO8 ... 48 C1
Coppleflat La
Rowley HU17 ... 55 D6
Walkington HU17 ... 43 C1
Copse Cl 1 DN40 ... 87 C2
Copse Mead YO25 ... 124 D5
Copse Rd DN16 ... 151 B1
Copse The
Beverley HU17 ... 137 B3
Bigby DN20 ... 98 D1
28 Grimsby DN33 ... 113 E8
Copwood Gr 7 YO32 ... 127 C8
Coral Dr 2 DN37 ... 113 D7
Corban La YO32 ... 13 B6
Corban Way 21 YO32 ... 13 D5
Corbridge Cl 2 HU9 ... 142 E1
Corby Pk HU14 ... 69 A5
Corby Rd DN16 ... 151 C6
Cordeaux Cl DN21 ... 107 C4
Cordella Cl 1 HU3 ... 145 A5
Coriander Cl HU17 ... 154 A1
Corinthian Ave DN34 ... 152 B2
Corinthian Way HU9 ... 146 D6
Corlett Ct
Woodthorpe YO24 ... 132 C8
York YO24 ... 132 C8
Cormorant Cl 2 HU7 ... 141 D8
Cormorant Dr 1 DN37 ... 102 B4
Cornaught Ct YO10 ... 133 D8
Cornborough Ave YO31 ... 130 F6
Cornelius Cswy YO8 ... 49 E8
Cornelius Wlk YO43 ... 135 E4
Corner Cl 17 YO32 ... 13 D5
Cornfield Cl 5 DN33 ... 113 D8
Cornfield Cres YO16 ... 122 B2
Cornflower Cl 17 DN41 ... 101 F5
Cornhill Dr DN18 ... 85 A8
Cornlands Rd YO24 ... 129 B1
Cornley Rd DN10 ... 116 A6
Cornmill Cl YO8 ... 48 B8
Cornwall Dr YO10 ... 133 E8
Cornwall Rd
2 Keadby DN17 ... 95 D6
Scunthorpe DN16 ... 151 C1
Cornwall St
7 Kirton in Lindsey DN21 ... 108 B1
New Village HU16 ... 139 C6
Stoneferry HU8 ... 141 A1
Cornwell Cl 5 DN33 ... 102 E2
Cornwood Way 11 YO32 ... 127 C8
Corona Dr
Kingston upon Hull HU8 ... 141 C4
8 Thorne/Moorends DN8 ... 79 A1
Coronation Cl HU17 ... 154 C3
Coronation Cotts DN35 ... 153 F1
Coronation Cres 10 DN9 ... 105 D6
Coronation Gdns 4 DN20 ... 97 E3
Coronation Rd
Cleethorpes DN35 ... 153 F1
Stainforth DN7 ... 92 C6
7 Ulceby DN39 ... 86 A1
Coronation Road N HU5 ... 139 C2
Coronation Road S HU5 ... 139 B1
Coronation St 10 DN14 ... 149 C4
Coronet Cl 5 HU6 ... 140 B8
Corporation Bridge DN31 ... 152 E4
Corporation Rd
Beverley HU17 ... 154 A3
Grimsby DN31 ... 152 C5
Kingston upon Hull HU9 ... 147 A7
Scunthorpe DN15 ... 151 A7
Corpslanding Rd YO25 ... 33 A7
Corran Garth 6 HU4 ... 144 A3
CORRINGHAM ... 118 B2
Corringham CE Prim Sch DN21 ... 118 B2
Corringham Rd DN21 ... 117 D1
Corsair Gr 4 HU3 ... 145 A4
Corunna Ct 5 YO8 ... 148 D5
Cosford Garth 5 HU7 ... 57 A5
Cosgrove St DN35 ... 153 F2
Cosmo Ave YO31 ... 131 A5
Costello Stadium HU4 ... 144 C5
Cotham Gdns 6 DN41 ... 101 A4
Cotness La DN14 ... 65 F3
Cotswold Ave DN14 ... 149 D5
Cotswold Dr 20 DN37 ... 113 D6
Cotswold Rd DN8 ... 93 A7
Cotswolds The HU9 ... 142 D2
Cotswold Way YO32 ... 128 A5
Cottage Beck Rd DN16 ... 151 B6
Cottage Cl DN20 ... 108 F5
Cottage Dr HU10 ... 143 B8
Cottage Field 1 HU17 ... 43 A2
Cottage Gn HU16 ... 139 A5
Cottage Mews HU17 ... 154 B3
COTTAGERS PLOT ... 102 B2
Cottage Yard La DN36 ... 114 C7
Cottam La YO25 ... 8 C5
Cottam Wlk HU11 ... 139 A5
Cotterdale HU7 ... 140 E7
Cotterdale Cl 7 YO16 ... 123 A7
Cotterdale Gdns LS25 ... 61 A6
Cottesmore Rd
Cleethorpes DN35 ... 103 C1
6 Kingston upon Hull HU13 ... 144 A2
COTTINGHAM ... 139 A5
Cottingham Croxby Prim Sch HU5 ... 139 D4
Cottingham Gr 2 HU6 ... 139 F4
Cottingham High Sch HU16 ... 138 E8
Cottingham Playsport Pavillion HU16 ... 139 A7
Cottingham Rd HU5 ... 139 E4
Cottingham St DN14 ... 149 C1
Cottingham Sta HU16 ... 139 B6
Cottom La YO42 ... 38 C2
Coulam Pl 8 DN36 ... 114 D8
Coulbeck Dr DN35 ... 153 D1
Coulman Rd 4 DN8 ... 93 B8
Coulman Road Ind Est DN8 ... 79 B1
Coulman St 5 DN8 ... 93 B8
Coulson Cl
Hibaldstow DN20 ... 109 A5
5 Strensall YO32 ... 14 C8
Coulson Dr HU13 ... 143 F2
Coultas Ct 3 HU3 ... 145 A6
Council Ave HU4 ... 144 E3
Council Terr 9 DN18 ... 69 E1
Council Villas DN19 ... 85 F8
Count De Burgh Terr 4 YO23 ... 130 B1
Countess Cl* DN15 ... 82 B8
Countess Cl
6 Kingston upon Hull HU6 ... 140 B8
New Waltham DN36 ... 114 A7
County Road N HU5 ... 139 E1
County Road S 2 HU5 ... 144 C8
Couper Gr DN14 ... 149 D1
Coupland Cl 27 DN21 ... 117 C1
Coupland Gdns 2 HU5 ... 140 E2
Coupland Rd 1 YO8 ... 148 C6
Courcey Gr YO26 ... 129 C4
Court Dr YO8 ... 148 A4
Court Gdns 8 DN14 ... 78 C8
Courtland Rd HU6 ... 139 E6
Courtneys
Selby YO8 ... 148 B4
Wheldrake YO19 ... 38 A8
Courtney St HU8 ... 146 B8
Courtneys The YO8 ... 148 B4
Courtpark Rd HU6 ... 139 F7
Courts Cl 7 DN14 ... 64 E4
Courtway Rd HU6 ... 139 E7
Courtyard The YO23 ... 133 B4
Courtyard The* DN14 ... 149 B4
COVENHAM ST BARTHOLOMEW ... 121 F5
COVENHAM ST MARY ... 121 F5
Coventry Ave DN34 ... 152 A1
Coventry Cl DN17 ... 150 D3
Coventry Rd
Kingston upon Hull HU5 ... 139 C1
12 Thorne/Moorends DN8 ... 93 B8
Cove Rd DN9 ... 104 F3
Coverdale HU7 ... 140 F7
Coverdale Garth 2 YO16 ... 122 F7
Coverdale Rd DN16 ... 151 E1
Covert Rd DN16 ... 151 B1
Covert The
Kingston upon Hull HU16 ... 139 C5
York YO24 ... 132 F7
Covington 21 HU15 ... 68 C6
Covin's La LN11 ... 121 F8
Cowden Gr 2 HU9 ... 142 A2
Cowden La HU11 ... 46 E4
Cowgate
Elloughton-cum-Brough HU15 ... 68 D6
18 Welton HU15 ... 68 D6
Cowick CE Prim Sch DN14 ... 78 E8
Cowick Rd
Fishlake DN8 ... 78 F1
Snaith DN14 ... 78 C8
Cowie Dr YO8 ... 148 D5
Cow La
Knottingley WF11 ... 61 A2
Twin Rivers DN14 ... 81 C6
Womersley DN6 ... 76 D6
Cowlings Cl 16 YO14 ... 3 A8
Cow Marsh La DN36 ... 114 E5
Cow Pasture La YO42 ... 38 C3
Cowper Ave DN17 ... 150 D3
Cowper Cl DN36 ... 115 B2
Cowper La YO23 ... 36 C8
Cowslam La YO25 ... 21 E1
Cowslip Ct DN41 ... 101 F5
Cowton La YO14 ... 3 C6
Cow Wold Rd HU17 ... 42 E1
Cox La 1 DN17 ... 94 D8
Coxlea Gr YO31 ... 131 B6
Cox's Ct DN20 ... 109 A5
Cox's Hill DN21 ... 117 B1
Coxwold Gr HU4 ... 144 E5
Crabley La HU15 ... 67 E7
Crabtree Gr 1 YO32 ... 127 D3
Crabtree La YO25 ... 32 B4
Crab Tree La HU11 ... 57 F7
Crabtree Rd DN7 ... 92 C4
Crackle Hill 6 DN9 ... 105 B2
Cradley Rd HU5 ... 139 C3
Cragston Ave 19 DN33 ... 102 E2
Craig Cl 5 DN20 ... 97 D3
Craikewells YO15 ... 5 A3
Craik Hill Ave 18 DN40 ... 87 C1
Craithie Rd 11 DN35 ... 103 C2
Crake Ave DN33 ... 102 E1
Crakedale Rd DN15 ... 83 B5
Crake Wells HU17 ... 55 C8
Crampin Rd DN35 ... 153 E3
Cranbeck Cl YO16 ... 122 B1
Cranberry Way HU4 ... 144 C4
Cranbourne Cl 23 DN35 ... 103 C1
Cranbourne St HU3 ... 145 C8
Cranbrook Ave
Kingston upon Hull HU6 ... 140 B6
York YO26 ... 129 C5
Cranbrook Rd YO26 ... 129 C5
Cranbrooks The YO19 ... 37 F8
Crane Rd HU9 ... 146 C6
Cranfield Pl 4 YO24 ... 132 C8
Cranham Gr HU7 ... 141 A7
Cranidge Cl 2 DN17 ... 94 D8
Cranswick Cl 8 HU17 ... 43 E6
Cranswick Gr HU9 ... 142 B1
Cranswick Ind Est YO25 ... 32 D6
Cranwell Cl 6 DN21 ... 119 C8
Cranwell Dr 10 DN37 ... 102 C5
Cranwell Rd YO25 ... 124 E4
Cranwell St YO25 ... 124 E4
Crapple La DN21 ... 107 C2
Crathorne Rd HU17 ... 154 C4
Craven Ct 6 HU9 ... 146 D7
Craven Garth 5 DN14 ... 61 D4
Craven Park (Hull Kingston Rovers RFC) HU8 ... 142 (
Craven Prim Sch HU9 ... 146 (
Craven Rd
Cleethorpes DN35 ... 153
Hatfield DN7 ... 92 (
Craven Street N HU9 ... 146 (
Craven Street S HU9 ... 146 [
Crawley Way YO31 ... 131
Crawshaw Ave HU17 ... 136
Craycroft Rd DN9 ... 105
Crayford Cl 6 HU9 ... 142
Crayke The YO16 ... 122
Credenhill Cl 13 HU7 ... 57
Crescent St
Grimsby DN31 ... 152 (
Kingston upon Hull HU16 ... 139 A
Crescent The
Beckingham DN10 ... 116
9 Bridlington YO15 ... 122
Brough HU15 ... 68 D
Burton Fleming YO25 ... 2 E
Hatfield DN7 ... 92 (
Holton le Clay DN36 ... 114 A
Hornsea HU18 ... 134 D
Huggate YO42 ... 18 (
1 Kelfield YO19 ... 36 D
Kexby YO41 ... 27 (
2 Kirk Sandall DN3 ... 92 A
Monk Fryston LS25 ... 61 A
13 Patrington HU12 ... 74 D
6 Riccall YO19 ... 48 F
Stamford Bridge YO41 ... 15 D
York YO10 ... 131 (
York YO24 ... 156 A
Cressey St DN31 ... 152 E
Cresswell Cl HU2 ... 155 A
Cresta Dr 10 DN17 ... 96 C
Cresta The DN34 ... 152 C
Creyke Cl 6 HU16 ... 139 E
Creyke La 7 HU15 ... 68 D
Creyke View DN14 ... 64 A
Crichton Ave YO30 ... 130 E
Cricklewood Wlk HU8 ... 141 E
Cridling Gdns DN6 ... 76 F
Cridling Pl 5 DN35 ... 103 E
CRIDLING STUBBS ... 76 C
Crinan Ct 3 YO32 ... 127 F
Crinan Dr 1 HU6 ... 140 E
Crispin Cl 5 HU4 ... 144 A
Crispin Way DN16 ... 96 D
CROCKEY HILL ... 26 A
Croft Ave 8 WF11 ... 61 A
Croft Cl
Eastrington DN14 ... 51 F
Market Weighton YO43 ... 135 D
Swanland HU14 ... 69 B
Croft Ct YO23 ... 133 A
Croft Dr HU10 ... 143 C
Crofters Dr HU16 ... 139 C
Crofters Gr 25 DN36 ... 114 A
Croft Farm Cl YO23 ... 132 B
Croft La DN17 ... 96 C
Croftlands 7 WF11 ... 61 A
Croft Lodge DN9 ... 94 E
Croft Pk HU14 ... 69 A
Croft Rd
Camblesforth YO8 ... 63 D
Finningley DN9 ... 104 A
Crofts Hill YO15 ... 4 F
Croftside 1 YO26 ... 129 B
Crofts La
Hollym HU19 ... 74 F
Stainforth DN7 ... 92 B
Croft's La DN9 ... 106 B
Crofts The
9 Humberston DN36 ... 114 C
Scunthorpe DN16 ... 151 B
Ulrome YO25 ... 23 A
Croft The
Beverley HU17 ... 136 C
Crowle Park DN17 ... 94 C
Kingston upon Hull HU7 ... 140 E
Knottingley WF11 ... 61 A
22 Thorne/Moorends DN8 ... 93 B
1 West/East Butterwick DN17 ... 106 D
Croft View
Bransholme HU7 ... 141 C
Kirk Ella HU10 ... 143 C
Market Weighton YO43 ... 135 D
Croftway
Camblesforth YO8 ... 63 C
Selby YO8 ... 148 C
2 York YO26 ... 129 B
Cromarty Cl HU9 ... 142 A
Crombie Ave YO30 ... 130 B
Cromer Ave DN34 ... 152 A
Cromer St
4 Kingston upon Hull HU5 ... 140 D
York YO30 ... 130 B
Cromford St 13 DN21 ... 117 B
Crompton Terr YO32 ... 127 D
Cromwell Ave
Grimsby DN31 ... 152 C
Scunthorpe DN16 ... 151 B
Cromwell Cl
2 Kingston upon Hull HU3 ... 145 D
16 Patrington HU12 ... 74 D
Cromwell Ct 1 HU10 ... 143 E
Cromwell Rd
Cleethorpes DN35 ... 103 D
Grimsby DN31 ... 152 A
35 Hedon HU12 ... 72 D
York YO1 ... 156 B
Cromwell View 25 LN7 ... 111 B

rooked Billet St 5
DN21 117 A2
rookes Broom Ave DN7 92 D4
rookes Broom La DN7 92 D4
rookesbroom Prim Sch
DN3 92 A1
rook Hill HU15 68 C8
rook La HU11 58 D7
rookland La YO32 13 F5
rook Mill Rd DN40 86 D5
rook Tree La DN7 92 F5
roome Dale La YO17 7 C6
roome Rd YO25 7 B4
room Medieval Village*
YO25 7 B4
ropton Rd HU5 139 E2
ROSBY 150 F8
rosby Ave DN15 96 C7
rosby Prim Sch DN15 151 A8
rosby Rd
Grimsby DN33 102 D1
Scunthorpe DN15 151 B8
rosland Rd DN37 102 B4
rossall Hill Lane HU15 68 E6
rossbeck Rd 2 DN16 96 D2
ross Carr Rd DN20 109 A5
ross Coates Rd DN34 152 A2
rossfield Cres YO19 133 E6
rossfield Rd HU13 143 E3
ross Gate YO43 41 E6
ross Gates YO25 21 F8
ross Gordon St 1
DN14 149 C4
ross Hill
5 Brandesburton YO25 34 B2
Driffield YO25 124 E4
Haxey DN9 105 C3
Hayton YO42 40 C8
rosshill La DN14 77 E6
ross Hills La YO8 148 A5
rossings The 13 DN14 64 E4
ross Keys Ct YO25 32 E7
rosskill Cl HU17 154 C4
ross La
Alkborough DN15 82 C8
3 Amcotts DN17 81 F1
Flaxton YO60 14 E8
Flixborough DN15 82 A2
Fulford YO19 133 F5
Hutton Cranswick YO25 32 F6
Leven HU17 44 F7
North Frodingham YO25 33 F7
North Kelsey LN7 110 B5
rosslands La HU15 53 B3
rosslands Rd 2 YO10 133 E8
rossmoor Bank DN14 80 C5
rossmoor La YO32 13 E6
ross Rd
Hatfield DN7 93 B4
North Frodingham YO25 33 F7
Ulceby DN39 86 B3
ross Slack 8 DN17 94 D8
ross St
8 Aldbrough HU11 47 C1
3 Barrow upon Humber
DN19 85 D8
Beverley HU17 154 A2
Bridlington YO15 122 F2
13 Brigg DN20 98 C2
Cleethorpes DN35 153 E2
Crowle DN17 94 D8
35 Gainsborough DN21 117 B1
Garthorpe & Fockerby DN17 81 E6
Goole DN14 149 D3
Grimsby DN31 152 F6
Hatfield HU11 46 C6
Kingston upon Hull HU1 155 A2
2 Scunthorpe DN15 151 B8
Skipsea YO25 23 A2
3 Waltham DN37 113 E6
West Halton DN15 82 E8
5 York YO24 129 C3
oss Street W DN14 149 B4
oss Tree Rd DN17 107 D7
ossways
10 Stainforth DN7 92 C6
York YO10 131 C2
ossway The
29 Grimsby DN34 102 B2
2 York YO31 130 E8
osswood Cl 6 HU7 57 A7
owberry Dr DN16 151 D1
ow Croft La DN14 78 A5
ow Hill Ave DN35 153 E2
owland Ave
Grimsby DN34 102 C2
Scunthorpe DN16 151 A3
owland Cl 2 HU8 142 C7
owland Rd 9 DN17 94 D7
ROWLE 94 D8
owle Bank Rd DN17 95 C4
owle Dr DN33 102 D2
owle Moor Nature
Reserve* DN17 94 B8
ROWLE PARK 94 D7
owle Prim Sch DN17 94 C7
owle Rd DN17 80 F2
owle St HU9 146 D7
owle Sta DN17 94 E6
own Gdns 21 DN21 107 C3
owther Cl HU17 137 A6
owther Way 5 HU14 69 B7
ow Tree Bank DN8 93 D4
ROXBY 112 C1
oxby Ave DN33 113 E8
oxby Gr 14 DN33 113 E8
ROXBY TOP 112 B1
ROXTON 99 F7
Croxton Rd
Croxton DN39 99 F7
Kirmington DN39 100 A5
Cruckley Animal Farm*
YO25 21 E1
Cruckley La YO25 21 E1
Crudhall La YO42 40 A8
Crummock 8 YO24 132 C7
Crumpton Rd YO43 135 C3
Crystal St HU3 145 C7
Cuckoo La DN7 92 E6
Cudworth Gr 1 HU8 141 B1
Cullen Cl HU8 141 C5
Cullingworth Ave 2
HU6 140 C7
Cumberland Ave DN32 152 D1
Cumberland Cl
Goole DN14 149 A4
6 Strensall YO32 14 B6
Cumberland Rd DN35 103 D1
Cumberland St
Kingston upon Hull HU2 155 C4
York YO1 156 B2
Cumbrian Ave 4 YO32 14 B6
Cumbrian Way HU7 56 F7
Cundall Cl
Kingston upon Hull HU9 141 E1
6 Strensall YO32 14 C8
Cundall Dr 6 YO32 36 C7
Cunningham Rd 3 DN7 104 A8
Cupid's Alley YO17 6 B6
Cupola Way DN15 96 C8
Curlew Cl
Beverley HU17 136 E6
Driffield YO25 125 A5
Kingston upon Hull HU7 141 D8
Curlew Ct 27 DN18 84 E8
Curlew Glebe 8 YO19 26 E7
Curlew Gn YO15 11 B4
Curry Rd DN34 102 C4
Curson Terr YO8 49 E3
Curtis Cl DN18 84 F8
Curzen Cres 5 DN3 92 A2
Curzon Ave DN35 153 D1
Curzon Ct 3 DN35 103 B2
Curzon St
4 Gainsborough DN21 117 B1
Kingston upon Hull HU3 144 F7
Curzon Terr YO23 130 B1
Cushman Cres 10 DN40 87 C1
Custance Wlk YO23 156 A1
Cuthbert Ave 6 DN38 99 B4
CUXWOLD 112 B4
Cuxwold Rd
Scunthorpe DN16 151 C4
Swallow LN7 112 B5
Cycle St 4 YO10 131 A3
Cygnet Cl HU18 134 B6
Cygnet St YO23 156 A1
Cynthia Rd DN32 153 C1
Cyprus Gr 37 YO32 13 E5
Cyprus St HU9 147 B8
Cyrano Way DN37 102 B4
Cyril Cooper Ct DN32 152 E2

D

Dacre Lakeside Pk*
YO25 34 B1
Dagger La HU1 155 B2
Daggett La YO25 21 F8
Daggett Rd DN35 103 D2
Dairycoates Ave HU3 145 A4
Dairycoates Ind Est HU4 144 F3
Dairycoates Rd HU4 144 E3
Dairy House La HU12 73 A8
Daisy Cl DN16 96 F2
Daisyfield Dr HU11 142 D6
Dalby Gr HU9 142 B2
Dalby Mead YO32 127 F1
Dale Cl
Selby YO8 148 C3
8 Swanland HU14 69 B7
Dale Dike Gr YO30 126 F2
Dale Garth YO43 135 E5
Dale Gate HU17 43 A1
Dalehouse Dr 2 HU10 143 F6
Dale Pit Rd DN7 92 F3
Dale Pk Ave DN15 83 A5
Dale Rd
Brantingham HU15 68 C8
Bridlington YO16 122 D4
Elloughton-cum-Brough
HU15 68 C6
Swanland HU14 69 B7
Welton HU15 68 E6
Dales Ct YO19 36 D3
Dale's La YO31 130 F6
Dale St
Scunthorpe DN15 151 A8
York YO23 156 A1
Dales The
Kingston upon Hull HU9 142 D2
Scunthorpe DN17 96 C2
Willerby HU16 138 D6
Dale Street N DN15 150 F8
Dalesway HU10 143 B6
Dale View 27 DN33 102 C2
Dalguise Gr YO31 156 C4
Dalkeith Cl 16 HU7 57 A6
Dallisons Rd DN20 109 A5
Dalmais Cl 1 YO42 28 F4
Dalmally Cl YO24 132 B6
Dalmatian Way DN20 97 E4
Dalsetter Rise HU8 141 F6
Dalton Cl YO25 124 D3
Dalton Hill YO19 38 A8
Dalton La HU12 73 F6
Dalton St HU8 141 A1
Dalton Terr YO24 130 A3
Dalwood Cl HU7 141 B8
Dam Bank YO8 148 C6
Dame Kendal Gr 29
DN33 102 D2
Dam Green La HU15 68 C7
Dam Hill YO23 24 B4
Dam La
Ottringham HU12 73 D2
Selby YO8 48 B3
Thornton Curtis DN39 85 E4
Dam Rd DN18 69 E1
Damson Cl YO26 129 E4
Damson Garth YO25 31 F2
Danby Cl HU8 141 E7
Danby Rd DN17 107 D7
Dancing La
Riston HU11 45 C5
Swine HU11 57 D7
Dane Ave
Thorpe Willoughby YO8 48 B1
York YO26 129 C5
Danebury Cres YO26 129 C4
Danebury Ct YO26 129 C4
Danebury Dr YO26 129 C4
Dane Cl 13 DN20 97 E4
Danepark Rd HU6 139 E7
Danes Cl DN32 153 A1
Danescroft YO8 148 C2
Danes Croft
Bridlington YO16 122 D5
2 York YO10 133 D8
Danes Ct 5 YO19 49 A8
Danes Dr HU13 69 F4
Danes' Dyke* YO15 4 F3
Danes Dyke Nature
Reserve* YO15 123 E8
Danesfield Ave DN37 113 E7
Danesfort Ave YO24 129 D2
Danesgate YO26 129 C4
Dane's Graves (Tumuli)*
YO25 8 D2
Danes Hills (Tumuli)*
YO8 37 E2
Danesmead YO10 133 D8
Danes Rd DN21 117 C1
Danesway HU17 136 D6
Daneswell Cl 3 YO41 15 D2
Dann Ct 42 HU12 72 D7
Dansom La HU8 141 B1
Dansom Lane S HU8 146 B8
Danson Cl DN18 85 A8
DANTHORPE 59 C3
Danthorpe Rd HU11 59 B4
Danube Rd HU5 144 C8
Danum Cl 14 DN8 93 B8
Danum Dr YO10 133 E8
Danum Rd
2 Hatfield DN7 92 D3
Scunthorpe DN17 150 F4
York YO10 133 E8
Dar Beck Rd DN21 107 C4
Darbie Cl YO32 127 D4
Darby Rd DN15 82 B4
D'arcy Rd YO8 148 E4
Darfield Cl YO32 14 B8
Dark La
5 Amcotts DN17 81 F1
Paull HU12 72 D4
Darley Cl
Kilham YO25 9 B3
7 Stamford Bridge YO41 15 D2
Darling La YO23 36 C8
Darlington Gr DN8 79 B2
Darnborough St YO23 156 B1
Darnbrook Wlk YO31 131 B5
Darneley Ct HU18 134 D6
Darnholm Ct 14 HU8 141 E7
Darnholme Cres DN17 107 D7
Darrismere Villas 4
HU3 145 A5
Dartford Wlk HU9 142 E1
Dart Gr HU8 142 B5
Dartmouth Rd DN17 150 D5
Dartmouth Wlk HU4 144 A3
Darwin Cl YO31 127 E1
Darwin Ct DN34 102 C3
Darwin Dr YO25 125 A3
Darwin Rd YO16 122 E6
Darwin St 4 DN21 108 B1
Datchet Garth 3 HU4 144 B2
Daubney St DN35 153 B4
Dauby La YO41 27 B3
Davenport Ave HU13 143 D1
Davenport Dr DN35 153 D1
Davey Cl YO25 124 E4
David Lister Sch HU9 141 E1
David Lister Sch East
HU9 142 D1
David Pl DN36 114 A7
David's Cl HU16 138 B8
David St DN32 152 F1
Davidstow Cl HU7 140 F8
Davie Pl DN35 153 B3
Daville Cl HU5 139 B1
Davisons Ave DN31 152 D4
Davis's Cl HU10 143 C8
Davy Ave DN15 150 E8
Davy Cres 2 DN20 98 C3
Davygate YO1 156 B2
Dawes La 1 DN15 151 C7
Daw La YO23 36 A5
Dawlish Rd DN33 113 E7
Dawnay Dr HU10 144 A6
Dawnay Garth
Shipton YO30 12 E5
Dawnay Garth *continued*
2 Snaith DN14 63 B1
Dawnay Rd HU11 58 A4
Dawnhill La DN21 119 B2
Dawson City Claypits Nature
Reserve* DN19 71 C4
Dawson Dr HU6 140 D8
Dawson Rd YO43 135 D5
Day Cl
Keadby DN17 95 D6
Wrawby DN20 98 E4
Daysfoot Ct 8 YO10 130 E3
Dayton Rd HU5 139 D1
Deacon Ct 3 YO8 148 B6
Deacon Dr DN15 150 B6
Deacons Ct YO23 132 B2
Dead La
Bainton YO25 31 E7
Foggathorpe YO8 51 A8
Kirkburn YO25 20 A2
Lockington YO25 32 B2
Deal Cl HU8 141 E8
Dealtry Ave 1 YO32 127 C8
Deane Rd 12 DN40 87 C1
Deangate YO1 156 B3
Deanhead Gr 7 YO30 126 E2
Dean La YO43 53 D4
Dean Park Ind Est HU17 137 C4
Dean Rd DN17 150 E2
Deans Cl
Bishopthorpe YO23 132 F4
5 Misterton DN10 116 C5
Deansgate 1 DN34 152 C2
Deansgrove DN32 152 D3
Dean's La 7 YO42 29 A3
Dearne Ct 9 HU15 68 D5
Dearne Gr 1 HU8 141 C1
De Aston Sq DN15 150 E7
Deaton La DN36 114 A7
Deben Gr HU8 142 C7
Dee Cl YO24 132 B7
Deene Cl 8 DN34 102 B2
Deepdale 5 YO24 132 D8
Deepdale Cl YO16 122 E7
Deepdale Gr 2 HU9 146 E8
Deeping Way YO8 148 A6
Deep The (Aquarium &
Marine Research Ctr)*
HU9 155 C1
Deer Hill Gr YO30 126 F3
Deerhurst Gr HU7 141 A7
Deer Park Ct 1 LS25 61 A8
Deer Park Way 6 HU17 55 F8
Deerstone Way 22 YO19 26 F7
Dee St 5 HU3 145 B4
Defender Dr DN37 102 A4
De Grey Ct YO30 156 A4
De Grey Pl 2 YO23 133 B3
De Grey St HU5 140 C2
De Grey Terr YO30 156 A4
DEIGHTON 37 A7
Deighton Grove La YO19 26 A1
Deira Ct YO25 124 F5
De Lacy La DN35 153 F2
De Lacy Way DN15 83 A5
Delamere Cl 6 YO32 13 D5
Delamere Ct 24 DN35 103 C1
Delamere Wlk DN14 149 F5
De La Pole Ave HU3 144 F7
Delhi St HU9 147 B7
Delius Cl HU4 144 B4
Dell The
Beverley HU17 137 B2
9 Broughton DN20 97 D3
Langtoft YO25 8 C5
Scunthorpe DN17 150 D1
5 Skelton YO30 126 B5
Del Pyke YO31 156 C4
Delwood YO10 133 D7
De Mowbray Ct YO23 24 D3
Dempster Ave DN14 149 C1
Denaby Ct HU8 146 B8
Denby Cl DN15 150 D8
Denby Dr DN36 103 B2
Dene Cl
Dunswell HU6 56 D5
Hensall DN14 62 C2
Denehall Rd DN3 92 A2
Dene Park Sports Club
HU6 56 D5
Dene Rd
Grimsby DN32 102 F2
Kingston upon Hull HU16 138 F6
Dene St HU9 141 D1
Denesway HU13 143 D2
Dene Wlk DN14 149 F6
Denholme Ave 3 HU6 140 C7
Denison Rd
Pocklington YO42 29 A4
Selby YO8 148 E4
Denmark Ct 7 HU9 146 C7
Denmark Rise 5 HU15 53 D3
Dennett Rd HU17 137 B5
Dennison St YO31 156 C4
Dennis St YO1 156 C2
Denton La YO43 53 D6
Denton St HU17 137 B3
Denton's Way DN20 109 A5
Dent Rd HU5 139 D3
Denver Rd 6 DN6 76 F2
Deramore Dr YO10 131 C3
Deramore Drive W YO10 131 C3
Derby Cl DN32 153 A5
Derby Rd DN15 150 B6
Derby St HU3 145 D8
Derringham Ave 5 HU4 144 B6
Derringham St HU3 145 C7
Derrymore Rd HU10 138 C2
Derrythorpe Rd DN17 95 D4
Derry Way 27 DN33 113 E8
Derwent Ave
18 North Ferriby HU14 69 A4
York YO31 130 F4
Derwent Chase DN14 64 B7
Derwent Cl
East Cottingwith YO42 38 C5
Elvington YO41 27 B3
Kingston upon Hull HU16 139 D6
2 Stamford Bridge YO41 15 D2
Derwent Cres DN14 65 B7
Derwent Ct YO41 27 C2
Derwent Dr
4 Barlby YO8 49 B5
12 Humberston DN36 103 C1
9 Kirk Sandall DN3 92 A2
Wheldrake YO19 37 F7
Derwent Est YO19 26 E7
Derwent Gdns YO16 122 E7
Derwent Inf Sch YO10 131 B4
Derwent Jun Sch YO10 131 B4
Derwent La YO19 26 E7
Derwent Pk YO19 38 A8
Derwent Rd
Goole DN14 149 D1
1 Howden DN14 65 B7
Scunthorpe DN16 151 D2
York YO10 133 D8
Derwent St HU8 141 B1
Derwent Wlk YO32 127 F5
Desmond Ave
4 Hornsea HU18 134 C4
Kingston upon Hull HU6 140 D4
Despatch Rd DN16 97 A5
Detuyll St DN15 96 C7
Detuyll Street W DN15 96 C7
Deveron Way YO24 132 B7
Devon Pl YO10 130 F3
Devonshire Ave DN32 102 E2
Devonshire Ct YO30 127 A1
Devonshire Dr DN14 149 B5
Devonshire Rd DN17 150 F2
Devon St
Cottingham HU16 139 C7
Gipsyville HU4 144 F3
Dewberry Ct HU4 144 D4
Dewsbury Ave DN15 150 C8
Dewsbury Ct YO1 156 A1
Dewsbury Terr YO1 156 A1
Deyne Ave DN15 151 A7
Diadem Gr HU9 142 C5
Dial Sq DN31 152 E3
Diamond St YO31 156 C4
Diana Princess of Wales
Hospl DN33 102 E2
Diana St DN15 96 D7
Dibsdane HU6 139 E8
Dickens Cl 1 YO32 127 F1
Dickey La YO8 48 D5
Dickinson Cl DN20 108 F5
Dickinson's La DN36 114 B1
Dick La DN14 65 E7
Didsbury Cl YO30 126 E2
Didscourt HU6 139 E6
DIG* YO1 156 C2
Digby Garth HU7 57 A5
Digby Gdns DN34 152 A1
Digby St DN15 150 F8
Dijon Ave YO24 129 C2
Dikelands Cl 19 YO26 12 F1
Dikelands La YO26 12 F1
Dike Ray Cl YO32 127 C7
Dikes Marsh La DN8 78 F4
Dill Dr HU17 154 B1
Dilys Gr 5 YO26 129 E4
DIMLINGTON 90 F7
Dimlington Bglws 5
HU12 90 F6
Dimlington Rd HU12 90 F6
Dingley Cl HU6 140 B6
Dinostar (Dinosour
Experience)* HU1 155 B1
Dirty La DN7 92 D8
Disraeli Cl YO32 127 E1
Distaff La 33 HU12 72 C7
Ditmas Ave 9 HU4 144 B6
Division Rd 1 HU3 145 B4
Dixon Ave
Broughton DN20 97 D3
Grimsby DN32 102 F2
Dixon Cl
Beverley HU17 154 A3
4 Brigg DN20 98 C2
Market Weighton YO43 135 D2
4 Tetney DN36 114 D4
Dixon Ct
Kingston upon Hull HU16 139 A5
Selby YO8 148 B6
Dixon Gdns YO8 148 B6
Dixons Yd YO1 156 C2
Dobella Ave DN14 64 A1
Dobella La DN14 79 B8
Dock Office Row HU1 155 C3
Dock St
Goole DN14 149 C2
Kingston upon Hull HU1 155 B2
Dodgson Terr YO26 129 D4
Dodswell Gr HU9 147 E8
Dodsworth Ave YO31 130 E7
Dodthorpe HU6 140 A8
Doe Park La YO41 16 B4
Doe Pk YO30 126 F2
Dog & Duck La
Beverley HU17 154 A3

Dog & Duck La *continued*
12 Gainsborough DN21 117 A2
Dog & Duck Sq 13 YO15 5 A2
Dog Kennel La HU17 43 C3
Doherty Wlk YO24 132 C8
Dolby Vale 23 DN34 102 C2
Dolegate YO41 15 F4
Dole Rd DN17 80 B1
Doll La 2 DN20 98 F7
Dollyth Howe* YO17 6 F6
Dolman Cres 11 DN17 96 C2
Dolphin St DN35 153 F2
Dominican Wlk HU17 154 B2
Dominion Cl 9 DN36 114 A7
Don Ave YO24 132 E8
Doncaster Coll DN8 93 B8
Doncaster Rd
Brayton YO8 148 B3
Gunness DN15 95 E6
Hatfield DN7 92 D3
Haxey DN9 104 F2
North Elmsall WF8 76 A1
Scunthorpe DN15 150 A7
Stainforth DN7 92 B6
Doncaster St HU3 145 B6
Don Cl DN14 78 B8
Donna Fields YO25 9 F6
Donnington Gdns DN15 150 F7
Donnington St DN32 152 F3
Don St DN14 149 D1
Donville Rd DN17 81 A3
Dooks Cl DN21 107 C1
Doon Garth HU4 144 A3
Dorado Cl 2 HU3 145 A5
Dorchester Prim Sch
HU7 141 B6
Dorchester Rd
Kingston upon Hull HU7 141 B7
Scunthorpe DN17 150 C4
Doriam Ave YO31 127 F2
Doriam Dr YO31 127 F2
Dorking Cl HU8 142 A4
Dornoch Dr HU8 141 C3
Dorothy Ave
Thorne/Moorends DN8 92 F8
6 Waltham DN37 113 E7
Dorrington Cl 23 YO42 29 A3
Dorr La DN14 78 A8
Dorset Ave HU11 45 E2
Dorset Close E 2 DN15 82 B4
Dorset Close W 1 DN15 82 B4
Dorset St HU4 144 F3
Dorsey Way 5 HU15 68 C7
Dot Hill Cl 3 YO43 53 F7
Double Bridges Rd DN8 93 B6
Doughty Cl 2 DN37 113 E7
Doughty Rd DN32 152 E3
Douglas Ave DN31 152 A4
Douglas Rd
Cleethorpes DN35 153 D4
Kingston upon Hull HU8 142 C6
Douglas St 3 YO8 148 C5
Dove Cl HU12 74 A8
Dovecote Garth 5 YO41 27 B2
Dove Cote Gdns DN14 62 D2
Dovecote Mdws DN20 98 D3
Dovedale Cl DN15 83 A6
Dovedale Ct YO16 122 F7
Dovedale Dr 18 DN33 113 E8
Dovedale Gr 1 HU9 146 E8
Dovedale Rd DN16 151 D1
Dove La HU12 74 B8
Dover St
Grimsby DN31 152 C4
Kingston upon Hull HU3 145 C8
Dove St YO23 156 A1
Dower Chase YO19 37 A6
Dower Pk YO19 37 B6
Dower Rise 11 HU14 69 B7
Downe Cl DN14 78 D7
Downe St YO25 124 E4
Downfield Ave HU6 140 B8
Downhill Dr 7 HU7 57 B5
Downing Cl 7 DN34 102 C3
Downing Cres 11 DN16 96 D2
Downing Gr HU9 142 A1
Downland Cres WF11 61 A1
Downs Cres HU5 139 D2
Dowse Ave DN15 150 E8
Dowsons La DN14 78 E8
DRAGONBY 82 E1
Dragonby Rd 3 DN17 96 C2
Dragon La YO16 122 C5
Drain Bank HU15 67 B8
Drain La
Gilberdyke HU15 52 D2
Holme-on-Spalding-Moor
YO43 51 F8
Drake Ave DN32 153 B2
Drakes Cl YO32 127 F5
Drake St 2 YO23 156 B1
Dr Anderson Ave 9 DN7 92 C6
Drapers Croft YO23 132 B4
Draper's La 17 HU12 72 C7
DRAX 63 F5
Drax Castle Earthworks*
YO8 63 F4
Drax Prim Sch YO8 63 F5
Draycot LN7 111 A2
Draycott Ave HU18 134 C5
Dray Dr HU17 43 E5
Drayton Cl 5 HU8 142 C5
Dressay Gr HU8 141 F7
Drew Ave DN32 102 F2
Drewry La 7 DN9 105 A2
Drewton Ct 8 DN14 65 A7
Drewton La HU15 54 A4
DRIFFIELD 124 C5
Driffield Bsns Ctr YO25 124 F2
Driffield CE Inf Sch
YO25 124 E4
Driffield Cl HU16 138 E6
Driffield Jun Sch YO25 124 F5
Driffield L Ctr YO25 125 A5
Driffield Rd
Beverley HU17 136 C6
Huggate YO42 18 C1
Kilham YO25 9 C2
Langtoft YO25 8 C4
Molescroft HU17 136 B8
Nafferton YO25 125 E7
Skerne & Wansford YO25 21 A2
Driffield Sch YO25 125 A5
Driffield Showground*
YO25 124 D2
Driffield Spellowgate
YO25 124 B7
Driffield Sports Ctr
YO25 125 A5
Driffield Sta YO25 124 F3
Driffield Terr YO24 130 A2
Driffil Way DN15 83 A4
Drill Hall La 28 DN21 117 B1
Dringfield Cl 2 YO24 132 D8
DRINGHOUSES 132 E8
Dringhouses Prim Sch
YO24 132 F8
Dringhouses Sports Club
YO24 132 F8
Dring La DN21 118 A7
Dringshaw HU6 139 F8
Dringthorpe Rd YO24 132 F7
Drive The
Cherry Burton HU17 43 A4
Kirk Sandall DN3 92 A1
Waltham DN37 113 E6
Drome Rd YO23 132 C2
Dronfield Ct DN15 150 B7
Drove La HU7 44 E1
Drovers Rise 1 HU15 68 C6
Drummer's Well* YO25 21 F8
Drummond Ct 5 HU7 57 B5
Drummond View YO23 133 B4
Drury Cl 1 DN37 113 D6
Drury La 3 DN36 114 A7
Drydales HU10 143 C6
Dryden Rd DN17 150 D2
Dryden St HU8 141 C2
Dryham La HU15 53 C3
Dryhurst Cl 9 DN6 76 F2
Drypool Way HU9 146 B6
Duchess St DN32 152 D2
Duck La
Ganton YO12 1 A8
Kirton in Lindsey DN21 108 B1
Duckthorpe La DN36 115 B2
Duddon Gr HU8 142 B6
Dudley Ct YO31 156 C4
Dudley Mews YO31 156 C4
Dudley Pl DN35 103 B2
Dudley Rd
28 Brigg DN20 98 C2
Scunthorpe DN16 151 E2
Dudley St
Grimsby DN34 152 C3
York YO31 156 C4
Dudley Wlk HU4 144 B3
Duesbery St HU5 145 C8
Duesbury Cl HU17 154 A3
Dugard Rd DN32 153 B3
DUGGLEBY 6 B6
Duggleby Howe* YO17 6 C5
Dukes Ct 3 YO26 129 D6
Duke's La YO25 2 A1
Duke St
Grimsby DN32 153 A5
13 Stainforth DN7 92 C6
Dukes Wharf YO23 156 B1
Dulverton Cl 4 HU7 56 F5
Dumfries Wlk HU8 142 C7
Dunbar Ave 5 DN36 114 A7
Dunbar Cl 6 DN21 117 C1
Duncan Dr DN18 69 E1
Dunce Mire Rd LS25 61 A8
Duncombe Ct HU12 72 E7
Duncombe Dr
Great Driffield YO25 124 D3
Strensall YO32 14 B8
Duncombe Gdns DN32 152 F5
Duncombe La YO32 14 B8
Duncombe Pl YO1 156 B3
Duncombe St DN32 152 F4
Dundas St YO1 156 C2
Dundee St HU5 145 A8
Dunelm Cl 3 HU8 141 C1
Dunelm Cres 13 DN8 79 B2
Dunflat Gate HU17 55 D6
Dunflat La HU16 55 B5
Dunflat Rd HU17 55 D6
Dunhill Rd DN14 149 B4
Dunkeld Dr 4 HU6 140 B8
Dunken Hill Highgate
HU17 42 F4
Dunlin Cl HU7 141 D8
Dunlin Dr DN16 151 F1
Dunlop Way DN16 151 E3
Dunmires La DN14 80 E8
Dunmow Cl 1 HU8 142 C5
Dunmow St DN31 152 B5
DUNNINGTON
Driffield 26 F7
Hornsea 34 F7
Dunnington La
Beeford YO25 34 D7
Skipsea YO25 22 F1
Dunnington Prim Sch
YO19 26 E7
Dunnock Cl
7 Kingston upon Hull
HU8 141 D7
26 Yaddlethorpe DN17 96 D1
Dunnscroft YO15 5 A2
Dunn's La 6 YO25 124 F4
Dunns Paddock 3 DN20 98 F7
Dunscombe Pk HU8 141 B2
DUNSCROFT 92 C3
Dunstall St DN15 151 A7
Dunstan Dr
30 Canal Side DN8 93 A8
26 Thorne/Moorends DN8 93 A8
Dunstan Hill DN21 108 B1
Dunstan Villas 17 DN21 108 B1
Dunstan Wlk 34 DN8 93 A8
Dunster Rd DN21 117 C1
Dunston Dr HU13 143 D1
Dunston Rd HU5 144 D7
DUNSVILLE 92 B3
Dunsville Prim Sch DN7 92 D3
DUNSWELL 56 D5
Dunswell Cl HU6 140 A7
Dunswell La HU6 56 C6
Dunswell Prim Sch HU6 56 D6
Dunswell Rd
Cottingham HU16 56 B6
Kingston upon Hull HU16 139 C8
Dunvegan Rd HU8 141 F6
Durban Rd DN32 153 B3
Durban St HU8 155 C3
Durham Ave
Grimsby DN34 152 A3
10 Thorne/Moorends DN8 93 A8
Durham Cl 18 YO8 49 F1
Durham Mews HU17 154 A1
Durham Rd
Cleethorpes DN35 153 C1
Hatfield DN7 92 D4
Durham St HU8 141 C1
Durlston Dr YO32 14 A7
Dursley Ave 1 DN36 113 F7
Dyer La HU17 154 A3
Dyke Cl 2 HU13 69 F4
Dykelands Cl YO19 37 F7
Dyke Rd DN36 115 C5
Dykes La YO23 132 A1
Dymoke Dr DN37 102 B3
Dyon La YO8 50 B3
Dyon Rd YO8 50 D7
Dyon Way YO8 50 D7

E

Eadon Pl DN14 78 B8
Eagle Bsns Ctr HU2 155 C4
Eagle Terr HU8 155 C4
EALAND 94 E6
Ealand Rd DN17 95 C6
Ealdane HU6 139 E8
Ealing Cl HU8 141 F5
Earfit La YO23 36 A8
Earl Ave 24 DN36 114 A8
Earlescourt HU6 139 E7
Earle's Rd
Kingston upon Hull HU9 146 D7
North Cotes DN36 115 C5
Earle St YO31 156 C4
Earlsborough Terr YO30 156 A3
Earlsgate Gdns DN15 82 F5
Earlsgate Rd DN15 83 A5
Earl St
Grimsby DN31 152 C3
Scunthorpe DN16 151 B6
Earls Wlk DN16 151 B6
Earsham Cl HU8 142 C6
EARSWICK 128 A7
Earswick Chase YO32 127 F7
Earswick Village YO32 127 F7
Easby Ct HU5 139 C2
Easedale Ave HU9 142 D3
Easenby Ave HU10 143 C6
Easenby Cl 3 HU14 69 C7
EASINGTON 91 A6
Easington CE VC Prim Sch
HU12 90 F5
Easington Rd
Easington HU12 91 B2
Skeffling HU12 90 E6
Easingwood Way YO25 125 A4
Eason Rd
8 Grimsby DN33 102 D1
York YO24 132 E8
Eason View YO24 132 E8
East Acridge 7 DN18 84 F8
East Back Side YO25 10 C3
East Bank DN7 92 C7
East Boundary Rd DN16 151 F6
Eastbourne Gr YO31 130 F5
Eastbourne Rd HU18 134 D4
Eastbourne St HU3 145 A5
Eastbourne Way 12
DN33 113 E8
EASTBURN 20 B2
EAST BUTTERWICK 106 E8
EAST CARLTON 47 A2
East Carr Rd
Keyingham HU12 73 D5
Kingston upon Hull HU8 141 F7
East Cl HU17 136 D6
East Comm La
Brumby DN16 151 D3
East Comm La *continued*
Scunthorpe DN16 151 B4
Selby YO8 148 F4
EAST COMMON 148 E4
EAST COTTINGWITH 38 C5
EAST COWICK 78 D8
East Cross St 15 DN21 108 B1
East Dale Dr DN21 108 B2
East Dale Rd HU14 68 E5
East Dock Rd DN40 87 E2
EAST ELLA 144 D7
East Ella Dr HU4 144 C6
East End
Humberside Airport
DN39 100 A6
Walkington HU17 55 C8
East End Cl DN33 102 E1
East End Rd HU12 58 D1
Easterfield Ct 10 YO25 124 F4
Eastern Ave DN21 117 C1
Eastern Inway DN34 152 A1
Eastern Terr YO31 130 E6
Easterwood Cl 12 HU7 57 B5
East Ferry Rd
Laughton DN21 106 D1
Wildsworth DN21 117 A8
Eastfield
5 Humberston DN36 114 D8
Hunmanby YO14 2 F8
Eastfield Ave
Grimsby DN33 113 E8
Haxby YO32 127 C7
Eastfield Cl
3 Beverley HU17 137 A6
North Frodingham YO25 34 A8
Eastfield Cres YO10 131 C2
Eastfield Ct
Northfield HU15 144 A2
York YO10 131 C2
Eastfield Est HU12 60 B1
Eastfield La
Dunnington YO19 26 F8
Kellington DN14 61 F4
Rise HU17 45 F6
Eastfield Prim Sch
Immingham DN40 87 C1
Kingston upon Hull HU4 144 D6
Eastfield Rd
Barton-upon-Humber
DN18 84 F7
Brandesburton YO25 34 C2
Bridlington YO16 122 E5
Brigg DN20 98 C2
Easington HU12 91 A5
Epworth DN9 105 E6
Fangfoss YO41 28 D7
Great Driffield YO25 124 E5
1 Keelby DN41 101 A5
Keyingham HU12 73 D4
Kingston upon Hull HU4 144 D6
Market Weighton YO43 135 E3
Messingham DN17 107 D7
North Killingholme DN40 86 F4
Scunthorpe DN16 151 C1
East Field Rd DN7 92 C8
Eastfield Rise 4 DN36 114 A5
Eastgate
Beverley HU17 154 B2
2 Goole DN14 149 D4
Grimsby DN32 152 E4
Hornsea HU18 134 C5
Kingston upon Hull HU13 143 E2
Lund YO25 31 F2
Nafferton YO25 125 F7
North Newbald YO43 53 F7
Patrington HU12 74 D1
Scotton DN21 107 C2
East Gate
Rudston YO25 9 F6
Thorne/Moorends DN8 79 B2
Eastgate Ct HU18 134 C5
East-Gate N YO25 124 E5
East-Gate S YO25 124 F4
Eastgate View HU18 134 B4
East Gn DN17 107 D7
East Gr
Barton-upon-Humber
DN18 69 F1
Kingston upon Hull HU4 144 D4
Easthall Rd LN7 110 B4
EAST HALTON 86 E7
East Halton Prim Sch
DN40 86 D6
East Halton Rd DN40 86 E3
East Hann La DN19 70 E1
Eastholme Cl YO25 124 F5
Eastholme Dr YO30 126 E1
Eastholme Gdns 9 DN15 82 B4
Eastholme La HU12 73 C7
Easthorpe Dr YO26 126 A1
East Hull Pools HU9 146 C8
East La
Beverley HU17 136 D5
Corringham DN21 118 B2
Sigglesthorne HU11 45 F8
Stainforth DN7 92 C6
East Lambwath Rd HU11 46 D3
Eastland Ave YO24 129 E2
Eastlands YO25 125 F7
Eastlands Rd YO25 19 E2
EAST LOUND 105 E3
East Lound Rd
Haxey DN9 105 D2
Owston Ferry DN9 106 A3
EAST LUTTON 7 C8
EAST MARSH 152 F5
East Marsh Rd DN19 71 C3
East Mid Mere Rd DN40 86 F4
East Moor Gdns YO19 133 F
East Mount 8 HU14 69 A
East Mount Ave HU8 142 B
East Mount Rd YO24 156 A
Eastmount Recn Ctr
HU8 142 B
EAST NEWTON 59 F
East Newton Rd HU11 47 D
EASTOFT 81 A
Eastoft CE Prim Sch
DN17 81 A
Eastoft Rd
Crowle DN17 94 D
Luddington & Haldenby
DN17 81 C
Easton Ave HU8 141 A
Easton Rd YO16 122 A
Easton Wlk YO16 122 B
East Parade
Brigg DN20 98 C
Goole DN14 149 D
York YO31 130 F
East Park Ave HU8 141 E
East Pk HU17 45 B
EAST RAVENDALE 113 C
East Ravendale CE Prim Sch
DN37 113 B
East Rd
Bridlington YO15 122 D
Keadby with Althorpe DN17 95 C
East Riding Bsns Pk
HU17 137 C
East Riding Coll @ Beverley
HU17 136 C
East Riding Coll @
Bridlington YO16 122 D
East Riding Coll @ Carnaby
YO25 10 D
East Riding Coll @ Hull
HU3 145 C
EASTRINGTON 51
Eastrington Ponds Nature
Reserve* DN14 65 E
Eastrington Prim Sch
DN14 51 F
Eastrington Sta DN14 66 A
East Riverside DN40 87 E
East St Mary's Gate 3
DN31 152 D
East Scar YO15 5 A
Eastside Rd
Grimsby DN31 152 F
Scunthorpe DN16 151 F
East St
Dalton Holme HU17 31 E
Grimsby DN31 152 E
Hibaldstow DN20 108 F
Kilham YO25 9 C
5 Kingston upon Hull
HU9 146 B
Leven HU17 45 A
Roxby cum Risby DN15 83 A
EAST STOCKWITH 116 F
East View
7 Campsall DN6 76 E
10 Knottingley WF11 61 A
Eastville Rd 10 DN33 102 D
Eastward Ave YO10 133 E
East Way YO31 127 E
East Wlk DN15 151 E
Eastwold 2 YO43 53 F
Eastwood Ave DN32 102 E
Eastwood Ct DN15 150 B
Eastwood Dr 8 DN20 97 E
Eaton Ct
Grimsby DN34 152 C
7 York YO24 132 B
Eaton Rd 13 DN40 87 C
Ebberston Gr 5 HU5 139 E
Ebor Ave HU18 134 D
Ebor Cl HU8 142 E
Ebor Ct 7 YO8 148 C
Ebor Ind Est YO31 156 C
Ebor Manor 1 HU12 73 C
Ebor Prep Sch YO30 130 A
Ebor St
Selby YO8 148 C
York YO23 156 E
Ebor View YO43 135 E
Ebor Way YO26 126 A
Ebsay Dr YO30 127 A
Eccles Cl YO30 126 D
Eccles Ct DN20 98 D
Ecclesfield Ave HU9 142 D
Eccleston Rd DN3 92 A
Eddlemere La YO25 32 E
Eden Ave YO8 148 D
Eden Cl
Beverley HU17 136 D
York YO24 132 C
Edencroft Dr 14 DN3 92 A
Edendale HU7 140
Eden Dene DN16 151 D
Eden Dr HU8 141 C
Edenfield Ave HU18 134 C
Eden Field Rd 12 DN3 92 A
Eden Gdns YO15 4 D
Eden Gr Rd 1 DN3 92 A
Eden Rd HU17 136 D
Eden Rise HU10 138 C
Edenthorpe Hall Prim Sch
DN3 92
Edgar Cl DN21 107 C
Edgar St HU3 145 D
Edgbaston Ave 27 DN17 96 C
Edge Ave DN33 102
Edgecliffe Villas 4
YO15 122

dgecumbe St HU5 140 C2
dgemere DN15 150 B7
dgeware Ave 1 HU9 141 F1
dgware Rd YO10 130 E2
dinburgh Dr 4 DN36 114 A6
dinburgh Rd 3 DN17 95 D6
dinburgh St
Goole DN14 149 C4
Kingston upon Hull HU3 145 A5
dison Gr HU9 141 E2
dith Cavell Ct 4 HU5 139 F4
dmonds Way DN31 152 D4
dmund Cl DN21 118 A1
dmund Wilson Swimming
Pool YO24 129 D1
dward Collins Sq 2
HU9 146 C7
dward Ct 6 DN8 79 B1
dward Heneage Prim Sch
DN32 152 F3
dwardian Dr YO15 122 C1
dward Rd 11 DN21 117 B1
dwards Rd DN15 150 F8
dward St
Beverley HU17 154 B3
Cleethorpes DN35 153 E1
Grimsby DN32 152 F3
Kingston upon Hull HU13 143 F1
1 Pocklington YO42 29 A4
6 Withernsea HU19 74 F7
dwins Garth YO43 135 F6
elmere La HU11 47 A5
GGBOROUGH 61 F2
gginton Cl HU10 143 C7
gginton St HU2 155 B3
glins Rd DN8 79 C1
glinton Ave HU8 141 F3
gremont Cl 11 YO41 15 D2
grom's La HU19 75 A5
gton Ave DN17 107 D7
gton St HU8 155 C4
gypt St HU9 147 B7
ighth Ave
Bridlington YO15 122 F4
Fixborough Stather DN15 82 A1
York YO31 130 F5
ildon Hills Cl HU7 57 B5
lba St HU9 147 C7
lderberry Dr HU4 144 D4
lderberry Way 4 DN35 103 B1
lder Gr 38 YO32 13 E5
lderwood Ct 6 HU3 145 D5
ldon Dr 11 HU12 58 C1
ldon Gr
Kingston upon Hull HU5 140 D2
Thorne/Moorends DN8 79 C2
'don St YO31 156 C4
don Terr YO31 156 C4
dwick Cl YO30 126 F2
eanor Ct HU9 142 B2
eanor St DN32 152 F4
gar Cl YO31 127 E1
gar Rd HU4 144 B4
izabeth Ave 6 DN3 92 A2
izabeth Cl
Bridlington YO15 122 C1
4 Gainsborough DN21 117 B2
14 Grimsby DN33 113 D8
Scotter DN21 107 C4
izabeth Ct 7 YO8 148 B6
izabeth Dr YO25 124 D3
izabeth St DN15 151 A8
la Ct HU10 143 C8
la Pk HU10 143 D7
la St HU5 140 B2
len Way 9 DN36 113 F8
lerbeck Ct HU8 141 D7
lerburn Ave HU6 140 A7
lerburn Dr 3 YO16 122 C5
lerby Gr
4 Kingston upon Hull
HU9 141 F2
2 Summergangs HU9 141 F2
lerby Rd HU11 45 F2
lerington La HU17 42 F6
LERKER 68 A8
lerker La HU15 53 F1
lerker Rd HU17 154 A2
lerker Rise HU10 138 D2
lerker Wold La HU15 54 B1
LERTON 38 C2
lesmere Ave HU8 142 A4
lesmere Gr DN7 92 D6
lesmere Rise DN34 102 B2
letson Mews HU12 73 C4
lifoot La HU12 73 B7
lingham Cl HU8 142 B6
liot Cl YO43 135 D3
liot Ct YO10 133 D7
liot Way YO43 135 D3
lis Cl 4 HU12 58 D1
lison Ave DN16 96 D1
lison St DN8 93 A7
lis St HU9 146 C8
liston Inf Sch DN35 153 D4
liston Jun Sch DN35 153 C4
liston St DN35 153 C3
lis Way
Grimsby DN31 152 E4
Hibaldstow DN20 108 F6
lmore La LN7 110 B4
LOUGHTON 68 C7
loughton Dale HU15 68 D8
loughton Gr 4 HU16 138 E6
loughton Prim Sch
HU15 68 C7
loughton Rd HU15 68 C5
Elloughtonthorpe Way 26
HU15 68 D5
Ellwood Ct YO10 130 D2
Elma Ave YO16 122 D2
Elma Gr 3 YO30 126 E2
Elm Ave
15 Brough HU15 68 C6
Burstwick HU12 73 A6
Cleethorpes DN35 153 E2
Goole DN14 149 B4
Grimsby DN34 152 A2
Kingston upon Hull HU8 141 C2
Elm Avenue 10 YO32 36 C7
Elma Villas 3 YO16 122 D2
Elmbridge Par 3 HU9 142 E1
Elm Cl HU17 136 D5
Elmdale 16 DN18 84 E8
Elm Dr HU17 43 A5
Elm End 9 YO32 13 E5
Elmfield HU6 140 B6
Elmfield Ave YO31 130 F8
Elmfield Dr
16 Brandesburton YO25 34 B2
Kingston upon Hull HU16 139 A6
Elmfield Terr YO31 130 F7
Elm Garth HU12 60 B1
Elm Gdns DN35 153 E2
Elm Gr
1 Aldbrough HU11 47 C1
Healing DN41 102 A5
Scunthorpe DN16 151 B4
York YO31 127 F2
Elmhirst Rd DN8 93 B8
Elm La
Goxhill DN19 71 A1
Laceby DN37 101 E1
Elmlands Gr YO31 130 F8
Elmpark Vale YO31 131 A8
Elmpark View YO31 131 A8
Elmpark Way YO31 131 A8
Elm Rd
Cleethorpes DN35 153 E2
Great Driffield YO25 124 F2
Waltham DN37 113 E6
Elmsall Dr HU17 136 C6
Elms Cl 2 YO19 36 F1
Elms Dr HU10 143 C8
Elm St
Kingston upon Hull HU5 140 D2
Selby YO8 148 D6
Elms The
4 Gilberdyke HU15 66 D7
Stockton on the Forest
YO32 14 D2
ELMSWELL 20 B5
Elmswell Spellowgate
YO25 20 B6
Elmswood HU13 143 C2
Elm Terr HU5 140 D2
Elmtree Ave 9 HU14 69 A4
Elm Tree Ave
9 Poppleton YO26 12 F1
5 Thorngumbald HU12 72 E5
Elm Tree Cl
Keyingham HU12 73 C4
6 Thorngumbald HU12 72 E5
Elm Tree Ct HU16 139 B6
Elm Tree Farm Rd 1
HU12 73 A6
Elmtree Gdns 3 YO24 129 C3
Elm Tree Gr 4 DN8 93 B7
Elm Way
Brigg DN20 98 B2
Messingham DN17 107 C7
Elsenham Rd DN31 152 B5
ELSHAM 98 F7
Elsham Dr DN37 113 D6
Elsham Gr 21 DN33 102 D2
Elsham Hall Gardens &
Country Pk* DN20 98 F6
Elsham Rd DN20 98 D7
Elsham Rise HU13 143 D1
Elsham Wold Ind Est
DN20 99 A8
Elsiemere Wlk 6 HU4 144 B6
Elsie St DN14 149 C5
Elsternwick Ave HU8 141 B2
Elston Cl
Kingston upon Hull HU6 140 D6
York YO30 130 A8
Elston Pl YO8 148 C6
ELSTRONWICK 59 A3
Elswick Gardens 16 DN18 69 E1
Elvaston Ave HU18 134 C5
Elvaston Pk 10 HU7 56 E5
Elveley Dr HU10 143 A7
ELVINGTON 27 B2
Elvington CE Prim Sch
YO41 27 B3
Elvington Cl HU6 140 A6
Elvington Cres HU17 43 D5
Elvington Ind Est YO41 27 A3
Elvington La YO19 26 E5
Elvington Pk YO41 27 A3
Elvington Terr YO10 130 E4
Elwell Ave HU17 154 A2
Elwes St 9 DN20 98 C2
Elwick Gr YO10 131 C4
Elwyn Pl 2 DN35 103 B1
Elwyn Way 40 HU12 72 D7
Ely Pk HU5 139 E3
Embankment The YO25 124 B3
Emberton Pk 12 HU7 56 F6
Embleton Dr 1 YO30 126 F1
Emerald Gr 8 HU3 145 A4
Emerald St YO31 156 C4
Emerson Ave DN7 92 C5
Emfield Gr DN33 113 E7
Emfield Rd DN33 113 D8
Emily Mews YO10 130 E4
Emily St 8 HU9 146 C7
Emmanual Rd DN16 151 F2
Emmanuel Ct
Grimsby DN34 152 A2
Scunthorpe DN16 151 B2
Emmanuel Dr 18 DN16 96 D2
Emmerson St 2 YO31 130 E5
Emmery Cl DN20 97 D4
Emmott Rd HU6 140 C7
Empringham St 5 HU9 146 D7
Empson Ave DN14 149 B6
Empson Terr HU17 154 A2
Emsdale Wlk YO16 122 B4
Ena St HU3 145 B6
Enclosure Gdns 1 YO10 131 B1
Endcliffe Ave DN17 96 C1
Endeavour Cres
3 Kingston upon Hull
HU9 142 B1
Marfleet HU9 147 B8
Endeavour High Sch
HU3 140 E1
Endeavour Sports Ctr
HU3 140 E1
Endell Dr 23 DN21 108 B1
Enderby Rd DN17 150 D1
Enderby Road Inf Sch
DN17 96 C2
Endfields Rd 1 YO10 133 E8
Endike La HU6 140 A6
Endike Prim Sch HU6 140 C6
Endsleigh RC Prim Sch
HU6 140 C4
Endsleigh St HU3 145 A7
Endyke La HU16 139 D6
Endymion St HU8 141 B1
Enfield Ave DN36 114 A7
Enfield Cres 1 YO24 130 A3
Enfield Mews HU17 154 B3
Enfield Prim Sch DN36 114 A7
Engelhart Cl YO8 148 A2
Engine La HU11 58 D7
Engine St 19 DN20 98 B2
England Rd HU11 142 F7
English Cl HU3 145 E4
English Martyrs RC Prim Sch
YO24 129 F3
English St HU1 155 A1
Ennerdale HU7 140 E7
Ennerdale Ave YO31 131 B5
Ennerdale Cl 13 DN36 103 C1
Ennerdale Ct 6 YO16 122 E7
Ennerdale L Ctr HU6 140 E6
Enstone Garth 20 HU7 57 A5
Enterprise Pk HU17 137 B3
Enterprise Rd LN7 111 A4
Enterprise Way
Bridlington YO16 122 C2
Grimsby DN32 153 A2
Winterton DN15 82 F5
Ephams La DN41 101 E7
Epping Cl HU8 141 E6
EPPLEWORTH 138 A4
Eppleworth Rd HU16 138 D6
Epsom Pl 33 DN35 103 C1
EPWORTH 105 D6
Epworth County Prim Sch
DN9 105 D6
Epworth L Ctr DN9 105 D6
Epworth Old Rectory*
DN9 105 E6
Epworth Rd
Hatfield DN7 92 F4
Haxey DN9 105 D3
Owston Ferry DN9 106 A4
Epworth St HU5 140 D1
EPWORTH TURBARY 105 C6
Epworth Turbary Nature
Reserve* DN9 105 B6
Eric Bielby Cl HU17 154 B3
Ermine St
Appleby DN15 97 D8
Kirton in Lindsey DN21 108 E3
Winteringham DN15 83 B8
Ernest Hill Ct 1 HU5 140 A2
Ernest Kirkwood Cl 4
HU5 139 D1
Eryholme Cres DN15 150 F7
Escart Ave DN32 153 B2
ESCRICK 37 B5
Escrick CE Prim Sch
YO19 37 A5
Escrick Ct YO19 37 B5
Escrick Park Gdns YO19 37 B5
Escrick St YO10 156 C1
Escrick Terr YO10 156 C1
Eskdale Ave
2 Kingston upon Hull
HU9 141 E1
York YO10 131 C3
Eskdale Dr YO16 122 F8
Eskdale Way 12 DN37 102 B4
Esk Dr YO26 129 B8
Eske Cl HU17 44 C5
Eske La HU17 44 C5
ESKHAM 115 C1
Eskham Cl 19 DN35 103 C2
Eskholme La DN14 78 B4
Eskwood Wlk DN14 149 F6
Esmond St HU6 140 D5
Esplanade
Bridlington YO15 122 F2
Hornsea HU18 134 D5
York YO26 156 A2
Esplanade Ct YO30 156 A3
Essex Dr 7 DN15 82 B4
Essex St HU4 144 E3
Estate Ave DN20 97 D3
Estate Rd No 1 DN31 152 A6
Estate Rd No 2 DN31 152 A5
Estate Rd No 3 DN31 102 C5
Estate Rd No 4 DN31 102 C5
Estate Rd No 5 DN31 152 A6
Estate Rd No 6 DN31 102 C5
Estate Rd No 7 DN31 102 C5
Estate Rd No 8 DN31 102 C5
Estcourt Prim Sch HU9 146 D8
Estcourt St
Goole DN14 149 D4
Kingston upon Hull HU9 146 D8
Estcourt Terr DN14 149 D4
Estuary Way DN31 152 B6
Ethel Ct 3 DN15 151 B7
Ethelstone Rd DN34 152 A3
Etherington Cl 5 HU12 73 C4
Etherington Ct HU17 137 B3
Etherington Dr HU6 140 D5
Etherington La YO25 124 E4
Etherington Rd HU6 140 C5
Etive Pl YO24 132 B7
Eton Dr
7 Haxby YO32 13 D5
Scunthorpe DN17 96 C2
Eton Rd DN14 149 B5
Eton St HU3 145 C4
ETTON 42 F6
Etton Cl HU16 138 E5
Etton Dikes HU17 43 A6
Etton Gr HU6 139 F5
Etton Rd HU17 43 A5
Etty Ave YO10 131 A4
Etty Cl 24 YO41 15 D2
Europa Bsns Pk DN31 152 A6
Europarc Innovation Ctr
DN37 102 B6
Europa Way
Brigg DN20 98 B2
Immingham DN41 87 E1
Eva Ave YO30 126 D2
Evelyn Cres YO30 130 B7
Evelyn Gdns 9 HU14 69 A5
Evelyn Grove N DN32 153 B2
Evelyn Grove S DN32 153 B2
Evendine Ct 2 DN36 114 B5
Everest Rd DN16 151 C1
Evergreen Dr 1 HU6 56 D5
Evergreen Way 1 YO8 48 D1
EVERINGHAM 40 A5
Everingham La YO42 40 A7
Everingham Wlk HU5 139 C2
Eversfield Cl 21 HU7 56 F5
EVERTHORPE 53 E3
Everthorpe Cl 33 HU15 68 D5
Ever Thorpe Cl 5 HU3 145 C5
Everthorpe Rd HU15 53 D3
Evesham Ave DN34 102 C3
Evesham Croft 1 YO16 122 D5
Exchange Pl 6 DN20 98 B2
Exchange St
Great Driffield YO25 124 E4
Kingston upon Hull HU5 140 E2
Exeter Ct 11 DN34 102 B2
Exeter Gr HU9 142 A2
Exeter Rd DN15 150 F7
Exeter St HU16 139 C7
Exhibition Sq YO1 156 B3
Exmoor Ave DN15 96 B8
Exmoor Rd DN17 150 C4
Exmouth St HU5 140 C3
Exton Cl HU7 56 F5
Eyre Ave DN16 151 B1
Eyre Cl
Brayton YO8 148 A2
Selby YO8 148 A2

F

Faber Cl YO23 132 B3
Faber St YO31 130 E5
Faceby Wlk HU5 139 E3
Fairbourne Cl 1 HU7 57 A7
Faircourt HU6 139 E7
Fairfax 15 YO41 15 D2
Fairfax Ave
Kingston upon Hull HU5 139 F3
Selby YO8 148 B4
Fairfax Croft YO23 132 B2
Fairfax Dr HU12 72 C8
Fairfax House* YO1 156 C2
Fairfax Rd DN34 152 B3
Fairfax St YO1 156 B1
Fairfield
Goole DN14 149 F6
North Cave HU15 53 D2
Rawcliffe DN14 79 B8
Fairfield Ave
Grimsby DN33 113 E8
Kingston upon Hull HU10 138 C1
Fairfield Cl
5 Broughton DN20 97 E3
Nafferton YO25 125 F7
Fairfield Croft 8 DN9 105 E6
Fairfield Ct 4 DN35 103 D1
Fairfield Dr
25 Barton-upon-Humber
DN18 84 F8
Messingham DN17 107 D7
Fairfield La LS25 61 A6
Fairfield Pit Nature
Reserve* DN19 70 D3
Fairfield Prim Sch DN33 113 E8
Fairfield Rd
Bridlington YO15 122 D1
Fairfield Rd *continued*
Grimsby DN33 113 E8
Kingston upon Hull HU5 139 F3
Scunthorpe DN15 150 C8
Fairfields 21 DN21 108 B1
Fairfields Dr YO30 126 B5
Fairfield View 5 HU15 68 D5
Fairholme La HU7 56 F7
Fairisle Rise 5 DN40 101 C8
Fairlawn HU17 136 C6
Fairmont Cres DN16 151 B6
Fairmont Rd DN32 153 A3
Fair Pl HU18 134 B4
Fairtree Wlk 21 DN8 93 A8
Fair View DN20 97 E4
Fair View Ave DN35 153 E2
Fair View Cl HU15 66 D8
Fairway
Selby YO8 148 A4
Waltham DN37 113 E7
York YO30 130 A8
Fairway Ave DN21 117 B2
Fairway Ct DN35 103 E1
Fairway Dr 18 YO26 12 F1
Fairways The
Kingston upon Hull HU8 142 A6
Scunthorpe DN15 150 B6
Fairway The
Kingston upon Hull HU10 143 A8
Thorne/Moorends DN8 79 B2
Falcon Cl 10 YO32 13 F5
Falcon Ct HU4 144 D2
Falconer St 1 YO24 129 F3
Falconers The DN21 108 F2
Falcon Gr 32 DN21 117 C1
Falcon Mews DN35 153 F1
Falkirk Cl 7 HU7 57 A7
Falkland Rd HU9 142 D1
Falklands Ct HU12 90 F6
Falkland St YO1 156 B1
Falkland Way DN18 69 F1
Fallowfield Rd DN33 113 D8
Falmouth St HU5 140 C3
Falsgrave Cres YO30 130 B7
Falsgrave Gr HU5 144 D7
Fangdale Ct 9 YO16 122 F7
FANGFOSS 28 C7
Fangfoss Pottery* YO41 28 C8
Fannystone Rd DN34 152 B3
Faraday St HU9 141 E2
Far Bank La DN7 92 C8
Far Bell Pl HU9 142 C2
Farbridge La HU12 72 C6
Fardell Rd DN16 151 D3
Farebrother St DN32 152 E1
Farfield YO26 129 C6
Far Field Cl 15 DN3 92 A2
Farfield La YO19 26 E8
Farfield lane YO19 14 E1
Far Field Rd DN3 92 A2
Far Grange L Pk TO25 35 C8
Faringdon Rd DN31 153 A6
Far Ings La DN18 69 C1
Far Ings National Nature
Reserve* DN18 69 D2
Far Ings Rd DN18 69 D1
Far La YO25 35 A5
Farlington Cl HU9 142 C5
Farm Cl
4 Edenthorpe DN3 92 A1
Gunness DN15 95 E6
Farm Ct YO43 135 C5
Farmers Way YO23 132 B3
Farmhouse Mews 11
DN36 114 A7
Farm La 2 DN17 106 D8
Farmlands Rd 1 YO24 132 D8
Farmstead Rise YO32 127 D7
Farm Way YO8 148 B7
Farndale Ave
Kingston upon Hull HU9 141 E1
York YO10 131 D4
Farndale Cl 1 YO32 13 F5
Farndale Rd 1 YO16 122 E7
Farndale St YO10 130 D2
Farndale Way
2 Grimsby DN31 152 D4
1 Winterton DN15 83 A5
Farnella Cl HU3 145 A5
Faroes Cl 1 HU9 142 A3
Farrand Rd HU12 72 C7
Farrar St YO10 130 E3
Farriers Croft 2 YO23 132 B3
Farriers Fold 13 DN9 105 D2
Farriers Wlk HU17 45 A8
Farringdon St 2 HU5 140 E1
Farrishes La DN18 84 A8
Farrows Pond DN19 71 A1
Farthing Ave DN15 150 E8
Farthing Dr 2 HU7 56 E5
Farthing La YO25 125 C4
Fauconberg Ave 6
DN33 102 E1
Faulding La DN40 86 F2
Faulding Way DN37 102 B4
Faversham Ave HU4 144 B6
Fawcett Cl HU5 140 D1
Fawcett Gdns 9 YO25 124 F4
Fawcett St
26 Gainsborough DN21 117 B1
York YO10 156 C1
Fawkes Dr YO26 129 C4
Fawley Cl HU5 140 E3
Faxfleet La DN14 67 A3
Feasegate YO1 156 B2

Featherbed La YO42 29 C4
Feather La 5 DN19 85 C7
Felbridge Cl 1 HU9 142 E2
Feldane HU6 139 E8
Fellbrook Ave YO26 129 B4
Felstead Rd DN34 102 C3
Fenby Cl 3 DN37 102 B3
Fenchurch St 1 HU5 140 E1
Fen La DN36 114 D1
Fenland Rd 12 DN8 93 B7
Fenners Ave 29 DN17 96 C2
Fenton St DN15 151 B7
FENWICK 77 D3
Fenwick Comm La DN6 77 D2
Fenwick Ct DN36 114 A5
Fenwick La DN6 77 B1
Fenwick Rd 10 DN33 102 D1
Fenwick's La YO10 133 D7
Fenwick St YO23 130 C2
Fen Wlk DN36 115 C5
Feoffee La YO42 28 C5
Ferens Art Gall* HU1 155 B2
Ferens Ave HU6 140 B4
Ferens Ct 2 HU9 141 D1
Ferens Gdns HU16 138 F8
Ferensway HU2 155 A3
Ferguson Rd 2 HU17 55 B7
Ferguson Way YO32 127 F1
Fernbank 1 DN9 105 D7
Fern Cl
Driffield YO25 124 D2
Kingston upon Hull HU2 155 A4
York YO32 128 A4
Fern Croft 18 DN9 105 E6
Fern Ct HU13 144 A1
Ferndale Ave HU10 138 D1
Ferndale Dr DN8 79 B1
Ferndale Gr DN14 149 C6
Ferndale Rd YO8 148 C4
Ferndale Terr 11 YO15 122 E2
Ferndown DN37 102 B5
Ferndown Dr DN40 87 C2
Fernhall Cl 17 DN3 92 A2
Fernhill 5 DN37 102 B4
Fernhill Rd HU5 139 D3
Fernland Cl 15 HU15 68 C5
Fernlea Cl YO8 148 D4
Fernley Green Cl 6 WF11 61 A2
Fern St YO31 156 C4
Ferns The YO19 36 D1
Fernway YO10 131 C3
Ferriby Gr HU6 139 F5
Ferriby High Rd HU14 69 B5
Ferriby La DN33 102 E1
Ferriby Rd
Barton-upon-Humber DN18 84 E8
Hessle HU13 143 B1
Scunthorpe DN17 150 E1
FERRIBY SLUICE 83 F7
Ferriby Sta HU14 69 A4
Ferries St HU9 146 D7
Ferry Cl 11 YO8 49 F1
Ferry Farm Cl 2 YO19 36 D8
Ferry La
Airmyn DN14 149 A8
Bishopthorpe YO23 133 B4
Bubwith YO8 50 C5
Goole DN14 65 B5
Snaith & Cowick DN14 63 C1
Thorganby YO19 38 B5
Winteringham DN15 68 B1
Woodmansey HU17 56 C7
Ferryman Pk HU12 72 A5
Ferrymans Wlk YO26 12 F2
Ferry Meadow Pk 24 HU7 56 F5
Ferry Rd
Barrow upon Humber DN19 70 C1
Fishlake DN8 78 F1
Goxhill DN19 85 F8
Haxey DN9 105 D1
Keadby with Althorpe DN17 95 D4
Kilpin DN14 65 B5
Kingston upon Hull HU13 143 E1
Scunthorpe DN15 150 D8
South Cave HU15 53 E1
Wawne HU7 56 D8
Wold Haven YO42 29 A3
Ferry Road E DN19 85 C8
Ferry Road W DN15 96 A7
Ferry Row DN14 65 B5
Ferry View
Keyingham HU12 73 C4
Thorngumbald HU12 72 E5
Fetherston Cl 19 YO42 29 A3
Fetter La YO1 156 B2
Feversham Cres 4 YO31 130 C7
Fewson Garth 26 HU12 72 D7
Fewster Way YO10 156 C1
Fewston Dr 9 YO30 126 F1
Field Ave YO8 48 B1
Field Cl
10 Laceby DN37 101 F1
Snaith DN14 78 C8
Fieldend La HU12 59 B2
Fieldfare YO25 125 B5
Field Head
Laceby DN37 101 E1
Wilberfoss YO41 27 F6
Fieldhouse Rd 7 DN36 103 D1
Fielding Way 19 DN21 117 C1
Field La
Eastoft DN17 81 A4
Field La *continued*
Gowdall DN14 77 F8
Hambleton YO8 48 B1
Hensall DN14 62 D2
Heslington YO10 131 C2
Morton DN21 116 F3
Rawcliffe DN14 64 A1
Thornton YO42 39 A8
Wistow YO8 48 C7
Wroot DN9 104 D5
Field La Sports Club YO8 48 B1
Field Rd
Bridlington YO16 122 C4
Crowle DN17 94 D7
Stainforth DN7 92 C6
Thorne/Moorends DN8 93 A8
West Haddlesey YO8 62 A5
Field Reeves Wlk 14 DN9 105 D6
Fields Cl 2 DN9 105 D7
Fields Cl Rd HU12 73 E4
Fields End
9 Misterton DN10 116 C5
North Killingholme DN40 86 E4
Ulceby DN39 86 B2
Fieldside
Blyton DN21 117 F5
Crowle DN17 94 D7
Epworth DN9 105 D6
Field Side DN8 93 A8
Fieldside Garth 3 HU6 56 D5
Fields Rd DN9 105 E2
Field St HU9 146 B7
Field The DN32 153 C2
Field View YO31 130 C7
Fifth Ave
Bridlington YO15 123 A4
Fixborough Stather DN15 82 A1
Goole DN14 149 C5
Scunthorpe DN17 150 B2
Ulrome YO25 23 B3
York YO31 130 F4
Figham Rd HU17 137 D3
Figham Springs Way HU17 154 B1
Fildes St DN31 152 D3
Filey Rd
Grimsby DN32 153 A1
Hunmanby YO14 3 A8
Filey Terr YO30 130 C7
Fillingham Cres
Cleethorpes DN35 103 C2
Gunness DN15 150 B7
FIMBER 18 D7
Fimber Ave HU16 139 A5
Finch Croft 5 HU8 141 D7
Finchcroft La HU17 43 B2
Finchley Cl
26 Barton Waterside DN18 69 E1
Kingston upon Hull HU8 141 F5
Finchley Ct DN31 152 A4
Finch Pk HU17 136 D5
Findlay Cres DN36 114 A7
Findon Cl 28 HU7 56 F6
Fingall Mews 1 HU5 139 D3
Finkle Ct YO43 135 D4
Finkle La DN18 69 F1
Finkle St
2 Bishop Burton HU17 43 A2
Hensall DN14 62 D2
Kingston upon Hull HU2 155 B1
Kingston upon Hull HU16 139 A6
Market Weighton YO43 135 D4
2 North Cave HU15 53 D3
Selby YO8 148 C5
Stainforth DN7 92 C7
Finningley Garth 14 HU7 57 A5
Finnley's La DN14 78 C7
Finsbury Ave YO23 130 C1
Finsbury Dr 7 DN33 102 D1
Finsbury St YO23 130 C1
Firbank Cl 9 YO32 14 A7
Fir Cl
11 Brough HU15 68 D5
Scunthorpe DN16 96 D2
Fircroft Way DN34 152 A3
Firethorn Cl 3 HU3 145 D5
Firglades Cl 10 HU3 145 C5
Fir Heath Cl 5 YO24 129 C1
Firsby Cres DN33 102 D1
First Ave
Bridlington YO15 122 F4
Flixborough DN15 82 A1
3 Goole DN14 149 C4
Grimsby DN33 102 E2
Scunthorpe DN17 150 C2
York YO31 130 F6
First Comm La YO8 48 D4
First La
Kingston upon Hull HU10 144 A5
South Cave HU15 54 A2
Firth Field Rd DN7 92 E4
Firth La DN9 104 D5
Firtholme Rd HU12 91 A4
Firtree Cl
4 Earswick YO32 127 F7
York YO24 129 E3
Fir Tree Cl YO8 48 B2
Firtree Dr DN20 98 F7
Fir Tree Dr 11 DN6 76 E2
Fir Tree La YO8 48 B2
Fir Trees HU10 143 D6
Fir Trees The YO8 48 B2
Fir Tree Way YO8 48 B2
Firwood Whin 5 YO31 127 F3
Fish Dock Rd DN31 152 F6
Fishemore Ave HU13 143 F2
Fisher Cl HU10 138 D2
Fishergate YO10 156 C1
Fishergate Prim Sch YO10 156 C1
Fisher La YO25 22 E5
Fisherman's Wharf DN31 152 D4
Fishermans Wlk 2 HU3 145 C4
Fisher Pl DN35 153 D3
Fisher Sq HU17 154 A2
Fishing Heritage Ctr* DN31 152 D4
Fish La HU15 52 D2
FISHLAKE 92 E8
Fishlake Nab DN7 92 C7
Fishpond Hill YO42 29 C4
Fish St HU1 155 B1
Fishwick Ave 5 HU13 143 E1
Fiskerton Cl 20 DN34 102 C2
Fiskerton Way DN37 102 C6
FITLING 59 C5
Fitling Gr
5 Kingston Upon Hull HU9 142 A2
1 Summergangs HU9 141 F2
Fitling Rd HU11 59 B5
Fitties La DN36 115 C5
Fitzroy St HU5 140 D2
Fitzwilliam Mews 2 DN35 103 C1
Five Rivers DN14 149 C5
Flaen Cl YO15 5 A2
Flaen Rd YO15 5 A2
Flag Wlk 1 HU6 140 C8
Flag Yd YO16 122 C4
FLAMBOROUGH 5 B2
Flamborough CE VC Prim Sch YO15 5 A2
Flamborough Outer Headland Nature Reserve* YO15 5 D2
Flamborough Rd
Dempton YO15 4 E1
Bridlington YO15 122 F4
Flanders Red HU7 140 E7
Flarepath The DN20 99 A8
Flashley Carr La DN6 77 F1
Flatgate DN14 65 B7
Flat La YO42 28 D4
Flavian Gr YO30 129 F8
Flaxdale Ct HU5 139 E1
Flaxley Ct YO8 148 B5
Flaxley Rd YO8 148 A7
Flaxman Ave YO10 131 A4
Flaxman Croft YO23 132 B3
Flaxmill Wlk 2 HU15 66 D7
Flaxton Rd
Kingston upon Hull HU5 139 D1
Strensall YO32 14 B7
Fleet Garth 11 HU12 72 D7
Fleetgate 11 DN18 69 E1
Fleet La DN14 64 A7
Fleets Cl DN7 92 C7
Fleetway DN36 115 A3
Fleetwood Cl 4 DN33 113 E8
Flemingate HU17 154 C2
Flemingate Ct HU17 154 B2
Fleming Ave 3 YO31 130 E5
Flemingdale HU7 140 F7
Fleming Wlk
Cottingham HU16 139 A4
Gipsyville HU4 144 D2
Fletcher Cl
Kingston upon Hull HU13 143 E2
6 Scunthorpe DN15 96 B7
Fletcher Ct 14 YO32 13 E5
Fletcher Gate HU12 72 C7
Fletcher Rd DN34 102 C4
Fletcher's Croft YO23 132 C3
Fletchers Ct 12 YO25 124 F4
FLINTON 59 A7
Flinton Gr HU9 142 A1
Flinton Rd
Aldbrough HU11 58 F8
Humbleton HU11 59 A7
Flinton St HU3 145 B3
FLIXBOROUGH 82 B1
Flixborough Rd DN15 82 A4
FLIXBOROUGH STATHER 82 A1
Floral Hall HU18 134 D5
Florence Ave HU13 143 F1
Florence Gr YO30 126 D2
Florence Nightingale 8 HU5 139 F4
Florence St DN32 152 E1
Florida Ct HU5 140 E3
Florin Dr 3 HU7 56 E5
Flottergate Mall 8 DN31 152 D3
Flour Sq DN31 152 E5
FOCKERBY 81 E5
FOGGATHORPE 51 B8
Fog La YO42 38 E4
Fold Wlk YO32 14 B8
Folkestone St HU5 140 D2
Folk Mus* HU18 134 C4
Folks Cl 13 YO32 13 F5
Folkton Ave HU16 139 A4
Follies The DN15 97 E7
Follifoot Dr HU4 144 E4
Folly La LN7 110 C5
Football Gn HU18 134 C3
Forber Ave HU9 142 C2
Forbes Ave HU6 140 C8
Ford Cl HU17 136 F4
Ford La DN20 108 F5
Fordlands YO8 48 B2
Fordlands Cres YO19 133 E5
Fordlands Rd YO19 133 E6
FORDON 2 A6
Fordon La
Willerby YO12 1 E7
Wold Newton YO25 2 A6
Ford's Ave 9 DN41 101 F5
Foredyke Ave HU7 141 A4
Foredyke Prim Sch HU9 142 A1
Forest Cl 27 YO32 13 E5
Forest Dr DN36 103 D1
Foresters Way YO16 123 A7
Foresters Wlk YO41 15 C1
Forester's Wlk YO24 129 B1
Forester Way HU4 144 D3
Forestgate YO32 127 C7
Forest Gr
Barlow YO8 63 D7
York YO31 130 F6
Forest La
Fulford YO19 26 A2
Strensall YO32 14 A8
Forest of Galtres Prim Sch YO30 12 F5
Forest Way
24 Humberston DN36 103 D1
York YO31 130 F6
Forge Cl
Bempton YO15 4 D4
Huntington YO32 128 A2
Melbourne YO42 39 B6
South Kelsey LN7 110 A1
8 Thorngumbald HU12 72 E5
Wheldrake YO19 38 A7
Forge Cres 3 DN39 86 A1
Forge Ct 18 HU12 72 E6
Forge Dr DN9 105 D7
Forge La YO19 37 A7
Forge Pl HU16 138 B7
Forge The YO25 124 E3
Forge Way 3 DN36 114 A6
Forkedale DN18 84 E8
Formby Cl HU16 139 E5
Forrester's Cl 2 DN6 76 E2
Forrester St 20 DN20 98 B2
Forster St 25 DN21 117 B1
Forsythia Ave 14 DN41 101 F5
Forsythia Dr 14 DN33 102 E1
Forth St YO26 129 F6
Fort Paull Battery* HU12 72 B4
Fort Terr 6 YO15 122 F2
Fortuna Way 2 DN37 102 B4
Fortune Cl HU8 141 F4
Forty Acre HU10 143 F7
Fortyfoot YO16 122 F4
Fortyfoot Ct YO16 122 E4
Fortyfoot Gr 1 YO16 122 F4
Forty Foot La DN39 99 F6
Forty Stps HU10 143 F7
Fosham Rd HU11 46 D2
Foss Bank YO31 156 C3
Foss Ct YO31 127 E1
Fossdale Cl HU8 141 E6
Fosse Hill Jet Ski Ctr* YO25 34 C1
Fossel Island Retail Park YO31 130 E5
Fosseway 29 DN21 117 C1
Foss Field La YO23 36 B8
Foss Garth YO41 27 F5
Fossgate YO1 156 C2
Foss Gr HU8 142 B6
Foss Islands Rd YO31 156 C3
Fossland View 4 YO32 14 A7
Fossway
Stamford Bridge YO41 15 D1
York YO31 130 D7
Foss Wlk YO26 129 B8
Fostergate YO8 48 A8
Foster Gate YO8 148 D4
FOSTERHOUSES 78 C1
Foster Rd 9 DN8 93 A8
Foster St HU8 141 A2
Foston Gr
Kingston upon Hull HU9 142 A1
4 York YO31 130 F8
Foston La
Beeford YO25 22 B1
North Frodingham YO25 21 F1
FOSTON ON THE WOLDS 22 A2
Fotherbie Garth 11 HU12 72 C7
FOTHERBY 121 D2
Fotherby Rd 4 DN17 96 C2
Fotherby St DN31 152 E5
Fotherby Wlk HU17 154 C4
Fothergill Dr 16 DN3 92 A2
Foundry Garth HU12 59 D1
Foundry La 5 WF11 61 A2
Foundry Sh Ctr The DN15 151 B7
Foundry The DN36 114 A1
Fountain Cl
Kingston upon Hull HU2 155 A4
Northfield HU13 143 C3
6 Waltham DN37 113 D7
Fountain Ct DN40 87 D1
Fountain Hill DN10 116 B3
Fountain Hill Rd DN10 116 B4
Fountain Rd HU2 140 E1
Fountain Road Ind Est HU2 155 C4
Fountains Ave YO16 122 D7
Fountain St
16 Caistor LN7 111 B4
Kingston upon Hull HU3 145 D6
Fountains Way HU15 53 D3
Fountayne Rd 13 YO14 2 F8
Fountayne St
Goole DN14 149 E5
Fountayne St *continued*
York YO31 130 C
Four Acre Cl HU10 143 C
Fourth Ave
Bridlington YO15 123 A
Fixborough Stather DN15 82 A
Goole DN14 149 C
Scunthorpe DN17 150 C
Ulrome YO25 23 B
York YO31 130 E
Fourways 9 DN36 114 D
Fowler Ct 3 DN15 83 A
Fowler Rd DN16 151 C
Fox Covert
Hibaldstow DN20 108 F
York YO31 127 F
Fox Covert La DN10 116 D
Fox Covert Rd WF8 76 C
Foxcroft 3 YO32 127 C
Fox Ct DN17 94 D
Foxdale Ave YO8 48 B
Fox Garth YO26 126 A
Fox Glade YO41 15 C
Foxglove Cl
22 Brigg DN20 98 B
16 Kingston upon Hull HU7 56 F
Foxglove Gdns 5 DN34 102 C
Foxhill DN37 102 E
Foxhill Cl HU9 142 E
Foxhill La YO8 148 A
Fox Hill La YO8 148 A
Foxhill Rd DN8 93 E
Foxhills Ind Pk DN15 96 C
Foxhills Rd DN15 96 C
Foxhills Sch & Tech Coll DN15 96 C
Fox Hill (Tumulus)* YO25 21 D
FOXHOLES 1 D
Foxholme Rd HU7 141 D
Fox La
Chapel Haddlesey YO8 62 C
Hambleton LS25 61 D
Laxton DN14 65 E
Thorpe Willoughby YO8 48 E
Fox St DN15 150 F
Foxthorn Paddock YO10 131 D
Foxton Cl YO24 132 C
Foxton Way DN20 98 C
Foxwood La 3 YO24 129 C
Foynes Gn 6 HU8 142 C
FRAISTHORPE 22 F
Frampton Cl HU7 141 E
Frances Ct 8 DN37 113 D
Frances St
Scunthorpe DN15 151 A
York YO10 130 D
Francis Askew Prim Sch HU4 144
Francis Ave 10 HU19 75 A
Francis Ct 7 YO8 48
Francis Scaipe Sports Ctr YO42 29 A
Francis St HU2 155
Francis Terr YO25 124
Francis Way 3 HU12 74 D
Frankfield DN14 78
Frankland Cl DN20 98
Frankland Pl DN35 153 D
Franklin Coll DN34 152
Franklin Cres DN16 151
Franklin Mews 17 DN18 69
Franklin Rd DN21 107
Franklin St HU9 146
Franklin Way DN39 99
Frank Walsham Ct DN32 153
Fraser St DN32 152
Frazer Ct YO30 129
Frederick Gough Sch DN16 96
Frederick Holmes Sch HU6 140
Frederick St
Cleethorpes DN35 153
Goole DN14 149
Grimsby DN31 152
Frederick Ward Way DN31 152
Frederic St YO30 156
Freehold St HU3 145
Freeman Ave 4 HU15 68
Freeman Ct DN36 114
Freemans La DN20 84
Freeman St DN32 152
Freeman Way 1 DN32 152
Freeport Hornsea Outlet Village HU18 134
Freeschool La or Gr DN14 52
Freeston St DN35 153
Freetown Ct HU6 140
Freetown Way HU2 155
Freightliner Rd HU3 144
Fremantle Ave HU9 142
Frensham Cl 9 HU7 56
Fresh Fields 12 HU15 68
Freshney Bog* DN34 102
Freshney Dr DN31 152
Freshney Pl 9 DN31 152
Freshney Place Sh Ctr DN31 152
Friargate YO1 156
Friargate Theatre YO1 156
Friars Cl YO19 26
Friars La HU17 154
Friars Mdw YO8 148
Friars Rd DN17 150
Friar's Wlk YO31 130
Friary Ct 5 HU3 140

riary Walk HU17 154 B2
RIDAYTHORPE 18 B6
riendship Ct 2 YO8 148 C6
rith Mews 4 YO8 148 C6
robisher Ave DN32 153 B2
RODINGHAM 151 B6
rodingham Inf Sch DN15 151 B6
rodingham La HU12 74 D4
rodingham Nature Reserve* DN15 150 E6
rodingham Rd
Brandesburton YO25 34 B4
Scunthorpe DN15 151 A8
rodingham South Rd DN16 151 E5
rodsham St HU9 147 B7
roebel House Sch HU5 140 C1
rome Rd HU8 142 C7
ront La HU12 59 A3
ront St
Alkborough DN15 82 C8
Burton Fleming YO25 2 E3
East Stockwith DN21 116 E5
Elsham DN20 98 F7
Gainsborough DN21 117 A2
Grasby DN38 110 E7
Langtoft YO25 8 C5
Laxton DN14 65 E4
Lockington YO25 32 B2
Middleton YO25 31 C4
Naburn YO19 36 D8
Ulceby DN39 86 A1
Wold Newton YO25 2 A4
York YO24 129 C3
roscoles Cl 6 HU15 53 D3
rusher Ave 7 DN33 102 E2
ryston 11 HU15 68 C6
ryston Comm La LS25 61 A8
uchsia Croft DN15 150 F6
uchsia Dr HU4 144 B2
ulbeck Rd DN16 151 C2
ULFORD 133 E7
ulford Cres
Kingston upon Hull HU10 144 A8
1 New Holland DN19 70 E2
ulford Cross YO10 130 D1
ulfordgate YO10 133 E7
ulford Gr HU9 142 E2
ulford Ind Est YO10 130 C1
ulford Mews YO10 133 E6
ulford Pk YO10 133 D7
ulford Rd YO10 133 D8
ulford Sch YO10 133 E7
ulham La DN14 76 E7
ulham Pk 2 DN33 102 D1
uller St DN35 153 D4
ULL SUTTON 16 A2
ulmar Cl HU7 141 D8
ULSTOW 121 E8
ulstow Gr 22 DN33 102 D2
ulstow Prim Sch LN11 121 E8
urlong Rd 23 YO41 15 D2
urness Cl 8 HU7 57 A7
urness Dr YO30 126 E1
urniss Ct 25 DN18 84 E8
urnwood 2 YO32 127 D7
urze Rd HU12 60 B2
ussey Gdns DN20 84 C1
ylingdales Ave 6 YO30 126 E1

G

able Pk YO23 24 C6
ables Cl 8 DN14 61 D4
adwall Cl 2 HU15 52 F1
adwall Way DN16 151 F1
ainas Ave DN21 117 B1
ainford Gr HU9 142 E2
ainford Rd DN8 79 B2
ainford Sq 18 DN8 79 B2
ain Hills Balk YO16 10 D4
AINSBOROUGH 117 C2
ainsborough Castle* DN21 117 C2
ainsborough Cl YO32 14 B8
ainsborough La DN20 108 F8
ainsborough Rd
Blyton DN21 117 E4
20 Kirton in Lindsey DN21 108 B1
Scotter DN21 107 B3
ainsthorpe Road E DN21 108 D4
ainsthorpe Road W DN21 108 C4
alecarr La YO42 39 E6
ale Farm Ct 6 YO24 129 C3
alegate YO43 53 E7
alegate Mews 13 YO43 53 F7
ale La
Thorganby YO19 37 F4
York YO24 129 C2
ale The YO19 36 D4
alfrid Rd HU11 142 F7
allagher Ret Pk DN15 150 A7
allands Cl HU14 69 A7
alleon Ct HU9 145 C6
alley Ct HU9 146 C6
alliard Cl 11 HU3 145 A4
alligap La YO10 131 C4
allops The YO24 132 B8
alloway Ct 4 YO25 124 F4
alloway La 3 YO25 124 F4
allows Bridge Rd HU11 59 A7
allows Hill* YO25 9 A2
allows La HU17 136 D5
almanhoe La YO30 156 A3

Galtres Ave YO31 131 B7
Galtres Gr YO30 129 F7
Galtres Rd YO31 131 B7
Gandhi Wy HU1 155 C2
GANSTEAD 57 F5
Ganstead Gr HU9 142 A2
Ganstead La HU11 142 D6
GANTON 1 A8
Ganton Ave HU16 139 A5
Ganton Ct 3 HU8 142 B5
Ganton Hill YO12 1 B7
Ganton Pl YO24 132 E7
Ganton Rd YO25 1 C4
Ganton Sch HU5 144 A7
Ganton Way HU10 143 F8
Gant Wlk 7 YO8 148 D5
Gap Cres YO14 3 D7
Gap Rd YO14 3 D8
Garbett Way 1 YO23 133 B3
Garburn Gr 3 YO30 126 E1
Garbutt Cl 2 HU12 58 D1
Garbutt Gr YO26 129 D5
Garbutt Pl 3 DN35 103 D2
Garden Ct
Selby YO8 148 B6
York YO26 129 C5
Garden Dr DN36 114 A8
Gardeners Cl 8 YO23 132 B3
Gardeners Row YO25 7 B3
Garden Flats La YO19 26 E7
Garden La 11 WF11 61 A3
Garden Pl YO1 156 C2
Garden Rd 23 DN8 79 B2
Garden St
14 Brigg DN20 98 C2
Grimsby DN32 152 D3
York YO31 156 B4
Gardens The HU3 145 C5
Garden Way YO26 129 C5
Garden Wlk 12 YO15 122 E2
GARDHAM 42 D5
Gardham La YO25 35 A6
Gardham Rd HU17 42 E5
Gare La DN14 66 A6
Garends Rd 4 YO15 5 A2
Garfield Cl HU9 142 D1
Garfield St 21 DN21 117 B1
Garfield Terr YO26 129 F5
Garibaldi St DN32 152 F5
Garland Cl HU9 142 C4
Garland St 2 YO26 129 E4
Garlands The YO30 130 A8
Garman Carr La YO8 48 D6
Garner St DN32 152 E2
Garnet Gr 6 HU3 145 A4
Garnet Terr YO26 129 E5
Garnett St DN35 153 D4
Garrick Cl
Brayton YO8 148 B1
Kingston upon Hull HU8 141 F4
15 Pocklington YO42 29 A3
Garrick La 21 DN36 114 A8
Garrison Rd HU9 155 C1
Garrison St YO15 122 F2
Garroway Way YO10 26 A4
Garrowby Hill YO41 16 F3
Garrowby Rd YO42 16 F2
Garrowby St YO41 16 E3
Garrowby View 5 YO41 15 D2
Garrowby Wlk HU5 139 C2
Garrow Hill YO10 130 F2
Garrow Hill Ave YO10 131 A3
Garth Ave
Kingston upon Hull HU11 58 A3
4 North Duffield YO8 50 A7
Garth Cl 6 YO8 48 D6
Garth Ct YO32 128 A4
Garth End YO32 127 F4
Garthends La
3 Hemingbrough YO8 49 F1
Mappleton HU11 47 B5
Garth Ends Rd HU17 43 A2
Garth La
Goole DN14 65 C4
Grimsby DN31 152 D4
Garth Mill 1 DN14 61 D4
GARTHORPE 81 F6
Garthorpe Rd
Luddington & Haldenby DN17 81 C4
Twin Rivers DN14 81 E7
Garth Rd YO32 127 F4
Garths End
20 Haxby YO32 13 F5
Pocklington YO42 29 A4
Garth's End YO10 133 E8
Garths End La YO42 29 A8
Garth Terr YO30 130 B7
Garth The HU16 139 A5
Garthway
13 Holton le Clay DN36 114 A5
4 York YO32 127 D3
GARTON 59 E6
Garton Balk YO25 20 D8
Garton Gr
Grimsby DN32 153 A1
3 Kingston upon Hull HU5 144 C7
Garton Hill YO25 19 E7
Garton La 2 YO14 2 F8
GARTON-ON-THE-WOLDS 20 A6
Garton-on-the-Wolds CE Prim Sch YO25 20 A6
Garton Rd HU11 47 C1
Garton Slack YO25 19 D6
Garvey Way 34 HU12 72 D7
Gascoigne Wlk YO23 156 B1

Gashouse La DN9 106 B3
Gas House La 16 DN14 65 B7
GATEFORTH 62 A7
Gateforth Mews YO8 61 F8
Gateforth New Rd YO8 62 A8
Gate-Goole Arts Theatre The* DN14 149 B4
Gatehead La YO42 38 D7
GATE HELMSLEY 15 B2
Gatehouse* DN39 86 B5
Gatehouse Rd DN19 85 F7
Gatehowe Rd YO17 17 A7
Gate La 11 DN33 102 E1
Gateland Cl YO32 127 C7
Gateland Field La DN14 64 B6
Gatesby Rd DN14 149 C6
Gate Way DN31 152 C6
Gateway to Humberside Trading Est HU15 66 E7
Gatewood La DN7 92 E2
Gatherums The DN35 153 E1
Gatwick Garth 15 HU7 57 A5
Gaufer Hill YO43 41 D3
Gautry La DN9 106 B4
Gayles Mews 3 HU5 139 D3
Gay Mdws YO32 14 D2
Gayton Rd DN35 103 D2
Gdns The HU7 141 D5
Gdn Village The YO32 128 A8
Gedney Cl 8 DN37 102 B4
Geeseness La DN7 78 D2
Gee St HU3 145 C5
Geldof Rd YO32 127 F1
GEMBLING 22 A3
Gembling La YO25 22 A4
Gembling Prim Sch YO25 22 A3
Gemel Rd HU12 59 C2
Gemsbok Way 3 HU4 144 D2
Gemtec Ctr The HU3 145 A7
General La YO42 38 E6
Genesis Way DN31 102 B6
Geneva Sq DN8 79 C2
Geneva Way
Kingston upon Hull HU7 141 B5
Sutton-on-Hull HU7 141 C5
George Ave DN17 95 D5
George Butler Cl 16 DN37 101 F1
George Cayley Dr YO30 127 A3
George Ct YO31 156 C3
George Hudson St YO1 156 B2
George Janney Ct DN32 153 A5
George La HU17 55 D8
George Mews 8 LN7 111 B4
George Odey Ct HU17 154 B2
George St
2 Barton-upon-Humber DN18 84 F8
Beverley HU17 154 B3
Bridlington YO15 122 C1
Broughton DN20 97 D3
Cleethorpes DN35 153 E1
Cottingham HU16 139 A7
Gainsborough DN21 117 A1
Great Driffield YO25 124 E4
Grimsby DN31 152 D3
28 Hedon HU12 72 C7
Keadby DN17 95 D5
Kingston upon Hull HU1 155 B2
11 Kirton in Lindsey DN21 108 B1
Pocklington YO42 29 A4
Scunthorpe DN15 151 A8
4 Selby YO8 148 D6
Snaith DN14 63 C1
7 Wistow YO8 48 D6
3 Withernsea HU19 74 F7
York YO1 156 C1
George Terr 1 YO8 49 B4
Georgian Mews
Bridlington YO15 122 C1
4 Great Driffield YO25 124 F3
Georgian Way YO15 122 C1
Georgina Ct 8 DN18 84 E8
Gerard Ave YO31 131 A5
Germain Rd YO8 148 E4
German Nook La HU17 56 D8
Germany La YO10 133 E6
Gershwin Ave HU4 144 B4
Gertrude St DN32 152 E1
Gervase St DN15 151 A7
Gibbon La DN8 92 F7
Gibraltar La DN37 101 F1
Gibraltar Way HU7 56 E5
Gibson La
36 Hedon HU12 72 D7
Welton HU14 68 E4
Gibson Lane N HU14 68 F5
Gibson Lane S HU14 68 F5
Gibson Rd
Caenby Corner Estate DN21 119 C1
4 Moorland Prison DN7 104 A8
Gibson St
Great Driffield YO25 124 E5
Kingston Upon Hull HU2 155 B4
Gifford Cl HU7 57 A6
GILBERDYKE 66 C8
Gilberdyke Prim Sch HU15 66 D8
Gilberdyke Sta HU15 66 D7
Gilbert St YO16 122 D3
Gilbey Rd DN31 152 B5
Gildane HU6 139 E8
Gilderidge Park 20 HU7 56 E5
Giles Ave YO31 131 A5
Giles St DN35 153 E2
Gillamoor Ave YO31 131 B5
Gillamoor Cl 16 HU8 141 E7

Gillann St 15 WF11 61 A2
Gillatts Cl DN20 98 D4
Gill Ct 25 DN33 102 D1
Gillett St HU3 145 B4
Gilliatt St DN15 151 A7
Gilling Mews 4 HU5 139 D3
Gillingwood Rd YO30 126 F3
Gillshill Prim Sch HU8 141 D5
Gillshill Rd HU8 141 D4
Gillus La 5 YO15 4 D3
Gillygate YO31 156 B3
Gillyon Cl 3 HU17 137 B3
Gipsey Cnr YO19 26 E3
Gipsy La DN9 116 F8
GIPSYVILLE 144 E3
Girton Cl 5 DN16 96 D2
Girton Rd 9 DN34 102 C3
Girvan Cl YO24 132 B7
Gisburn Rd HU13 143 F2
Givendale Cl 2 YO16 122 F7
Givendale Gr 3 YO10 131 C4
Givendale Hill YO42 29 C6
Givendale La YO42 29 A8
Glade Rd YO19 37 B2
Glade The
Beverley HU17 137 B3
Escrick YO19 37 A6
Owthorne HU19 74 F6
York YO31 131 B7
Gladstone Dr DN16 151 C5
Gladstone St
Hessle HU13 143 E1
Kingston upon Hull HU3 145 C6
York YO24 129 D3
York YO31 156 C4
Gladstone Terr 6 YO15 122 F3
Glaisby Ct YO31 131 A6
Glaisdale YO24 132 D7
Glaisdale Cl 6 YO16 122 F7
Glaisdale Gr HU9 146 F8
Glaisdale Rd
Knapton YO26 24 F7
Scunthorpe DN16 151 E1
Glamis Rd HU13 143 F2
Glanford Gr 6 DN19 85 D8
Glanford Park (Scunthorpe United FC) DN15 150 A6
Glanford Rd
23 Brigg DN20 98 C2
Scunthorpe DN17 96 C2
Glanford Way DN15 150 B7
Glanville Ave DN17 150 F4
Glanville Cres DN17 150 F4
Glasgow St HU3 145 A5
Glass House Row HU8 141 A1
Glebe Ave
Full Sutton YO41 16 A2
York YO26 129 D5
Glebe Cl
Burton upon Stather DN15 82 A5
5 Holton le Clay DN36 114 A6
3 Strensall YO32 14 B7
2 Wawne HU7 56 E7
Glebe Farm HU7 56 E7
Glebe Garth 3 YO8 49 B5
Glebe Gdns YO25 22 D1
Glebelands HU12 59 D2
Glebe Lands The 4 YO43 135 E4
Glebe Rd
Brigg DN20 98 C2
Campsall DN6 76 E1
Cleethorpes DN35 153 E2
Grimsby DN33 102 F1
Humberston DN36 114 C8
Kingston upon Hull HU7 141 A4
Scunthorpe DN15 151 B8
Thorne/Moorends DN8 93 B8
Wawne HU7 56 E7
Glebe Retail Park DN15 151 B8
Glebe Way
Barton-upon-Humber DN18 85 A8
26 Haxby YO32 13 E5
Glede Farm Way LN7 111 B3
Glen Almond HU11 142 D6
Glen Ave YO31 130 E5
Glen Cl YO10 133 E6
Glencoe Cl 22 DN7 92 D4
Glencoe St
Kingston upon Hull HU3 144 F6
1 York YO30 130 B7
Glencourt HU6 139 E6
Glen Cres YO42 39 A7
Glendale Cl HU10 138 C1
Gleneagles 15 DN37 113 D6
Gleneagles Cres 4 DN19 70 E2
Gleneagles Pk HU8 141 F6
Glenfell Cl HU7 141 D5
Glenfield Ave YO43 135 D4
Glenfield Dr HU10 138 B1
Glenfield Rd DN37 102 B4
Glen Hall Rise 11 DN19 85 C8
Glenham Dr HU10 143 E7
Glenholme Ct YO25 32 E7
Glen Rd YO31 130 E5
Glenridding YO24 132 D7
Glenrock Pk HU15 68 B6
Glen The
Beverley HU17 137 B2
Kingston upon Hull HU10 138 B1
Glenville Cl YO25 33 F8
Glenwood Cl HU8 141 C3
Glenwood Dr 2 HU4 144 B6
Glews Hollow Bsns Enterprise Pk DN14 149 B2
Glimpse The YO16 123 A7
Globe Mews HU17 154 A3

Gloria Way 3 DN37 102 B4
Glossop Rd DN15 150 B6
Gloucester Ave
Grimsby DN34 102 D2
Scunthorpe DN16 151 B3
Gloucester Ct 4 DN15 96 D7
Gloucester Rd HU10 138 E2
Gloucester St HU4 144 E3
Glover Rd DN17 150 E4
Glovers Ave DN17 95 D4
Goathead La DN14 78 E8
Goathland Cl HU3 145 A6
Goble Cl DN18 85 A8
Godbold Cl HU17 154 C3
Goddard Ave HU5 140 B2
Goddard Cl 9 DN18 84 E8
Godfrey Rd 11 DN8 93 A8
Godman's La HU10 143 B8
Godnow Rd DN17 94 C6
Godwinsway 18 YO41 15 D2
Goldcrest Cl
1 Kingston upon Hull HU7 141 D8
Scunthorpe DN15 96 B7
Golden Ct 10 HU9 142 A3
Golden Gr HU11 142 D6
Goldgarth DN32 153 A1
Goldings The DN9 105 D2
Gold Thread La 5 YO8 48 B8
Golf Course La DN37 113 E5
Golf Links Dr HU15 68 B6
Golf Links Rd HU6 139 E5
Gollands La DN9 105 B2
Goodfell Rd HU17 137 A6
Goodhand Cl DN18 85 A8
Goodhart Rd HU7 141 B8
GOODMANHAM 135 F7
Goodmanham Rd
Market Weighton YO43 135 D5
Middleton YO25 31 C3
Goodmanham Way 6 HU16 138 E6
Goodramgate YO1 156 B2
Goodrich Cl HU2 140 E1
Goodricke Way 5 YO10 131 A1
Goods Yd The YO8 148 D5
Goodwin Par 1 HU3 145 D5
Goodwood DN17 96 B2
Goodwood Cl HU17 136 E6
Goodwood Gr YO24 129 F1
Goodwood La 32 DN35 103 C1
GOOLE 149 C3
Goole Coll DN14 149 B4
Goole & District Hospl DN14 149 C6
Goole L Ctr DN14 149 D3
Goole Mus* DN14 149 D4
Goole Rd
Goole DN14 65 C3
Swinefleet DN14 80 C8
Goole Sta DN14 149 C4
Gooseacre DN17 107 D7
Goosenook La HU17 45 A8
Gordan Pk HU16 139 C6
Gordon Gdns DN33 113 E8
Gordon Rd YO16 122 C4
Gordon St
Goole DN14 149 C4
4 Kingston upon Hull HU3 145 B5
York YO10 130 E3
Gordons Terr YO25 124 E4
Gore La DN14 77 B5
Goring Pl DN35 153 D3
Gormire Ave 2 YO31 127 E2
Gorse Cl
32 Bottesford DN16 96 E2
Hatfield DN7 92 C3
Selby YO8 148 C2
Gorsedale HU7 140 E7
Gorse Hill 1 YO19 26 F7
Gorse Paddock YO32 127 F2
Gorthorpe HU6 140 A8
Gorton Rd HU10 143 E7
Gorton St DN31 152 F6
Gosport Rd DN34 152 A2
Gosport Wlk HU4 144 A4
Gossips Wood Rd DN14 79 B8
Gothenburg Way HU7 140 E6
Goths La HU17 154 B4
Gott Cl YO25 124 C2
Gouldesborough Ct 2 HU5 140 C3
Goulding Ct HU17 154 A3
Goulton St HU3 145 B3
Gouthwaith Cl YO30 126 F2
Government House Rd YO30 130 A6
Government St 1 DN14 149 D4
GOWDALL 63 A1
Gowdall Broach DN14 77 E8
Gowdall La
Pollington DN14 77 F7
Snaith & Cowick DN14 63 B1
Gowdall Rd DN14 62 E2
Gowdall Way 1 DN14 65 A7
Gower Rd
Kingston upon Hull HU4 144 B3
York YO24 132 E8
GOWTHORPE 16 C1
Gowthorpe YO8 148 C5
Gowthorpe La DN14 66 E4
GOXHILL 86 B8
Goxhill Gdns 17 DN34 102 C2
Goxhill Prim Sch DN19 86 A8

Goxhill Rd DN19 85 E8
Goxhill Sta DN19 85 F8
Grafton St
Grimsby DN32 153 A5
Kingston upon Hull HU5 140 C2
Gragdale Cl HU8 141 E7
Graham Ave HU4 144 C2
Graingers Rd HU18 134 D3
GRAINSBY 113 F2
Grainsby Ave
Cleethorpes DN35 103 B2
Holton le Clay DN36 114 B5
Grainsby Healing* DN36 113 F3
Grainsby La
Grainsby DN36 113 E1
Tetney DN36 114 D3
Grains Gate LN11 115 E1
GRAISELOUND 105 C1
Graizelound Fields Rd DN9 105 D1
Grammar School La DN20 98 C3
Grammar School Rd
Brigg DN20 98 C2
Kingston upon Hull HU5 139 E2
Grammar School Road S 7 DN20 98 C2
Grammar School Wlk DN16 96 E2
Grammar School Yd HU1 155 B1
Grampian Cl 4 YO32 127 F5
Grampian Way
23 Grimsby DN33 113 E8
Kingston upon Hull HU7 57 A6
Thorne/Moorends DN8 93 A7
Grampion Sh Ctr HU7 57 A6
Granary Cl DN21 117 A3
Granary Croft 7 DN9 105 D2
Granary Ct
Elloughton HU15 68 C7
York YO1 156 B3
Granary Fold DN21 107 C4
Granary The DN21 107 C4
Grandale HU7 140 E7
Grand Opera House York* YO1 156 B2
GRANGE 152 A1
Grange Ave
12 Barton-upon-Humber DN18 84 E8
Hatfield DN7 92 D4
14 Laceby DN37 101 F1
Misterton DN10 116 D5
Grange Cl
2 Buckton/Bempton YO15 4 C3
Full Sutton YO41 16 A2
5 Hatfield DN7 92 D4
Kingston upon Hull HU2 155 B4
Misterton DN10 116 D4
Skelton YO30 126 B5
Grange Cres
Kingston upon Hull HU10 143 E6
Tickton HU17 137 F8
Grange Ct 7 DN9 105 B2
Grange Dr
Kingston upon Hull HU16 139 A7
Misterton DN10 116 D4
Grange Farm Cl YO8 49 B5
Grange Farm La 20 DN36 114 A7
Grange Field DN20 98 D8
Grange Garth
10 Wistow YO8 48 D6
York YO10 130 D2
Grange Gr 3 DN8 79 B2
Grange Ind Est DN15 151 D4
Grange Ind Est The DN14 149 B4
Grange Jun & Inf Sch DN34 102 C3
Grange La
Covenham St Bartholomew LN11 121 F6
Molescroft HU17 137 A7
North Kelsey LN7 110 A3
Rufforth YO26 129 A2
Utterby LN11 121 C4
Grangeland Wlk YO42 28 E3
Grange Lane Inf Sch DN16 151 D1
Grange Lane Jun Sch DN16 151 D1
Grange Lane N DN16 151 D3
Grange Lane S
25 Bottesford DN16 96 E2
Scunthorpe DN16 151 D1
Grange Park La HU10 138 B2
Grange Pk
1 Brough HU15 68 C5
Gainsborough DN21 117 A3
2 Kirk Sandall DN3 92 A2
Swanland HU14 69 B6
Granger Ave YO26 129 C4
Grange Rd
3 Bridlington YO16 122 D5
8 Campsall DN6 76 E1
Gainsborough DN21 117 D1
Garthorpe & Fockerby DN14 81 E8
Goole DN14 149 B4
7 Leconfield HU17 43 D6
North Frodingham YO25 34 B6
Snaith DN14 78 C8
Thorne/Moorends DN8 79 B2
Thorngumbald HU12 72 F5
Granger's Yd 8 HU18 134 C4
Grangeside Ave HU6 139 F5
Grange St YO10 130 D2
Grange Way HU17 136 E7
Grange Wlk
Grimsby DN34 152 A2
Misterton DN10 116 D5
GRANSMOOR 22 C6
Gransmoor La YO25 22 A5
Gransmoor Rd YO25 22 D5
Grantchester Cl HU5 139 C1
Grantham Ave
Grimsby DN33 102 E1
11 Kingston upon Hull HU7 56 F6
Grantham Dr YO26 129 E4
Grantley Gr HU9 142 C2
Grants Ave YO10 133 E8
Grant St
Cleethorpes DN31 153 E3
Grimsby DN31 153 B5
GRANT THOROLD 153 A4
Granville Rd 1 DN15 96 D7
Granville St
Grimsby DN32 152 F2
1 Kingston upon Hull HU3 145 A6
Granville Terr 4 YO10 130 E3
Grape La YO1 156 B3
GRASBY 110 E7
Grasby All Saints CE Prim Sch DN38 110 E8
Grasby Cres DN37 102 B4
Grasby Rd
Great Limber DN37 100 C3
Kingston upon Hull HU8 142 A4
North Kelsey LN7 110 D5
Scunthorpe DN17 150 E1
Grasby Wold La DN38 110 F8
Grasmere Cl
Gainsborough DN21 117 C1
Goole DN14 149 D5
Grasmere Dr YO10 131 B4
Grasmere Gr
Bridlington YO16 122 E7
11 Humberston DN36 103 C1
5 York YO30 126 F1
Grassam Cl 3 HU12 58 D1
Grassdale Pk 3 HU15 68 B5
Grassholme YO24 132 C7
Grassington Cl 11 HU7 57 A6
Grassmoor Ct 2 DN15 150 B6
Gravelhill La DN14 76 F7
Gravelholes La DN10 116 C4
Gravel Pit Hill DN20 109 D6
Gravelpit La
Kirkburn YO25 19 F1
Sancton YO43 41 E2
Gravel Pit La
Kirmington DN39 100 A6
Yaddlethorpe DN17 96 C1
Gravel Pit Rd
Barton-upon-Humber DN18 84 D8
Scotter DN21 107 C4
Graves La YO42 39 B6
Grayburn Ct HU17 154 A3
Grayburn La HU17 154 A2
Gray Friars DN37 102 B4
GRAYINGHAM 119 B7
Grayingham Rd 19 DN21 108 B1
Grayling Cl 15 DN37 102 B4
Gray Rd DN17 150 D2
Grays Croft HU12 59 C2
Grayshon Dr YO26 129 B5
Gray St
Goole DN14 149 C5
York YO23 156 A1
Greame Rd YO16 123 A5
Great Barn St 4 YO16 122 D5
Great Cl YO8 48 B8
GREAT COATES 102 B5
Great Coates Prim Sch DN37 102 B5
Great Coates Rd
Grimsby DN37 102 B4
Healing DN41 101 F5
Great Coates Sta DN37 102 B5
GREAT COWDEN 47 A5
Great Field La HU9 147 C7
GREAT GIVENDALE 29 B8
Great Grimsby Bsns Pk DN37 102 C6
Great Gutter La HU10 55 C1
Great Gutter Lane E HU10 138 C2
Great Gutter Lane W HU10 138 A2
GREAT HATFIELD 46 D6
Great Hatfield Rd HU11 46 D4
GREAT HECK 77 D7
GREAT KELK 22 A5
GREAT KENDALE 20 D7
GREAT LIMBER 100 D3
Great Meadow Rd YO16 122 E5
Great North Way YO26 129 B8
Great Passage St HU1 155 A1
Great Stather Cl DN15 82 A5
Great Thornton St HU3 145 D6
GREAT TOWS 120 A1
Great Union St HU9 155 C3
Grebe Rd HU15 52 F1
Greek St HU3 144 F5
Greenacre 23 HU12 73 C4
Greenacre Cl
Dunsville DN7 92 D2
Pocklington YO42 29 B3
Greenacre Pk
Gilberdyke HU15 66 D8
Greenacre Pk *continued*
Hornsea HU18 134 C1
Greenacres
4 Swanland HU14 69 C7
York YO32 127 F4
Green Acres HU10 143 C6
Greenacres Cl 8 YO8 48 D1
Greenacres Cres 7 YO8 48 D1
Greenacres Dr 4 YO8 48 D1
Greenacres Gr 3 YO8 48 D1
Greenacres Pk HU12 60 B1
Green Balk YO42 17 D1
Green Bank DN8 93 D6
Green Cl
Kingston upon Hull HU6 139 F6
York YO30 130 A8
Greencliffe Dr YO30 130 A6
Greencroft Ct 14 YO19 26 F7
Greencroft La 17 YO19 26 F7
Greendale DN17 107 D7
Greendale Ct HU16 138 E5
Green Dike YO32 127 C8
Green Dikes La YO25 8 F1
Green Dykes La YO10 130 F3
Greenfield Cl 6 DN3 92 A3
Greenfield Dr
6 Brayton YO8 48 D1
Hibaldstow DN20 109 A5
Greenfield Garth 5 HU6 56 D5
Greenfield La YO25 31 C4
Greenfield Park Dr YO31 131 A7
Greenfield Rd
Bridlington YO16 122 B2
Middleton-on-the-Wolds YO25 31 C4
Greenfields
Pollington DN14 77 F6
York YO31 130 D7
Greenfinch Dr 8 DN35 103 C1
Greengales Ct YO19 38 A8
Greengales La YO19 38 A8
Greengarth DN17 96 C1
Greengate DN9 105 E6
Greengate La
Cliffe YO8 49 F6
2 Goxhill DN19 86 A8
Greengate Rd WF8 76 C1
Greenhill 8 DN20 97 D3
Green Hill 10 DN35 103 B2
Greenhill Rd DN9 105 C2
Green Hills YO60 15 B7
Greenhoe Rd DN17 96 B2
Greenholme Bank DN9 105 A6
Greenhow Cl HU8 141 E7
Green Island HU11 142 E5
Green La
Acomb YO24 129 D2
Appleton Roebuck YO23 36 B6
Barmby on the Marsh DN14 64 A6
Barrow upon Humber DN19 85 D8
Belton DN9 94 D2
Brigsley DN37 113 D4
Broughton DN20 97 E3
Buckton/Bempton YO15 4 D3
Cottingham HU16 138 E6
Cottingwith YO42 38 C5
Fimber YO25 18 F6
Hatfield DN7 92 E1
Heck DN14 77 D8
Kingston upon Hull HU2 155 B4
Langtoft YO25 8 D5
Ludborough DN36 121 B6
Moor Monkton YO26 24 A8
Nafferton YO25 125 D7
North Duffield YO8 49 F8
North Kelsey LN7 110 A4
Pilham DN21 118 A4
Rawcliffe YO30 127 A1
Selby YO8 148 A3
Skidby HU10 138 B4
South Cave HU15 53 D1
Sutton Ings HU13 144 A1
Swine HU11 57 E7
Tibthorpe YO25 19 D2
Tickton HU17 137 F8
Weaverthorpe YO25 8 A8
Wetwang YO25 18 D5
Wigginton YO32 13 D5
Wressle DN14 64 D8
Greenland La DN14 78 F7
Greenlands YO25 124 F5
Greenlands Ave 13 DN36 114 A7
Greenlands La YO8 48 C3
Green Lane Trading Est YO30 127 A1
Green Marsh Rd HU12 72 E4
Green Mdws YO31 131 A7
Greenoak La DN14 66 B7
Green Rd
Gringley on the Hill DN10 116 A1
15 Hedon HU12 72 C7
Greensborough Ave 3 YO26 129 B5
Greens Cl 9 DN15 151 B7
Greenshaw Dr YO32 127 C8
Greenshaw La HU12 74 D1
Greenside
18 Dunnington YO19 26 F7
8 Flamborough YO15 5 A2
Greenside Cl 24 YO19 26 F7
Greenside Wlk 23 YO19 26 F7
Greens La
Burstwick HU12 73 B8
Burton Pidsea HU12 59 C1
Wawne HU7 56 E7
Green's Rd DN7 92 C3
Greenstiles La HU14 69 C7
Green Sward YO31 131 A8
Green The
Barmby Moor YO42 28 D3
5 Brough HU15 68 D6
20 Dunnington YO19 26 F7
Great Driffield YO25 125 A4
Lund YO25 31 F3
7 Market Weighton YO43 135 D4
Rawcliffe DN14 64 A1
20 Scotter DN21 107 C3
1 Skelton YO30 126 B5
Sproatley HU11 58 D5
Stillingfleet YO19 36 D3
1 Swanland HU14 69 B7
20 Thorne/Moorends DN8 93 A8
Wistow YO8 48 D6
York YO26 129 C3
Green Top Prim Sch 14 DN8 93 A7
Greenway
8 Barton-upon-Humber DN18 69 F1
10 Waltham DN37 113 E6
Green Way YO32 127 F4
Green Way Prim Sch The HU6 140 A6
Greenways
Great Driffield YO25 124 F5
2 North Ferriby HU14 69 A5
Greenways Cl YO16 122 F6
Green Ways Ct 2 YO8 48 D6
Greenways Dr 1 YO8 48 D6
Greenways Wlk YO16 122 F6
Greenway The
2 Haxby YO32 127 C7
Hornsea HU18 134 C2
1 Kingston upon Hull HU4 144 C6
Greenwich Ave HU9 142 C4
Greenwich Cl
3 Frodingham DN15 96 D7
5 York YO30 126 E3
Greenwood Ave
Beverley HU17 154 C3
Inglemire HU6 139 F6
Kingston upon Hull HU6 139 E5
Greenwood Gdns HU17 136 F7
Greenwood Gr YO24 132 C8
Greetham's La DN32 153 B1
Greet's Hill YO17 16 F7
GREETWELL 108 C7
Gregory Cl YO30 126 C5
Grenley St 8 WF11 61 A2
Grenville Bay HU11 142 D6
Gresley Ct 3 YO26 129 B4
Gresley Way DN40 87 D2
Greville Rd HU12 72 D7
Greyfriars Cres HU17 154 A1
Greyfriars Rd DN20 97 E3
Greygarth Cl 14 HU7 56 F6
GREY GREEN 94 E2
Greylees Ave 6 HU6 56 D5
Grey St
Gainsborough DN21 117 A1
Kingston upon Hull HU2 145 D7
Greystoke Rd YO30 126 E1
Greystone Ave HU5 144 E7
Greystone Ct YO32 127 C7
Greystones Rd DN21 117 A2
GRIBTHORPE 51 B6
Griffin Prim Sch HU9 142 C3
Griffin Rd HU9 142 C3
Griffiths Way 18 HU12 73 C4
Grime St DN31 152 E4
GRIMSBY 152 E2
Grimsby Auditorium* DN31 152 A4
Grimsby Docks Sta DN32 152 F5
Grimsby Institute of FE & HE DN34 152 C1
Grimsby Institute (The Towers International Ctr) The DN34 152 C2
Grimsby L Ctr DN31 152 A4
Grimsby Rd
Caistor LN7 111 C4
Cleethorpes DN35 153 D4
Fotherby LN11 121 D1
Humberston DN36 103 B1
Laceby DN37 101 F1
Swallow LN7 112 B6
Waltham DN37 113 E7
Grimsby Swimming Pool DN33 102 E2
Grimsby Town Sta DN31 152 D3
Grimscott Cl 2 HU7 56 F5
GRIMSTON 131 E3
Grimston Bar YO19 131 F4
Grimston Dr HU1 155 B3
Grimston Rd
12 Hunmanby YO14 3 A8
5 Kingston upon Hull HU10 143 F6
Grimston St HU1 155 B3
Grimthorpe Hill YO42 29 B7
Grimwith Garth YO30 126 F2
GRINDALE 3 D2
Grindale La YO16 122 A7
Grindale Rd
Bempton YO16 4 A3
Grindale YO16 3 E2
Grindell St HU9 146 D8
Gringley Rd DN10 116 B4
Grinsdale Rise YO25 125 F7
Grizedale HU7 140 F7
Grosmont Cl HU8 141 E7
Grosvenor Ave DN14 149 A5
Grosvenor Cres 2 DN32 152 D3
Grosvenor Ct DN7 92 D
Grosvenor House YO30 156 A
Grosvenor Pk YO30 156 A
Grosvenor Pl HU17 136 D
Grosvenor Rd
Hornsea HU18 134 D
York YO30 156 A
Grosvenor St
Grimsby DN32 152 D
Kingston upon Hull HU3 145 D
Grosvenor Street N DN15 151 A
Grosvenor Street S DN15 151 A
Grosvenor Terr YO30 156 A
Grove Cl HU17 154 B
Grove Cres DN35 153 C
Grove Ct YO25 124 F
Grove Gdns 12 YO26 12 F
GROVEHILL 137 C
Grovehill HU17 137 C
Grove Hill HU13 143 E
Grovehill Ind Est HU17 137 C
Grovehill Rd HU17 154 C
Grove House View HU5 140 D
Grove La DN37 113 E
Grovenor Ct 11 DN35 103 D
Grove Pk
7 Barlby YO8 49 B
Beverley HU17 154 A
Misterton DN10 116 C
Grove Rd DN7 92 D
Groves Ct YO31 156 C
Groves La YO31 156 C
Grove St DN21 108 A
Groves The
Great Driffield YO25 125 A
Kingston upon Hull HU4 144 B
Northfield HU4 144 B
Grove Terr La YO31 156 C
Grove The
Barrow upon Humber DN19 85 D
Beckingham DN10 116 D
Kellington DN14 62 A
York YO24 132 E
Grove View YO30 130 A
Grove Wharf* DN15 95 E
Grove Wood Rd DN10 116 C
Grove Wood Terr DN10 116 C
Grundale HU10 143 C
Grundell's Yd 4 YO16 122 D
Grundill La
Hatfield HU11 46 A
Seaton HU11 35 A
Guardians Rd 2 HU12 74 D
Guernsey Gr 1 DN40 101 C
Guest Field HU11 47 B
Guildford Ave HU8 141 D
Guildford Cl HU17 136 E
Guildford St 20 DN32 153 A
Guildhall Rd HU1 155 B
Guilicarr La LN7 109 E
Guisefield Rd 5 DN9 105 D
Gullane Dr 7 HU6 56 D
Gull Nook YO15 5 A
GUNBY 50 D
Gunby Pl 9 DN35 103 C
Gunby Rd
Bubwith YO8 50 D
Scunthorpe DN17 150 E
Gunbywood Rd YO8 50 D
GUNNESS 95 E
Gunness & Burringham CE Prim Sch DN17 95 E
Gunness La DN15 95 F
GUNTHORPE 117 A
Gunthorpe Rd DN9 116 F
Gurnell St DN15 151 A
Gurth Ave DN3 92 A
Gus Walker Dr YO42 29 B
Guy Garth 3 HU12 72 D
Guy's Cres 8 HU9 142 A
Gypsey Rd YO16 122 B

H

HABROUGH 100 E
Habrough Ct 9 DN40 86 E
Habrough La DN39 100 C
Habrough Rd
Immingham DN40 87 A
South Killingholme DN40 86 E
Habrough Sta DN40 100 E
Hackforth Wlk HU5 139 D
Hackness Gr 2 HU5 144 D
Haddlesey Rd WF11 61 D
Haddon Cl YO24 129 C
Haddon Rd YO16 122 D
Haddon St HU3 144 F
Hadds La DN8 78 F
Hadds Nook Rd DN8 78 F
Hadleigh Cl 4 HU2 140 E
Hadleigh Ct DN15 151 A
Hadleigh Gn 4 DN17 95 D
Hadleigh Rd DN40 87 C
Hadrian Ave YO10 131 B
Hagg La
Belton DN9 94 E
Cottingwith YO42 38 E
Dunnington YO19 26 F
Hemingbrough YO8 49 F
Haggs La
Fenwick DN6 77 D
Kingston upon Hull HU10 138 E
Haggwood Wlk YO19 26 F
Hag La YO42 38 C

ague Park La 12 YO25 . . 124 F4
aig Ave DN16 . . . . 151 B5
aigh Ct DN32 . . . . 102 F2
aigh La DN14 . . . . 77 A6
aigh St DN35 . . . . 103 D3
aig Rd DN8 . . . . 79 B2
aig St YO8 . . . . 148 B6
aile Rd DN36 . . . . 103 D1
ailgate DN14 . . . . 65 A7
ailgate Cl 8 DN14 . . . . 65 B7
ainsworth Pk HU6 . . . . . . 139 E5
ainton Ave DN32 . . . . 152 F2
AISTHORPE 10 C3
aith's La DN36 . . . . 114 B1
aldane Ct HU4 . . . . 144 D2
aldane St DN21 . . . . 117 A1
alecroft 24 HU7 . . . . 56 E5
ale Hill La DN7 . . . . 92 E3
ales Cl 3 DN16 . . . . 96 D1
ales Cres 12 HU12 . . . . 72 C7
ales Entry HU9 . . . . 146 C6
ales La YO8 . . . . 63 E5
aley's Terr YO31 . . . . 130 D8
alfacres La YO42 . . . . 40 A6
alf Acre Wood 1 DN17 . . 95 D4
alifax App DN20 . . . . 99 A8
alifax Ave DN14 . . . . 149 C6
alifax Cl
Full Sutton YO41 . . . . 16 A2
8 Pocklington YO42 . . . . 28 F4
alifax Ct 7 YO30 . . . . . . 127 A1
alifax Way
Elvington YO41 . . . . 27 A3
Pocklington YO42 . . . . 28 E3
alkon Cl DN17 . . . . 81 D3
alladale Cl 1 YO24 . . . . . 132 B7
ALLANDS THE 85 F7
allard Way 7 YO32 . . . . . . 14 B7
allbrook Ct 4 DN16 . . . . . 96 D1
all Cl
5 Airmyn DN14 . . . . 64 E4
Cawood YO8 . . . . 36 D1
Nafferton YO25 . . . . 125 E7
7 Snaith DN14 . . . . 78 C8
allcroft 1 DN39 . . . . 86 A1
allcroft La YO23 . . . . 132 A3
allcroft Rd 1 DN9 . . . . . 105 D2
all Ct DN17 . . . . 81 A3
aller St HU9 . . . . 146 E8
all Farm Cl 4 YO19 . . . . . 48 F8
all Farm Ct YO42 . . . . 16 F2
allfield Rd YO31 . . . . 130 E5
ALL GARTH 26 F6
allgarth DN36 . . . . 115 B2
all Garth YO8 . . . . 49 C4
allgarth Ave DN16 . . . . . . 151 B6
allgarth Way HU17 . . . . . 154 B2
allgate
Kingston upon Hull HU16 . 139 A6
10 Pocklington YO42 . . . . . . 29 A4
allgate Prim Sch HU16 . 139 B7
all Gdns
Rawcliffe DN14 . . . . 64 B2
Winterton DN15 . . . . 83 B5
alliwell Cl HU9 . . . . 147 E8
all La
Elsham DN20 . . . . 98 F7
Stainforth DN7 . . . . 92 A6
all Leys Park 22 HU7 . . . . 56 E5
all Mdw DN20 . . . . 84 C2
all Park Rd
Hunmanby YO14 . . . . 2 F8
Immingham DN40 . . . . 87 C2
all Pk
Swanland HU14 . . . . 69 C6
Wistow YO8 . . . . 49 A5
York YO10 . . . . 131 B1
all Rd
Goole DN14 . . . . 149 D1
Hornsea HU18 . . . . 134 D5
Kingston upon Hull HU6 . . 139 E5
Market Weighton YO43 . . . 135 D4
Sproatley HU11 . . . . 58 D5
all Rise
12 Haxby YO32 . . . . 13 F5
Messingham DN17 . . . . 107 D7
all Road Prim Sch HU6 . 139 F4
alls La
13 Keelby DN41 . . . . 101 A4
North Kelsey LN7 . . . . 110 A4
all Spinney The 5 DN14 . 65 B7
all Spout YO42 . . . . 28 D3
all's Rd DN10 . . . . 116 A2
all St HU2 . . . . 145 D7
all View DN17 . . . . 107 D7
all Way DN39 . . . . 99 F5
all Wlk
1 Brough HU15 . . . . 68 D6
Kingston upon Hull HU16 . . 139 B6
Walkington HU17 . . . . 55 B8
allytreeholme Rd YO25 . . 33 E3
ALSHAM 73 F6
altemprice L Ctr HU10 . . 143 E7
altemprice St HU3 . . . . . . 144 F5
alton Cl 5 DN21 . . . . 119 C8
alton Pl DN35 . . . . 103 B2
alton Way DN34 . . . . 102 D2
alyard Croft HU1 . . . . 155 B1
ambledon Cl HU7 . . . . 141 B6
ambleton Ave YO10 . . . . 131 C4
ambleton Terr YO31 . . . . 130 C7
ambleton View 10 YO32 . . 13 D5
ambleton Way YO32 . . . . 127 F3
ambling Dr HU17 . . . . . . 136 E7
amburg Rd HU7 . . . . 141 A5
amden Rd YO42 . . . . 28 E3
amerton Cl 11 YO14 . . . . . . 3 A8
amerton Rd 10 YO14 . . . . . . 3 A8

Hamilton Cl 7 DN34 . . . . . 102 B2
Hamilton Dr
Kingston upon Hull HU8 . . . 141 F6
York YO24 . . . . 129 E2
Hamilton Drive E YO24 . . . 129 F2
Hamilton Drive W YO24 . . 129 D2
Hamilton Hill Rd YO25 . . . . 23 A6
Hamilton Rd
Bridlington YO15 . . . . 122 D2
Scunthorpe DN17 . . . . 150 F4
Hamilton St DN32 . . . . 153 B5
Hamilton Way YO24 . . . . . 129 E2
Hamish Wlk 27 DN40 . . . . . . 87 B1
Hamlet The 8 DN14 . . . . . . 61 F2
Hamling Way HU4 . . . . . . 144 D2
Hamlyn Ave HU4 . . . . 144 E7
Hamlyn Dr HU4 . . . . 144 E6
Hammersike Rd YO8 . . . . . . 48 A4
Hammersmith Rd 1
HU8 . . . . 141 F5
Hammerton Cl 3 YO26 . . . 129 B3
Hammerton Rd 25 DN17 . . . 96 C2
Hammond Rd HU17 . . . . . . 154 C4
Hamont Rd DN32 . . . . 153 B3
Hampden Cres 1 DN7 . . 104 A8
Hampden St YO1 . . . . 156 B1
Hampshire St HU4 . . . . 144 E3
Hampson Gdns
19 Kirk Sandall DN3 . . . . 92 A2
York YO30 . . . . 130 B8
Hampstead Ct 6 HU3 . . . . 140 D1
Hampstead Pk 6 DN33 . . 102 D1
Hampston Cl HU6 . . . . 140 A7
Hampton Cl 18 DN35 . . . . 103 C1
Hampton Gdns YO30 . . . . 130 C8
Hampton Rd
Hatfield DN7 . . . . 92 C4
Scunthorpe DN16 . . . . 151 B4
Hamshaw Ct HU3 . . . . 145 C4
Handel Ct DN21 . . . . 117 B1
Handel House Prep Sch
DN21 . . . . 117 B1
Handley Cl YO30 . . . . 127 A2
Hands on History Mus*
HU1 . . . . 155 B2
Hanger La DN14 . . . . 63 B3
Hankins La YO42 . . . . 38 D1
Hanley Rd HU5 . . . . 139 D3
Hanover Ct
Beverley HU17 . . . . 154 C3
Kingston upon Hull HU1 . . 155 A2
Hanover Dr 25 HU15 . . . . . . 68 C5
Hanover Gdns DN16 . . . . . 151 C2
Hanover Grange 6 HU6 . . 122 D4
Hanover St W 7 YO26 . . . 129 F5
Hanover Sq HU1 . . . . 155 B2
Hanover Street E 5
YO26 . . . . 129 F5
Hansard Cres
6 Caistor LN7 . . . . 111 B4
5 Gilberdyke HU15 . . . . 66 D8
Hansard Dr 6 HU15 . . . . . . 66 D8
Hansom Pl YO31 . . . . 130 C7
Hanson Cl YO43 . . . . 135 D3
Hanson Way DN32 . . . . . . 153 B4
Ha'penny Bridge Way
HU9 . . . . 146 B5
Harborough Cl 20 YO14 . . . . 2 F8
Harbour Rd YO15 . . . . 122 F2
Harbour Way HU9 . . . . 146 C6
Harcourt Cl
Bishopthorpe YO23 . . . . . . 133 A4
Wheldrake YO19 . . . . 37 F7
Harcourt Dr HU9 . . . . 146 C8
Harcourt St YO31 . . . . 130 E5
Hardane HU6 . . . . 139 E8
Harden Cl YO30 . . . . 126 F2
Hardenshaw La YO8 . . . . . . 63 B4
Hardington Cl HU8 . . . . . . 142 B7
Hardisty Mews YO26 . . . . 130 A4
Hardmoor La YO43 . . . . 53 C5
Hardrada Way 3 YO41 . . . . 15 D1
Hardwick St HU5 . . . . 145 B8
Hardy Rd DN17 . . . . 150 D2
Hardy's Ct DN32 . . . . 153 A2
Hardys Rd HU12 . . . . 72 C7
Hardy's Rd DN35 . . . . 103 C2
Hardy St
Kingston upon Hull HU5 . . 140 C3
Selby YO8 . . . . 148 E4
Hare St DN32 . . . . 152 F2
Harewood HU17 . . . . 136 B6
Harewood Ave
Bridlington YO16 . . . . 122 D6
Kingston upon Hull HU9 . . 142 A3
4 Kirk Sandall DN3 . . . . 92 A2
Harewood Cl
Rawcliffe YO30 . . . . 126 D2
5 Wigginton YO32 . . . . 13 D5
Harewood Crest 21 HU15 . 68 D5
Harewood Gr 17 DN35 . . . 103 C1
Harewood Way YO10 . . . . 131 A2
Harfry Wlk DN14 . . . . 149 F6
Hargrave St DN31 . . . . 152 B5
Hargreave Cl HU17 . . . . . 136 E6
Hargreaves Way DN15 . . . . 96 D7
Hariff La HU12 . . . . 73 B4
Harington Ave YO10 . . . . . 130 F4
Harker St 12 WF11 . . . . 61 A2
Harland La YO25 . . . . 124 E4
Harland Rd
Bridlington YO16 . . . . 122 F5
6 Brough HU15 . . . . 68 C6
Harland Way HU16 . . . . . . 138 E8
Harlech Cl 1 HU7 . . . . 57 A6
Harlech Way DN32 . . . . . . 152 F4
Harleigh Ave
Kingston upon Hull HU7 . . 141 A5

Harleigh Ave *continued*
Stoneferry HU7 . . . . 141 B5
Harlequin Dr 15 HU7 . . . . . . 56 F5
Harleston Cl 5 HU8 . . . . . 142 B5
Harlestone Ct 8 DN34 . . . 102 B3
Harley St HU2 . . . . 155 A4
Harlow Cl
2 Kingston upon Hull
HU8 . . . . 142 C6
1 York YO24 . . . . 129 F2
Harlow Rd YO24 . . . . 129 F2
Harlow St DN31 . . . . 152 B5
HARLTHORPE 51 A8
Harlthorpe Gn YO8 . . . . 51 A8
Harneis Cres DN37 . . . . . . 101 F1
Harold Ct YO24 . . . . 129 D3
Harold St
Grimsby DN32 . . . . 153 A4
Selby YO8 . . . . 148 F4
Harolds Way 1 YO41 . . . . . 15 D1
Harome Gr HU5 . . . . 144 C7
Harpenden Cl 12 DN7 . . . . . 92 D3
Harpendon Dr 6 DN7 . . . . . 92 D3
Harper Cl YO42 . . . . 29 A3
Harper St
8 Great Driffield YO25 . . . . 124 F4
2 Selby YO8 . . . . 148 C5
HARPHAM 21 F8
Harpham Gr HU9 . . . . 142 A1
Harpham La YO25 . . . . 9 D2
Harpham Rd DN36 . . . . 115 B2
Harpings Rd HU5 . . . . 139 F1
Harpswell Hill DN21 . . . . . 119 B1
Harpswell La DN21 . . . . . . 118 F1
Harrier Ct YO41 . . . . 27 A3
Harrier Rd 2 DN18 . . . . 69 F1
Harrington Ct 33 HU12 . . . . 72 D7
Harrington Pl DN16 . . . . . . 151 A1
Harrington Rd YO16 . . . . . 122 B2
Harrington St DN35 . . . . . . 153 B5
Harrison Cl
Sproatley HU11 . . . . 58 D5
Winteringham DN15 . . . . 83 B8
Harrison St
Grimsby DN31 . . . . 152 C3
York YO31 . . . . 130 F6
Harris St HU3 . . . . 144 F5
Harrow Cl 12 DN21 . . . . . . 117 C1
Harrowdyke 10 DN18 . . . . . 84 E8
Harrow Gdns 12 DN17 . . . . 96 C2
Harrow Glade 5 YO30 . . . 127 A1
Harrow St HU3 . . . . 145 B4
Harrybeck La YO43 . . . . 53 D4
Harry Moor La YO8 . . . . 48 B2
Harry's Ave HU8 . . . . 141 B3
Harrys Dream 3 DN20 . . . . 97 E3
Harsell La HU11 . . . . 34 F2
HARSWELL 40 C3
Harswell La
Everingham YO43 . . . . 40 D5
Holme-on-Spalding-Moor
YO42 . . . . 40 C2
Hart Dr 26 YO42 . . . . 29 A3
Hartendale Cl 22 YO15 . . . . . 5 A2
Hartford Wlk HU8 . . . . 142 C7
Harthill YO25 . . . . 31 B7
Harthill Ave HU17 . . . . 43 D6
Hart Hill Cres YO41 . . . . . . 16 A2
Harthill Dr HU3 . . . . 145 C5
Hart La DN15 . . . . 83 B5
Hartland Cl HU7 . . . . 140 F8
Hartley Bridge HU9 . . . . . 146 C6
Hartley Ct YO15 . . . . 122 D1
Hartley St HU18 . . . . 134 D5
Hartoft Rd HU5 . . . . 139 E2
Hartoft St YO10 . . . . 130 D2
HARTON 15 C8
Harts Cl HU18 . . . . 134 B4
Hartshead Ave DN15 . . . . 150 C7
Hartshead Wlk YO16 . . . . 122 B4
Hartsholme Pk 27 HU7 . . . . 56 F5
Hart St DN35 . . . . 153 C4
Harvest Ave 19 DN18 . . . . . 84 E8
Harvest Cl
13 Kirk Sandall DN3 . . . . 92 A2
11 Strensall YO32 . . . . 14 B7
Harvest Cres 4 DN37 . . . . 113 D6
Harvester Cl DN9 . . . . 105 F6
Harvest Rise 1 DN19 . . . . . 85 C8
Harwood Dr 1 HU4 . . . . . . 144 B6
Harwood Rd YO26 . . . . 24 F7
Hase Wlk HU13 . . . . 143 E1
Haslemere Ave YO15 . . . . 122 E3
Hassacarr La YO19 . . . . 26 F6
Hastings Ave 1 HU5 . . . . . 140 E2
Hastings Cl 4 YO30 . . . . . 127 A1
Hastings Gr HU5 . . . . 144 E7
Hastings Wlk YO16 . . . . . . 122 C2
HATCLIFFE 112 F3
Hatcliffe Cl 20 DN33 . . . . . 102 D2
HATFIELD 92 D5
Hatfield Cl 3 YO30 . . . . . . 126 E3
Hatfield La
Barnby Dun DN3 . . . . 92 A4
Edenthorpe DN3 . . . . 92 A1
Hatfield Manor CE Jun Sch
DN7 . . . . 92 E4
Hatfield Pl DN14 . . . . 149 C1
Hatfield Rd DN7 . . . . 93 A6
Hatfield & Stainforth Sta
DN7 . . . . 92 C5
Hatfield Travis VA CE Inf Sch
DN7 . . . . 92 E4
Hatfield Visual Arts Coll
DN7 . . . . 92 D4
Hatfield Water Pk* DN7 . . 92 E5
Hatfield Wlk
Kingston upon Hull HU8 . . 141 C1

Hatfield Wlk *continued*
York YO24 . . . . 132 B8
HATFIELD WOODHOUSE . . 93 A3
Hatfield Woodhouse Prim
Sch DN7 . . . . 93 A3
Hathersage Ct DN15 . . . . . 150 B6
Hathersage Rd HU7 . . . . . 141 C4
Hatkill La YO41 . . . . 16 B1
Hatters Cl YO23 . . . . 132 B3
Hatton Gr 32 DN33 . . . . . . 102 D2
Haugh La YO8 . . . . 61 F8
Haugh Pk 14 HU7 . . . . 56 E5
Haughton Rd YO30 . . . . . . 130 C7
Hauling La YO23 . . . . 36 C8
Hauxwell Gr 6 HU8 . . . . . 142 A5
Havelock Acad DN32 . . . . 153 C2
Havelock Cres YO16 . . . . . 122 D3
Havelock Mews DN32 . . . 153 C2
Havelock Pl YO16 . . . . 122 D3
Havelock St
Bridlington YO16 . . . . 122 D3
Kingston upon Hull HU3 . . 145 A4
Haven Ave
2 Brough HU15 . . . . 68 B5
Grimsby DN31 . . . . 152 C4
Haven Basin Rd HU12 . . . . 72 C6
Haven Cl DN21 . . . . 117 F5
Haven Garth
1 Brough HU15 . . . . 68 B5
2 Hedon HU12 . . . . 72 D7
Haven Gdns DN31 . . . . 152 A5
Haven Rd
Barton-upon-Humber
DN18 . . . . 69 E1
North Killingholme DN40 . . . 87 A6
Patrington HU12 . . . . 89 C8
Haven Staithes 24 HU12 . . . 72 C7
Haven Terr DN31 . . . . 152 C4
Haven The
Kingston upon Hull HU9 . . . 146 B6
Selby YO8 . . . . 148 D5
2 Walkington HU17 . . . . 55 D8
Haverah Ct YO30 . . . . 126 F1
Havercroft Rd 15 YO14 . . . . . 3 A8
Haverflats Cl 3 HU5 . . . . . 139 F1
Haverstoe Pl 7 DN35 . . . . 103 B2
Hawdon Ave YO8 . . . . 148 D5
Hawerby Rd DN37 . . . . 101 F1
Haweswater Way HU6 . . . 140 D8
Hawes Wlk HU5 . . . . 139 D3
Hawke Garth 5 YO14 . . . . . . 3 A8
Hawkesbury St HU8 . . . . . 141 E3
Hawkins Gr DN32 . . . . 153 B2
Hawkins Way 3 DN40 . . . . 86 E3
Hawkshead Cl 3 YO24 . . . 132 B8
Hawling Rd YO43 . . . . 135 C2
Haworth Cl DN15 . . . . 150 D8
Haworth St HU6 . . . . 140 C4
Haworth Wlk YO16 . . . . . . 122 B4
Hawse Rd YO8 . . . . 63 E8
Hawthorn Ave
2 Brigg DN20 . . . . 98 C2
1 Immingham DN40 . . . . . . 87 D2
Kingston upon Hull HU3 . . . 144 F5
Hawthorn Cl
Burstwick HU12 . . . . 73 B6
Healing DN41 . . . . 101 F6
5 Newport HU15 . . . . 52 F1
Wootton DN39 . . . . 85 E2
Hawthorn Ct 1 HU3 . . . . . 144 F6
Hawthorn Dr
Wilberfoss YO41 . . . . 27 E5
Wistow YO8 . . . . 49 A5
Hawthorne Ave
Cleethorpes DN35 . . . . 153 D4
29 Grimsby DN33 . . . . 113 E8
Hatfield DN7 . . . . 92 C2
12 Haxby YO32 . . . . 13 E5
Kingston upon Hull HU10 . 138 D1
5 New Waltham DN36 . . . . 113 F7
Scunthorpe DN17 . . . . 150 F4
4 Thorne/Moorends DN8 . . 79 A1
Hawthorne Cl
10 Thorpe Willoughby
YO8 . . . . 48 B2
12 Winterton DN15 . . . . 83 A5
Hawthorne Cres DN17 . . . . 150 F4
Hawthorne Dr YO43 . . . . . . 40 A1
Hawthorne Garth HU17 . . 136 F7
Hawthorne Gdns DN19 . . . . 86 A8
Hawthorne Gr
5 Thorne/Moorends
DN8 . . . . 79 A1
York YO31 . . . . 130 E5
Hawthorne Mews YO32 . . . . 14 B7
Hawthorne Rd DN8 . . . . 79 A1
Hawthorne Rise HU13 . . . . 143 B3
Hawthorn Garth DN14 . . . . . 61 F4
Hawthorn Gate 17 DN18 . . . 84 F8
Hawthorn Gr
Gainsborough DN21 . . . . . . 117 B1
York YO31 . . . . 130 E5
Hawthorn Pl YO32 . . . . 127 E4
Hawthorn Rd YO8 . . . . 148 D3
Hawthorn Rise 6 DN19 . . . . 85 C8
Hawthorns 2 YO19 . . . . 48 F8
Hawthorn Spinney YO31 . . 127 E3
Hawthorn St 1 YO31 . . . . 130 E5
Hawthorns The
12 Kingston upon Hull
HU8 . . . . 141 E7
5 Long Riston/Arnold
HU11 . . . . 45 C5
Hawthorn Terr
Goole DN14 . . . . 149 F5
York YO32 . . . . 127 D4
Hawthorn Terrace N
YO32 . . . . 127 D4

Hawthorn Terrace S
YO32 . . . . 127 D3
Hawthorn Terr Cent 2
YO32 . . . . 127 D3
Hawthorn Way
6 Althorpe DN17 . . . . 95 D4
9 Gilberdyke HU15 . . . . 66 D7
Hawton Cl 1 DN21 . . . . . 117 C1
HAXBY 127 D7
Haxby Moor Rd
Haxby YO32 . . . . 13 F7
Towthorpe YO32 . . . . 14 A7
Haxby Rd
Clifton YO31 . . . . 127 D1
New Earswick YO32 . . . . . . 127 D6
York YO31 . . . . 156 B4
Haxby Rd Prim Sch
YO31 . . . . 130 D7
HAXEY 105 C3
HAXEY CARR 105 B4
Haxey CE Prim Sch DN9 . 105 D3
Haxey Gate Rd DN10 . . . . 116 C7
Haxey Grange 8 DN9 . . . 105 D2
Haxey La DN9 . . . . 105 D2
Haxey Rd DN10 . . . . 116 C6
Hayburn Ave HU5 . . . . 139 F2
Haycroft Ave
Grimsby DN31 . . . . 152 C3
West Marsh DN31 . . . . 152 C3
Haycroft St DN31 . . . . 152 C3
Haydock Garth 6 HU7 . . . . 57 A5
Haydon Cl HU10 . . . . 143 D8
Hayes La DN7 . . . . 78 D1
Hayfield Cl
Barnby Dun DN3 . . . . 92 A4
9 Haxey DN9 . . . . 105 D2
Hayforth Cl YO30 . . . . 127 A2
Hayling Mere 29 DN35 . . . 103 C1
Haymarket Cl HU8 . . . . . . 141 F4
Haymer Dr 43 HU12 . . . . . . 72 D7
Haynes Cl 2 DN8 . . . . 93 B7
Haynes Gdns 15 DN8 . . . . . 93 B8
Haynes Gn 9 DN8 . . . . 93 B8
Haynes Gr 1 DN8 . . . . 93 B7
Haynes Rd DN8 . . . . 93 B8
Hays Cl 3 DN36 . . . . 114 A5
HAYTON 40 C8
Hayton Cl DN15 . . . . 83 A5
Hayton Gr HU4 . . . . 144 D4
Hayton's La DN15 . . . . 83 D2
Hayward Cl 3 HU17 . . . . . . 55 D8
Hazel Ave
Crowle DN17 . . . . 94 D8
Withernsea HU19 . . . . 75 A5
Hazelbarrow Dr HU10 . . . . 143 F7
Hazel Cl
Great Driffield YO25 . . . . . 124 E3
Messingham DN17 . . . . 107 C7
York YO32 . . . . 127 D2
Hazel Cres 12 HU15 . . . . . . 66 D7
Hazel Croft 5 DN40 . . . . . . 87 B1
Hazel Ct
23 Brough HU15 . . . . 68 C5
York YO10 . . . . 130 E4
Hazel Garth YO31 . . . . 131 B7
Hazel Gr
Goole DN14 . . . . 149 D1
2 Kingston upon Hull
HU3 . . . . 145 D5
20 Yaddlethorpe DN17 . . . . . 96 D1
Hazelmere Ct YO32 . . . . . . 127 E3
Hazelnut Gr YO30 . . . . 127 B2
Hazel Old La DN14 . . . . 62 C2
Hazel Rd DN7 . . . . 92 C5
Hazelwood Ave YO10 . . . . 131 D4
Hazing La DN14 . . . . 77 B6
Headingley Ave 20 DN17 . . 96 C2
Headingley Rd 7 DN6 . . . . 76 E2
Headland Cl 30 YO32 . . . . . 13 E5
Headlands Cl YO16 . . . . . . 122 F6
Headlands Dr
Aldbrough HU11 . . . . 47 C1
Bridlington YO16 . . . . 122 F6
Kingston upon Hull HU13 . 143 C2
Headlands Prim Sch
YO32 . . . . 127 D8
Headlands Rd HU11 . . . . . . 47 C1
Headlands Sch YO16 . . . . . 122 F5
Headlands Wlk YO16 . . . . 122 E6
Headland View HU18 . . . . 134 D5
Headley Cl 2 YO30 . . . . . . 127 B1
Heads La HU13 . . . . 143 C1
Healey Gr YO31 . . . . 130 F8
Healey Rd DN16 . . . . 151 C4
HEALING 102 A5
Healing Prim Sch DN41 . . 101 F5
Healing Rd DN41 . . . . 101 D6
Healing Sch DN41 . . . . 101 F5
Healing Sta DN41 . . . . 101 F6
Health Pl 29 DN20 . . . . 98 C2
Heanor Ct DN15 . . . . 150 B7
Heapham Rd DN21 . . . . . . 117 C1
Hearfield Terr HU13 . . . . . 143 E1
Heater Cnr HU17 . . . . 31 F1
Heath Cl 2 YO24 . . . . 129 F2
Heathcote St HU6 . . . . 140 D4
Heath Croft YO10 . . . . 133 F7
Heather Bank
13 Stamford Bridge YO41 . . . 15 D2
York YO10 . . . . 131 C4
Heather Cl
31 Gainsborough DN21 . . . 117 C1
7 Kingston upon Hull
HU5 . . . . 139 D1
Selby YO8 . . . . 148 C3

Heather Cl *continued*
York YO32 ... 128 A4
Heather Croft 4 YO31 ... 127 E2
Heatherdale Cl 9 DN33 .. 113 E8
Heather Garth YO25 ... 124 E2
Heather Gr 1 DN16 ... 96 F2
Heatherwood Cl 11 HU7 ... 57 B5
Heathfield Cl 8 DN3 ... 92 A3
Heathfield Ct DN34 ... 152 B1
Heathfield Rd 1 YO10 .. 131 A3
Heath Moor Dr YO10 ... 133 F8
Heath Ride YO32 ... 14 B8
Hebden Ave HU8 ... 142 C5
Hebden Rd DN15 ... 150 C8
Hebdon Rise 2 YO26 ... 129 D4
Heber St DN14 ... 149 C2
Hebrides Cl HU9 ... 142 A3
Heckdyke La DN10 ... 116 F7
Heck La
Heck DN14 ... 77 C7
Hensall DN14 ... 62 D1
Heck & Pollington Lake
DN14 ... 77 E7
Hedgerow Cl 4 DN19 ... 85 C8
Hedgerow Ct 10 HU6 ... 140 B8
Hedgerow La 24 DN20 ... 98 C2
Hedgerows The YO8 ... 49 E3
Hedley Cl 7 HU15 ... 53 F1
HEDON ... 72 C8
Hedon Mus★ HU12 ... 72 C7
Hedon Prim Sch HU12 ... 72 C7
Hedon Rd
Kingston upon Hull HU9 ... 146 B6
Marfleet HU9 ... 147 D7
Heigholme La HU17 ... 44 F8
Heigholm La YO25 ... 34 A1
Height Lands La YO23 ... 24 D6
Heimdal Rd DN33 ... 102 E1
Helen Cres 9 DN40 ... 87 B1
Helene Gr DN32 ... 153 B3
Hellyer Cl HU14 ... 69 A5
Hellyers Ct HU4 ... 144 D2
Helm Dr HU9 ... 146 C6
Helms Ave 6 HU12 ... 58 C1
Helmsdale YO24 ... 132 C6
Helmsley Gr
16 Haxby YO32 ... 13 D5
Kingston upon Hull HU5 .. 144 C7
Helperby Wlk HU5 ... 139 E3
Helsinki Rd HU7 ... 140 F5
Helston Wlk DN17 ... 150 C4
Helvellyn Cl 10 HU7 ... 57 A6
Hemble Way HU7 ... 56 F5
HEMINGBROUGH ... 49 F1
Hemingbrough Prim Sch
YO8 ... 49 F1
Hemlock Ave YO31 ... 127 E1
Hemmingway Wlk HU13 .. 143 E3
Hempbridge Cl YO8 ... 148 A5
Hempbridge Rd YO8 ... 148 A5
Hempdyke Rd DN15 ... 150 E8
Hempland Ave YO31 ... 130 F6
Hempland Dr YO31 ... 131 A7
Hempland La YO31 ... 131 A7
Hempland Prim Sch
YO31 ... 131 B6
HEMSWELL ... 119 A1
Hemswell Ave HU9 ... 147 D8
HEMSWELL CLIFF ... 119 D1
Hemswell Dr 6 DN37 ... 102 C4
Hemswell La DN21 ... 119 A1
Henderson Ave DN15 ... 150 F8
Henderson Ave Prim Sch
DN15 ... 150 F8
Henderson Cres DN15 ... 150 F8
Henderson St DN31 ... 153 A6
Henderson Way DN15 ... 83 A5
Hendon Garth YO30 ... 127 A1
Heneage Rd DN32 ... 152 F2
Hengate HU17 ... 154 A3
Henley Ct 6 DN21 ... 117 B1
Henley Dr HU9 ... 141 E1
Henlow Cl 4 DN21 ... 119 C8
Henry Boot Way HU4 ... 144 C2
Henry Ct 8 DN8 ... 79 B1
Henry St
Goole DN14 ... 149 B4
Grimsby DN31 ... 152 C4
Scunthorpe DN15 ... 150 F7
Henry Verone Ct HU2 ... 155 B1
HENSALL ... 62 D2
Hensall Prim Sch DN14 ... 62 C1
Hensall Sta DN14 ... 62 C1
Henwick Hall La YO8 ... 148 C1
Hepscott Wlk HU8 ... 142 D6
Hepworth's La DN14 ... 63 C2
Herbert St 6 YO10 ... 130 E3
Herberts Way YO31 ... 130 F7
Herdsman Dr YO23 ... 132 C3
Herdsman Rd 3 YO24 ... 132 D8
Herdwick Cl 1 YO30 ... 127 B1
Hereford Ave DN34 ... 152 C1
Hereford Cl 4 HU17 ... 136 E1
Hereford Rd YO42 ... 28 E3
Hereford St HU4 ... 144 E3
Hereford Tech Sch DN34 .152 B1
Hereward Pl DN16 ... 151 E3
Herman Wlk YO24 ... 132 C8
Hermes Cl HU9 ... 142 C4
Hermitage Rd YO16 ... 122 C4
Hermitage The 5 DN8 ... 79 B2
Heron Ave YO24 ... 132 C8
Heron Cl
Grimsby DN32 ... 103 A2
10 Scunthorpe DN15 ... 96 B7
Heron Dr DN21 ... 117 C1
Heron Gate DN16 ... 151 F1
Heron Holt 1 DN20 ... 97 D4
Heron Mews YO15 ... 11 B4
Heron Rise YO32 ... 127 F5
Heron St HU3 ... 145 B5
Heron Way
26 Barton Upon Humber
DN18 ... 84 E8
6 Holton le Clay DN36 ... 114 A6
Herrick Rd DN17 ... 150 D3
Herriot Way DN15 ... 150 C7
Hersey Rd 24 LN7 ... 111 B4
Hertfordshire Cl 2 HU5. 139 D1
Hesketh Bank YO10 ... 131 D3
Hesketh Dr DN3 ... 92 A2
Heslerton Ave HU16 ... 139 A4
Heslin Cl 8 YO32 ... 127 C8
HESLINGTON ... 131 B1
Heslington Croft YO10 ... 133 F7
Heslington Ct 2 YO10 ... 131 B1
Heslington La
Heslington YO10 ... 131 A1
York YO10 ... 130 F3
Heslington Rd YO10 ... 130 E3
HESSAY ... 24 C8
Hessay Ind Est YO26 ... 24 C8
Hessay Pl 2 YO26 ... 129 A3
HESSLE ... 143 E1
Hessle All Saints CE Inf Sch
HU13 ... 143 F2
Hessle All Saints CE Jun Sch
HU13 ... 143 F2
Hessle High Sch HU13 .. 143 C2
Hessle Mount Sch HU13. 143 C3
Hessle Rd HU1 ... 155 A1
Hessleskew La YO43 ... 42 A4
Hessle Station HU13 ... 69 E4
Hessle View 22 DN18 ... 84 E8
Hetherton St YO30 ... 156 A3
Hewde La DN15 ... 83 A8
Hewitt's Ave DN36 ... 114 A8
Hewitts Ave Bsns Pk
DN36 ... 103 B1
Hewitt's Cir DN36 ... 103 B1
Hewitts Cir Ret Pk DN35 .103 B1
Hewitts Manor
3 Cleethorpes DN35 ... 103 B1
New Waltham DN36 ... 114 B8
Hewley Ave YO10 ... 131 A4
HEWORTH ... 130 F6
Heworth YO31 ... 131 A6
Heworth CE Prim Sch
YO31 ... 130 F6
Heworth Gn YO31 ... 156 C4
Heworth Hall Dr YO31 ... 130 F6
Heworth Mews YO31 ... 130 E6
Heworth Pl YO31 ... 130 F6
Heworth Rd YO31 ... 130 F6
Heworth Village YO31 ... 131 A6
Hewson Rd DN36 ... 114 D8
Hewson's La DN18 ... 69 E1
Hewson St DN17 ... 107 D7
Heyford Rd YO42 ... 28 E3
Hey St DN35 ... 153 F1
Heythrop Rd DN35 ... 103 C2
HIBALDSTOW ... 108 F5
Hibaldstow Cl 21 DN34 .. 102 C2
Hibaldstow Prim Sch
DN20 ... 109 A5
Hickleton Cl HU8 ... 141 C1
Hickman Cres DN21 ... 117 B2
Hickman Gr DN21 ... 117 E5
Higham Cl HU8 ... 141 E7
Higham Way HU15 ... 68 D5
Highbields YO42 ... 28 F7
High Bridge Rd DN8 ... 93 C7
High Brighton St 18 HU19 75 A6
High Burgage 2 DN15 ... 68 B1
HIGH CATTON ... 27 D8
High Catton Rd YO41 ... 27 D8
Highcliffe Ct YO30 ... 130 A6
Highcliff Gdns DN15 ... 150 F8
Highcourt HU6 ... 139 E7
Highcroft HU17 ... 43 A5
High Croft 7 YO14 ... 2 F8
Highdales HU10 ... 143 C8
High Eggborough La
DN14 ... 62 A1
High Farm Ct HU11 ... 142 F7
HIGHFIELD ... 50 E7
Highfield
Kingston upon Hull HU7 .. 141 D6
Pollington DN14 ... 77 F7
Withernsea HU19 ... 75 A6
High Field YO10 ... 131 D4
Highfield Ave
Great Driffield YO25 ... 124 E6
Grimsby DN32 ... 152 E1
22 Immingham DN40 ... 87 B1
Scunthorpe DN15 ... 150 E7
Highfield Cl
Barnby Dun DN3 ... 92 A4
Fangfoss YO41 ... 28 C8
Gainsborough DN21 ... 117 C1
Hatfield DN7 ... 92 D5
Kingston upon Hull HU7 .. 141 D6
North Frodingham YO25 ... 34 A8
5 North Thoresby DN36 ... 114 B1
Wold Newton YO25 ... 2 A4
Highfield Cres
Barlby with Osgodby YO8 ... 49 B5
15 Barton-upon-Humber
DN18 ... 84 F8
Kingston upon Hull HU11 .. 142 F7
9 Thorne/Moorends DN8 ... 79 A1
2 Westwoodside DN9 ... 105 B2
Highfield Ct YO8 ... 148 B1
Highfield Dr 1 DN21 ... 108 B1
Highfield Gr
4 Brigg DN20 ... 98 C3
Highfield YO8 ... 50 E7
Highfield La
Fangfoss YO41 ... 16 B1
Womersley DN6 ... 76 D5
Highfield Rd
Beverley HU17 ... 136 F6
Highfield YO8 ... 50 D7
North Thoresby DN36 ... 114 B1
High Field Rd DN20 ... 98 D3
Highfield Rise 1 HU12 ... 58 D1
Highfields
10 Barrow upon Humber
DN19 ... 85 C8
Crowle DN17 ... 94 D8
South Cave HU15 ... 54 A2
Highfield View 3 YO8 ... 49 B4
Highfield Way HU14 ... 69 A4
High Garth
Earswick YO32 ... 128 A7
Scunthorpe DN17 ... 96 C1
Highgate
Balne DN14 ... 77 D6
Cherry Burton HU17 ... 42 E4
Cleethorpes DN35 ... 153 E1
Highgate Cl HU8 ... 142 A5
High Gn YO16 ... 122 D5
Highgrove DN17 ... 107 D7
Highgrove Cl 7 YO30 ... 126 E3
Highgrove Way HU7 ... 56 F6
High Hazel Rd DN8 ... 79 B2
HIGH HUNSLEY ... 54 D6
High La
Carnaby YO25 ... 10 C3
Sutton upon Derwent YO41 .27 D3
Highlands Ave 5 YO32 ... 14 B7
Highlands Prim Sch HU7 .57 A6
Highland Tarn 31 DN40 ... 87 B1
High Levels Bank
Belton DN8 ... 94 A4
Hatfield DN8 ... 93 A6
High Leys Rd DN17 ... 96 C2
High Mdw
Gowdall DN14 ... 63 A1
Selby YO8 ... 148 B6
High Mdws HU10 ... 143 C8
Highmoor Cl YO24 ... 132 D8
High Moor La YO30 ... 12 C8
Highmoor Rd YO24 ... 132 D8
HIGH MOWTHORPE ... 6 D7
High Newbiggin St YO31 .156 B3
High Oaks YO31 ... 131 B7
High Ousegate YO1 ... 156 B2
High Petergate YO1 ... 156 B3
High Peter La YO25 ... 20 D7
High Point Ret Pk DN31 .152 E5
High Rd
Elloughton-cum-Brough
HU15 ... 68 D6
North Cave HU15 ... 53 E3
HIGH RISBY ... 82 F1
High Risby Medieval
Village★ DN15 ... 83 A1
High Row YO41 ... 16 D4
High Sewerby Rd YO15 .. 123 C7
High Side YO25 ... 34 A8
High St
Airmyn DN14 ... 64 E3
Aldbrough HU11 ... 47 C1
Barmby on the Marsh DN14 .64 A7
Barrow upon Humber DN19 .85 D8
Barton-upon-Humber DN18 .69 E1
Beckingham DN10 ... 116 D1
Belton DN9 ... 94 E1
Blyton DN21 ... 117 F5
Boynton YO16 ... 10 D7
Bridlington YO16 ... 122 C4
Broughton DN20 ... 97 D3
Buckton/Bempton YO15 ... 4 C3
Burringham DN17 ... 95 D4
Burton upon Stather DN15 .. 82 B4
Caistor LN7 ... 111 B4
Carlton DN14 ... 63 C2
Cawood YO8 ... 48 B8
Cleethorpes DN35 ... 153 E2
Corringham DN21 ... 118 A1
Cottam YO25 ... 7 E5
4 Crowle DN17 ... 94 D7
Easington HU12 ... 90 F6
East Butterwick DN17 ... 106 D8
East Ferry DN21 ... 106 B2
Eastoft DN17 ... 81 A3
Eastrington DN14 ... 65 F8
Epworth DN9 ... 105 E6
7 Flamborough YO15 ... 5 A2
Flixborough DN15 ... 82 B1
Garthorpe & Fockerby DN17 81 E5
Goole DN14 ... 65 C4
Great Limber DN37 ... 100 D3
Gringley on the Hill DN10 . 116 A1
Hatfield DN7 ... 92 C2
Haxey DN9 ... 105 D2
Holme-on-Spalding-Moor
YO43 ... 40 A1
Humberside Airport DN39. 100 A6
Kilham YO25 ... 9 A8
Kingston upon Hull HU1 .. 155 C1
Kirby Grindalythe YO17 ... 6 D8
Kirton in Lindsey DN21 ... 108 B1
Laceby DN37 ... 101 F1
Langtoft YO25 ... 8 C8
Luddington & Haldenby
DN17 ... 81 C4
Market Weighton YO43 ... 135 D4
Messingham DN17 ... 107 D7
Misterton DN10 ... 116 C5
High St *continued*
Nafferton YO25 ... 125 E7
Nettleton LN7 ... 111 C2
North Ferriby HU14 ... 69 A5
North Kelsey LN7 ... 110 A4
North Thoresby DN36 ... 114 A1
14 Norton DN6 ... 76 E1
Owston Ferry DN9 ... 106 B3
Rawcliffe DN14 ... 64 A1
Redbourne DN21 ... 108 F2
Roxby cum Risby DN15 ... 82 E1
Sancton YO43 ... 41 D2
Scotter DN21 ... 107 C3
Scotton DN21 ... 107 C1
Scunthorpe DN15 ... 151 A7
Snaith DN14 ... 63 B1
South Ferriby DN18 ... 84 A7
Swinefleet DN14 ... 65 D1
Ulceby DN39 ... 86 A1
Walkeringham DN10 ... 116 C3
Waltham DN37 ... 113 E6
West/East Butterwick
DN17 ... 95 D1
Wharram YO17 ... 6 A6
Winterton DN15 ... 83 A5
Withernwick HU11 ... 46 D3
Wootton DN39 ... 85 E2
Wroot DN9 ... 104 D6
High Stile HU17 ... 45 B8
High Street E DN15 ... 151 C7
High Street W DN21 ... 107 C4
Highthorn Rd YO31 ... 127 E2
High Thorpe Cres DN35 .. 103 B2
High Trees Mount HU8 .. 141 E6
Highwood YO25 ... 124 E6
Higrove Way 32 HU7 ... 56 F6
Hilary Gr HU4 ... 144 B2
Hilary Rd 11 DN33 ... 113 E8
Hilbeck Gr YO31 ... 131 B6
Hilbra Ave YO32 ... 127 D6
Hilda St
Goole DN14 ... 149 C5
Grimsby DN32 ... 153 A4
6 Selby YO8 ... 148 C5
3 York YO10 ... 130 E3
HILDERTHORPE ... 11 B4
Hilderthorpe Inf Sch
YO15 ... 122 C1
Hilderthorpe Jun Sch
YO15 ... 122 C1
Hilderthorpe Rd YO15 ... 122 D2
Hildyard Cl
19 Hedon HU12 ... 72 D7
1 Kingston upon Hull
HU10 ... 143 F6
Hildyard St DN32 ... 153 A4
Hiles Ave DN15 ... 83 A5
HILLAM ... 61 A7
Hillam Comm La LS25 ... 61 B7
Hillam Hall La 4 LS25 ... 61 A7
Hillam Hall View 3 LS25 .. 61 A7
Hillam House Cl 5 LS25 .. 61 A7
Hillam La LS25 ... 61 A7
Hillam Rd YO8 ... 61 F8
Hillary Garth 9 YO26 ... 129 E4
Hillary Rd DN16 ... 151 B1
Hillary Way DN37 ... 102 C4
Hill Brow HU10 ... 143 B6
Hillcrest
Beverley HU17 ... 136 C6
8 Monk Fryston LS25 ... 61 A8
Hill Crest YO19 ... 14 F1
Hillcrest Ave
Kingston upon Hull HU13 . 143 C2
Poppleton YO26 ... 126 A2
Hillcrest Dr
Beverley HU17 ... 136 D6
Burton upon Stather DN15 .. 82 A4
Hill Crest Gdns YO24 ... 129 F1
Hillerby La HU18 ... 134 B4
Hill Field YO8 ... 148 B8
Hillfield Dr HU11 ... 45 D2
Hillfoot Dr 22 DN17 ... 96 C2
Hillgarth Ct 4 YO41 ... 27 B2
Hillman Rd HU13 ... 143 F3
Hill Rd DN21 ... 118 B1
Hill Rise
Brough HU15 ... 68 C6
Market Weighton YO43 ... 135 E4
Hill Rise Cl YO43 ... 135 E4
Hill Rise Dr YO43 ... 135 E4
Hillsborough Terr 5
YO30 ... 130 C7
Hills Dr 6 DN36 ... 114 D4
Hillside Cl
Bootham Stray YO30 ... 127 B2
9 Monk Fryston LS25 ... 61 A8
Hillside Cres DN38 ... 99 B5
Hillside Dr DN18 ... 84 E8
Hillside Gdns YO25 ... 8 D5
Hillside Rd DN20 ... 97 E4
Hillside Way YO17 ... 7 B8
Hillsmere Gr 5 DN15 ... 83 A5
Hill St
Bridlington YO16 ... 122 D3
Kingston upon Hull HU8 .. 141 A2
York YO24 ... 129 E3
Hillstead Cl 6 DN36 ... 114 D4
Hillsway Cl HU8 ... 141 D4
Hillsyde Ave DN10 ... 116 C5
Hill The DN20 ... 98 D8
Hilltop Ave DN15 ... 150 E8
Hilltop Gdns DN17 ... 107 C7
Hill Top La DN21 ... 117 E5
Hill Top Pl DN34 ... 102 B2
Hill Top Rd 4 YO8 ... 48 D6
Hill Top View HU11 ... 57 F6
Hill View YO31 ... 131 C7
HILSTON ... 60 B
Hilston Gr HU9 ... 142 B
Hilton Ave DN15 ... 150 B
Hilton Cl DN9 ... 94 E
Hilton Ct DN35 ... 103 D
Hinch Garth HU12 ... 60 B
Hinderwell St HU5 ... 140 C
Hindon Wlk DN17 ... 150 C
Hinkler St DN35 ... 153 E
Hinkley Dr 2 DN40 ... 87 B
Hinman Wlk DN15 ... 151 B
Hinsley La DN14 ... 63 C
Hinton Ave 1 YO24 ... 132 C
Hirncroft Cl 10 HU8 ... 141 E
HIRST COURTNEY ... 62 F
Hirst Courtney & Temple
Hirst Prim Sch YO8 ... 62 E
Hirst Rd DN14 ... 63 A
HIVE ... 52 C
Hive La HU15 ... 52 B
Hobart St HU3 ... 155 A
Hobb La 14 DN21 ... 107 C
Hobby Cl DN31 ... 102 B
Hobgate YO24 ... 129 D
Hobman La YO25 ... 32 E
Hob Moor Dr YO24 ... 129 E
Hob Moor Oaks Sch
YO26 ... 129 D
Hob Moor Prim Sch
YO24 ... 129 E
Hobmoor Terr YO24 ... 129 F
Hobson Cl YO23 ... 132 B
Hobson Ct HU17 ... 154 B
Hobson Rd 5 HU15 ... 68 C
Hobson Way DN41 ... 101 F
Hodder Gr HU8 ... 142 C
Hoddesdon Cres 13 DN7 .. 92 D
Hoddy Cows La YO15 ... 4 C
Hodge Ct 3 HU9 ... 146 C
Hodge La WF8 ... 76 B
Hodgson Ave HU17 ... 154 B
Hodgson La
Roos HU12 ... 60 A
Upper Poppleton YO26 ... 24 F
Hodgson's Fields Nature
Reserve★ HU12 ... 90 D
Hodgson St HU8 ... 155 C
Hodsow Fields YO42 ... 28 E
Hodsow La YO42 ... 28 F
Hoggard La DN14 ... 81 E
Hogg La HU10 ... 143 B
Hogsea La HU11 ... 60 B
Holbeck Pl 17 DN40 ... 87 B
Holborn St HU9 ... 146 B
Holbrook Cl 2 HU7 ... 141 B
Holburns Croft 3 YO10 .. 131 B
Holcombe Cl HU8 ... 142 B
Holcroft Garth 10 HU12 ... 72 D
Holden Gdns YO8 ... 48 D
Holderness Cres HU17 ... 154 B
Holderness Rd HU9 ... 146 C
HOLGATE ... 129 F
Holgate Bridge Gdn 7
YO24 ... 130 A
Holgate Cl 2 HU17 ... 137 B
Holgate Lodge Dr YO26 .. 129 E
Holgate Pl 12 HU14 ... 69 B
Holgate Rd
Scunthorpe DN16 ... 151 D
York YO24 ... 156 A
Holland Ave
Crowle DN17 ... 94 D
Scunthorpe DN15 ... 150 E
Holland Dr DN38 ... 110 E
Holland St HU9 ... 146 C
Holland Way HU9 ... 146 C
Holles St DN32 ... 152 E
Hollicarrs Cl YO19 ... 37 A
Hollies The
Barlby with Osgodby YO8 ... 49 C
Beverley HU17 ... 137 A
Hornsea HU18 ... 134 D
Kingston upon Hull HU10 .. 138 E
Snaith & Cowick DN14 ... 78 C
Stockton on the Forest
YO19 ... 14 D
Hollin Bridge La DN7 ... 93 A
Hollingsworth Ave 12
DN40 ... 87 B
Hollingsworth Cl 14
DN35 ... 103 B
Hollingsworth La 22
DN9 ... 105 E
Hollis Cres YO32 ... 14 B
Hollowgate Hill DN21 ... 119 A
Hollows The 9 YO16 ... 122 C
Holly Bank Gr 3 YO24 ... 129 F
Holly Bank Rd YO24 ... 129 F
Hollybush Cl DN14 ... 77 A
Hollybush Way HU17 ... 136 D
Holly Cl
Acaster Malbis YO23 ... 36 C
Full Sutton YO41 ... 16 A
13 Scunthorpe DN16 ... 96 E
Stallingborough DN41 ... 101 D
Hollycroft YO25 ... 23 A
Holly Dr HU16 ... 138 E
Hollygarth La DN14 ... 61 D
Holly Gr
11 Gilberdyke HU15 ... 66 D
Selby YO8 ... 148 B
Summergangs HU8 ... 141 C
8 Thorpe Willoughby YO8 .. 48 B
Holly Hill HU15 ... 68 E
HOLLYM ... 75 A
Hollym Rd
Patrington HU19 ... 74 F
Withernsea HU19 ... 75 A

olly Rd 11 DN8 79 B1
ollyrood Rd YO30 126 E3
olly Terr YO10 130 D1
ollytree Ave 2 HU4 144 B7
olly Tree Croft 2 YO19 26 F7
olly Tree Garth YO32 14 E3
olly Tree La
Dunnington YO19 26 F7
Haxby YO32 127 D8
ollytree Way YO8 48 D1
olly Wlk 10 DN8 79 B1
ollywood YO8 148 B7
OLME 97 A1
olme Ave DN36 114 A7
olmechurch La HU17 154 C2
olme Cl
19 Brigg DN20 98 C2
Holme-on-Spalding-Moor YO43 40 A1
Paull HU12 72 A5
olme Cres HU16 138 E6
olme Ct YO43 135 D4
olme Dene DN9 105 C2
olme Dr DN15 82 B5
olme Farm Cl DN37 102 B5
olmefield Cl 3 YO8 148 A1
olmefield Ct 2 YO8 148 A1
olmefield La YO10 131 A1
olme Gdns 11 DN7 92 C6
olme Hall Ave DN16 96 D2
OLME HILL 152 F3
olme Hill DN17 94 D8
olme Hill La YO10 26 C4
olme Ind Est YO43 52 C6
olme La
Holme DN16 96 E2
Messingham DN17 107 D8
Scunthorpe DN16 96 D2
Selby YO8 148 D6
OLME-ON-SPALDING-MOOR 40 B1
olme on Spalding Moor Prim Sch YO43 40 A1
OLME ON THE WOLDS 31 E1
olme Rd YO43 135 B3
olmes Ave YO8 148 C6
olmes Dr 2 YO19 37 A1
olmes Ind Est YO8 148 D6
olmes La
Bilton HU11 58 A4
Roxby cum Risby DN15 83 D5
olmes Pk DN14 51 F1
olme St DN32 152 E3
olme Valley Prim Sch DN16 96 E2
olmfirth Rd DN15 150 C8
olm Garth Dr HU8 142 B4
OLMPTON 75 C2
olmpton Gr HU9 142 B1
olmpton Rd
Patrington HU12 74 E1
Withernsea HU19 75 A5
olm Rd DN9 105 B2
olmshaw Cl 18 DN3 92 A2
olms La YO43 53 E7
olray Pk DN14 63 C2
olroyd Ave YO31 131 A5
olstein Dr 2 DN16 96 D1
OLTBY 14 F1
oltby Cl HU9 142 C5
oltby Gdns HU18 134 C6
oltby La
Holtby YO19 14 D1
Stockton on the Forest YO19 128 F2
oltby's Yd YO16 122 C4
olton Ct 8 DN36 114 A5
OLTON LE CLAY 114 B5
olton le Clay Inf Sch DN36 114 A5
olton le Clay Jun Sch DN36 114 B5
olton Mount 7 DN36 114 A5
olton Rd
Holton le Moor LN7 110 F1
Tetney DN36 114 C5
olt The 26 DN21 117 C1
olwell Rd HU7 141 A5
olwick Mews HU5 139 D4
olydyke DN18 84 E8
oly Family RC High Sch The DN14 63 C3
oly Family RC Prim Sch DN7 92 D6
oly Name RC Prim Sch HU6 139 E7
olyoake Rd DN32 153 C2
olyroad Dr DN15 96 B7
olyrood Ave YO15 122 F3
oly Well La LN11 121 D4
ome Beat Dr DN20 97 C3
ome Cl HU4 144 C5
ome Farm Cl DN14 62 D2
omefield Ave 8 DN33 102 E2
omefield Cl YO23 132 A2
ome Gn HU16 139 A5
omelea YO32 14 A6
ome Paddock 5 DN37 113 E6
omerton Pl 11 DN34 102 C3
ome St DN15 151 B8
omestead Cl
Eggborough DN14 62 A2
2 York YO32 127 F1
omestead Garth 3 DN7 92 D4
omestead Rd HU12 72 F5
omethorpe HU6 140 A8
oney Pot 5 YO8 50 D7
oneypots La HU12 59 A2
Honeysuckle Cl
20 Brough HU15 68 C5
Selby YO8 148 C2
Honeysuckle Ct
24 Bottesford DN16 96 E2
Humberston DN35 103 C1
Honeysuckle Farm* HU18 35 C3
Honeysuckle Pl 15 HU15 68 D5
Honiton Rd HU7 141 A8
Honleywood Cl 15 HU7 57 B5
Hood Croft DN9 105 D2
Hood Gr DN14 149 B6
Hood Rd DN17 150 D2
Hood St HU8 155 C4
Hook CE Prim Sch DN14 65 B4
Hook La DN14 149 C8
Hook Pasture La DN14 149 C1
Hook Rd DN14 149 E4
Hooks La
Holmpton HU19 75 B2
Thorngumbald HU12 72 E4
Hoop End DN36 114 D4
Hope St
Cleethorpes DN35 103 D3
Grimsby DN32 152 F4
York YO10 156 C1
Hopewell Rd HU9 142 C3
Hopfield DN20 109 A5
Hopgarth DN9 105 D2
HOPGROVE 128 D2
Hopgrove Lane N YO32 128 C3
Hopgrove Lane S YO32 128 E3
Hop Hills La DN7 92 D5
Hopkins Ave DN17 151 A3
Hopkins St HU9 142 A3
Hopwood Cl HU3 145 D8
Hopwood La HU15 52 F1
Hopyard Ct 15 DN14 65 B7
Horbury Ave HU9 142 B2
Horbury Cl DN15 150 D8
Hords La YO25 21 D4
HORKSTOW 84 A5
Horkstow Bridge* DN18 83 F6
Horkstow Rd DN18 84 A6
HORKSTOW WOLDS 84 B6
Hornbeam Ave DN16 151 A1
Hornbeam Cl YO30 127 B2
Hornbeam Dr HU16 139 C5
Hornbeams Ct HU7 141 D6
Hornbeam Wlk HU16 139 B5
Hornby Gr HU9 142 C3
Horner St YO30 130 B7
Hornsby Cres DN15 96 C7
Hornscroft Park 16 HU7 56 E5
HORNSEA 134 D5
Hornsea Bridge Ind Est HU18 134 C2
HORNSEA BURTON 134 D2
Hornsea Burton Prim Sch HU18 134 C4
Hornsea Burton Rd HU18 134 D3
Hornsea & District War Memorial Cottage Hospl HU18 134 C5
Hornsea L Ctr HU18 134 D4
Hornsea Prim Sch HU18 134 C4
Hornsea Rd
Aldbrough HU11 47 B2
Atwick HU18 134 A8
Hatfield HU11 46 D6
Leven HU17 45 B8
Seaton HU11 35 B1
Skipsea YO25 23 B1
Hornsea Sch & Language Coll HU18 134 B4
Hornsey Garth 25 YO32 13 E5
Hornsey Hill Rd DN21 106 D1
Horse Carr La YO25 10 B1
Horse Fair Gn 21 DN8 93 A8
Horsefair La YO25 124 B5
Horsefair The YO25 124 C5
Horsegate Field Rd DN19 86 A8
Horseman Ave YO23 132 A3
Horseman Cl 2 YO23 132 A3
Horseman Dr YO23 132 A3
Horseman La YO23 132 A3
Horse Mkt 17 LN7 111 B4
Horseshoe Cres YO43 40 A1
Horseshoe Dr YO15 123 C6
Horseshoe The
Great Driffield YO25 124 E3
3 Little Leven HU17 44 F6
York YO24 132 E7
Horsfield Way YO19 26 F7
Horsforth Ave YO15 122 D1
Horsley Rd 15 DN21 117 A2
Horsman Ave YO10 156 C1
Horstead Ave DN20 98 C3
Horton House Sch HU5 140 A2
Hospital Fields Rd YO10 130 D1
Hospital Hill 4 YO25 10 A2
Hospital La YO8 48 B4
Hospitium The* YO1 156 A3
HOTHAM 53 D4
Hotham Ave YO26 129 B2
Hotham Dr HU5 144 B8
Hotham Rd
Hutton Cranswick YO25 32 E7
Kingston upon Hull HU5 144 A8
North Cave HU15 53 D4
Hotham Road N HU5 139 E3
Hotham Road S HU5 144 B8
Hothams Ct YO1 156 C2
Hotham Sq HU17 137 B4
Hotham St HU9 146 D7
Hotspur Rd 1 DN21 117 B1
Hotton Cl HU9 142 C1
Houghton La YO43 41 C1
Houghton Wlk HU5 139 C2
Houndale La YO25 125 E8
Houndsway 6 YO24 132 B8
Houps Rd 10 DN8 93 B8
Hourne Ct HU13 143 E2
Hourne The HU13 143 E2
House Ct DN16 96 E2
Housemartin Dr 4 HU8 141 D8
Houston Dr HU5 140 D3
Hovedene Dr DN14 65 A6
Hove Rd HU5 139 D1
Hovingham Cl 17 HU8 141 E7
Howard Dr YO30 126 E2
Howard Gr DN32 153 B2
Howard Link YO30 126 D2
Howard Rd YO32 14 B6
Howard St YO10 130 D2
Howdale Rd HU8 141 E7
HOWDEN 65 A7
Howden Croft Hill HU15 68 A8
Howden Jun & CE Inf Sch DN14 65 B7
Howden La YO19 133 E1
Howden Marsh Nature Reserve* DN14 65 A7
Howden Rd
4 Barlby YO8 49 B4
Eastrington DN14 65 F8
Holme-on-Spalding-Moor YO43 51 F6
Howden Sch DN14 65 B7
Howdens Hill
Scunthorpe DN15 151 A6
Scunthorpe DN15 151 A6
Howdenshire Way DN14 64 F6
Howden Sta DN14 51 B1
Howe Hill Cl YO26 129 E4
Howe Hill Rd YO26 129 E4
Howe La
Goxhill DN19 85 F8
Kirby Underdale YO41 17 A5
Nafferton YO25 125 F7
Howes La YO25 33 E8
Howes Rd 8 YO14 3 A8
Howe St YO24 129 D3
Howgate La YO43 41 A8
Howlett Rd 4 DN35 103 D2
Howl Gate YO41 27 E8
Howl La YO25 32 E8
HOWSHAM 110 A7
Howsham Cl HU9 142 D5
Howsham La DN38 110 C8
Howville Ave DN7 92 F3
Howville Rd DN7 92 F3
Hoylake Cl
Gainsborough DN21 117 C2
Kingston upon Hull HU6 139 E5
Hoylake Dr 6 DN40 87 C2
Hoylake Rd DN17 96 B2
Hubert St
1 Withernsea HU19 74 F7
2 York YO23 130 B1
Huby Ct YO10 130 E3
Hucknall Garth 16 HU7 57 A5
Huddleston Rd DN32 153 B3
Hudson Ave DN15 96 C7
Hudson Cl YO41 15 D2
Hudson Cres 2 YO30 130 A7
Hudson Ct
Kingston upon Hull HU13 143 D1
Market Weighton YO43 135 D4
Hudson Gdns 2 HU5 140 D1
Hudson's La YO25 31 B7
Hudson St
Kingston upon Hull HU3 145 D8
6 York YO30 130 C7
Hudson Way YO26 129 C8
HUGGATE 18 B2
Huggate Dikes* YO42 17 F2
Huggate Hill YO17 17 E7
Huggate La YO25 18 B5
Huggin Carr Rd DN7 92 F1
Hugh Field La YO8 50 A8
Hugh Field North La YO8 38 A1
Hugh Hill La DN7 92 D6
Hull Arena HU1 155 A1
Hull Bridge Rd
Beverley HU17 154 B4
Tickton HU17 137 C7
Hull Bsns Pk HU8 142 A1
Hull Coll (Cannon St) HU2 155 B4
Hull Coll (Construction Ctr) HU2 155 C3
Hull Collegiate Sch HU10 143 C5
Hull Coll of Further Ed HU1 155 C3
Hull Coll (Park Street Ctr) HU2 145 D7
Hull Coll (The Learning Zone) HU3 145 B6
Hull & East Riding Mus* HU1 155 C2
Hull & East Yorkshire Hospl (Artificial Limb Unit) HU2 155 B3
Hull Maritime Mus* HU1 155 B2
Hull New Theatre HU1 155 B3
Hull Rd
Aldbrough HU11 59 B7
Barmby Moor YO42 28 B4
Beverley HU17 137 B3
Cliffe YO8 49 E2
Hull Rd *continued*
Coniston HU11 57 F5
Easington HU12 90 E6
Hatfield HU11 46 C5
Hemingbrough YO8 50 B1
Hornsea HU18 134 B1
Howden DN14 65 B7
Keyingham HU12 73 C4
Marfleet HU12 147 F6
Northfield HU13 143 F1
Osbaldwick YO10 131 D3
Preston HU12 72 A7
Rimswell HU19 74 E6
Woodmansey HU17 137 B2
York YO10 131 B3
Hull Road Ave 4 DN14 65 B7
Hull Royal Infmy HU3 145 C6
Hull Sch of Art & Design HU1 155 C2
Hull Sta HU1 155 A2
Hull Trinity Ho Sch HU1 155 B2
Hull Truck Theatre* HU2 145 D7
Humber Bank S DN31 153 A6
Humber Bridge Ctry Pk* HU13 69 D4
Humber Bridge Ind Est DN18 70 A1
Humber Bridge Rd DN31 153 A5
Humber Cres
5 Brough HU15 68 C5
Scunthorpe DN17 150 F2
Humberdale Cl 4 HU14 69 B6
Humberdale Dr HU14 69 C5
Humber Dock St HU1 155 B1
Humber Dr 5 YO32 14 B6
Humber Ind Est HU14 68 E4
Humber La
Patrington HU12 74 D1
Skeffling HU12 90 D5
Welwick HU12 90 A7
Humber Pl HU1 155 B1
Humber Rd
Barton-upon-Humber DN18 69 E1
North Ferriby HU14 69 A4
South Killingholme DN40 86 F3
Humberside Airport DN39 99 F5
Humber Side La
Easington HU12 90 F4
Welwick HU12 89 F6
Humber Side Rd HU12 90 B6
Humber St
Cleethorpes DN35 153 F1
Goole DN14 149 D1
Grimsby DN31 153 A5
Kingston upon Hull HU9 155 C1
Market Weighton YO43 135 F4
HUMBERSTON 114 E8
Humberston Ave 13 DN36 114 D8
Humberston CE Prim Sch DN36 114 D8
Humberston Comp Sch DN36 114 C8
Humberstone Rd DN32 153 A2
HUMBERSTON FITTIES 114 F8
Humberston Park Special Sch DN36 114 C8
Humberston Rd DN36 103 B1
Humber Terr DN31 152 C4
Humber View
23 Barton-upon-Humber DN18 84 E8
Kingston upon Hull HU13 143 C2
5 Swanland HU14 69 B6
Humberville Rd DN40 87 C1
HUMBLETON 59 B5
Humbleton Rd
East Garton HU12 59 C6
Elstronwick HU12 58 E3
Hume Brae DN40 87 B1
Hume St DN31 152 C3
Hund Oak Dr DN7 92 D4
Hungate
13 Barton-upon-Humber DN18 69 E1
York YO1 156 C2
Hungate Ct
11 Hunmanby YO14 2 F8
Market Weighton YO43 135 D5
Hungate La YO14 2 F8
Hunger Hills Balk YO25 10 C4
Hungerhills Dr HU11 58 A4
HUNMANBY 2 F8
Hunmanby Ind Est YO14 3 A1
Hunmanby Prim Sch YO14 2 F8
Hunmanby Rd
Burton Fleming YO25 2 E3
Reighton YO14 3 C6
Hunmanby Sta YO14 3 A7
Hunsley Ave 3 HU5 139 B1
Hunsley Cres DN32 103 A2
Hunsley Dr DN41 101 E6
Hunsley Rd HU17 55 A7
Huntcliffe Sch DN21 108 C1
Hunt Ct YO31 156 C3
Hunter Cl
1 Patrington HU12 74 D1
5 Preston HU12 58 D1
Hunter Dr YO41 27 A2
Hunter Gr HU3 145 A4
Hunter Rd HU15 68 C6
Hunters Cl
Dunnington YO19 26 E7
Grimsby DN37 102 B5
10 Haxby YO32 127 C8
Hunter's Croft DN9 105 D3
Hunters Way
Selby YO8 148 B4
York YO24 132 F7
Hunters Wlk YO8 63 D7
Hunters Wood Way 21 YO19 26 F7
Huntingdon Cres 5 DN15 82 B4
Huntingdon St HU4 144 E3
HUNTINGTON 127 E3
Huntington Mews YO31 130 D7
Huntington Prim Sch YO32 127 F4
Huntington Rd YO31 156 C4
Huntington Sch YO32 127 E3
Huntington Stadium (York City Knights RLFC) The YO32 128 A2
Huntley Dr HU5 140 A1
Hunt Rd DN16 151 C1
Hunts Cl 7 DN20 97 E4
Hunts La DN20 108 F5
Huntsmans Chase 8 DN36 113 F8
Huntsmans La YO41 15 C2
Huntsman's Wlk YO24 129 B1
Hurd's Farm DN20 98 D8
Hurford Pl DN37 113 E7
Hurley Cl HU8 141 F3
Hurlstone Cl 20 DN3 92 A2
HURN 136 C4
Hurn Cl HU8 141 E6
Hurns La YO30 126 A7
Hurricane Way YO30 126 E3
Hurst La DN17 96 C2
Hurstlea Dr 19 DN36 103 D1
Hurst's Yd YO1 156 C2
Hurton's La LN11 121 F6
Hushells La DN7 78 C2
Husthwaite Rd 27 HU15 68 D5
Hustler Rd YO16 122 F5
Hutchinson Rd DN35 153 D3
Hutchinson St 1 YO8 148 B6
Hutchinson Way DN14 65 A6
Hutch La DN14 66 C3
Huteson La DN15 82 C8
HUT GREEN 62 A2
HUTTON 32 E8
Hutton Balk YO25 32 D8
Hutton Cl
Kingston upon Hull HU5 139 E2
Poppleton YO26 126 A2
HUTTON CRANSWICK 32 D7
Hutton Cranswick Prim Sch YO25 32 E7
Hutton Cranswick Sta YO25 32 E7
Hutton Rd
Grimsby DN31 153 A6
Hutton Cranswick YO25 32 E7
Hutton St YO26 24 A5
HUTTON WANDESLEY 24 A5
Hutt St HU3 145 D7
Huzzard Cl 5 HU17 55 D8
Hyde Pk Cl 15 DN33 102 D1
Hykeham Cl 12 HU7 56 F6
Hymers Ave HU3 145 B7
Hymers Cl 11 YO25 32 B2
Hymers Coll HU3 145 B7
Hyperion St HU9 155 C3
Hyrst Gr YO31 130 E6
Hytec Way 7 HU15 68 B5

I

Icehouse Rd HU3 145 D6
Icelandic Cl HU3 145 C5
Idas Cl HU9 155 C1
Idle Bank
Epworth DN9 94 A2
Haxey DN9 104 F4
Ikin Way YO32 127 F6
Ilchester Cl HU7 141 B5
Ilford Rd HU5 139 C1
Ilkeston Ave DN14 149 B5
Ilkeston Ct DN15 150 B7
Ilthorpe HU6 140 A8
Ilton Garth YO30 127 A2
IMMINGHAM 87 B2
Immingham Medieval Village* DN40 87 B2
Immingham Mus* DN40 87 C1
Immingham Rd DN40 86 F1
Immingham Sports Ctr DN40 87 C1
Immingham Swimming Pool DN40 87 C1
Impala Way HU4 144 D2
Imperial Ave DN35 153 C4
Imperial Ct 12 HU9 142 A3
Inghams La 12 DN36 114 D4
Inghams Rd DN36 114 D4
Ingland Ct HU9 142 B1
Ingleborough Ave YO10 131 B4
Ingleby Cl HU8 141 F7
Ingleby Rd DN17 107 D7
Inglefield Cl 7 HU17 55 E8
INGLEMIRE 139 F6
Inglemire Ave HU6 140 C5
Inglemire La HU6 139 E5
Inglenook Dr 1 DN8 93 B8
Ingleton 25 HU15 68 C6
Ingleton Ave HU4 144 C6
Ingleton Wlk 3 YO31 131 A5
Inglewood Dr 4 HU4 144 B5

Ingmires 3 HU15 68 D6
Ing Nook Rd HU15 52 C2
Ingram Ave HU11 142 F6
Ingram Cres DN7 92 C4
Ingram Gdns DN20 108 E8
Ingram Gr DN7 92 C4
Ingram Pl DN35 103 B2
Ingram Rd DN7 92 C3
Ingrish La YO23 24 C1
Ings Ct DN14 61 F4
Ings Dr YO43 53 F7
Ings La
Beal DN14 61 D4
Bishop Wilton YO42 16 D2
Brough HU15 68 C5
Carlton DN14 63 E2
Cawood YO19 48 D8
Cottingwith YO42 38 C5
Dunswell HU6 56 D2
Ellerker HU15 67 F8
Hensall DN14 62 D2
Hibaldstow DN20 109 A5
Immingham DN40 87 D1
Kellington DN14 61 F4
Keyingham HU12 73 C4
Kirk Bramwith DN7 92 C7
Nether Poppleton YO26 126 B1
North Coates DN36 115 A3
North Ferriby HU14 69 A4
Patrington HU12 74 C1
Riccall YO19 48 E8
Riston HU11 45 C2
South Cave HU15 67 E7
Spaldington DN14 51 C4
Thorganby YO19 38 B5
Utterby LN11 121 E4
Walkerith DN21 116 F3
Waltham DN37 113 E6
West Stockwith DN10 116 F6
Wheldrake YO19 38 B7
Whitton DN15 67 E3
Winterton DN15 83 D7
Wistow YO8 49 A6
Ings Prim Sch HU8 141 F4
Ings Rd
Cliffe YO8 49 D2
Kingston upon Hull HU7 141 D5
Kirton in Lindsey DN21 107 F1
Molescroft HU17 136 D7
Thorganby YO19 38 B4
Wilberfoss YO41 27 E6
Ings View YO30 126 D2
Inmans Prim Sch HU12 72 D7
Inmans Rd HU12 72 D7
Inman Terr YO26 129 D4
Innescourt HU6 139 E7
Innovation Cl YO10 131 B2
Innovation Way
Great Coates DN31 102 B6
York YO10 131 B2
Innsworth Garth 17 HU7 57 A5
Inrea Hill YO42 29 F5
Intake Ave YO30 130 C8
Intakefield Rd YO8 50 D7
Intake Hill YO43 135 C8
Intake La
Acaster Malbis YO23 36 C7
Beal WF11 61 D5
Dunnington YO19 26 F7
Heck DN14 77 C8
West Haddlesey YO8 61 F6
Intakes La YO42 39 A6
Intax Farm Mews DN32 152 F2
Inverewe Way 2 HU16 138 F5
Inverness Rd 24 DN7 92 D4
Invicta Ct YO24 132 B8
Iona Cl
8 Gainsborough DN21 117 C1
Kingston upon Hull HU8 141 E7
Iona Dr DN36 114 D8
Iona Rd YO16 122 F4
Irby Ct 8 DN35 103 B2
Irby Rd DN17 150 E1
IRBY UPON HUMBER 112 D7
Ireland Wlk HU4 144 B4
Iridium Ct HU13 144 A1
Irvine Rd DN16 151 C1
Irvine Way YO24 132 B7
Irwin Ave YO31 130 E6
Irwin Rd DN21 117 F6
Isaac's Hill DN35 153 E2
Isis Ct HU9 146 B5
Island Carr Rd DN20 98 B2
Island Rd DN17 81 E6
Isle Cl DN17 94 D8
Isledane HU6 139 E8
Itlings La HU13 143 F1
Itterby Cres DN35 103 B2
Ivanhoe Rd DN16 151 C5
Iver Cl YO26 129 C5
Iveson Cl 27 HU12 72 C7
Ivy Cl DN7 92 E4
Ivy Farm Ct 6 DN41 101 F5
Ivy House Ct 23 DN16 96 E2
Ivy La
Grainthorpe LN11 115 E1
Hedon HU12 72 C7
Snaith & Cowick DN14 78 D8
Ivy Mdw HU12 59 C2
Ivy Park Rd DN14 149 E6
Ivy Pl YO32 127 D3
Ivy Rd DN8 79 A1

J

Jackey La HU11 58 B8
Jacklin La DN17 81 C3
Jacklins App DN16 96 D2
Jack Rd YO43 53 C8
Jack Row La DN7 92 B8
Jackson La YO41 27 E4
Jackson Mews 7 DN40 87 B1
Jackson Pl DN36 103 B1
Jackson Rd DN15 150 E7
Jackson's La WF8 76 A4
Jackson's Pl DN36 103 B1
Jackson St
Goole DN14 149 C4
Grimsby DN31 152 C4
Kingston upon Hull HU3 145 D4
York YO31 156 C4
Jackson's Wlk YO23 24 D3
Jacksonville DN14 149 C5
Jack Taylor La HU17 137 B4
Jacobi Cl YO30 130 A7
Jacobs Cl LN11 121 C4
Jade Gr 1 HU3 145 A4
Jalland St HU8 141 C1
James Backhouse Pl
YO24 129 E3
James Cl 1 HU19 75 A6
James Ct 5 DN8 79 B1
James Ingle Mews HU17 154 C2
James Nicolson Link
YO30 127 A2
James Niven Ct 1 HU9 141 D1
Jameson Rd YO16 122 C4
Jameson St HU1 155 A2
James Pl DN39 86 B1
James Reckitt Ave HU8 141 B1
James St
21 Brigg DN20 98 B2
Goole DN14 149 D2
Grimsby DN31 152 C4
Selby YO8 148 C5
York YO10 130 E4
James Way
29 Immingham DN40 87 B1
York YO10 131 A1
Jamieson Terr YO23 130 B1
Janton Ct 23 DN36 114 A8
Japan Rd DN21 117 A1
Japonica Hill 8 DN40 87 C1
Jaque's Bank DN8 94 A5
Jarratt Hill La HU15 67 C8
Jarratt St HU1 155 B3
Jasmine Cl
10 Snaith DN14 63 C1
York YO32 127 D2
Jasmine Ct 8 DN19 86 A8
Jasmine Garth 6 YO41 27 C2
Jasmine Gr 17 HU7 56 F5
Jasmine Way DN40 87 C1
Jason Cl YO16 122 E6
Jason Garth 1 HU7 57 B5
Jaywick Cl YO32 14 B8
Jedwell Cl YO32 127 D5
Jefferson Cl
Goole DN14 65 C4
Molescroft HU17 136 E6
Jefferson Dr HU15 68 C6
Jefferson St DN14 149 C4
Jeffrey La DN9 94 E1
Jellicoe Ct DN16 151 C5
Jendale HU7 140 F8
Jenkings Cl 30 YO42 29 A3
Jenkinson La YO25 32 D8
Jenner Ct DN35 153 B4
Jenner Pl DN35 153 B4
Jennifer Gr 4 YO24 129 F2
Jenning St HU8 155 C4
Jenny Brough La HU13 143 B3
Jenny Brough Mdws
HU13 143 B3
Jenny Cl HU13 143 B3
Jenny La DN14 77 B5
Jenthorpe HU6 140 A8
Jericho La DN40 86 D7
Jervis Ct YO41 27 C1
Jervis Rd
Kingston upon Hull HU9 142 D5
York YO24 132 E8
Jesmond Ave 28 DN17 96 C2
Jesmond Gdns HU9 141 D1
Jesmond Rd HU16 139 C6
Jetcourt HU6 139 E7
Jetty Cl DN14 65 B5
Jevans Ct 2 YO25 124 F4
Jewbury YO31 156 C3
Jewison La
Bempton YO16 4 D1
Flamborough Maltings
YO15 123 B8
Jill Gr HU13 143 F1
Jipdane HU6 139 F8
Jobsons Cl 11 HU15 53 F1
Joby La HU17 43 A2
Jockey La YO32 127 F2
John Bull World of Rock*
YO15 10 F3
John Coupland Hospl
DN21 117 A2
John Gray Ct HU10 138 D1
John Harrison CE Prim Sch
DN19 85 C8
John Harrison's Cl 1
DN19 85 D8
John Leggott Coll DN17 150 E4
John Newton Way HU7 56 E5
Johnny Moor Long La
DN14 79 B6
Johnson Cl DN9 94 E2
Johnson Dr
21 Bottesford DN16 96 E2
Scotter DN21 107 C4
Johnson's La DN17 94 C7
Johnson St
Cleethorpes DN35 153 B4
Selby YO8 148 B6
John St
Kingston upon Hull HU2 155 B3
Scunthorpe DN15 151 B7
Selby YO8 148 D6
York YO31 130 E6
Johnston Ct HU17 136 D7
Joiners La YO25 19 B6
Jonathans Garth DN36 114 D4
Jonquil Ave 16 DN16 96 E2
Jorvik Cl YO26 129 C5
JORVIK Viking Ctr*
YO1 156 C2
Joscelyn Ave HU7 141 B5
Joseph Ogle Cl 6 DN36 113 F8
Joseph Rowntree Sch The
YO32 127 E5
Joseph St DN31 152 C4
Jowland Winn La YO8 63 A4
Jubber Gate YO1 156 B2
Jubilee Ave YO16 122 D4
Jubilee Cl
50 Hedon HU12 72 D7
Shiptonthorpe YO43 40 F6
Jubilee Cres 34 DN21 117 B1
Jubilee Ct YO32 127 D8
Jubilee Gr 8 YO16 122 D5
Jubilee La HU12 59 C2
Jubilee Rd YO8 48 D6
Jubilee Sq HU2 155 B3
Jubilee Terr YO26 129 F5
Jubilee Way
Frodingham DN15 151 B7
6 Scunthorpe DN15 151 B7
Jubilee Wlk YO16 122 D5
Julia Ave YO32 128 B2
Julian Cl HU5 144 A7
Julian St DN32 153 A3
Julians Wlk 8 HU10 143 F6
Junction Rd DN7 92 C6
Junella Cl HU3 145 A4
Jungle Zoo The* DN35 103 D2
Juniper Chase HU17 136 D4
Juniper Cl
Crosby DN15 96 B7
York YO32 127 D3
Juniper Dr YO8 148 D2
Juniper Way
Gainsborough DN21 117 B1
Grimsby DN33 102 E1
Justice Hall La 3 DN17 94 D8
Justice La DN14 81 B8
Jute Rd YO26 129 B5
Jutland Ct 13 DN36 114 A8

K

Karelia Ct HU4 144 B5
Karen Ave 10 DN41 101 A4
Kathleen Ave
Cleethorpes DN35 153 D4
Scunthorpe DN16 151 B1
Kathleen Gr DN32 153 C3
Kathleen Rd HU8 141 B2
Kathleen Rice Cl DN32 153 A4
Kathryn Ave YO32 128 A2
Katrine Cl HU7 141 D5
Kaye Dr YO8 49 B4
Kay Kendall Ct 16 HU19 75 A6
Kaymile Cl 15 DN36 114 A7
KEADBY 95 D6
Kealholme Rd DN17 107 D7
Keats Ave DN17 150 D3
Keats Cl YO30 129 F8
Keb La DN15 83 D2
Keble Cl YO23 133 B3
Keble Dr YO23 133 A2
Keble Gdns YO23 133 B2
Keble Park Cres YO23 133 A2
Keble Park N YO23 133 A3
Keble Park S YO23 133 A2
Keddington Rd 18 DN17 96 C2
Kedrum Rd HU9 141 F1
KEELBY 101 B5
Keelby Prim Sch DN41 101 A5
Keelby Rd
Scunthorpe DN17 150 F1
Stallingborough DN41 101 C6
Keel Ct HU17 137 B3
Keel Rd HU6 140 C8
Keeper's Hill YO25 7 A1
Keepers Way 11 YO19 26 F7
Keeper's Way 2 DN9 94 E1
Keirhardie Wlk 4 DN32 152 E3
Keir Hardie Wlk 13
DN32 152 D3
Keith Ave YO32 128 A4
Keith Cres DN37 101 E1
Kelberdale Cl 30 HU7 56 F6
Keldale 4 YO32 13 F5
Keld Cl 55 HU12 72 D7
Keldgarth YO25 32 F6
Keldgate HU17 154 A2
Keldgate Bar HU17 154 A2
Keldgate Cl HU17 154 A2
Keldgate Rd
Beverley HU17 136 C2
Cottingham HU16 138 D7
Keldmarsh Nature Reserve*
HU17 154 B1
Keldmarsh Prim Sch
HU17 154 A1
Keldspring La YO42 28 E4
KELFIELD 36 D1
Kelfield Rd 9 YO19 48 F8
Kelgate Cl 11 HU8 141 E7
Kelham Rd DN32 153 D2
Kelk La YO25 22 B6
KELLEYTHORPE 124 C1
Kelleythorpe Ind Est
YO25 124 B3
KELLINGLEY 61 C2
KELLINGTON 61 F4
Kellington Ct 9 DN14 61 F2
Kellington La DN14 61 F2
Kellington Prim Sch DN14 61 F3
Kelsey Ave DN15 150 B7
Kelsey Cl YO43 135 D2
Kelsey Dr 3 HU12 73 C4
Kelsey La DN17 95 D4
Kelsey Rd LN7 110 D1
KELSTERN 120 D1
Kelstern Ct DN34 152 A1
Kelston Dr 2 HU13 144 A3
Kelvin Hall Sch HU5 139 E3
Kelvin St HU9 141 E2
Kemp Rd
Grimsby DN31 153 A7
North Ferriby HU14 69 B6
Kempton Cl
Beverley HU17 136 E6
2 York YO24 129 D1
Kempton Dr DN7 92 C2
Kempton Rd HU3 144 E6
Kendal Cl 6 YO19 26 F7
Kendal Ct DN16 151 C2
Kendale Rd DN16 151 E4
Kendale View YO25 124 E6
Kendal Rd DN40 87 D1
Kendal Way HU4 144 C7
Kendon Gdns DN8 93 B8
Kendrew Cl 8 YO32 127 F3
Kenerdales La YO43 53 E8
Kenford Ct 1 DN36 114 A8
Kenilworth Ave HU5 139 F3
Kenilworth Rd
6 Cleethorpes DN35 103 B2
Scunthorpe DN16 151 C5
Kenlay Cl YO32 127 D4
Kenmar Rd DN37 101 F1
Kenmore Dr 4 HU6 56 D5
Kennedy Cl DN20 98 D2
Kennedy Dr
Goole DN14 149 D5
32 Haxby YO32 13 E5
Kennedy Way Sh Ctr
DN40 87 C1
Kenneth Ave 5 DN7 92 C6
Kennet Rd HU8 142 C6
Kennington Wlk HU16 139 D6
Kenrick Pl 5 YO26 129 B5
Kensal Rise YO10 130 D2
Kensington Ct 1 YO24 132 F8
Kensington Gdns 14 DN14 65 A7
Kensington Pl 3 DN33 113 F8
Kensington Rd
Rawcliffe YO30 126 D2
Scunthorpe DN15 150 B7
Kensington St YO23 130 B1
Kent Cl HU9 146 C7
Kent Dr DN20 109 A5
Kentmere Cl 2 HU7 57 A7
Kentmere Dr YO30 126 F1
Kent Rd
Bridlington YO16 122 A2
Goole DN14 149 B4
Kingston upon Hull HU16 139 A5
Selby YO8 148 A6
Kents Gdns 14 DN8 79 B2
Kent Sq YO16 122 A2
Kent St
Grimsby DN32 152 F5
York YO10 156 C1
Kenwardly Rd HU10 143 E8
Kenwood HU19 75 A5
Kenya Dr 3 DN17 96 C1
Kenyon Cl 28 DN8 93 A8
Keppel Dr YO16 123 A8
Kerdane HU6 139 F8
Kerries Wlk DN17 150 C2
Kerrside YO30 129 E8
Kerry Dr HU10 143 C6
Kerry Pit Way HU10 143 C6
Kerver La YO19 26 F7
Kesgrave St DN31 153 A5
Kesteven Ct 6 DN40 100 E8
Kesteven Gr 9 DN17 94 D8
Kesteven Way HU7 56 F5
Kestrel Ave
33 Gainsborough DN21 117 C1
Kingston upon Hull HU7 141 D8
Kestrel Cl YO25 125 A5
Kestrel Dr YO15 123 B7
Kestrel Rd DN17 150 E2
Kestrel Wood Way YO31 127 F2
Keswick Gdns HU6 139 E6
Keswick Way 5 YO32 127 F5
Kettering Rd DN16 151 C6
Kettlebridge La DN40 86 D6
Kettleby La DN20 98 E3
Kettleby View DN20 98 D2
Kettlestring La YO30 127 A3
Kettlethorpe Hill HU15 53 F4
Kettlewell Cl 2 HU7 56 F6
Kettlewell St DN32 152 E1
Ketwell La 19 HU12 72 C7
Kew Rd DN35 153
KEXBY 27
Kexby Ave YO10 130
Kexby Stray YO41 27
Keyholme La DN36 115
KEYINGHAM 73
Keyingham Prim Sch
HU12 73 C
Keyingham Rd HU12 73
Keynes Pk 22 HU7 56
Key Way YO19 133
Keyworth Dr 5 LN7 111
Kiddier Ave 12 DN33 113
Kidd La
Brough HU15 68
Melbourne YO42 39
Kidhill La HU11 45
Kilburn Ave HU2 155
Kilburn Rd YO10 130
Kildale Cl HU8 141
KILHAM 9 C
Kilham CE Prim Sch YO25 9 C
Kilham La
Kilham YO25 9
Thwing YO25 9
Kilham Rd YO25 8
Kilkoy Dr 4 HU7 56
Killingholme Haven Pits
Nature Reserve* DN40 87
Killingholme Prim Sch
DN40 86
Killingholme Rd DN40 86
Killingwoldgraves La
HU17 43
Kiln Beck Bsns Pk HU17 137 C
Kilnhouse La HU12 60 C
Kiln La
17 Brigg DN20 98
Patrington HU12 74
Kiln Lane Ind Est DN40 101
Kiln Lane Trading Est
DN40 87
KILNSEA 91
Kilnsea Gr HU9 141
KILNWICK 32
Kilnwick Ave HU5 139 C
Kilnwick Garth 2 YO42 29
Kilnwick La YO25 32
KILNWICK PERCY 29 C
Kilnwick Percy Hill YO42 29 D
Kilnwick Rd YO42 29
KILPIN 65 D
Kilpin Broad La DN14 65 E
KILPIN PIKE 65 C
Kilton Ct 12 HU8 141 D
Kilvin Dr HU17 137
Kimberley Ct 33 DN15 96
Kimberley St HU3 145 C
Kimberlows Wood Hill 3
YO10 131 C
Kimmeridge Cl HU7 141
Kinbrace Dr YO24 132
Kinderscout Cl 15 HU7 56
King Charles Cl HU10 143
King Edward Cres 9 DN8 79
King Edward Rd DN8 93
King Edward St
Belton DN9 94 E
Grimsby DN31 152 E
Kingston upon Hull HU1 155 A
12 Kirton in Lindsey DN21 108
Scunthorpe DN16 151 A
King Edwards Terr 4
HU15 68
Kingerby Rd DN17 150
Kingfisher HU7 141 D
Kingfisher Cl
22 Barton Waterside
DN18 69
Brigg DN20 98
Kingston upon Hull HU7 141 D
1 Leven HU17 45 A
Scunthorpe DN15 96 B
Kingfisher Dr YO15 11
Kingfisher Rise HU7 141
Kingfisher Way DN16 151
King Georges Ct DN7 92 C
King George V Athletic
Stadium DN32 153 B
King Oswald Rd DN9 105 D
King Rudding Cl 6 YO19 49
King Rudding La YO19 49 B
Kings Acre YO31 131 B
King's Ave DN20 98 C
King's Bench St HU3 145 B
Kingsbury Way 7 HU7 56
Kings Cl
5 Barlby YO8 49
24 Pocklington YO42 29
King's Cl 7 DN7 92
Kingsclere YO32 127
Kingscott Cl 10 HU7 56
Kings Court Rd 4 DN8 79
Kings Croft 3 DN17 94
King's Cross Cl 2 HU3 145
King's Cswy
Reedness DN14 80
Swinefleet DN14 65
Kings Ct
Market Weighton YO43 135
Scawby DN20 108
Scunthorpe DN15 151
York YO1 156
Kingsdale DN17 96
KINGSFORTH 84
Kings Garth YO25 125
Kingsgate
Bridlington YO15 122

ngsgate *continued*
Carnaby YO15 10 F2
Cleethorpes DN32 153 A3
ngsgate Mews DN32 153 A3
ngsland Terr 11 YO26 129 F5
ngs Lea YO8 50 A8
ngs Leigh 1 HU3 145 C6
ngsley Ave HU9 141 E2
ngsley Cl 6 HU15 68 B5
ngsley Dr HU10 138 D1
ngsley Gr 4 DN33 102 E2
ngs Mdw YO25 124 D4
ngsmead 20 DN8 79 B2
ngs Mead
Great Driffield YO25 124 D4
Woodmansey HU17 137 D1
ngs Mews DN35 103 E1
ngs Mill Cl YO25 124 D4
ngs Mill Pk YO25 124 D4
ng's Mill Rd YO25 124 D3
ngs Mill Sch YO25 124 E4
ngs Moor Rd YO32 14 D2
ng's Pl 29 HU12 72 C7
ngsport Cl HU3 145 A7
ngs Rd DN40 87 D1
ng's Rd
Barnetby le Wold DN38 99 B5
Cleethorpes DN35 103 D2
ng's Sq
Beverley HU17 154 B3
York YO1 156 C2
ng's Staith YO1 156 B2
ng St
1 Barton-upon-Humber DN18 84 F8
Bridlington YO15 122 E2
6 Cawood YO8 48 B8
Cottingham HU16 139 B6
East Halton DN40 86 D7
Goxhill DN19 86 A8
Great Driffield YO25 124 F4
1 Hornsea HU18 134 C3
19 Keelby DN41 101 A4
Sancton YO43 41 E2
Scunthorpe DN15 151 B8
Thorne/Moorends DN8 93 A8
Winterton DN15 83 A5
17 Withernsea HU19 75 A6
Woodmansey HU17 137 D1
York YO1 156 B2
ngsthorpe YO24 129 D2
ngsthorpe Pk 11 YO8 48 D6
ngston Ave
Grimsby DN34 152 A2
Kingston upon Hull HU13 143 F1
ngston Cl
Hilderthorpe YO15 11 B4
8 Humberston DN35 103 D1
ngston Communications Stadium (Hull City AFC & Hull RLFC) HU3 145 B7
ngston Cres YO15 11 B4
ngston Rd
Bridlington YO15 11 B4
Kingston upon Hull HU10 138 D1
Scunthorpe DN16 151 A3
ngston Ret Pk HU1 155 A1
ngston Rise
Kingston upon Hull HU10 138 C1
Willerby HU10 138 C1
ngston Sq HU2 155 B3
ngston St
Goole DN14 149 C2
Kingston upon Hull HU1 155 B1
NGSTON UPON HULL 155 B2
ngston View 27 DN18 84 F8
ngston Way HU7 140 F5
ngston Wharf HU1 155 A1
ngsway
2 Brigg DN20 98 B2
Cleethorpes DN35 103 D3
Goole DN14 149 D4
Kingston upon Hull HU16 139 B5
Scunthorpe DN15 150 C7
14 Stainforth DN7 92 C6
6 Stamford Bridge YO41 15 D2
ngsway N YO30 130 B7
ngsway Prim Sch DN14 149 E5
ngsway Sta DN35 103 D2
ngsway W YO24 129 D1
ngswood College of Arts HU7 57 A5
ngswood Gr YO24 129 D3
ngswood Ret Pk HU7 56 E5
ngtree Ave HU16 139 B6
nloch Way 28 DN40 87 B1
nloss Garth 2 HU7 57 B5
nsbourne Gn 37 DN7 92 D4
nsley Wlk 5 DN15 151 B7
nthorpe HU6 140 A8
plin Dr 14 DN6 76 E2
pling Ave DN17 150 D3
pling Cl YO25 31 C4
plingcotes Chalk Pit Nature Reserve* YO43 41 F6
plingcotes La YO43 42 A5
pling Cotes Medieval Village* YO25 30 D2
plingcotes Racecourse* YO25 30 E1
plington Cl HU3 145 A7
pling Wlk 1 HU4 144 D2
rby Cl YO43 135 E2
rby Dr
Cottingham HU16 139 B6
Kingston upon Hull HU16 139 B6
IRBY GRINDALYTHE 6 E6
Kirby La YO25 7 A4
KIRBY UNDERDALE 17 A5
Kir Cres YO24 129 C3
Kirk Balk YO17 16 E8
Kirk Balk La YO60 15 B7
KIRK BRAMWITH 92 A6
KIRKBURN 20 A2
Kirkby Ave YO8 148 B7
Kirkby Cl DN14 149 C5
Kirkby Rd
Scunthorpe DN17 96 C2
Selby YO8 148 B7
Kirkby St HU2 155 B4
Kirk Cl HU7 141 D6
Kirkcroft YO32 127 C8
Kirk Croft HU16 139 A6
Kirkdale Rd YO10 131 D4
Kirkden Paddocks DN9 94 C2
KIRK ELLA 143 D8
Kirkfield Rd HU19 75 A6
Kirkgate
Bridlington YO16 122 D4
8 Pocklington YO42 29 A4
Kirk Gate DN37 113 E6
Kirkgate Mews YO16 122 D5
Kirkham Ave 1 YO31 130 E8
Kirkham Cl HU13 143 F2
Kirkham Ct DN14 149 E6
Kirkham Dr HU5 140 B2
Kirkham Rd YO16 122 D7
Kirkholme Way HU17 137 B4
Kirkhouse Green Rd DN7 92 A8
Kirk La
Sykehouse DN14 78 B4
Walkington HU17 55 B7
Kirkland Cl YO8 148 D4
Kirklands YO32 14 B6
Kirklands La YO41 16 C2
Kirklands Rd HU5 144 E8
Kirkland St YO42 29 A4
Kirk Rd 2 HU12 58 C1
Kirk Rise HU10 143 C7
Kirkside 2 DN37 113 E6
KIRK SMEATON 76 B3
Kirk Smeaton CE Prim Sch WF8 76 B3
Kirkstead Cres DN33 102 D2
Kirkstead St HU8 141 A2
Kirkstone Dr YO31 131 A6
Kirkstone Rd HU5 139 D2
Kirk View 1 YO26 129 C3
Kirkway HU10 143 B7
Kirkwell YO23 133 A4
Kirman Cres 18 DN17 96 C2
KIRMINGTON 100 A6
Kirmington CE Prim Sch DN39 100 A6
Kirmington Gdns DN34 152 A2
Kirncroft Cl 16 HU12 73 C4
KIRTON IN LINDSEY 108 B1
Kirton in Lindsey Prim Sch DN21 108 A1
Kirton La DN7 92 E6
Kirton Lane Prim Sch DN7 92 D7
Kirton Lindsey Sta DN21 108 B2
Kirton Rd
Blyton DN21 117 F6
Holme DN16 97 B2
Kirton in Lindsey DN21 108 A3
Messingham DN17 107 E6
Scawby DN20 108 C8
Scotton DN21 107 D2
Kishorn Ct 30 DN40 87 B1
Kissing Gate HU12 59 D2
Kitchen Dr YO8 148 D4
Kitchener Cl YO8 148 B5
Kitchener St
Selby YO8 148 B6
York YO31 130 D7
Kitchen La HU17 154 A1
Kitemere Pl 2 YO24 132 B8
Kit Kat Crescent (York City FC) YO31 130 B7
Kitty Garth YO19 38 A7
Kitty Hill (Tumulus)* YO41 16 E3
Klondyke DN16 151 D7
KNAPTON 129 A5
Knapton Ave 7 HU5 139 E3
Knapton Cl 1 YO32 14 B6
Knapton Ct LN7 111 C4
Knapton La YO26 129 B4
KNAVESMIRE 133 A7
Knavesmire Cres YO23 130 B1
Knavesmire Prim Sch YO23 130 B1
Knavesmire Rd
Nunthorpe YO23 133 B8
York YO23 130 A1
KNEDLINGTON 64 E6
Knedlington Rd DN14 65 A6
Knedlington Wlk 7 DN14 65 A6
Knightly Way HU7 56 E5
Knightsbridge 7 DN36 114 A8
Knightsbridge Ct 7 HU3 140 D1
Knightsbridge Rd DN17 107 D7
Knights Cl
Belton DN9 94 E2
8 Laceby DN37 101 F1
Knightscourt HU6 139 E7
Knights Ct HU17 154 B2
Knight's Ct 16 DN16 96 D2
Knight St DN32 153 B2
Knights Way HU17 154 B3
Knole Pk HU7 56 F5
Knoll St DN35 153 F2
Knoll The YO24 129 B2
KNOTTINGLEY 61 B2
Knottingley High Sch WF11 61 A2
Knowle Rd 25 HU7 56 F5
Knowles Ave HU6 140 C8
Knowle Way 54 HU12 72 D7
Knowsley Ave HU16 139 A7
Kyffin Ave HU9 142 D2
Kyle Cl HU8 142 C6
Kyle Way YO26 129 B8
Kyme St YO1 156 B1

L

Labrador Dr 11 DN20 97 E4
Laburnham Ave 21 DN37 113 D6
Laburnham Cl 22 DN37 113 D6
Laburnum Ave
18 Gainsborough DN21 117 B1
Gunness DN15 95 E6
Hutton Cranswick YO25 32 E7
Kingston upon Hull HU8 141 C2
11 Thorne/Moorends DN8 79 B2
Laburnum Cl
Rufforth YO23 24 C6
7 Snaith DN14 63 C1
3 Thorpe Willoughby YO8 48 B1
Laburnum Ct
Barlow YO8 63 D7
4 Bridlington YO16 123 A6
Kingston upon Hull HU13 143 D1
Laburnum Dr
Beverley HU17 137 A7
7 Church Town DN9 94 E1
Grimsby DN34 102 C4
3 Kingston upon Hull HU4 144 B7
Laburnum Farm Cl YO26 24 C8
Laburnum Garth 6 YO31 130 F8
Laburnum Gr
Burton upon Stather DN15 82 B5
10 Crowle DN17 94 D7
Scunthorpe DN16 151 B3
Stillingfleet YO19 36 D4
Laburnum Wlk 17 HU15 66 D8
LACEBY 101 E2
LACEBY ACRES 102 B2
Laceby Acres Prim Sch DN34 102 B3
Laceby Rd
Grimsby DN34 102 C2
Laceby Acres DN34 102 B2
Scunthorpe DN17 150 E1
Lady Anne Ct YO1 156 B1
Ladybower Cl 4 HU8 141 E7
Lady Frances Cres DN35 153 C1
Ladygate HU17 154 A3
Lady Hamilton Gdns YO24 129 E2
Lady Kell Gdns YO32 127 E8
Lady Mill Garth YO30 130 B8
Lady Peckitts Yd YO1 156 B2
Lady Rd YO30 130 B7
Ladyside Cl 11 HU7 57 A6
Ladysmith Ind Est DN32 153 A2
Ladysmith Mews 13 YO32 14 A7
Ladysmith Rd
Grimsby DN32 152 F3
Kingston upon Hull HU10 138 E1
Lady's Well* YO43 135 F7
Ladywell Gate 3 HU15 68 E6
Lady Wortley Pl YO23 133 B6
Laforey Rd DN37 102 C6
Lagoon Dr HU7 141 D8
Lagoon Rd DN17 150 B2
Lairgate HU17 154 A2
Lairs La YO42 30 A5
Lake Dr HU8 141 E3
Lakeside
Acaster Malbis YO23 36 C7
Great Coates DN31 102 B6
Little Leven HU17 44 F6
Lakeside County Prim Sch YO30 126 F2
Lakeside Dr DN17 150 C1
Lakeside Gr
Kingston upon Hull HU4 144 D4
1 Strensall YO32 14 B8
Lakeside Parkway DN16 151 F1
Lakeside Ret Pk DN16 151 F1
Lakeside Sta DN35 103 E2
Lakeview 6 HU17 44 F6
Lake View HU8 141 E3
Laking La YO25 2 A3
Lalrgate Pl 20 DN36 103 C1
Lambert Ave 16 HU15 68 C6
Lambert Cl YO43 135 E3
Lambert Ct YO1 156 B1
Lambert Park Rd 23 HU12 72 C7
Lambert Rd
Bridlington YO16 122 F5
Grimsby DN32 152 E2
Lambert St HU5 140 D2
Lamb Inn Rd 9 WF11 61 A2
Lamb La
Newport HU15 67 B8
Roos HU12 60 A1
Lambourn Ct 25 DN35 103 C1
Lambourne Rise 7 DN16 96 D1
Lambton St HU5 140 C3
Lambwath Hall Ct HU7 141 C8
Lambwath La HU11 46 A3
Lambwath Rd HU8 141 C4
Lambwell Hill HU15 54 E2
Lamel St YO10 131 A3
Lamorna Ave HU8 141 B3
Lamplugh Cres YO23 133 B3
Lamplugh La 7 YO15 122 F4
Lamplugh Rd YO15 122 F4
Lamplugh Sq 6 YO15 122 F4
Lampton Gr DN32 152 D2
Lanark St 3 HU5 145 B8
Lancar Cl 18 YO32 13 D5
Lancaster App DN40 86 D4
Lancaster Ave DN31 152 B3
Lancaster Ct 13 DN33 102 D1
Lancaster Dr
Kingston upon Hull HU8 141 D4
2 Moorland Prison DN7 104 A8
7 South Killingholme DN40 86 E3
Lancaster Gate DN36 114 A4
Lancaster La HU18 134 A4
Lancaster Rd
Carnaby YO15 10 D2
Gringley on the Hill DN10 116 A1
Pocklington YO42 28 E3
Scunthorpe DN16 151 A1
Lancaster Way
26 Brough HU15 68 C5
York YO30 127 A1
Lancelot Ct HU9 146 C6
Lancing Way 24 DN33 113 E8
Landalewood Rd YO30 126 F2
Landau Cl YO30 129 F8
Land Dike LN11 115 A1
Landeck Ave DN34 152 B2
Land Ends Rd DN8 78 F1
Landing La
Asselby DN14 64 D6
Barlby with Osgodby YO8 148 F8
Broomfleet HU15 67 A7
Gilberdyke HU15 52 D1
Haxby YO32 127 E7
Hemingbrough YO8 63 F8
Newport HU15 52 E1
Riccall YO19 48 F8
York YO26 129 E6
Landing Rd YO8 62 A7
Landings The 21 YO32 13 F5
Land of Green Ginger HU1 155 B2
Landor Ave DN17 150 D3
Landress La HU17 154 A2
Laneham St DN15 151 A7
Lanes End 24 DN21 108 B1
Lanes The 7 DN36 114 D4
Lane The YO41 15 B2
Lang Ave YO10 131 A4
Langdale Ave
Beverley HU17 154 B3
Grimsby DN33 113 D8
Kingston upon Hull HU5 139 E2
York YO31 131 B6
Langdale Cres HU16 139 A5
Langdale Dr 4 HU12 73 C4
Langdale Gr YO8 148 B3
Langdale Mews YO16 122 E7
Langdale Rd YO43 135 E4
Langford Wlk 1 HU4 144 B7
Langham Rd 13 HU12 72 E5
Langholm Cl HU17 136 D5
Langholme Dr YO26 129 C6
Langholme La DN9 116 B8
Langley Ct 1 YO32 127 F6
Langley Dr DN16 96 D1
Langley Garth
11 Driffield YO25 124 F4
Great Driffield YO25 124 F4
Langley Pk 25 HU7 56 F5
Langley Pl 5 DN35 103 D2
Langleys Rd 6 DN6 76 E1
Langold Dr 15 DN6 76 E2
Lang Rd
Bishopthorpe YO23 132 F4
York YO32 127 F6
Langrick Ave 9 DN14 65 B7
Langrickgate La YO42 38 C5
Langsett Gr YO30 126 F3
Langsett Rd HU8 141 D7
Langthorpe Rd HU11 45 F2
Langthwaite Cl 18 HU15 68 D5
LANGTOFT 8 D5
Langtoft Gr HU6 139 F5
Langtoft Prim Sch YO25 8 C5
Langton Cl 16 DN33 102 D2
Langton Ct 1 YO32 14 A6
Langton Dr DN33 102 D2
Langton Rd DN36 114 B5
Langtree Cl HU7 140 F8
Langwith Stray YO10 26 C2
Lansdowne Ave DN33 102 E2
Lansdowne Cres 9 YO15 122 F3
Lansdowne Rd YO15 122 F2
Lansdowne St HU3 145 C6
Lansdowne Terr 5 YO10 130 E3
Lansdown Link 17 DN35 103 C2
Lansdown Rd
Goole DN14 149 A5
13 Immingham DN40 87 B1
Lansdown Way 7 YO32 13 F5
Lanshaw Croft YO30 126 F1
Lanyon Cl HU7 141 C7
Laporte Rd DN40 87 E2
Lapwing Cl HU7 141 D8
Lapwing Rd YO25 125 B5
Lapwing Way 17 DN18 69 E1
Larard Ave 2 HU6 140 C8
Larch Cl
2 Immingham DN40 87 D2
Kingston upon Hull HU5 140 D2
Larch Ct 11 DN21 117 C1
Larch Dr HU12 72 E5
Larchfield YO31 131 C7
Larch Gr
Scawby DN20 108 F8
Scunthorpe DN16 151 B3
Larchmont Cl 7 HU15 68 C6
Larch Rd 6 DN35 103 B1
Larch Road YO8 148 E2
Larch Way
35 Haxby YO32 13 E5
Selby YO8 148 D2
Larden Ave 1 DN33 113 E8
Larkfield Cl 1 YO23 132 A3
Larkfield Rd YO8 148 A4
Lark Rise 2 DN21 107 B3
Larkspur Ave DN41 101 F5
Larmour Rd DN37 102 B4
Larne Rd HU9 142 B4
Larsen Pk DN14 149 A3
Larsen Rd DN14 149 A3
Lascelles Ave HU19 74 F6
Lasenby Cl YO32 127 D5
Lashbrook Garth HU4 144 B4
Lastingham 12 HU15 68 C6
Lastingham Cl HU6 139 F6
Lastingham Terr YO10 130 D2
LAUGHTON 117 F8
Laughton Rd
Beverley HU17 154 B4
Blyton DN21 117 B4
Laundry La YO25 124 E5
Laura St DN14 149 C5
Laurel Ave DN8 79 B2
Laurel Cl
Earswick YO32 128 A7
10 Gainsborough DN21 117 C1
Gateforth YO8 48 B1
3 Grimsby DN33 102 E1
Kingston upon Hull HU5 144 B7
Laurel Gr LN7 110 A1
Laurels Cl 1 DN40 100 E8
Laurels The
Barlby YO8 49 B5
Barmby Moor YO42 28 D3
Laurel Way 19 DN16 96 E2
Laurence Gr YO8 148 D3
Lauridson Cl 2 DN37 101 E1
Laurier St DN35 153 D4
Laurold Ave DN7 93 A3
Lauty La HU11 45 C5
Lavender Cl
23 Dunswell HU7 56 F5
Goole DN14 149 E7
Lavender Gr
10 New Waltham DN36 113 F8
York YO26 129 E5
Lavender Way DN15 151 B6
Lavender Wlk
Beverley HU17 154 A1
1 Kingston upon Hull HU5 144 C7
Lavenham Rd DN33 113 D8
Laveracks Ind Est YO41 27 B3
Lawn La DN6 77 E3
Lawnsgarth HU16 139 A7
LAWNS THE 138 F7
Lawns The
Beverley HU17 136 C6
Bridlington YO16 122 E7
Grimsby DN34 152 C2
Kirk Ella HU10 143 D7
Sutton-on-Hull HU7 141 D6
Lawnswood HU13 143 D2
Lawnswood Cl HU7 141 D5
Lawnswood Dr YO30 129 F8
Lawnway YO31 131 A7
Lawrence Ave
Bewholme HU11 34 E3
Kingston upon Hull HU8 141 F3
Lawrence Ct 11 YO10 130 E3
Lawrence Sq YO10 130 F3
Lawrence St
Grimsby DN31 152 C4
York YO10 130 E3
Lawson Ave
Grimsby DN31 152 B3
Kingston upon Hull HU16 139 B7
Lawson Cl
Kingston upon Hull HU6 140 B5
1 Walkington HU17 55 B7
Lawson Rd
Bridlington YO16 122 D4
York YO24 132 F7
Lawsons Cl YO14 2 F7
Laxthorpe HU6 140 A8
LAXTON 65 F4
Laxton Garth HU10 138 B1
Laxton Gr 5 DN16 96 D1
Laybourne Garth YO25 125 A4
LAYERTHORPE 130 E4
Layerthorpe YO31 156 C3
LAYTHAM 39 B2
Laytham Gr 6 HU9 142 A2
Leaburn Rd DN17 107 D7
Lea Cres HU16 139 A5
Lea Croft 2 YO43 135 E4
Leadhills Way 6 HU7 57 B5
Leadley Croft YO23 36 A1
Lead Mill La YO1 156 C1
Lea Dr DN32 102 F2
Leads Rd HU7 141 C6
Lea Field Rd YO25 31 E6
Lea Garth DN17 107 D7
Leake St 12 YO10 130 E3
Lealand Cl 1 DN37 101 E1
Lealholm Ct 11 HU8 141 D7

Leame Cl HU3 145 A7
Leamington Cl DN16 151 C5
Leamington Ct DN16 151 C5
Leander Rd HU9 142 B3
Learmans Way YO23 132 C3
Learning La DN14 61 F1
Leas Cl 12 DN37 113 E7
Lease La DN40 86 D6
Leases The HU17 154 A2
Leas Jun & Inf Sch The
DN37 113 E7
Leas La HU11 34 F1
Lea The HU15 54 A2
Leathley Cl 1 HU17 136 E1
Leavens La HU15 52 D2
Lea Way YO32 128 A4
LECONFIELD 43 D6
Leconfield Cl HU9 142 D1
Leconfield Prim Sch
HU17 43 D6
Ledbury Dr 10 DN36 114 A8
Ledbury Rd HU5 139 D2
Lee Ave HU19 75 A6
Lee Ct DN14 77 A7
Leeds Rd YO8 148 A4
Lee Fair Gdns DN17 96 C1
Leek Hill 9 DN15 83 A5
Leeman Rd YO26 156 A2
Leeming Garth 3 HU7 57 B5
Leeside YO24 132 E8
Lee Smith St HU9 146 E7
Lees Rest Houses HU4 144 D6
Lee St HU8 141 D3
Lees Wlk HU3 145 A7
Lee View DN14 77 A7
Legard Ave DN16 151 B2
Legard Dr HU10 143 F6
Legarde Ave HU4 144 C6
Leggott Way 1 DN41 101 E6
Legion Cl 11 HU15 68 C5
Legsby Ave DN32 152 E2
Legsby Pl DN32 102 F2
Leicester St HU3 145 D8
Leicester Way YO1 156 C1
Leighton Croft 3 YO30 126 F1
Leighton Gr 2 DN33 102 E2
Leitholm Cl 2 HU7 57 A6
LELLEY 58 F3
Lelley Rd
Humbleton HU11 58 F5
Preston HU12 58 D2
Lendal YO1 156 B2
Lenham La HU1 155 A2
Leningrad Rd HU7 140 F6
Lennox Cl 2 YO14 3 A8
Leonard Cl HU12 72 A5
Leonard Cres DN15 150 F7
Leonard St
4 Kingston upon Hull HU3 145 D8
Kingston upon Hull HU3 155 A4
Leopold Cl DN16 151 A2
LEPPINGTON 16 C8
Lerecroft Rd YO24 132 D8
Lesley Ave YO10 133 E8
Leslie Ct 4 DN15 151 B7
Lestrange St DN35 153 C3
Levels La DN9 104 A4
Levels The
Hornsea HU18 134 C4
Wrawby DN20 98 E3
LEVEN 45 A8
Leven CE Prim Sch HU17 45 B7
Leven Rd
Little Burton YO25 34 B1
Scunthorpe DN16 151 D2
York YO24 132 D7
Leverstock Gn 36 DN7 92 D4
Levington St DN32 153 A5
Levisham Cl HU6 139 F6
Levisham St YO10 130 D2
Levita Ave HU9 142 C2
Levitt Lanes YO25 31 F2
Lewis Rd DN35 153 D4
Lexington Dr HU4 144 C5
Leyburn Ave
Hornsea HU18 134 C2
Kingston upon Hull HU6 139 E4
Leyden Cl 18 DN40 87 B1
Leyes The YO10 131 C4
Leyfield Cl 1 YO32 14 A7
Leyland Ave 6 DN7 92 E4
Leyland Rd YO31 131 A5
Leys Ct YO16 122 B4
Leys Farm Jun Sch DN17 96 C2
Leys La
Darrington WF11 76 A8
Little Smeaton WF8 76 B4
Skipsea YO25 23 A1
Winterton DN15 83 B6
Leys Rd
Bridlington YO16 122 B4
Darrington WF11 76 A7
Leys The HU18 134 B4
Liberty La HU1 155 C2
Library Sq YO1 156 B3
Lichfield Ave DN17 150 C3
Lichfield Cl
Beverley HU17 136 E1
Kingston upon Hull HU2 155 A4
Lichfield Ct
Cleethorpes DN32 153 B2
6 York YO23 130 B1
Lichfield Rd
Grimsby DN32 153 B2
Lichfield Rd *continued*
40 Hatfield DN7 92 D4
Liddell St HU2 155 A3
Lidgard Rd DN36 103 D1
Lidgett Cl DN20 108 E8
Lidgett Gr YO26 129 B6
Lidgett The 7 DN9 105 D6
Lidice Rd DN14 64 E2
Lighthouse Rd YO15 5 B2
Lilac Ave
Beverley HU17 136 F7
Scunthorpe DN16 151 C5
Summergangs HU8 141 B2
Willerby HU10 138 D1
York YO10 131 B3
Lilac Cl YO25 124 D3
Lilac Gr YO32 127 D4
Lilac Rd 20 HU15 68 C5
Lilacs The 10 YO42 29 A3
Lilbourne Dr YO30 130 A8
Lilling Ave 3 YO31 130 E8
Lily La YO15 5 A2
Lilywood Rd DN20 97 D3
Limber Ct DN34 152 A2
Limber Hill LN8 120 A4
Limber Rd
Humberside Airport DN39 100 A6
Swallow LN7 112 A7
Limber Vale DN34 152 A2
Lime Ave
Brough HU15 68 C5
Kingston upon Hull HU10 138 E1
Scunthorpe DN16 97 A3
York YO31 130 F7
Lime Cl YO25 124 F2
Limedale View 3 DN3 92 A3
Limedane HU6 139 F8
Limegarth 10 YO26 12 F1
Lime Gr
Goxhill DN19 86 A8
Holton le Clay DN36 114 A5
Humberston DN36 114 C7
Scunthorpe DN16 151 B3
Limekiln Hill YO25 7 B3
Limekiln La YO16 123 A5
Limerick Cl HU8 142 B6
Limes Ct YO31 130 F6
Lime St
Grimsby DN31 152 C4
Kingston upon Hull HU8 155 C4
Limes The
2 Beckingham DN10 116 D1
3 South Cave HU15 53 F1
3 Stallingborough DN41 101 D6
Stockton on the Forest YO32 14 D2
Limes Wlk YO25 124 F5
Lime Tree 6 HU15 66 D7
Limetree Ave
12 Grimsby DN33 102 E2
Kingston upon Hull HU7 141 D6
Lime Tree Ave
Beverley HU17 137 A6
20 Gainsborough DN21 117 B1
Goole DN14 149 D5
Northfield HU13 143 F2
Summergangs HU8 141 C2
York YO32 127 D3
Limetree Cl 2 YO8 48 B1
Lime Tree Dr
Little Burton YO25 34 B2
Whitley DN14 77 A7
Lime Tree Gdns DN14 149 D5
Lime Tree Gr
Selby YO8 148 A6
4 Thorne/Moorends DN8 93 A8
Lime Tree La HU11 142 F6
Lime Tree Mews 15 YO19 26 F7
Lime Tree Villas HU7 141 D6
Lincoln Bvd DN31 152 B3
Lincoln Castle Way DN19 70 D2
Lincoln Cl 13 DN17 94 D7
Lincoln Cres 2 DN21 119 C8
Lincoln Ct DN16 151 B3
Lincoln Dr
24 Barton-upon-Humber DN18 84 F8
Caistor LN7 111 B4
Winterton DN15 83 A5
Lincoln Gate DN36 121 A5
Lincoln Gdns DN16 151 A2
Lincoln Gdns Prim Sch
DN16 151 A2
Lincoln Gn HU4 144 C7
Lincoln Rd
Barmby Moor YO42 28 F3
Cleethorpes DN35 153 C1
Moorland Prison DN7 104 A8
Lincolnshire Wolds Rly*
DN36 121 C7
Lincoln St
22 Gainsborough DN21 117 B1
Kingston upon Hull HU2 155 B4
York YO26 129 F5
Lincoln Way 9 HU17 55 E8
Lindale 2 YO24 132 C7
Lindale Ave HU18 134 B2
Lindale Gdns DN16 151 C3
Linden Ave HU16 139 C7
Linden Cl
6 Hatfield DN7 92 D4
19 Scalby HU15 66 D8
York YO32 127 F5
Lindengate Ave HU7 141 B4
Lindengate Way HU7 141 B5
Linden Gr 1 YO30 130 A8
Linden Way 9 YO8 48 B1
Linden Wlk HU15 66 D8
Lindholme DN21 107 C3
Lindholme Bank Rd DN7 93 B1
Lindisfarne Ave 4 DN36 113 F7
Lindley Rd YO30 126 F1
Lindley St
Scunthorpe DN16 151 A2
York YO24 129 F3
Lindley Wood Gr YO30 126 E3
Lindrick Wlk 8 DN37 113 D6
Lindsey DN36 114 A6
Lindsey Ave YO26 129 D4
Lindsey Ct 21 DN9 105 E6
Lindsey Dr
Crowle DN17 94 D8
Healing DN41 102 A5
Holton le Clay DN36 114 A6
Lindsey Pl HU4 144 D6
Lindsey Rd DN35 153 F1
Lindsey Rise 30 DN33 113 E8
Lindsey St 2 DN16 151 C6
Lindum Ave 23 DN40 87 B1
Lindum Cres 27 DN20 98 B2
Lindum Gr DN17 94 C7
Lindum Rd DN35 103 C2
Lindum St DN15 151 B7
Lindum Wlk LN7 110 A4
Linecroft La DN10 116 E4
Linegate 4 YO43 135 D4
Lingcourt HU6 139 F7
Ling Croft HU15 68 D5
Lingcroft Cl YO8 63 D4
Lingcroft La YO19 133 E3
Lingdale Rd HU9 142 E3
Ling Dr 34 DN21 117 C1
Lingfield Cres YO24 129 F1
Ling House La DN7 92 A5
Ling La YO41 27 F6
Lings La DN7 92 D3
Lings Rd HU17 42 E3
LINGS THE 92 D3
Link Ave YO30 130 C8
Link Bsns Pk YO10 131 D4
Linkfield Rd HU5 139 E4
Link Rd
Huntington YO32 127 E2
Kingston upon Hull HU16 139 B5
Link Rd Ct YO10 131 D4
Link Road Ct YO10 131 D4
Links Rd DN35 103 D2
Link The
Copmanthorpe YO23 132 A3
Kingston upon Hull HU4 144 C5
Selby YO8 148 A4
York YO10 133 E8
Linkway
Hatfield DN7 92 F3
Norton DN6 76 E2
Linley Cl HU17 45 A8
Linleyhill Rd HU17 33 C1
Linnaeus St HU3 145 C6
Linnet Cl DN15 96 B7
Linnet Dr HU8 141 D7
Linnet Way YO24 132 C8
Linn Park 13 HU7 56 E5
Linthorpe Gr HU10 143 E8
Linton 23 HU15 68 C6
Linton Cl
Beverley HU17 154 A1
Upperthorpe DN9 105 A2
Linton Garth HU17 43 A5
Linton on Ouse Prim Sch
YO30 12 A7
Linton Rd YO26 126 A1
Linton Rise DN15 82 A4
Linton St 5 YO26 129 E5
Linton Woods YO30 12 A7
Linton Woods La YO30 12 A8
Linwith La DN14 63 C3
Linwood Ave 17 DN33 113 E8
Lisburn Gr DN33 102 E1
Lisle Ct HU2 155 B1
Lisle Marsden CE Prim Sch
DN32 102 F2
Lismore Ave HU9 142 A3
LISSETT 22 E4
Lissett Cl HU17 43 D6
Lissett Gr HU6 140 C7
Lissett La YO25 22 D4
Lister Rd DN15 150 C7
Lister St
Grimsby DN31 152 B4
Kingston upon Hull HU1 155 A1
York YO31 156 C3
Lister Way YO30 130 A7
Litondale Ct 3 YO16 122 F7
LITTLE AIRMYN 64 E4
Little Ave YO30 130 B8
Littlebeck Cl HU3 145 A7
Littlebeck Rd 4 DN36 114 C8
Little Beck Rd YO16 122 B4
Little Belt The DN21 117 B2
LITTLE BURTON 34 B2
Little Burton 3 YO25 34 B2
LITTLE CATWICK 45 D7
Little Clover HU17 136 F6
LITTLE COATES 102 C3
Littlecoates Prim Sch
DN31 152 B5
Little Coates Rd DN34 102 C2
Little Comm La DN14 77 C5
Little Dam La HU12 88 B8
LITTLE DRIFFIELD 124 C4
LITTLE END 40 A1
Littlefair Rd HU9 147 A7
LITTLEFIELD 152 C2
Littlefield Cl 5 YO26 12 F1
Littlefield La
Grimsby DN34 152 B2
Littlefield La *continued*
Marsh Chapel DN36 115 B1
Little Garth YO26 126 A2
Little George St HU8 155 C4
LITTLE GRIMSBY 121 E2
Little Grimsby La LN11 121 D1
Little Hallfield Rd YO31 130 E5
Littleham Cl HU7 141 B8
LITTLE HATFIELD 46 B6
LITTLE HECK 62 D1
Little Heck Comm La
DN14 62 D1
Little John St DN34 152 B3
Little La
Broomfleet HU15 67 C6
Ellerton YO42 38 C1
11 Haxby YO32 13 E5
Little Smeaton WF8 76 D4
Mappleton HU11 47 A5
Shipton Thorpe YO43 40 E5
Watton YO25 32 E5
Wrawby DN20 98 D3
LITTLE LEVEN 45 A7
LITTLE LIMBER 100 C5
Little London La DN14 78 D8
Little Mason St HU2 155 C3
Little Mdws YO32 127 D8
Little Michael St DN34 152 B3
Littlemoor Cl HU15 53 D3
Little Moor La YO8 148 A8
Little Orch DN14 65 C4
Little Queen St HU1 155 A2
LITTLE REEDNESS 66 A1
Little Reed St HU2 155 A3
Little Shambles YO1 156 B2
Little Shore HU11 45 E2
LITTLE SKIPWITH 37 D1
LITTLE SMEATON 76 C3
Little Stonegate YO1 156 B3
Littlethorpe Cl 6 YO32 14 B8
LITTLE WEIGHTON 55 A4
Little Weighton Prim Sch
HU20 55 A4
Little Weighton Rd
Skidby HU16 138 A8
Walkington HU17 55 B7
Little Westfield YO25 8 C3
Little Wlk DN21 116 E5
Little Wold La HU15 54 A2
Littlewood Rd
Rowley HU17 54 D7
11 Thorne/Moorends DN8 93 B8
Littondale
Kingston upon Hull HU7 140 F7
15 Welton HU15 68 D6
Liverpool St HU3 145 A3
Livesey Rd DN36 121 B6
Livingstone Rd HU13 69 F4
Livingstone St YO26 129 F5
Lloyd Cl YO10 131 B1
Lloyds Ave DN17 150 F4
Loatley Gn HU16 139 C5
Lobelia Dr DN16 96 C1
Lob La YO41 15 D2
Lochrin Pl 2 YO26 129 B4
Lock Cl DN14 77 F6
Lockey Croft YO32 127 C8
Lockgate Rd DN14 77 C4
Lockham Rd HU12 90 F4
Lockhill DN31 152 E6
Lock Hill DN8 93 A8
Lock House La YO32 127 F8
Locking Garth LN11 121 F5
LOCKINGTON 32 B2
Lockington CE Sch YO25 32 B2
Lockington Rd YO25 31 F3
Lock Keepers Ct HU9 146 B6
Lock La
Holme-on-Spalding-Moor YO43 52 C8
Thorne/Moorends DN8 93 A8
Lock Rd DN36 115 A4
Lockside Rd DN40 87 D3
Lockton Gr 1 HU5 144 D8
Lockwood Bank DN9 105 E6
Lockwood Cl 6 DN8 93 B8
Lockwood Ct DN15 150 E8
Lockwood Dr HU17 136 E7
Lockwood Rd HU17 136 D7
Lockwood St
Great Driffield YO25 124 E3
Kingston upon Hull HU2 155 B4
York YO31 156 C3
Lockyer Cl 4 YO30 130 A8
Lodge Ave DN18 84 F8
Lodge Cl
Elloughton HU15 68 C7
Kingston upon Hull HU13 143 F1
Lodge Ct 35 DN7 92 D4
Lodge Farm Ct YO42 39 B6
Lodge Gdns
Northfield HU13 143 C2
5 Snaith DN14 63 C1
Lodge La
Flixborough DN15 82 B2
Gowdall DN14 62 F1
Kirk Bramwith DN7 92 A8
Snaith DN14 78 D8
Lodge Rd DN15 150 C6
Lodge St HU9 141 E2
Lofthouse La YO41 27 D7
Loftsome Way 11 DN14 65 B7
Loftus Gr HU9 142 E3
Loganberry Dr HU4 144 C4
Logan Cl HU7 141 C7
Lombard St DN34 152 A3
Lombardy Cl 8 HU5 144 C7
Lomond Gr 1 DN36 114 C8
Lomond Rd HU5 144
LONDESBOROUGH 41
Londesborough Ct YO25 124
Londesborough Gr 5
YO8 48
Londesborough Hill YO43 41
Londesborough Rd
Hutton Cranswick YO25 32
Market Weighton YO43 135
Londesborough St
Kingston upon Hull HU3 145
5 Selby YO8 148
London La DN6 77
London St 15 YO42 29
Longbrough La HU12 59
Long Cl La YO10 156
Longcroft 2 YO32 13
Longcroft Lower Sch
HU17 136
Longcroft Pk HU17 136
Longcroft Sch HU17 136
Longdales La HU11 142
Longden St HU3 145
LONG DRAX 64
Long Field Dr DN3 92
Longfield Rd 4 DN34 102
Long Field Rd DN3 92
Longfield Terr YO30 156
Longford Gr HU9 142
Long Furrow YO32 127
Long Hill YO42 29
Longhill Prim Sch HU8 142
Longhorn Cl 1 DN37 113
Long La
Atwick YO25 35
Beverley HU17 154
Bridlington YO16 122
Catton YO41 27
Cawood YO8 48
Driffield YO25 124
Eastrington DN14 65
Ellerby HU11 58
Ellerton YO42 38
Foston YO25 22
Great Driffield YO25 124
Heck DN14 77
Heslington YO10 26
Humbleton HU11 58
Kirk Smeaton WF8 76
Market Weighton YO43 41
Nafferton YO25 20
Pollington DN14 78
Skeffling HU12 90
Willoughton DN21 119
Woodmansey HU17 154
Longleat Ave YO16 122
Long Mann Hills Rd YO8 148
Longmans Hill Sch YO8 148
Longmans La HU16 139
LONG MARSTON 24
Long Marston CE Prim Sch
YO26 24
Longmeadow Rise 7
DN41 101
Longmeadows Dr DN37 101
Long Rampart YO42 38
Long Rd DN15 150
Long Ridge Dr YO26 126
Longridge Gdns 27 YO26 12
Long Ridge La YO26 126
LONG RISTON 45
Long St YO25 9
Long Toft Prim Sch DN7 92
Longton Rd 13 DN3 92
Long Trods 5 YO8 148
Longwood Link 8 YO30 126
Longwood Rd YO30 126
Long Wood Rd DN21 117
Lonsdale Cl DN36 114
Lonsdale St 5 HU3 145
Lopham La DN37 101
Lord Deramores Prim Sch
YO10 131
Lord Dr 27 YO42 29
Lord Mayor's Wlk YO31 156
Lord Porter Ave DN7 92
Lord Roberts Rd HU17 154
Lordship La
5 Barlby YO8 49
Wistow YO8 148
Lords La
Barrow upon Humber DN19 85
Upper Poppleton YO26 12
Lords Moor La YO32 14
Lord St
Grimsby DN31 152
Stainforth DN7 92
Lorenzo Way HU9 141
Loriners Dr 7 YO23 132
Lorne Cl HU2 155
Lorne St YO23 130
Lorraine Ave 3 YO41 27
Lorraine St HU8 141
Losely Park 19 HU7 56
Loten Dr HU18 134
Lothian Way HU7 57
Lotting's La YO42 28
Louis Dr HU5 144
Louis St HU3 145
Louth Rd
Fotherby LN11 121
Grimsby DN33 102
5 New Waltham DN36 113
Louville Ave HU19 75
Lovat Cl HU3 145
Loveden Ct 7 DN35 103

ve La
Gainsborough DN21 117 B1
Hedon HU12 72 C7
Londesborough YO43 41 A8
Nunthorpe YO10 133 C8
South Cave HU15 54 A2
York YO24 130 A2
well Rd 8 DN17 96 C2
veridge Ave HU5 140 A2
vett St DN35 153 B4
w Balk Rd HU17 42 F2
w Burgage DN15 68 B1
W BURNHAM 105 D5
W CATTON 27 C8
w Catton Rd YO41 27 C8
w Croft 6 YO32 14 A7
wcroft Ave 3 DN9 105 D2
wcroft Cl 4 DN9 105 D2
wcroft Mdw 10 DN9 105 D2
w Cross St 7 DN17 94 D8
wdale Cl HU5 139 E1
w Deeps La DN10 104 C1
wer Bridge St DN14 149 C3
werdale 18 HU15 68 D6
wer Darnborough St
YO23 156 B1
wer Derwent Valley Nat Nature Reserve* YO42 50 C8
wer Friargate YO1 156 B2
wer Kenyon St 6 DN8 93 A8
wer Mdws DN18 69 F1
wer Priory St YO1 156 A1
wer Spring St DN31 152 E5
weswater Rd 5 YO30 126 E1
w Farm Cl YO25 34 A8
w Farm Rd HU11 57 E5
wfield YO43 40 B1
wfield Cl
10 Barnby Dun DN3 92 A3
18 Kirton in Lindsey DN21 108 B1
wfield Dr YO32 13 E5
wfield House HU10 143 E6
wfield La
East Garton HU12 59 C5
Nunburnholme YO42 29 D3
Rufforth YO26 129 A4
Scrayingham YO41 16 A7
ow Field La
Carnaby YO25 10 C3
Welton HU14 68 E5
owfield Rd
Barlby with Osgodby YO8 49 B5
Beverley HU17 137 A7
Hillam LS25 61 C8
Kingston upon Hull HU10 143 E5
ow Fields Dr YO24 129 C3
OW FOSHAM 46 F1
ow Garth DN17 96 C1
owgate
Balne DN14 77 D5
Kingston upon Hull HU1 155 C2
ow Gate DN36 115 C1
ow Gn
Copmanthorpe YO23 132 B2
13 Knottingley WF11 61 A2
owhill DN8 78 F1
owick YO24 132 C7
ow La
Heslington YO10 131 D1
Kirk Bramwith DN7 92 A6
owland Cl 3 HU7 141 D8
ow Levels Bank DN8 93 E3
ow Leys Rd DN17 96 C1
ow Mdw YO8 148 C6
ow Mill Cl YO10 131 D3
ow Mill La HU15 53 C2
ow Moor Ave 3 YO10 133 F8
ow Moor La
Askham Richard YO23 24 D3
Hessay YO26 24 C8
owmoor Rd YO8 49 E6
OWNDES PARK 124 D6
owndes Pk YO25 124 D5
own Hill YO24 129 C2
owood Dr YO16 122 B4
ow Ousegate YO1 156 B2
ow Petergate YO1 156 B3
ow Peter La YO25 20 D7
ow Poppleton La YO26 129 B7
ow Rd
Blyborough DN21 119 B6
Gowdall DN14 63 A1
Healing DN41 101 F5
Kellington DN14 61 E4
Kirby Grindalythe YO17 6 F7
Marsh Chapel DN36 115 A1
North Cave HU15 53 E2
Worlaby DN20 98 C8
OW RISBY 83 B1
ow Risby Medieval Village*
DN15 83 A2
ow St
Beckingham DN10 116 E1
Carlton DN14 63 C2
Haxey DN9 105 D2
North Ferriby HU14 69 A5
Sancton YO43 41 D2
South Ferriby DN18 84 A7
Winterton DN15 83 A5
owther Ct YO31 156 C4
owther Dr YO8 148 E3
owther St
Kingston upon Hull HU3 145 A7
York YO31 156 C4
owther Terr YO24 130 A3
OWTHORPE 21 E7
owthorpe La YO25 125 F7
ow Well Pk YO19 37 F7
Low Westfield Rd YO23 132 A1
Loxley Cl YO30 126 F2
Loxley Gn HU4 144 B7
Loyalty Way 7 HU15 68 D5
Loyalty La DN18 69 F2
Loyds Cl 12 HU15 53 F1
Loyd St HU10 143 F6
Lucas Ave YO30 130 C8
Lucas Ct DN41 101 F5
Lucerne Cl YO19 37 A1
Lucian Wlk HU4 144 A2
Luck La HU12 58 C1
Lucombe Way YO32 127 D4
LUDBOROUGH 121 C6
Ludborough Pk DN36 121 B6
Ludborough Rd DN36 121 B8
Ludborough Way 21
DN35 103 C2
LUDDINGTON 81 C3
Luddington & Garthorpe
Prim Sch DN17 81 C4
Luddington Rd DN17 81 E5
Ludford St DN32 152 E2
Ludgate Cl 4 DN37 113 D6
Ludlow Ave DN34 152 A3
Ludlow Pl DN35 153 E1
Lulworth Ave HU4 144 A3
Lulworth Ct DN17 150 D4
Lumby Hill LS25 61 A8
Lumby La LS25 61 A8
Lumley Rd YO30 130 B7
Lumsden Cl YO25 124 B2
LUND
Beverley 31 F3
Selby 49 D3
Lund Ave HU16 138 E6
Lund Cl YO32 127 C8
Lund La
Bubwith YO8 50 C4
Cliffe YO8 49 D4
Lund Rd YO25 32 A2
Lunds The HU10 143 C6
Lundy Cl 10 YO30 127 A1
Lundy Ct DN40 101 C8
Luneburg Pl 14 DN15 96 B7
Luneburg Way DN15 96 B7
Lunedale Cl HU8 141 E7
Lunedale Rd DN16 151 D1
Lunn La DN14 61 D3
Lunn's Cres DN18 84 E8
Luton Rd HU5 144 F8
Luttons Prim Sch YO17 7 B8
Lycett Rd YO24 132 F6
Lych Gate DN20 97 D3
Lydbrook Rd DN16 151 A5
Lydford Rd DN40 87 C1
Lydham Ct 2 YO24 132 C8
Lydia Ct 6 DN40 87 B1
Lygon St DN16 151 B5
Lymington Garth HU4 144 A3
Lyndale Ave
8 Kirk Sandall DN3 92 A1
York YO10 131 C3
Lynden Way YO24 129 D3
Lyndhurst Ave
17 Grimsby DN33 102 E2
Kingston upon Hull HU16 139 D6
Lyndhurst Cl
Beverley HU17 137 B4
2 Norton DN6 76 F2
Thorne/Moorends DN8 92 F8
Lyndhurst Dr 1 DN6 76 F2
Lyndhurst Rise 3 DN6 76 F2
Lynhams Rd
Bempton YO15 4 E1
Bridlington YO15 123 B8
Lynmouth Cl 9 HU7 57 A5
Lynmouth Dr DN17 150 C4
Lynngarth Ave HU16 139 C6
Lynton Ave HU4 144 B3
Lynton Cl
Brayton YO8 148 B1
Scunthorpe DN15 150 D8
Lynton Gdns YO8 148 B1
Lynton Par DN31 152 B3
Lynton Rise 10 DN35 103 C2
Lynwith Cl DN14 63 C3
Lynwith Ct DN14 63 C3
Lynwith Dr DN14 63 C3
Lynwood Ave
3 Copmanthorpe YO23 132 A3
Kingston upon Hull HU10 143 E6
Lynwood Cl YO32 14 A7
Lynwood View 4 YO23 132 A3
Lyric Cl 1 HU3 145 C5
Lysaghts Way DN15 82 C1
Lysander Bsns Pk YO30 127 A3
Lysander Cl YO30 127 A3
Lysander Dr YO43 135 E4
Lytham Dr
Barnoldby le Beck DN37 113 D6
Kingston upon Hull HU16 139 D6
Lyth Cl 5 YO16 123 A7
Lythe Ave HU5 139 E4

M

M62 Trad Est DN14 149 A3
Mablethorpe Rd DN36 115 A3
Mcan Cl YO10 131 D4
MacArthy Cl 20 DN33 102 D1
MacAulay Sch DN31 152 B4
MacAulay St DN31 152 B4
MacAulay Way DN31 152 C4
MacDonald Ct 12 YO42 29 A3
Mace View HU17 154 B1
McGrath Cl 25 YO42 29 A3
Machray Pl DN35 153 D3
MacKender Ct 3 DN16 151 B2
Mackenzie Pl 24 DN40 87 B1
McKintosh Dr YO25 125 A3
MacLagan Rd YO23 132 F4
MacLure St DN31 152 F6
McShane Ct 11 YO42 29 A3
McVeigh Ct 10 DN41 101 F5
Madeira Ct
Kingston upon Hull HU5 140 A1
Sculcoates HU5 140 A1
Madeley St HU3 145 C4
Madison Gdns 4 HU5 140 A1
Madron Cl HU7 141 B8
Maegan Way DN35 153 E2
Magazine La YO8 49 C4
Magazine Rd YO8 49 B4
Magdalen Cl 3 DN16 96 D2
Magdalen Ct 8 HU12 72 D7
Magdalene Rd 8 DN34 102 C3
Magdalen Gate HU12 72 D7
Magdalen La HU12 72 D7
Magnolia Cl YO25 124 D3
Magnolia Dr DN36 114 A5
Magnolia Gr YO32 127 D2
Magnolia Rise 9 DN40 87 C1
Magnolia Way DN16 151 A3
Magrath Ct 3 DN20 98 C2
Maida Gr YO10 130 D2
Maiden Cl 1 DN40 87 B1
Maiden Ct 8 HU7 57 B5
Maidensgrave Henge*
YO25 2 F1
Maidenwell La LN7 110 A4
Maidwell Way 1 DN34 102 B2
Main Approach Rd DN15 151 C7
Main Ave
Scunthorpe DN17 150 C2
York YO31 130 F5
Maine Ave DN15 96 A7
Main Rd
Ashby cum Fenby DN37 113 D3
Aylesby DN37 101 E2
Bilton HU11 58 A3
Burton Agnes YO25 10 C3
Burton Pidsea HU12 59 C2
Drax YO8 63 F5
Gilberdyke DN14 66 B7
Holmpton HU19 75 C2
Kilpin DN14 65 D7
Kingston upon Hull HU11 142 E6
Mappleton HU11 47 A4
Newport HU15 53 A1
Skeffling HU12 90 D6
Thorngumbald HU12 72 F5
Ulrome YO25 22 E6
Utterby LN11 121 C4
Mains La YO42 39 E3
Main St
Askham Bryan YO23 24 F3
Asselby DN14 64 D7
Bainton YO25 31 E7
Barmby Moor YO42 28 D3
3 Beal DN14 61 D4
Beeford YO25 22 C1
Beswick YO25 32 C4
Bilbrough YO23 24 C1
Bishopthorpe YO23 133 A4
Bonby DN20 84 C2
Boynton YO16 10 D6
Brandesburton YO25 34 B2
Bridlington YO16 122 A1
Broomfleet HU15 67 C6
Brough HU15 68 C6
Bubwith YO8 50 C7
Buckton/Bempton YO15 4 C3
Bugthorpe YO41 16 D4
Burstwick HU12 73 A6
Burton Agnes YO25 10 A1
Cadney DN20 109 D6
Carnaby YO16 10 E4
Catwick HU17 45 C8
Cherry Burton HU17 43 A5
Cliffe YO8 49 E2
Coniston HU11 57 F6
Copmanthorpe YO23 132 A2
Cottingwith YO42 38 C5
Crowle DN17 94 E6
Dalton Holme HU17 42 E8
Deighton YO19 37 A7
East/West Stockwith
DN10 116 F6
Ellerker HU15 68 A8
Ellerton YO42 38 C1
Elvington YO41 27 C2
Escrick YO19 37 B5
Etton HU17 42 F6
Fishlake DN7 92 D8
Foston YO25 22 A4
Fulstow LN11 121 F8
Ganton YO12 1 A8
Garton HU11 59 F6
Garton YO25 19 F6
Goodmanham YO43 41 D6
Gowdall DN14 63 A1
Graiselound DN9 105 D1
Grasby DN38 110 E7
Harpham YO25 21 F8
Hatfield DN7 92 F3
Hatfield HU11 46 C5
Heck DN14 77 C8
Hemingbrough YO8 49 F1
Hensall DN14 62 D2
Heslington YO10 131 B1
Hessay YO26 24 B8
Horkstow DN18 84 A5
Hotham YO43 53 D5
Humberside Airport DN39 100 A6
Main St *continued*
Hutton Cranswick YO25 32 E7
Keadby with Althorpe DN17 95 D4
Kelfield YO19 36 D1
Kelk YO25 21 F6
Kellington DN14 61 F3
Keyingham HU12 73 C4
Kirkburn YO25 19 F1
Kirk Smeaton WF8 76 B3
Knapton YO26 129 A5
Leconfield HU17 43 D6
Long Riston/Arnold HU11 45 C5
Monk Fryston LS25 61 A8
1 Naburn YO19 36 D8
North Duffield YO8 50 A8
North Frodingham YO25 33 F8
Nunthorpe YO10 133 D8
Ottringham HU12 73 E3
Patrington HU12 89 C8
Paull HU12 72 A5
Pollington DN14 77 F6
Poppleton YO26 12 F1
Preston HU12 58 C1
Reighton YO14 3 E5
Riccall YO19 49 A8
Roos HU12 60 A1
Scawby DN20 108 E7
Sculcoates HU2 140 F1
Searby cum Owmby DN38 110 D8
Seaton HU11 35 A1
Shipton YO30 12 F5
Sigglesthorne HU11 45 F8
Skerne & Wansford YO25 21 A2
Skidby HU16 138 B8
Skipsea YO25 23 A1
Stamford Bridge YO41 15 D2
Swanland HU14 69 B7
Swine HU11 57 D6
Thornton Curtis DN39 85 E5
Thwing YO25 2 B1
Tibthorpe YO25 19 D2
Tickton HU17 137 E8
Ulrome YO25 22 E5
Watton YO25 32 D5
Wawne HU7 56 F7
Welwick HU12 90 A7
Wheldrake YO19 37 F7
Whitton DN15 67 E3
Wilberfoss YO41 27 E5
Willerby HU10 138 C2
Withernwick HU11 46 D3
Womersley DN6 76 C6
Worlaby DN20 98 D8
Maister Rd 12 HU12 73 C4
Majestic Ct 7 HU9 142 A3
Malbys Gr YO23 132 B2
Malcolm Rd DN34 102 C2
Maldon Dr HU9 146 C6
Malet Lambert Sch Lang Coll
HU8 141 E4
Malham Ave HU4 144 C6
Malham Gr YO31 131 B5
Malkinson Cl 11 DN15 83 A5
Mallalieu Ct DN15 150 E8
Mallard Ave
Barnby Dun DN3 92 A4
2 Leven HU17 45 A8
Mallard Cl
Beverley HU17 136 F6
Driffield YO25 125 A4
2 Healing DN41 101 F5
Ulrome YO25 23 A3
Mallard Dr LN7 111 A4
Mallard Landings YO31 130 D8
Mallard Mews DN32 152 E2
Mallard Rd
Kingston upon Hull HU9 142 B4
Scunthorpe DN17 150 E2
Mallards Reach HU16 139 C8
Mallard Way 11 YO32 13 F5
Malling Wlk 13 DN16 96 D1
Mallory Cl YO32 127 D4
Mallory Rd DN16 151 D1
Malmesbury Dr DN34 152 C2
Malmo Rd HU7 140 E5
Malm St HU3 145 B6
Malpas Cl 8 HU7 56 F5
Maltby Ave DN37 102 B2
Maltby La 12 DN18 69 E1
Maltby Rd DN17 150 E1
Malthouse La 5 YO16 122 D5
Malthouse Row DN14 149 C3
Maltings Ct 6 YO8 148 C6
Maltings Ind Est The
DN14 61 F1
Maltings The
Beverley HU17 154 C3
Cliffe YO8 49 E3
Kingston upon Hull HU2 155 B3
Nafferton YO25 125 F6
Maltings Way DN31 152 E4
Maltkiln La 4 DN20 98 F7
Maltkiln Rd DN18 69 F1
Malt Kilns The DN14 149 D4
Maltings The 5 YO43 135 D4
Malton Ave YO31 130 E6
Malton La YO17 7 A8
Malton Mews HU17 137 B3
Malton Rd
Hunmanby YO14 2 F8
Huntington YO32 128 A1
Molescroft HU17 136 B6
York YO31 130 F7
Malton St HU9 155 C3
Malton Way YO30 129 F8
Malt Shoval Ct YO1 156 C2
Malvern Ave
Grimsby DN33 102 D2
Malvern Ave *continued*
York YO26 129 D5
Malvern Cl
Huntington YO32 128 A5
4 Thorne/Moorends DN8 93 A7
Malvern Cres 9 HU5 139 D2
Malvern Rd
Goole DN14 149 D5
Kingston upon Hull HU5 139 D2
Scunthorpe DN17 150 F3
Manby Rd
Immingham DN40 87 B3
Scunthorpe DN17 96 C2
Manchester Rd YO42 28 E3
Manchester St
Cleethorpes DN35 153 D4
Kingston upon Hull HU3 145 A4
Mancklin Ave HU8 141 D5
Mancroft YO32 127 C8
Mandela Link DN31 152 C3
Manderville Cl 18 HU12 72 D7
Manet Rd HU8 141 C1
Manifold Rd DN16 151 E1
Manilla La DN18 69 F2
Manlake Ave DN15 83 A5
Manley Cl YO32 127 D4
Manley Ct
1 Epworth DN9 105 D6
Messingham DN17 107 D7
Manley Gdns
Brigg DN20 98 B2
Cleethorpes DN35 103 C2
Manley St 10 DN15 151 B7
Mannaberg Way DN15 96 D7
Manningtree Cl DN32 152 E2
Mann La DN9 94 D2
Manor Ave DN32 152 D2
Manor Barn Ct YO42 29 D6
Manor Barns HU20 55 A4
Manor Beeches The 3
YO19 26 E7
Manor CE Sch YO26 129 C7
Manor Cl
Beverley HU17 154 A4
Great Driffield YO25 124 F4
5 Hemingbrough YO8 49 F1
4 Keelby DN41 101 A5
Kirk Smeaton WF8 76 B3
Nafferton YO25 125 F6
6 North Duffield YO8 50 A7
12 Norton DN6 76 E2
Skipsea YO25 23 A2
Sproatley HU11 58 D5
Upper Poppleton YO26 24 F8
Manor Croft YO42 16 F1
Manor Ct
6 Bubwith YO8 50 D7
Kingston upon Hull HU10 69 C8
Stallingborough DN41 101 E7
York YO10 130 F3
2 York YO32 127 F6
Manor Ct Rd 7 DN9 105 E6
Manor Dr
Beeford YO25 22 C1
Bonby DN20 84 C2
Brough HU15 68 C6
Camblesforth YO8 63 C4
4 Dunnington YO19 26 E7
10 Gilberdyke HU15 66 D8
5 North Duffield YO8 50 A7
Scawby DN20 108 E8
Waltham DN37 113 E7
Manor Drive N YO26 129 D4
Manor Drive S YO26 129 D4
Manor Farm Cl
1 Brayton YO8 148 A1
Carlton DN14 63 C2
Copmanthorpe YO23 132 A2
Kellington DN14 61 F3
Messingham DN17 107 D6
Manor Farm Ct
Chapel Haddlesey YO8 62 C4
Huggate YO42 18 C2
9 Leconfield HU17 43 D6
Manor Farm La DN14 78 A3
Manor Farm Rd DN17 150 E2
Manorfield Ave YO25 124 F5
Manorfield Rd YO25 124 F4
Manor Fields
Kingston upon Hull HU10 69 C8
Market Weighton YO43 135 D4
Rawcliffe DN14 64 B2
14 Welton HU15 68 D6
Manor Garth
Barmby Moor YO42 28 D3
Fridaythorpe YO25 18 B5
Haxby YO32 127 B8
Kellington DN14 61 F3
Keyingham HU12 73 C4
7 Norton DN6 76 F2
1 Riccall YO19 49 A8
Skidby HU16 55 C4
Manor Gdns
8 Hatfield DN7 92 E4
6 Hunmanby YO14 3 A8
Manor Gn
Bolton YO41 28 D7
Church End YO25 33 F8
Manor Heath YO23 132 A3
Manorhouse La HU17 55 B8
Manor House La 6 DN17 81 F1
Manor House St HU1 155 A1
Manor La
Barrow upon Humber
DN19 85 D8

Manor La *continued*
Goxhill DN19 85 F8
Grayingham DN21 119 B7
Hollym HU19 75 A4
Rawcliffe YO30 126 D2
MANOR PARK 150 D2
Manor Park Cl YO30 126 E2
Manor Park Gr 2 YO30 126 E2
Manor Park Rd YO30 126 E2
Manor Pk
Beverley HU17 154 A4
Preston HU12 58 D1
Seaton HU11 35 A1
Manor Rd
Beal DN14 61 C4
Beverley HU17 154 A3
Crowle DN17 94 C7
Goole DN14 149 C1
Hatfield DN7 92 E4
Kingston upon Hull HU5 144 B8
9 North Cave HU15 53 D3
Northorpe DN21 118 D8
Preston HU12 58 C1
Reedness DN14 65 F1
Scunthorpe DN16 96 D2
South Cliffe YO43 53 B7
Stainforth DN7 92 C7
Swanland HU14 69 B6
Thorngumbald HU12 72 F5
Twin Rivers DN14 81 E7
Manor St
6 Bridlington YO15 122 E2
6 Keelby DN41 101 A5
Kingston upon Hull HU1 155 B2
Manor Way
Kingston upon Hull HU10 143 F6
York YO30 126 E2
Mansell Cl YO8 148 A2
Mansel St DN32 153 B4
Mansfield Ct 6 DN32 153 A5
Mansfield Pk HU5 140 B3
Mansfield Rd DN15 150 B6
Mansfield St YO31 156 C3
Mansgate Hill LN7 111 B3
Mansion Court Gdns DN8 93 A8
Manson Cl 13 DN34 102 B2
Manston Garth 4 HU7 57 B5
MANTON 108 B5
Manton Ct DN20 108 F6
Manton La DN20 108 E6
Manton Rd DN21 108 A4
Manuel St DN14 149 B4
Manvers St HU5 140 C3
Maple Ave
Bishopthorpe YO23 133 A3
Crowle DN17 94 D7
18 Crowle Park DN17 94 D7
Flixborough DN15 96 B7
Grimsby DN34 102 C4
Keelby DN41 101 A4
Kingston upon Hull HU10 143 F8
Maple Cl
2 Bridlington YO16 123 A6
Brigg DN20 98 D2
Gainsborough DN21 117 A2
Hambleton YO8 48 B1
12 Keelby DN41 101 A4
5 Kingston upon Hull HU5 144 C7
Messingham DN17 107 D6
Maple Ct
30 Gainsborough DN21 117 C1
Wheldrake YO19 37 D8
York YO10 133 E6
Maple Dr
Beverley HU17 136 F6
Goole DN14 149 F5
Maple Gr
12 Brayton YO8 48 D1
8 Healing DN41 101 F5
3 Immingham DN40 87 C2
6 New Waltham DN36 113 F7
Northfield HU13 143 B3
Summergangs HU8 141 C2
York YO10 130 D1
Maplehurst Ave YO31 130 D7
Mapleleaf Ct 9 HU16 138 F5
Maple Pk HU12 72 D8
Maple Rd
Bridlington YO16 123 A6
12 Thorne/Moorends DN8 79 B1
Maple St HU5 140 D2
Maple Tree Ave 10 YO8 49 B4
Maple Tree Close E
DN16 151 A5
Maple Tree Close W
DN16 151 A5
Maple Tree Way DN16 151 A5
Maple Wlk
8 Brandesburton YO25 34 B2
Goole DN14 149 F5
Maplewood Ave HU5 144 B7
Maplewood Paddock 2
YO24 129 C1
MAPPLETON 47 A7
Mappleton Gr HU9 142 A2
Mappleton Rd HU11 46 D6
Marbury Pk 29 HU7 56 F5
Marchant Cl HU17 136 D7
March St
6 Kirton in Lindsey DN21 108 B1
York YO31 156 C4
Marcus St
Goole DN14 149 B4
Marcus St *continued*
Grimsby DN34 152 A2
MARFLEET 147 C8
Marfleet Ave HU9 147 B7
Marfleet Cnr DN36 114 B1
Marfleet La HU9 142 B3
Marfleet Prim Sch HU9 147 C8
Margaret Ave DN17 95 D5
Margaret Gr 1 HU13 143 F1
Margaret Philipson Ct
YO1 156 C3
Margaret Pl 18 DN36 114 A7
Margaret St
Grimsby DN32 152 F3
Immingham DN40 101 C8
York YO10 156 C1
Margrave La
Garthorpe & Fockerby DN17 81 E5
Reedness DN14 80 E7
Marian Way DN37 113 C6
Marigold Cl YO8 148 C2
Marigold Wlk 22 DN35 103 C1
Marina Ave 3 DN14 63 B1
Marina Ct HU2 155 B1
Marina View 6 DN8 93 A7
Marin Ct 7 HU17 137 B3
Marine Ave HU14 69 A4
Marine Dr HU18 134 D5
Mariners Arms Flats
DN17 95 D6
Mariners Cl HU9 146 C6
Mariners Ct HU17 154 C2
Mariners St 9 DN14 149 C4
Marine Valley 2 YO15 5 B3
Marine Wharf HU1 155 B1
Marjorie Waite Ct YO30 130 B7
Markeaton Park 21 HU7 56 E5
Marketbridge La YO42 39 E7
Market Cross Sh Ctr 13
YO8 148 C5
Market Ct 5 DN17 94 D7
Market Gn HU16 139 B6
Market Hill
36 Hedon HU12 72 C7
Scunthorpe DN15 151 B8
Market Hill Ct 37 HU12 72 C7
Market La
12 Barton-upon-Humber DN18 84 F8
5 Brigg DN20 98 B2
14 Selby YO8 148 C5
Market Pl
11 Barton-upon-Humber DN18 84 F8
Bridlington YO16 122 C5
8 Brigg DN20 98 B2
11 Caistor LN7 111 B4
2 Cawood YO8 48 B8
5 Epworth DN9 105 E6
Great Driffield YO25 124 E4
31 Hedon HU12 72 C7
Hornsea HU18 134 B4
Kingston upon Hull HU1 155 C1
22 Kirton in Lindsey DN21 108 B1
Market Weighton YO43 135 D4
Owston Ferry DN9 106 B2
Patrington HU12 74 D1
Pocklington YO42 29 A3
11 Selby YO8 148 C5
9 Snaith DN14 63 C1
South Cave HU15 54 A2
Market St
Cleethorpes DN35 153 F2
East Marsh DN31 152 E4
9 Pocklington YO42 29 A4
14 Winterton DN15 83 A5
York YO1 156 B2
MARKET WEIGHTON 135 B4
Market Weighton Inf Sch
YO43 135 D3
Market Weighton Rd
Barlby with Osgodby YO8 49 B6
Holme-on-Spalding-Moor YO43 40 B2
Market Weighton YO43 135 A2
Sancton YO43 41 D3
Market Weighton Sch
YO43 135 F4
Market Wlk YO25 124 E4
Markham Cres YO31 156 B4
Markham Mews DN37 113 E6
Markhams Orch DN33 113 E8
Markham St YO31 156 B4
Markham Way DN20 98 E4
Marklew Ave DN34 152 B3
Markman La YO25 125 D5
Mark Rise DN21 117 F5
Marlborough Ave
Goole DN14 149 C5
2 Haxey DN9 105 D2
Hornsea HU18 134 C1
Kingston upon Hull HU5 145 A8
Northfield HU13 143 D2
Marlborough Cl
15 Cleethorpes DN32 153 A5
Rawcliffe YO30 126 D3
Marlborough Dr DN16 151 B4
Marlborough Gr YO10 130 D2
Marlborough Rd 9 DN8 93 B7
Marlborough Terr
8 Bridlington YO15 122 F2
Kingston upon Hull HU2 155 A3
Marlborough Villas
YO10 130 D2
Marlborough Way DN35 103 C1
Marlowe Rd DN17 150 D3
Marlowe St HU8 141 C2
Marlow Rd DN21 117 C1
Marmaduke St 3 HU3 145 C4
Marmiam Dr 2 YO32 14 D2
Marmion Dr DN15 83 A5
Marmion Rd DN16 151 C3
Marne St HU5 145 A8
Marples Mews DN35 153 F1
Marquis Ave DN36 114 A8
Marquis Ct 2 YO26 129 D6
Marris Dr DN15 83 B5
Marritt Way 9 HU12 73 C4
Marr La HU15 66 F7
Marsdale HU7 140 F7
Marsden Dr DN15 150 D8
Marsden Gr 3 DN8 93 A8
Marsden Landing HU6 140 D8
Marsden Rd DN31 153 A5
Marshall Ave
Bridlington YO15 122 E2
Grimsby DN34 152 B3
Kingston upon Hull HU10 143 E8
Preston HU12 72 C8
Marshall Cl 3 DN37 101 E1
Marshall Hill YO25 19 D2
Marshall St HU5 140 C2
Marshall Way 47 HU12 72 D7
MARSHCHAPEL 115 B2
Marshchapel Cl 20 DN35 103 C2
Marshchapel Prim Sch
DN36 115 B2
Marsh Dr HU17 154 A1
Marsh End
17 Howden DN14 65 A7
Knottingley WF11 61 A3
Marshfield Ave DN14 149 E4
Marshfield Rd
Goole DN14 149 E4
Scunthorpe DN16 151 C1
Marsh Hill La DN14 78 C4
Marsh La
Asselby DN14 64 D7
Barlow YO8 63 B8
Barnetby le Wold DN38 99 B4
Barrow upon Humber DN19 70 C2
Barton-upon-Humber DN18 69 F1
2 Beal DN14 61 D4
Cawood YO8 48 D8
Keyingham HU12 73 B3
Knottingley WF11 61 A2
Misterton DN10 116 D5
New Holland DN19 70 E2
Ryehill HU12 73 A4
South Killingholme DN40 87 B4
Thorne DN8 79 A2
Thorngumbald HU12 73 A4
West Haddlesey YO8 61 F5
Winteringham DN15 68 A1
Marshland Rd DN8 79 B2
Marshlands Prim Sch
DN14 149 D1
Marsh Lane Gdns DN14 61 F4
Marsh Rd
Crowle DN17 94 B7
Keyingham HU12 73 A2
Ottringham HU12 88 C8
Walkeringham DN10 116 E3
Marsh Way DN36 115 C5
Marske Wlk 1 HU5 139 E3
Marston Ave YO26 129 B3
Marston Cres YO26 129 B3
Marston La
Long Marston YO26 24 A8
Moor Monkton YO26 12 A1
Martello Way YO32 128 A1
Marten Cl 2 YO30 130 A8
Martin Cheeseman Ct 3
YO24 132 C8
Martin Cl HU9 142 B3
Martin La YO42 29 C6
Martin's Alley HU2 155 B1
Martin's Cl DN19 85 D8
Martins Ct YO26 130 A5
Martinson Dr DN14 78 C8
Martins Rd DN39 86 B1
Martin St HU17 137 B3
Martin Way 7 DN36 113 F8
MARTON
Bridlington 123 D8
Hornsea 46 B2
Marton Ave YO16 122 E5
Marton Ct 6 YO16 123 A7
Martongate YO16 123 A7
Martongate Prim Sch
YO16 122 F6
Marton Gr
8 Grimsby DN33 102 D2
43 Hatfield DN7 92 D4
Kingston upon Hull HU6 139 F5
Marton La YO25 9 F6
Marton Rd
Bridlington YO16 122 D5
Ellerby HU11 46 B1
Marton View YO15 123 B8
Martyn Rd DN35 153 D2
Marvelgarth La HU11 35 A2
Marvel St HU9 146 B7
Marydene Dr HU6 140 C5
Marygate YO30 156 A3
Marygate La YO30 156 A3
Marylebone Wlk 3
DN33 102 D1
Mary St DN15 151 A7
Mary Sumner Way DN15 150 E8
Mascotte Gdns HU18 134 D3
Mask La YO41 27 D4
Mason Dr DN17 96 C2
Masons Ct
6 Barton-upon-Humber DN18 84 E8
Crowle DN17 94 D8
Mason St HU2 155 B3
Maspin Cl 19 HU7 56 F5
Maspin Moor Rd LS25 61 C7
Massey Cl
8 Epworth DN9 105 D6
Kingston upon Hull HU3 145 A5
Massey St
Kingston upon Hull HU3 145 A4
Selby YO8 148 C5
Mast Dr HU9 146 C6
Mathews St DN35 153 C3
Matlock Ct DN15 150 B6
Matlock Dr DN37 102 C4
Matson Cl YO16 122 C2
Matson Rd YO16 122 B1
Matthew Humberstone CE Sch DN35 103 B2
Mattison Way YO24 129 E2
Mattocks La HU12 72 D8
Matty La 10 YO43 53 F7
Maude Cl 10 HU12 73 C4
Maulson Dr HU11 58 A3
Maurice Ave HU8 141 A2
Mavis Rd DN17 150 E2
Mawson Green La DN14 78 C3
Maxwell Ct 9 DN34 102 B3
Maxwell Rd YO42 29 A4
Maxwell St HU8 141 A2
Maybury Prim Sch HU9 142 B3
Maybury Rd HU9 141 F3
May Ct 23 YO42 29 A3
Maye Gr
Kingston upon Hull HU2 155 C4
Summergangs HU8 141 B1
Mayfair Cres 18 DN37 113 D6
Mayfair Ct
3 Humberston DN35 103 D1
Kingston upon Hull HU5 140 C2
Mayfair Drive W DN37 102 B4
Mayfield DN14 149 E6
Mayfield Ave
2 Gainsborough DN21 117 B2
South Killingholme DN40 86 F2
Stainforth DN7 92 D7
Mayfield & Broompark Nature Reserve* DN14 149 F6
Mayfield Cl DN33 113 D8
Mayfield Ct YO8 63 C7
Mayfield Dr 5 YO8 148 A1
Mayfield Gr YO24 132 E8
Mayfield Rd
Brayton YO8 148 A1
Bridlington YO15 122 D1
Mayfield St HU3 145 C8
Mayflower Ave 6 DN40 87 C1
Mayflower Cl 2 DN40 86 E3
May Gdns HU7 141 A4
May Gr HU13 143 D2
Mayland Ave HU5 144 A8
Mayland Dr HU16 138 E6
Maypole Gdns YO8 48 B8
Maypole Gr 3 YO19 36 D8
Maypole St DN21 119 A2
Maysfield Ct DN20 109 A5
May St
Cleethorpes DN35 153 D4
Kingston upon Hull HU5 140 D3
Maythorn Rd YO31 127 E2
Maythorpe YO23 24 C6
Maythorpe Cl HU3 145 A7
May Tree Ave HU8 141 C2
Mayville Ave HU8 141 B3
Mead Garth DN15 96 A7
Meadlands YO31 131 B6
Meadley Ct HU17 137 C4
Meadow Ave DN39 86 A2
Meadowbank
4 Belton DN9 94 E1
Grimsby DN37 102 B4
Meadow Bank 2 HU17 136 F7
Meadowbank Rd HU3 144 E7
Meadowbeck Cl YO10 131 B4
Meadow Cl
Barrow Upon Humber DN19 85 C7
5 Beeford YO25 22 D1
North End DN19 71 A1
Thorpe Willoughby YO8 48 C2
Meadow Croft
Brayton YO8 148 A2
16 Kirk Sandall DN3 92 A2
Waltham DN37 113 D7
Meadowcroft Rd YO25 125 A6
Meadow Ct
Grayingham DN21 119 B7
Grimsby DN37 102 C4
Hibaldstow DN20 108 F5
3 York YO24 132 E8
Meadow Ct Greyhound Stadium DN7 92 C5
Meadow Dr
Barton-upon-Humber DN18 84 F8
Burstwick HU12 73 B6
Grimsby DN33 113 D8
Healing DN41 102 A5
Market Weighton YO43 135 E4
Misterton DN10 116 C5
Thorpe Willoughby YO8 48 B2
Meadowfield 1 YO8 50 D7
Meadow Field YO43 40 A1
Meadowfield Cl 6 YO42 28 F4
Meadowfield Dr YO8 50 A4
Meadowfield Rd YO15 122 D1
Meadow Field Rd DN3 92
Meadowfields Dr YO31 127
Meadow Garth
2 Kingston upon Hull HU6 56
Thorpe Willoughby YO8 48
Meadow La
Driffield YO25 125
1 Haxby YO32 127
9 Newport HU15 52
Meadow Lands DN21 117
Meadow Pl 5 YO8 148
Meadow Rd
Bridlington YO16 122
Great Driffield YO25 125
Scunthorpe DN17 150
Meadow Rise
Aldbrough HU11 47
Barnby Dun DN3 92
Blyton DN21 117
Meadows The
Beverley HU17 137
Brandesburton YO25 34
Bransholme HU7 140
4 Buckton/Bempton YO15 4
Burringham DN17 95
Carlton DN14 63
Cherry Burton HU17 43
Dunswell HU6 56
Great Driffield YO25 125
Howden DN14 65
Leven HU17 45
Messingham DN17 107
7 Monk Fryston LS25 61
Riccall YO19 48
2 Skelton YO30 126
13 South Cave HU15 53
West Ella HU10 69
5 Westwoodside DN9 105
Meadow The LN7 111
Meadow Vale DN20 108
Meadow View
Bainton YO25 31
Bridlington YO16 122
28 Humberston DN35 103
Patrington HU12 74
Meadow Way
Heworth YO31 130
Huntington YO32 127
Kingston upon Hull HU16 138
3 Walkington HU17 55
Meadow Wlk 6 HU14 69
Mead St HU8 141
Mead The 1 DN37 101
Meadway YO8 48
Meadway Dr YO8 48
Mead Wlk HU4 144
Meam Cl YO10 131
Measham Dr DN7 92
MEAUX 44
Meaux Abbey (Site of)* HU17 44
Meaux La HU17 44
Meaux Rd HU7 56
Mechanic La 9 HU3 145 D
Meden Ave 8 HU15 68 D
Medforth Rd YO16 122 C
Medina Ave YO16 122 D
Medina Rd HU8 142 C
Medium Section Rd DN16 97 A
Medlar Ct 25 DN8 93 E
Medlar Dr 2 HU15 68 D
Medway Pl DN34 152 A
Meggison's Turnpike
YO25 32 F
Meggitt La DN15 68 A
Megson Way
Thorngumbald HU12 72 E
Walkington HU17 55 D
Melander Cl YO26 129 B
Melander Gdns 5 YO32 127 D
MELBOURNE 39 E
Melbourne Ave
Bridlington YO16 122 D
18 Grimsby DN33 102 E
Melbourne Pk YO42 39 A
Melbourne Prim Sch
YO42 39 A
Melbourne Sq HU17 43 D
Melbourne St
4 Kingston upon Hull HU5 140 C
York YO10 130 D
Melbury Wlk DN17 150 C
Melcombe Ave 11 YO32 14 A
Melford Ct DN16 151 E
Melior Com Coll DN17 150 E
Mellor Way 28 DN36 114 A
Mellwood View DN9 106 A
Melrose Cl 1 YO31 131 A
Melrosegate YO31 130 F
Melrose Pk HU17 154 A
Melrose Rd 5 DN21 117 B
Melrose St HU3 144 F
MELTON 68 F
Melton Ave YO30 129 F
Melton Bottom HU14 68 E
MELTONBY 28 F
Meltonby Ave HU5 139 C
Meltonby La YO42 28 E
Melton Coll YO24 129 F
Melton Dr
Bishopthorpe YO23 133 A
York YO30 129 F
Melton Fields HU14 68 F
Melton Gallows DN38 99 A
Melton Old Rd HU14 68 E

elton Rd
orth Ferriby HU14 69 A5
rawby DN20 98 F4
ELTON ROSS 99 C5
elville Cl 19 HU12 73 C4
elville St HU1 155 A1
elwood Cl DN9 105 F6
elwood Gr
ingston upon Hull HU5 140 D2
ork YO26 129 B5
elwood Hill DN9 105 F6
elwood View DN9 105 F6
emorial Ave 14 HU19 75 A6
enasha Way DN16 151 E3
endip Ave
oole DN14 149 D5
rimsby DN33 113 E8
endip Cl 2 YO32 127 F5
endip Rd DN17 150 D4
enson Dr DN7 92 D4
ENTHORPE 50 C5
ercer Rd 1 DN21 117 A1
erchant Adventurers' Hall★
O1 156 C2
erchantgate YO1 156 C2
erchants Ct YO31 130 E5
erchant Way
opmanthorpe YO23 132 B3
ew Village HU16 139 E5
ercia Way DN15 96 C8
ere Cres DN16 151 D3
eredith Ave DN17 150 C2
eredyke Rd DN17 81 D3
ere Garth HU18 134 B4
ere Grange YO25 18 B6
ere La
alton Holme HU17 42 F8
denthorpe DN3 92 A1
interton DN15 83 A7
ereside 9 YO15 5 A2
ereside Terr HU18 134 B4
ereside View YO15 5 A2
ere View Ave HU18 134 B2
ere Way HU14 69 B7
ere Wlk 6 HU18 134 C4
eridian Point Ret Pk
N35 103 D2
erlin Cl HU7 141 D7
erlin Covert 4 YO31 127 F3
erlin Dr DN20 99 A8
erlin Rd DN17 150 E2
errick St HU9 146 B7
erryman Garth HU12 72 C7
erryweather Ct 14 DN16 96 D1
ersey Prim Sch HU8 141 C1
ersey St HU8 141 C1
erton Gr 5 HU9 141 F1
erton Rd DN16 96 D2
ESSINGHAM 107 C7
essingham La DN20 108 C7
essingham Prim Sch
N17 107 D7
essingham Rd
ast Butterwick DN17 106 D8
cotter DN21 107 C4
6 Scunthorpe DN17 96 C2
etcalfe La YO19 131 C5
etham La DN14 65 F4
ews The
ransholme HU7 29 B3
ingston upon Hull HU3 145 C5
eynell St DN21 117 A8
icklegate
1 Selby YO8 148 D5
ork YO1 156 A2
icklegate Bar Mus★
O24 156 A1
icklethwaite Gr 2 DN8 79 B2
icklethwaite Rd 1 DN8 79 B2
ickley Gr HU9 142 C2
iddle Banks 24 YO32 13 E5
iddle Barn Hill DN20 84 D1
iddlebrook Gdns YO8 148 A2
iddlebrook La 23 DN8 93 A8
iddleburg St HU9 146 D8
iddlecroft YO41 27 F5
iddlecroft Dr YO32 14 A7
iddlecroft Gr 2 YO32 14 B7
iddle Ct DN31 152 E4
iddle Dike La HU16 139 D7
iddledyke La HU16 139 D6
iddlefield La WF8 76 A2
iddle Garth Dr HU15 54 A2
iddlegate Cl 9 DN19 85 C8
iddlegate La
axby All Saints DN20 84 B4
outh Ferriby DN18 84 B7
iddlegate Mews DN38 99 D5
iddleham Ave YO31 130 E8
iddleham Cl 3 HU9 146 E8
iddlehowe Gn 2 HU17 55 B8
iddlehowe Rd HU17 55 A8
iddle La
mcotts DN17 95 E8
rayton YO8 148 C1
14 Knottingley WF11 61 A2
reston HU12 58 B1
5 Seaton HU11 35 A1
iddlemarsh Cl 3 HU7 141 B4
iddleplatt Rd DN40 87 D2
iddlesex Rd HU8 141 F5
iddle St
orringham DN21 118 B2
oggathorpe YO42 39 A2
ilham YO25 9 B3
afferton YO25 125 F7
orth Kelsey LN7 110 A4
udston YO25 9 F6

Middle St *continued*
Scotton DN21 107 C1
Wilberfoss YO41 27 F5
Willoughton DN21 119 B3
Middle Street N YO25 124 E4
Middle Street S YO25 124 F3
MIDDLETHORPE 133 B6
Middlethorpe Dr YO24 132 E7
Middlethorpe Gr YO24 132 F7
Middlethorpe Prim Sch
DN35 103 B2
Middle Thorpe Rd DN35 103 B2
Middleton CE Prim Sch
YO25 31 C4
Middleton Cl
Beverley HU17 154 C4
Messingham DN17 107 D7
Middleton Ct
Bridlington YO16 122 D5
Kingston upon Hull HU5 145 B8
Middleton Hall★ HU6 140 B4
MIDDLETON-ON-THE-WOLDS 31 B4
Middleton Rd
Bainton YO25 31 D5
Scunthorpe DN16 96 D2
York YO24 129 C2
Middleton St HU3 145 C8
Middlewood Cl YO23 24 C6
Midfield Pl DN36 114 D8
Midfield Rd DN36 114 D8
Midfield Way 1 DN41 101 A4
Midgley Cl
Kingston upon Hull HU3 145 C5
21 Stamford Bridge YO41 15 D2
Midland Ind Est DN15 151 D5
Midland Rd DN16 151 D5
Midland St HU1 155 A2
Midmere Ave HU7 141 B7
Midway Ave
Bridlington YO16 122 D2
Poppleton YO26 126 A1
Midway Gr HU4 144 E4
Milcroft Cres 13 DN7 92 D4
Mildred Gr 5 YO24 129 F2
Mile End Ave DN7 92 D3
Mile End Pk YO42 29 A4
MILE HOUSE 141 E2
Miles La HU17 43 C6
Milestone Ave YO23 24 C6
Mile The YO42 29 A4
Milford Ave YO16 122 C5
Milford Cres 5 YO16 122 C5
Milford Ct 19 DN31 153 A5
Milford Gr HU9 142 E1
Milford Mews 7 YO32 127 D7
Milford Way 8 YO32 127 D7
Millard Ave DN7 92 D4
Millard Nook 18 DN7 92 D4
Mill Ave DN31 152 C4
Mill Balk DN14 77 C8
Mill Balk Pl DN14 78 B8
Millbank 11 YO16 122 C5
Millbank St DN14 149 F5
Mill Baulk Rd DN10 116 C3
Millbeck Bank HU15 67 E8
Millbeck Cl YO43 135 D5
Mill Beck La HU16 139 B8
MILLBROOK PARK 135 C3
Millbrook Way 23 DN18 84 F8
Mill Cl
Blyton DN21 117 F5
Bridlington YO16 122 C5
15 Broughton DN20 98 B2
Great Driffield YO25 124 D4
Marshchapel DN36 115 C2
Monk Fryston LS25 61 A8
7 Waltham DN37 113 E6
Mill Cres 11 DN21 107 C3
Millcroft 15 YO8 48 D1
Mill Croft
Scawby DN20 108 F8
11 Scunthorpe DN16 96 E2
Millcroft 32 DN8 93 A8
Mill Ct 10 YO16 122 C5
Milldane HU16 139 E8
Mill Dr HU17 45 A8
Millennium Way DN14 149 F5
Miller Ave DN32 153 C2
Miller Cl
Barmby Moor YO42 28 F4
10 Thorne/Moorends DN8 93 B7
Miller La
Thorne/Moorends DN8 93 B7
Yapham YO42 29 A6
Miller Rd DN21 117 D1
Millers Brook DN9 94 E1
Millers Cl 3 DN21 108 B2
Millers Croft 6 YO23 132 B3
Millers Quay 14 DN20 98 B2
Millers Way DN20 97 E3
Miller's Wlk HU5 139 F2
Mill Falls YO25 124 D4
Millfield Ave
16 Grimsby DN33 102 E2
York YO10 130 F3
Millfield Cl YO41 27 E5
Millfield Ct YO19 37 F7
Mill Field Ct 5 DN3 92 A3
Millfield Dr YO8 63 D4
Millfield Garth YO25 31 C4
Millfield Gdns YO26 126 A2
Millfield Ind Est YO19 37 F7
Millfield La
Nether Poppleton YO26 129 B8
Poppleton YO26 126 A2
York YO10 131 A3

Millfield Rd
4 Bridlington YO16 122 C5
17 Hemingbrough YO8 49 F1
Hemingbrough YO8 63 F8
Thorne/Moorends DN8 93 A8
York YO23 130 B2
Mill Field Rd
Chapel Haddlesey YO8 62 B5
Fishlake DN7 92 C8
Scunthorpe DN16 151 E7
Millfields
Barton-upon-Humber
DN18 84 E8
23 Caistor LN7 111 B4
Millfields Way 7 DN19 85 C8
Millfield The DN20 109 A6
Mill Garth
12 Cleethorpes DN35 103 B2
14 Hemingbrough YO8 49 F1
Millgate YO8 148 C6
Mill Gate YO16 122 C5
Millgate Mews 3 YO8 148 C6
Millgates YO26 129 C6
Mill Hill
Ellerker HU15 68 A8
Escrick YO19 37 B5
Mill Hill Cres DN35 153 E1
Mill Hill Dr
6 Scunthorpe DN16 96 E2
York YO32 127 F4
Millhill Rd DN14 149 E5
Mill Hill Rd DN7 92 E3
Millhouse La DN14 149 F5
Mill House La DN15 83 B5
Millhouse St Rise 3
DN40 87 B1
Mill House Way HU11 45 D2
Millhouse Woods La
HU16 139 B8
Millias Cl 13 HU14 68 D5
MILLINGTON 29 C6
Millington Woods Nature
Reserve★ YO42 29 D8
Mill La
Acaster Malbis YO23 36 C8
Askham Richard YO23 24 D2
Barlow YO8 63 B7
Barrow upon Humber DN19 85 C8
Beverley HU17 154 B4
Bielby YO42 39 E6
Bishop Burton HU17 43 B2
Brandesburton YO25 34 B2
Brayton YO8 62 C8
Bridlington YO16 122 C5
Brigg DN20 98 B1
Brough HU15 68 C6
Broughton DN20 97 E3
Caistor LN7 111 C4
Carlton DN14 63 D3
Drax YO8 63 F5
East Halton DN40 86 D6
Eastrington HU15 52 A1
Elstronwick HU12 58 F3
Foston YO25 21 F1
Gainsborough DN21 117 A2
Gilberdyke HU15 52 D1
Goxhill DN19 71 A1
Harpham YO25 21 E7
Haxby YO32 13 D5
Haxey DN9 105 B2
Hayton YO42 29 D1
2 Hemingbrough YO8 49 F1
Hessay YO23 24 B7
Holton le Clay DN36 114 B4
Hornsea HU18 134 B4
Huggate YO42 18 B1
Immingham DN40 87 A1
Inglemire HU16 138 E7
14 Keelby DN41 101 A4
Kilpin DN14 65 D5
Kirk Ella HU10 143 C6
Kirton in Lindsey DN21 108 C1
Langtoft YO25 8 C7
Laxton DN14 65 F3
Marshchapel DN36 115 C2
Newbald YO43 53 E6
Newland YO8 64 A3
Newport HU15 52 E1
3 North Cave HU15 53 D3
North Dalton YO25 31 C7
North Kelsey LN7 110 A4
Rawcliffe DN14 63 F1
1 Riccall YO19 37 A1
Rise HU17 45 E6
Scawby DN20 108 F8
Seaton HU11 35 A2
Seaton Ross YO42 39 D4
Skipsea YO25 23 B2
Sledmere YO25 6 F3
Snaith & Cowick DN14 78 C8
South Ferriby DN18 84 A7
Walkeringham DN10 116 C3
Warter YO42 30 A4
Watton YO25 32 D4
Welwick HU12 90 A7
Wilberfoss YO41 27 E6
Wrawby DN20 98 E3
York YO31 130 E6
Mill Lane Ct HU17 154 B3
Mill Lane W HU15 68 B6
Mill Mere Rd DN21 118 A2
Mill Mount YO24 130 A3
Mill Mount Ct YO24 130 A3
Millom Way DN32 152 F4
Mill Pl DN35 153 F2
Millport Dr HU4 144 B2
Mill Race DN36 114 E4

Mill Rd
Aldbrough HU11 47 C2
Burton Constable HU11 58 D7
Burton Fleming YO25 2 D4
Cleethorpes DN35 153 E1
Crowle DN17 94 D8
Hibaldstow DN20 108 E4
Keadby DN17 95 D5
Keyingham HU12 73 C4
Luddington & Haldenby
DN17 81 C4
Skidby HU16 138 C7
Sproatley HU11 58 D5
Swanland HU14 69 A6
Mill Rise
Great Driffield YO25 124 D4
Skidby HU16 138 B8
Swanland HU14 69 A6
Mills Dr DN7 104 A8
Millside YO25 9 C3
Mill Side Cl 6 YO25 9 C3
Mills Service Rd DN16 97 A4
Mill St
Great Driffield YO25 124 E4
Hutton Cranswick YO25 32 E8
Kingston upon Hull HU1 155 A2
York YO1 156 C1
Millstone Cl 4 DN21 108 B2
Millthorpe Sch YO23 130 B2
Mill View
Hut Green DN14 62 A2
Waltham DN37 113 D6
Mill View Cl DN9 105 D7
Mill View Cres YO25 22 C1
Mill View Ct DN14 149 E4
Millview Gdns DN20 98 E3
Mill View Pl 5 HU17 137 B3
Mill View Rd HU17 154 C2
Mill Wlk HU16 139 C5
Milne Rd HU9 142 C4
Milner Pl YO16 122 D4
Milner Rd YO16 122 D4
Milner St YO24 129 D3
Milson Cl
4 Barton-upon-Humber
DN18 84 E8
Broughton DN20 97 D4
Milson Gr YO10 131 A3
Milson Rd 8 DN41 101 A4
Milton Carr 8 YO30 126 F1
Milton Cl
5 Gainsborough DN21 117 C1
12 Howden DN14 65 A7
Milton Rd
3 Gainsborough DN21 117 C1
Grimsby DN33 102 D2
Scunthorpe DN16 151 B1
Milton St
Goole DN14 149 C4
York YO10 130 F3
Mimosa Ct DN15 96 F2
Minchin Cl 3 YO30 127 B1
Minehead Rd HU7 57 A5
Mineral Quay Rd DN40 87 C3
Minnow Cl 14 DN37 102 B4
Minshull Rd 12 DN35 103 C2
Minster Ave
Beverley HU17 154 B2
York YO31 127 F2
Minster Cl
3 Haxby YO32 127 C8
Kingston upon Hull HU8 141 D5
40 Wigginton YO32 13 E5
York YO1 156 B3
Minster Ct
Beverley HU17 154 A2
11 Howden DN14 65 A7
York YO1 156 B3
Minster Moorgate HU17 154 A2
Minster Moorgate W
HU17 154 A2
Minster Rd
Misterton DN10 116 C5
Scunthorpe DN15 150 B6
Minster Sch The YO1 156 B3
Minster View YO32 127 C8
Minster Yard N HU17 154 B2
Minster Yard S HU17 154 B2
Minster Yd YO1 156 B3
Minter Cl 2 YO24 129 B1
Mintfields Rd HU17 154 C3
Minton St HU5 140 D3
Mint Wlk HU17 154 B1
Mires La HU15 53 D2
Mires The YO43 53 F7
Mirfield Gr HU9 142 C1
Mirfield Rd
Grimsby DN32 102 F2
Scunthorpe DN15 150 C8
Mirkhill Rd YO8 148 B6
Misson Bank DN9 104 C3
MISTERTON 116 C5
Misterton Prim Sch
DN10 116 C4
Mistral Ct YO31 130 E8
Mitcham Rd HU8 142 A5
Mitchell Cl DN7 92 D5
Mitchell La YO41 27 D8
Mitchell Way 11 YO30 126 E3
Mitchel's La YO10 133 F8
Miterdale 4 YO24 132 C7
Mitford Cl 3 YO14 2 F8
Mitford Rd 2 YO14 2 F8
Mitten Ave 10 DN14 78 C8
Mizzen Rd HU6 140 B8
MLS Bsns Centres YO30 127 A2
Moat Field YO10 131 C4
Moat House Rd DN21 108 A1

Moat La 4 DN40 86 E3
Moat Rd DN15 82 C1
Moatside Ct YO31 156 B3
Moat The 45 HU12 72 D7
Moat Way YO8 148 A2
Modder St DN16 151 B2
Model Farm La DN39 86 B1
Moffat Cl HU8 141 C4
Moins Ct YO10 131 D4
Moira Cl DN7 92 D7
Moiser Cl YO32 127 D4
MOLESCROFT 136 B5
Molescroft Ave 3 HU17 136 D6
Molescroft Dr HU17 136 D6
Molescroft Gdns 5
HU17 136 D6
Molescroft Mews HU17 136 C6
Molescroft Pk 4 HU17 136 D6
Molescroft Prim Sch
HU17 136 D6
Molescroft Rd HU17 136 C6
Molescroft West Cl 2
HU17 136 D6
Mollison Ave DN35 153 F1
Mollison Rd HU4 144 A3
Monarch Way YO26 129 D6
Monckton Rise YO43 53 F6
Mond Ave DN14 149 D5
Money Hill (Tumulus)★
YO43 42 A8
Monic Ave HU13 143 F2
Monk Ave YO31 130 F7
Monk Bar Ct YO1 156 B3
Monkbridge Ct YO31 156 C4
MONK FRYSTON 61 B8
Monk Fryston CE Prim Sch
LS25 61 A8
Monkgate YO31 156 C3
Monkgate Cloisters
YO31 156 C3
Monk La YO8 148 C7
Monks Cl DN7 92 D5
Monks Cross Dr YO32 128 A3
Monks Cross Link YO32 128 B4
Monks Cross Sh Pk
YO32 128 B3
Monks Rd DN17 150 F2
Monks Way (West) HU14 68 F5
Monks Wlk The HU17 154 B2
Monkton 11 HU15 68 D6
Monkton Cl 10 HU16 138 F5
Monkton Rd 5 YO31 127 F1
Monkton Wlk HU8 142 C6
Monmouth St HU4 144 E3
Monson Rd DN21 118 D8
Mons St HU5 145 A8
Montague Rd YO23 133 A3
Montague St
Cleethorpes DN35 153 B5
Goole DN14 149 C4
York YO23 130 C1
Montague Wlk 6 YO26 12 F1
Montbretia Dr 25 DN16 96 D1
Montcalm Wlk 8 HU16 138 F5
Montgomery Rd DN35 153 D1
Montgomery Sq YO25 124 C2
Montreal Cres 4 HU16 138 F5
Montrose Ave YO31 130 D8
Montrose Ct DN14 149 F5
Montrose Dr DN14 149 F5
Montrose St
Kingston upon Hull HU8 141 B1
Scunthorpe DN16 151 B6
Monument Cl YO24 129 E3
Moody La DN31 152 A7
Mook St YO60 16 B8
Moorbeck Cl HU6 139 F4
Moor Carr La
Barlby with Osgodby YO8 49 B5
Barlby YO8 49 B5
Moor Cl YO19 37 F8
Moor Cottage Rd YO25 34 D5
Moorcroft Rd YO24 132 D7
Moor Dike Rd DN7 104 A8
Moore Ave YO10 131 B4
Moor Edges Rd DN8 93 B8
MOOR END 52 B8
Moor End YO43 52 B8
MOORENDS 79 C2
Moorends Rd DN8 79 A4
Moorfield Dr YO41 27 E6
Moorfield Rd YO16 122 D3
Moorfields 3 YO8 48 D6
Moorfields La DN14 65 D3
Moorfield Way YO41 27 E6
Moorfoot Cl 8 HU7 57 A6
Moorgarth Ave 10 YO24 129 F2
Moorgate YO24 129 D3
Moor Gn HU4 144 B7
Moor Gr YO24 132 E8
Moorhouse Rd 1 HU5 139 B1
Moorings Ct DN14 65 C4
Moorings The DN20 98 A2
Moor La
6 Barlby YO8 49 B5
Bilbrough LS24 24 B1
Bishopthorpe YO23 132 E2
Burton Agnes YO25 10 C2
Caistor LN7 111 A4
Carnaby YO16 10 E4
Cliffe YO8 49 F4
Copmanthorpe YO23 132 A1
Earswick YO32 128 C8
Full Sutton YO41 15 F1
Harpham YO25 22 A8

Moor La *continued*
Hatfield DN8 93 D3
Haxby YO32 13 D7
Humbleton HU11 58 E6
Kelfield YO19 36 E2
Knapton YO26 24 E6
Murton YO19 131 F8
Naburn YO19 36 D8
Newton-on-Ouse YO30 12 C7
Rufforth YO26 24 E6
Skelton YO30 126 D6
Strensall YO32 14 B7
Sykehouse DN14 78 A4
Thorne DN8 79 B1
Thornholme YO25 10 B2
Wroot DN9 104 C6
York YO24 132 C6
Moorland Ave 3 DN10 116 C3
Moorland Cl 4 DN10 116 C3
Moorland Dr 16 DN36 114 A8
Moorland Garth 2 YO32 14 A7
Moorland Gdns
Copmanthorpe YO23 132 A1
York YO23 132 A1
Moorland Rd
Goole DN14 149 D1
York YO10 133 D8
Moorlands
Skelton YO32 13 B5
6 Westwoodside DN9 105 A2
Moorlands Cl YO10 131 C4
Moorlands Fields YO10 133 E8
Moorlands La YO30 126 C6
Moorlands Nature Reserve* YO32 13 B5
Moorlands The HU15 53 E1
Moorland Way 12 DN9 105 E6
Moor Lee La
Eggborough DN14 77 B8
Heck DN14 62 B1
MOOR MONKTON 12 A3
Moor Owners Rd DN8 93 D8
Moor Rd
Bottesford DN17 96 B1
Bridlington YO15 123 D7
15 Brough HU14 68 D5
Crowle DN17 94 C8
Hunmanby YO14 3 B7
Rawcliffe DN14 79 B7
Sancton YO43 53 C8
Stamford Bridge YO41 15 D2
Thorne DN8 93 C7
Moorside Ct 22 DN8 79 B2
Moors La HU15 53 E2
Moors Rd DN15 150 C7
MOORTOWN 110 D2
Moortown Rd
Brandesburton YO25 34 B4
Nettleton LN7 111 A3
Moor Way YO32 128 A4
Moorwell Bsns Pk DN17 96 C1
Moorwell Rd
Scunthorpe DN17 96 C1
Yaddlethorpe DN17 96 B1
Moot Hill* YO25 124 E5
Morcar Rd YO41 15 D1
Mordacks Dr YO16 123 B8
Mordacks Rd YO16 123 A7
Mordaunt Ave DN33 113 D8
Morecambe Ave DN16 151 A1
Morehall Cl YO30 126 F2
More Hall Dr HU8 141 D7
Moreton Bay HU11 142 E5
Morfield Gr 3 DN9 105 D6
Morgan Cl 32 YO42 29 A3
Morgan Way DN19 70 D2
Morley Rd DN17 150 F1
Morley St
Goole DN14 149 D1
Kingston upon Hull HU8 141 A2
Morley's Yd HU17 154 A3
Morpeth St HU3 145 D7
Morpeth Wlk DN34 152 A3
Morrell Ct
Woodthorpe YO24 132 B8
York YO24 132 B8
Morrell Garth YO8 148 C2
Morrell Way YO10 131 A2
Morrets La YO8 48 A1
Morrill St HU9 141 D1
Morris Rd HU3 144 E7
Morritt Cl 3 YO31 130 F8
Morrow Ave HU18 134 D5
Mortimer Dr HU10 143 F6
Mortimer Wlk YO25 125 A3
Mortlake Cl HU8 141 E5
MORTON 117 A3
Morton Cl
4 Gainsborough DN21 117 A2
Immingham DN40 87 B2
Morton La
Beverley HU17 154 B3
Hambleton YO8 62 A8
Morton Rd
Gainsborough DN21 117 B2
Grimsby DN34 152 B3
Laughton DN21 117 E8
Morton St HU3 145 C8
Morton Terr DN21 117 B1
Morton Trentside Prim Sch DN21 117 A2
Moseley Hill HU11 142 E6
MOSS 77 D1
Mosscroft La DN7 92 E2
Mosscroft Way DN7 92 E3
Moss Green Cl YO8 148 A2
Moss Green La
Brayton YO8 148 A2
Hirst Courtney YO8 62 F3
Moss Haven DN6 77 D1
Moss Rd
Grimsby DN32 152 E3
Kirk Bramwith DN7 92 A8
Moss DN6 77 B1
Moss St YO23 156 A1
Motherwell Cl HU7 141 C4
Moulton Cl 6 DN34 102 B2
Mount Ave
13 Barton-upon-Humber DN18 84 E8
Bridlington YO16 122 E6
Kingston upon Hull HU13 143 D2
Selby YO8 148 B3
Winterton DN15 83 B5
Mountbatten Cl 7 DN16 96 D2
Mountbatten Mews DN14 149 C5
Mountbatten Prim Sch HU9 142 E3
Mount Cres YO16 122 E6
Mount Dr YO16 122 E6
Mount Ephraim 6 YO24 130 A3
Mount Gr YO8 148 B3
Mount Par YO24 130 A3
Mount Pk YO19 49 A8
Mount Pleasant
Aldbrough HU11 47 D2
Harpham YO25 9 D3
9 Holton le Clay DN36 114 A5
1 Hornsea HU18 134 B4
Kingston upon Hull HU8 141 A1
New Holland DN19 70 E2
Waltham DN37 113 D7
Worlaby DN20 98 D8
Mount Pleasant CE Jun Sch YO43 135 D3
Mount Pleasant Rd
Goole DN14 149 D5
21 Moorends DN8 79 B2
North Frodingham YO25 34 A7
Thorne DN8 79 A2
Mount Pleasant Windmill* DN21 108 B2
Mount Ret Pk The HU9 146 C8
Mount Royale Cl 4 DN39 86 A1
Mount Sch The YO24 130 A3
Mount Terr YO24 130 A3
Mount The
Great Driffield YO25 124 F5
7 Kirk Sandall DN3 92 A1
Selby YO8 148 B3
York YO24 156 A1
Mount Vale YO24 130 A2
Mount Vale Dr YO24 130 A2
Mount Vernon HU11 142 E6
Mount View HU14 69 A5
Mowbray Cl DN9 105 D3
Mowbray Ct 20 DN9 105 E6
Mowbray Dr YO26 129 C4
Mowbray Rd 18 DN8 93 B7
Mowbray St
Epworth DN9 105 E6
3 Gainsborough DN21 117 B1
Mowthorpe Medieval Village* YO17 6 C6
Moy Ct HU6 140 A6
Mucky La HU12 59 C6
Muirfield 16 DN37 113 D6
Muirfield Croft 4 DN40 87 C1
Muirfield Pk HU5 140 A1
Muirfield Way 6 YO26 129 B5
Mulberry Ave 12 DN8 79 B2
Mulberry Cl
Bridlington YO16 123 A8
Great Driffield YO25 124 D3
11 Keelby DN41 101 A4
North Thoresby DN36 114 B1
Mulberry Ct YO32 127 F6
Mulberry Dr
11 Crowle DN17 94 D7
7 Haxby YO32 13 E5
Mulberry Gdns DN15 96 F2
Mulberry La HU11 45 E2
Mulcourt HU6 139 F7
Mulgrave St HU8 155 C4
Mulgrave Street S DN15 151 A8
Mullion Cl HU7 141 C7
Mull Way DN40 101 C8
Mulwith Cl YO31 131 A6
Mumby Cl 7 DN36 114 B1
Muncastergate YO31 130 E7
Munroe Cl HU8 141 C4
Munster Ct 5 DN31 153 A5
Murham Ave DN14 149 C6
Murray Cl 3 YO42 29 A4
Murray Cres HU16 138 F5
Murrayfield Rd HU5 139 F1
Murray St
Grimsby DN31 152 F6
York YO24 129 F3
Murrough Wilson Pl 3 YO31 130 C7
MURTON 26 D7
Murton Garth YO19 131 F6
Murton La YO19 26 D7
Murton Way YO19 131 E5
Museum St YO1 156 B2
Muston Ave HU16 139 A5
Muston Rd YO14 2 F8
Muswell Ct HU8 142 A5
Mutton La DN10 116 C1
Mylor Cl 13 HU7 57 A5
Myrtle Ave
Bishopthorpe YO23 133 B3
Selby YO8 148 B3
Myrtle Rd DN7 92 C4
Myrtle Way 14 HU15 68 D5
Mytongate HU1 155 A1
Myton St HU1 155 A2

N

Nab Dr DN14 149 C6
Nab La DN7 92 C8
NABURN 36 D8
Naburn CE Prim Sch YO19 36 D8
Naburn La
Deighton YO19 37 A7
Fulford YO19 133 D4
Naburn Park Mews YO19 36 E8
Naburn St HU3 145 A4
Nacton St DN31 152 F5
NAFFERTON 125 E7
Nafferton Prim Sch YO25 125 E6
Nafferton Sta YO25 125 F6
Nairn Cl YO24 132 C6
Nairn Way DN34 152 C1
Nalton Cl YO23 132 A1
Nalton Ct HU16 139 A5
Nalton St YO8 148 C5
Nandike Cl 4 HU10 143 F6
Nan Sampson Bank DN9 104 B4
Napier Cl HU17 154 A4
Narborough Ct 7 HU17 55 F8
Narrow Boats The 13 DN20 98 B2
Narrow La
Cottingwith YO42 38 D7
Eastrington DN14 52 A2
Kilpin DN14 65 D6
17 North Ferriby HU14 69 A5
Skipwith YO8 37 E3
Twin Rivers DN14 81 C8
Narvick Rd HU7 140 E5
Naseby Cl 14 DN7 92 D3
Naseby Dr DN31 152 B3
Naseby Gr DN31 152 B4
Nashcourt HU6 139 F7
National Ave HU5 144 F8
National Ctr for Early Music* YO1 156 C2
National Rly Mus* YO26 130 A4
Navensby Cl DN31 102 C5
Navigation La LN7 111 A4
Navigation Rd YO1 156 C2
Navigation Way HU9 146 C6
Nayfield Cl 7 YO25 124 F4
Naylor's Row 3 HU9 146 B7
Neap House Rd DN15 95 E6
Neasden Cl HU8 141 E5
Neasden Prim Sch HU8 141 E5
Neatgangs La DN19 71 A3
Neath Rd DN16 151 A5
NEAT MARSH 58 A2
Neat Marsh Rd HU12 58 B1
Neatshead Garth 9 HU7 57 B5
Needham Cl HU17 137 B4
Nelson Ct HU1 155 B1
Nelson Rd HU5 144 B7
Nelson's La YO24 129 F1
Nelson St
Bridlington YO15 122 E2
Gainsborough DN21 117 B1
Grimsby DN32 152 F5
Kingston upon Hull HU1 155 C1
York YO31 156 C4
Nelson Way DN34 102 B3
Nelthorpe Cl 6 DN39 86 A1
Neptune Dr YO16 122 C4
Neptune St
Bridlington YO15 122 E1
Cleethorpes DN35 153 E3
Kingston upon Hull HU3 145 D4
Nessgate YO1 156 B2
Ness La
Garthorpe & Fockerby DN17 81 E6
1 Preston HU12 58 C1
Ness Rd 5 YO8 148 D6
Nestlings The HU8 141 D4
Nestor Gr HU9 142 C5
Neswick La YO25 31 F7
Nethergate
Nafferton YO25 125 F7
Westwoodside DN9 105 B2
Netherlands Way DN41 87 E1
NETHER POPPLETON 126 A2
Netherton Rd HU4 144 B4
Nether Way 20 YO26 12 F1
Netherwindings 13 YO32 13 F5
Netherwoods 5 YO32 14 B8
Nettle Hill 12 HU15 52 F1
Nettleholme 2 DN7 92 D4
NETTLETON 111 A2
Nettleton Garth 3 HU12 73 A6
Nettleton Prim Sch LN7 111 A3
Nettleton Rd LN7 111 B3
Neville Ave HU17 154 C3
Neville Cl
2 Keadby with Althorpe DN17 95 D4
Kingston upon Hull HU3 145 D5
Neville Cres DN15 83 A5
Neville Dr YO23 133 A3
Neville Garth 27 HU12 72 D7
Neville La DN7 92 A8
Neville Pits La DN14 77 B4
Neville Rd DN16 151 C6
Neville St
Cleethorpes DN35 153 D4
York YO31 156 C4
Neville Terr YO31 156 C4
Neville Turner Way 9 DN37 113 D6
Nevinson Gr YO10 133 E8
Nevis Way YO24 132 B7
NEW ARRAM 43 F7
Newbald Gr HU6 139 F6
Newbald Prim Sch YO43 53 F8
Newbald Rd HU17 136 A2
Newbald Way 1 HU16 138 E6
NEW BARNETBY 99 D5
Newbegin
Beverley HU17 154 A3
Hornsea HU18 134 C4
Newbigg
Crowle DN17 94 C8
Westwoodside DN9 105 B2
Newbolt Ave DN17 150 D3
Newbolt Cl LN7 111 A3
Newborn Ave DN15 150 E8
Newborough St YO30 156 A4
Newbridge La YO41 28 A7
New Bridge La YO25 125 F5
Newbridge Rd HU12 73 B6
New Bridge Rd HU9 146 C8
New Burlington Rd 2 YO15 122 D2
Newbury Ave
Grimsby DN37 102 C5
York YO24 129 D1
Newbury Gr 2 DN34 102 C2
Newby La DN14 77 F8
Newby Rd DN31 152 C3
Newby Terr YO31 130 C7
New Carr La DN14 52 A3
New Cartergate 5 DN31 152 D3
New Chapel La 6 DN37 101 F1
New Church Terr 12 YO8 148 C5
New Cl
1 Grimsby DN33 102 E2
Nunsthorpe DN33 102 E2
New Clee Sta DN31 153 B5
New Cleveland St HU8 155 C4
Newclose La DN14 149 D6
New College Nottingham DN10 116 D5
Newcomen St HU9 141 D1
Newcroft YO8 148 B4
New Cut YO25 22 E5
Newdale 3 YO32 13 F5
New Delights DN36 114 F3
Newdown Rd DN17 96 B2
NEW EARSWICK 127 D3
New Earswick Prim Sch YO32 127 D4
New Earswick Sports Club YO32 127 D3
NEW ELLERBY 46 A2
Newfield Cl DN3 92 A3
Newfield La
Burstwick HU12 58 F2
South Cave HU15 53 E1
Newfields Ave DN8 79 B1
Newfields Cl DN8 79 B1
Newfields Dr DN8 79 B1
New Fields Ind Est HU12 72 A8
New Finkle Ct HU16 139 A6
New Forge Ct 15 YO32 13 F5
New Garden St HU1 155 B3
Newgate YO1 156 B2
Newgate Ct YO1 156 B2
Newgate St HU16 139 B6
New George St HU2 155 B3
New Gn 2 DN7 92 C6
Newhall Rd 8 DN3 92 A2
New Haven Terr DN31 152 B5
Newhay La YO8 49 E1
NEW HOLLAND 70 E2
New Holland CE & Methodist Prim Sch DN19 70 E2
New Holland Rd DN19 85 D8
New Holland Sta DN19 70 E3
Newholme Cl HU6 139 F6
Newholme Dr 8 DN8 79 B2
Newington Ave HU4 144 E5
Newington Prim Sch HU3 145 A4
Newington St HU3 144 F4
New Inn La DN7 92 C7
New La
Beal DN14 61 D3
Bishopthorpe YO23 133 A4
Holgate YO24 129 E3
Humbleton HU11 59 A5
Huntington YO32 127 F1
Laxton DN14 65 E4
Long Marston YO23 24 B3
Newland YO8 64 A3
Rawcliffe DN14 79 A8
Reedness DN14 80 E8
Selby YO8 148 C5
Strensall YO32 14 B8
New Laids La HU12 73 B7
NEWLAND
Goole 64 B3
Howden 66 A8
Hull 140 C3
Newland Ave
Great Driffield YO25 124 D4
Kingston upon Hull HU5 140 C2
Scunthorpe DN15 150 E6
Newland Cl YO25 124 D4
Newland Dr DN15 150 D7
Newland Gr 1 HU5 140
Newland Park Ave HU6 140
Newland Park Cl YO10 131
Newland Park Dr YO10 130
Newland Pk HU5 140
Newland Rd DN14 149
Newlands 17 DN21 117
Newland St Johns CE Prim Sch HU6 140
Newland Sch for Girls HU6 140
Newlands Dr YO26 129
Newlands La
Paull HU12 72
Upper Poppleton YO26 24
Newlands Pk 23 DN36 103
Newlands Rd
Bishopthorpe YO23 132
Sunk Island HU12 89
Newlands The HU6 140
Newland View 11 DN9 105
Newland Wlk DN15 150
Newlyn Cl
4 Kingston upon Hull HU13 144
New Waltham DN36 114
Sutton-on-Hull HU7 141
Newmarch Ct 26 DN33 102
Newmarket St DN32 152
New Michael St HU1 155
New Mill Field Rd DN7 92
New Millgate YO8 148
Newnham Cres 12 DN16 96
New Options Barton Sch DN18 85
New Park Est DN7 92
New Pasture Cl 6 YO16 122
New Pasture La YO16 122
New Pasture Lane Prim Sch YO16 122
New Pastures YO42 39
New Pasture Wlk YO16 122
NEWPORT 53
Newport Ave YO8 148
Newport Cl 4 HU3 145
Newport Dr DN15 83
Newport Prim Sch HU15 52
Newport Rd HU15 53
Newport St
Barton-upon-Humber DN18 69
Goole DN14 149
New Potter Grange Rd DN14 64
New Rd
Beningborough YO30 12
Brandesburton YO25 33
Burton Pidsea HU12 59
Cleethorpes DN35 153
Etton HU17 43
Foggathorpe YO42 39
Great Driffield YO25 124
Heck DN14 62
Hedon HU12 72
Hessay YO26 24
Holme-on-Spalding-Moor YO43 40
Hornsea HU18 134
Hunmanby YO14 2
Keyingham HU12 73
Kirby Grindalythe YO17 6
Laceby DN37 113
Long Drax YO8 63
Nafferton YO25 125
Norton DN6 76
Ottringham HU12 73
Reighton YO14 3
Roos HU12 59
Scunthorpe DN17 150
Stapleton WF8 76
Swinefleet DN14 80
Waltham DN37 113
Wheldrake YO19 37
Worlaby DN20 98
Newroad End WF8 76
New Row DN17 107
Newsam Cl 4 YO25 22
Newsham Abbey (Site of)* DN39 100
Newsham Dr DN34 152
Newsham Garth HU4 144
Newsham Gdns HU19 75
Newsham Hill La YO16 4
Newsham La DN40 100
NEWSHOLME 64
New St
18 Brigg DN20 98
Gainsborough DN21 117
Grimsby DN31 152
Pocklington YO42 29
York YO1 156
Newstead Ave DN36 114
Newstead Cres YO16 122
Newstead Rd DN35 103
Newstead St HU5 145
Newthorpe Rd 2 DN6 76
Newtondale HU7 140
Newtondale Garth YO16 122
Newton Dr HU17 154
Newton La LN8 120
Newton Marsh La DN36 114
NEWTON-ON-OUSE 12
Newton Pk YO30 12
Newton Rd DN16 151
Newton St 3 HU3 145
Newton Terr YO1 156
NEWTON UPON DERWENT 27

ewtown Ct HU9 .... 146 E7
ewtown Sq HU9 .... 146 E7
ew Trent St DN17 .... 94 E6
EW VILLAGE 139 D6
ew Village Rd
Kingston upon Hull HU16 . 139 C7
Little Weighton HU20 .... 55 A4
ew Walkergate HU17 .. 154 A3
EW WALTHAM 114 A7
ew Waltham Prim Sch
DN36 .... 114 A8
ew Wlk
Beverley HU17 .... 136 D5
Great Driffield YO25 ..... 124 F4
North Ferriby HU14 .... 69 A4
ew Wlk Cl YO25 .... 124 F4
ew Wlk Terr YO10 ..... 130 D2
icholas Ct 7 DN18 ..... 84 E8
icholas Gdns YO10 ..... 130 F3
icholas St YO10 .... 130 F3
icholson Cl HU17 ..... 137 B4
icholson Ct
31 Pocklington YO42 ..... 29 A3
Wold Haven YO42 .... 29 A3
icholson La 2 HU11 ..... 35 A1
icholson Rd DN41 ..... 102 A5
icholsons Ct HU16 ..... 139 A6
icholson's La HU12 ..... 74 B3
icholson St
Cleethorpes DN35 .... 153 F1
5 Kingston upon Hull
HU5 .... 140 E2
icholson Way 6 DN9 .. 105 D7
ickerson Way DN36 ... 114 A5
ickey Nackey La YO8 ..... 48 B8
icolgate La 27 DN20 ..... 98 C2
icolson Dr 16 DN18 ..... 84 F8
idd Cl YO26 .... 129 B8
idderdale HU7 .... 140 F6
idderdale Cl 1 YO16 .. 123 A7
idd Gr YO24 .... 132 E8
idd St DN14 .... 149 D1
igel Gr 7 YO24 .... 129 F2
ightingale Cl
28 Barton Upon Humber
DN18 .... 84 F8
Scunthorpe DN15 .... 96 B7
4 Walkington HU17 ..... 55 D8
York YO32 .... 127 E1
ightingale Dr YO16 ..... 122 F5
ightingale Rd YO16 ..... 122 F5
ine Dikes Rd YO25 .... 9 D8
inescores La DN9 ..... 104 B4
inth Ave
Fixborough Stather DN15 ... 82 A1
York YO31 .... 130 F5
isa Way DN15 .... 82 C1
ithdale Gdns HU5 ..... 140 E2
ith Gr HU8 .... 142 C6
oddle Hill Way HU7 ..... 141 D8
oel St 2 DN21 .... 117 B1
olloth Cres HU17 ..... 154 B4
oodle Hill Way HU7 ..... 57 B5
ooking La DN37 ..... 101 D2
ookings Dr DN20 ..... 109 A5
ooking The DN9 ..... 105 D3
ook The YO8 .... 148 D6
ordale Cl 9 HU8 ..... 141 E7
ordham HU15 .... 53 D3
orfolk Ave DN15 .... 82 B4
orfolk Bank La HU15 ..... 67 E8
orfolk Ct 11 DN32 ..... 153 A5
orfolk La DN35 .... 153 E3
orfolk St
Beverley HU17 .... 136 D5
Kingston upon Hull HU2 .. 155 A3
York YO23 .... 130 C2
orland Ave HU4 ..... 144 C6
orlands La
Bempton YO16 .... 4 A1
Norlands YO16 .... 4 A1
ORMANBY 82 B3
ormanby Ent Pk DN15 . 151 B8
ormanby Hall Ctry Pk*
DN15 .... 82 C3
ormanby Rd
Burton upon Stather DN15 .. 82 B4
Nettleton LN7 .... 111 B2
Scunthorpe DN15 .... 151 A8
orman Cl
Barton-upon-Humber
DN18 .... 84 F8
7 Thorpe Willoughby YO8 ... 48 B1
orman Cres DN17 ..... 150 F4
orman Dr
3 Hatfield DN7 .... 92 D3
York YO26 .... 129 B6
ormandy Ave HU17 ..... 55 E8
ormandy Cl 4 YO8 ..... 148 B6
ormandy Rd DN35 ..... 153 D1
ormandy Way DN14 ..... 149 A3
orman Rd
Grimsby DN34 .... 152 B3
Hatfield DN7 .... 92 D3
orman St 5 YO10 ..... 131 A3
ormanton Rise HU4 ..... 144 C7
ornabell Dr HU17 ..... 136 E7
ornabell St 1 HU8 ..... 146 C8
orris Ave YO42 .... 28 E4
orrison Ave HU6 ..... 140 C8
orsefield Ave 1 DN37 .. 113 E7
orseman Cl 7 YO19 ..... 48 F8
orseway 2 YO41 .... 15 D1
orthampton Rd DN16 .. 151 C5
orth Axholme Comp Sch
DN17 .... 94 D6
orth Back La
2 Bridlington YO16 ..... 122 D4

North Back La *continued*
Kilham YO25 .... 9 B3
North Bar Within HU17 .. 154 A3
North Bar Without HU17 136 D4
North Burton La YO14 ..... 3 B4
North Carr Dales Rd HU19 74 F4
North Carr La
Saxby All Saints DN20 ..... 83 F3
Tickton HU17 .... 44 D3
North Carr Rd
Scotter DN17 .... 106 E5
West Stockwith DN10 ..... 116 E5
NORTH CAVE 53 D3
North Cave CE Prim Sch
HU15 .... 53 D3
North Cave Rd YO43 ..... 53 D4
North Cave Wetland Nature
Reserve* HU15 .... 53 C3
North Church Side
1 Easington HU12 .... 90 F6
Kingston upon Hull HU1 .. 155 B2
NORTH CLIFFE 53 B8
North Cliffe Wood Nature
Reserve* YO43 .... 53 A8
North Cliff Rd DN21 ..... 108 C2
North Coates Rd DN36 .. 115 A4
North Comm Rd DN8 ..... 78 F2
Northcote Ave YO24 ..... 129 E3
NORTH COTES 115 A3
North Cotes CE Prim Sch
DN36 .... 115 B3
North Cotes Rd
Hunmanby YO25 .... 2 C5
Wold Newton YO25 .... 1 E5
Northcott Sch HU7 ..... 56 F5
Northcroft 5 YO32 ..... 13 F5
Northcroft Dr 13 HU8 .. 141 E7
North Ctry Ct 2 HU9 .. 141 F1
North Cty Prim Sch
DN21 .... 117 A1
North-Dale Ct 2 DN21 .. 108 B2
Northdale Pk 3 HU14 ..... 69 B7
NORTH DALTON 31 B7
North Dr
Kingston upon Hull HU10 .. 143 E6
Swanland HU14 .... 69 B7
NORTH DUFFIELD 50 A8
North Duffield Prim Sch
YO8 .... 50 A8
North Eastern Rd DN8 ..... 93 A8
North Eastern Terr YO24 . 132 E8
NORTH ELKINGTON 121 A1
North Elkington La LN11 . 121 B1
North Ella Dr HU4 ..... 144 E6
NORTH END
Goxhill 71 A1
Withernwick 46 D4
North End
5 Flamborough YO15 .... 5 A2
Goxhill DN19 .... 86 A8
Seaton Ross YO42 .... 39 D4
South Ferriby DN18 .... 84 A8
North End Cres 13 DN36 114 D4
North End La LN7 ..... 110 A2
North End Rd
Halsham HU12 .... 73 F5
Roos HU12 .... 60 A2
1 Tetney DN36 .... 114 D4
Northern Acad of Performing
Arts HU1 .... 155 A2
Northern Ave 3 DN20 ..... 98 C3
Northern Gateway HU9 .. 147 A7
Northern Gateway Rd
HU9 .... 147 A7
North Farm Rd DN17 ..... 96 B2
NORTH FERRIBY 69 B4
North Ferriby CE Prim Sch
HU14 .... 69 A5
Northferry La DN9 ..... 94 C1
NORTHFIELD 143 F2
Northfield
3 Barlby YO8 .... 49 B5
Bridlington YO16 ..... 122 C5
22 Keyingham HU12 ..... 73 C4
Rimswell HU19 .... 74 F7
Swanland HU14 .... 69 B7
Northfield Ave
Great Driffield YO25 ..... 124 F6
Kingston upon Hull HU13 .. 143 E3
Northfield Cl
Driffield YO25 .... 124 F6
Laughton DN21 .... 117 E8
12 Pocklington YO42 ..... 28 F4
1 Scunthorpe DN16 ..... 151 C2
5 South Cave HU15 ..... 53 F1
2 Tetney DN36 ..... 114 D4
West Butterwick DN17 ..... 95 D1
Womersley DN6 .... 76 C6
Northfield Cotts DN16 ..... 96 D1
Northfield Cres YO25 ..... 124 E5
Northfield Inf Sch YO25 .. 124 F6
Northfield La
Amcotts DN17 .... 81 F2
Kirton in Lindsey DN21 ..... 119 B8
3 Riccall YO19 .... 36 F1
Thornton Curtis DN39 ..... 85 D5
Welwick HU12 .... 90 A8
Willoughton DN21 ..... 119 A4
Womersley DN6 .... 76 C7
North Field La
Askham Bryan YO23 ..... 24 F3
Upper Poppleton YO26 ..... 24 F7
Northfield Rd
Beverley HU17 .... 136 C6
Bubwith YO8 .... 50 E8
Coniston HU11 .... 57 F7
Great Driffield YO25 ..... 124 E6
Kingston upon Hull HU3 .. 144 F6

Northfield Rd *continued*
Market Weighton YO43 ..... 135 E4
Messingham DN17 .... 107 D8
Pocklington YO42 .... 28 F4
Wetwang YO25 .... 19 A6
Northfield Rise 7 YO42 ... 28 F4
Northfields
Barmby Moor YO42 .... 28 D4
4 Strensall YO32 .... 14 B8
Northfield Terr YO24 ..... 132 E8
Northfield Wlk YO25 ..... 124 F6
NORTH FRODINGHAM 34 A8
North Frodingham Prim Sch
YO25 .... 33 F8
North Frodingham Rd
YO25 .... 34 B8
Northgate
Cottingham HU16 .... 139 A7
Hornsea HU18 .... 134 C5
Hunmanby YO14 .... 2 F8
Northfield HU13 .... 143 E2
Thorne/Moorends DN8 ..... 79 B2
Walkington HU17 .... 55 B8
Northgate Gr YO43 ..... 135 C4
Northgate La YO41 ..... 15 A3
Northgate Mews HU16 .. 139 A7
Northgate Vale YO43 ... 135 C4
North Grange Ct YO30 ... 156 A4
North Holme 8 DN36 ... 114 D4
NORTH HOWDEN 51 B1
North Ings Rd DN7 ..... 92 E5
North Intake La DN9 ..... 117 A8
NORTH KELSEY 110 A5
North Kelsey Prim Sch
LN7 .... 110 A4
North Kelsey Rd LN7 ..... 110 F4
North Kelsey Road Ind Est
LN7 .... 110 A4
NORTH KILLINGHOLME 86 D4
North La
Dringhouses YO24 .... 132 E8
Huntington YO32 .... 127 F5
Marsh Chapel DN36 ..... 115 C2
Sykehouse DN14 .... 78 B4
Wheldrake YO19 .... 37 F7
Northlands Ave
1 Earswick YO32 .... 127 F7
2 Winterton DN15 .... 83 A5
Northlands Rd DN15 ..... 83 A6
Northlands Road S DN15 .. 83 A5
North Leas Ave YO16 ..... 122 E7
North Leas Dr YO16 ..... 122 E7
North Leas Wlk YO16 ..... 122 E7
North Leys Rd HU19 ..... 75 B4
North Lincoln Rd DN16 .. 151 D6
North Lincolnshire Mus
DN15 .... 151 A6
North Lindsey Coll DN17 . 150 E4
North Marine Dr YO15 .. 123 A4
North Marine Prom
YO15 .... 123 A4
North Marine Rd 1 YO15 .. 5 B3
North Marsh Rd HU12 ..... 91 B3
Northminster Bsns Pk
YO26 .... 24 F7
North Moor 7 YO32 ..... 127 F5
Northmoor Cl 8 YO32 ... 127 F5
North Moor Dr 1 DN10 . 116 C3
North Moor Gdns YO32 .. 127 F5
North Moor La
Bottesford DN17 .... 96 B1
Cottingham HU16 .... 139 D8
Messingham DN17 .... 107 B8
North Moor Rd
3 Flamborough YO15 .... 5 B3
Messingham DN17 .... 107 C6
Walkeringham DN10 ..... 116 C3
York YO32 .... 127 F5
North Moss La DN41 ..... 101 E8
North Moss Lane Ind Est
DN41 .... 86 F1
NORTH NEWBALD 53 E8
North Newbald Becksies
Nature Reserve* YO43 .. 53 F8
Northolmby St 20 DN14 ... 65 A7
Northolme DN21 .... 117 B1
Northolme Circ 2 HU13 .143 E2
Northolme Cres
Kingston upon Hull HU13 .. 143 E2
Scunthorpe DN15 .... 150 F7
Northolme Dr YO30 ..... 126 E1
Northolme Rd HU13 ..... 143 E2
Northolt Cl HU8 .... 141 E6
NORTH ORMSBY 121 B3
North Ormsby Medieval
Village* LN11 .... 121 A3
NORTHORPE 118 D8
Northorpe Cl HU9 ..... 142 C1
Northorpe Gr 3 HU9 ..... 141 F2
Northorpe Rd DN21 ..... 107 D1
Northorpe Rise YO16 ..... 122 B5
Northorpe Wlk YO16 ..... 122 B5
North Parade
Scunthorpe DN16 .... 151 D2
York YO30 .... 156 A3
North Pinfold Way 2
YO16 .... 122 D6
North Pk HU12 .... 58 F2
North Point Sh Ctr HU7 .. 141 B8
North Promenade
Cleethorpes DN35 .... 153 E3
Withernsea HU19 .... 75 A7
North Quay DN31 ..... 153 A7
North Rd
Atwick YO25 .... 35 C6
Bewholme YO25 .... 35 A5
Halsham HU12 .... 73 F6
Hatfield HU11 .... 46 C5

North Rd *continued*
Keadby with Althorpe DN17 . 95 C6
Kingston upon Hull HU4 ... 144 E4
Lund YO25 .... 31 F3
Ulrome YO25 .... 23 A4
Withernsea HU19 .... 74 F7
North Rise 2 HU12 .... 73 A6
North Sea La DN36 ..... 103 D1
Northside
Haxey DN9 .... 105 C2
Laxton DN14 .... 65 F4
Patrington HU12 .... 74 D1
Northside Ct 6 HU12 ..... 74 D1
Northside Ind Pk DN14 ..... 61 F1
Northside Rd HU19 ..... 75 A4
North's La DN37 .... 112 D8
North St
Aldbrough HU11 .... 47 C1
Barmby on the Marsh DN14 . 64 A7
Barrow upon Humber DN19 . 85 D8
Bridlington YO15 .... 122 E2
Caistor LN7 .... 111 B4
Cleethorpes DN35 .... 153 F2
Crowle DN17 .... 94 D8
6 Gainsborough DN21 ... 117 A2
Goole DN14 .... 149 D4
Great Driffield YO25 ..... 124 E5
Kingston upon Hull HU2 .. 155 A3
Kirk Ella HU10 .... 143 E6
Leven HU17 .... 45 A8
Nafferton YO25 .... 125 E8
Owston Ferry DN9 .... 106 B3
Roxby cum Risby DN15 ..... 83 A4
1 Scunthorpe DN15 ..... 151 B8
West Butterwick DN17 ..... 95 D1
West/East Butterwick
DN17 .... 106 D8
York YO1 .... 156 B2
Northstead Cl HU10 ..... 138 E1
North Street Retail Park
DN14 .... 149 D3
NORTH THORESBY 114 A1
North Thoresby Prim Sch
DN36 .... 114 A1
North Townside Rd YO25 .. 33 F8
North Turnpike YO25 ..... 23 A4
Northumberland Ave
Hornsea HU18 .... 134 B5
Kingston upon Hull HU2 .. 155 B4
Northumberland Cl
DN34 .... 152 B2
North View
Beverley HU17 .... 137 C4
Skidby HU20 .... 55 B4
North View Terr YO15 ..... 122 F3
North Walls HU1 .... 155 C2
North Warren Rd DN21 .. 117 A1
Northway
Fulstow LN11 .... 121 E8
Goole DN14 .... 149 B6
North Way DN36 .... 115 B2
Northwood Cl HU8 ..... 142 C6
Northwood Dr HU13 ..... 143 B3
NORTON 76 E2
Norton Comm La DN6 ..... 76 F2
Norton Comm Rd DN6 ..... 77 A1
Norton Gr HU4 .... 144 D4
Norton Jun & Inf Schs
DN6 .... 76 E2
Norton & Kirk Smeat
WF8 .... 76 C3
Norton La LN8 .... 119 F2
Norton Mill La DN6 ..... 76 E2
Norton Priory DN6 ..... 76 E2
Norton Rd DN16 .... 151 B1
Norton St HU17 .... 154 A2
Norway Dr YO10 .... 133 D8
Norwich Ave 3 DN34 ..... 102 D2
Norwich Ct HU17 .... 136 E1
Norwood HU17 .... 154 B4
Norwood Ave DN15 ..... 150 F6
Norwood Cl 3 HU10 ..... 143 E7
Norwood Ct HU17 .... 154 B4
Norwood Dale HU17 ..... 154 A3
Norwood Far Gr HU17 ..... 154 B4
Norwood Gr HU17 .... 154 B4
Norwood Rd DN7 .... 92 C5
Norwood St HU3 .... 145 C7
Noseley Way 31 HU7 ..... 56 F6
Nostell Gr YO16 .... 122 D7
Nostell Rd DN16 .... 151 D5
Nostell Way YO16 ..... 122 D7
Nottingham Rd 6 HU11 ..... 47 C1
Nouth-Dale Cl 2 DN21 .. 108 B2
Nova Scotia Way 4 YO19 . 49 A8
Novello Garth HU4 ..... 144 B4
Nuffield Cl 6 DN16 ..... 96 D2
NUNBURNHOLME 29 E3
Nunburnholme Ave HU14 . 69 A4
Nunburnholme Hill YO42 .. 29 F3
Nunburnholme Pk HU5 .. 144 B7
Nunmill St YO23 .... 130 C2
NUN MONKTON 12 A4
Nun Monkton Prim Sch
YO26 .... 12 A5
Nunnerley Pl DN37 ..... 113 E7
Nunnery La YO23 .... 156 B1
Nunnery Wlk 4 HU15 ..... 53 F1
Nunnington Cl HU5 ..... 140 B2
Nuns Rd DN17 .... 150 F2
NUNSTHORPE 102 D1
Nunsthorpe Com Sch 36
DN33 .... 102 D2
NUNTHORPE 133 C8
Nunthorpe Ave YO23 ..... 130 B2
Nunthorpe Cl 17 DN7 ..... 92 D4
Nunthorpe Cres YO23 ..... 130 B1
Nunthorpe Gr YO23 ..... 130 B2

Nunthorpe Rd YO23 ..... 156 A1
Nurseries The
Asselby DN14 .... 64 D7
Molescroft HU17 ..... 136 D7
Nursery Cl
3 Barton-upon-Humber
DN18 .... 69 F1
19 Hemingbrough YO8 ..... 49 F1
Kingston upon Hull HU4 .. 144 B5
Scunthorpe DN17 .... 96 C2
Thorngumbald HU12 ..... 72 E5
Nursery Ct
14 Brough HU15 .... 68 C5
Low Catton YO41 .... 27 C8
Nether Poppleton YO26 ... 126 A2
Nursery Dr YO24 .... 129 E3
Nursery Gdns
Beverley HU17 .... 154 A1
17 Holton le Clay DN36 ... 114 A5
York YO10 .... 131 C3
Nursery Gr
Bridlington YO16 .... 122 B5
Kingston Upon Hull HU9 ... 142 B2
Nursery La HU6 .... 139 E4
Nursery Rd YO26 .... 126 A2
Nursery Vale DN21 ..... 117 A3
Nursery View HU16 ..... 139 C7
Nursery Wlk
Kingston upon Hull
HU16 .... 139 D6
Little Leven HU17 .... 45 A7
Nutana Ave HU18 ..... 134 C7
Nutfields Gr 8 DN7 ..... 92 C6
Nuttles La HU12 .... 58 E2
Nutwell Ct 27 DN15 ..... 96 E2
Nutwood View 22 DN16 ... 96 E2

O

Oak Ave
Brough HU15 .... 68 C6
Goole DN14 .... 149 D1
Grimsby DN32 .... 102 F2
Kingston upon Hull HU10 . 138 D1
Scawby DN20 .... 108 F8
Withernsea HU19 .... 75 A5
Oak Cl
Beverley HU17 .... 137 A6
Sproatley HU11 .... 58 C5
Oak Cres
Little Leven HU17 .... 44 F6
7 Thorne/Moorends DN8 .. 79 A1
Oakdale Ave 3 HU10 ..... 143 E8
Oakdale Cl 6 DN14 ..... 78 C8
Oakdale Rd YO30 .... 126 F2
Oakdene HU16 .... 139 B6
Oak Dene DN14 .... 149 E6
Oak Dr
8 Acaster Malbis YO32 ..... 36 C7
Kingston upon Hull HU5 .. 144 B7
Messingham DN17 .... 107 D7
Newport HU15 .... 52 F1
5 Thorpe Willoughby YO8 .. 48 B1
Oak Farm YO8 .... 48 D6
Oak Field YO8 .... 148 A1
Oakfield Cl DN20 .... 98 D2
Oakfield Ct 1 HU6 ..... 139 F4
Oakfield La 21 YO8 ..... 49 F1
Oakfield Prim Sch DN16 . 151 A1
Oakfield Sch HU6 ..... 140 A5
Oakford Cl DN17 ..... 150 D4
Oak Glade 6 YO31 ..... 127 F3
Oak Gr
9 Barnetby le Beck DN38 .. 99 B4
Barrow upon Humber DN19 . 85 C7
9 Hedon HU12 .... 72 C7
Oak Hill HU10 .... 138 C2
Oakhill Cres 3 YO32 ..... 14 A6
Oakington Garth HU7 ... 141 C8
Oakland Ave
33 Hatfield DN7 .... 92 D4
York YO31 .... 131 A7
Oakland Dr YO31 ..... 131 A7
Oaklands
Beckingham DN10 ..... 116 D1
Camblesforth YO8 .... 63 C5
Gilberdyke HU15 .... 66 D8
Hornsea HU18 .... 134 D2
Hutton Cranswick YO25 ..... 32 E6
6 Strensall YO32 .... 14 B7
Oaklands Ave 3 DN14 ..... 65 B7
Oaklands Cres YO8 ..... 63 C5
Oaklands Dr
Northfield HU13 .... 143 D3
Willerby HU10 .... 138 C1
Oaklands Rd DN40 .... 87 C2
Oaklands Sports Ctr
YO24 .... 129 C2
Oakleigh 9 DN16 .... 96 E2
Oakmoor Gr DN8 .... 79 B2
Oakmoor Rd DN8 .... 79 B2
Oakney Wood Dr YO8 ... 148 D1
Oak Rd
Healing DN41 .... 101 F5
Kingston upon Hull HU6 .. 140 E4
2 North Duffield YO8 ..... 50 A7
Scunthorpe DN16 .... 151 B3
Thorne/Moorends DN8 ..... 79 A1
Oak Rise 4 YO24 .... 129 C3
Oaks La DN10 .... 116 C2
Oaksley Carr HU17 ..... 137 C1
Oak Sq 3 HU7 .... 56 E7
Oak St 3 YO26 .... 129 E5
Oak Tree Ave 14 DN21 ... 117 C1

Oak Tree Cl
Beverley HU17 136 D6
Strensall YO32 14 B7
Oak Tree Ct
Bubwith YO8 50 D7
4 Wigginton YO32 127 D7
Oaktree Dr 4 HU8 141 D7
Oak Tree Dr HU17 136 D6
Oak Tree Est 10 HU12 58 C1
Oak Tree Gr YO32 127 D3
Oak Tree La YO32 127 C7
Oak Tree Way
Little Burton YO25 34 B2
10 Strensall YO32 14 B7
Oak Tree Wlk DN17 94 D7
Oakville St YO31 130 D7
Oak Way
Cleethorpes DN35 103 B1
Selby YO8 148 D2
Oakwell Ave YO16 123 A6
Oakwell Gr 2 HU8 141 B1
Oakwood Cl HU5 144 A7
Oakwood Dr DN37 102 B3
Oakwood Pk DN14 77 F6
Oakwood Rise 1 DN16 96 D2
Oasis Acad Immingham DN40 87 C1
Oasis Acad Wintringham DN32 102 F2
Oatfield Cl 16 DN33 113 D8
Oatlands Rd YO16 123 A6
Oban Ave HU9 142 A2
Oban Ct 32 DN40 87 B1
Occupation La
North Kelsey LN7 110 A4
Swanland HU14 69 B8
Ulceby DN39 86 B1
Ocean Bvd HU9 146 B6
Ocean Dr 7 HU15 52 F1
Ochrepit Hill YO42 17 A2
Octagon The HU10 138 D1
OCTON 8 F8
Octon Rd YO25 9 A8
Oderin Dr DN36 114 B8
Odin Ct DN31 102 D2
Ogilvy Dr DN17 96 C2
Ogleforth YO1 156 B3
Ogle Rd 11 YO15 5 B2
O'hanlon Ave DN20 98 C2
Old Annandale Rd HU10 143 C8
Old Barn La DN15 83 A3
Oldbeck Rd HU17 137 C4
Old Boys Sch La 4 YO8 48 B8
Old Bridge Rd HU18 134 C2
Old Brumby St DN16 151 A4
Old Carpenter's Yd DN7 92 B6
Old Chapel Cl 2 HU11 45 C5
Old Chapel La DN37 101 F1
OLD CLEE 153 C2
Old Clee Jun & Inf Sch DN32 153 B2
Old Coppice 14 YO32 13 F5
Old Courts Rd 6 DN20 98 C2
Old Crosby DN15 96 D7
Old Ct HU17 136 D5
Old Dairy DN19 85 D8
Old Dairy Cl DN8 93 A8
Old Dike Lands YO32 127 C8
OLD ELLERBY 58 A8
Old Epworth Road E DN7 92 F4
Old Epworth Road W 9 DN7 92 E4
Old Farm Cl HU12 73 E3
Old Farm Ct 5 DN37 113 D6
Old Farm Way YO8 148 B2
Oldfield Ave HU6 140 C6
Oldfield Cl
Barnby Dun DN3 92 A4
Stainforth DN7 92 B6
Oldfield Cres DN7 92 C6
Oldfield La DN7 92 B6
Old Field La DN7 92 A5
Oldfield Rd 11 DN8 93 B7
Old Fleet 2 DN37 102 B3
Oldfleet Prim Sch HU9 142 E2
Old Forge Rd 4 DN10 116 C5
Old Forge Way
North Frodingham YO25 34 C8
Skirlaugh HU11 45 D2
OLD GOOLE 149 C1
Old Green La YO41 28 A5
Old Hall La YO41 27 C5
Old Haxey Rd DN10 116 C6
Old Highway The 9 YO32 14 B6
Old House Gdns YO8 62 A5
Old Howe La YO25 22 A3
Old Ironside Rd DN15 151 D7
Old La
Blacktoft DN14 66 C4
Hirst Courtney YO8 62 F3
Long Marston YO26 24 A6
Reedness DN14 80 E7
Sigglesthorne HU11 45 F8
Oldlane Gate DN14 80 D4
Old Lea YO43 40 B1
Old Leys La DN21 119 C3
Old Main Rd
Barnetby le Beck DN37 113 B6
Irby DN37 112 D7
Oldman Ct
Woodthorpe YO24 132 C8
York YO24 132 C8
Old Manor Dr DN20 108 E8
Old Manor Lawns HU17 154 B2
Old Mill Cl YO43 135 F3
Old Mill La
7 Broughton DN20 97 E3
Whitton DN15 67 E3
Wrawby DN20 98 D4
Old Mkt Pl 6 DN31 152 D3
Old Moorings The DN17 81 A3
Old Moor La YO24 132 E7
Old Nursery Yd 24 DN8 93 B7
Old Orchard YO32 127 D8
Old Orchard The
Fulford YO10 133 E7
Shipton YO30 12 F5
Old Paddock Ct DN36 114 B7
Old Penny Memories* YO15 122 F2
Old Plumtree La 2 DN36 114 B1
Old Pond Pl 16 HU14 69 A4
Old Post Office La
Barnetby le Wold DN38 99 B4
5 South Ferriby DN18 84 A7
Old Quarry The DN38 110 E7
Old Rd
Healing DN37 102 B5
Holme-on-Spalding-Moor YO43 40 B1
Leconfield HU17 43 C6
Ottringham HU12 73 E3
Old Rectory Gdns DN17 151 A1
Old Row The DN15 82 A5
Old Rugby Pk DN14 149 C5
Old School Cl
Osbaldwick YO10 131 B4
Sykehouse DN14 78 B4
Old School Dr DN20 108 F5
Old School La
Allerthorpe DN17 95 D5
Barlby with Osgodby YO8 49 B5
Keadby DN17 95 D5
North Kelsey LN7 110 A4
20 Scunthorpe DN16 96 D2
Old School Yd 8 DN21 108 B1
Old Showfields 8 DN21 117 B1
Old Smithy & Heritage Ctr The* DN9 106 B3
Old Stack Yd The DN20 98 D3
Oldstead Ave HU6 139 F5
Old Sunderlandwick La YO25 20 D1
Old Tatham YO43 40 B1
Old Thorne Rd DN7 92 E4
OLD TOWN 122 E5
Old Trent Rd DN10 116 F1
Old Trough La HU15 52 C2
Old Vicarage Dr DN15 83 D1
Old Vicarage La 5 LS25 61 A8
Old Vicarage Pk DN20 108 E8
Old Village Rd HU20 55 A4
Old Village St DN15 95 E6
Old Village The YO32 127 F5
Old Warp La DN18 84 A7
Old Waste HU17 154 A3
Old Woodyard The 23 HU19 75 A6
Olinda Rd 2 YO15 122 E2
Olive Dr DN16 96 F2
Olive Gr DN14 149 F5
Oliver Ct DN31 152 D4
Oliver's Cl 18 YO14 2 F8
Olivers La YO16 122 E3
Oliver St DN35 153 D4
Olivier Ct HU4 144 E3
Olympia Cres YO8 148 E6
Olympian Ct YO10 130 F4
Ombler Cl 11 HU12 73 C4
Omega Bsns Pk HU3 145 D4
Omega Bvd DN8 92 F8
Omega Cl YO16 123 A5
Omega Rd YO16 122 F5
On Hill HU14 69 B6
Ontario Rd DN17 96 B2
Onyx Gr 2 HU3 145 A4
Oole Rd DN35 153 F2
Opsa Bsns Ctr YO1 156 B2
Opus Ave YO26 126 C1
Orb La DN15 96 D8
Orby Gr 6 DN33 102 D2
Orchard Ave 8 DN21 107 C3
Orchard Cl
2 Barrow upon Humber DN19 85 C7
13 Barton-upon-Humber DN18 84 F8
Blyton DN21 117 F5
Bridlington YO16 122 E7
3 Burringham DN17 95 D4
Burton upon Stather DN15 82 B5
Driffield YO25 125 E7
Eggborough DN14 61 F2
Great Driffield YO25 124 D5
Hatfield DN7 92 C3
Kingston upon Hull HU10 143 F7
2 Kirton in Lindsey DN21 108 B1
Messingham DN17 107 D7
6 Monk Fryston LS25 61 A8
Morton DN21 117 A3
9 Norton DN6 76 E2
10 Pocklington YO42 28 F4
Roos HU12 74 A8
2 Scunthorpe DN16 151 B2
Selby YO8 148 A4
13 Snaith DN14 63 C1
Wilberfoss YO41 27 E6
York YO24 129 E1
Orchard Cotts 4 YO19 26 F7
Orchard Croft
3 Epworth DN9 105 D7
10 Grimsby DN33 113 E8
Orchard Croft *continued*
Kingston upon Hull HU16 139 B8
Orchard Ct
3 Market Weighton YO43 135 E4
10 Waltham DN37 113 D6
Orchard Dr
Burton upon Stather DN15 82 B5
Goole DN14 65 C4
Gunness DN15 95 E6
Hatfield DN7 92 C3
Kingston upon Hull HU13 143 E1
Middleton-on-the-Wolds YO25 31 C4
1 Winteringham DN15 68 B1
Orchard End 20 YO8 49 F1
Orchard Garth
Beverley HU17 136 D6
Copmanthorpe YO23 132 B2
Orchard Gdns
4 Pocklington YO42 28 F4
York YO31 127 E2
Orchard Gr
Hatfield DN7 92 D5
Misterton DN10 116 D4
Orchard Grange 8 DN9 94 E1
Orchard La
Great Driffield YO25 124 E5
Hutton Cranswick YO25 32 E8
Thorne/Moorends DN8 79 B2
Orchard Paddock 3 YO32 127 D8
Orchard Park Rd HU6 139 F8
Orchard Pk YO42 39 B6
Orchard Rd
Kingston upon Hull HU4 144 B5
Selby YO8 148 A4
Skidby HU16 138 A8
Upper Poppleton YO26 126 A1
Orchard St DN8 93 A8
Orchards The YO25 32 E8
Orchard The
Beverley HU17 137 F8
Bishopthorpe YO25 133 A3
Cherry Burton HU17 43 A5
Fangfoss YO41 28 C8
Heslington YO10 131 A1
Kingston upon Hull HU9 142 B4
Leven HU17 45 A7
14 New Waltham DN36 114 A7
Orchard View 3 YO30 126 B5
Orchard Way
1 Gilberdyke HU15 66 D7
Hensall DN14 62 C2
Howden DN14 65 A6
7 Long Riston HU11 45 C5
9 Pocklington YO42 28 F4
Selby YO8 148 A4
Skirlaugh HU11 45 D2
1 Strensall YO32 14 B7
Thorpe Willoughby YO8 48 B2
York YO24 129 E1
Orchid Rise DN15 150 F6
Ordnance La YO10 130 D1
Ore Blending Rd DN16 97 A4
Oribi Cl HU4 144 C2
Oriel Cl 6 HU17 55 D8
Oriel Gr
Kingston upon Hull HU9 142 A1
York YO30 130 A8
Oriole Rd DN17 150 E2
Orion Cl 8 HU3 145 B5
Orion Way DN34 102 B2
Orkney Cl 7 HU8 141 E7
Orkney Pl 11 DN40 87 C1
Ormerod Cres 7 HU5 139 D2
Ormerod Rd HU5 139 D2
Ormesby Wlk 9 HU5 139 D3
Ormonde Ave HU6 140 D4
Ormsby Cl 9 DN35 103 B2
Ormsby Rd DN17 150 E1
Orniscourt HU6 139 F7
Orrin Cl YO24 132 C7
Orwell St DN31 152 F5
OSBALDWICK 131 C4
Osbaldwick Ind Est YO19 131 D5
Osbaldwick La YO10 131 B4
Osbaldwick Link Rd YO10 131 D4
Osbaldwick Prim Sch YO10 131 C4
Osbaldwick Village YO10 131 C4
Osborne Dr DN36 114 A5
Osborne Rd DN41 101 E8
Osborne St
Cleethorpes DN35 153 F2
Grimsby DN31 152 D3
Kingston upon Hull HU1 155 A2
Osbourne Dr
Keyingham HU12 73 D4
4 York YO30 126 E3
OSGODBY 49 C4
OSGODBY COMMON 49 C6
Oshawa Dell YO42 29 A2
Oslear Cres DN35 153 E1
Oslo Rd HU7 140 F6
Osmington Gdns 10 YO32 14 A7
Osprey Cl
Kingston upon Hull HU6 140 B8
4 York YO24 132 B8
Osprey Dr DN31 102 B5
Ossett Cl HU8 141 C1
Ostler's Cl YO23 132 C3
Ostler's La DN18 84 A5
Ostman Rd YO26 129 C5
Oswald Rd DN15 151 A7
Otley Cl HU9 142 C2
Ottawa Cl 6 HU16 138 F5
Ottawa Rd 6 DN17 96 C2
Otterbirch Wharf HU17 137 B3
Otterburn St 6 HU3 145 A5
Otterwood Bank 5 YO24 129 B1
Otterwood La YO24 129 B1
Otterwood Paddock YO41 15 C2
OTTRINGHAM 73 F3
Ottringham Rd HU12 73 D4
Oubrough La HU11 57 F8
Oundle Cl 5 DN16 96 E2
Our Ladys RC Prim Sch YO24 129 E1
Ouse Acres YO26 129 D6
Ouse Bank YO8 148 E5
Ouseburn Ave YO26 129 C6
Ousecliffe Gdns YO30 130 A6
OUSEFLEET 66 D2
Ousegate YO8 148 D5
Ousegate Mills Business Centre YO8 148 D5
Ouse Lea YO30 130 A7
Ouse Way DN14 78 B8
Outer Trinities HU17 154 B2
Outgaits Cl 4 YO14 2 F8
Outgaits La YO14 3 A8
Outgang La YO19 131 D6
Outgang The
Brantingham HU15 68 B7
South Cliffe YO43 53 B6
Outgate DN17 94 E6
Out Gates
Foston YO25 22 B3
Harpham YO25 21 E6
Out Holme La DN36 114 E3
Outlands Rd HU16 139 D5
OUT NEWTON 90 E8
Out Newton Rd
Holmpton HU19 75 C1
Skeffling HU12 90 D6
Outram Cl HU2 155 A4
Outstray Rd HU12 89 C7
Oval The
Brough HU15 68 C6
Grimsby DN33 102 E1
Hatfield DN7 92 C5
Kellingley DN14 61 C3
Kirk Ella HU10 143 E8
Pocklington YO42 29 A4
23 Scunthorpe DN17 96 C2
Summergangs HU8 141 C2
Overdale Cl YO24 132 D8
Overland Rd HU16 139 C5
Overstrand Dr HU7 141 D6
OVERTON 12 F2
Overton Ave HU10 143 E8
Overton Ct 6 DN18 69 F1
Overton Rd YO30 12 F3
Ovington Terr YO23 130 B2
Owbridge Ct HU2 155 A2
Owen Ave HU13 144 A1
Owlet Nature Reserve* DN21 117 C6
Owlwood Ct 7 YO19 26 E7
Owlwood La 6 YO19 26 E7
OWMBY 110 D7
Owmby Cl DN40 87 A1
Owmby Hill DN38 110 D8
Owmby La LN7 110 C5
Owmby Mount DN38 110 D8
Owmby Rd DN38 110 D8
Owmby Wold La DN38 110 E8
Owsthorpe La DN14 52 A1
Owston Ave 2 YO10 131 A3
Owston Castle* DN9 106 A3
OWSTON FERRY 106 A2
Owston Ferry Castle Nature Reserve* DN9 106 A3
Owston Ferry Rd DN9 116 E8
Owston Rd
1 Hunmanby YO14 2 F8
West Stockwith DN10 116 E6
Owst Rd HU12 73 C4
OWSTWICK 59 E3
OWTHORNE 74 F7
Owthorne Cl YO16 122 B6
Owthorne Gr 3 HU9 142 A2
Owthorne Grange HU19 74 F6
Owthorne Wlk
Bridlington YO16 122 B5
Withernsea HU19 74 F7
Ox Calder Cl 10 YO19 26 F7
Ox Carr La YO32 14 B6
Ox Cl YO41 15 D2
Ox Close La YO10 26 C4
Oxcombe Cl DN37 113 D8
Oxenhope Rd HU6 140 D7
Oxen La YO8 49 E3
Oxford Cl 6 HU17 136 E1
Oxford Rd DN14 149 C5
Oxford St
Bridlington YO16 122 D3
Cleethorpes DN35 153 F1
Grimsby DN32 153 A4
Kingston upon Hull HU2 155 C4
Scunthorpe DN16 151 D2
5 York YO24 130 A3
Oxford Violet HU7 140 E6
Oxmardyke La HU15 66 E6
Oxmarsh La DN19 70 E2
Ox Pasture La DN17 81 C2
Oyster Ct DN35 153 F1
Oyster Way YO14 3 C8

P

Packman La HU10 143 B
Paddock Cl
Askham Richard YO23 24 D
Copmanthorpe YO23 132 A
Huntington YO32 127 F
Paddock Ct
Bridlington YO16 122 E
Great Driffield YO25 124 F
33 Immingham DN40 87 B
Paddock La
Blyton DN21 117 F
West Butterwick DN17 95 C
Paddock Lane E DN21 117 F
Paddock Rise 8 DN19 85 C
Paddocks The
Barnoldby le Beck DN37 113 B
Beckingham DN10 116 D
6 Crowle DN17 94 D
Great Driffield YO25 124 D
Hutton Cranswick YO25 32 E
Kingston upon Hull HU10 143 B
Middleton YO25 31 C
Wheldrake YO19 38 A
Paddock The
14 Airmyn DN14 64 E
Beverley HU17 136 D
1 Buckton/Bempton YO15 4 D
3 Burton upon Stather DN15 82 E
Cottingham HU16 139 C
East Ella HU4 144 B
Fangfoss YO41 28 C
13 Gilberdyke HU15 66 D
1 North Ferriby HU14 69 A
8 Selby YO8 148 C
2 Swanland HU14 69 C
Wilberfoss YO41 27 E
York YO26 129 C
Paddock View HU11 58 B
Paddock Way YO26 129 C
Pademoor Terr DN17 81 A
Padstow Cl 7 HU7 56 F
Padstow Wlk DN17 150 C
Pagehall Cl DN33 102 E
Paghill Est HU12 72 A
Pagnell Ave YO8 148 E
Paignton Ct DN33 113 E
PAINSTHORPE 17 B
Painsthorpe La YO41 17 B
Paisley Prim Sch HU3 145 A
Paisley St HU3 145 A
Palace Ave YO15 122 E
Palanza Terr 8 YO15 122 E
Pale La YO8 61 F
Palmcourt HU6 139 F
Palmer Ave HU10 143 D
Palmer Gr YO8 148 A
Palmer La
Barrow upon Humber DN19 85 D
York YO1 156 C
Palmes Cl YO19 36 E
Palm Farm* DN39 85
Pam Cl 19 DN40 87 C
Pamela Rd DN40 87 C
Panama Dr HU11 45 D
Panman La YO19 26 F
Paper Mill Rd DN14 79 E
Parade Ct YO31 130
Parade The
Hunmanby YO14 3 E
Kingston upon Hull HU5 140 D
Paradise Cotts YO17 17
Paradise Pl
9 Brigg DN20 98 E
3 Goole DN14 149 D
Paradise Sq HU17 154
Paragon Sq HU1 155 A
Paragon St
Kingston upon Hull HU1 155 A
York YO10 156 C
Parcevall Dr 32 HU7 56 F
Parish Church Prim Sch DN21 117
Parishes Sh Ctr The 12 DN15 151
Park Ave
Barlow YO8 63 C
Barton-upon-Humber DN18 84 E
Beverley HU17 154 A
1 Brandesburton YO25 34 E
Bridlington YO15 122
Cottingham HU16 139 A
Crowle DN17 94 D
Goole DN14 149 E
Great Driffield YO25 124
Grimsby DN32 152 D
Misterton DN10 116 C
New Earswick YO32 127 D
Northfield HU13 143
Scunthorpe DN17 96 C
Snaith DN14 78 D
Withernsea HU19 75 A
Park Avenue W HU5 140 A
Park Cl
6 Airmyn DN14 64
Great Driffield YO25 124
Immingham DN40 87 C
Melbourne YO42 39 A
Skelton YO30 126
Westwoodside DN9 105 A
Park Cres
11 Thorne/Moorends DN8 93 A
York YO31 156 C

ark Ct DN15...151 B8
arkdale 15 DN18...84 E8
ark Dr
Campsall DN6...76 E1
Grimsby DN32...152 E1
4 Westwoodside DN9...105 A2
arker Ave YO26...129 B2
arker Cl DN37...101 E2
arker Rd DN36...114 D8
arker's La DN16...151 C2
arker St DN35...153 F1
ark Est YO32...127 D8
ark Farm Rd DN15...96 C8
arkfield Ave HU14...69 A4
arkfield Dr
Bridlington YO16...122 B5
Kingston upon Hull HU3...144 F6
ark Gate YO32...14 B8
ark Gdns 5 DN14...78 C8
ark Gr
Kingston upon Hull HU5...140 C1
Manor Park DN17...150 B2
Selby YO8...148 B3
York YO31...156 C4
ark Grove Prim Sch
YO31...156 C4
ark Hill DN21...108 B1
arkhill Cres DN3...92 A4
arkhill Rd DN3...92 A4
arkhill Rise DN15...83 B5
arkhurst Cl 4 HU8...142 C6
arkin Ave YO8...148 E4
arkin Rd DN17...96 C2
arkinson Ave DN15...151 A7
ark La
Balne DN14...77 C5
Barlow YO8...63 C7
Bishop Wilton YO42...16 F1
Burn YO8...62 D7
31 Humberston DN35...103 C1
Luttons YO17...7 C8
Redbourne DN21...108 F3
Rowley HU17...55 B6
Saxby All Saints DN20...84 A3
Scawby DN20...108 F8
Snaith & Cowick DN14...78 C6
Westwoodside DN9...105 A2
Wilberfoss YO41...27 E5
Womersley DN6...76 D6
York YO24...129 F3
arklands
Beeford YO25...34 C8
Goole DN14...149 B5
3 West/East Butterwick
DN17...106 D8
arklands Cres 10 HU14...69 A5
arklands The 2 HU15...54 A2
arkland Way YO32...127 D8
ark Lane Cl
Bishop Wilton YO42...16 F1
Hatfield DN7...92 C2
ark Lane E HU4...144 C6
ark Lane Rd DN7...92 C2
ark Lane W HU4...144 C5
ark Lodge YO32...127 D4
ark Pl YO31...156 C4
ark Rd
Airmyn DN14...64 E4
Barlow YO8...63 C7
Brough HU15...68 E5
Dalton Holme HU17...42 C8
Kingston upon Hull HU3...140 D1
Sproatley HU11...58 C5
Thorne/Moorends DN8...79 B2
ark Rise 17 YO14...2 F8
ark Rose Owl Sanctuary*
YO15...10 E3
ark Row
Hornsea HU18...134 D4
Kingston upon Hull HU2...145 D7
Northfield HU13...143 E2
Selby YO8...148 D5
Sproatley HU11...58 C5
arks Cl 8 DN39...86 A1
arkside YO43...135 D4
arkside Cl
Cottingham HU16...138 F6
Newland HU5...140 B1
York YO24...129 E3
arkside Commercial Ctr
YO23...156 C1
arkside Prim Sch DN14...149 B6
arks Prim Sch The HU6...139 E7
ark Sq DN15...151 A6
arks Rd DN7...92 C4
ark St
Cleethorpes DN35...153 B4
Hotham YO43...53 D5
Kingston upon Hull HU3...145 D6
Messingham DN17...107 D7
Selby YO8...148 D5
Swinefleet DN14...80 D8
Winterton DN15...83 B5
York YO24...156 A1
ARKS THE...92 C4
arkstone Gr 8 DN7...92 D4
arkstone Prim Sch
HU6...140 D7
arkstone Rd HU6...140 C7
ark Terr YO32...127 D5
ark The HU14...69 B6
ark View
Barton-upon-Humber
DN18...84 F8
2 Bridlington YO16...122 F4
Cleethorpes DN35...153 C3
Crowle DN17...94 D6
Kingston upon Hull HU4...144 E4

Park View *continued*
Messingham DN17...107 D7
10 Thorne/Moorends DN8...93 A7
Park View Cl DN19...85 C7
Park View Terr DN17...106 C8
Parkways
12 Hatfield DN7...92 D4
Selby YO8...148 B3
Parkway The
Cottingham HU16...139 A5
Kirk Ella HU10...143 E8
9 Snaith DN14...78 C8
Park Wlk HU4...144 B5
Parkwood Prim Sch
DN17...150 C4
Parkwood Rise DN3...92 A3
Parliament St
8 Brough HU15...68 D6
Goole DN14...149 C4
York YO1...156 B2
Parris Pl DN35...153 D3
Parsonage Cl YO25...125 E7
Parsons Cl 10 DN14...64 E4
Parsons La YO26...12 E1
Parson's La DN14...65 A7
Parson's Wlk 11 DN14...64 E4
Parthian Rd HU9...142 C3
Partridge Cl
Caistor LN7...111 B4
Hilderthorpe YO15...11 B4
Scunthorpe DN17...150 E2
Partridge Dr LN7...111 F2
Parva Rd HU18...134 D4
Pashley Rd 20 DN8...93 B7
Pashley Wlk DN9...94 E1
Paston Wlk YO23...156 B1
Pasture Ave
5 Burringham DN17...95 D4
Goole DN14...149 D5
Pasture Cl
Kilham YO25...9 B3
2 Leconfield HU17...43 D6
Market Weighton YO43...135 E4
Owthorne HU19...74 F6
Skelton YO30...126 B5
2 Strensall YO32...14 B6
Wistow YO8...48 D6
Pasture Farm Cl YO10...133 D6
Pasture Gdns DN6...76 F2
Pasture Hill YO17...16 E8
Pasture House Mews
HU17...136 D4
Pasture La
Amcotts DN17...81 D1
Beverley HU17...136 D4
Ellerton YO42...38 C1
Garthorpe & Fockerby DN17 81 D6
Heworth YO31...131 B8
Sproatley HU11...58 D6
Pasture Rd
Barton-upon-Humber
DN18...69 F1
Goole DN14...149 C4
Hornsea HU18...134 D4
Pasture Rise YO16...122 B5
Pasture Road N DN18...69 F1
Pasture Road S DN18...69 F1
Pastures Ct DN17...107 D7
Pastures La HU11...60 B4
Pasture St DN32...152 E3
Pastures The
Carlton DN14...63 C3
Hutton Cranswick YO25...32 F7
4 York YO24...132 E8
Pasture Terr HU17...136 D4
Pasture Way YO8...48 D6
Pasture Wharf Nature
Reserve* DN18...70 A1
Patchett Cl 24 DN33...102 D1
Pately Pl 1 YO26...129 D4
Patrick Pool YO1...156 B2
Patricks Cl LN7...110 A4
Patrick St DN32...152 E1
PATRINGTON...74 E1
Patrington CE Prim Sch
HU12...74 D1
Patrington Garth HU7...141 C8
PATRINGTON HAVEN...89 C8
Patrington Rd
Holmpton HU19...75 C2
Ottringham HU12...73 F3
Patrington Haven HU12...89 B7
Patterdale Dr YO30...126 E1
Patterdale Rd HU5...144 E8
Paul Cres 5 DN36...114 C8
PAULL...72 A5
Paul La DN15...83 D1
Paull Prim Sch HU12...72 A5
Paull Rd HU12...72 B6
Paul's Wlk DN17...150 B3
Pavement YO1...156 B2
Paver La YO1...156 C2
Pavilion Cl HU8...141 B2
Pavilion Gdns DN17...150 F6
Pavilion L Ctr 20 HU19...75 A6
Pavilion Row YO10...133 D7
Pavilion Way 18 DN36...114 A5
Paxdale HU7...140 E8
Paynter Wlk 22 DN33...102 D1
Payton Cl 17 YO42...29 A4
Peace Haven 3 DN37...113 D7
Peacehaven Cl 2 HU7...141 B7
Peace Wlk 6 HU12...58 D1
Peach Tree Ct 5 HU3...145 D5
Peacock Pl 35 DN21...117 C1
Peacock St DN17...150 F1
Peaks Ave DN36...114 A8
Peaksfield Ave DN32...152 F1

Peaks La
Grimsby DN32...152 F1
New Waltham DN36...114 A8
Peaks Parkway DN32...152 E2
Peaks Parkway Ret Park
DN32...152 E3
Pearcy La (Smook Hills Rd)
HU19...75 A4
Pearson Ave HU5...140 D1
Pearson Pk HU5...140 D1
Pearson Prim Sch HU3...145 D8
Pearson Rd DN35...103 C2
Pearson St HU2...155 A3
Pearson Way HU6...140 F3
Pear Tree Ave
Long Drax YO8...63 F7
8 Poppleton YO26...12 F1
Pear Tree Cl
Kingston upon Hull HU8...141 D4
11 Waltham DN37...113 D6
York YO32...127 F4
Peartree Ct YO1...156 C3
Pear Tree La
Covenham St Bartholomew
LN11...121 E6
Kirk Bramwith DN7...92 A8
Utterby DN36...121 B5
Peartree Pk 19 DN14...65 A7
Peaseholme HU13...143 C1
Pease St HU3...155 A2
Peasholme Gn YO1...156 C2
Peckham Cl HU8...141 E5
Peckitt St YO1...156 B1
Peel Castle Rd 8 DN8...93 B7
Peel Cl YO10...131 A1
Peel Hill Rd 5 DN8...93 B7
Peel Pl
Beverley HU17...136 D4
Kingston Upon Hull HU3...145 D8
Peel St
Kingston upon Hull HU3...145 D8
York YO1...156 C1
Pefham La YO25...17 F4
Pegasus Rd DN20...99 A8
Pegasus Way DN31...102 B6
Pelham Ave 8 DN33...102 E1
Pelham Cl
5 Barton-upon-Humber
DN18...84 E8
5 Beverley HU17...55 F8
Pelham Cres 15 DN41...101 A4
Pelham Dr 1 HU9...146 C7
Pelham Ind Est DN40...87 C2
Pelham Pl
9 Grimsby DN33...102 E1
15 Strensall YO32...14 A7
Pelham Rd
Cleethorpes DN35...153 D3
Grimsby DN34...152 C2
1 Holton le Clay DN36...114 A5
Immingham DN40...87 C1
10 Immingham DN40...87 C2
Pelham's Pillar* DN37...111 C6
Pelham Sq DN35...153 E3
Pelham View DN20...108 F5
Pemberton Dr 3 DN36...113 F7
Pemberton St 1 HU8...146 B7
Pembroke Ave
Grimsby DN34...152 A3
13 Scunthorpe DN16...96 D2
Pembroke Gr HU9...142 A1
Pembroke Rd DN34...152 A1
Pembroke St YO30...130 B7
Pembroke Terr YO15...122 E1
Pem La 7 YO42...29 A4
Pendeen Cl 7 DN21...117 C1
Pendeen Gr HU8...141 B3
Pendle Cl 18 HU7...57 A6
Pendreth Pl DN35...153 D3
Pendrill St HU3...140 E1
Penistone Ct 2 HU9...146 D7
Penley's Grove St YO31...156 C4
Pennine Cl
Immingham DN40...87 B2
York YO32...127 F4
Pennine Rd DN8...93 A7
Pennine Way HU7...57 A6
Pennington St HU8...146 B7
Pennyholme Cl 34 HU7...56 F6
Penny La YO25...2 E2
Penny La Ct YO1...156 C3
Pennyman Rd HU17...154 C4
Penrose Cl 9 HU7...56 F5
Penshurst Ave HU13...143 F3
Penshurst Mews HU13...143 F3
Penshurst Prim Sch
HU13...143 F3
Penshurst Rd DN35...103 B2
Pentire Cl 11 YO30...127 A1
Pentland Ave DN14...149 D5
Pentland Cl HU8...141 F7
Pentland Dr YO32...127 E3
Penwith Dr HU10...143 F7
Penyghent Ave YO31...131 A5
Peploe Cres 6 DN19...70 E2
Peploe Ct DN19...70 E2
Peploe La DN19...70 E2
Peppercorn Cl 6 YO26...129 E4
Peppercorns The 2
HU15...66 D8
Peppercorn Wlk
Grimsby DN32...152 E3
11 Holton le Clay DN36...114 A5
Peppermint Way YO8...148 A5
Peppin La LN11...121 D2
Peppleton Cl HU8...141 C4
Percival St DN15...151 A8
Percy Cl HU17...43 C6

Percy Dr 4 DN14...64 E4
Percy Rd
14 Hunmanby YO14...3 A8
Pocklington YO42...29 A4
Percy's La YO1...156 C2
Percy St
Goole DN14...149 C1
Kingston upon Hull HU2...155 A3
Scunthorpe DN16...151 B6
York YO31...156 B3
Peregrine Cl HU4...144 D2
Perivale Cl HU8...142 A5
Periwinkle Ct DN14...149 E6
Perkins Cl DN37...102 C4
Permain Cl DN33...102 F1
Perran Cl HU7...141 B7
Perry St HU3...145 A6
Pershore Ave DN34...102 B2
Perth St HU5...144 F8
Perth Street W HU5...145 A8
Perth Way 3 DN40...101 B8
Petchell Way DN32...152 E4
Peterborough Rd DN16...151 B3
Petercroft Cl 5 YO19...26 F7
Petercroft La YO19...26 F7
Peter Hill Dr YO30...130 A8
Peterhouse Ct 23 DN16...96 D2
Peterhouse Rd DN34...152 A1
Peter La YO1...156 B2
Peter Nevill Way 9 HU11...45 C5
Petersfield Cl HU7...141 B6
Petersham Cl 1 HU8...142 A5
Peterson Dr 26 DN36...114 A8
Petersway YO30...156 A4
Petre Ave YO8...148 E3
Petuaria Cl HU15...68 B6
Petula Ct 18 HU8...141 E7
Pevensey Cl 1 HU7...141 B7
Peveril Ave DN17...150 F4
Pew Tree Cl YO41...27 E6
Pexton Rd YO25...124 B3
Pheasant Cl DN17...150 E2
Pheasant Ct 1 LN7...111 B4
Pheasant Dr 5 YO24...132 B8
Phelps Pl DN32...153 C1
Phelps St DN35...153 B5
Pheonix Bsns Pk HU17...154 A4
Philadelphia Terr 2
YO23...130 B2
Philip Ave
Cleethorpes DN35...103 B2
5 Waltham DN37...113 E7
Philip Gr DN35...103 B2
Philip Larkin Cl HU6...140 C4
Philips Cres DN15...150 F7
Phillips La 4 DN37...101 F1
Phoenix Bsns Ctr DN14...149 D2
Phoenix Bvd YO26...130 A4
Phoenix Cl HU8...141 F4
Phoenix House Sch
DN32...153 B4
Phoenix Parkway DN15...96 B7
Phoenix Parkway Nature
Reserve* DN15...96 B8
Phoenix St
Goole DN14...149 D4
Grimsby DN32...152 E3
Phyllis Ave DN34...152 B3
Phyllis Taylor Gdns
DN32...152 D3
Picadilly Ct YO1...156 C2
Piccadilly
8 New Waltham DN36...114 A7
York YO1...156 C2
Pickering Ave HU18...134 D2
Pickering Gr 9 DN8...93 A7
Pickering Grange 22
HU14...68 D5
Pickering High Sch Sports
Coll HU4...144 C4
Pickering Pk YO25...31 C4
Pickering Rd HU4...144 C3
Pickerings The 17 HU14...69 A4
Pickering View HU3...144 D3
Pick Haven Garth DN14...61 F3
Picksley Cres DN36...114 A5
Pidgeon Cote La 3 DN19...86 A8
Pier Rd HU19...75 A6
Pier St HU1...155 B1
Piggy La 4 HU19...75 A6
Pighill La HU17...136 D7
Pighill Nook Rd LS25...61 C7
Pike Hills Mount YO23...132 A3
Piker Thorn La YO19...14 D1
Pilgrim Ave DN40...87 C1
Pilgrim's Cl 5 DN40...86 E3
Pilgrim St YO31...156 B4
Pilgrims Way DN40...87 B1
PILHAM...118 A4
Pilham La DN21...117 E4
Pilmar La HU12...60 B1
Pilot's View DN18...69 F2
Pilots Way HU9...155 C1
Pimpernel Way 15 DN16...96 E2
Pinchbeck Ave DN16...151 C6
Pincheon Green La DN14...78 D4
Pindars Way YO8...49 B4
Pinderfield Cl 7 HU9...142 A5
Pine Cl DN37...102 B5
Pine Ct 3 DN35...103 B1
Pinefield Ave 4 DN3...92 A3
Pinefield Pl 27 HU15...68 C6
Pinefield Rd DN3...92 A3
Pine Hall Rd DN3...92 A3
Pinelands 4 YO32...127 D7
Pinelands Way YO10...131 C3
Pine Mdws HU10...143 B8
Pinetree Ave 5 DN21...107 C3

Pinetree Cl 4 DN20...97 E4
Pine Tree Cl
Thorpe Willoughby YO8...48 B2
Wroot DN9...104 D6
Pine Tree La 1 LS25...61 A7
Pine Wlk
4 Brough HU15...68 C6
Healing DN41...102 A5
Pinewood DN16...96 E2
Pinewood Cl 5 YO42...29 A3
Pinewood Cres DN33...102 C2
Pinewood Ct 4 YO42...29 A3
Pinewood Dr YO8...63 D4
Pinewood Gr
2 Kingston upon Hull
HU5...144 C7
6 York YO31...127 E2
Pinewood Hill 4 YO10...131 C3
Pinewood Rd 3 YO42...29 A3
Pinfold
10 Epworth DN9...105 E6
South Cave HU15...53 F1
Pinfold Cl
4 Bridlington YO16...122 D6
Hutton YO25...32 E8
5 Riccall YO19...37 A1
Pinfold Ct
3 Bridlington YO16...122 D6
4 Preston HU12...58 C1
4 York YO30...130 A7
Pinfold Gdns
Bridlington YO16...122 D6
14 Holton le Clay DN36...114 B5
Pinfold Gr YO16...122 C6
Pinfold Hill YO8...48 D6
Pinfold Ind Est YO16...122 D6
Pinfold La
Bempton YO16...4 B1
Bridlington YO16...122 C7
Burstwick HU12...73 A6
Fishlake DN7...92 D8
10 Grimsby DN33...102 E1
Holton le Clay DN36...114 A5
Kirk Smeaton WF8...76 B3
Misterton DN10...116 C5
Moss DN6...77 D1
Norton DN6...76 E2
Pollington DN14...77 F6
Roos HU12...60 A1
Stallingborough DN41...101 D6
25 Thorne/Moorends DN8...93 A8
Pinfold Mdws YO16...122 C6
Pinfold Mews HU17...154 B3
Pinfold St
Bridlington YO16...122 D5
Eastrington DN14...51 F1
Howden DN14...65 A6
Pinfold View DN14...77 F6
Pinfold Way N 2 YO16...122 D5
Pingley La DN20...98 C1
Pingley Mdw DN20...98 C1
Pinkney's La YO25...124 D4
Pink Pig The* DN16...96 E1
Pinney's Ct 7 DN41...101 F5
Pinsent Ct 4 YO31...130 E8
Pioneer Bsns Pk YO30...126 F3
Piper Rd YO25...32 E8
Piper's La HU11...46 C2
Pippin Cl DN10...116 D4
Pippin Ct 11 DN15...96 B7
Pippin Dr 16 DN16...96 D1
Pitbalk Hill HU15...53 E4
Pitman Ave DN18...84 E8
Pitmoor La 5 DN39...86 A1
Pitsfold Cl 11 HU7...57 A5
Pitt La HU12...73 A4
Pitt St HU3...144 F7
Plains La DN8...93 F3
Plane St HU3...145 A5
Plantain Cl 14 DN16...96 E2
Plantation Cl HU17...137 B4
Plantation Dr
Barlby with Osgodby YO8...49 B5
1 South Cave HU15...53 F1
Welton HU14...68 F5
York YO26...129 C6
Plantation Gr YO26...129 C6
Plantation Rd 22 DN8...93 A8
Plantation View YO16...123 A8
Plantation Way 23 YO32...13 E5
Platform 17 HU17...154 B3
Plaxton Bridge Rd HU17...56 C7
Pleasure Island Theme Pk*
DN35...103 E1
Plimsoll Way HU9...146 B6
Plough Garth The DN14...61 F3
Plough Hill 12 LN7...111 B4
Ploughlands 1 YO32...127 C7
Ploughman's Cl YO23...132 C3
Ploughmans' La YO32...127 C7
Plover Dr 9 HU15...68 C6
Plover Sq 2 LN7...111 B4
Plowden Rd HU3...144 F5
Plowright Theatre DN15...151 A6
Plume Cl YO43...135 D5
Plumer Ave YO31...131 A5
Plum Tree Dr DN36...115 C2
Plumtree Hill Rd DN7...92 C7
Plumtree La 1 DN36...114 B1
Plumtree Rd HU12...72 E4
Plum Tree Rd HU11...58 D5
Plum Tree Way DN16...151 A5
Plum Tree Wlk HU15...54 A2
Plym Gr HU8...142 C6
Plymouth Cl 8 DN15...83 A5

Plymouth Rd DN17 . . . 150 D4
Poacher's Croft 3 DN9 . . . 94 E1
Poachers The YO8 . . . 50 C5
Pochard Cl 3 HU15 . . . 52 F1
Pochards Drive DN16 . . . 151 F1
POCKLINGTON . . . 29 A4
Pocklington CE Inf Sch
YO42 . . . 29 A4
Pocklington Com Jun Sch 24
YO42 . . . 29 A4
Pocklington Ind Est YO42 . 28 F3
Pocklington La
Bishop Wilton YO42 . . . 16 F2
Huggate YO42 . . . 18 A1
Pocklington & Lyndhurst
Schs YO42 . . . 28 F3
Pocklington Montessori
School YO42 . . . 29 A1
Pockthorpe La YO25 . . . 8 F2
Poffinder Wood Rd DN8 . . . 92 E7
Poles Bank DN9 . . . 104 E6
POLLINGTON . . . 77 F6
Pollington Balne CE Prim
Sch DN14 . . . 77 F6
Polton Cl DN7 . . . 92 D7
Polton Toft DN7 . . . 92 D7
Pomona Way YO25 . . . 124 D3
Pond Side DN39 . . . 85 E3
Pond St 3 YO8 . . . 148 D6
Ponds Way 6 DN18 . . . 69 E1
Pontefract Rd DN14 . . . 78 A8
Poolbank La HU15 . . . 68 E5
Pool Ct 7 DN14 . . . 149 C4
Pool Dr DN17 . . . 96 C2
Pools Brook Park 15 HU7 . 56 E5
Poorhouse La HU9 . . . 142 C1
Poplar Cl
Burstwick HU12 . . . 73 A6
Kingston upon Hull HU4 . . 144 A5
Skirlaugh HU11 . . . 45 E2
Poplar Cres 7 DN17 . . . 95 D4
Poplar Ct
Drax YO8 . . . 63 F5
Kingston upon Hull HU7 . . 141 C6
Poplar Dr
Beverley HU17 . . . 136 F6
Bridlington YO16 . . . 123 A6
Brigg DN20 . . . 98 C3
3 Broughton DN20 . . . 97 D3
Goole DN14 . . . 65 C3
21 Humberston DN36 . . . 103 D1
Poplar Gdns
Drax YO8 . . . 63 F5
Scunthorpe DN16 . . . 151 B3
Poplar Gr
Cleethorpes DN35 . . . 153 E3
10 Hedon HU12 . . . 72 C7
1 Scotter DN21 . . . 107 C3
York YO32 . . . 127 E3
Poplar La DN21 . . . 118 A2
Poplar Rd
Cleethorpes DN35 . . . 153 E3
Hatfield DN7 . . . 92 C4
Healing DN41 . . . 101 F5
Poplar St YO26 . . . 129 E5
Poplars The
15 Brandesburton YO25 . . . 34 B2
11 Brayton YO8 . . . 48 D1
Knottingley WF11 . . . 61 A1
5 Leconfield HU17 . . . 43 D6
Shiptonthorpe YO43 . . . 40 F6
Poplars Way HU17 . . . 136 D1
Popple St HU9 . . . 146 B6
Poppleton Hall Gdn
YO26 . . . 126 A3
Poppleton Ousebank Prim
Sch YO26 . . . 12 F1
Poppleton Rd YO26 . . . 129 E4
Poppleton Rd Prim Sch
YO26 . . . 129 E5
Poppleton Sta YO26 . . . 24 F8
Popplewell Cl DN9 . . . 94 E2
Popplewell Terr 14 DN9 . . 105 E6
Poppy Cl
2 Scunthorpe DN15 . . . 96 B7
Selby YO8 . . . 148 C2
Poppyfield Way 23 DN20 . . 98 B2
Poppy Mews 20 DN41 . . . 101 F6
Porlock Dr HU7 . . . 57 A5
Portal Rd
Knapton YO26 . . . 129 B7
York YO26 . . . 129 B6
Port Ave HU6 . . . 140 C8
Porter Cl YO25 . . . 125 A3
Porter St
Kingston upon Hull HU3 . . 155 A1
Scunthorpe DN15 . . . 151 A8
Portholme Cres 7 YO8 . 148 C5
Portholme Ct YO8 . . . 148 C4
Portholme Dr YO8 . . . 148 C4
Portholme Rd YO8 . . . 148 C5
PORTINGTON . . . 51 E2
Portington Rd DN14 . . . 51 F1
Portisham Pl 12 YO32 . . . 14 A7
Portland Ave DN32 . . . 152 E1
Portland Mews YO16 . . . 122 C3
Portland Pl
Bridlington YO16 . . . 122 C3
Grimsby DN32 . . . 102 F2
Kingston upon Hull HU2 . . 155 A3
Portland St
Kingston upon Hull HU2 . . 155 A3
Rawcliffe DN14 . . . 79 B8
York YO31 . . . 156 B4
Portmadoc Cl 5 HU7 . . . 56 F7
Portman Rd DN15 . . . 96 C7
Portobello St HU9 . . . 141 F3
Port Royal YO43 . . . 52 B8
Portsmouth Wlk HU4 . . . 144 B4
Postern Cl YO23 . . . 156 B1
Posterngate HU1 . . . 155 B2
Postern La YO42 . . . 38 D6
Postill Sq YO16 . . . 122 D4
Post Office La
Ashby cum Fenby DN37 . . . 113 D3
Humberside Airport DN39 . 100 A6
Whitton DN15 . . . 67 E3
Post Office Row DN14 . . . 64 A1
Post Office St 12 YO15 . . . 5 A2
Potter Cl YO43 . . . 135 D3
Potterdale Dr HU20 . . . 55 A4
Potterill La HU7 . . . 141 D6
Potters Dr 4 YO23 . . . 132 B3
Potters Way HU18 . . . 134 C1
Pottery La
Strensall YO32 . . . 14 A8
York YO31 . . . 130 E7
Pottinger Gdns LN7 . . . 111 A2
Potts La DN17 . . . 94 D7
Poultney Garth 4 HU12 . . . 72 D7
Powells Cres DN16 . . . 151 B2
Powell St YO8 . . . 148 B6
Pratt's La HU11 . . . 46 D3
Prebendal Cl 11 LS25 . . . 61 A8
Precentor's Ct YO31 . . . 156 B3
Precinct The DN17 . . . 150 D3
Prescott Ave 9 HU15 . . . 68 C5
Prescott Gr 23 DN7 . . . 92 D4
PRESTON . . . 58 C1
Preston Dr 1 DN20 . . . 98 C2
Prestongate HU13 . . . 143 E1
Preston La DN18 . . . 84 F8
Preston Prim Sch HU12 . . . 58 D1
Preston Rd
Bilton HU11 . . . 58 A3
Hedon HU12 . . . 72 C8
Kingston upon Hull HU9 . . . 141 F1
Prestwick Ct YO26 . . . 129 B5
Pretoria St HU3 . . . 144 F5
Pretymen Cres DN36 . . . 114 A7
Price's La YO23 . . . 156 B1
Prickett Rd YO16 . . . 122 C4
Priest Cl YO14 . . . 2 F8
Priestgate
3 Barton-upon-Humber
DN18 . . . 84 F8
Kingston upon Hull HU7 . . 141 D6
Nafferton YO25 . . . 125 F6
Priestgate Cl YO25 . . . 125 F6
Priest La YO19 . . . 26 F5
Primitive Chapel La DN40 . 86 F2
Primrose Ave YO14 . . . 3 B8
Primrose Cl 19 DN41 . . . 101 F5
Primrose Dr 1 HU5 . . . 144 C8
Primrose Gr YO8 . . . 148 A6
Primrose Hill 9 WF11 . . . 61 A3
Primrose Pk HU17 . . . 137 D1
Primrose Vale 1 WF11 . . . 61 A2
Primrose Way
Humberston DN35 . . . 103 C1
1 Scunthorpe DN15 . . . 96 B7
Prince Albert Gdns
DN31 . . . 152 E5
Prince Andrew Dr DN40 . . . 87 E1
Prince Charles Dr
20 Barton-upon-Humber
DN18 . . . 84 F8
Immingham DN40 . . . 87 D1
Prince Edward Dr DN40 . . . 87 E1
Prince Henry Dr DN40 . . . 87 E1
Prince Philip Dr 21 DN18 . . 84 F8
Princes Ave
Grimsby DN31 . . . 152 C3
1 Hedon HU12 . . . 72 C7
Hessle HU13 . . . 143 E1
Kingston upon Hull HU5 . . 145 C8
Prince's Ave HU19 . . . 75 A6
Princes Dock St HU1 . . . 155 B2
Princes Gdns HU17 . . . 154 A2
Princes Quay Sh Ctr
HU1 . . . 155 B2
Prince's Rd
Cleethorpes DN35 . . . 153 E2
Kingston upon Hull HU5 . . 140 C2
Princess Alexandra Co 14
DN17 . . . 96 C2
Princess Ave DN7 . . . 92 C6
Princess Cl YO43 . . . 135 D3
Princess Dr
22 Barton-upon-Humber
DN18 . . . 84 F8
West Haddlesey YO8 . . . 62 A5
York YO26 . . . 129 D6
Princess Mary Prom
YO15 . . . 122 D1
Princess Par YO43 . . . 135 D3
Princess Rd
Market Weighton YO43 . . . 135 D3
Strensall YO32 . . . 14 B7
Princess Royal Hospl The
HU8 . . . 142 A6
Princess St
4 Bridlington YO15 . . . 122 F2
Goole DN14 . . . 149 C2
Immingham DN40 . . . 87 C1
Kingston upon Hull HU2 . . . 155 B3
Princes St 17 DN20 . . . 98 C2
Princess Terr 5 YO15 . . . 122 F2
Princess Way
8 Beverley HU17 . . . 55 E8
Woodmansey HU17 . . . 136 D1
Prince St
Bridlington YO15 . . . 122 F2
Prince St *continued*
Kingston upon Hull HU1 . . . 155 B2
Principal Trading Pk 3
HU3 . . . 145 A3
Printing Office La 6
DN17 . . . 94 D8
Priors Cl DN36 . . . 114 A7
Prior's Wlk YO26 . . . 129 D6
Priory Ave 13 HU14 . . . 69 A4
Priory Cell (Rems of)*
DN37 . . . 113 A2
Priory Cl
Bridlington YO16 . . . 122 E5
10 Swanland HU14 . . . 69 B7
Wilberfoss YO41 . . . 27 F6
Priory Cres
Bridlington YO16 . . . 122 E4
Kingston upon Hull HU16 . . 139 B5
Scunthorpe DN17 . . . 151 A3
Ulceby DN39 . . . 86 A2
Priory Dr HU5 . . . 139 D2
Priory Farm Dr 4 HU4 . . 144 D2
Priory Gr HU4 . . . 144 D3
Priory La
Barrow upon Humber
DN19 . . . 85 D8
Scunthorpe DN17 . . . 150 E2
1 Snaith DN14 . . . 63 C1
Priory Lane Inf Sch
DN17 . . . 150 A2
Priory Lane Jun Sch
DN17 . . . 150 F2
Priory Park Cl 3 LS25 . . . 61 A8
Priory Park Gr 2 LS25 . . . 61 B8
Priory Pk HU13 . . . 144 A1
Priory Prim Sch HU5 . . . 139 D1
Priory Rd
Beverley HU17 . . . 154 C2
Cottingham HU5 . . . 139 C3
Grimsby DN37 . . . 102 B3
Kingston upon Hull HU16 . . 139 B5
Scunthorpe DN17 . . . 151 A2
Priory Rise DN17 . . . 150 F2
Priory Road Ind Est
HU17 . . . 154 C2
Priory Road or House
DN6 . . . 76 E2
Priory St YO1 . . . 156 A1
Priory Way
Kingston upon Hull HU4 . . 144 A1
1 Snaith DN14 . . . 63 B1
Priory Wlk YO16 . . . 122 D4
Priory Wood Way YO31 . . . 127 F2
Proctor's Way DN20 . . . 109 A5
Promenade YO15 . . . 122 F2
Promenades Sh Ctr The
YO15 . . . 122 F2
Promenade The 15 HU19 . . 75 A6
Prospect Cl
Camblesforth YO8 . . . 63 D5
Monk Fryston LS25 . . . 61 A8
Pollington DN14 . . . 77 F6
Swinefleet DN14 . . . 65 D1
Prospect La
Alkborough DN15 . . . 82 C8
Withernwick HU11 . . . 46 D3
Prospect Pl
Kingston upon Hull HU9 . . . 146 B7
Wistow YO8 . . . 48 D6
Prospect Rd
22 Pocklington YO42 . . . 29 A4
Rawcliffe DN14 . . . 79 B8
Prospect Sh Ctr HU2 . . . 155 A3
Prospect St
Bridlington YO15 . . . 122 E2
Kingston upon Hull HU2 . . 155 A3
Prospect Terr
Fulford YO10 . . . 133 D6
York YO1 . . . 156 B1
Prospect Way YO8 . . . 148 D4
Prospect Way Ind Est
YO8 . . . 148 D4
Providence Cres DN18 . . . 84 E8
Providence Pl
10 Bridlington YO15 . . . 122 F3
1 Great Driffield YO25 . . . 124 F4
Providence Row HU3 . . . 155 A4
Prunus Ave HU10 . . . 143 F8
Pryme Rd DN16 . . . 151 C4
Pryme St
Anlaby HU10 . . . 143 F6
Kingston upon Hull HU2 . . 155 A3
Prystie Pl 1 DN35 . . . 103 B1
Puddiners La DN14 . . . 80 E7
Pudding & Dip La 47 DN7 . 92 D4
Pudding Gate 8 HU17 . . . 43 A2
Pulcroft Rd HU13 . . . 143 D2
Pulfin Bog Nature Reserve*
HU17 . . . 44 A7
Pulham La YO25 . . . 19 B5
Pulleyn Cl 3 YO32 . . . 14 C8
Pulleyn Dr YO24 . . . 129 F1
Pulman St HU3 . . . 145 A7
Pump Hill DN20 . . . 109 D6
Pump La YO15 . . . 4 C3
Punton Wlk DN14 . . . 78 B8
Purbeck Rd
Grimsby DN33 . . . 113 E8
Scunthorpe DN17 . . . 150 C5
Purey Cust Nuffield Hospl
The YO31 . . . 156 B3
Purton Gr HU7 . . . 141 A7
Putney Cl HU8 . . . 141 E5
PYEWIPE . . . 152 A8
Pyewipe Rd DN31 . . . 152 C5
Pykestone Cl 15 HU7 . . . 57 A6
Pyruss Dr HU4 . . . 144 B2
Pytchley Wlk 1 DN35 . . . 103 C1

Q

Quadrant The HU6 . . . 139 F4
Quaker Gn 1 YO24 . . . 132 C7
Quaker La HU17 . . . 136 D4
Quaker Rd HU12 . . . 59 F4
Quakers' La HU15 . . . 53 D3
Quales Mews 2 HU18 . . 134 C4
Quant Mews YO10 . . . 131 B3
Quantock Cl
7 Kingston upon Hull
HU3 . . . 145 D5
Scunthorpe DN17 . . . 150 D4
5 Thorne/Moorends DN8 . . . 93 A7
Quantock Rd DN33 . . . 113 E8
Quarrington Gr 19 HU7 . . . 56 F6
Quarry Ave 20 WF11 . . . 61 A2
Quarry Rd DN6 . . . 76 F2
Quart La
Eastrington DN14 . . . 65 F7
Reedness DN14 . . . 80 D6
Quay La DN14 . . . 80 C7
Quay Prim Sch YO16 . . . 122 D3
Quay Rd
Bridlington YO16 . . . 122 D3
4 Thorne DN8 . . . 78 F1
Quayside 1 DN8 . . . 78 F1
Quay St HU1 . . . 155 B2
Quay The YO8 . . . 148 D6
Quebec Dr HU16 . . . 138 E5
Quebec Rd DN17 . . . 96 C2
Queen Annes Rd YO30 . . 156 A3
Queen Elizabeth Ave 4
DN18 . . . 84 A7
Queen Elizabeth Rd 6
DN36 . . . 114 C8
Queen Elizabeths High Sch
DN21 . . . 117 B2
Queen Elizabeth Way 19
DN18 . . . 84 F8
Queen Margarets Sch
YO19 . . . 37 A5
Queen Mary Ave DN35 . . 153 C3
Queen Mary Ave Inf Sch
DN35 . . . 153 C3
Queen's Alley HU1 . . . 155 C1
Queen's App DN16 . . . 151 F6
Queen's Ave 5 DN18 . . . 69 F1
Queensbury Way 2 HU14 . 69 B6
Queen's Cl
Goole DN14 . . . 149 C4
2 Kingston upon Hull
HU16 . . . 139 B7
Queens Cres DN17 . . . 95 D6
Queen's Cres DN7 . . . 92 C6
Queen's Ct
17 Thorne/Moorends
DN8 . . . 93 A8
York YO1 . . . 156 B2
Queens Dock Ave HU1 . . . 155 B2
Queens Dr
7 Crowle DN17 . . . 94 D7
Goole DN14 . . . 149 D6
Queen's Dr HU16 . . . 139 A7
Queensfield LN7 . . . 110 A1
Queensgate
Beverley HU17 . . . 154 A1
Bridlington YO16 . . . 122 E4
Queen's Gate HU16 . . . 139 B7
Queensgate Sq YO16 . . . 122 D3
Queen's Gate St HU3 . . . 145 B5
Queens Gdns HU18 . . . 134 B3
Queensmead
Aldbrough HU11 . . . 47 C1
Beverley HU17 . . . 55 E8
Lund YO25 . . . 31 F2
Queens Par DN31 . . . 152 C3
Queen's Par DN35 . . . 153 F1
Queens Rd
Beverley HU17 . . . 154 C4
Immingham DN40 . . . 87 D1
Kingston upon Hull HU5 . . 140 C2
Queen's Rd DN38 . . . 99 B4
Queens Sq 13 YO16 . . . 122 E2
Queens Staith Mews
YO1 . . . 156 B1
Queen's Staith Rd YO1 . . . 156 B2
Queen St
Barton-upon-Humber
DN18 . . . 69 F1
Bridlington YO15 . . . 122 E2
15 Brigg DN20 . . . 98 C2
13 Epworth DN9 . . . 105 E6
Great Driffield YO25 . . . 124 F4
Grimsby DN31 . . . 152 E3
Kingston upon Hull HU1 . . 155 C1
Kirton in Lindsey DN21 . . . 108 B1
Scunthorpe DN16 . . . 151 C6
16 Thorne/Moorends DN8 . . . 93 A8
15 Winterton DN15 . . . 83 A5
Withernsea HU19 . . . 75 A6
York YO24 . . . 156 A2
Queen Street N HU19 . . . 74 F7
Queen's View Cres DN16 151 D3
Queensway
Goole DN14 . . . 149 D4
Grimsby DN37 . . . 102 C4
Scunthorpe DN16 . . . 151 A5
Woodmansey HU17 . . . 56 B8
Queen's Way HU16 . . . 139 B7
Queensway Court Bsns Pk
DN16 . . . 151 E2
Queensway Ind Est DN15 151 E2
Queensway The HU6 . . . 140 B8
Queenswood Gr YO24 . . . 129 D2
Queenswood Rd 7 DN16 . . 96 E2
Queen Victoria Sq HU1 . . . 155 B2
Queen Victoria St YO23 . . . 130 B
Quillcourt HU6 . . . 139 E
Quilter Ave HU4 . . . 144 B
Quilter Dr HU11 . . . 142 F
Quilt Mus & Gall The*
YO1 . . . 156 C
Quinton Rd DN32 . . . 102 F
Quorn Mews 26 DN35 . . . 103 C
Quorum The HU4 . . . 144 D

R

Racca Ave 11 WF11 . . . 61 A
Racca Gn WF11 . . . 61 A
Racecourse Rd YO23 . . . 133 B
Race La
Carlton DN14 . . . 63 E
Wootton DN39 . . . 85 C
Rachel Cl 3 DN21 . . . 117 B
Radcliffe Ct DN16 . . . 151 D
Radcliffe Garth HU15 . . . 54 A
Radcliffe Rd DN41 . . . 101 F
Radcroft La YO43 . . . 53 D
Radstock Wlk HU8 . . . 142 C
RAF Holmpton &
Underground Bunker*
HU19 . . . 75 C
Raglan St HU5 . . . 140 C
Raich Carter Way HU6 . . . 56 D
Railway Cres 2 HU19 . . . 75 A
Railway Pl DN31 . . . 152 F
Railway St
Barnetby le Wold DN38 . . . 99 B
Beverley HU17 . . . 154 B
Grimsby DN32 . . . 152 F
Hornsea HU18 . . . 134 D
Kingston upon Hull HU1 . . . 155 B
Railway Terr
Grimsby DN32 . . . 152 D
York YO24 . . . 130 A
Railway View YO24 . . . 132 E
Raincliffe St 4 YO8 . . . 148 C
Raines Cl 5 HU12 . . . 73 A
Rainham Cl HU8 . . . 141 E
Rainhill Ct 3 HU5 . . . 140 A
Rainhill Rd 2 HU5 . . . 140 A
Rainsborough Way 3
YO30 . . . 130 A
Rainsburgh La YO25 . . . 2 A
Rainsbutt Rd DN17 . . . 94 C
Rainswood Cl 8 HU7 . . . 56 F
Raithby Ave 3 DN41 . . . 101 A
Raithby Gr 12 DN33 . . . 102 D
Rake Bridge Bank DN7 . . . 92 D
Raker Cl YO19 . . . 37 F
Rakes Rd HU17 . . . 42 E
Raleigh Dr
Kingston upon Hull HU9 . . 146 D
Sproatley HU11 . . . 58 D
Ralph Butterfield Prim Sch
YO32 . . . 13 F
Ramblers La 18 DN18 . . . 69 E
Ram Bvd DN15 . . . 96 C
Ramsay Cl YO31 . . . 156 C
Ramsden Ave DN18 . . . 84 E
Ramsden Cl YO25 . . . 124 A
Ramsden Ct HU17 . . . 154 C
Ramsden Pl 11 HU16 . . . 138 F
Ramsey Ave YO23 . . . 133 B
Ramsey Cl YO16 . . . 122 C
Ramsey Rd YO16 . . . 122 E
Ramsgate Cl HU8 . . . 141 E
Ramskir La DN7 . . . 92 C
Ranby Cres HU18 . . . 134 C
Ranby Dr HU18 . . . 134 C
Ranby Rd DN17 . . . 150 E
Randall Garth YO25 . . . 125 A
Rands Est 7 HU12 . . . 58 D
Randsfield Ave 17 HU15 . . . 68 C
Rangely Cl 9 HU7 . . . 57 A
Rannoch Cl 6 HU7 . . . 57 A
Ransom Ct DN39 . . . 100 A
Ransome Way 14 HU15 . . . 68 C
RASCAL MOOR . . . 52 E
Ratcliffe Ct YO30 . . . 126 C
Ratcliffe St YO30 . . . 130 B
Rattan Row YO25 . . . 8 C
Ratten Row
4 Bishop Burton HU17 . . . 43 A
11 North Newbald YO43 . . . 53 F
Rauceby Cl 10 HU7 . . . 56 F
Raven Cl DN20 . . . 97 D
Ravencroft La 1 DN10 . . 116 D
Ravendale 18 DN18 . . . 84 F
Ravendale Cl 1 DN36 . . . 114 B
Ravendale Rd 10 DN35 . . 103 D
Ravendale Street N
DN15 . . . 151 E
Ravendale Street S
DN15 . . . 151 E
Raven Gr YO26 . . . 129 C
Ravenhall HU17 . . . 43 B
Ravenhill Cl 14 DN35 . . . 103 B
Ravenscar Rd 9 DN37 . . 102 C
Ravensfleet Rd DN21 . . . 116 F
Ravenspurn YO16 . . . 122 E
Ravenspurn Gr 1 HU9 . . 142 A
Ravenspurn Rd HU12 . . . 89 C
Ravenspurn St DN31 . . . 152 D
Ravenspurn Way 1
DN31 . . . 152 D
Ravenspur Rd HU11 . . . 58 A
Raven St HU9 . . . 146 C
Raventhorpe Medieval
Village* DN16 . . . 97 E
RAWCLIFFE
Goole . . . 64 A

AWCLIFFE *continued*
York 126 E2
awcliffe Ave YO30 129 F8
AWCLIFFE BRIDGE 79 C8
awcliffe Bridge Prim Sch DN14 79 B8
awcliffe Cl 5 YO30 126 E2
awcliffe Croft YO30 126 D2
awcliffe Dr YO30 129 F8
awcliffe Gr HU4 144 D5
awcliffe Ind Est YO30 126 E3
awcliffe Inf Sch YO30 126 E1
awcliffe La YO30 126 F1
awcliffe Landing YO30 126 C3
awcliffe Prim Sch DN14 64 A1
awcliffe Rd DN14 149 A4
awcliffe Sta DN14 79 A8
awcliffe Village YO30 126 E3
awcliffe Way YO30 126 E2
awdale Cl HU15 54 A2
awdon Ave YO10 130 F4
awling Way HU3 145 C5
awlinson Ave 22 LN7 111 B4
aymond Rd DN16 151 C3
aynard Cl YO25 32 E7
aywell Cl HU10 143 F7
aywell St HU2 155 A3
ead Cl YO8 63 F5
eading Gate
Reedness DN17 80 C3
Swinefleet DN14 80 D7
eading Room Yd 4
HU14 69 A4
ead Sch YO8 63 F5
eangamoor La YO42 39 D2
eaper's Rise 15 DN9 105 E6
eaper's Way 6 DN9 105 D2
ecreation Club La
HU17 154 A4
ecreation Rd 2 YO8 148 D6
ecto Ave DN32 152 F1
ectory Ave 33 DN21 117 B1
ectory Cl YO25 125 F7
ectory Gdns
3 Beckingham DN10 116 D1
York YO23 130 B1
ectory La
Beeford YO25 22 C1
Preston HU12 58 C1
Roos HU12 60 C3
ectory Rd HU12 74 A8
ectory St DN9 105 E6
ectory View
9 Beeford YO25 22 D1
Lockington YO25 32 C2
ectory Way YO43 40 B1
ectory Wlk YO16 122 B4
edbarn Dr YO10 131 D4
edbourn Cl DN16 151 B5
EDBOURNE 108 F3
edbourn East Rd DN16 97 A6
edbourne Mere DN21 108 E2
edbourne Rd
Grimsby DN33 102 D2
Hibaldstow DN20 108 F4
Waddingham DN21 119 F8
edbourne St
Kingston upon Hull HU3 145 B5
3 Scunthorpe DN16 151 C6
edbourn Way DN16 151 B6
edcap La YO42 38 C5
edcar Gr DN32 153 A1
edcar St HU8 155 C4
edcliff Dr 19 HU14 69 A4
edcliff Rd
Kingston upon Hull HU13 69 E4
Melton HU14 68 F5
edcoat Way 1 YO24 132 B8
edcombe La DN20 98 B2
edeness St YO31 130 E5
edfern Cl HU3 145 D5
edgates HU17 55 B7
edgrave Cl 4 YO31 130 E8
edhall Cl 7 DN3 92 A2
edhill Field La YO23 24 D1
edhill Pk HU6 139 E5
edhouse La YO8 63 F6
ed House La YO43 135 A4
ed La
Market Weighton YO43 135 E5
South Ferriby DN18 83 F7
edland Cres 2 DN8 93 B8
edland Dr HU10 143 C8
ed Lion St 2 DN14 149 C4
edman Cl
15 Gainsborough DN21 117 C1
York YO10 133 C8
edmayne Sq YO32 14 B8
edmire Cl HU7 57 A6
edmires Cl YO30 127 A2
edruth Cl HU7 141 C6
edthorn Dr YO31 127 F1
ed Twr* YO1 130 E4
edwing Dr YO25 125 A5
edwood Cl YO16 122 E6
edwood Ct DN16 96 E2
edwood Dr
7 Cleethorpes DN35 103 B1
6 Haxby YO32 13 E5
edwood Gdns YO25 124 F3
edwoods The HU10 138 C2
edwood Way YO16 122 D6
ed Ct DN14 149 D4
edham Garth HU4 144 A3
edholme La DN8 78 F4
EDNESS 65 F2
edness Prim Sch DN14 66 A1
ed St HU2 155 A3
Reedsway 12 YO25 34 B2
Rees Cl YO43 135 D5
Reeth Wlk HU5 139 D3
Reeves The YO24 129 C1
Refinery Rd DN16 151 F6
Reform St HU2 155 B3
Regency Ct 8 DN18 69 E1
Regency Mews 2 YO24 132 F8
Regent Arc DN32 152 D3
Regent Cl
Kingston upon Hull HU3 145 C6
Willerby HU10 138 E1
Regent Dr 15 DN17 94 D7
Regent Gdns DN34 152 C1
Regents Ct
Cottingham HU16 139 A6
14 York YO26 129 F5
Regents Mews 1 YO26 129 D6
Regent St
Beverley HU17 154 B2
Pocklington YO42 29 A3
York YO10 130 E3
Regent Street Pavement 8
YO42 29 A3
Regent Terr 7 YO15 122 F2
Regimental Mus* YO1 156 B1
Regina Cres 2 HU5 140 A1
Reginald Gr YO23 130 C1
Reginald Rd DN15 96 C7
Reginald Terr YO8 148 D4
Regis Ct HU9 142 B3
Register Sq HU17 154 A2
Reid Pk YO32 13 E5
Reigate Cl HU8 142 A4
REIGHTON 3 D6
Reighton Ave YO30 129 F8
Reighton Dr 10 YO30 126 F1
Reilly Way YO42 28 E4
Reina Dr YO25 124 C4
Rein The DN9 105 A2
Reldene Dr HU5 144 B7
Remembrance Ct YO16 122 A2
Remillo Ave DN32 152 F1
Remington Ave HU11 34 E3
Remple Ave DN7 93 A3
Remple Comm Rd DN7 92 F2
Remple La DN7 93 A3
Rendel St DN31 152 D5
Rensburg St HU9 141 D1
Renshaw Gdns 8 YO26 129 E4
Renton Ct HU13 143 F6
Reporto Ave DN32 152 F1
Repton Dr
Kingston upon Hull HU7 141 D5
21 Scunthorpe DN16 96 D2
Reservoir Rd HU6 140 F3
Responso Ave DN32 152 F1
Reston Ct 8 DN35 103 D2
Reston Gr 25 DN33 102 D2
Retford Gr HU9 142 E1
Retreat Hospl The
York YO10 130 F2
York YO10 130 F2
Revenser Ct 53 HU12 72 D7
Revesby Ave
13 Grimsby DN34 102 C2
Scunthorpe DN16 151 A3
Revesby Ct DN16 151 A4
Revigo Ave DN32 152 F1
Revill Cl 17 DN21 107 C3
Reygate Gr YO23 132 B2
Reynolds Cl HU14 68 E5
Reynoldson Ct HU5 140 B2
Reynoldson St HU5 140 C2
Reynolds Prim Sch
DN35 153 D3
Reynolds St DN35 153 D2
Rhodena Ave YO16 122 D2
Rhodes St HU3 144 F5
Rhyl Cl 4 HU7 56 F7
Rialto Ave DN32 152 F1
Ribblesdale 3 HU7 141 A6
Ribblesdale Cl YO16 122 F7
Ribble St 4 HU3 145 B4
Ribston Cl 9 DN16 96 D1
Ribstone Gr YO31 131 B6
RIBY 101 C2
Ribycourt HU6 139 E7
Riby Ct DN36 114 B5
Riby Rd
Cabourne LN7 111 D6
Keelby DN41 101 A4
Scunthorpe DN17 150 E1
Stallingborough DN41 101 C4
Swallow LN7 112 A7
Riby Sq DN32 152 F5
Riby St DN31 153 A5
RICCALL 49 A8
Riccall Cl HU6 140 A6
Riccall La YO19 36 D1
Riccall Prim Sch YO19 36 F1
Richard Cooper St DN14 149 E4
Richard III Mus* YO31 156 C3
Richardson Cl DN36 114 D8
Richardson Rd 35 HU12 72 C7
Richardson St YO23 130 C2
Richard St
Grimsby DN31 152 C4
Selby YO8 148 B5
Richdale Ave DN21 108 B1
Richmond Cl YO43 135 F3
Richmond Dr
Goole DN14 149 F5
10 Scunthorpe DN16 96 E2
Richmond Gdns HU17 136 D1
Richmond La HU7 56 E6
Richmond Rd
Cleethorpes DN35 153 E1
Richmond Rd *continued*
Grimsby DN34 152 A2
Kingston upon Hull HU13 143 E2
24 Thorne/Moorends DN8 79 B2
Richmond St
Bridlington YO15 122 D1
2 Kingston upon Hull
HU5 145 B8
York YO31 130 E5
Richmond Way
2 Beverley HU17 55 E8
Dunswell HU6 56 E6
Richmond Wlk HU17 136 D1
Rickaby Cl YO16 122 D4
Ridding Cres DN14 64 A1
Ridding La DN14 64 A1
RIDDINGS 150 F1
Riddings Inf Sch DN17 96 C2
Riddings Jun Sch DN17 96 C2
Riddings Pool DN17 96 B2
Ridgestone Ave HU11 142 E7
Ridge View DN20 98 C2
Ridgeway YO26 129 B3
Ridge Way DN17 150 E5
Ridgeway Rd HU5 144 B7
Ridgeway The DN34 102 B2
Ridgewood Ave 6 DN3 92 A1
Ridgewood Dr DN15 82 A4
Riding Fields Sq HU17 154 C3
Riding Mews HU17 154 B3
Ridings The
Beverley HU17 136 C6
Cottingham HU16 138 E6
East Ella HU5 144 A8
Great Driffield YO25 125 A6
15 North Ferriby HU14 69 A4
Ridsdale HU7 140 F7
Rifle Butts Quarry Nature
Reserve* YO43 41 D5
Rigby Cl HU17 136 D7
Rileston Pl 12 DN16 96 D1
Rillington Ave HU16 139 A5
RIMSWELL 74 D7
Rimswell Gr HU9 142 A2
Ring Beck La HU15 68 A8
Ringley Mdws 5 YO15 4 C3
Ringrose La HU10 143 E6
Ringrose St HU3 144 F5
Ringstead Garth 4 HU7 57 A5
Ringstone Rd
Bishopthorpe YO23 133 B5
York YO30 126 F3
Ringwood Cl DN16 151 B1
Ripley Cl
Bridlington YO16 122 D5
Kingston upon Hull HU6 140 B7
Ripley Ct DN15 150 B6
Ripley Gr 3 YO32 13 E5
Ripley Pl YO43 135 D4
RIPLINGHAM 54 E2
Riplingham Rd
Kingston upon Hull HU10 143 A8
Skidby HU10 138 A1
Ripon Ave HU17 136 E1
Ripon Cl DN17 150 C3
Ripon St DN31 152 C3
Ripon Way HU9 146 C8
RISBY 55 C5
Risby Garth HU16 55 C4
Risby Gr HU6 139 F5
Risby Hill HU20 55 A4
Risby La HU17 55 B7
Risby Pl HU17 154 A1
Risby Rd DN15 82 F1
RISE 45 F5
Rise Cl HU11 45 C5
Risedale 21 LN7 111 B4
Rise La
Catwick HU17 45 D8
Rise HU11 45 D5
Rise Rd HU11 45 F7
Rise The
Hornsea HU18 134 C4
7 North Ferriby HU14 69 A5
Scunthorpe DN17 96 C2
South Ferriby DN18 84 A8
Riseway HU11 45 C5
Risewood YO41 15 B2
Rishworth Cl 5 HU7 57 A6
Rishworth Gr YO30 126 F2
Riston CE Prim Sch HU11 45 C5
Riston Rd HU17 45 C7
Riston St HU3 145 C5
Rivan Ave 5 DN33 113 E8
Rivan Gr 6 DN33 113 E8
Rivelin Cres DN16 151 A4
Rivelin Park 23 HU7 56 E5
Rivelin Pl DN16 151 A4
Rivelin Rd DN16 151 A3
Rivelin Way YO30 126 F2
Riverbank Cl DN17 95 D5
Riverbank Rise
24 Barton-upon-Humber
DN18 84 E8
20 Barton upon Humberside
DN18 69 E1
River Cl
2 Barlby YO8 49 B5
Goole DN14 149 F5
Riverdale 4 DN14 61 D4
Riverdale Rd
Kilpin DN14 65 C1
Scunthorpe DN16 151 A3
River Gr HU4 144 E3
Riverhead* DN31 152 E3
River Head YO25 124 F3
River Head Dr 3 YO25 124 F3
Riverhead Gdns YO25 124 F3
River La
Fishlake DN7 92 D8
Market Weighton YO43 40 F2
West Haddlesey YO8 62 A5
River Mdw DN20 98 B1
Riversdale 17 YO32 13 F5
Riversdale Dr DN14 149 F5
Riversdale Rd HU6 140 D6
Riverside
11 Broughton DN20 98 B2
Great Driffield YO25 124 F3
Rawcliffe DN14 64 A2
Scotter DN21 107 C4
Riverside App 5 DN21 117 A1
Riverside Cl
1 Elvington YO41 27 C2
6 Great Driffield YO25 124 F3
West Haddlesey YO8 62 A5
Riverside Cres YO32 127 F6
Riverside Ct
5 Hessle HU13 69 E4
Rawcliffe DN14 64 A2
Riverside Dr DN35 103 D1
Riverside Gdns
2 Elvington YO41 27 C2
2 Poppleton YO26 12 F1
Riverside Mews 5 YO25 124 F3
Riverside Sch DN14 149 E5
Riverside Wlk
1 Poppleton YO26 12 F1
5 Strensall YO32 14 A7
River St
1 Selby YO8 148 D6
York YO23 156 B1
Riversvale Dr 21 YO26 12 F1
River View
1 Barlby YO8 49 B5
26 Barton-upon-Humber
DN18 84 F8
Goole DN14 65 C3
Kingston upon Hull HU13 143 F1
Riverview Ave HU14 69 A4
Riverview Gdns HU7 140 E7
Riverview Rd HU17 137 C4
River Wlk DN14 65 C4
Rivesby Ave DN16 151 A3
Riviera Dr YO15 123 B6
Rix Rd HU7 141 A3
Roall La DN14 61 F4
Robert Cl
Immingham DN40 87 B1
3 Withernsea HU19 75 A6
Robertson Cl YO42 29 A3
Roberts St DN32 153 A3
Robert St
Scunthorpe DN15 151 B7
Selby YO8 148 C5
Robert Wilkinson Prim Sch
YO32 14 A7
Robert Wood Ave HU17 154 A2
Robin Cl 28 HU15 68 D5
Robin Gr 6 YO24 129 F3
Robin Hood Cres 5 DN3 92 A1
Robin Hood Rd 3 DN3 92 A1
Robinia Dr HU4 144 C2
Robinson Cl DN15 150 E8
Robinson Ct YO1 156 C2
Robinson Dr YO24 129 B2
Robinson La DN31 153 A6
Robinson Rd DN40 87 E2
Robinson Row HU1 155 B2
Robinson's Gr DN20 109 A5
Robinson's La DN36 114 B1
Robinson Street E DN32 152 E3
Robin Wlk DN31 102 B5
Roborough Cl HU7 141 B8
Robson Ave HU6 140 B8
Robson Rd DN35 153 D3
Robson Way
Kingston upon Hull HU8 141 D7
6 Preston HU12 72 C7
Rochdale Rd DN16 151 A1
Roche Ave YO31 130 E8
Roche Dr DN14 149 E6
Rochester Ave HU4 144 A3
Rochester Cl DN17 150 C3
Rochester Ct 2 DN35 103 D1
Rockford Ave HU8 141 B3
Rockford Gr HU8 141 B3
Rockingham Ave YO31 131 A5
Rockingham Ct 10 DN34 102 B2
Rockley Ct HU10 143 F6
Rod Mill Rd DN16 151 E5
Rodney Cl HU2 155 A4
Roecliffe Ct YO26 24 C8
Roe La LS25 61 C7
Rogers Ct
Woodthorpe YO24 132 C8
York YO24 132 C8
Rokeby Ave HU4 144 B5
Rokeby Cl
Beverley HU17 154 A4
Kingston upon Hull HU4 144 B5
Rokeby Park Prim Sch
HU4 144 B4
Rokeby Pk HU4 144 B5
Roladan Cl 27 DN36 114 A8
Roland Ct YO32 127 E3
Roland Simpson Cl 1
DN14 78 C8
ROLSTON 46 E8
Rolston Ave 3 YO31 127 E2
Rolston Cl HU9 142 C1
Rolston Rd HU18 134 C2
Roman Avenue N 17 YO41 15 D2
Roman Avenue S YO41 15 D1
Roman Cl YO42 40 C8
Roman Rd DN20 108 D8
Roman Rigg YO43 53 D8
Romans Cl YO19 48 F8
Roman Way
Riddings DN17 150 F2
Scunthorpe DN17 150 F2
Rombalds Croft 26 HU15 68 C6
Romford Gr HU9 142 E1
Romney Gdns 4 HU5 140 E2
Romsey Ct 11 DN34 102 B3
Romwood Cl 17 HU15 68 D6
Romyn Cl YO16 122 B2
Ronaldsway Cl 6 HU9 142 A3
Ronson Cl HU9 142 D3
Rookery Ave 10 DN33 102 E2
Rookery Croft 9 DN9 105 E6
Rookery Rd 18 DN41 101 F5
Rookery The
Scawby DN20 108 F8
22 Scotter DN21 107 C3
Rooklands 2 DN21 107 C3
Rookley Cl 3 HU8 142 C5
Rook's La DN10 116 C5
ROOS 60 A1
Roos CE Prim Sch HU12 60 B1
Roos Cl HU17 136 F7
Rootas La HU17 43 A6
Ropers Ct YO23 132 C3
Roper St HU1 155 A2
Ropery Cl
Beverley HU17 137 B4
Keyingham HU12 73 D3
3 Kilham YO25 9 C3
Thorngumbald HU12 72 E5
Ropery La 1 DN18 69 E1
Ropery Rd DN21 117 A2
Ropery St
Grimsby DN32 152 F3
Kingston upon Hull HU3 145 D5
Ropery Walk 36 YO42 29 A3
Ropery Wlk YO42 29 A3
Ropewalk The* DN18 69 F1
Ropewalk The
9 Caistor LN7 111 B4
York YO31 130 E5
Rope Wlk
Bridlington YO15 122 E2
Thorne/Moorends DN8 93 A8
Rosaire Pl DN33 113 E8
Rosalind Ave DN34 152 B3
Rosamond St 6 HU3 145 B4
Rosbrook Way 11 DN19 86 A8
Roseacres DN14 65 C4
Roseberry Ave
Bridlington YO15 122 C1
15 Hatfield DN7 92 D4
Roseberry Gr YO30 126 F3
Rosebery St YO26 129 F6
Rose Carr Wlk HU18 134 D6
Rosecomb Way 6 YO32 127 D7
Rosecroft Way YO30 129 E8
Rosedale
Leven HU17 45 B8
Scunthorpe DN17 96 C1
Skipsea YO25 23 B2
Waltham DN37 113 D7
Rosedale Ave
Kingston upon Hull HU9 141 E1
York YO26 129 C4
Rosedale Gr HU5 144 D7
Rosedale St YO10 130 D2
Rosedale Wlk
Beverley HU17 136 E1
Bridlington YO16 122 B4
Rosefields DN21 117 C1
Rose Gdns 4 DN40 87 C2
Rose La HU17 43 C5
Rose Lea Cl 2 LS25 61 A7
Rosemary Ave DN34 102 C3
Rosemary Ct YO1 156 C2
Rosemary Pl YO1 156 C2
Rosemary Way
Beverley HU17 154 C1
Humberston DN36 103 C1
Rosemoor Cl 19 YO14 2 F8
Rosemount Cl 3 HU6 140 B8
Rosemount Dr DN16 151 B2
Rosemount Grange
HU13 143 C3
Rose St YO31 130 C7
Rose Tree Gr YO32 127 D4
Rosetta Way YO26 129 D6
Roseveare Ave DN34 152 A3
Rose Wlk DN15 151 C7
Rosewood Cl
3 Bridlington YO16 123 A6
4 Kingston upon Hull
HU4 144 B7
Rosewoods DN14 65 C8
Rosewood Way 25 DN16 96 D2
Rosewood Wlk YO16 123 A6
Rosey Row 4 HU9 146 C7
Rosina Grove N DN32 153 B2
Rosina Grove S DN32 153 B2
Roslyn Cres HU12 72 C7
Roslyn Rd HU3 144 E7
Rosmead St HU9 146 D8
Rosper Rd DN40 87 A4
Rossall Cl 4 DN16 96 E2
Ross La
Bainton YO25 31 D7
Winterton DN15 83 B5
Rosslyn St 1 YO30 130 A6
Ross Rd DN31 153 B5
Rostun Rd HU12 60 B2
Rothbury Rd DN17 150 F3

Rothesay Cl 1 HU9 141 E1
Roth Hill La YO19 37 E3
ROTHWELL 111 F2
Rothwell Ave 15 DN33 102 D2
Rothwell Rd
Cabourne LN7 111 C3
Scunthorpe DN15 150 D8
Rotsea La YO25 33 B7
Rotterdam Rd HU7 141 A5
Rotton Sykes La DN15 67 F2
Rougier St YO1 156 A2
Roundhay Rd YO15 122 D1
Round Hill Link YO30 126 F2
Roundway
Grimsby DN34 152 C1
7 Immingham DN40 87 C1
Roundway The HU4 144 C5
ROUTH 44 F5
Routh Ave HU17 154 C3
Roval Dr DN40 87 B1
Rowan Ave
Beverley HU17 136 F7
York YO32 127 D4
Rowan Cl
3 Barrow upon Humber DN19 85 C8
Gateforth YO8 48 B1
4 Hut Green DN14 62 A2
2 Keelby DN41 101 A4
10 Thorne/Moorends DN8 79 B2
Rowan Cres 2 DN16 96 E2
Rowan Ct
7 Goxhill DN19 86 A8
Little End YO43 40 A1
Rowan Dr
Blyton DN21 117 F5
Healing DN41 101 F5
6 Humberston DN36 114 D8
Rowan Garth HU16 55 C4
Rowan Pl YO32 127 D4
Rowans The
23 Gainsborough DN21 117 C1
Holme-on-Spalding-Moor YO42 40 A1
11 Little Leven HU17 44 F6
1 Westwoodside DN9 105 A2
Rowan Wlk HU18 134 D2
Rowedale Cl 15 YO14 2 F8
Row La HU12 90 A7
Rowlandhall La DN14 50 E1
Rowland Rd DN16 151 A6
Rowlandson St DN31 152 F6
Rowley Ct 2 YO32 127 F7
Rowley Gr HU6 139 F5
Rowley Mews
Pocklington YO42 29 A3
37 Pocklington YO42 29 A3
Rowley Rd HU20 54 F3
Rowlston Gr HU9 142 A2
Rowmans The YO30 126 C4
Rowmills Rd DN16 151 C4
Rowntree Ave YO30 130 C8
Rowpit La HU17 45 C8
Rowston Cl 7 DN21 117 B1
Rowston St DN35 103 D3
Rowton Dr HU11 45 D2
Roxburgh St 1 HU5 145 B8
ROXBY 83 A3
Roxby Cswy DN15 83 C4
Roxby Rd DN15 82 F4
Roxton Ave DN41 101 A5
Roxton Hall Dr 13 HU14 69 A5
Roxton Medieval Village* DN40 101 A7
Royal Chase YO24 132 F8
Royal Cres YO15 122 F2
Royal Ct 25 DN35 103 D1
Royal Dr DN14 79 A8
Royale Ct HU9 141 F3
Royal Garth HU17 154 A1
Royal Prince's Par 11 YO15 122 F2
Royal St DN31 152 E6
Royal Wlk HU16 139 D5
Royd's Rd YO8 61 F6
Royston Gr HU8 141 B1
Ruard Rd DN19 86 B8
Ruards La DN19 71 A1
Ruby St 3 YO23 130 B1
Rudcarr La YO19 14 E1
Rudding Dr YO16 122 D7
Ruddings YO19 38 A8
Ruddings Cl 9 YO32 127 C8
Ruddings La YO42 38 E2
Ruddings The
Selby YO8 148 A4
Wheldrake YO19 38 A8
Rudgate La DN14 78 E4
Rudham Ave DN32 102 F2
RUDSTON 9 F6
Rudston Beacon* YO25 9 F4
Rudston Gr HU9 142 A1
Rudston Monolith* YO25 9 F6
Rudston Rd YO25 9 F2
Rue de Nozay 2 DN20 97 E4
Ruffhams Cl YO19 37 F8
Rufford Rd 3 DN35 103 C2
RUFFORTH 24 C6
Rufforth Dr HU17 43 D5
Rufforth Garth HU7 141 C8
Rufforth Prim Sch YO23 24 C6
Rugby Cl 21 HU19 75 A6
Rugby Rd DN16 151 A4
Ruislip Cl HU8 142 A5
Runcorn Garth HU4 144 B3
Rundle Ct 29 YO42 29 A3
Runner End YO43 40 A1
Runnymede Ave 1 HU7 56 E6
Runnymede Way HU7 56 E5
Runswick Ave YO26 129 B4
Runswick Ct DN32 153 A2
Runswick Rd DN32 153 B2
Rupert Rd 9 DN33 102 E2
Rushcarr La DN17 95 C1
Rushes The 14 DN18 69 E1
Rusholme La YO8 64 A5
Rushtons Way DN20 108 F5
Rushwood Cl 6 YO32 13 F5
Ruskington Cl DN31 102 C5
Ruskin St HU3 145 B6
Ruskin Way 20 HU14 68 D5
Russel Cl 6 DN15 96 D7
Russell Ct 13 DN35 103 D1
Russell Dr
20 Keyingham HU12 73 C4
York YO30 129 E8
Russell Rd DN14 149 B4
Russell St
Kingston upon Hull HU2 155 A3
York YO23 130 B2
Russell Wlk DN17 107 D7
Russet Cl
12 Scunthorpe DN15 96 B7
Wrawby DN20 98 D3
Russet Dr YO31 131 B5
Rustenburg St HU9 141 D1
Rustic La DN21 117 F6
Ruston Ct 18 HU12 74 D1
RUSTON PARVA 21 C8
Ruston Terr 17 HU12 74 D1
Ruswarp Gr HU6 139 E6
Rutherglen Dr HU9 142 A3
Rutland Cl YO23 132 A3
Rutland Dr 16 DN36 114 A7
Rutland Rd
Goole DN14 149 D6
Kingston upon Hull HU5 144 E8
Scunthorpe DN16 151 D3
Rutland St DN32 153 A4
Ryburn Cl YO30 126 F2
Rydal Ave
11 Grimsby DN33 113 D8
York YO31 131 A6
Rydale Ct HU5 140 E3
Rydales The HU5 140 E3
Rydal Gr HU16 138 E6
Ryde Ave HU5 140 D3
Ryde St HU5 140 D2
Rye Cl YO32 127 C8
Rye Cres 31 HU15 68 D5
Ryecroft 2 YO32 14 A6
Ryecroft Ave
10 Norton DN6 76 E2
York YO24 132 C7
Ryecroft Cl YO31 131 C8
Ryecroft Dr HU19 75 A6
Ryecroft Gdns DN14 62 A2
Ryecroft Rd DN6 76 E1
Ryedale 12 HU15 68 D6
Ryedale Ave DN15 83 A6
Ryedale Way YO8 148 C3
RYEHILL 73 A4
Ryehill Cl YO32 127 D5
Ryehill Gr HU9 141 F2
Ryehill La HU12 73 A4
Ryelands Ave YO16 123 A6
Ryemoor Rd YO32 127 C8
Rylatt Pl YO26 129 B3
Rymer Pl DN35 103 D2
Rysome La HU19 75 C1
Rysome Rd HU12 90 B7
Rythergate 8 YO8 48 B8

S

Sabina Ct HU8 141 E7
Sable Cl HU4 144 C2
Sabrina Ct 15 HU8 141 E7
Sackville Cl
5 Beverley HU17 55 E8
14 Immingham DN40 87 C1
Sackville Rd 15 DN40 87 C1
Sackville St DN34 152 C3
Sacred Gate HU12 72 D6
Sadberge Ct YO10 131 C3
Saddleback La YO25 31 B7
Saddle Cl DN19 86 A8
Saddlers Cl
1 Copmanthorpe YO23 132 B3
Huntington YO32 127 F2
Saddlers Way YO26 24 A6
Saddler's Way DN9 105 D3
Saddlers Wlk YO19 37 A5
Saddleworth Cl 19 HU7 57 A6
Saffre Cl 17 DN15 83 A5
Saffrondale HU10 143 E7
Saffron Dr 6 DN14 63 C1
Saffron Garth 15 HU12 74 D1
Saffron Way 16 DN17 94 D7
Sage Cl HU17 154 B1
Sagefield Cl 6 DN33 113 D8
Sailors Wharf HU9 146 C6
Sails Dr YO10 131 B3
Sainsbury Way HU13 144 A1
St Abbs Cl HU9 155 C1
St Aelreds Cl YO31 130 F4
St Aelreds RC Prim Sch YO31 131 B5
St Aidan Cres YO16 122 E4
St Aidan Ct YO16 122 E5
St Aidan Rd YO16 122 E4
St Aiden Cl YO43 135 E3
St Aiden's Way HU9 141 F2
St Alban Cl YO16 122 E4
St Alban Rd YO16 122 E4
St Albans Ave DN31 152 A4
St Albans Cl
7 Beverley HU17 136 E1
Hibaldstow DN20 108 F5
Scunthorpe DN17 150 C3
St Alban's Cl HU11 46 D3
St Albans Mount HU6 140 C4
St Ambrose Ct 23 HU7 57 A5
St Andrewgate YO1 156 B2
St Andrew Pl YO1 156 C2
St Andrew Rd YO16 122 E4
St Andrews Ave DN17 96 C1
St Andrews CE Prim Sch HU7 140 E8
St Andrews Cl YO25 31 E7
St Andrew's Cl
Middleton-on-the-Wolds YO25 31 C4
Paull HU12 72 A5
Redbourne DN21 108 E3
St Andrews Ct
Goole DN14 149 C4
Northfield HU4 144 A3
St Andrew's Dr DN15 82 A4
St Andrews Gr 10 DN7 92 D4
St Andrews La 5 DN40 87 B2
St Andrew's Mount HU10 143 C8
St Andrews Prim Sch HU10 143 C7
St Andrew's St DN21 108 A1
St Andrew St HU17 154 B2
St Andrew's Terr 6 DN14 149 C4
St Andrews Way HU8 141 C3
St Andrew's Way
2 Barnby Dun DN3 92 A3
Epworth DN9 105 E7
St Andrews Wlk YO25 22 A2
St Ann Ct YO10 130 E2
St Anne's Cl HU17 137 B5
St Anne's Dr HU16 139 D6
St Annes Rd YO15 122 F3
St Anne's Rd 8 DN41 101 A5
St Annes Sch HU15 68 E5
St Anne's Wlk
9 Brough HU15 68 D6
Driffield YO25 125 A3
St Ann's Ave DN34 152 B2
St Ann's Ct YO10 130 D2
St Anthony Rd YO16 122 E4
St Anthony's Dr 24 HU12 72 D7
St Anthony's Pk 25 HU12 72 D7
St Athony's Cl HU6 140 B4
St Aubyn's Pl YO24 130 A2
St Augustine Ave DN32 152 E1
St Augustine Cres DN16 151 B1
St Augustine Dr HU11 45 E2
St Augustines Ct 40 HU12 72 C7
St Augustine's Ct 2 HU5 140 D3
St Augustine's Dr YO16 122 E5
St Augustine's Gate 30 HU12 72 C7
St Augustine's Gr YO16 122 E5
St Augustine Webster RC Prim Sch DN15 150 D8
St Austells Cl HU9 141 F2
St Barbara's Cres 8 DN15 82 B4
St Barnabas CE Prim Sch
Barnetby le Wold DN38 99 B4
Clifton Park YO26 129 F5
St Barnabas Ct
4 Kingston upon Hull HU3 145 C4
13 York YO26 129 F5
St Barnabas Dr HU14 69 C7
St Barnabas Rd
Barnetby DN38 99 C4
Barnetby le Wold DN38 99 B4
St Bartholemew's Way HU8 142 A5
St Bartholomew's Cl 17 DN41 101 A4
St Bede Ct
East Ella HU4 144 E5
Kingston upon Hull HU4 144 E5
St Bedes RC Comp Sch DN16 151 B2
St Benedict Cl 21 HU7 57 B5
St Benedict Rd YO23 156 A1
St Bernadettes RC Prim Sch DN16 151 C2
St Bernard's Cl 9 DN20 97 E4
St Boltophs Cl 4 WF11 61 A2
St Botolph's Rd DN16 151 C3
St Bridget's Ct YO23 156 B1
St Catherines Cl YO30 126 C5
St Catherines Cres 8 DN16 96 D2
St Catherines Ct
6 Grimsby DN34 102 C3
Kingston upon Hull HU5 140 E2
Scunthorpe DN16 151 D2
St Catherines Dr HU17 43 C6
St Catherine's Dr DN7 92 C2
St Catherines Pl YO24 130 A3
St Chad DN19 85 D8
St Chad Cres YO16 122 E4
St Chad Gr YO16 122 E4
St Chad Rd YO16 122 E4
St Chad's Rd DN16 151 D3
St Chads Wharf YO23 133 C8
St Charles' RC Prim Sch HU2 155 A3
St Christopher Rd YO16 122 E4
St Christopher's Rd DN36 114 C8
St Clares Wlk 12 DN20 98 C2
St Clement's Field DN20 98 D8
St Clements Gr YO23 130 C2
St Clements Pl HU2 155 A4
St Clements Way
17 Holton le Clay DN36 114 A5
Kingston upon Hull HU9 141 F2
St Columba Rd YO16 122 F5
St Crispins Cl DN40 86 E4
St Cuthbert Rd YO16 122 E4
St David Cl HU17 154 B2
St David La YO15 5 B3
St David's Cl HU16 139 D6
St Davids Cres DN17 96 C2
St David's View 9 DN14 64 E4
St Deny's Cl 1 DN40 86 E3
St Denys' Rd YO1 156 C2
St Edmunds YO41 15 D2
St Edmund's Ct 4 HU5 139 D2
St Edward's Cl YO24 132 F8
St Edwin Reach DN7 92 C5
St Edwins Cl 27 DN7 92 D4
St Ellens Ct HU17 154 B2
St Francis Ave DN31 152 A4
St Francis Ct 1 HU5 139 D2
St Francis Gr DN37 101 E1
St George's Ave
Bridlington YO15 122 E3
Hatfield DN7 92 C3
St Georges Cl 19 DN8 93 B7
St George's Ct DN21 108 F3
St George's Gn DN14 149 D6
St George's Pl YO24 129 F2
St Georges Prim Sch HU3 145 A6
St Georges RC Prim Sch YO10 130 D2
St Georges Rd 16 DN8 93 B7
St George's Rd HU3 145 A5
St George's Wlk HU9 142 B2
St Giles' Ave DN33 102 E1
St Giles Croft HU17 154 A2
St Giles Ct
Kingston upon Hull HU9 142 C1
York YO31 156 B3
St Giles Rd YO30 126 B5
St Giles Way YO23 132 A2
St Gregory's Mews YO1 156 A2
St Hedda's Ct 6 HU5 139 D2
St Helena Gdns 3 HU5 140 E2
St Helens Ave 13 DN33 102 E2
St Helen's Ave YO42 29 B4
St Helen's Cl YO42 29 B4
St Helen's Cres DN37 113 D5
St Helen's Dr 10 HU15 68 D6
St Helen's La YO14 3 C6
St Helen's Rd
Brigg DN20 98 C2
Pocklington YO42 29 B4
5 York YO24 132 E8
St Helen's Rise YO19 38 A7
St Helen's Sq
Barmby Moor YO42 28 D4
3 Market Weighton YO43 135 D4
York YO1 156 B2
St Helens Way DN21 119 B2
St Helen's Well* YO43 41 D5
St Helier's Rd DN35 153 E3
St Hilda's Ave DN34 152 B2
St Hildas Mews YO10 131 B4
St Hilda St
3 Bridlington YO15 122 E2
Kingston upon Hull HU3 140 E1
St Hugh's Ave DN35 153 D2
St Hugh's Cres DN16 151 C4
St Hughs Hospl DN32 102 F2
St Hughs Sch DN16 151 B5
St Hybald's Gr DN20 108 F7
St Ives Cl HU7 141 C7
St Ives Cres DN34 102 C3
St James Ave
Grimsby DN34 152 A2
Hatfield DN7 92 C3
St James CE Prim Sch HU7 141 C6
St James Cl
12 Crowle DN17 94 D7
Kingston upon Hull HU7 141 D7
York YO30 126 E3
St James Croft YO24 129 D1
St James Ct
Rawcliffe DN14 64 A1
Scunthorpe DN15 151 A6
St James' Ct DN34 152 C2
St James Mount YO23 130 A2
St James Pl
31 Bottesford DN16 96 E2
5 York YO24 129 D1
St James Rd
Bridlington YO15 122 D1
22 Brigg DN20 98 C2
Welton HU14 68 F5
St James' Sch DN34 152 C2
St James's Rd DN20 108 E8
St James St HU3 145 D5
St James Terr YO8 148 C5
St Joan's Dr DN20 108 E8
St John Mews YO8 148 B7
St John's Ave YO16 122 C3
St John's Avenue W YO16 122 C2
St Johns Bsns Pk HU9 141 F1
St Johns Cl
1 Beverley HU17 55 F8
12 Goxhill DN19 86 A8
St John's Cl
Bridlington YO16 122
11 Pocklington YO42 28
St John's Cres YO31 156
St Johns Ct
Goole DN14 149
Grimsby DN34 152
Kingston upon Hull HU6 140
St John's Gdns YO25 124
St John's Gr HU9 141
St John's Pl 2 YO25 124
St John's Rd
Great Driffield YO25 124
8 Humberston DN36 114
Scunthorpe DN16 151
9 Stamford Bridge YO41 15
St John's St
Bridlington YO16 122
15 Howden DN14 65
St John St
Beverley HU17 154
York YO31 156
St John's Well* YO25 21
St John's Wlk
Bridlington YO16 122
1 Great Driffield YO25 124
Kingston upon Hull HU13 143
St Joseph Dr HU4 144
St Josephs Ct 9 YO24 129
St Josephs RC Prim Sch
Cleethorpes DN35 103
Goole DN14 149
St Jude Gr YO16 122
St Jude Rd YO16 122
St Jude's Ct 3 HU5 139
St Julian's Wells HU10 143
St Katherine's Rd 2 HU15 53
St Lawrence Acad The DN15 150
St Lawrence Ave
Kingston upon Hull HU16 138
Snaith DN14 78
St Lawrence Rd DN7 92
St Lawrences CE Prim Sch YO10 130
St Lawrence's Pl DN16 151
St Lawrence Sq HU11 45
St Lawrence's Rd DN16 151
St Leonards Ave YO8 49
St Leonard's Ave DN31 152
St Leonard's Cl 2 YO25 22
St Leonard's Pl YO30 156
St Leonard's Rd
Beverley HU17 136
Kingston upon Hull HU5 140
St Luke's Cl DN7 92
St Luke's Cres 12 DN36 114
St Lukes Ct HU10 143
St Luke's Ct DN32 152
St Luke's Gr YO30 130
St Lukes Sch DN16 151
St Luke's St
6 Kingston Upon Hull HU3 145
Kingston upon Hull HU3 155
St Margarets Ave HU16 138
St Margarets Cl
Driffield YO25 124
Kingston upon Hull HU16 138
St Margaret's Cl 9 DN37 101
St Margaret's Cres 4 DN40 100
St Margarets Ct 3 HU8 142
St Margaret's Terr YO1 130
St Margarets View 4 HU11 45
St Margaret's Wlk DN16 151
St Mark's Gr YO30 126
St Mark's Rd 13 DN36 114
St Mark's Sq HU3 145
St Mark St HU8 155
St Martins Ave 2 HU4 144
St Martins CE Prim Sch
Fangfoss YO41 28
Owston Ferry DN9 106
St Martin's Cl
Blyton DN21 117
2 Burton Agnes YO25 10
Fangfoss YO41 28
St Martin's Cres
6 Grimsby DN33 102
Scawby DN20 108
St Martin's Ct HU17 154
St Martins Dr YO16 122
St Martin's Dr 1 YO25 10
St Martin's Gr YO16 122
St Martin's La YO1 156
St Martins Pk 1 DN9 106
St Martin's Pl 16 DN41 101
St Martins Prep Sch DN32 152
St Martin's Rd
Scawby DN20 108
Thorngumbald HU12 72
St Mary Queen of Martyrs Prim Sch HU7 141
St Mary's YO30 156
St Mary's Abbey* YO1 156
St Mary & St Josephs RC Prim Sch 20 YO42 29
St Mary's Ave
1 Barnetby le Wold DN38 99
12 Hemingbrough YO8 49
Kingston upon Hull HU5 139
St Marys CE Prim Sch
Askham Richard YO23 24
Beverley HU17 136

St Mary's CE Prim Sch DN20 98 E3
t Marys Cl
Cottingwith YO42 38 C5
6 South Field HU13 69 E5
t Mary's Cl
Beverley HU17 136 D5
Brough HU15 68 C7
Grimsby DN32 153 C2
15 Haxby YO32 13 E5
Strensall YO32 14 A7
7 Thorngumbald HU12 72 E5
t Marys Coll HU6 140 C5
t Mary's Cres YO16 122 D4
t Mary's Ct
23 Pocklington YO42 29 A4
9 Scunthorpe DN15 96 B7
York YO23 156 A1
t Mary's Dr
Hatfield DN7 92 C2
38 Hedon HU12 72 D7
t Mary's Gr YO10 131 C4
t Marys La HU17 154 A3
t Mary's La
5 Barton-upon-Humber DN18 84 F8
York YO30 156 A3
t Marys Mount HU16 139 C6
t Mary's Mus* YO1 156 B2
t Mary's RC High Sch 35 DN33 102 D2
t Marys RC Prim Sch
Bridlington YO15 122 C2
Brigg DN20 98 C3
Grimsby DN32 152 F4
Market Weighton YO43 135 E3
Selby YO8 148 B2
t Mary's Rd DN7 92 C2
t Marys Terr YO30 156 A3
t Mary's Terr
Beverley HU17 154 A3
York YO30 156 A3
t Marys View YO8 148 B2
t Mary's Wlk 15 HU14 69 B7
t Mary's Wlk
Beverley HU17 154 A4
Bridlington YO16 122 D4
t Matthews Cl HU17 154 B2
t Matthew's Cl 4 YO19 36 D8
t Matthew's Ct HU17 154 B2
t Matthew's Rd 11 DN36 114 C8
t Matthew St HU3 145 B5
t Maurice's Rd YO31 156 C3
t Mawes Cres DN34 152 A3
t Mews 34 HU12 72 C7
t Michael's Cl
Kingston upon Hull HU8 142 B5
Skidby HU16 138 A8
13 Thorne/Moorends DN8 93 B7
t Michael's Cres DN16 151 C4
t Michaels Ct 10 YO24 129 B1
t Michael's Ct DN19 86 A8
t Michael's Dr
39 Hedon HU12 72 D7
Thorne DN8 93 B7
t Michael's Mount
Kingston upon Hull HU6 140 C5
14 Swanland HU14 69 B7
t Michael's Rd DN34 102 B2
t Michael's Wlk 15 YO15 4 D3
t Monicas Cl YO42 39 B6
t Monica's Ct 3 HU5 140 C3
t Nectan Cl 9 HU3 145 A4
t Nicholas Ave
Kingston upon Hull HU4 144 C2
York YO19 133 E4
t Nicholas CE Prim Sch DN39 86 A1
t Nicholas Cl
Copmanthorpe YO23 132 A3
8 Newbald YO43 53 F7
t Nicholas CP Sch HU17 154 C2
t Nicholas Cres YO23 132 A3
t Nicholas Croft YO23 24 E3
t Nicholas Ct DN16 96 F2
t Nicholas Dr
Beverley HU17 154 C2
Grimsby DN37 102 B3
Hornsea HU18 134 C6
t Nicholas Fields* YO10 130 F4
t Nicholas Gate HU12 72 D7
t Nicholas Gdns HU4 144 C3
t Nicholas Pk 6 HU19 75 A6
t Nicholas Pl 1 YO10 130 F3
t Nicholas Prim Sch HU6 140 C4
t Nicholas Rd
Beverley HU17 154 C2
Copmanthorpe YO23 132 A3
Thorne/Moorends DN8 93 A8
t Nicholas Way 22 YO32 13 E5
t Norberts RC Prim Sch DN17 94 D7
t Olaf's Gr DN32 152 D2
t Olave's Rd YO30 156 A4
t Olaves Sch YO30 156 A3
t Oswald Ct 5 HU5 139 D2
t Oswald Rd YO16 122 E4
t Oswalds CE Prim Sch YO10 133 E7
t Oswald's Cl YO41 27 F6
t Oswalds Ct YO10 133 E7
t Oswald's Rd YO10 133 D8
t Patrick's Gn 14 HU12 74 D1
t Paulinus Cres 20 HU15 68 C6
St Pauls CE Prim Sch YO24 130 A3
St Pauls Dr HU17 137 E8
St Paul's Gdns 4 DN16 151 B2
St Pauls Mews YO24 130 A3
St Paul's Rd
Gainsborough DN21 117 A2
Scunthorpe DN16 151 B2
St Paul's Sq YO24 130 A3
St Paul St HU2 155 A4
St Paul's Terr YO24 130 A4
St Pauls Way HU17 137 E8
St Peter's Ave
Cleethorpes DN35 153 E2
Kingston upon Hull HU10 143 E6
Scunthorpe DN16 96 D2
St Peter's CE Prim Sch DN35 153 F2
St Peter's Church* DN18 84 F8
St Peters Cl
East/West Stockwith DN21 116 E5
Hutton Cranswick YO25 32 E8
Rufforth YO26 129 A5
St Peter's Cl
10 Holton le Clay DN36 114 A5
16 Howden DN14 65 A7
St Peter's Court 27 DN18 69 E1
St Peter's Cres 7 DN36 114 C8
St Peters Ct YO30 156 A4
St Peters Gr DN37 101 E1
St Peter's Gr
9 Scotter DN21 107 C3
York YO30 156 A4
St Peters Orch DN18 69 F1
St Peter's Rd
Drax YO8 63 F5
19 Scotter DN21 107 C3
St Peters Sch YO30 156 A4
St Peter's Sq 14 YO42 29 A4
St Peter St HU9 155 C2
St Peters View HU11 142 F6
St Peters Wlk
Burton Pidsea HU12 59 D2
7 Wawne HU7 56 F7
St Philip's Gr YO30 130 A8
St Philips Rd HU12 73 C4
St Quintin Field YO25 125 F7
St Quintin Pk 9 YO25 34 B2
St Quintins Cl 4 HU9 146 C8
St Richards RC Prim Sch HU9 142 C1
St Sampsons Sq YO1 156 B2
St Saviourgate YO1 156 C2
St Saviour's Pl YO1 156 C2
Saints Cl HU9 141 F2
St Silas St HU2 155 B4
St Stephen Rd YO16 122 E4
St Stephen's HU11 145 D6
St Stephens Cl YO25 124 E3
St Stephen's Cl HU10 138 C2
St Stephen's Cres 4 HU15 66 D8
St Stephens Mews YO30 127 A2
St Stephen's Rd YO24 129 C2
St Stephens Shop Ctr HU2 155 A1
St Stephen's Sq YO24 129 C1
St Stephens St HU2 145 D6
St Swithin's Wlk YO26 129 E4
St Thomas Moore Rd HU4 144 A4
St Thomas More RC Prim Sch HU4 144 B4
St Thomas' Pl YO31 156 B4
St Thomas Rd YO16 122 E4
St Thomas' Rd 14 DN36 114 C8
St Thomas's Cl 2 YO10 131 C4
St Thomas's Grange 2 HU5 139 D2
St Vincent's Ave DN15 96 D7
St Vincents RC Prim Sch HU5 140 D2
St Wilfred Rd YO16 122 E3
St Wilfreds RC Prim Sch YO31 156 C3
St Wilfrids Cl HU12 73 E3
St Wilfrid's Cl 7 YO32 14 B6
St Wilfrid's Cres 9 YO8 48 D1
St Wilfrid's Ct YO31 156 C3
St Wilfrid's Rd 8 YO32 14 B6
St Williams Coll YO1 156 B3
St Wulstan Cl YO31 130 E7
Salacon Way 1 DN32 153 A5
Saladine Ct 16 DN41 101 F5
Salamander Cl DN31 152 B4
Salcey Cl 23 HU7 56 F6
Salents La YO17 6 B6
Sales La DN14 78 B3
Salisbury Ave
Beverley HU17 136 E1
Goole DN14 149 E4
Hornsea HU18 134 C2
24 Waltham DN37 113 D6
Salisbury Cl
Morton DN21 117 A3
Scunthorpe DN17 150 C3
Salisbury Rd YO26 129 F5
Salisbury St
6 Gainsborough DN21 117 B2
Northfield HU13 143 D1
Sculcoates HU5 140 B2
Salisbury Ter YO26 129 F5
Salmonby Rd
1 Scunthorpe DN17 96 C2
Scunthorpe DN17 150 E1
Salmond Rd 4 YO24 129 B1
Salmon Gr HU6 140 B4
Salsbury Ave DN34 152 B2
Saltash Rd HU4 144 A2
Saltaugh Rd HU12 88 B8
Saltburn Gr DN32 153 A1
Saltburn St HU3 145 A4
SALT END 72 A8
Salt End La HU12 72 A7
Saltergate Rd DN17 107 D7
Salters' La DN36 120 E4
Saltford Ave HU9 147 F8
Saltgrounds Rd HU15 68 B5
Salthouse La HU1 155 C2
SALTMARSHE 65 F3
Saltmarshe Delph Nature Reserve* DN14 65 D1
Saltmarshe Sta DN14 65 E4
Salton Ave 4 HU5 139 E3
Saltshouse Rd HU8 141 E6
Saltwell Pk 29 HU7 56 F6
Salvesen Rd DN31 153 B5
Salvesen Way HU3 145 A3
Samman Cl HU10 143 D6
Samman Rd HU17 154 C4
Samphire Cl DN36 115 C4
Sample Ave HU17 154 B4
Sampson St DN17 81 A3
Samuel Ave DN32 153 B2
Sanbeds La DN9 105 B2
SANCTON 41 E2
Sancton Cl HU16 138 E6
Sancton Rd YO43 135 E3
Sanctuary Way DN37 102 B3
Sandacre Ct YO26 129 D5
Sandale Ct HU5 139 E1
Sandars Cl 2 DN9 106 A3
Sandbeck La DN21 117 E6
Sandcroft Cl 4 YO24 132 D8
Sandcroft Rd YO24 132 D8
Sanderling Way DN16 151 F1
Sanderson Cl
Driffield YO25 124 D2
Newland HU5 140 B2
Scunthorpe DN16 151 A5
Sanderson Ct YO26 129 B3
Sanderson's Bank DN10 104 C2
Sandfield Cl
Market Weighton YO43 135 B3
Scunthorpe DN17 150 D1
Sandfield Dr 3 HU15 68 C5
Sandfield Gn YO43 135 B3
Sandford Cl HU7 56 F5
Sandford St DN31 152 B4
Sandgate Rd YO16 123 A6
Sandhall Dr DN14 149 F5
Sandhall Rd DN14 65 C3
Sandhill La
Brayton YO8 48 D2
Sutton upon Derwent YO41 27 E2
Sandhill Rd DN14 81 B6
SAND HOLE 52 B8
SANDHOLME 52 C1
Sandholme
2 Haxby YO32 13 F5
Market Weighton YO43 135 C3
Sandholme Bsns Pk HU15 52 D1
Sandholme Cl 1 HU15 66 D8
Sandholme La HU17 44 F8
Sandholme Pk HU15 66 D8
Sandholme Rd HU15 66 C8
Sandholme Way 4 DN14 65 A7
Sandhouse Cres DN16 151 C5
SAND HUTTON 15 B5
Sand Hutton CE Prim Sch YO41 15 B5
Sand Hutton Ct YO41 15 B5
Sandiacres 5 YO8 48 D1
Sand La
Barlby with Osgodby YO8 49 B4
Broughton DN20 97 D3
Bubwith YO8 50 D5
Caistor LN7 110 E4
Manton DN21 108 A5
Messingham DN17 107 A7
Newton on Derwent YO41 28 B5
North Cave HU15 53 D2
Sancton YO43 53 D8
South Cliffe YO43 52 E8
Thornton YO42 39 D7
Wistow YO8 48 E6
Wroot DN9 104 C6
Sandlemere Cl 3 HU3 145 A5
Sandmartin Ct YO24 132 D8
Sandmoor Cl HU8 142 B6
Sandown Cl YO24 129 E2
Sandpiper Ct HU18 134 D6
Sandpiper Dr HU4 144 B1
Sandpiper Way 25 DN18 69 E1
Sandpits La HU11 47 C1
Sand Rd DN17 106 B8
Sandringham Cl
6 Bridlington YO16 122 D6
Haxby YO32 127 C7
Kingston upon Hull HU16 139 A7
Sandringham Cres 15 DN17 96 C2
Sandringham Dr DN14 149 B6
Sandringham Rd
28 Brough HU15 68 C5
Cleethorpes DN35 103 B2
Sandringham St
2 Kingston upon Hull HU3 145 A6
York YO10 130 D2
Sandsacre Ave YO16 123 A6
Sandsacre Dr 1 YO16 123 A6
Sandsacre Rd YO16 123 A6
Sandsacre Way YO16 122 F6
Sands Cl
Keadby DN17 95 D6
Reighton YO14 3 D7
Sands Ct 3 HU14 69 A4
Sandsfield Ave YO43 40 E6
Sands La
Barmston YO25 22 F5
Bridlington YO15 122 F3
Brough HU15 68 C6
Ellerker HU15 67 F6
Holme-on-Spalding-Moor YO43 39 F1
Hornsea HU18 134 D4
Hunmanby YO14 3 A8
Scotter DN21 107 C3
South Ferriby DN18 84 A7
Ulrome YO25 23 B3
Sands Rd YO14 3 B7
Sandstock Rd
Pocklington YO42 29 A4
York YO31 131 B7
Sands Top YO43 53 E7
SANDTOFT 94 A3
Sandtoft Rd
Epworth DN9 94 B3
Hatfield DN7 93 A4
Sandwalk YO43 135 C3
Sandway Ave 12 YO8 48 B1
Sandway Cl 11 YO8 48 B1
Sandway Dr
Camblesforth YO8 63 D4
1 Thorpe Willoughby YO8 48 B1
Sandwith Ct HU17 154 B4
Sandwith La DN14 63 B4
Sandy Cl DN36 115 C5
Sandycroft Cl HU10 139 A1
Sandy Gap YO32 127 C7
Sandy La
Harpham YO25 9 E2
Harton YO60 15 B8
16 Haxby YO32 13 E5
North Duffield YO8 49 F8
Stockton on the Forest YO32 14 E4
Sandyland 29 YO32 13 E5
Sandy Point HU11 142 E5
Sandyridge YO26 126 A1
Sandy Rise YO8 148 C3
Saner's Cl HU16 139 B5
Saner St HU3 145 B6
Santolina Way HU4 144 C2
SANTON 97 B7
Santon Bsns Pk DN16 97 A7
Sapperton Cl 16 HU7 56 F6
Sapphire Gr 7 HU3 145 A4
Sarah Rhodes La DN14 65 C3
Sarah's Wlk DN17 150 B2
Sarge Cl 10 DN36 114 A5
Sargent Ave YO23 132 F4
Sargent's Way 8 DN20 108 F5
Sargon Way DN37 102 C6
Sassaby Cl HU4 144 C3
Saunby Gr DN35 153 E3
Saunders Cres 21 YO42 29 A3
Saunders Croft 4 HU17 55 B8
Saunders La HU17 55 B7
Saunders St DN31 152 C4
Savage Rd YO15 122 D2
Savery St HU9 141 D1
Savile Cl HU17 136 E6
Saville Gr YO30 130 A8
Saville St HU1 155 B2
Savoy Ct 12 DN36 114 A7
Savoy Rd HU8 141 F4
Sawcliffe Ind Pk DN15 96 D7
Sawcliffe Medieval Village* DN15 82 F1
Sawcliffe Nature Reserve* DN15 96 E8
Sawley Cl HU18 134 C5
Sawmill Yd 5 YO15 122 E2
Sawston Ave HU5 139 C2
Sawyer's Cres YO23 132 C2
Sawyers Wlk 9 YO19 26 F7
SAXBY ALL SAINTS 84 A3
Saxby Gr 17 DN33 102 D2
Saxby Hill DN20 84 B3
Saxby Rd
Bonby DN20 84 B2
Kingston upon Hull HU8 142 A5
Scunthorpe DN17 150 E1
Saxcourt HU6 139 E7
Saxford Way 8 YO32 13 D5
Saxon Cl
Barton-upon-Humber DN18 84 F8
Shipton YO30 12 F5
6 Thorpe Willoughby YO8 48 B1
Saxon Cres DN35 153 D2
Saxon Ct
Blyton DN21 117 F5
Scunthorpe DN16 96 D2
Saxondale HU4 144 B7
Saxonfield LN7 111 A4
Saxon La DN9 94 C2
Saxon Pl YO31 130 E7
Saxon Rd YO41 15 D2
Saxon Rise HU17 136 D7
Saxon Vale YO30 12 F5
Saxon Villas 10 HU3 145 A4
Saxon Way
4 Caistor LN7 111 B4
Kingston upon Hull HU13 143 F1
Saxton Cl DN17 150 E2
Scafell Cl 4 YO30 126 E1
Scaggiethorpe La YO26 12 D2
Scaife Cl HU17 154 C2
Scaife Garth YO42 28 F3
Scaife Gdns YO31 130 C7
Scaife Mews
Beverley HU17 137 B3
York YO31 130 C7
Scaife St YO31 130 C7
SCALBY 66 E8
Scalby Gr HU5 144 D8
Scalby La HU15 66 D8
Scalby Pl HU18 134 B4
Scale La HU1 155 C2
Scale Lane Staith HU1 155 C2
Scallow La DN17 107 D6
Scalm La YO8 48 A4
SCAMLAND 39 C7
Scampton Cl DN34 152 A1
Scampton Garth HU7 141 C8
Scandinavian Way DN41 87 E1
Scarborough Cres 8 YO16 122 C5
Scarborough Rd
Bempton YO16 4 A1
Blyton DN21 117 E5
7 Bridlington YO16 122 C5
Great Driffield YO25 124 E6
Langtoft YO25 8 C7
Scarborough St HU3 145 A4
Scarborough Terr YO30 156 B4
Scarcroft Hill YO24 130 B2
Scarcroft La YO23 156 A1
Scarcroft Prim Sch YO23 156 A1
Scarcroft Rd YO24 156 A1
Scarcroft View YO23 156 A1
Scardale Ct YO8 148 A2
Scargate Cl YO16 123 A7
Scarrington Cres HU4 144 B6
Scarrow Cl HU3 145 A7
Scarsea Way YO15 4 C3
SCARTHO 102 F1
Scartho Jun & Inf Sch DN33 102 E1
Scartho Pk DN33 102 D1
Scartho Rd DN33 102 E2
Scaudercroft 13 YO19 26 F7
SCAWBY 108 E8
Scawby Hall* DN20 108 F8
Scawby Prim Sch DN20 108 E8
Scawby Rd
Brigg DN20 98 A1
Broughton DN20 97 E2
13 Grimsby DN33 102 D2
Scunthorpe DN17 150 E1
Scawton Ave 1 YO31 127 E2
Schiphol Way DN39 99 E5
Schofield Ave HU17 154 C3
Schofield Cl 5 DN19 85 C8
Scholars Way YO16 122 D4
Scholefield Ave HU17 56 B8
School Cl
Selby YO8 148 B3
16 Stamford Bridge YO41 15 D2
School Croft 8 DN9 105 B2
School Dr DN17 107 D7
School Hill YO16 10 E4
School House La 2 DN10 116 C3
School Houses 6 DN20 97 E4
School La
Appleby DN15 83 D1
Askham Richard YO23 24 D3
Beswick YO25 32 B4
Beverley HU17 154 B3
Bishopthorpe YO23 133 A4
Bonby DN20 84 C2
Buckton/Bempton YO15 4 C3
Burton Fleming YO25 2 E3
Cabourne LN7 111 D5
Copmanthorpe YO23 132 A2
Corringham DN21 118 D1
10 Flamborough YO15 5 A2
Goxhill DN19 86 A8
Grayingham DN21 119 B7
Heslington YO10 131 B1
Holmpton HU19 75 D2
Irby DN37 112 D7
15 Keyingham HU12 73 C4
Kingston upon Hull HU10 143 C8
New Holland DN19 70 E2
5 North Ferriby HU14 69 A4
North Kelsey LN7 110 A5
5 Pocklington YO42 29 A4
23 Poppleton YO26 12 F1
Redbourne DN21 108 F2
Rothwell LN7 111 E2
South Ferriby DN18 84 A7
Tetney DN36 114 C3
West/East Butterwick DN17 106 D8
York YO10 133 E7
School La Mews HU17 154 B3
School Rd
Hemingbrough YO8 49 F1
7 Preston HU12 58 C1
Scunthorpe DN16 151 B2
South Killingholme DN40 86 E3
Winteringham DN15 68 A1
School Rise YO43 53 F7
School St
Kingston upon Hull HU1 155 A2
York YO24 129 D3
School Wlk DN35 153 C1
Schooner Ct HU4 144 B3
Schubert Cl HU9 142 A3
SCORBOROUGH 43 D8
Scorborough La YO25 43 D8

Scoreby La
Gate Helmsley YO41 ....15 B2
Kexby YO41 ....15 B1
Low Catton YO41..........27 B8
Scotchman La YO60.......15 A8
Scotney Cl 5 HU3........140 E1
Scott Ave DN17..........150 C2
Scott Cl 7 DN37.........102 C4
SCOTTER 107 D3
Scotter Prim Sch DN21...107 C3
Scotter Rd
Laughton DN21...........117 F8
Messingham DN17.........107 D5
Scotton DN21............107 C2
Scunthorpe DN17.........150 C3
Scotter Road S
Bottesford DN17..........96 B1
Scunthorpe DN17.........150 C1
SCOTTERTHORPE..........107 B5
Scotterthorpe Rd DN21 ..107 B4
Scott Gdns 7 HU19........75 A6
Scott Moncrieff Rd YO32 ..14 B6
SCOTTON 107 D2
Scotton Rd DN21 ....107 C3
Scott Rd YO8 ....148 C6
Scotts Croft YO43.......135 D3
Scotts Garth Cl HU17 ....137 F8
Scotts Garth Dr HU17 .....44 C5
Scott St
27 Gainsborough DN21....117 B1
Kingston upon Hull HU2 ...155 B3
York YO23 ....130 C2
Scrap Bay Rd DN16 ....97 A3
SCRAYINGHAM.............15 F7
Scrivelsby Ct 9 DN35....103 D2
Scriven Gr 8 YO32 ....13 F5
Scrope Ave 4 YO31.......130 E5
Scrub La DN40............86 E5
Scrubwood La HU17 ......136 E6
SCULCOATES 140 F2
Sculcoates La HU5.......140 E2
SCUNTHORPE.............150 F5
Scunthorpe CE Prim Sch
DN15 ....151 A8
Scunthorpe General Hospl
DN15 ....150 E6
Scunthorpe L Ctr DN15...151 B7
Scunthorpe Sta DN16 ...151 A6
Seabrook Dr DN16.........96 D1
Seacroft Rd
Cleethorpes DN35........103 D3
Withernsea HU19..........75 A6
Seafield Ave HU9........141 F3
Seafire Cl YO30.........127 A3
Seaford Rd DN35 ....103 D1
Seagate YO15............123 C6
Seagate View YO15.......123 E6
Seagull Cl HU4..........144 E2
Seakel La YO23...........24 C2
Sea La DN36.............115 B3
Seamer Gr DN32.........153 A1
Sean La DN14.............65 F4
SEARBY 110 C8
Searby Hill DN38........110 D8
Searby Rd DN17...........96 C2
Searby Wold La DN38......99 E1
Sea Rd
Cleethorpes DN35........153 F2
Holmpton HU19............75 D3
Seascale Wlk DN32 ......152 F4
Seaside La HU12..........60 C2
Seaside Rd
Aldbrough HU11...........47 C2
Easington HU12...........91 A5
Holmpton HU19............75 C2
Withernsea HU19..........75 A7
Seathorne HU19...........74 F7
Seathorne Rd 1 YO16 ...122 C5
Seathorne Wlk YO16 .....122 B5
SEATON...................35 A1
Seaton Cl YO10 ....131 C4
SEATON COMMON...........39 D4
Seaton Gr
Grimsby DN32............153 A1
Kingston upon Hull HU4 ...144 E5
Seaton La YO25...........35 A4
Seaton Rd
Bewholme YO25............35 A4
Hornsea HU18............134 A4
Kingston upon Hull HU13 ..143 F2
Scunthorpe DN17.........150 D4
SEATON ROSS..............39 E4
Sea View St DN35........153 F1
Seavy Rd DN14...........149 B3
Seawall La DN36.........115 C5
Second Ave
Bridlington YO15.........123 A4
Fixborough Stather DN15 ...81 F1
4 Goole DN14.............149 C4
Grimsby DN33.............102 D2
Scunthorpe DN17..........150 C2
Ulrome YO25...............23 B3
York YO31.................130 F6
Second Comm La YO8 ....48 C4
Sedbergh Ave HU5........139 D3
Sedbury Cl 5 HU7.........56 F6
Sedgebrook Gr 18 HU7.....56 F6
Sedge Cl 4 DN18..........69 F1
Sedgewood Way 13 DN15 ..96 B7
Seed Close La 3 DN37...101 F1
Sefton Ave YO31.........130 F8
Sefton St 2 HU3.........145 B4
Seg La YO8...............63 F3
Segmere St DN35.........103 D3
Segrave Gr HU5..........144 D8
Segrave Wlk 10 YO26 ....129 E4
Selbourne Rd 5 DN34 ..102 C2
SELBY...................148 C6
Selby Abbey* YO8 ....148 D5
Selby Abbey CE Prim Sch
YO8 ....148 C5
Selby Bsns Pk YO8.......148 D1
Selby Cl 16 DN9 ....105 D6
Selby Coll YO8...........148 F3
Selby Coll (1811 Ctr)
YO8 ....148 C5
Selby Com Prim Sch
YO8 ....148 B5
Selby Ct DN17...........150 D3
Selby High Sch YO8......148 B4
Selby Ironworks Bsns Ctr
YO8 ....148 D5
Selby Rd
Eggborough DN14..........61 F1
Fulford YO19.............133 E6
Holme-on-Spalding-Moor
YO43......................39 F1
Howden DN14...............65 A7
Riccall YO19..............49 A8
Snaith DN14...............63 C1
Thorne DN8................92 F8
Wistow YO8................48 D6
Womersley DN14............77 A4
Selby Rly Sports Club
YO8 ....148 D5
Selby St HU3............145 A5
Selby Sta YO8...........148 D5
Selby War Memorial Hospl
YO8 ....148 B4
Seldon Rd YO26..........129 E5
Selge Way DN33..........102 C1
Selkirk St HU5..........145 A8
Sellers Dr HU17..........43 D6
Selmeston Ct DN34.......152 C2
Selset Way HU7..........140 D8
Selsey Cl 2 HU5.........140 D2
Selvage La DN14..........78 A6
Selwick Dr YO15...........5 D2
Selworthy Cl 3 HU7.......57 A5
Selwyn Ave 14 HU14.......69 A4
Selwyn Ct 10 DN34.......102 C3
Sennefleet Rd DN21......107 B4
Sequana Ct HU9..........146 B6
Seraphim Approach Rd
DN16 ....151 E5
Seraphim Rd
Brumby DN16..............151 E5
Scunthorpe DN16..........151 F4
Service Rd 1 12 DN37 ...102 C4
Service Rd 2 15 DN37 ...102 C4
Service Rd 3 17 DN37 ...102 C4
Service Rd 4 3 DN37 ....102 C4
Service Rd 5 4 DN37 ....102 C4
Service Rd 6 8 DN37 ....102 C4
Service Rd 7 9 DN37 ....102 C4
Service Rd 8 1 DN37 ....102 C5
Service Rd 9 2 DN37 ....102 C5
Service Rd 10 3 DN37 ...102 C5
Service Rd 11 4 DN37 ...102 C5
Service Rd 12 5 DN37 ...102 C5
Service Rd 13 6 DN37 ...102 C5
Service Rd 14 7 DN37 ...102 C5
Service Rd 15 19 DN37 ..102 C4
Service Rd 16 18 DN37 ..102 C4
Service Rd 17 10 DN37 ..102 C4
Service Rd 18 11 DN37 ..102 C4
Service Rd 19 13 DN37 ..102 C4
Service Rd 20 14 DN37 ..102 C4
Service Rd 21 13 DN37 ..102 B4
Service Rd 22 1 DN37 ...102 C4
Service Rd 23 2 DN37 ...102 C4
Service Rd 25 5 DN37 ...102 C4
Service Rd 26 8 DN37 ...102 C5
Service Rd No 1 DN32 ...152 F5
Service Rd No 2 DN32 ...152 F5
Services Rd DN16.......151 E6
Setterwood Garth 2
HU10 ....143 E8
Setting Cres 8 HU5 .....139 D2
Setting Rd HU5..........139 D2
Seven Corners La HU17 .136 D4
Seven Lakes Country Pk*
DN17 ....94 D6
Seven Quay Rd DN40.......87 D3
Seventh Ave
3 Bridlington YO15.......122 F4
Ulrome YO25...............23 B3
York YO31.................130 F5
Severn Gn YO26..........129 C8
Severn St HU8...........141 C1
Severus Ave YO24........129 D4
Severus St YO24.........129 D3
SEWERBY................123 A5
Sewerby Ave YO16........122 E5
Sewerby Cres YO16.......122 D5
Sewerby Ct 6 YO16......122 D5
Sewerby Hall & Gdns*
YO15 ....123 C7
Sewerby Headlands
YO16 ....122 F5
Sewerby Heads YO16......122 F5
Sewerby Park Cl YO15 ...123 C7
Sewerby Rd YO16.........122 D5
Sewerby Rise YO16.......122 E5
SEWERBY VILLAGE.........123 C6
Sewer La HU1............155 B1
Sextant Rd HU6..........140 C8
Seymour Gr YO31.........130 F6
Seymour Rd 6 HU12........73 C4
Seymour St HU3..........144 F5
Shadwell Rise 5 DN18.....69 E1
Shady La 3 YO25..........10 A2
Shaftesbury Ave
Goole DN14...............149 A5
Grimsby DN34.............152 B3
Hornsea HU18.............134 C5
Kellingley DN14............61 C3
Kingston upon Hull HU8 ...141 F4
Shaftesbury Mews 1
DN36 ....114 A7
Shaftesbury Rd YO15.....122 C1
Shakespeare Ave
2 Campsall DN6............76 E1
Scunthorpe DN17..........150 C2
Shakespeare Cl 6 HU3 ..145 D8
Shallowdale Gr 1 YO10 ..131 C3
Shannon Rd HU8..........142 C6
Shape Cl 52 HU12..........72 D7
Shardeloes HU11.........142 E5
Shardeloes Ct HU16......139 B6
Shardlow Rd HU18........134 C5
Sharow Dr HU4...........144 E4
Sharp Ave HU12...........73 A6
Sharpe Cl 20 DN18........84 E8
Sharpe Howe* YO11..........2 A8
Sharp Hill La YO8........63 F6
Sharps La HU17...........55 B7
Sharp St HU5............140 B2
Shaw Dr 1 DN33..........113 F8
Shawfield Cl 7 DN3.......92 A3
Shaw La DN6..............77 D2
Shaw Rd DN10............116 A2
Shaw St HU9.............146 B7
Shaw's Terr YO24........156 A1
Shears Ct DN37..........113 E7
Sheep Cote La DN7........92 D2
Sheepdike La YO25........21 F2
Sheep Dip La DN7.........92 C4
Sheep Dip Lane Prim Sch
DN7 ....92 D4
Sheepdyke La
Bonby DN20................84 C2
Hunmanby YO14...............3 A8
Sheepfold St DN32.......152 E3
Sheepman La YO25.........32 F7
Sheep Marsh La DN36.....115 B3
Sheeprake La YO15.......123 B8
Sheep Rake La YO25........8 F4
Sheepswarth La HU20......54 F3
Sheep Trod La HU12.......89 F6
Sheepwalk La YO17.........7 B7
Sheepwash La DN14........77 A7
Sheffield Park Ave DN15 ..96 C7
Sheffield St DN15.......151 A8
Sheffield Street E DN15 .151 A8
Sheffield Street W DN15 .150 F8
Sheldon Cl HU7..........141 B8
Sheldrake Way HU17......136 F6
Shelford Ave DN14........65 A7
Shelford St DN15........151 A7
Shelley Ave
Grimsby DN33.............102 D2
Kingston upon Hull HU9 ..142 C2
Shelley Gr YO30.........126 F1
Shelroy Cl DN15..........96 B7
Shenley Cl 11 DN7.........92 D3
Shepherd La HU17.........55 F8
Shepherd's Croft DN9....105 D7
Shepherds Lea 6 HU17.....55 E8
Shepherds Well HU15......54 A2
Shepherdton Mere YO25 ....9 B1
Sheraton Dr 3 DN36......114 D8
Sherbrooke Ave HU5......139 E4
Sherburn Cres DN15......150 D8
Sherburn Rd YO8.........148 A8
Sherburn St
1 Cawood YO8..............48 B8
Cleethorpes DN35.........153 F1
Kingston upon Hull HU9 ..146 D8
Sherbuttgate Dr 13 YO42 ..28 F4
Sherbuttgate Rd 14 YO42 ..28 F4
Sheriff Highway HU12.....72 C6
Sherringham Dr YO24.....132 D8
Sherwood Ave HU9........141 E1
Sherwood Cl
13 Norton DN6..............76 E1
4 Walkington HU17.........55 C8
Sherwood Ct HU11........142 D5
Sherwood Dr HU4.........144 A7
Sherwood Gr
Huntington YO32..........127 F1
York YO26................129 B6
Sherwood Rd DN34........102 C2
Sherwood Vale DN15......150 D7
Shetland Cl 6 HU8.......141 E7
Shetland Way 4 DN40.....101 C8
Shevington Wlk HU8......142 C6
Shields Rd 5 HU12........72 C7
Shildon Gr DN8...........79 C2
Shilling Cl 26 HU7........56 F5
Shilton Garth Cl 3 YO32 127 F7
Shinewater Park 18 HU7 ...56 E5
Shipcote Rd DN14........149 D1
Shipley Cl HU9..........142 C2
Shipman Rd YO43.........135 D3
SHIPTON..................12 F5
Shipton Cl HU9..........142 C5
Shipton Cres 6 HU17......43 D6
Shipton La YO43..........40 E3
Shipton Low Rd YO30......12 E5
Shipton Rd
Clifton YO30.............129 F8
Rawcliffe YO30...........126 D2
Scunthorpe DN16..........151 C1
York YO30................130 A7
Shipton St 3 YO30.......130 B7
SHIPTONTHORPE............40 F6
Shipyard Ind Est YO8....148 E5
Shipyard Rd YO8.........148 E5
Shirbutt La YO26..........24 C8
Shirley Ave YO26........129 C6
Shirley Cres DN16.......151 B4
Shoemaker's La DN21.....107 D5
Shopeth Way HU17.........56 B8
Shoreditch Cl 2 HU8.....141 F5
Shore Rd DN17............81 F5
Shorne Wood Park 2
HU7 ....56 E6
Shortacre La YO42........38 E2
Shorthill Croft HU17....154 A1
Short La
Acaster Selby YO23.........36 A4
Bempton YO16................4 C1
12 Bridlington YO16 .....122 C5
Fotherby LN11.............121 C2
West Haddlesey YO8.........61 F6
West Halton DN15...........82 E8
Short St DN35...........153 E2
Shorwell Cl 2 HU8.......142 C5
Shotel Cl YO30..........129 F8
Shropshire Cl HU5.......139 D1
Shrubberies The YO8......49 E2
Shuttleworth Ct HU18....134 D4
Sibelius Rd HU4.........144 B4
Sicey La HU6.............56 D7
Sidebottom St DN31......152 F6
Side La DN33............113 F8
Siding La YO8............49 B5
Sidings Ct HU15..........68 B5
Sidings The YO32.........14 B7
Sidmouth Prim Sch HU5 .140 B3
Sidmouth St HU5.........140 C3
Sidney Ct DN35..........153 B4
Sidney Pl DN35..........153 B4
Sidney Rd
Grimsby DN34..............152 B3
Scunthorpe DN17...........150 D2
Sidney St DN35..........153 B4
Sidney Way DN35.........153 B4
Sidsaph Hill 2 DN10.....116 D3
SIGGLESTHORNE............45 F8
Sigglesthorne CE Prim Sch
HU11 ....45 F8
Sigglesthorne Rd HU11 ...46 B6
Sigglesthorne Sta Nature
Reserve* HU11 ....46 B6
Signhills Ave 1 DN35....103 D2
Signhills Jun & Inf Sch
DN35 ....103 D2
Sigston Rd HU17.........154 C4
Silica Cres DN17........150 D1
Silkstone Oval 15 DN8 ....79 B2
Silkstone Wlk HU8.......141 C1
Sills La YO30.............12 B6
Silsden Ave 5 HU6.......140 C7
Silverbell Cl 2 DN16.....96 F2
Silver Birch Rise 22 DN16 .96 D2
Silverdale Ct YO24......132 D7
Silverdale Rd HU6.......140 C6
Silvergarth DN32........153 A1
Silversides La DN20......98 A1
Silver St
Barnetby le Wold DN38......99 B4
Barrow upon Humber DN19 .85 C7
Holton le Clay DN36 ......114 A5
Huggate YO42...............18 C2
Kingston upon Hull HU1 ...155 B2
Owston Ferry DN9..........106 B2
3 Riccall YO19..............49 A8
1 Stainforth DN7............92 C6
24 Thorne/Moorends DN8....93 A8
Whitley DN14................77 A7
Winteringham DN15...........68 B1
York YO1....................156 B2
Silvertree Wlk DN14.....149 F6
Silvester St HU1........155 B3
Sim Balk La YO23........132 E5
Simon Howe YO12...........1 A5
Simons Pl DN35..........153 D3
Simpson Ave 6 YO14........2 F8
Simpson Cl DN19...........85 D8
Simpson's Fold Ct 8
DN36 ....113 F7
Simson Ct HU17..........154 B4
Sinclair Cres HU8.......141 F6
Sinderby Wlk HU5........139 D4
Sinderson Rd 18 DN36 ...103 D1
Sir Henry Cooper Sch
HU6 ....56 D5
Sirius Cl 3 HU3.........145 B5
Sirius Ct YO16..........122 C4
Sir James Reckitt Haven
HU8 ....141 C1
Sir John Nelthorpe Sch
DN20 ....98 C2
Sirocco Ct YO31.........130 D8
Siskin Cres DN16..........96 D1
Sissons La HU15..........53 B1
Sissons Way HU5.........140 E3
Sittingbourne Cl HU8....141 E8
Sitwell Gr YO26.........129 C5
Sitwell St HU8..........155 C4
Siwards Howe* YO10........131 B1
Siward St YO10..........131 A3
Siward's Way YO10.......131 A2
Sixhills St DN32........152 F3
Sixth Ave
Bridlington YO15...........122 F4
Fixborough Stather DN15 ...82 A1
Scunthorpe DN17...........150 B2
Ulrome YO25.................23 B3
York YO31..................130 E5
Skeckling Cl HU12.........73 A6
SKEFFLING..................90 C6
Skeffling Rd HU12.........90 B7
Skeldergate YO1.........156 B2
SKELTON
Goole........................65 C4
SKELTON *continued*
York........................126 C
Skelton Ave HU5..........139 E
Skelton Broad La DN14.....65 C
Skelton Cres YO43........135 C
Skelton Ct 3 YO30........130 A
Skelton La YO32...........126 D
Skelton Park Trading Est
YO30 ....127 B
Skelton Prim Sch YO30...126 C
Skelton Rd DN17..........150 C
SKERNE.....................21 A
Skerne Rd YO25...........124 F
Skern Gr HU9.............142 A
Skewsby Gr YO31..........127 F
SKIDBY....................138 B
Skidby Carr La HU6.........56 C
Skidby CE Prim Sch
HU16 ....138 A
Skidby Gr HU6............139 F
Skidby Rd HU20............55 A
Skidby Windmill & Mus of
East Riding Rural Life*
HU16 ....138 C
Skiddaw YO24.............132 C
Skiff La YO43..............52 C
Skilgate Cl 7 HU7..........57 A
Skillings La HU15..........68 C
Skinners La
3 South Ferriby DN18........84 A
Waltham DN37...............113 E
Skipper La YO25.............1 E
Skippingdale Rd DN15......96 C
SKIPSEA....................23 B
Skipsea Castle* YO25.......23 A
Skipsea La YO25............23 A
Skipsea Prim Sch YO25 ....23 B
Skipsea Rd
Atwick YO25..................35 C
Beeford YO25.................22 D
Bewholme YO25...............35 A
SKIPWITH...................37 E
Skipwith Cl HU6...........140 B
Skipwith Comm* YO8.........49 E
Skipwith Rd YO19...........37 B
Skirbeck Rd HU8...........141 D
SKIRLAUGH..................45 E
Skirlaugh CE Prim Sch
HU11 ....45 E
Skirlaugh Rd
Ellerby HU11..................45 F
Swine HU11...................57 E
Skirlaw Cl 18 DN14.........65 A
SKIRPENBECK................16 A
Skitter Rd DN40.............86 D
Skylark Cl YO25...........125 A
Skylark Dr DN16.............96 D
Slack The DN17..............94 D
Slay Pit Cl DN7.............92 F
Slay Pit La DN7.............92 F
Sleaford Ave 3 HU9........142 E
SLEDMERE....................7 B
Sledmere CE Prim Sch
YO25 ....7 B
Sledmere Gr HU4...........144 E
Sledmere House* YO25........7 B
Sledmere Rd YO25............8 B
Sleightholme Cl 21 HU7....56 F
Sleights Cl HU3...........145 A
Sleights La
Acklam YO17..................16 E
Broomfleet HU15..............67 B
Eastrington DN14.............51 E
Slessor Rd YO24...........129 B
Slingsby Cl HU5...........139 D
Slingsby Gr YO24..........132 E
Sloe La HU17..............136 D
Sluice La DN15..............83 D
Sluice Rd DN18..............83 F
Smales' St YO1............156 B
Smary La YO19...............26 D
Smeatley's La WF8...........76 C
Smeaton Gr YO26...........129 C
Smeaton Rd YO41.............27 D
Smedley Cl HU17...........154 C
Smithall Rd HU17..........136 E
Smith Cl YO10.............133 F
Smith Field 4 DN36........114 B
Smithfield Rd DN16........151 D
Smithie Cl YO32...........127 D
Smith St
Grimsby DN31................152 F
Scunthorpe DN15.............150 F
Smithy La 7 DN38............99 B
Smitton St DN31............153 A
Smook Hills Rd (Pearcy La)
HU19 ....75 A
Smythy La YO25...............1 D
Snainton Gr 4 HU5.........144 D
SNAITH......................63 C
Snaith Prim Sch DN14.......78 C
Snaith Rd
Pollington DN14...............77 F
Rawcliffe DN14................64 A
Snaith DN14...................78 D
Snaith Sch The DN14.........78 B
Snaith Sta DN14..............63 C
Snatchells La DN14..........78 C
Snowdon Cl YO23..............24 D
Snowdonia Ave DN15..........96 B
Snowdon Way HU7..............57 A
Snowdrop Garth YO42..........40 A
Snowhill Cl 4 HU7............57 A
Snuff Mill La HU16..........139 B
Sober Hill Dr YO43...........40 A
Soft La DN19..................86 A
Solomon Ct DN35.............153 D
SOMERBY......................99 B

merby Dr 3 DN9 106 A3
merby Gn DN38 99 C1
merby Rd DN17 150 D1
merby Wold La DN38 99 C1
merden Rd HU9 147 E7
mersby St DN31 152 D4
merscales St HU3 155 A4
merset Cl 6 YO30 126 E3
merset Dr 6 DN15 82 B4
merset Rd YO31 130 D8
merset St HU3 145 A5
merton Dr DN7 92 F4
merton Rd DN40 87 C1
mervell Rd DN16 151 C1
nia Crest DN40 87 B1
phia Ave 7 DN33 102 E1
phia Cl HU2 155 A4
rbus Ct 5 HU3 145 D6
rbus View 4 HU5 144 C7
rrel Cl HU17 136 E1
rrel Dr 5 HU5 144 D8
rrell La DN14 78 D1
rrel Way DN15 96 B7
ss La DN10 116 D5
therton St DN14 149 D4
ur La DN8 92 E8
utergate 12 DN18 69 F1
uth Ave YO25 31 F2
outh Axholme Com Sch DN9 105 D6
outh Back La YO16 122 B4
OUTH BANK 130 A1
outh Bank DN17 95 D6
outh Bank Ave YO23 130 B1
OUTH BRAMWITH 92 B6
outh Bridge Rd HU9 155 C1
OUTHBURN 20 B1
outhburn Ave HU5 144 E7
outhburn Rd
Bainton YO25 32 A8
Kirkburn YO25 20 A1
outh Carr Dales Rd HU19 75 A4
outh Carr La DN20 109 B4
outh Carr Rd DN20 109 A4
outh Carrs HU17 45 A8
OUTH CAVE 54 A2
outh Cave CE Prim Sch HU15 53 F1
outh Cave Sports Ctr HU15 53 F1
outh Church Side
2 Easington HU12 90 F6
Kingston upon Hull HU1 155 B2
outh Cl
7 Kilham YO25 9 C3
Kingston upon Hull HU6 140 C6
OUTH CLIFFE 53 B7
outhcliffe Rd 12 DN21 107 C3
outhcliff Rd HU19 75 A6
outh Cliff Rd
4 Bridlington YO15 122 E2
Kirton in Lindsey DN21 108 B1
outhcoates Ave HU9 141 E2
outhcoates La HU9 146 E8
outhcoates Prim Sch HU9 141 F1
outhcote Cl 4 HU15 54 A2
outhcroft Dr 8 HU8 141 E7
outh Dale LN7 111 B4
outh-Dale Cl 1 DN21 108 B2
OUTH DALTON 42 E8
outh Down Rd 3 YO32 127 F5
outh Dr YO25 31 C4
OUTH DUFFIELD 50 A4
outh Duffield Rd YO8 49 C4
outh Ella Dr HU10 143 D7
outh Ella Farm Ct HU10 143 D6
outh Ella Way HU10 143 D7
OUTH END
Hornsea 46 D3
Patrington 90 F5
outh End
Seaton Ross YO42 39 E3
South Ferriby DN18 84 A7
Thorne/Moorends DN8 93 A7
Wike Well End DN8 93 B7
outh End La DN14 77 B4
outh End Rd
Ottringham HU12 73 E3
Roos HU12 60 B1
Southern Dr HU4 144 C5
Southern Way DN40 87 C3
Southern Wlk DN33 113 E8
South Esplanade YO1 156 B1
South Farm Rd HU12 88 D5
SOUTH FERRIBY 84 B7
South Ferriby Prim Sch DN18 84 A7
SOUTH FIELD 69 E4
Southfield
1 Belton DN9 94 E1
Kingston upon Hull HU13 69 E4
Southfield Cl
Great Driffield YO25 124 F6
Rufforth YO23 24 D6
14 Thorne/Moorends DN8 93 B7
Ulceby DN39 86 B1
Wetwang YO25 19 B5
Southfield Cres 2 YO24 132 E8
South Field Ct 5 HU16 138 F5
Southfield Dr
1 Beverley HU17 137 A6
4 Epworth DN9 105 D6
North Ferriby HU14 69 A4
Southfield La
Barmston YO25 23 A6
Southfield La *continued*
Elstronwick HU12 59 C3
Everingham YO42 40 B4
Kellington DN14 61 E2
Roos HU12 60 C1
Seaton Ross YO42 39 D1
Skipsea YO25 23 B2
Willoughton DN21 119 A3
Southfield Pk YO43 135 D3
Southfield Rd
1 Broughton DN20 97 D3
8 Crowle DN17 94 D7
Elstronwick HU12 59 A2
Great Driffield YO25 124 F6
Grimsby DN33 113 E8
15 Holton le Clay DN36 114 A5
Kingston upon Hull HU5 140 A2
North Kelsey LN7 109 E2
Pocklington YO42 28 F4
Scunthorpe DN16 151 C1
Thorne/Moorends DN8 93 B7
Wetwang YO25 19 A5
Winterton DN15 82 F5
Southfields HU15 52 E1
Southfields Rd YO32 14 B7
Southfield Well Balk YO25 19 B5
South Furlong Croft 17 DN9 105 E6
Southgate
Hornsea HU18 134 C3
Kingston upon Hull HU13 143 E1
Market Weighton YO43 135 E3
2 Scunthorpe DN15 151 B7
South Gate YO25 32 E6
Southgate Cl HU10 138 E2
Southgate Ct YO43 135 D4
Southgate Gdns 2 HU18 134 C3
South Glebe YO25 32 B1
South Gr 8 YO25 9 C3
South Holderness Sports Ctr HU12 72 D8
South Holderness Tech Coll HU12 72 D8
South Humberside Ind Est DN31 152 A5
South Hunsley Sch HU14 68 E5
South Ings La HU15 53 C2
South Intake La DN9 116 F7
SOUTH KELSEY 110 A1
SOUTH KILLINGHOLME 86 E3
South La
Bishop Wilton YO42 16 F1
Burton Fleming YO25 2 E2
Cawood YO8 48 B7
Kingston upon Hull HU13 143 E1
South Landing Nature Reserve* YO15 5 A1
Southlands
4 Haxby YO32 13 E5
16 Hemingbrough YO8 49 F1
Southlands Ave 1 DN21 117 A2
Southlands Cl YO19 37 B6
Southlands Dr 3 DN21 117 A2
Southlands Gdns 2 DN21 117 A2
Southlands Rd YO23 130 B2
South Lawn Way HU14 68 F5
South Leys Rd HU19 75 A4
South Marine Dr YO15 122 D1
South Marsh Rd DN41 101 F7
Southmoor La WF11 61 B1
Southmoor Rd
Crowle DN17 94 C8
Thorganby YO19 37 F5
South Moor Rd DN10 116 C3
SOUTH NEWBALD 53 F6
South Newbald Rd YO43 53 F7
Southolme Dr 7 YO30 126 F1
South Orbital Trading Pk HU9 146 C7
Southorpe Cl YO16 122 B5
Southorpe La DN21 118 D7
Southorpe Nature Reserve* HU11 46 D8
Southorpe Rd HU11 134 A1
South Osbourne Way DN40 87 C2
South Parade
Grimsby DN31 152 D4
Leven HU17 45 A7
8 Selby YO8 148 C5
Thorne DN8 93 A7
York YO23 156 A1
South Park Rd DN17 96 B2
South Parkway 4 DN14 78 C8
South Pk HU12 60 B1
South Prom HU18 134 D4
South Rd
Keadby with Althorpe DN17 95 C6
Thorne/Moorends DN8 79 B2
South Rise HU16 138 B8
South Rise Cres 20 DN17 96 C2
South Ruddings La YO19 37 F7
South St Mary's Gate 4 DN31 152 D3
South Sea Ave 26 YO15 5 A2
South Sea La DN36 114 D7
South Sea Mews YO15 5 A2
South Sea Rd YO15 5 A2
Southside HU12 74 D1
South Side
Kilham YO25 9 B3
Winteringham DN15 68 A1
South Side La YO25 9 F6
Southside Rd HU12 73 F5
South St
Barmby on the Marsh DN14 64 A7
Barnetby le Wold DN38 99 B4
Bridlington YO15 122 E1
Burton Fleming YO25 2 E2
Cottingham HU16 139 A6
8 Gainsborough DN21 117 A2
Goole DN14 149 C2
Keelby DN41 101 A5
Kingston upon Hull HU1 155 A2
Leven HU17 45 A7
Middleton-on-the-Wolds YO25 31 C4
North Kelsey LN7 110 A4
Owston Ferry DN9 106 B2
Roxby cum Risby DN15 82 F3
West Butterwick DN17 106 D8
Winterton DN15 83 A5
South Townside Rd YO25 34 A8
South View
Broughton DN20 97 D4
Grimsby DN34 152 A2
Healaugh LS24 24 A2
Holton le Clay DN36 114 B5
6 Humberston DN36 103 D1
Kingston upon Hull HU4 144 B6
South View Ave
Brigg DN20 98 C2
Burringham DN17 95 D4
Southwell Ave HU9 147 E8
Southwell Cl HU17 136 E1
South Wold HU20 55 A4
Southwold Cres 25 DN33 113 E8
Southwood Ave HU16 138 F6
Southwood Dr HU16 139 A6
South Wood Dr 12 DN8 93 A7
Southwood Gdns HU16 138 F5
Southwood Pk YO25 20 D2
Southwood Rd
Kingston upon Hull HU16 138 F5
Sutton upon Derwent YO41 38 C8
Soutter Gate HU12 72 C7
Sovereign Cl 14 DN34 102 B2
Sovereign Way 7 HU7 56 E5
Sowerby Rd YO26 129 D4
Sowers La DN15 83 A5
Sow Hill Rd HU17 154 A3
Spa Hill DN21 108 B1
Spalding Ave YO30 130 B7
Spalding Rd DN16 151 B4
SPALDINGTON 51 C4
Spa Prom The YO15 122 E1
Spark Mill La HU17 154 C1
Sparkmill Terr HU17 154 C2
Spark St DN34 152 A3
Sparrowcroft La DN14 66 E3
Spa The* YO15 122 E1
Spawd Bone La 27 WF11 61 A2
Spa Well La DN14 78 C8
Speculation St YO1 130 E4
Speedwell Cres DN15 96 B7
Speedwell La 1 HU17 55 D8
SPEETON 3 F5
Speeton Gate YO15 4 B4
Spellowgate YO25 20 C7
Spellowgate Cl YO25 124 D5
Spencer Ave DN15 150 F8
Spencer Cl
22 Hedon HU12 72 C7
Kingston upon Hull HU16 138 F6
Spencers Mead YO25 124 E3
Spencer St
Beverley HU17 154 A3
Grimsby DN31 153 B5
Kingston upon Hull HU2 155 A3
3 York YO23 156 B1
Spencers Way YO25 124 E4
Spencer Way 1 HU16 139 B7
Speng La YO23 24 B4
Spen La
Holme-on-Spalding-Moor YO43 39 F2
York YO1 156 C3
Spenser St DN14 149 C5
Sperrin Cl 2 HU9 142 A3
Spey Bank YO24 132 C6
Spicer's Rd HU12 72 C6
Spilsby Rd DN17 150 E1
Spindle Cl YO24 132 C8
Spindlewood 1 HU15 68 C7
Spinnaker Cl HU3 145 D5
Spinney Cl 2 DN40 87 C1
Spinney Croft Cl 12 HU14 69 A5
Spinney The
1 Barnby Dun DN3 92 A3
8 Barrow upon Humber DN19 85 D8
Brigg DN20 98 C1
28 Gainsborough DN21 117 C1
Grimsby DN34 152 C3
Kingston upon Hull HU16 139 A5
6 Newport HU15 52 F1
7 Swanland HU14 69 B7
York YO24 132 F7
Spinney Wlk HU4 144 C6
Spire Hull & East Riding Hospl HU10 143 E5
Spire View
21 Hemingbrough YO8 49 F1
1 Kingston upon Hull HU13 143 E1
Spital Hill DN21 117 B1
SPITAL IN THE STREET 119 E1
Spital Terr DN21 117 B1
Spittlerush La DN6 76 D2
Sport Rd DN16 151 E6
Spout Hill HU15 68 C8
Spratton Ct 2 DN37 102 B2
Springbank DN20 98 C2
Spring Bank
Grimsby DN34 152 A3
Kingston upon Hull HU3 155 A3
4 North Newbald YO43 53 F7
Springbank Ave
Dunnington YO19 26 E7
Hornsea HU18 134 B4
Spring Bank W HU5 144 D7
Springbok Cl HU4 144 D2
Springburn St HU3 145 A5
Spring Cl YO25 124 D5
Spring Cottage Prim Sch HU8 141 F6
Springdale Cl HU10 143 F8
Springdale Rd YO43 135 E5
Springdale Way HU17 154 A1
Springfield
Holme-on-Spalding-Moor YO43 40 A1
6 Howden DN14 65 B7
Springfield Ave
Bridlington YO15 122 E2
18 Brough HU15 68 C6
5 Hatfield DN7 92 E4
Springfield Cl
Barlby with Osgodby YO8 49 B5
Heworth YO31 131 C7
2 Scunthorpe DN16 151 C2
Spring Field Cl HU11 45 F8
Springfield Cres 3 WF8 76 C3
Springfield Dr
9 Barlby YO8 49 B5
Beverley HU17 137 A6
Springfield Gdns YO43 40 A1
Springfield Prim Sch DN33 113 D8
Springfield Rd
26 Brigg DN20 98 C2
Grimsby DN33 113 D8
Kingston upon Hull HU3 144 F6
Pocklington YO42 29 B3
4 Poppleton YO26 12 F1
Springfield Rise DN20 98 D2
Springfields 18 WF11 61 A2
Springfields Ave 17 WF11 61 A2
Springfield Way
Hook DN14 149 F6
Kingston upon Hull HU10 143 F7
York YO31 131 B7
Spring Gardens E HU4 144 B6
Spring Gardens S HU4 144 B5
Spring Gardens W HU4 144 B6
Spring Gdns
Goole DN14 149 E4
Kingston upon Hull HU8 141 D5
Spring Gr HU3 145 A7
Springhead Ave HU5 144 A7
Springhead Cl 6 DN14 65 A7
Springhead Ct HU10 144 A6
Springhead Gdns HU5 144 A7
Springhead La HU5 144 A7
Springhead Prim Sch HU10 143 F7
Spring La
2 Buckton/Bempton YO15 4 D3
11 Laceby DN37 101 F1
Long Marston YO26 24 A5
York YO10 131 A1
Spring Rd 1 YO43 135 E4
Springs Rd DN10 104 C1
Spring St
Immingham DN40 87 C1
Kingston upon Hull HU2 155 A3
Springs Way DN20 98 B2
Springthorpe Rd DN21 118 B1
Spring Vale HU11 142 D5
Springville Ave HU13 143 F2
Springway Cres DN34 152 A3
Spring Wlk YO8 148 A1
Springwood YO32 127 D7
Springwood Cres 7 DN33 113 D8
Springwood Gr
Knapton YO26 129 C6
16 Welton HU15 68 D6
SPROATLEY 58 C5
Sproatley Endowed Prim Sch HU11 58 D5
Sproatley Rd HU12 58 D3
Spruce Cl YO32 127 D2
Spruce La DN39 86 A1
Spruce Rd
Kingston upon Hull HU1 155 A1
Leven HU17 45 B8
Spurn Ave 16 DN33 113 E8
Spurn Lightship* YO23 155 B1
Spurn National Nature Reserve* HU12 91 D6
Spurn Rd HU12 91 B2
Spurr Ct YO24 132 C8
Spurriergate YO1 156 B2
Spurr Rd DN39 99 F5
Spyvee St HU8 155 C3
Square The
4 Easington HU12 90 F6
Goxhill DN19 86 A8
Kingston upon Hull HU10 138 D1
Kingston upon Hull HU13 143 E1
Skerne & Wansford YO25 21 C3
Yapham YO42 28 E7
Squire La YO16 122 C4
Stable La 4 DN18 69 E1
Stabler Cl 15 YO32 13 D5
Stable Rd YO8 63 D7
Stablers Wlk YO32 127 F7
STADDLETHORPE 66 D7
Staddlethorpe Broad La HU15 66 D7
Stafford St
6 Kingston upon Hull HU2 140 E1
Kingston upon Hull HU2 155 A4
Staindale Cl YO30 126 E2
Staindale Rd DN16 151 E1
Staines Cl HU8 142 A4
STAINFORTH 92 C7
Stainforth Moor Rd DN7 93 C3
Stainforth Rd DN7 92 A5
Stainton Dr
Grimsby DN33 102 D2
15 Immingham DN40 87 B1
9 Scunthorpe DN17 96 C2
Staithes Cl 4 YO26 129 B4
Staithes Rd HU12 72 B8
Staithe St 3 YO8 50 D7
STALLINGBOROUGH 101 E6
Stallingborough CE Prim Sch DN41 101 E6
Stallingborough Rd
Healing DN41 101 E5
Immingham DN40 87 B1
Keelby DN41 101 A5
Stallingborough Sta DN41 101 E6
Stalybridge Ave HU9 142 E1
STAMFORD BRIDGE 15 E2
Stamford Bridge Prim Sch YO41 15 D2
Stamford Bridge Rd YO19 26 E7
Stamford Bridge W YO41 15 C2
Stamford Gr HU9 142 E1
Stamford Street E 10 YO26 129 F5
Stamford Street W 8 YO26 129 F5
Stamford Wlk YO16 122 C2
Stanage Wlk DN32 152 F4
Stanbury Rd HU6 140 C7
Standage Rd 12 HU12 72 E5
Standidge Dr HU8 142 A5
Standish La 1 DN40 87 B2
Stanfield Rd 2 DN9 105 D6
Stanford Cl DN37 101 F1
Stanford Jun & Inf Sch DN37 101 F1
Stanholme La DN36 114 A1
Stanhope Ave HU9 141 E2
Stanhope Pl DN35 153 C3
Stanhope St DN14 149 C4
Staniland Dr YO8 148 A5
Staniland Way 1 DN36 114 D8
Staniwell Rise DN17 150 D3
Staniwells Dr 9 DN20 97 D3
Stanley Ave
Haxby YO32 127 D7
Hornsea HU18 134 C2
Stanley Gdns
Bridlington YO16 122 D6
15 Stainforth DN7 92 C6
Stanley Rd
Scunthorpe DN15 150 C7
16 Stainforth DN7 92 C6
Stanley St
Goole DN14 149 D4
Grimsby DN32 153 A4
Kingston upon Hull HU3 145 C7
York YO31 156 C4
Stannington Dr HU8 142 D6
Stansfield Cl HU9 142 D1
Stansted St DN31 152 B5
Stan Valley 2 WF8 76 C3
Stapleford Cl 4 HU9 142 E2
Staple Rd DN40 86 F3
Starboard Ave HU6 140 C8
Starcarr La YO25 34 A1
Star Carr La DN20 98 C4
Starella Gr HU3 145 A4
Starham Rd LN7 109 C4
Star Hill Rd YO25 124 F5
Starkbridge La DN14 78 A3
Starkey Cres YO31 131 A5
Startforth Wlk HU5 139 E3
Stather Rd
Burton upon Stather DN15 82 A5
Flixborough DN15 82 A1
Stathers Wlk 3 HU10 143 F6
Station App
Bridlington YO15 122 E2
Cleethorpes DN35 153 F3
Station Ave
10 Bridlington YO16 122 D3
New Earswick YO32 127 D3
New Waltham DN36 114 A7
York YO1 156 A2
Station Bsns Pk YO26 129 F4
Station Ct
33 Canal Side DN8 93 A8
46 Hatfield DN7 92 D4
Hornsea HU18 134 D4
Station Dr HU3 140 D1
Station Hill YO25 19 B6
Station La
Barmby on the Marsh DN14 64 B7
Cliffe YO8 49 E3
Hedon HU12 72 C8
Holme-on-Spalding-Moor YO43 39 F1
Searby cum Owmby DN38 110 D7
Shipton YO30 12 E5
Station Mews HU18 134 D4

Station Rd
Bainton YO25 ..... 31 E6
Blyton DN21 ..... 117 F6
Bridlington YO15 ..... 122 D2
Brough HU15 ..... 68 B5
Burringham DN17 ..... 95 D4
7 Burstwick HU12 ..... 73 A6
Burton Agnes YO25 ..... 10 A1
Carlton DN14 ..... 63 C3
Cleethorpes DN35 ..... 153 E3
Copmanthorpe YO23 ..... 132 B2
Cottingham HU13 ..... 143 E1
East Halton DN40 ..... 86 D7
Eastrington DN14 ..... 65 F8
Epworth DN9 ..... 105 D7
Fulstow LN11 ..... 121 D7
Garthorpe & Fockerby DN17 81 E6
Garton YO25 ..... 20 A5
Gilberdyke HU15 ..... 66 D8
Grasby DN38 ..... 110 E6
Grimsby DN37 ..... 102 B5
Gunness DN15 ..... 95 E5
Habrough DN40 ..... 100 E8
Harpham YO25 ..... 21 E8
Hatfield DN7 ..... 92 D4
Haxby YO32 ..... 13 F5
Haxey DN9 ..... 116 C7
Healing DN41 ..... 101 F5
Hensall DN14 ..... 62 C1
Holton le Clay DN36 ..... 114 A4
Howden DN14 ..... 65 B8
Hutton Cranswick YO25 ..... 32 E7
Keadby with Althorpe DN17 .95 D6
Keyingham HU12 ..... 73 C4
Killingholme High DN40 ..... 87 B5
Kingston upon Hull HU16 . 139 C7
Kirton in Lindsey DN21 ..... 108 B2
Lockington YO25 ..... 32 D1
Ludborough DN36 ..... 121 B6
Market Weighton YO43 ... 135 D4
Middleton YO25 ..... 31 C5
Misterton DN10 ..... 116 D5
Nafferton YO25 ..... 125 F6
New Waltham DN36 ..... 114 A7
North Cave HU15 ..... 53 D3
North End DN19 ..... 71 A1
North Ferriby HU14 ..... 69 A4
North Kelsey LN7 ..... 110 A4
North Thoresby DN36 ..... 114 B1
Norton DN6 ..... 76 F2
Ottringham HU12 ..... 73 F4
Owston Ferry DN9 ..... 106 A2
Patrington HU12 ..... 74 C2
Pocklington YO42 ..... 29 A3
24 Poppleton YO26 ..... 12 F1
Preston HU12 ..... 72 C8
Rawcliffe DN14 ..... 64 A1
Riccall YO19 ..... 49 A8
Scawby DN20 ..... 108 F7
Scunthorpe DN15 ..... 151 B6
Selby YO8 ..... 148 D5
South Cave HU15 ..... 54 A2
South Kelsey LN7 ..... 110 D2
South Killingholme DN40 ..... 87 A5
Stallingborough DN41 ..... 101 D6
Thorngumbald HU12 ..... 73 A5
Thornton Curtis DN39 ..... 85 F5
Ulceby DN39 ..... 86 B1
Walkeringham DN10 ..... 116 D3
Waltham DN37 ..... 113 E7
Wharram YO17 ..... 6 A4
Whitton DN15 ..... 67 D3
Wistow YO8 ..... 48 C6
5 Withernsea HU19 ..... 75 A6
Womersley DN6 ..... 76 D5
York YO24 ..... 156 A2
Station Rise YO1 ..... 156 A2
Station Sq 4 YO32 ..... 14 B7
Station St DN10 ..... 116 C5
Station View
Cliffe YO8 ..... 49 D3
Little Weighton HU20 ..... 55 A4
Staunton Pk HU7 ..... 56 E5
Staveley Rd HU9 ..... 142 C3
Staves Ct 10 DN36 ..... 114 D4
Staxton Ct HU9 ..... 146 D8
Staxton Hill YO12 ..... 1 C8
Staynor Ave YO8 ..... 148 E3
Steadings The DN15 ..... 82 B1
Steele Cl YO43 ..... 135 D3
Steep Hill HU15 ..... 54 B2
Steeping Dr 11 DN40 ..... 87 B1
Steeple Cl 4 YO32 ..... 13 D5
Steeton Ave 4 HU6 ..... 140 C7
Stembridge Cl 1 HU9 ..... 142 E1
Stephen Cl 2 DN39 ..... 86 A1
Stephen Cres
14 Barton-upon-Humber DN18 ..... 84 F8
Grimsby DN34 ..... 102 C2
10 Humberston DN36 ..... 114 C8
Stephenson Cl
37 Hedon HU12 ..... 72 D7
Market Weighton YO43 ... 135 C3
York YO31 ..... 127 E1
Stephenson St HU9 ..... 141 E1
Stephenson's Wlk HU16. 139 D6
Stephenson Way YO26 ..... 129 F5
Stephen's Wlk YO8 ..... 148 B1
Stephenwath La YO41 ..... 16 C5
Stepney Ave 13 YO16 ..... 122 C5
Stepney Gr YO16 ..... 122 C4
Stepney Ind Est HU17 ..... 137 B4
Stepney La HU5 ..... 140 E1
Stepney Prim Sch HU5 ..... 140 E1
Sterling Cres DN37 ..... 113 D6
Sterling Pk YO30 ..... 127 A3
Sterne Ave
7 Broughton DN20 ..... 97 D3
York YO31 ..... 131 A5
Stevenson Pl DN35 ..... 153 D1
Stevenson's Way 18 DN18 .84 E8
Steward Cl YO8 ..... 48 D1
Stewart Garth HU16 ..... 138 E6
Stewart La YO19 ..... 36 C4
Steynburg St HU9 ..... 141 D1
STILLINGFLEET 36 C3
Stirling Cl 2 DN21 ..... 117 C1
Stirling Gr YO10 ..... 133 F8
Stirling Rd
Barmby Moor YO42 ..... 28 E3
York YO30 ..... 126 F3
Stirling St
Grimsby DN31 ..... 153 B5
Kingston upon Hull HU3 ... 144 F6
Stirrup Cl YO24 ..... 132 B8
Stockbridge Ave HU9 ..... 142 E1
Stockbridge La YO25 ..... 32 F6
Stockbridge Pk 2 HU15 ..... 68 C7
Stockbridge Rd HU15 ..... 68 B7
Stockham Ct 21 DN33 ..... 102 D1
Stockhill Cl 1 YO19 ..... 26 E7
Stockholm Cl 1 YO10 ..... 133 D8
Stockholm Pk 23 HU12 ..... 72 D7
Stockholm Rd
Kingston upon Hull HU7 ... 140 E5
16 Thorngumbald HU12 ..... 72 E5
Stocking La
Hillam LS25 ..... 61 B7
Knottingley WF11 ..... 61 B2
Stockleigh Cl HU7 ..... 140 F8
Stocks Dr DN14 ..... 79 B8
Stocks Hill
Belton DN9 ..... 94 E1
Huggate YO42 ..... 18 C1
Ludborough DN36 ..... 121 B6
Stockshill Rd DN16 ..... 151 C2
Stockton Hall Hospl YO32 .14 D3
Stockton La
Heworth YO32 ..... 128 D1
York YO31 ..... 131 A7
STOCKTON ON THE FOREST 14 D3
Stockton on the Forest Prim Sch YO32 ..... 14 D3
Stockwell Gr HU9 ..... 147 E8
Stockwell La 13 YO25 ..... 34 B2
Stockwell Prim Sch HU9 .147 E8
Stockwith La DN14 ..... 63 A4
Stockwith Rd
Haxey DN9 ..... 105 E1
Owston Ferry DN9 ..... 116 E8
Walkeringham DN10 ..... 116 D3
Walkerith DN21 ..... 116 E4
Stoke St HU2 ..... 155 A4
Stonebow The YO1 ..... 156 C2
Stonebridge Ave HU9 ... 142 D1
Stone Bridge Dr YO41 ..... 27 F5
Stonecarr Ct 2 HU7 ..... 56 F7
Stone Creek HU12 ..... 88 C5
Stone Dale YO42 ..... 17 D3
STONEFERRY 141 B3
Stoneferry Prim Sch HU8 ..... 141 A3
Stoneferry Rd HU8 ..... 141 A2
Stonegate
Hunmanby YO14 ..... 2 F8
Thorne/Moorends DN8 ..... 93 A8
York YO1 ..... 156 B3
Stonegate Cl 3 HU8 ..... 141 D7
Stone Hill DN7 ..... 93 A4
Stone Hill Rd DN7 ..... 93 A4
Stoneknowle Hill YO43 ..... 54 A8
Stone La DN17 ..... 95 D4
Stonelands Ct 2 YO30 .. 127 A1
Stonepit Balk YO17 ..... 6 C5
Stonepit Hill YO17 ..... 6 C4
Stonepit La YO15 ..... 4 E3
Stonepit Rd HU15 ..... 54 A1
Stone Riggs YO32 ..... 14 D2
Stones Cl YO24 ..... 129 E2
Stonesdale HU7 ..... 141 A6
Stones Mount HU16 ..... 139 A7
Stonethwaite 5 YO24 ... 132 C7
Stonewall Cottage La 25 YO41 ..... 15 D2
Stoney La HU15 ..... 53 A3
Stoney Way DN36 ..... 114 D4
Stony Cl DN7 ..... 92 C7
Stony La HU15 ..... 53 A2
Stool Close Rd DN9 ..... 94 E1
Stoop Cl YO32 ..... 127 C8
Storkhill Rd HU17 ..... 154 C4
Storking La YO41 ..... 27 F6
Stornaway Sq HU8 ..... 141 F7
Stortford St DN31 ..... 152 B5
Story St HU1 ..... 155 A3
Stothards La 1 DN19 ..... 86 A8
Stottlebink 17 YO15 ..... 5 A2
Stovin Cres DN15 ..... 83 A5
Stow Cl 11 DN37 ..... 102 B4
Stow Ct YO32 ..... 127 E3
Stowe Garth 1 YO16 ..... 122 F7
Stowgarth 29 DN18 ..... 84 F8
Stow Rd
Atwick YO25 ..... 35 D5
Scunthorpe DN16 ..... 151 B3
Straight La YO19 ..... 26 F8
Straits Rd HU11 ..... 46 D2
Strand Cl HU3 ..... 155 A4
Strand Com Sch DN32 .. 153 A5
Strand St DN32 ..... 152 F5
Stratford Ave 4 DN33 ... 102 D2
Stratford Dr DN16 ..... 151 C5
Stratford Way YO32 ..... 127 E3
Stratford Wlk HU9 ..... 142 E1
Strathcona Ave HU5 ..... 139 E4
Strathearn St 1 HU5 ... 140 D3
Strathmore Ave
Burstwick HU12 ..... 73 A7
Kingston upon Hull HU6 .. 140 C6
Strathmore Ct DN36 ..... 114 A7
Stratton Cl HU8 ..... 142 B7
Stratton Pk 3 HU14 ..... 69 B6
Strawberry Gdns
Hornsea HU18 ..... 134 C1
Kingston upon Hull HU9 ... 145 B7
Strawberry Hill 2 DN37. 113 C6
Strawberry St HU9 ..... 146 B7
Stray Garth YO31 ..... 130 F7
Straylands Gr YO31 ..... 130 F8
Stray Rd
Sunk Island HU12 ..... 89 B6
York YO31 ..... 131 B6
Stray The HU15 ..... 54 A2
Street La
Bubwith DN14 ..... 50 F5
North Kelsey LN7 ..... 110 B4
Streetlife Mus* HU1 ..... 155 C2
Streets The' DN15 ..... 151 A7
Street The YO42 ..... 28 A2
STRENSALL 14 A7
STRENSALL CAMP 14 B6
Strensall Comm Nature Reserve* YO60 ..... 14 D8
Strensall Pk YO32 ..... 14 A5
Strensall Rd
Earswick YO32 ..... 128 A7
Kingston upon Hull HU5 .. 139 C1
York YO32 ..... 127 F6
Strickland Rd
Eastoft DN17 ..... 81 A2
13 Hunmanby YO14 ..... 3 A8
Strickland St HU3 ..... 145 C4
Strines Gr 9 HU8 ..... 141 D7
Stripe La YO30 ..... 126 B5
Stromness Way HU8 ..... 141 F7
Stroud Crescent E HU7 .. 141 A7
Stroud Crescent W HU7. 141 A8
Strouther Cl YO42 ..... 29 A3
Stroykins Cl DN34 ..... 102 C3
Strubby Cl 6 DN35 ..... 103 D2
Stuart Cl
Bridlington YO15 ..... 122 C1
Scunthorpe DN17 ..... 96 C1
4 Strensall YO32 ..... 14 C8
Stuart Gr
Eggborough DN14 ..... 62 A2
9 Thorpe Willoughby YO8 ... 48 B1
Stuart Rd YO24 ..... 129 D1
Stuart Wortley St DN31 .. 152 F6
Stubbs Cl 30 HU15 ..... 68 D5
Stubbs La
Cridling Stubbs WF11 ..... 76 A8
Norton DN6 ..... 76 E2
Stubbs Rd WF8 ..... 76 D3
Stubden Gr YO30 ..... 126 F2
Studcross DN9 ..... 105 D6
Studio 2 Theatre* HU1 .. 155 A2
Studley Mdws YO16 ..... 122 D7
Studley St HU8 ..... 146 B8
Sturdee Gr YO31 ..... 130 D7
Sturmer Ct 15 DN16 ..... 96 D1
STURTON 108 F7
Sturton Gr 23 DN33 ..... 102 D2
Sturton La DN20 ..... 108 E7
Stygate La DN6 ..... 76 E1
Stylefield Rd 15 YO15 ..... 5 A2
Styles Croft HU14 ..... 69 C7
Subway St HU3 ..... 145 B3
Subway The DN16 ..... 97 A4
Suddaby Cl HU9 ..... 141 F2
Suddle Way 4 DN41 ..... 101 A4
Sudforth La DN14 ..... 61 C3
Suffolk Ct 13 DN32 ..... 153 A5
Suffolk St HU5 ..... 140 D3
Sugar Mill Ponds Nature Reserve* DN14 ..... 79 B8
Suggitt's Ct DN35 ..... 153 D4
Suggitt's La DN35 ..... 153 D4
Suggitt's Orch DN35 ..... 153 D4
Sullivan Rd HU4 ..... 144 B4
Summerdale DN18 ..... 84 E8
Summerfield Ave 3 DN37 ..... 113 E7
Summerfield Cl
Great Driffield YO25 ..... 124 D5
4 Waltham DN37 ..... 113 E7
Summerfield Rd
Bridlington YO15 ..... 122 D1
York YO24 ..... 132 C7
SUMMERGANGS 141 C2
Summergangs Dr 17 HU12 ..... 72 E5
Summergangs Rd HU8 .. 141 C3
Summer Gdns YO30 ..... 129 F8
Summergroves Way HU4 ..... 144 B2
Summer Hill DN21 ..... 117 C1
Summermeadows HU11 . 142 D6
Sunbeam Rd HU4 ..... 144 D5
Sundrew Ave DN14 ..... 149 D6
Sunk Island Rd HU12 ..... 88 E8
Sunningdale 12 DN37 ... 113 D6
Sunningdale Ave 1 DN20 .98 C3
Sunningdale Cl
Knapton YO26 ..... 129 B5
1 York YO26 ..... 129 B5
Sunningdale Dr 7 DN40 .. 87 C2
Sunningdale Rd
Gipseyville HU4 ..... 144 E4
Sunningdale Rd *continued*
Northfield HU13 ..... 143 F2
Scunthorpe DN17 ..... 96 B2
Sunningdale Way DN21 . 117 C2
Sunnybank 1 DN18 ..... 84 E8
Sunny Bank
Kingston upon Hull HU3 ... 145 B7
3 Knottingley WF11 ..... 61 A2
Sunny Cnr 13 DN33 ..... 102 E1
Sunnydale 3 YO32 ..... 127 D7
Sunny Hill 9 DN21 ..... 108 B1
Sunnyside Cl HU12 ..... 73 C4
Sunrise Dr YO14 ..... 3 C8
Sunway Gr DN16 ..... 151 A1
Surbiton Cl HU8 ..... 141 F5
Surrey Ct 12 DN32 ..... 153 A5
Surrey Garth HU4 ..... 144 B4
Surrey Way YO30 ..... 129 F8
Surtees St
Grimsby DN31 ..... 152 F6
York YO30 ..... 130 B7
Sussex Cl
5 Kingston upon Hull HU5 ..... 139 D1
York YO10 ..... 131 C2
Sussex Ct 14 DN32 ..... 153 A5
Sussex Rd YO10 ..... 131 C2
Sussex St DN35 ..... 153 B4
Sussex Way 14 YO32 ..... 14 A7
Susworth Rd DN17 ..... 106 D4
Sutcliffe Ave 18 DN33 ... 102 D2
Sutherland Ave HU6 ..... 140 B6
Sutherland St YO23 ..... 130 B1
Sutor Cl YO23 ..... 132 B3
Sutton Bridge* YO41 ..... 27 C2
Sutton Cl HU7 ..... 141 B8
Sutton Ct HU8 ..... 141 E6
Sutton Fields Ind Est
Kingston upon Hull HU2 .. 155 C4
West Carr HU7 ..... 140 F5
Sutton Gdns HU7 ..... 141 B7
Sutton House Rd HU8 ... 141 D5
SUTTON INGS 141 F4
Sutton La
Barmby Moor YO42 ..... 28 B3
Byram cum Sutton WF11 ..... 61 A4
SUTTON-ON-HULL 141 D6
Sutton Park Prim Sch HU7 ..... 140 F7
Sutton Pl DN20 ..... 108 F7
Sutton Rd
Howden DN14 ..... 65 A6
Kingston upon Hull HU6 .. 140 D6
12 Kirk Sandall DN3 ..... 92 A3
Wawne HU7 ..... 56 F7
Wigginton YO32 ..... 13 D7
Sutton St DN14 ..... 149 D4
SUTTON UPON DERWENT 27 C1
Sutton upon Derwent CE Prim Sch YO41 ..... 27 C2
Sutton Way
Kingston upon Hull HU9 ... 142 B2
York YO30 ..... 130 B8
Swaby Cl DN36 ..... 115 B2
Swaby Dr DN35 ..... 103 B2
Swaby's Yd HU17 ..... 154 A3
Swaddale Ave HU10 ..... 138 F2
Swainby Cl HU8 ..... 141 D7
Swale Ave YO24 ..... 132 E8
Swaledale Ave HU9 ..... 141 E1
Swaledale Mews YO16 ... 122 F6
Swaledale Pl DN16 ..... 151 D2
Swale Rd 29 HU15 ..... 68 D5
Swales Dr YO43 ..... 135 D3
Swales Rd DN36 ..... 114 D8
SWALLOW 112 B5
Swallow Cl HU18 ..... 134 B6
Swallow Ct 4 DN9 ..... 105 D7
Swallow Dr 3 DN41 ..... 101 F5
Swallowfield Dr HU4 ..... 144 B2
Swallow Grange 6 HU8. 141 D7
Swallow La DN39 ..... 85 E2
Swallow Rd YO25 ..... 125 B5
Swanage Wlk HU4 ..... 144 B4
Swan Cl YO19 ..... 37 A7
Swan Ct
Gainsborough DN21 ..... 117 D1
Hornsea HU18 ..... 134 C6
Swanella Gr HU3 ..... 145 A4
Swan Farm Ct YO19 ..... 37 A7
Swanfield Rd HU9 ..... 142 C2
Swan La DN14 ..... 149 D6
SWANLAND 69 B6
Swanland Ave 3 YO15 ... 122 F3
Swanland Butts Cl HU10 143 C6
Swanland Cl 17 DN8 ..... 93 B7
Swanland Ct 23 DN8 ..... 93 B7
Swanland Dale HU14 ..... 69 B8
Swanland Garth 4 HU14 .. 69 A5
Swanland Hill 16 HU14 ..... 69 A5
Swanland Prim Sch HU14 .69 B6
Swanland Rd HU13 ..... 143 C2
Swanland Way 3 HU16 .. 138 E6
Swannacks View DN20 ... 108 F7
Swann St
Kingston upon Hull HU2 .. 155 C4
York YO23 ..... 156 A1
Swan Syke Dr 8 DN6 ..... 76 F2
Sweep Cl YO43 ..... 135 D3
Sweet Briar Cl 7 DN37 . 113 D7
Sweet Dews Gr HU9 ..... 146 D8
Sweyne Garth DN14 ..... 65 D1
Swift Ave YO25 ..... 125 B5
Swift Cl HU18 ..... 134 B6
Swift Dr DN20 ..... 98 B2
Swift Rd DN17 ..... 150 D2
Swiftsure Cres 16 DN34 .. 102 B2
Swinburne La DN17 150
Swinburne Rd DN17 150
Swinburne St HU8 141
Swinderby Garth 19 HU7 .. 57
Swinderby Gdns DN34 .. 152
Swindon St YO16 122
SWINE 57
Swine Bank HU5 139
SWINEFLEET 65
Swinefleet Prim Sch DN14 65
Swinefleet Rd
Goole DN14 149
Goole Fields DN14 80
Swinegate
Kingston upon Hull HU13 .. 143
York YO1 156
Swinegate Court E YO1 .. 156
Swine La HU11 57
Swinemoor La HU17 137
Swinemoor Prim Sch HU17 154
Swine Rd HU11 45
Swineridge Hill YO42 29
Swineridge La YO42 29
Swinescaif Hill Swine HU15 ..... 54 A
Swinescaif Rd
South Cave HU15 ..... 54 A
South Cave HU15 ..... 54 E
Swinster La DN40 ..... 86 E
Swinsty Ct YO30 ..... 126 F
Swinton Cl 8 YO30 ..... 126 E
Switchback LN8 ..... 120 A
Swithin Cl HU13 ..... 144 A
Sycamore Ave
15 Grimsby DN33 ..... 102 E
1 Hut Green DN14 ..... 62 A
York YO32 ..... 127 D
Sycamore Cl
3 Barnetby le Wold DN38 ..... 99 B
2 Broughton DN20 ..... 97 D
East Ella HU5 ..... 144 C
14 Gilberdyke HU15 ..... 66 D
Goole DN14 ..... 149 E
1 Haxby YO32 ..... 127 D
Hessle HU13 ..... 143 C
Nafferton YO25 ..... 125 F
8 Preston HU12 ..... 58 C
Selby YO8 ..... 148 A
Skelton YO30 ..... 126 C
12 Snaith & Cowick DN14 .. 78 C
Sycamore Cres
Bottesford DN16 ..... 96 F
Hutton Cranswick YO25 ..... 32 E
Sycamore Ct
Kingston upon Hull HU5 .. 140 C
Sproatley HU11 ..... 58 D
Sycamore Dr
9 Gainsborough DN21 ... 117 C
3 Thorngumbald HU12 ..... 72 E
Sycamore Mews YO8 ..... 148 D
Sycamore Pl
New Earswick YO32 ..... 127 D
York YO30 ..... 156 A
Sycamore Rd YO8 ..... 49 B
Sycamores The HU17 ..... 137 B
Sycamore Terr YO30 ..... 156 A
Sycamore View 17 YO26 ... 12 F
Sydney Smith Sch HU10. 144 A
SYKEHOUSE ..... 78 B
Sykehouse Rd DN14 ..... 78 C
Sykes Balk YO25 ..... 21 E
Sykes Cl
6 Kingston upon Hull HU10 ..... 143 F
Swanland HU14 ..... 69 B
Sykes La
Garton YO25 ..... 124 A
Goxhill DN19 ..... 71 A
Sykes St HU2 ..... 155 B
Sylvan Falls YO25 ..... 124 C
Sylvan Lea YO25 ..... 124 C
Sylvan Mead YO25 ..... 124 C
Sylvester La HU17 ..... 154 A
Sylvester Sq HU1 ..... 155 B
Sylvester St 13 DN21 ..... 108 B
Sylvia Cl HU6 ..... 139 F
Symmons Cl 4 HU17 ... 137 A
Symons Cl HU2 ..... 155 A
Symons Way 13 YO42 ..... 29 A

T

Tabard Hamlet 5 DN14 ... 61 F
Tabard Rd 6 DN14 ..... 61 F
Tabards The 7 DN14 ..... 61 F
Tadcaster Rd
Copmanthorpe YO23 ..... 132 C
York YO24 ..... 129 F
Tadcaster Rd Dringhouses YO23 ..... 132 E
Tadman Cl HU17 ..... 136 E
Tadman St HU3 ..... 145 D
Tailler Rd 44 HU12 ..... 72 D
Talbot Circ DN3 ..... 92 A
Talbot Rd DN40 ..... 87 C
Talbot Wlk DN16 ..... 151 B
Talisman Dr 6 DN16 ..... 96 D
Tallert Way 28 DN33 ..... 102 C
Tall Trees HU13 ..... 143 C
Tamar Dr 14 DN36 ..... 114 A
Tamar Gr HU8 ..... 142 C
Tamarisk Way 18 DN16 ..... 96 E
Tamar Wlk DN17 ..... 150 C
Tamworth Rd 9 YO30 ... 127 A

an Dyke Way HU17 154 C2
anfield Gr HU9 142 C2
ANG HALL 130 F5
ang Hall La YO31 131 A5
ang Hall Prim Sch
YO31 130 F5
anner Row YO1 156 A2
anner's Moat YO1 156 A2
anner St YO1 156 B2
annery Cl 12 DN37 113 E6
annery The 10 YO10 130 E3
anpit La DN6 76 E3
ansley Ct DN15 150 B7
ansley La HU18 134 D1
ANSTERNE 59 A8
ansterne La HU11 59 A7
ara Ct HU5 140 E3
arbert Cres 2 YO24 132 B7
ardrew Cl HU17 136 E6
arget La 16 YO42 29 A4
arleton Cl 3 DN3 92 A2
arran Ave HU6 140 B8
asburgh St DN32 152 F2
ate Cl YO8 48 D6
attersall Cl DN17 150 D1
attersall Dr 1 HU17 137 B3
attershall Ave 14 DN34 102 C2
attershall Cl HU2 140 E1
atton Cl YO30 127 A1
atton Pk 28 HU7 56 F5
aunton Rd HU4 144 A3
aunton Way 19 DN33 113 E8
aurus Ct YO23 156 A1
avella Ct 1 DN9 105 B2
avistock St HU5 140 C3
awny Owl Cl 18 DN36 114 D8
aylor Ave HU9 142 C3
aylor Cl DN9 94 E2
aylor's Ave DN35 103 C2
aylors Cl 5 HU17 55 B7
aylors Field YO25 124 E4
aylor's La HU19 75 C2
aylor St DN35 153 B5
ealby Gr 19 DN33 102 D2
Tealby Rd DN17 150 D1
Teal Cl
12 Broughton DN20 98 B2
Walkington HU17 55 B7
Teal Dr YO24 132 C8
Teale St DN15 151 A8
Teal Garth YO15 11 B4
Teal Pl LN7 111 A4
Teal Rd 1 HU15 52 F1
Team Gate 1 DN37 102 B3
Teanby Dr DN15 83 A5
Tedder Rd YO24 129 B1
Teddington Cl HU8 141 E6
Tedworth Rd HU9 142 C5
Tee La DN15 82 B5
Teesdale Ave HU9 146 E8
Teesdale Mews YO16 122 F7
Tees Gr HU8 142 C7
Telford Pl DN34 152 A3
Telford St HU9 141 E2
Telford Terr 1 YO24 130 B2
Temperance Ave DN17 107 D7
Temper Rd DN16 151 F4
Temperton's La DN9 106 A2
Templar Cl DN14 61 F1
Templar Ct 17 DN16 96 D2
Templar Way YO8 148 C2
Temple Ave YO10 131 B4
Temple Cl
Belton DN9 94 E2
Welton HU15 68 E6
Templefield Rd DN21 119 A3
Temple Garth YO23 132 C1
TEMPLE HIRST 62 E4
Temple La
Aylesby DN37 101 E1
Carnaby YO16 10 E5
Copmanthorpe YO23 132 C1
Welton HU15 68 E6
Templemans La DN36 114 A1
Templemead YO31 130 E8
Temple Rd
Bishopthorpe YO23 132 F4
Riddings DN17 150 F2
Temple St HU5 140 E1
Templewaters 31 HU7 56 F5
Temple Wlk 2 HU15 68 E6
Temsdale 2 HU7 141 A6
Tennant St YO8 148 B6
Tennent Rd YO24 129 B2
Tennison Ct HU16 139 A7
Tennyson Ave
Bridlington YO15 122 E3
1 Campsall DN6 76 E1
Kingston upon Hull HU5 140 A1
7 Thorne/Moorends DN8 93 B8
York YO30 130 C7
Tennyson Cl
Brigg DN20 98 C1
Caistor LN7 111 A3
Tennyson Ct HU12 72 D7
Tennyson Mews 4
DN31 152 D4
Tennyson Rd
Cleethorpes DN35 153 E3
Scunthorpe DN16 151 D3
Tennyson St
32 Gainsborough DN21 117 B1
Goole DN14 149 C5
Grimsby DN31 152 D4
Tensing Rd DN16 151 C1
Tenterden Cl HU7 141 A6
Ten Thorn La YO26 129 A4
Tern Gr HU8 142 C5
Terrington Cl YO32 14 B8
Terrington Pl 4 DN35 103 B2
Terry Ave YO1 156 B1
Terry St
Kingston upon Hull HU3 140 D1
York YO23 130 C1
Tetley Rd DN16 151 C3
Tetley View 2 DN17 94 E6
TETNEY 114 D4
Tetney La DN36 114 B5
TETNEY LOCK 115 A5
Tetney Lock Rd DN36 114 D4
Tetney Prim Sch DN36 114 D4
Tetney Rd DN36 114 C8
Tewkesbury Dr DN34 152 C2
Thamesbrook HU7 141 D5
Thanet Prim Sch HU9 142 D6
Thanet Rd
Kingston upon Hull HU9 142 D5
York YO24 129 D1
Thatch Cl YO8 148 C4
Thatchers Croft YO23 132 C3
Thaxted Cl HU8 142 B6
Theaker Ave DN21 117 C1
Theakston Mews HU17 136 D1
THEALBY 82 D4
Thealby La DN15 82 D5
THEARNE 56 D7
Thearne Cl 7 HU5 140 C3
Thearne La HU17 56 D7
Theasby Way HU17 45 A7
Theatre Mews HU2 155 B3
Theodore Rd DN15 150 E8
Theresa Cl 6 YO31 127 F1
Therm Rd HU8 155 C4
Thesiger St DN32 152 F5
Thesiger Wlk 2 DN32 152 F5
Thief La
Barlow YO8 148 F1
York YO10 130 F3
Thimblehall La HU15 52 E2
Thinholme La DN9 105 A1
Third Ave
Bridlington YO15 123 A4
Fixborough Stather DN15 82 A1
Goole DN14 149 C4
Scunthorpe DN17 150 C2
Ulrome YO25 23 B3
York YO31 130 F5
Third La DN37 113 D3
Thirkleby Cres DN32 103 A2
Thirkleby Walk 1 YO10 131 D3
Thirkleby Way YO10 131 C4
Thirlby Wlk HU5 139 D3
Thirlmere Ave DN33 113 E8
Thirlmere Dr YO31 131 A6
Thirlmere Wlk DN14 149 E6
Thirsk Mews HU5 139 D4
Thirtle Bridge La HU19 74 C8
THIRTLEBY 58 B5
Thirtleby La HU11 57 F6
Thirty Acre La 13 HU12 72 D7
Thiseldine Cl 6 YO43 53 F7
Thistle Cl YO8 148 C2
Thistleton Gdns 6 HU5 140 E2
Thistlewood Court 14
HU7 57 B5
THIXENDALE 17 E7
Thixendale Rd
4 Bridlington YO16 122 F7
Fridaythorpe YO25 18 A7
Thomas Clarkson Way
HU7 140 E8
Thomas Rd
Scunthorpe DN17 150 F4
17 Stainforth DN7 92 C5
Thomas St
Grimsby DN32 152 F3
Kingston upon Hull HU9 146 B7
6 Selby YO8 148 D6
2 York YO10 130 E3
Thompson Ave HU17 154 C3
Thompson Cl 9 YO8 49 B4
Thompson Dr
16 Hatfield DN7 92 D4
2 Strensall YO32 14 B8
Thompson Nook 14 DN7 92 D4
Thompson Pl 6 YO26 129 E5
Thompson Rd HU12 72 B7
Thompson St
Bridlington YO16 122 D3
Scunthorpe DN15 151 B7
Thonock Rd DN21 117 D4
Thoresby Ave YO16 122 D6
Thoresby Cl YO16 122 D6
Thoresby Mews 7 YO16 122 D6
Thoresby Pl 2 DN35 103 C2
Thoresby Prim Sch HU5 145 B8
Thoresby Rd
Fulstow LN11 121 D8
North Coates DN36 115 A2
Scunthorpe DN17 150 D1
Tetney DN36 114 D3
York YO24 129 B1
Thoresby St HU5 145 B8
Thoresway Gr 9 DN33 102 D2
Thorgam Ct DN31 152 C3
THORGANBY 38 B4
Thorganby Rd DN35 103 D2
Thorgill Gr HU5 139 E3
Thorn Bank DN9 104 E4
Thorn Barn Cl HU12 72 F5
Thornbeck YO19 26 E6
Thornbridge Cl HU9 142 B3
Thornbury Rd DN40 87 C1
Thorncroft 8 YO19 26 F7
Thorndale HU7 140 E8
Thorndale Croft YO25 19 B5
Thorndale La YO25 19 A5
Thornden Bldgs YO8 148 D5
Thorndike Way DN21 117 D1
THORNE 93 A8
Thorne & Dikesmarsh
DN8 79 A2
Thorne King Edward Prim
Sch DN8 93 B8
Thorne Moorends
Marshlands Prim Sch 26
DN8 79 B2
Thorne North Sta DN8 93 A8
Thorne Rd
Hatfield DN7 92 F5
Kirk Sandall DN3 92 A1
3 Stainforth DN7 92 C6
Thorne South Sta DN8 93 B7
Thorne Sports Ctr DN8 93 B8
Thorne Waste Drain Rd
DN8 79 D1
Thorneycroft Rd 14 HU12 72 E5
Thornfield Ave 5 YO31 130 F8
Thornfield Dr 7 YO31 127 E2
Thorn Fields HU12 72 D5
Thorngarth La 9 DN19 85 C8
THORNGUMBALD 72 E5
Thorngumbald Prim Sch
HU12 72 E5
Thorngumbald Rd HU12 72 B4
Thornham Cl HU15 53 F1
Thornham's Way 6 HU15 68 C7
Thornhill Ave HU8 141 C4
Thornhill Cres 19 DN17 96 C2
Thornhill Gdns DN34 152 A3
Thornhills 19 YO32 13 F5
THORNHOLME 10 B2
Thornholme Dr 14 DN16 96 D2
Thorn La DN19 86 A8
Thorn Leigh 3 HU3 145 C6
Thornleys HU17 43 A4
Thorn Marsh Rd HU12 72 E2
Thorn Nook YO31 130 F8
Thorn Rd HU12 72 D7
THORNTON 39 B8
Thornton
10 Brough HU15 68 C6
Market Weighton YO43 135 D5
Thornton Abbey &
Gatehouse* DN39 86 B5
Thornton Abbey Sta DN39 86 A5
Thornton Ave DN16 151 A3
Thornton Cl HU13 143 D1
Thornton Cres DN35 103 C2
Thornton Ct 22 DN36 114 A8
THORNTON CURTIS 85 E5
Thorntondale Dr YO16 122 F7
Thornton Dam La HU15 66 D8
Thornton Gdns 5 DN41 101 A6
Thornton Gr
7 Grimsby DN34 102 C2
3 Preston HU12 58 C1
Thornton La YO25 20 A1
Thornton Moor Cl YO30 126 F2
Thornton Pl DN40 87 B1
Thornton Rd
Barrow upon Humber
DN19 85 D6
Bridlington YO16 122 B2
Goxhill DN19 85 F6
South Kelsey LN7 110 A1
Thornton St DN19 85 C7
Thorntree Cl DN14 149 E6
Thorntree Gr YO30 127 B2
Thorntree La
Balne DN14 77 C6
Goole DN14 149 E6
Thornwick Ave HU10 143 E8
Thornwick Cl 2 HU3 145 C5
Thornwick Rd YO15 5 B3
Thornwood Covert 1
YO24 129 C1
Thorny La YO42 16 F2
Thorold Pl 11 DN3 92 A3
Thorold St DN31 153 A5
THORPE 32 B1
Thorpe YO25 32 B1
Thorpehall Rd DN3 92 A2
Thorpe La YO8 48 B8
THORPE LE STREET 40 D7
Thorpe Leys YO25 32 B2
Thorpepark Prim Sch
HU6 140 A8
Thorpepark Rd HU6 139 F8
Thorpe Rd
6 Brough HU15 68 C5
Howden DN14 65 C8
Thorpe Road Ave 2 DN14 65 B7
Thorpe St
9 Bridlington YO15 122 E2
York YO23 130 B2
THORPE WILLOUGHBY 48 C2
Thorpe Willoughby Prim Sch
YO8 48 B2
Three Lakes Ind Est YO8 148 D2
Three Lakes Ret Pk YO8 148 D3
Thrislington Sq 19 DN8 79 B2
Thronton Cl YO43 135 D5
Throughleys La YO42 39 A5
Thrunscoe Prim Sch
DN35 153 E1
Thrunscoe Rd DN35 153 F1
Thrussendale Rd YO17 16 E8
Thurlow Ave
Beverley HU17 136 E6
22 Pocklington YO42 29 A3
Thurlow Garth YO25 125 F7
Thurlstone Cl 13 HU7 56 F6
Thurstan Cl
Beverley HU17 136 D2
Kingston upon Hull HU9 142 D2
Thurstan Rd HU17 154 A2
Thwaite Hall (University of
Hull Residence) HU16 139 C6
Thwaite St HU16 139 C6
THWING 2 B1
Thwing Rd
Burton Fleming YO25 2 E2
Kilham YO25 9 B5
Thyme Way HU17 55 F8
Tibby La YO25 32 C4
TIBTHORPE 19 D2
Tichbourne Cl 6 HU3 145 C5
TICKTON 137 E8
Tickton CE Prim Sch
HU17 137 F8
Tickton Gr HU6 139 F4
Tickton Mdws HU17 137 F8
Tideswell Ct DN15 150 B6
Tideworth Hague La
DN14 78 C3
Tiger La HU17 154 A3
Tilbury Prim Sch HU4 144 B3
Tilbury Rd HU4 144 B3
Tilia Cl
Kingston upon Hull HU4 144 B2
Scunthorpe DN16 96 E2
Tilmire Cl 2 YO10 133 F8
Tilworth Rd HU8 141 F4
Timberland 26 DN16 96 E2
Timberley Dr 7 DN37 102 B4
Tindale Bank Rd DN10 116 C7
Tinker La YO23 24 D6
Tinkler's La WF11 61 D6
Tinley Cl HU16 139 B7
Tintagel Way DN36 114 A8
Tintern Ave YO16 122 E6
Tippaty La WF11 61 A4
Tippet La HU17 44 F2
Tison Garth HU10 143 F6
Tithe Barn Cl 9 HU12 74 D1
Tithe Barn La
8 Patrington HU12 74 D1
13 Thorne/Moorends DN8 93 B8
Tithe Barn Rd 2 WF11 61 A2
Tithe Barn Way DN14 61 F3
Tithe Cl YO24 129 B1
Tithe La YO25 22 E5
Tithe Rd HU12 58 A1
Tiverton Rd HU7 141 A8
Tiverton St DN35 153 C4
Tivoli Gdns
East Marsh DN32 152 F4
Grimsby DN32 152 F4
TLS Community Arts Coll
DN35 103 C2
Toadham La DN14 77 C5
Toby Ct YO32 14 A7
Todd La DN21 117 F4
Todds Cl
Swanland HU14 69 C6
Tetney DN36 114 D3
Todds Ct DN17 107 D7
Todds La DN15 82 A4
Todd's La HU15 68 A8
Toft Gn YO1 156 A2
Tofts Rd 2 DN18 84 E8
Tokenspire Bsns Pk
HU17 137 C2
Toll Bar Ave DN36 113 F7
Toll Bar Sec Sch DN36 113 F7
Tollerton La YO30 12 B7
Tollesby La 9 DN7 92 D4
Toll Gavel HU17 154 A3
Tom Hammond Way
DN32 153 A4
Tom La LS25 61 B7
Tomline Rd 2 DN41 101 A5
Tomline St DN31 152 F5
Tomlinson Ave DN15 150 E7
Tonbridge Gr 2 HU9 142 E2
Tonbridge Wlk 21 DN33 113 E8
Tongue La HU15 66 E6
Tonnant Way 6 DN34 102 B3
Toogood St HU2 155 B4
Toothill Gdns 2 DN34 102 C3
Toothill Rd 1 DN34 102 C3
Topaz Gr 3 HU3 145 A4
Topcliff Ct YO8 148 B7
Topcliffe Garth HU7 141 C8
TOPHAM 78 A4
Tophill Low Nature
Reserve* YO25 33 D4
Top House Ct WF8 76 B3
Top La
Copmanthorpe YO23 132 B3
Kirk Bramwith DN7 92 A7
Top Rd
South Killingholme DN40 86 E3
Winterton DN15 82 F6
Worlaby DN20 98 D8
Torbay Dr DN33 113 E7
Torchil Cl HU10 143 C6
Toremill Cl YO32 127 D4
Torksey Dr DN33 102 D2
Torksey Pl 28 DN33 102 D2
Torksey St 25 DN21 108 B2
Tornville Cres DN14 79 B8
Torridge Gr HU8 142 C6
Torridge Rd HU8 142 C6
Torridon Pl YO24 132 B7
Torrington Rd DN17 150 C4
Torrington St
Grimsby DN32 152 F1
5 Kingston upon Hull
HU5 140 C3
Tostig Ave YO26 129 C5
Tostig Cl 14 YO41 15 D2
Totnes Rd DN33 113 E7
Tottenham Cl 3 HU8 141 F5
Tottering La DN14 51 B5
Tottermire La DN9 105 D7
Towan Cl 11 HU7 56 F5
Tower Ct YO30 127 A2
Tower Hill
Kingston upon Hull HU13 143 E1
Westwoodside DN9 105 B2
Tower Hill Dr HU13 143 E1
Tower Hill Mews 2
HU13 143 E1
Tower House La HU12 147 F7
Tower Mews HU15 68 C7
Tower Pl YO1 156 B1
Tower Rd
Rimswell HU12 74 C6
Roos HU11 60 A4
Tower St
Flamborough YO15 5 A2
31 Gainsborough DN21 117 B1
Kingston upon Hull HU9 155 C1
York YO1 156 B1
Tower View
Carlton DN14 63 C2
Kingston upon Hull HU10 143 C5
Towgarth Wlk DN14 51 F1
Town End Ave DN14 63 C3
Townend Cswy DN14 66 D2
Town End Gdns 3 YO32 13 D5
Townend La HU15 53 C3
Town End La YO42 18 C2
Townend Rd
Ellerton YO42 38 D1
12 Newbald YO43 53 F7
Walkington HU17 55 B8
Town End Rd HU12 72 A5
Townend St YO31 156 B4
Town Farm Cl YO25 23 A2
Town Hall Sq DN31 152 E3
Town Hall St 1 DN31 152 E3
Town Hill DN20 97 E4
Town Hill Dr DN20 97 E4
Town Rd DN36 114 D4
Townsend Cl DN36 103 E1
Townshend Dr 1 HU16 138 F5
Townside DN40 86 D6
Townside Cl 1 YO43 53 F7
Townside Rd YO43 53 F7
Town St
Hayton YO42 40 C8
Immingham DN40 86 E4
Nunburnholme YO42 29 F3
Shiptonthorpe YO43 40 F6
TOWTHORPE
Duggleby 6 D1
York 14 B5
Towthorpe YO43 135 D8
Towthorpe La YO43 135 B7
Towthorpe Medieval
Village* YO43 135 B8
Towthorpe Moor La YO32 14 C5
Towthorpe Rd YO32 13 F5
Towton Ave 9 YO24 129 F2
Toynton Rd 27 DN33 102 D2
Trafalgar Ave 10 DN34 102 B3
Trafalgar Cres YO15 11 B4
Trafalgar Pk DN36 114 A8
Trafalgar St
5 Kingston upon Hull
HU3 145 D7
York YO23 130 B1
Trafford Rd
Kingston upon Hull HU10 143 E8
4 Norton DN6 76 E2
Trafford St DN15 151 B8
Traffords Way DN20 108 F6
Train Ave HU6 140 C7
Train Gate DN21 108 B1
Tranby Ave
Kingston upon Hull
HU13 143 D2
York YO10 131 D4
Tranby Croft HU10 143 C5
Tranby Dr DN32 103 A2
Tranby La
Hessle HU10 143 B5
Swanland HU14 69 B6
Tranby Lodge Gdns
HU13 143 C1
Tranby Meadows Pk
HU13 143 C3
Tranby Ride HU10 143 C5
Trandy La DN14 65 D5
Tranmere Cl HU3 145 B5
Tranmere Pk HU18 134 D3
Tranmore La DN14 62 B3
Travis Ave 18 DN8 93 B8
Travis Cl 16 DN8 93 B8
Travis Gr 17 DN8 93 B8
Travis Rd HU16 138 F5
Traviss Cl DN16 151 B4
Travis St YO15 122 E3
Trawden Cl HU7 56 F6
Treasurer's House* YO1 156 B3
Treece Gdns 10 DN18 69 F1
Tree Cl 9 DN9 105 D6
Trees The
Kingston upon Hull HU6 140 C4
Newland HU6 140 C4
Treeton Rd DN14 65 A6
Tremayne Ave 2 HU15 68 C5
Trenchard Cl 3 DN40 87 D2

Trenchard Rd YO26 129 B6
Trenfield Ct YO24 129 F3
Trent Ave 4 YO32 127 F6
Trentham Cl YO16 122 D6
Trentham Dr YO16 122 D6
Trentham Mews 1 YO16 122 D6
Trentholme Dr
Messingham DN17 107 D7
2 York YO24 130 A2
Trenton Ave HU4 144 B6
Trent Pk 6 HU7 56 F6
Trent Rd DN17 95 D6
Trentside
Keadby with Althorpe DN17 95 D3
Morton DN21 117 A2
Trent Side
4 Amcotts DN17 81 F1
Keadby with Althorpe DN17 95 D6
Trent St DN16 151 B6
Trentvale Prep Sch DN17 95 D6
Trent View DN17 95 D5
Trent Way YO24 132 D7
Trent Wlk 32 HU15 68 D5
Trevor Cl 15 DN37 101 F1
Trevor Gr 8 YO24 129 F2
Trevor St HU2 155 B4
Triangle Dr HU14 69 A4
Triangle The 11 HU14 69 A4
Tribune Way YO30 127 B2
Trinity Academy DN8 93 B8
Trinity Ave YO15 122 F3
Trinity Cl
Burstwick HU12 73 A6
Goxhill DN19 86 A8
Leven HU17 45 B8
Trinity Ct
5 Broughton DN20 97 D4
Kingston upon Hull HU2 155 B1
Trinity Fields 22 HU19 75 A6
Trinity Fold 5 HU15 54 A2
Trinity Garth HU16 138 A8
Trinity Gr
Beverley HU17 154 B3
1 Bridlington YO15 122 F3
3 Kingston upon Hull HU9 141 F1
Kingston upon Hull HU13 143 E2
Trinity La
Beverley HU17 154 B2
York YO1 156 A2
Trinity Mdws YO32 14 D3
Trinity Mews 2 YO15 122 F3
Trinity Rd
Bridlington YO15 122 F3
Cleethorpes DN35 153 E1
Hornsea HU18 134 C2
10 Scunthorpe DN16 96 D2
Trinity St
Grimsby DN31 153 A5
Kingston upon Hull HU3 145 C7
Trinity Wharf HU1 155 C2
Trinity Wlk 2 DN18 69 E1
Trippett St HU1 155 C3
Triton Rd HU9 142 D3
Trolleybus Mus at Sandtoft The* DN8 94 A3
Trondheim Way DN41 101 E8
Troon Cl 2 YO26 129 B5
Troon Ct HU8 142 B6
Troon Rd DN7 92 D4
Troutbeck 7 YO24 132 C7
Troutsdale Ave YO30 126 E2
Troutsdale Cl YO16 122 F7
Troutsdale Gr HU9 146 F8
Trumfleet La DN6 77 D1
Trundle Gate YO43 53 F6
Trundle La DN7 92 C8
Trundles La 7 WF11 61 A2
Trunkass La DN37 112 D6
Trunk Rd DN17 95 D4
Trunscoe Jun Sch DN35 153 E1
Truro Cl HU7 141 C6
Tudor Cl
Bridlington YO15 122 C1
30 Brough HU15 68 C5
16 Humberston DN36 114 D8
10 Thorpe Willoughby YO8 48 B1
Tudor Ct HU10 138 C1
Tudor Dr HU6 140 B8
Tudor Rd YO24 129 C2
Tudor Way YO32 14 C8
Tudworth Field Rd DN7 93 B5
Tudworth Rd DN7 93 A5
Tuke Ave YO10 131 B4
Tulip Rd DN15 151 C7
Tummel Ct 4 DN40 101 B8
Tune St YO8 49 B4
Tunis St HU5 140 E2
Tunnard St DN32 153 A4
Tunnel Rd DN20 98 D4
TUNSTALL 60 C2
Turbary La YO32 128 E6
Turbary Rd
Epworth DN9 105 B6
Haxey DN9 105 C3
Turf Moor Rd DN7 93 A3
Turkey La YO16 10 E4
Turks Head Ct YO1 156 C3
Turks Head Gdns 10 HU15 52 F1
Turmarr Rd HU12 89 C8
Turmarr Villas 6 HU12 90 F6
Turmar View HU11 58 A4
Turmer Ave YO15 122 F3
Turnberry App DN37 113 D6
Turnberry Dr YO26 129 B4
Turnberry Mews 18 DN7 92 C6
Turnbull Dr 18 YO42 29 A3
Turner Ave HU19 75 A5
Turner Cl YO43 135 D3
Turner Ct HU3 155 A2
Turner Rd HU17 154 B4
Turner's Croft YO10 131 A1
Turner's La 15 HU14 69 A5
Turners Sq 9 YO8 148 C5
Turner St 5 DN21 108 B1
Turnham La YO8 49 C2
Turnhead Cres YO8 49 B5
Turnhead Ct YO8 49 B6
Turnmire Rd 1 YO24 132 E8
Turpin Cl DN21 117 C1
Turpin Ct YO1 156 C1
Turpit La HU12 72 A5
Turrets The 15 HU12 72 E5
Turver's La WF11 61 C2
Tuxford Gr HU9 142 E2
Tweed Gr HU8 142 B5
Tween Dykes Rd HU7 141 D6
Tweendykes Sch HU7 141 C6
Twickenham Cl 2 HU8 142 A5
Twin Pike Way 14 YO32 13 D5
Two Riggs HU17 43 A4
Twyford Cl 5 HU9 142 E2
Twyning Pl DN35 153 D3
Tydeman Cl 1 DN16 96 D1
Tyler Ave DN31 152 A3
Tynedale 1 HU7 141 A6
Tynedale Ct 1 DN3 92 A2
Tyne St HU3 145 B4
Tyn Garth YO19 36 D8
Tyrell Oaks 49 HU12 72 D7
Tysons Cl 7 DN18 69 F1
Tythe Garth 8 HU15 53 D3

U

ULCEBY 86 A1
Ulceby Rd
Scunthorpe DN17 96 B2
South Killingholme DN39 86 C2
Wootton DN39 85 F3
ULCEBY SKITTER 86 C2
Ulceby Sta DN39 86 C2
Ullswater YO24 132 D7
Ullswater Ave 5 YO16 122 E7
Ullswater Cl HU8 141 D4
Ullswater Gr DN14 149 E5
ULROME 23 A3
Ulrome Ct 1 HU9 142 B1
Ulster Ave 5 DN33 102 E1
Ulster Rd DN21 117 B1
Ulverston Rd HU4 144 A3
Ulyett La DN17 106 C8
Undercroft 7 YO19 26 F7
Underwit Rd YO8 63 C4
Unicorn Row 10 DN21 108 B1
Union La YO8 148 C4
Union Pl DN14 149 D6
Union Rd DN8 93 A8
Union St
Great Driffield YO25 124 E4
Kingston upon Hull HU2 155 B3
19 Pocklington YO42 29 A4
Union Terr YO31 156 B4
Unity Ave HU13 143 F1
Unity Rd DN32 153 C2
University of Hull HU6 140 A4
University of Lincoln (Derek Crothall Building) HU1 155 B3
University of Lincoln (Pacific Ct & 42 High St) HU1 155 C2
University of Lincoln (Queens Garden Building) HU1 155 C2
University of York (King's Manor) YO30 156 A3
University of York (Main Campus) YO10 131 A1
University Rd YO10 130 F2
Upavon Garth HU7 141 C7
Upper Burgess St DN31 152 D4
Uppercommon La DN14 61 F3
Uppercroft 4 YO32 127 C8
Upper Hanover St 6 YO26 129 F5
UPPER HELMSLEY 15 B3
Upper Kenyon St 5 DN8 93 A8
Upper Newborough St 1 YO30 130 C7
UPPER POPPLETON 12 F1
Upper Price St YO23 156 A1
Upper St Paul's Terr YO24 130 A4
UPPERTHORPE 105 B3
Upperthorpe Hill DN9 105 A2
Upper Union St HU1 155 A2
UPTON 22 E1
Upton St HU8 141 B1
Uredale Pl DN16 151 E1
Usher La YO32 13 F6
Utgard Way 4 DN33 102 D1
UTTERBY 121 D4
Utterby Dr DN34 152 C1
Utterby Prim Sch LN11 121 B5
Uxbridge Gr HU9 142 E1

V

Vagarth Cl 21 DN18 69 E1
Valda Vale 34 DN40 87 B1
Vale Cres YO42 16 F2
Valentine Cl
1 Kingston upon Hull HU4 144 A2
6 Pocklington YO42 29 A3
Vale of Ancholme Sch DN20 98 B2
Vale The
Beverley HU17 137 B2
Kingston upon Hull HU10 143 B7
Skelton YO30 126 B5
Vale Wood DN16 96 E2
Valiant Dr HU9 142 D4
Valletta St HU9 147 D7
Valley Dr HU10 143 B7
Valley View YO19 37 F7
Valley View Dr DN16 96 D1
Vanbrugh Dr YO10 131 C3
Vanbrugh Way YO10 131 A2
Vancouver Cres 5 DN17 96 C2
Vanessa Dr DN21 117 B2
Vane St HU3 145 D7
Varah Cl DN18 84 E8
Varlow Rd LN7 111 B4
Varsity Cl 6 DN7 104 A8
Vaughan Ave DN36 103 A2
Vaughan Rd
10 Campsall DN6 76 E1
1 Kingston upon Hull HU13 69 F4
Vavasour Ct YO23 132 B2
Veal St DN31 152 C3
Ventnor St HU5 140 C3
Venture Bsns Pk DN31 152 B6
Vere Terr DN31 152 C4
Verity Way YO25 125 A3
Vermont St HU5 140 D3
Vermuyden Rd DN8 79 C2
Vermuyden Sch DN14 149 B5
Vermuyden Terr DN14 149 D2
Vermuyden Villas DN8 94 A3
Vernon Cl YO23 133 A3
Vernon Rd
Bridlington YO15 122 F3
York YO30 126 E2
Vernon St HU1 155 B2
Vesper Dr YO24 129 B3
Vesper Wlk YO32 127 F6
Veterinary Cl YO25 9 A2
Vicarage Ave DN20 98 D3
Vicarage Cl
Beswick YO25 32 D4
2 Bubwith YO8 50 D7
12 Hunmanby YO14 2 F8
Vicarage Cres DN15 82 B5
Vicarage Gdns
2 Brough HU15 68 C6
Grimsby DN34 152 C2
Scunthorpe DN15 150 F6
Wrawby DN20 98 E4
1 York YO10 131 C4
Vicarage La
Beckingham DN10 116 D1
Bishop Wilton YO42 16 F2
8 Buckton/Bempton YO15 4 D3
Cadney DN20 109 D6
Elsham DN20 98 F7
Grasby DN38 110 E7
Immingham DN40 86 E4
3 Kingston upon Hull HU13 143 E1
Naburn YO19 36 E8
North Newbold YO43 53 F7
Redbourne DN21 108 F2
Scawby DN20 108 E8
Skirlaugh HU11 45 D2
Wootton DN39 85 E3
Vicarage Lawn DN34 152 C2
Vicarage Paddock DN20 108 E8
Vicarage Pk DN15 83 D1
Vicarage Rd
Willoughton DN21 119 B4
Wrawby DN20 98 D3
Vicarage View DN37 100 D3
Vicarage Wlk HU15 53 D3
Vicar La
Beverley HU17 154 A3
Eastrington DN14 51 F1
38 Hedon HU12 72 C7
Hollym HU19 75 A4
Kingston upon Hull HU1 155 B1
Vicars Cl YO23 132 B2
Vicars La HU12 91 A6
Vicar's La HU12 91 A6
Vicar's Wlk 1 DN17 94 D7
Viceroy Cl HU2 155 B4
Vickerman's La HU12 59 A3
Victor Charles Terr YO43 135 D4
Victoria Ave
Hatfield DN7 92 D4
Hornsea HU18 134 D5
Sculcoates HU5 140 A1
Willerby HU10 138 C2
12 Withernsea HU19 75 A6
Victoria Cl
Marshchapel DN36 115 C2
Stainforth DN7 92 C5
Wike Well End DN8 93 A7
Victoria Ct
Burton upon Stather DN15 82 B5
15 York YO26 129 F5
Victoria Dock Prim Sch HU9 146 B6
VICTORIA DOCK VILLAGE 146 B5
Victoria Dr
3 Barton-upon-Humber DN18 69 E1
3 Gilberdyke HU15 66 D8
Victoria Farm Cl YO23 24 C6
Victoria Gdns
Hornsea HU18 134 C6
1 Kingston upon Hull HU5 140 A1
Victoria Rd
Barnetby le Wold DN38 99 B4
Beverley HU17 154 A1
Bridlington YO15 122 E3
Great Driffield YO25 124 D5
5 Keelby DN41 101 A5
2 Pocklington YO42 29 A4
Scunthorpe DN16 151 A1
Woodmansey HU17 55 E8
Victoria Ret Pk DN31 152 E5
Victoria St
Goole DN14 149 D4
Kingston upon Hull HU13 144 A1
1 York YO23 156 B1
Victoria Street N DN31 152 E4
Victoria Street S 3 DN31 152 E3
Victoria Street W 2 DN31 152 E3
Victoria's Way HU16 139 B6
Victoria Way 2 YO32 130 F8
Victor St
Grimsby DN32 153 A4
2 Kingston upon Hull HU9 146 C8
York YO1 156 B1
Victory Way
1 Barton-upon-Humber DN18 69 F1
Bridlington YO16 122 C4
9 Grimsby DN37 102 B2
Viking Cl
2 Immingham DN40 87 B1
Kingston upon Hull HU10 138 C2
20 Stamford Bridge YO41 15 D2
Viking Dr 5 YO19 48 F8
Viking Rd
Bridlington YO16 123 B6
Stamford Bridge YO41 15 D2
York YO26 129 C5
Villa Cl YO8 49 F1
Villa Ct YO26 129 B7
Villa Fields 4 DN14 63 C1
Village Farm YO25 31 C4
Village Farm Cl
9 Beal DN14 61 D4
11 Newport HU15 52 F1
Village Farm Ct 7 DN14 61 D4
Village Farm Rd 5 HU12 58 C1
Village Garth 1 YO32 13 E5
Village Rd
Kingston upon Hull HU8 141 C1
Sunk Island HU12 88 E5
Village St YO30 126 E3
Village The
Haxby YO32 13 E5
Skelton YO30 126 B5
Stockton on the Forest YO32 14 D2
Strensall YO32 14 B7
York YO10 131 C4
Villa Gr 2 YO31 130 E6
Villa La HU12 72 D5
Ville Rd DN16 151 D2
Villiers Ct 7 HU12 72 D7
Vincent Cl 3 HU4 144 A2
Vincent Rd 19 DN33 102 D1
Vincent Way YO24 132 C8
Vine Cl HU16 139 A7
Vinegarth 2 DN9 105 E6
Vine Gdns YO8 50 D7
Vinehall Rd DN9 105 C2
Vinery The 13 DN14 65 A7
Vine St YO23 130 C2
Vineyards The 3 HU17 45 A8
Violet Cl 16 DN35 103 C1
Viscount Way 12 DN36 114 D8
Vivars Way YO8 148 D5
Vivian Ave DN32 153 B1
Voases Cl HU10 143 E6
Voases La HU10 143 E6
Volage Ct 13 YO42 29 A4
Volta St YO8 148 E4
Vulcan St HU6 140 F4
Vulcan Way DN7 93 A1
Vyner St YO31 130 C7

W

Waby Cl DN37 102 B4
Waddingham Pl
3 Habrough DN40 100 E8
19 New Waltham DN36 114 A7
Waddingham Rd LN7 109 F1
Waddington Ct HU5 140 B3
Waddington Dr 20 DN17 96 C2
Waddington Pl DN34 152 A1
Wade Ave HU18 134 C6
Wadebridge Gr 4 HU9 142 E1
Wade House La YO8 63 F4
Wadham Gr 4 HU9 141 F1
Wadhurst Cl HU7 141 A6
Wadsworth Ave HU6 140 C8
Wadsworth Rd YO25 124 B3
Waggoners Cl DN21 107 C4
Waggoners Dr 3 YO23 132 B3
Waggoners La YO25 20
Waincroft 8 YO32 14
Wainers Cl 5 YO23 132
Wainfleet Ave HU16 139
Wainfleet Rd 33 DN33 102
Wain's Gr YO24 132
Wain's Rd YO24 132
Waite Cl 17 YO42 29
WAITHE 114
Waithe La DN37 113
Wake Ave HU16 139
Wakefield Ave
Kingston upon Hull HU9 142
Scotter DN21 107
Wakefield La HU12 75
Wakerley Rd 13 DN21 107
WALCOT 82
Walcot Rd DN15 82
Walcott St HU3 145
Waldby Garth Rd HU12 73
Waldegrave Ave HU8 142 A
WALDEN STUBBS 76
Walden Stubbs Rd DN6 76
Waldorf Rd DN35 103
Waldo Way DN15 82
Walesby Cl 8 DN33 113
Walesby Rd DN17 150
Walgrave St HU5 140
Walker Ave DN33 113
Walker Cl DN15 82
Walker Dr
Winterton DN15 83 A
York YO24 132 C
Walkergate HU17 154 A
WALKERINGHAM 116 C
Walkeringham Prim Sch DN10 116 C
Walkeringham Rd
Beckingham DN10 116 D
Gringley on the Hill DN10 116 A
WALKERITH 116 E
Walkerith Rd 11 DN21 117 A
Walker La YO19 37 F
Walkers Cl 8 DN15 151 B
Walker's Cl 2 DN38 99 B
Walkers Ct DN17 107 D
Walker St HU3 145 C
Walkers Way DN39 86 B
WALKINGTON 55 B
Walkington Dr YO43 135 C
Walkington Heads HU17 54 D
Walkington La YO30 12 B
Walkington Prim Sch HU17 55 C
Walkington Rd
Beverley HU17 136 B
Rowley HU20 55 A
Walk La
Humberston DN36 114 C
Irby DN37 112 D
Waller St
3 Hornsea HU18 134 C
Kingston upon Hull HU9 146 C
Walliker St HU3 145 A
Wallingfen La HU15 53 A
Wallis Ct 9 DN33 102 D
Wall St DN34 152 A
Walmer Carr YO32 13 D5
Walmgate YO1 156 C
WALMGATE STRAY 130 F
Walmsgate DN33 102 D
Walmsgate Pl 24 DN33 102 D
Walmsley Cl 1 YO15 4 C3
Walmsley St HU3 145 D
Walney Rd YO31 131 A5
Walnut Cl
Kingston upon Hull HU16 139 D5
39 Wigginton YO32 13 E5
York YO10 131 A1
Walnut Cres
9 Cleethorpes DN35 103 B1
11 Snaith & Cowick DN14 78 C8
Walnut Dr DN20 108 F7
Walnut Gr YO25 125 F8
Walnut Rd 1 DN8 79 A1
Walnut Way DN17 107 C7
Walpole St YO31 130 D7
Walsall Garth HU4 144 A4
Walsh Gdn 23 DN33 102 D1
Walsh Way DN21 119 C8
Walter St 5 HU19 74 F7
Walter's Terr 6 HU5 140 C3
WALTHAM 113 D7
Waltham Cl YO32 14 B8
Waltham Ct HU17 154 B4
Waltham Grange 24 DN35 103 C2
Waltham La HU17 154 A3
Waltham Rd
Barnoldby le Beck DN37 113 C6
Brigsley DN37 113 D5
Grimsby DN33 113 E8
Waltham St HU1 155 B2
Waltham Tollbar Bsns & Ent Coll DN36 113 F7
Waltham Windmill & Rural Craft Ctr* DN37 113 D6
Walton Gr 3 DN33 102 E2
Walton La YO43 53 E6
Walton Pl YO26 129 B3
Walton Rd YO43 53 E6
Walton St HU3 145 A7
Walworth Cl HU8 141 E5
Walworth Street N 4 YO26 129 F5
Walworth Street S 9 YO26 129 F5

andell's View HU15 68 C8
andhill 31 YO32 13 E5
and La DN14 62 C3
andle The YO26 129 A2
anlass Dr HU16 139 C7
ansbeck 3 YO24 132 B7
ansbeck Prim Sch
HU8 142 D7
ansbeck Rd HU8 142 C7
ANSFORD 21 C3
ansford Gr HU9 142 A1
ansford Rd
Driffield YO25 125 B3
Nafferton YO25 125 F5
arblers Cl 23 DN18 69 E1
ardall St DN35 153 F1
ard Ave HU11 142 F7
ard Ct YO23 156 B1
ard Lea YO25 125 F7
ard St DN35 153 C4
aredale Cl YO16 122 F7
areham Cl HU7 141 B6
ares Way DN15 150 B7
arfield Rd YO25 124 B2
arley Ave DN16 151 C4
arley Dr DN16 151 C4
arley Rd DN16 151 C3
armer La HU19 90 E7
arn Ave 18 HU12 72 C7
arneford Gdns HU5 145 A8
arneford Rd DN35 153 D4
arping Way DN15 150 B7
arren Cl DN21 117 A1
arrendale DN18 84 E8
arren Farm Cl DN40 86 D7
arren Farm Cotts YO42 28 C1
arrenne Cl 31 DN7 92 D4
arrenne Rd DN7 92 D4
arren Rd DN15 96 D7
ARTER 30 A5
arter CE Prim Sch YO42 30 A5
arter Rd
Etton HU17 42 F6
Middleton YO25 31 A4
ARTHILL 14 F2
arthill CE Prim Sch
YO19 14 F2
arton Ave HU17 137 B4
arton Dr HU17 56 B8
arwick Ave 5 DN33 102 D2
arwick Cl DN7 92 F4
arwick Dr
Barton-upon-Humber
DN18 84 E8
Molescroft HU17 136 E6
arwick Rd
Cleethorpes DN35 153 D1
Scunthorpe DN16 151 C5
arwickshire Cl 6 HU5 139 D1
arwick St
Kingston upon Hull HU9 146 B7
York YO31 130 D7
ascana Cl HU4 144 B3
asdale Cl 2 YO30 126 E1
asdale Gn 4 HU16 139 B7
aseley Hill Way HU7 57 B5
ashdyke La
Elsham DN20 98 E6
Immingham DN40 87 B2
ashinghall La DN17 81 A2
ashington St
Great Driffield YO25 124 E4
Kingston upon Hull HU5 140 D3
assand Balk HU11 46 A8
assand Hall & Gdns*
HU11 35 B1
assand Rd HU11 35 B1
assand St HU3 145 C4
ater Bank DN9 104 E5
aterdale HU7 140 E8
aterdale Pk YO31 127 E1
ater End YO26 129 E5
ater Garth DN14 61 F4
aterhall 13 DN9 105 D6
ater Hill La YO8 148 D6
aterhills Ct 26 LN7 111 B4
aterhouse La HU1 155 A1
ateringdike La YO43 135 F7
aterings 19 YO32 13 D5
ater La
Bewholme YO25 35 A5
Camblesforth YO8 63 D5
8 Clifton YO30 127 A1
Dunnington YO19 26 F7
Eggborough DN14 62 A2
20 Flamborough YO15 5 A2
Goole DN14 65 C4
Harpham YO25 21 E7
Hemingbrough YO8 49 F1
Kirby Grindalythe YO17 6 B6
Kirby Underdale YO41 17 A5
Kirk Bramwith DN7 92 C7
Kirk Smeaton WF8 76 C3
Selby YO8 148 C6
South Cave HU15 53 F1
West Halton DN15 82 E8
Winterton DN15 83 A5
York YO30 130 A7
aterland Cl 15 HU12 72 D7
aterline Ind Est YO23 36 B7
aterloo Dr 14 DN33 102 D1
aterloo St HU2 155 A4
aterlow Dr 7 DN15 83 A5
aterman Ct 3 YO24 129 B1
atersedge YO25 124 F3
aters Edge DN20 98 B2
ater's Edge Ctry Pk*
DN18 69 F2

WATERSIDE 92 F8
Waterside
Goole DN14 65 C4
Hemingbrough YO8 49 F1
3 Thorne DN8 78 F1
Water Side DN15 68 A2
Waterside Dr DN31 152 C4
Waterside Gdns YO31 130 D8
Waterside Rd
Barton-upon-Humber
DN18 69 E2
Beverley HU17 137 B3
2 Thorne DN8 78 F1
Waterside The DN14 65 C4
Waterton La DN7 92 D2
Water Way Garth DN14 77 F6
Waterworks La HU11 142 E6
Waterworks St DN40 87 C2
Watford Ave DN34 102 C2
Watford Wlk HU9 142 E1
Wath Gr HU8 141 C1
Wath La YO41 27 C8
Watkinson Cl 8 HU12 58 D1
Watkin Street N DN31 152 C5
Watkin Street S DN31 152 D5
Watson Ave HU9 142 C2
Watson Cl 9 YO14 3 A8
Watson Dr
Beverley HU17 136 D1
30 Hedon HU12 72 D7
Watsons Ave YO16 122 D5
Watsons Croft DN7 92 D6
Watson's La YO14 3 D6
Watson St
Kingston upon Hull HU7 141 D6
York YO24 130 A3
Watson Terr 2 YO24 130 A3
Wattlers Cl YO23 132 C3
WATTON 32 D5
Watton Abbey* YO25 32 E4
Watton Carr Nature
Reserve* YO25 33 C2
Watton Gr HU6 140 B7
Watts Rd HU17 154 B4
Watt St HU9 141 E1
Waudby Cl 2 HU17 55 C8
Wauldby Cl 4 HU10 143 E7
Wauldby View 2 HU14 69 B7
Wavell St YO8 148 A6
Waveney Cl DN15 82 B5
Waveney Gr YO30 130 B8
Waveney Rd HU8 142 B6
Waverley Cl DN14 63 C2
Waverley St
Kingston upon Hull HU1 155 A1
York YO31 156 C3
WAWNE 56 E8
Wawne Lodge HU7 56 F6
Wawne Prim Sch HU7 56 E7
Wawne Rd HU7 141 C8
WAXHOLME 74 E8
Waxholme Rd
Owthorne HU19 74 F7
Rimswell HU19 74 E8
Waxwing Way DN31 102 B5
Wayfbain La 20 HU12 72 C7
Waynefleet Gr 3 YO10 131 A3
Wayside Cl
Holton le Clay DN36 114 A5
15 Scunthorpe DN16 96 D2
Wayside Cres YO16 122 B4
Wayside Dr DN36 114 A8
Wayside Rd YO16 122 B4
Weald Pk HU7 56 E6
Weardale HU7 140 F8
Weatherill St DN14 149 C4
Weaver Gr HU8 142 C7
Weavers Cl YO23 132 C3
Weavers Croft 8 DN9 105 A2
Weavers Pk
9 Copmanthorpe 132 B3
York YO23 132 B3
Webb Cl DN18 84 E8
Webster Ave DN15 150 E7
Weddall Cl YO24 129 F1
Wednesday Mkt HU17 154 B2
Weekes Rd 13 DN35 103 C2
WEEL 137 F3
Weeland Ct 16 WF11 61 A2
Weeland Rd DN14 61 E3
Weel Rd HU17 137 D8
WEELSBY 153 A1
Weelsby Ave DN32 152 E1
Weelsby Gr DN32 102 F2
Weelsby Prim Sch DN32 153 A4
Weelsby Rd DN32 152 E1
Weelsby St DN32 153 A4
Weelsby Street S DN32 153 A3
Weelsby View DN36 114 A8
Weelsby Way HU13 143 C2
Weeping Elm Way DN16 96 E2
WEETON 90 B7
Weeton Cl HU11 58 A4
Weeton Dr YO25 19 B5
Weeton North La HU19 90 B8
Weeton Rd HU12 90 C7
Weeton Way 5 HU10 143 E7
Weghill Rd HU12 58 D1
Weighton Ct 9 DN14 65 A7
Weighton Gr HU6 139 F5
Weighton Hill YO43 135 F4
WEIGHTON WOLD 135 F4
Weir Cl DN9 105 A2
Weir Rd DN9 105 A2
Weir The HU13 143 E1
Welbeck Pl 9 DN34 102 C2
Welbeck Rd DN35 153 C1
Welbeck St HU5 145 B8

Welborn Cl YO10 131 A4
Welbourn Wlk HU4 144 B6
Welburn Ct 8 YO25 22 D1
Welbury Gr HU5 139 E2
Welbury Gr HU9 142 C2
Weldon Rd DN21 119 B1
Welgarth YO25 31 B7
WELHAMBRIDGE 51 F5
Welham Cl 10 DN14 65 B7
Welholme Ave DN32 152 D1
Welholme Galleries*
DN32 152 F2
Welholme Prim Sch
DN32 152 F2
Welholme Rd DN32 152 E2
Welland Ave DN34 102 C2
Welland Dr DN15 82 B5
Welland Rd HU8 142 C7
Welland Rise YO26 129 D5
Wellbeck Cl 20 DN20 98 C2
Wellbeck Rd 8 DN34 102 C2
Wellesley Ave HU6 140 D4
Wellesley Cl YO30 127 A2
Wellgarth DN32 153 B1
Wellington Ave HU18 134 C2
Wellington Cl
5 Pocklington YO42 28 F4
6 South Killingholme DN40 86 E3
Wellington Ct DN32 153 A4
Wellingtonia Dr 5 DN6 76 E1
Wellington La HU3 145 D8
Wellington Rd
Beverley HU17 154 B4
Bridlington YO15 122 E2
Pocklington YO42 28 E3
Wellington Row YO1 156 A2
Wellington St
Grimsby DN32 152 F4
Kingston upon Hull HU1 155 B1
York YO10 130 E3
Wellington Street W
HU1 155 B1
Wellington Way DN20 99 A8
Well La
Beverley HU17 154 B2
Bridlington YO16 122 B4
Kingston upon Hull HU10 138 E2
Tibthorpe YO25 19 D2
WELLOW 152 D1
Wellowgate DN32 152 D3
Wellowgate Mews DN32 152 D2
Wells Cl YO8 148 A5
Wells Cres 3 DN35 103 C1
Wells Gr DN14 149 B6
Wells La DN14 61 E3
Wells Rd DN41 101 D4
Wells St
Grimsby DN31 152 B3
Kingston upon Hull HU3 145 A5
Scunthorpe DN15 151 B8
Well St
Messingham DN17 107 C7
Tibthorpe YO25 19 D2
Wellsted St HU3 145 C5
Well Vale 3 DN33 113 D8
Wellwick Saltmarsh Nature
Reserve* HU12 89 F6
Welshpool Cl 3 HU7 56 F7
WELTON 68 D6
Welton Ave
2 Kingston upon Hull
HU16 138 E6
York YO26 129 D5
Welton Cl
17 Barton-upon-Humber
DN18 84 E8
9 Beverley HU17 136 E1
Welton Gr HU6 139 F4
Welton Low Rd HU15 68 C6
Welton Old Rd HU15 68 E6
Welton Prim Sch HU15 68 D5
Welton Rd HU15 68 C5
Welton Wold View HU14 69 B7
WELWICK 90 A8
Welwick Rd HU12 74 D1
Welwyn Dr YO10 133 E8
Welwyn Park Ave HU6 140 C7
Welwyn Park Dr HU6 140 D7
Welwyn Park Rd HU6 140 C7
Wembley Park Ave HU8 141 E5
Wembley Rd DN8 79 B2
Wenchirst La DN7 78 D2
Wendan Rd 7 DN8 93 A7
Wendover Cl
Humberston DN36 114 D8
Messingham DN17 107 D7
Wendover La DN36 114 D8
Wendover Rd DN17 107 D7
Wendover Rise DN35 153 E1
Wendron Cl HU7 141 C6
Wenham Rd YO24 132 C8
Wenlock Dr YO19 37 B6
Wenlock St HU3 145 C7
Wenlock Terr
Kingston upon Hull HU9 141 E1
York YO10 130 D1
Wenning Gr HU8 142 D7
Wensley Ave HU6 139 E4
Wensleydale HU7 140 F8
Wensleydale Cl YO16 122 F6
Wensleydale Dr YO10 131 D4
Wensleydale Rd DN16 151 E2
Wentdale 1 WF8 76 C3
Wentworth Cl
3 Beverley HU17 55 E8
Camblesforth YO8 63 D4
Gainsborough DN21 117 C2
3 Kellington DN14 62 A2

Wentworth Cl *continued*
Kingston upon Hull HU10 143 F8
Wentworth Cres 1 DN19 70 E2
Wentworth Dr
Goole DN14 149 E5
Messingham DN17 107 D7
Wentworth Gr 5 HU11 47 C1
Wentworth Rd
Bottesford DN17 96 B1
Bridlington YO16 122 C4
Grimsby DN34 152 B3
York YO24 130 B2
Wentworth Way
5 Hunmanby YO14 2 F8
Kingston upon Hull HU9 146 C7
York YO10 130 F2
Werkdyke The YO1 156 C3
Werneth Rd DN32 152 F4
Wesley Cl
3 Epworth DN9 105 E6
South Cave HU15 54 A2
Winterton DN15 83 A5
Wesley Cres 15 DN35 103 C2
Wesley Ct
10 Cleethorpes DN32 153 A5
7 Kingston upon Hull
HU3 145 C5
Wesley Pl YO1 156 C2
Wesley Rd
5 Brigg DN20 98 C2
Scunthorpe DN16 151 E3
Wesley Sq 5 DN14 149 D4
Wesley St DN21 108 B1
West Acridge DN18 69 E1
West Ave
Burton Fleming YO25 2 E3
Stainforth DN7 92 C6
West Back Side YO25 10 C4
West Bank
Stainforth DN7 92 B7
York YO24 129 E3
Westbeck Hill YO42 30 A5
Westbeck La DN21 118 F5
Westborough Way HU4 144 B6
Westbourne Ave
Bridlington YO16 122 D3
3 Hessle HU13 143 E2
Kingston upon Hull HU5 140 A1
Westbourne Avenue W
HU5 140 A1
Westbourne Centre Hospl
HU5 140 B1
Westbourne Dr DN17 94 D7
Westbourne Gdns YO8 148 C4
Westbourne Gr
Goole DN14 149 D6
15 Grimsby DN33 113 E8
Kingston upon Hull HU13 143 D2
Selby YO8 148 C4
Westbourne Rd
Hornsea HU18 134 D4
Selby YO8 148 C4
Westbourne St 5 HU3 145 A4
Westbourne Terr YO8 148 C4
Westbrook Cres 3 HU15 66 D7
Westbrooke Gr 18 LN7 111 B4
Westbrook Rd 12 HU15 66 D8
Westburn Ave 2 DN19 70 E2
Westburn Way DN15 150 B7
Westbury Pk 10 DN35 103 D1
Westbury Rd DN35 103 C1
WEST BUTTERWICK 106 D8
West Butterwick CE Prim
Sch DN17 106 D8
WEST CARLTON 46 F1
WEST CARR 140 F5
West Carr La HU7 140 F6
West Cl
Fangfoss YO41 28 C8
Nafferton YO25 125 E6
Newport HU15 52 E1
WESTCLIFF 150 E3
Westcliffe Prim Sch
DN17 150 D2
Westcliffe Rd 16 DN21 107 C3
Westcliff Gdns DN17 150 F3
West Coates Rd DN31 152 B6
Westcombe Ct DN16 151 A4
West Common Cres
DN17 150 F4
West Common Gdns
DN17 150 F2
West Common La DN17 150 F3
West Common North Rd
DN17 107 A8
West Common Rd DN17 150 F3
Westcott Prim Sch HU8 141 C3
Westcott St HU8 141 D2
WEST COWICK 78 D8
West Crayke YO16 122 F6
Westcroft 11 YO43 53 F7
West Cross St 16 DN21 108 B1
West Ct
8 Riccall YO19 48 F8
8 Thorne/Moorends DN8 93 A7
West Dale Cres DN21 108 B2
West Dock Ave HU3 145 B4
West Dock St HU3 145 B3
West Dr YO25 125 F6
West Edge Rd WF8 76 A3
WEST ELLA 143 A7
West Ella Rd
Kingston upon Hull HU10 143 A7
Swanland HU10 69 C7
West Ella Way HU10 143 C7
WEST END 53 F2
West End
Bainton YO25 31 E7

West End *continued*
Dalton Holme HU17 42 E8
Garthorpe & Fockerby DN17 81 E6
Kilham YO25 9 B3
Lund YO25 31 E2
Pollington DN14 77 F6
Rawcliffe DN14 64 A2
Seaton Ross YO42 39 D4
South Cave HU15 53 F1
Strensall YO32 14 A7
Swanland HU14 69 B6
Swanland HU14 69 B6
Walkington HU17 55 B7
Winteringham DN15 68 A1
West End Cl
North Duffield YO8 50 A8
9 Strensall YO32 14 B7
Westenders Way HU1 155 A1
Westend Falls YO25 125 E6
West End Farm Cl 6
HU15 53 F1
West End Gdns
Driffield YO25 125 F6
Nafferton YO25 125 F6
Pollington DN14 77 F6
Westend La DN14 77 B6
West End La DN36 115 B1
West End Rd
Epworth DN9 105 C7
2 Habrough DN40 100 E8
Kingston upon Hull HU16 138 F7
Laughton DN21 117 E8
Norton DN6 76 E2
Ulceby DN39 85 F1
Westerby Ct LN7 110 A1
Westerdale 4 HU14 69 B7
Westerdale Cl 8 HU12 73 C4
Westerdale Ct 2 YO30 130 A6
Westerdale Gr HU9 146 E8
Westerdale Rd DN16 151 D1
Western Access Rd DN40 87 C3
Western Ave DN20 98 C3
Western Dr 7 DN18 69 E1
Western Gailes Way
HU8 142 B5
Western Gn DN15 68 A1
Western Outway DN34 102 D2
Western Prim Sch DN34 102 B3
Western Rd DN14 149 C6
Western Tech Sch The
DN34 102 C3
Western Terr YO32 127 D3
WESTFIELD 148 C4
WEST FIELD 129 A2
Westfield
Patrington HU12 74 C1
Scotter DN21 107 C1
Selby YO8 148 B4
Westfield Ave
Beverley HU17 136 D6
3 Eggborough DN14 61 F2
Goole DN14 149 D5
11 Grimsby DN33 102 E2
Rawcliffe DN14 64 A1
Selby YO8 148 B4
Westfield Cl
Easington HU12 90 F6
2 Eggborough DN14 61 F2
21 Haxby YO32 13 E5
Kingston upon Hull HU16 138 F6
Nafferton YO25 125 E6
3 Pocklington YO42 28 F4
Rawcliffe DN14 64 A1
Westfield Cres YO43 135 C4
Westfield Ct YO23 132 A2
Westfield Dr
Messingham DN17 107 D7
York YO10 133 D8
Westfield Garth
1 Crowle DN17 94 E6
1 Walkington HU17 55 B8
Westfield Gr
4 Eggborough DN14 61 F2
Grimsby DN35 153 D2
12 Haxby YO32 13 D5
Westfield La
East Garton HU12 59 D5
Eastrington DN14 51 E1
Fishlake DN7 92 B8
Hook DN14 149 D8
Kirk Bramwith DN7 78 B1
Norton WF8 76 C2
Preston HU12 58 B1
Thorganby YO19 38 A5
Wigginton YO32 13 D5
West Field La
1 Swanland HU14 69 B6
Upper Poppleton YO26 12 E1
Westfield Pk HU15 68 C6
Westfield Pl
19 Haxby YO32 13 E5
York YO24 129 A1
Westfield Prim Com Sch
YO24 129 B2
Westfield Prim Sch
HU16 138 F6
Westfield Rd
Barton-upon-Humber
DN18 69 C1
Cottingham HU16 138 F6
East Ella HU4 144 D5
1 Eggborough DN14 61 F2
4 Goxhill DN19 86 A8
4 Hatfield DN7 92 E4
20 Haxby YO32 13 E5

Westfield Rd *continued*
Kirk Bramwith DN7 92 A8
Market Weighton YO43 135 C4
3 North Duffield YO8 50 A7
Pocklington YO42 28 F4
Rawcliffe DN14 64 A1
Scunthorpe DN17 150 B2
Selby YO8 148 B4
Skidby HU16 138 A5
Waltham DN37 113 D6
Westfield Rise
Beeford YO25 34 B8
Kingston upon Hull HU13 143 D2
13 Withernsea HU19 75 A6
Westfields YO25 32 B4
Westfield Sq DN14 149 D6
Westfield Terr YO43 135 C4
Westfield Villas 3 DN7 92 E4
West Garth
Kilham YO25 9 B3
Rowley HU20 55 A4
Westgarth Ave HU6 139 F5
WESTGATE 94 D2
Westgate
Bridlington YO16 122 B4
Grimsby DN31 152 D5
Hornsea HU18 134 B4
Nafferton YO25 125 E6
North Cave HU15 53 D3
North Newbald YO43 53 E7
Patrington HU12 74 D1
Scotton DN21 107 C1
West-Gate YO25 124 E5
Westgate Gdns YO25 125 F6
Westgate Manor 4 HU12 74 D1
Westgate Mdws YO25 125 E6
Westgate Rd DN9 94 D2
West Gn
Kingston upon Hull HU10 69 C8
Messingham DN17 107 D7
Pocklington YO42 28 F3
West Gr
Barton-upon-Humber DN18 69 E1
Kingston upon Hull HU4 144 D4
West Green Dr YO42 29 A3
WEST HADDLESEY 62 A5
West Hall Garth 10 HU15 53 F1
WEST HALTON 82 E8
West Halton La DN15 82 C8
West Hann La DN19 70 C1
West Haven Way DN40 87 B3
WEST HILL 122 A1
West Hill 1 HU13 69 E4
Westhill Rd DN34 152 A1
Westholme Ave HU18 134 C7
Westholme Cl 10 DN15 82 B4
Westholme Dr YO30 126 E1
Westholme La DN38 99 C5
West Ings Cl 4 WF11 61 A3
West Ings Cres 5 WF11 61 A3
West Ings Ct 1 WF11 61 A3
West Ings La 2 WF11 61 A3
West Ings Mews 6 WF11 61 A3
West Ings Way 3 WF11 61 A3
Westkirke Ave 2 DN33 113 F8
West La
Burn YO8 62 C6
Burton Fleming YO25 2 E3
Keelby DN41 101 A4
Laxton DN14 65 D2
Sykehouse DN14 77 F2
Winterton DN15 83 B5
West Lambwath Rd HU11 46 D3
Westland Rd
Kingston upon Hull HU10 143 B7
3 Westwoodside DN9 105 B2
Westlands Ave
Grimsby DN34 152 C1
Tetney DN36 114 D4
Westlands Cl 13 HU12 72 C7
Westlands Dr HU12 72 C7
Westlands Gr YO31 130 F7
Westlands Mews YO25 124 D5
Westlands Rd
Hedon HU12 72 C7
Kingston upon Hull HU5 144 B8
Sproatley HU11 58 C5
Westlands Way HU17 45 A8
West Lea DN33 113 E8
West Leys Pk HU14 69 B6
West Leys Rd HU14 69 B6
WEST LUTTON 7 B8
WEST MARSH 152 B5
West Marsh Ind Est DN31 152 D5
West Marsh La
Barrow upon Humber DN19 70 B1
Goxhill DN19 71 A3
West Mid Mere Rd DN40 86 D3
West Mill Rise 4 HU17 55 B7
Westminster Ave HU8 141 E3
Westminster Bsns Ctr YO26 129 C8
Westminster Cl DN21 117 A3
Westminster Ct DN14 149 E6
Westminster Dr
Grimsby DN34 152 C2
Hatfield DN7 92 C2
Westminster Pl YO26 126 B1
Westminster Rd
2 Broughton DN20 97 D4
York YO30 130 A6
West Moor La YO10 26 A4
West Moor Rd DN10 116 C3
Westmoreland Ave 3 YO15 122 F2
Westmoreland Cl 9 DN9 105 A2
Westmoreland Gr 2 YO15 122 F2
Westmoreland St HU2 155 B4
WEST NEWTON 58 D8
West Newton Rd HU11 58 D8
Westoby La
Barrow upon Humber DN19 85 C7
Rowley HU20 54 E3
Weston Gr 3 DN40 87 B2
Westover Dr DN15 82 A4
West Parade
Grimsby DN31 152 C3
Kingston upon Hull HU3 145 C7
West Parade Rd HU3 145 D6
West Parklands Dr 8 HU14 69 A5
Westparkside DN14 149 A6
Westpit La YO32 14 A7
West Pk YO8 148 A4
West Point Trading Pk HU3 145 A3
West Point Trading Pk 2 HU3 145 A3
Westport Rd 27 DN35 103 C1
West Promenade YO25 124 D4
WEST RAVENDALE 113 A2
West Rd
Keadby with Althorpe DN17 95 C6
Sigglesthorne HU11 34 E1
Thorne/Moorends DN8 79 B2
West Rd Prim Sch 25 DN8 79 B2
Westridge Rd YO15 122 C1
West Riverside DN40 87 C3
WESTRUM 98 C1
Westrum La DN20 98 C1
West St Mary's Gate DN31 152 D3
Westside Rd DN31 152 C6
West St
Barnetby le Wold DN38 99 B4
Beverley HU17 137 C4
Bridlington YO15 122 E1
Cleethorpes DN35 153 F2
21 Flamborough YO15 5 A2
9 Gainsborough DN21 117 A2
Goole DN14 149 C5
Hibaldstow DN20 108 F5
Kingston upon Hull HU1 155 A2
Leven HU17 44 F8
North Kelsey LN7 110 A4
Roxby cum Risby DN15 82 F3
Scawby DN20 108 E8
Scunthorpe DN15 151 A7
Thorne/Moorends DN8 93 A7
West Butterwick DN17 106 C8
West Halton DN15 82 E7
Winterton DN15 83 A5
WEST STOCKWITH 116 F6
West Terr
Beverley HU17 154 C2
18 Brigg DN20 98 B2
West Terr St 3 DN17 94 D7
West Thorpe YO24 132 D8
West View
Messingham DN17 107 C7
12 North Ferriby HU14 69 A4
Scunthorpe DN17 96 C2
12 Snaith DN14 63 C1
Westview Cl YO26 129 B7
West View Cl 9 DN41 101 A4
Westward Cl DN34 152 C1
Westward Ho DN34 152 B1
Westway Ave HU6 139 F6
Westwick 25 HU12 72 C7
Westwinds Gdns DN15 83 A5
Westwinds Rd 10 DN15 83 A5
West Wold HU14 69 B6
Westwold Rd 20 LN7 111 B4
Westwood
Beverley HU17 136 D2
4 Broughton DN20 97 D4
Westwood Ave HU18 134 B4
Westwood Cl HU7 141 C6
Westwood Dr 3 HU4 144 B6
Westwood Gate HU17 154 A1
Westwood Hospl HU17 136 D3
West Wood La YO23 24 E4
Westwood Mews 12 YO19 26 F7
Westwood Rd
Beverley HU17 154 A3
12 Healing DN41 101 F5
WESTWOODSIDE 105 A2
Westwoodside CE Prim Sch DN9 105 B2
Westwood Terr YO23 130 B1
Westwood Way HU17 136 D4
Wetherall Rd YO8 63 F5
Wetherby Cl HU6 139 F7
Wetherby Rd YO26 129 B3
WETWANG 19 B6
Wetwang CE Prim Sch YO25 19 B5
Wexford Ave HU9 142 E1
Weyford Rd 9 DN35 103 D1
Weymouth Cl HU7 141 B6
Weymouth Cres DN17 150 C5
Whales La DN14 61 E3
Wharf Cl 10 DN10 116 C5
Wharfdale Cl DN15 95 E5
Wharfedale Ave HU9 141 E1
Wharfedale Dr YO16 122 F7
Wharfedale Pl DN16 151 D2
Wharfedale Way 3 DN31 152 D4
Wharfe Dr YO24 132 D8
Wharf Rd
Crowle DN17 94 D7
Misterton DN10 116 C5
Wharfside Ct DN15 82 A1
Wharf The DN36 115 A5
Wharncliffe Road N DN31 153 A7
Wharncliffe St HU5 145 A8
Wharnscliffe Dr YO30 126 F2
Wharram Field 3 YO25 22 D1
WHARRAM LE STREET 6 A4
Wharram St HU2 140 F1
WHARTON 117 E4
Wharton Ave YO30 130 B7
Wharton Rd
Blyton DN21 117 D5
8 Stamford Bridge YO41 15 D2
Wharton St DN31 152 B3
Wheatcroft 6 YO32 14 A6
Wheatcroft Ave HU10 138 E2
Wheatfield Cl
9 Barnby Dun DN3 92 A3
Epworth DN9 105 F6
2 Kingston upon Hull HU4 144 D2
Wheatfield Dr 2 DN37 113 D6
Wheatfield La YO32 127 C8
Wheatfields Wlk YO19 37 A1
Wheatland Cl YO42 29 B3
Wheatlands Dr HU17 136 C6
Wheatlands Gr YO26 129 C6
Wheatley Dr
Bridlington YO16 123 A6
Haxby YO32 127 C8
Wheatley Gdns HU8 141 D3
Wheeldale Cl 2 HU8 141 D7
Wheeldale Ct 7 YO16 122 F7
Wheeldale Dr YO32 128 E2
Wheeler Prim Sch HU3 144 F5
Wheeler St HU3 144 F6
Wheelhouse The 4 YO30 126 B5
Wheels La DN14 63 F3
Wheelwright Cl
Copmanthorpe YO23 132 B2
Sutton upon Derwent YO41 27 C1
Wheel Wright Cl YO23 132 B3
WHELDRAKE 38 A7
Wheldrake CE Prim Sch YO19 38 A8
Wheldrake Ings Nature Reserve* YO19 38 C7
Wheldrake La
Deighton YO19 26 B1
Escrick YO19 37 B5
Whenby Gr YO31 127 F1
Whernside Ave YO31 131 A5
Whernside Cl 12 HU7 57 A6
Whimbrel Ave HU18 134 C2
Whimbrel Way 12 DN36 114 A8
Whinchat Cl DN31 102 B5
Whin Cl
3 Strensall YO32 14 B6
York YO24 132 F7
Whincroft Ave DN14 149 C6
Whin Garth YO24 132 F6
Whinhill La HU12 73 F4
Whin La
Burstwick HU12 73 C7
South Cave YO43 54 B6
Whin Moor La HU15 68 A7
Whinns The HU17 154 C1
Whinny Hagg La YO8 48 A2
Whinny La YO60 15 A7
Whin Rd YO24 132 F6
Whins Gate DN17 81 A4
Whins La HU11 45 D6
Whip-ma-whop-ma-gate YO1 156 C2
Whisby Ct DN36 114 B5
Whispering Mdws DN14 78 B4
Whisperwood Way HU7 57 B5
Whistler Cl YO23 132 C3
Whiston Way 9 DN18 69 F1
Whitby Ave YO31 131 A7
Whitby Dr
Grimsby DN32 153 A1
York YO31 131 A7
Whitby St HU8 146 B8
Whitebeam Cl HU3 145 D5
Whitecarr La YO42 39 E8
White Cross* HU11 45 A6
Whitecross Gdns YO31 130 D7
Whitecross Rd HU11 45 B6
White Cross Rd YO31 130 D7
Whitecross St DN18 84 F8
White Cross Way YO41 16 A2
Whitefield Bglws DN14 76 F8
Whitefield La DN14 61 E1
Whitefields Cl HU17 136 E7
White Gap La HU20 54 E5
White Gap Rd HU20 54 F4
Whitegate Hill LN7 111 C3
Whitehall Gdns 3 HU5 140 A1
Whitehall Rd 5 DN35 103 D1
Whitehead Cl HU17 154 B2
Whitehope Cl 13 HU7 57 A6
White Horse Cl 6 YO32 127 F5
White Horse La HU12 73 E3
White House Cl
19 Hatfield DN7 92 D4
Kingston upon Hull HU10 138 C2
Kirk Bramwith DN7 92 C7
White House Dale YO24 129 F1
White House Dr YO24 129 F1
White House Garth
Bubwith YO8 50 D7
15 North Ferriby HU14 69 A5
White House Gdns 4 YO24 130 A2
White House Gr 1 YO41 27 B2
White House La DN15 82 E8
White House Mews 16 HU14 69 A5
White House Rise YO24 129 F1
Whitehouse Way 12 DN9 105 D6
Whitehouse Wlk HU6 56 D5
White La DN8 92 F8
Whitelands YO25 124 D5
White Ley Rd WF8 76 C1
White Lodge YO8 148 B4
Whitemoor La YO8 49 C6
White Rose Ave 3 YO32 127 D3
White Rose Cl YO26 126 C1
Whiterose Dr YO41 15 D2
White Rose Gr 5 YO32 127 D3
White Rose Way YO26 129 C8
White's Cl La HU12 59 A2
White Sprunt Hill YO17 1 A1
White's Rd DN35 153 F1
White St
Kingston upon Hull HU3 144 F5
Selby YO8 148 B6
Whitestone Dr YO31 127 E2
Whitestone Rd DN17 150 C2
Whitethorn Ave 11 HU19 75 A6
Whitethorn Cl YO31 127 E2
Whitethorn Way HU8 141 D4
Whitewell Cl 3 DN21 108 B1
White Wlk HU10 143 C6
Whitfield Rd DN17 150 D2
WHITGIFT 66 B1
Whitgift Cl 13 DN37 101 F1
Whitgift Sec Sch DN37 102 B4
Whiting Cl HU16 139 A6
WHITLEY 77 A7
Whitley Bridge Sta DN14 61 F1
Whitley Cl YO30 127 A1
Whitley & Eggborough Prim Sch DN14 61 F1
Whitley Farm Cl DN14 77 A8
Whitley Rd YO41 27 A3
WHITLEY THORPE 76 F7
Whitley Thorpe La DN14 76 F7
Whitman Rd DN17 150 C2
Whitstable Cl 3 HU8 141 E7
Whitstone Cl HU7 140 F8
WHITTON 67 E3
Whitton Pl YO10 131 C4
Whitton Rd DN15 82 C8
Whitworth St HU9 141 E2
Wickenby Cl 18 DN34 102 C2
Wickenby Garth HU7 141 C8
Wickham Rd DN31 153 A6
Wickham Way YO25 124 D3
Wicklow Ave 22 DN33 113 E8
Wickwane Rd HU17 137 A6
Wicstun Way YO43 135 C3
Wide La YO14 3 E5
Widford Gn 7 DN7 92 D3
Widop St DN14 149 C5
WIGGINTON 13 D5
Wigginton Prim Sch YO32 13 D5
Wigginton Rd YO31 156 B4
Wigginton Terr YO31 130 C8
Wike Gate Cl 7 DN8 93 B7
Wike Gate Gr 6 DN8 93 B7
Wike Gate Rd DN8 93 B8
WIKE WELL END 93 B7
Wilbar Gr HU5 140 B2
Wilberforce Ave YO30 130 B7
Wilberforce Coll HU8 142 A5
Wilberforce Cres HU17 154 C4
Wilberforce Dr HU1 155 C3
Wilberforce House Mus* HU1 155 C2
Wilberforce Mon* HU1 155 C3
Wilberforce St HU3 145 D6
WILBERFOSS 27 F5
Wilberfoss CE Prim Sch YO41 27 E6
Wilbert Ct HU17 154 B3
Wilbert Gr HU17 154 B3
Wilderspin National Sch* 15 DN18 69 F1
WILDSWORTH 117 A8
Wiles Ct HU17 154 C2
Wilfholme Rd YO25 32 F3
Wilflete Ct HU9 142 B3
Wilfreds Gr 8 YO8 49 B4
Wilkie Cl DN15 150 C7
Wilkinson Ave DN8 79 B1
Wilkinson Way
20 Bottesford DN16 96 E2
3 Strensall YO32 14 A7
Willans Gr YO26 129 E4
WILLERBY 138 C1
Willerby Bsns Pk HU10 138 C4
Willerby Carr Cl 2 HU5 139 B1
Willerby Dr 2 DN14 65 A7
Willerby Low Rd HU10 138 D3
Willerby Rd HU5 144 C8
Willesden Cl 4 HU8 141 F5
William Barcroft Jun Sch DN32 153 C3
William Ct YO10 156 C1
William Jacques Dr YO8 49 E2
William Plows Ave YO10 130 E2
William Rd YO8 49 B4
Williams Dr DN39 86 B1
Williamson St HU9 146
William St
Cleethorpes DN35 153
Kingston upon Hull HU1 155
Scunthorpe DN16 151
William Wright Dock HU1 145
Willingham Garth 4 HU12 72
Willingham St DN32 152
Willingham Way HU10 138
Willing Way DN32 152
Willis St YO10 130
WILLITOFT 51
Willitoft Rd DN14 50
Willoughby Gr 12 DN34 102
Willoughby Rd
Hibaldstow DN20 109
Scunthorpe DN17 150
Willoughby Way YO24 132
WILLOUGHTON 119
Willoughton Prim Sch DN21 119
Willow Ave
2 Misterton DN10 116
Thorne/Moorends DN8 79
Willow Bank
14 Brayton YO8 48
York YO32 127
Willowbridge Rd WF8 76
Willowbrook Dr DN20 98
Willow Cl
13 Gainsborough DN21 117
Laceby DN37 101
18 Little Burton YO25 34
Pollington DN14 78
Snaith DN14 78
Ulceby DN39 86
Willow Cres DN8 79
Willow Croft DN14 65
Willow Ct
Beverley HU17 136
Hutton Cranswick YO25 32
Kexby YO41 15
Kingston upon Hull HU10 138
9 Pocklington YO42 29
Selby YO8 148
Willowdale HU7 140
Willowdale Cl YO16 123
Willow Dr
11 Barton-upon-Humber DN18 69
Bridlington YO16 123
12 Brough HU15 68
Goole DN14 65
Kingston upon Hull HU10 143
Messingham DN17 107
1 North Duffield YO8 50
1 Thorngumbald HU12 72
Willowfield HU6 140
Willow Garth
Eastrington DN14 51
Pollington DN14 78
Willow Garth La DN6 77
Willow Gdns 2 DN19 85
Willow Glade YO32 127
Willow Gn 7 HU15 66
Willow Gr
3 Aldbrough HU11 47
5 Barnetby le Wold DN38 99
Beverley HU17 136
Earswick YO32 128
Keadby DN17 95
Kingston upon Hull HU5 140
Pollington DN14 78
Scawby DN20 108
Scunthorpe DN16 151
3 Thorne/Moorends DN8 79
York YO31 130
Willow La
Goxhill DN19 86
Pollington DN14 78
Woodmansey HU17 154
Willowmead Cl 18 DN15 96
Willow Park Rd YO41 27
Willow Pk DN37 113
Willow Rd
Burstwick HU12 73
9 Campsall DN6 76
10 Knottingley WF11 61
6 Thorne/Moorends DN8 79
Willow Rise YO8 48
Willows Ave HU9 141
Willows Dr HU18 134
Willows Prim Sch DN37 102
WILLOWS THE 102
Willows The
7 Acaster Malbis YO32 36
Bransholme HU7 140
Hornsea HU18 134
Howden DN14 65
Kingston upon Hull HU13 143
8 Strensall YO32 14
Willow Tree Cl 9 DN40 87
Willow Tree Garth 5 HU17 136
Willow View YO8 49
Willow Wlk 4 HU17 44
Willy Howe* YO25 2
Wilmore La DN38 110
Wilson Cl
Market Weighton YO43 135
7 North Ferriby HU14 69
Wilsons Cl 7 DN15 151
Wilson St
Cleethorpes DN35 153
Gainsborough DN21 117
5 Goole DN14 149